# Outsourcing and Offshoring in the 21st Century: A Socio-Economic Perspective

Harbhajan Kehal, University of Western Sydney, Australia

Varinder P. Singh, IT Consultant, Australia

IDEA GROUP PUBLISHING

Hershey • London • Melbourne • Singapore

Acquisitions Editor: Michelle Potter
Development Editor: Kristin Roth
Senior Managing Editor: Amanda Appicello
Managing Editor: Jennifer Neidig
Copy Editor: Dawne Brooks
Typesetter: Cindy Consonery
Cover Design: Lisa Tosheff
Printed at: Integrated Book Technology

Published in the United States of America by
Idea Group Publishing (an imprint of Idea Group Inc.)
701 E. Chocolate Avenue
Hershey PA 17033
Tel: 717-533-8845
Fax: 717-533-8661
E-mail: cust@idea-group.com
Web site: http://www.idea-group.com

and in the United Kingdom by
Idea Group Publishing (an imprint of Idea Group Inc.)
3 Henrietta Street
Covent Garden
London WC2E 8LU
Tel: 44 20 7240 0856
Fax: 44 20 7379 0609
Web site: http://www.eurospanonline.com



Library of Congress Cataloging-in-Publication Data

Outsourcing and offshoring in the 21st century : a socio-economic perspective / Harbhajan Kehal and Varinder P. Singh, editors.
p. cm.
Summary: "This book discusses the economic impacts of outsourcing and off shoring to the developing countries and developed countries and the short term and long term implications"--Provided by publisher.
Includes bibliographical references and index.
ISBN 1-59140-875-X (hardcover) -- ISBN 1-59140-876-8 (softcover) -- ISBN 1-59140-877-6 (ebook)
1. Contracting out. 2. Offshore outsourcing. I. Kehal, Harbhajan S., 1942- II. Singh, Varinder P., 1974-
HD2365.O9415 2006
658.4'058--dc22

2005032069

British Cataloguing in Publication Data
A Cataloguing in Publication record for this book is available from the British Library.

# Dedication

In memory of my parents,
Chaudhry Harkishan Singh Kehal and Sardarni Harnam Kaur Kehal.

**H. S. Kehal**

To my parents,
Who have guided me with wisdom and always supported me in every walk of life.

**Varinder P. Singh**

# Outsourcing and Offshoring in the 21st Century: A Socio-Economic Perspective

## Table of Contents

# Preface

The current stampede toward outsourcing and offshoring should come as no surprise. Today outsourcing and offshoring is one of the best ways for companies to cut application development and maintenance costs, deal effectively with the software demands and focus on more strategic work. Depending on whom you ask, anywhere from one-half to two-thirds of all Fortune 500 companies are already outsourcing and offshoring to China, India and other countries. If companies are not already sending some development or maintenance work to Beijing, Mumbai or Chennai, chances are they're either looking into it or their financial department is asking why they are not.

Now from the economic perspective, our interest in this world lies in analysing how these tools are used, how services are chosen, what level of prices and competition will prevail and ultimately whether a market exists or fails. There is another perspective on this issue, which corresponds to the traditional division of the world between the East and the West, that is, the rich West and the developing East.

This book will provide what are the economic impacts of outsourcing and offshoring to the developing countries and developed countries. It will discuss how it is helping developing countries or profits and how savings are just reaped by developed countries. What are the short-term and long-term implications? How is trust and the confidence of customers, as with the shift of call centres overseas, affected? How are telecoms taking advantage of the technology? Will this bring people close culturally? What will be its implications for the East-West countries and how their political-economic relations will unfold in the 21$^{st}$ century? Why are certain countries getting more contracts? How are the wage differentials affecting this equation? Are the outsourcings and offshoring really win-win situations? We will analyse all of these issues in this book. This book will provide information from a socio-economic angle. While paying attention to the current status of intertwined issues of such as technology, standards, policy and legal issues, the focus will be on many economic issues and aspects of the outsourcing and offshoring those other books do not cover. This book will cover various aspects of global production, trade and investment and the effects of technology on outsourcing and offshoring.

The change in the flow of information, computing and communication in the recent past has greatly influenced the world economy. In the emerging digital economy, the players, as well as the rules of the game, are changing fast. Along with those changes has come a lot of confusion and uncertainty. This era creates a borderless environment, which changes the responsibilities of the private sector and the governments. This book builds on the strength of our experience of editing an earlier book: *Digital Economy: Impacts, Influences and Challenges* for Idea Group in 2005. Please see the Idea Group Web site at www.idea-group.com for details on our first book.

Most of the books on the changes in ICTs have covered the experiences of advanced economies; however, the many economies of Asia and emerging economies of Eastern Europe and erstwhile the USSR are also producers and users of information technologies. The digital revolution has influenced the government as well as the private sector. The book aims to provide relevant theoretical frameworks and the latest empirical research findings in the area of outsourcing and offshoring. It will cater to the needs of professionals and many others as stated in the following section who would like to improve their understanding of outsourcing and offshoring in the digital economy.

In addition to the academics, students and other knowledge workers, this book is intended for business people who are thinking about outsourcing and moving offshore for suppliers and partners around the world. If a business person is already directly involved in international trade and business-to-business transactions, either as a manufacturer, distributor, exporter and importer, custom broker and freight forwarder, trade financer or diplomat, then this book will be for him or her. If he/she is involved in international trade, investments in ICTs and the related fields of outsourcing and offshoring — perhaps as a lawyer, management consultant, trade show organizer, site developer, business school professor, executive educator or someone who advises international companies about outsourcing and offshoring, then this book will also be for him or her.

The assembling of the chapters and editing of this volume was a very onerous task, but has proved to be highly worthwhile and rewarding in the end. The response to the call for chapters was overwhelming. We received proposals from top scholars, professionals and practitioners from various parts of the world. We have received chapters from the U.S., Canada, Germany, Australia, Croatia, Singapore, India and many other countries. Authors with backgrounds from various cultural groups and with firsthand knowledge of outsourcing and offshoring have contributed to this volume.

Choosing the chapters for this volume was a highly challenging task, as we received an overwhelming response. Which chapter to include and which to exclude was very difficult. Chapters included in this volume have gone through a very rigorous review process. The ultimate choices of the chapters for inclusion in this volume were guided by the quality, relevance and coverage of the vital issues and proper analysis and depiction of the subject. The brief summaries of the various chapters included in the book in the words of the contributors are provided below for the readers to make their own judgment.

*The first chapter of this book deals with Development of Outsourcing Theory and Practice: A Taxonomy of Outsourcing Generations written by Glauco De Vita and Catherine L. Wang.*

This chapter tracks the evolution of outsourcing theory and practice in order to develop a taxonomy of outsourcing generations. The authors begin by exploring the roots of outsourcing theory and by framing its development in the context of the "bigger-is-better:" vs. "small-is-beautiful" debate. This review is used to identify drivers for, as well as basic features and outcomes of, outsourcing. Then, a critical evaluation of models aimed at guiding the decision of what should be contracted out is undertaken, leading to an original classification of existing outsourcing frameworks, namely, matrix-type, factor-based and process-based models. Appraisal of these models allows to unveil several ambiguities and contradictions over the why and how of outsourcing, and hence uncover theoretical inadequacies on how firms determine what, and under what conditions, to outsource. The authors attribute these inadequacies to the inherent difficulties stemming from the analysis of what we see as a phenomenon "in motion", in that the very nature of outsourcing has kept changing over time. Given the evolutionary nature of outsourcing, the authors view the development of taxonomy of outsourcing generations as an essential tool for a better understanding of outsourcing activities. Indeed, although the existing literature has already pointed to a shift in the nature of outsourcing, from the procurement of support activities to that of more critical functions, to the authors' knowledge no formal taxonomy of different waves of outsourcing has yet been developed. Our taxonomy identifies three generations of outsourcing, articulated across five dimensions that help distinguish different waves of outsourcing practice. The first dimension relates to key drivers for outsourcing, ranging from basic efficiency motives to full blown business process transformation. The second dimension refers to the type of activity being outsourced (i.e., peripheral, near-core or core). The third dimension focuses on the characteristics of the relationship between the outsourcing firm and the supplier. The fourth dimension defines the different critical success factors pertaining to the different forms of outsourcing, whilst the fifth dimension highlights the alternative measures of performance across outsourcing generations. Case study evidence based on the operations of companies such as Rank Xerox, General Motors and Dell Inc., is found to be consistent with the taxonomy proposed and provides support to its efficacy as a valuable analytical platform for the study of outsourcing as a dynamic construct.

*The second chapter is about Making Sense of the Sourcing and Shoring Maze: Various Outsourcing and Offshoring Alternatives written by Subrata Chakrabarty.*

Many terminologies have grown out of the outsourcing and offshoring bandwagon. While the corporate world continues to experience these phenomena, the academic world continues to research the same. An attempt has been made to give an overview of the various alternatives in sourcing maze. The author first discusses the basic sourcing strategies (insourcing and outsourcing) and the shoring strategies (onshoring and offshoring). Then moves deep and wide into the maze and unravel the multiple alternatives that businesses exercise in order to get the best deal for their information system

(IS) needs. Approximately 50 terminologies that are related to this growing maze have been discussed. The literature was scanned for various sourcing alternatives and terminologies.

The two basic sourcing strategies are insourcing and outsourcing. Insourcing implies that the service provider is a client entity, while outsourcing implies that the service provider is a non-client entity. The primary shoring strategies are onshoring, nearshoring, and offshoring. In onshoring (onshore sourcing or domestic sourcing) the service provider is located in the same country as the client. In nearshoring (or nearshore sourcing) the service provider is located in a country that is geographically close to the client's country. And finally, in offshoring (or offshore sourcing) the service provider is located in country which is geographically far away from the client's country. Often, the term offshoring is used to broadly imply nearshoring too, and hence one may do away with the specific term nearshoring. Offshoring (or "global sourcing" or offshore sourcing) may therefore be defined as a scenario where the service provider is located in a country which is different from the client's country.

Furthermore, within this wide framework of sourcing and shoring, some of the various alternatives that are available and practiced are discussed in this chapter. The numerous similar, dissimilar, confusing, and not-so-confusing terminologies were analyzed, deciphered, and often grouped in the following 28 sections: (1) application service provision/application service providing/net-sourcing/on-demand, (2) backsourcing, (3) benefit-based relationships/business benefit contracting, (4) body shop outsourcing, (5) business process outsourcing, (6) complex sourcing, (7) cooperative sourcing, (8) co-sourcing, (9) creative contracting, (10) distributed consulting, (11) dyadic outsourcing arrangement, (12) facilities management, (13) facilities sharing, (14) general outsourcing, (15) global delivery, (16) managed offshore facilities, (17) multi-sourcing, (18) multi-vendor outsourcing/multiple-supplier sourcing/dual sourcing, (19) project management outsourcing, (20) selective/smart/right/flexible/modular sourcing, (21) spin-offs, (22) strategic alliances/partnerships/joint ventures/equity holdings/strategic sourcing, (23) tactical outsourcing/contracting-out/out-tasking, (24) total insourcing, (25) total outsourcing/traditional outsourcing, (26) transformational outsourcing, (27) transitional outsourcing, and (28) value-added outsourcing.

Hence, the purpose of this chapter is to compile and elucidate the various facets of domestic and global sourcing of IS needs. The reader will gain holistic perspective of a phenomenon that is continuously changing the way business is carried out globally

*The third chapter written by Ashima Goyal deals with Global Sourcing: East-West Divide or Synthesis?*

This chapter examines the implications of global sourcing for global inequities. Internet and communication technologies (ICTs) reduce frictions and search costs for labour, and allow market access to geographically separated entrants. Labour intensive components of production can be unbundled and sent where it is cheaper. The smaller scale of efficient production induces more entry of new firms; entry costs fall. The rise in scale of aggregate employment raises productivity, and induces more labour-using technological progress. Among the implications of improved matching are:

First, the horizontal splitting and matching of production processes into the least cost due to global sourcing makes jobs in different locations complements, raising aggregate productivity, and aiding the convergence of wages across the globe. Complementary local jobs will be created as profits and activities expand, reducing fears of sustained local unemployment due to some jobs going abroad.

Second, the importance of investing in new technology and in worker training, for business to benefit fully from future trends. A multiplier effect can occur from induced education and technology adoption. Policy that targets education and training of workers can have major effects by stimulating these self-reinforcing trends. Encouraging access to, and the provision of, ICT infrastructure should be a major aim. Regulation should reduce barriers to the entry of new firms and ensure open standards especially in the production of intermediates. Tax of transitory profits or insurance schemes can cover transitional unemployment.

Third, expected income distributional changes, over time, across countries, workers and firms. Although outsourcing is seen as benefiting firms while workers lose jobs or are offered low-wage jobs, the longer-term trends set in motion are exactly the opposite — they favour workers over firms as opportunities increase and more firms enter. There will be more global convergence of wages, but established Western firms will make considerable profits in the short-term. Advantages to the East will only reverse long-entrenched inequalities. Greater prosperity in the East and more intra-firm trade will increase exports from the West and create more jobs there in the medium-run. Again skilled labour gains relative to unskilled initially, but the multiplier effects of outsourcing jobs, the range from low to high end jobs created, and the boost given to education will create gains for unskilled labour in developing countries also. Unskilled labour in developed countries will gain because of a fall in physical migration combined with an expansion of traditional service sector jobs, a large proportion of which are not tradable. These trends will lower social and global tensions.

Fourth, ICTs will allow hitherto excluded segments, whether firms or workers in developing countries or women, to access new networks, thus reducing inequities in power. Modernization did not benefit women as much as it was expected to, since it raised relative returns to work outside the home, thus lowering women's status. ICTs by allowing flexi-time and distance work can change this state of affairs.

Finally, the analysis is used to understand the rapid changes taking place; these turn out to be consistent with the analysis.

*The fourth chapter is about the Strategies of Outsourcing: From De-Risking to Uncertainty written by Parthasarathi Banerjee.*

This chapter investigates conditions when economic profit can be made from outsourcing. Ordinarily outsourcing is undertaken in order to reduce cost. Other factors such as local sourcing, advantages of distributed logistics or of reduced labor problems can be ultimately reduced to the aspect of cost. Cost reduction and cost-based competition, however, fail to offer strategic advantage since all the competing firms would rather soon adopt outsourcing. In the absence of strategic advantage the incumbent firm fails to reap economic profit over and above the rent. In order to have such a profit a firm must pursue certain novel tricks. Strategies of cooperation undertaken in a certain manner, we argue, can generate the economic profit.

Under conditions of no-outsourcing an incumbent firm undertakes all necessary business activities in the vertical as well as in the horizontal dimension. Ordinarily the incumbent will have multiple divisions and a complex matrix structure. Such a large and complex structure necessarily suffers from structural risks. The latter arises from opportunism of managers and transactions of incomplete information. Moreover, managers are not strict followers of rules and do suffer from bounded rationality. This entire set combines to render the large structure of the incumbent risky. Unreliability of structural information leads to this risk.

When outsourcing business processes of the incumbent, a provider unlike the managers of the incumbent necessarily must provide de-risked and more reliable information as well as goods. In fact, rather often the provider suggests value-adding initiatives to the business process outsourced. A provider acts as it were as an extended arm of the incumbent, albeit with a significant difference. The provider is bound by enforceable contracts and liability claims while remaining free from authoritative controls. A very large degree of relative freedom allows this provider to suggest and sometimes allow it to effect changes that the managers of the incumbent would certainly fail to deliver. A provider, therefore while de-risking the incumbent challenges that structure, and through challenging brings the incumbent closer to uncertain business horizons. Outsourcing can then potentially bring the incumbents structure to an economic or the "Knightian" profit.

Strategic interdependence between the client and the provider firms has led us to look into the manoeuvrability of one structure by the other. The client firm in order to de-risk its business from risks generated by its own structure outsources part of the business. The structure of the outsourced partner, described sometimes as the extended enterprise, together with the structure of its client generate endogenous demand for outsourcing. Structures are the sources of demand here. Boundaries of the two structures become fuzzy, and transactions in intermediate outsourced goods shift the management of coordination between the two firms to a novel platform. Now each firm forms an expectation on what the counterparty expects, and through this the parties evolve norm. A norm-based transaction leads to uncertainty and this uncertainty is the source of an entrepreneurial profit. Outsourcing when undertaken strategically thus might lead to a profit solution.

*The fifth chapter explores the New Ethics for E-Business Offshore Outsourcing, which is written by Fjodor Ruzic.*

Historically, companies have moved activities from one place to another for various reasons, and their mobility has only increased in recent decades. In developing countries, this can encourage mass migration from villages to urban areas, practice development experts generally consider unsustainable. In an era of telecommunications, it is better to move jobs to people than to move people to jobs. Advances in technology and global networking of economies support this trend. Whether jobs move or people move, communities suffer losses. E-business companies with a commitment to corporate social responsibility must work to reduce the pain and stress of disruption in home countries while increasing the socio-economic benefits of these jobs in the receiving country — both done responsibly and to the best of the ability of the company. The particular insight in the e-business outsourcing as well as offshore outsourcing is the key of successful and sustained development in all countries and regions where the e-business firms work under globally accepted and harmonized rules and universal code of ethics. The idea of this work is to express why and how the role of the global ethics environment is important to e-business, and what is done to make harmonized and balanced platform for sustained development of e-business offshore outsourcing in all regions around the globe. It is obvious that we are considering business ethics. Ethics principally relates to morality of what well-behaved people do, and sometimes, ethical rules are binding as on regulated professionals, such as lawyers and accountants. Hence, ethical rules are generally not incorporated into outsourcing contracts, although e-business outsourcing and offshoring urgently need them.

These notions are introductory explained at the beginning of this chapter, and the author presume that ethics programs are of vital interest for most of current e-business companies especially when offshore outsourcing is in place. Besides the basics on ethics and outsourcing issues, this chapter is focused on finding directions of promoting ethics and social responsibility on regional and global scene.

Furthermore, the author states that e-business should develop outsourcing ethics program that presents the analysis of the nature and the social impact of information technology and the corresponding formulation and justification of policies for the ethical use of e-technologies. Ethics covers both social as well as personal policies for the ethical use of technology. It is a dynamic and complex field of study, which takes into account, the relationships between facts, conceptualization, policies and values with regard to the ever-changing information technology. These notions are considered in efforts to produce globally acceptable ethics program that would articulate both individual company and global interests in an appropriate way. In this context, the chapter is also covering the recent work on international scene in order to develop offshore outsourcing activities in accordance with globally accepted rules/codes of ethics — it will be the new age of global e-business ethics. The author examines e-business ethics development, and new standardization efforts toward unified, globally acceptable code of ethics. Thus, the chapter covers the analysis and discussion on the needs for such instrument and findings on how to reach unified global solution.

*The sixth chapter is a Perspective of Advanced Countries about Information Technology Offshore Outsourcing: A Perspective of Advanced Countries, authored by Narendra S. Chaudhari and Smita Gupta.*

Offshore outsourcing is a term covering a range of information technology (IT) and business services delivered to companies in developed countries by IT personnel based in developing countries. The widespread use of Internet, standardization of software development methodologies, efficient IT project management techniques, low cost of telecommunications, have provided the necessary thrust for global production of software and services. The significant cost savings achieved by the offshore model is the prime factor in its growing acceptance and use. IT software and service outsourcing is becoming a new reality for employers, employees, government and academicians.

Offshoring has support from the U.S. government. The chief economic advisor of President George W. Bush, Gregory N. Manikw, in his economic report has expressed that offshoring is just another form of trade and has economic benefits to the U.S. The rapid increase in offshore outsourcing of IT software and services has led the U.S. workforce to believe in widespread loss of "white-collar" IT jobs. Offshore developing countries invest considerably high amounts of their resources in science, mathematics, and engineering education. It is relatively less known that, as early as the 1960s and 1970s, countries like India have set up the educational institutions for providing very competitive learning environments; such efforts needed considerable investments in terms of their monitory and human resources. Large numbers of technically skilled students are graduating from such institutions work on the offshore projects.

In this chapter, the authors analyze the impact of today's offshore outsourcing movement to U.S. economy, education, jobs, wages and social issues. The authors suggest that offshoring is a viable economic model. It leads to improved productivity, lower inflation and eventually growth in jobs and wages. The U.S. will also see significant numbers of "insourced" jobs because of subsidiaries of foreign based companies. Future job growth in different areas of business and skills, require young students and present IT workforce to acquire them with education and training. Federal Reserve chairman Alan Greenspan has also expressed the need to produce highly skilled workers. The offshoring has a positive effect of creation of unstructured jobs requiring very high skills and higher level decision making.

Offshoring results in the loss of well-structured jobs. The jobs lost due to offshoring are typically characterized by their absence of higher level decision making. The loss of such jobs for IT workers is the difficult aspect of offshoring. In this chapter, the authors make some recommendations to reduce, minimize and overcome the hardships caused by the IT outsourcing. The recommendations involve suggestions for the basic educational system as well as social system. From the educational perspective, the higher level thinking skills, involving the balance of creativity as well as competition, should be encouraged. For comparison, the authors give the numbers of engineering degrees awarded in countries like China, Japan, South Korea and Taiwan. For doctorate degrees in the field of engineering, the authors note that, within America itself, American universities award more engineering doctorate degrees to foreigners as compared to Americans. In countries like Singapore, the educational system emphasizes both the aspects of creativity as well as competition from the primary level. From the social perspective, the authors suggest that the laid off workers should be provided assistance to find a new comparable job, both by the U.S. government and companies.

*The seventh chapter explores Business Process Outsourcing to Emerging Markets: A Knowledge Management Approach to Models and Strategies written by Jurgis Samulevièius and Val Samonis.*

A major phenomenon of globalization, outsourcing is a complex and controversial issue. It occurs when companies contract out activities previously performed in-house or in-country to foreign (usually offshore) companies globally. Couched in the terms of a SWOT analysis and using a modified Harvard-style case study that was subjected to the SWOT analysis, this chapter analyzes business process outsourcing (BPO) to emerging markets, frequently called outsourcing or offshoring in short. The overarching advantage of outsourcing is that it allows a business to focus on core activities as called for by core competence, strategic alliance, and competitive advantage theories of international business. Such a global restructuring of production has been sometimes called the true WMD (weapon of mass destruction) of jobs in the developed world. However, a more balanced approach could borrow the term "creative destruction" from the prominent Austrian economist Josef Schumpeter and emphasize the all-important transformational aspect of outsourcing. A transformational aspect of outsourcing is evidently very important for emerging markets but also for many companies in the developed world; therefore, BPO is sometimes called BTO (business transformational outsourcing).

The global digital/knowledge economy offers unprecedented opportunities to produce and sell on a mass scale, reduce costs, and customize to the needs of consumers, all at the same time. Whether one lives in a large country such as the U.S. or China, a mid-sized country such as Canada, or a smaller country such as Lithuania, their potential market is of the same global size. And one can source (netsource) inexpensively wherever one wishes. Added to that are immensely increased opportunities to access new knowledge and technologies, driving productivity and living standards further up. BPO to emerging markets is or should be driven by those fundamental reasons having to do with rapid organizational change, reshaping business models to make them viable in the long term, and launching new strategies. This is the essence of transformational outsourcing.

In this chapter, BPO is used in the broader, integrated, and comprehensive understanding of changes in the company's business models and strategies but first of all the company's changing core competencies and competitive advantages: partnering with another company to achieve a rapid, substantial, and sustainable improvement in company-level performance. A knowledge management approach is advocated in this research that is to be continued in the future. The chapter concludes that outsourcing is a wave of the future. Postcommunist and other emerging markets countries are well advised to jump to these new opportunities as they represent the best chance yet to realize the "latecomer's advantage" by leapfrogging to technologies and models of doing business which are new for Western countries as well. The chapter analyzes and outlines some of the ways in which contemporary and future business models are deeply transformed by the global digital/knowledge economy. Global outsourcing provides a compelling platform to research the issues of upgrading competitive advantage in developed countries and contract out non-core competencies to emerging markets. Therefore, suggestions for further research are included in the chapter as well.

*The eighth chapter deals with Outsourcing Decision-Making: A Review of Strategic Frameworks and Proposal of a Multi-Perspective Approach written by Luke Ho and Anthony S. Atkins.*

Outsourcing, which began as an arrangement of necessity and later a major cost cutting operation, has now evolved to become a mainstream management practice in a myriad of industries. In recent years, outsourcing deals have become prevalent in number and the strategic importance of the decision-making process has correspondingly increased. Like any other business operation, outsourcing involves a magnitude of risk. Research by Gartner indicated that as many as 80% of deals are unsuccessful and that European businesses lost as much as $7 billion on poorly managed contracts, which highlights the potential complexity in decision-making and the financial risks involved. This chapter reviews a number of strategic frameworks which practitioners have attempted to develop for use in outsourcing decision-making, and highlights the differences between proposed theories and current practice.

Outsourcing decision-making is multi-faceted in nature, requiring the consideration of issues within a wide range of domains, such as political (e.g., union pressures), economical (e.g., financial feasibility) and technological (e.g., performance metrics). However, the frameworks reviewed appear to be largely mono-faceted in coverage, which indicates potential inadequacies in existing capabilities. Analysis of the frameworks highlighted a lack of quantitative measures, financial costing and performance benchmarking, which is contradictory as cost savings and service level improvements are commonly identified as the top drivers behind the use of outsourcing. This indicates a possible misalignment between existing theoretical frameworks and current practices, which is the motivation behind developing a new framework.

This chapter proposes a framework to address such inadequacies by means of a tri-perspective approach, which extends the decision-making process to take into consideration various issues from multiple domains. This includes issues commonly overlooked in conventional frameworks, such as the need to maintain internal expertise (i.e., knowledge retention strategies) and the impact from national legislations.

Loss of internal expertise is a commonly cited risk of outsourcing, which increases the level of dependence that the organisation has on the service provider(s). The organisation risks being more locked into the service provider(s) and therefore is more vulnerable to business disruptions from service provision failures. Hence, organisations should take into account the degree of internal expertise which it intends to retain to ensure business continuity in the event of any complication in outsourcing arrangements. Legislations vary from country to country, resulting in different operating environments for organisations, which enforce a unique set of constraints on the outsourcing decision-making process. Examples include the U.S. Sarbanes-Oxley Act (2002), the UK Transfer of Undertakings (Protection of Employment) Regulations (1981), the UK Data Protection Act (1998) and the Basel II Capital Accord (2004).

Hence, in order to provide a more holistic approach which is required of current outsourcing decision-making practices, the framework incorporates both quantitative measurements (e.g., financial costing) and qualitative articulations (e.g., descriptive analysis of impact from internal policies). As outsourcing becomes an increasingly mainstream management practice, the role of such framework techniques in its decision-making process is anticipated to be increasingly significant.

*The ninth chapter is Outsourcing and Offshoring: Issues and Impacts on Venture Capital authored by Alev Efendioglu.*

Recently, outsourcing/offshoring has gained significant exposure in the popular as well as academic publications, with authors arguing the many different facets of the concept and its implications. The ongoing debates have revolved around issues related to cost of operations, benefits for outsourcing countries and countries that are recipients of outsourcing, the types of skills and associated unemployment, the types of industries that are being most effected, and even its political implications. A research study was undertaken to validate (or disprove) some of the most widely discussed and presented points of view. The findings are based on a survey of 364 individuals from 101 San Francisco Bay Area (California) venture capital firms. This chapter discusses various issues related to outsourcing/offshoring and presents the findings of the research study.

When one considers the major issues associated with the practice of outsourcing/offshoring, the findings of the survey provide a mixed picture. Some of the survey results reinforced the points of view that argue offshored outsourcing can create a competitive advantage and can yield very significant cost savings for the offshoring company. It also reinforced that there are major, identifiable costs associated with low quality product and information from the offshored-company, lost sensitive data and know-how, and investment risk posed by a host of other local environment factors. The results also show that venture capitalists do not view offshoring as a major impediment or negative for funding new or ongoing business enterprises, or see it as having a negative impact on the valuation of the offshoring company or increase its liability exposure. Even though they recognize the practice as an element that increases the "investment risk", this increased risk was not seen as a factor that would eliminate or significantly limit their funding of organizations that utilize offshoring as a business practice. Other findings were contrary to some of the claims made through various news programs and prevailing popular beliefs. The study respondents did not see increased government regulations, for example, Sarbanes-Oxley, as a compelling reason for offshoring or thought that a cultural connection to the offshored country was critical.

*The 10th chapter is about Outsourcing and Offshoring of Finance Activities written by Siri Terjesen.*

This chapter focuses on the outsourcing and offshoring of finance activities in the firm from firm, host country and home country perspectives. Globalisation, technology, regulation changes, stakeholder pressures and firm re-organisation changes present challenges and opportunities to firm finance functions to improve their contributions to the business. One of these opportunities is the outsourcing and offshoring of finance services. Finance services comprise 10% of the nearly $250 billion worldwide business process outsourcing (BPO) market (Gartner, 2003) and the total number of finance service outsourcing is expected to increase 71% over the next few years (Accenture & EIU, 2004). Firms are also offshoring these finance activities. A survey of 275 finance executives revealed that 21% send finance and accounting activities offshore (*CFO Magazine*, 2003). Finance services offshoring is more commonplace among firms based in the U.S. and Europe than those in Asia Pacific. While the offshoring of finance activities has key implications for firms, there are also socioeconomic issues at the home and host country level.

This chapter begins with an introduction to the hierarchy of firm finance activities, from strategic finance decisions such as corporate risk management, budgeting and forecasting to business partnering activities, group finance, tax and treasury, and transaction activities include credit, control, payroll, general ledger, accounts payable, and accounts receivable. The author reports the findings from the author's structured in-depth interviews with 37 managers at 25 U.S. and European headquartered multinational firms. This study was undertaken by the author and her team: Anne Evison (Organisational Edge), Julian Birkinshaw (London Business School) and Roy Barden (Catalise) in 2003 and 2004 (Evison et al., 2004). The study identified five drivers of finance activity outsourcing and offshoring: automation, disaggregation, consolidation, commercialization and relocation. A theoretical framework for evaluating location choice based on the codifiability and interdependence of finance activities is put forward and five location options are reviewed: co-location, virtual centre of excellence, nearshoring, offshoring and automation "lights out" processing. Case studies illustrate both successes and failures. Next, managers' perceptions of the costs and benefits of outsourcing and offshoring are reported. The author then turns to issues regarding the implementation of a finance services offshoring model, exploring four key elements of change: disaggregated jobs, loss of control, compromise and business interaction. The critical role of senior management commitment and the organisation's overall appetite for change are highlighted. The research identifies three important trends among the more sophisticated firms in the study: disaggregation, shifting and monitoring of finance activities.

The author then turns her attention away from the firm and to the country environment, exploring the socioeconomic issues faced by countries where firm finance activities have been relocated and to where they have been traditionally housed: India and the U.S. The increase in offshoring of finance and other BPO activities has led to fundamental changes across in the economy, education, social, cultural and political environment in both host and home countries. The author reviews key transformations in national and regional economic growth, education and training programmes, government initiatives and legislation, and career models.

*The 11th chapter is about Open Source and Outsourcing: A Perspective on Software Use and Professional Practices Related to International Outsourcing Activities written by Kirk St.Amant.*

International outsourcing practices have grown markedly in the past few years, and one of the more pronounced areas of growth is in the knowledge work sector. Now, activities such as computer programming, accounting, and medical transcription are regularly sent abroad as part of a practice known as business process outsourcing (BPO). Many of these BPO activities, however, require use of software either to perform a task or to provide the technologies that allow clients and outsourcing providers to interact. As a result, cost and copyright factors associated with the use of conventional, or "proprietary," software can affect who may participate in international BPO and how effective such activities can be. This software factor also affects the way in which international outsourcing can serve as a mechanism for providing access to emerging overseas markets. For this reason, software selection can be an important choice for companies considering the outsourcing of certain knowledge-based activities.

One solution to this situation might be the use of open source software (OSS), which is often free to use and is relatively easy to modify or to update. OSS, however, also has limitations and operating constraints related to areas such as product consistency, user support, and digital piracy. For this reason, companies need to understand and to weigh both the benefits and the limitations of OSS before planning their international outsourcing activities. Only though understanding these factors and making informed choices can organizations hope to reap the manifold benefits of integrating international BPO into their business practices.

This chapter examines the role of open source software (OSS) in international outsourcing practices that involve the transfer of knowledge work from one nation to another. In particular, this chapter focuses on the role of software in relation to the outsourcing of knowledge-based work through a process known as business process outsourcing (BPO). Included in this examination are discussions of the benefits and the limitations of OSS use in international outsourcing. This chapter also presents organization-specific and industry-wide strategies for effective OSS use in outsourcing situations. The chapter then concludes with a discussion of areas of international outsourcing where OSS might have important future applications or effects. The purpose of such an examination is to provide readers with the knowledge and the insights needed to make effective decisions related to the use of OSS in international outsourcing situations.

*Chapter XII is the Real Life Case Studies of Offshore Outsourced IS Projects: Analysis of Issues and Socio-Economic Paradigms written by Subrata Chakrabarty.*

The primary purpose of this chapter is to present descriptive case studies of two very different offshore outsourced custom software development projects. The case studies explain some contrasting and very effective approaches to offshoring and outsourcing of custom software development, and attempt to be of practical significance to managers and software professionals by analyzing the issues involved. The case studies discuss the business scenario, personnel distribution, project life-cycle, and provide insights into the practical and real life strategies adopted by managers to solve issues and problems in offshore outsourcing.

The first case study discusses the strategies used in two custom software development projects that were offshore-outsourced under fixed-term/fixed-price contracts by a client. The client is a UK/U.S. based telecommunications company and the vendor is a large India-based software service provider. The outsourcing initiative involved two projects, which developed customer relationship management (CRM) software for the client's Europe and North America operation respectively. The business scenario, stakeholders, specifics of IS systems being developed, contractual negotiations and relationship building issues, personnel distribution strategies (at client and vendor sites), personnel interaction and movement, project life cycle phases (requirements analysis and design, programming, integration, testing and delivery ), and a comparative analysis of the two projects (the maturity of relationships over time, importance of defining project scope and requirements, and verification of requirements and design) have been described.

The second case study discusses the strategies used in the offshore outsourcing of a custom software development project to multiple vendors under time-and-materials contracts, which involved simultaneous insourcing, onshore outsourcing and offshore outsourcing. The client is a leading Europe based provider of telecommunication services. The client outsourced simultaneously to four vendors: (1) a large offshore (India) based software service provider, (2) an onshore (Europe) based IS product and service provider, (3) a small onshore based software service provider, and a joint venture company (between the client and another offshore partner). The business scenario, stakeholders, specifics of IS system being developed, relationship building issues, contractual specifications, personnel distribution, reporting structure at onshore and offshore, cooperation and communication issues within the multiple vendors, issues in the client's competition inducing multiple-vendor sourcing strategy, and project life cycle (incremental evolutionary approach) have been described.

Furthermore, the observations and issues from these case studies are analyzed by comparing them with the paradigms of socio-economic theories that have been adopted extensively in the academic IS outsourcing literature (namely the agency theory, transaction cost theory, innovation diffusion theory, social exchange theory and power-politics theory). Most of the paradigms in literature resulting from the adoption of socio-economic theories for IS outsourcing research concurred with the observations in the real life case studies. The reasons behind the growth in offshoring of IS work, and also the primary factors that influence the choice of whether to insource or outsource are also addressed.

Offshoring and outsourcing is truly about delivering software that's value for money. "They come for the cost, and stay for the quality" seems to be an apt summary for the offshoring and outsourcing trend that is not only growing but also maturing.

*The 13th chapter deals with the dynamics of Growth of Outsourced IT-Enabled Services in India: A Systems Dynamics Approach, which is written by Varadharajan Sridhar and Sangeeta S. Bharadwaj.*

IT-enabled services (ITES) in India have registered tremendous growth in recent years. India controls 44% of the global offshore outsourcing market for IT services and ITES with revenues of US$17.2 billion in the year ended March 2005. At the end of March 2005, India's outsourcing industry employed 1.05 million programmers and other skilled workers, while giving indirect employment to 2.5 million people in support services such as transport and catering. Availability of English speaking trained manpower and low wages are some of the major factors that have contributed to the growth of ITES sector in India. However, recent political movements against outsourcing, quality concerns of the clients, higher cost and poorer quality of supporting infrastructure such as telecommunications and electricity, data theft, insufficient intellectual property protection have had negative effects retarding the growth of this sector.

In this chapter, the authors address the following issues: (1) determine various techno-economic factors that affect positively and negatively the growth of the ITES industry; (2) build a generic causal model that captures various interactions between these factors and growth of the industry which can be useful to various stakeholders such as the service providers and the government for formulating policies and strategies to augment growth of this sector; (3) illustrate the causal relationships with specific references to Indian ITES sector and outline factors of advantages and disadvantages India has in this sector.

Factors such as wages, transaction costs, trained manpower level, job quality, adoption by competitors, cost and quality of telecom and electricity infrastructure, data and intellectual property protection, maturity of the software industry, external medial influence, anti-outsourcing laws and competition from other countries are explored in detail and their positive/ negative effect on the growth of the ITES industry is explained.

The authors use the well-known finite difference equation methodology of system dynamics to develop a model of the mechanics of growth of the ITES industry. For this purpose, they develop a causal model of the growth of the ITES industry. Since the basic construct of a system dynamics model is the feedback loop, insights into cause-effect mechanisms of the growth can be obtained as a by-product of model structure.

Given the data limitations of this rapidly evolving industry, authors embark upon a qualitative rather than a quantitative approach in explaining the effect of various factors on the growth of the ITES industry. Factors of advantages and disadvantages India has in this sector are also discussed. The growth model they have developed in this chapter when calibrated against the available data on ITES industry revenue, can be used for sensitivity analysis of the various factors and their effect on growth. The authors draw some broad conclusions and give some examples as to how the stakeholders such as policy making bodies, the government and the industry associations can use this model to study the effects of these factors on the growth of the industry.

*An Overview of Service Level Agreements written by Nicholas B. Beaumont is the 14th chapter of this book.*

This chapter explains the increased commercial use of service level agreements (SLAs), advocates a methodology for their expression; proposes a taxonomy of service attributes, and recommends further research into SLAs. Preparing, negotiating, and monitoring performance as specified in an SLA require large amounts of managerial time. The proposed methodology and taxonomy will reduce that time requirement. This chapter draws on formal interviews with a small sample of outsourcing executives (mostly vendors); numerous informal discussions with executives involved in insourcing and outsourcing; examination of a number of SLAs; and negotiating an SLA at Monash University.

Direct and indirect evidence of increased use of SLAs in business (in part a consequence of outsourcing and a desire to formalize internal customer/supplier relationships) is presented. SLAs are contextualized as part of the outsourcing cycle. There is some evidence that well designed SLAs contribute to a fruitful and long-term relationship between business partners; a fruitful relationship will comprise cooperative and competitive aspects. The business advantages of using SLAs are summarized.

The bulk of an SLA comprises service level clauses (SLCs). Each SLC specifies, for a service or group of services: a definition of the service, the client's obligations, relevant fees, performance targets, ways in which performance will be measured, computation of penalties and/or bonuses, and possibly other causes pertaining to security and privacyand so forth.

Writing, negotiating, updating, and monitoring a SLA are demanding tasks. Writing entails precise and voluminous descriptions of business processes to be transferred to the vendor and methods of measuring the vendor's performance. The difficulties are exacerbated because, when a business process is performed in-house; the input data, computations, processes 'customers', and their requirements are often not explicitly expressed let alone formalized, and the real costs of the process may be unknown. Before serious negotiation can start, internal processes must be carefully defined and their costs ascertained.

The cost of preparing a SLA can be lessened by using the methodology and taxonomy expounded in this chapter. Hierarchical methods minimize repetition; in particular, it will be advantageous to write a general clause and vary it through parameterization. Less voluminous SLAs will facilitate negotiation and revision of documents.

Service level agreements are a live topic in industry but academic research lags practitioners' concerns. Ascertaining whether organisations use SLAs effectively, seeking better methods of expressing business requirements in an SLA, and ascertaining the effect of SLAs on business relationships is appropriate, even urgent. Especially considering the growing interest in and use of outsourcing and especially offshoring, SLAs have not received proportionate attention from academia.

*Understanding Consumer Reactions to Offshore Outsourcing of Customer Services written by Piyush Sharma, Rajiv Mathur and Abhinav Dhawan is the 15$^{th}$ chapter of this book.*

Offshore outsourcing is a fast-growing aspect of the world economy today with companies striving to reduce cost and improve productivity by shifting parts of their operations to overseas service providers in order to remain competitive (McCartney, 2003; Ross, 2003). Existing research on offshore outsourcing is primarily focused into the labor and ethical issues of outsourcing or on the effects of strategic outsourcing decisions on organizations (Clott, 2004; Razzaque & Sheng, 1998). There is little research on the influence of outsourcing on consumers, their perceptions, attitudes and behaviors. However, organizations are already facing concerns about offshore outsourcing resulting in dilution of their image, lower customer satisfaction, reduced brand loyalty and an increase in customer complaints due to real or perceived concerns about cultural differences, lower service standards and loss of privacy (Cornell, 2004; DataMonitor, 2004; *Economist*, 2001; Kennedy, 2002; Reilly, 1997; Roy, 2003).

Prior research in the country-of-origin area shows that consumers in developed countries tend to evaluate products and services from less developed countries unfavorably due to negative perceptions about their quality (Gronroos, 1999; Javalgi, Cutler, & Winans, 2001; Kotabe, Murray, & Javalgi, 1998; Ruyter, Birgelen, & Wetzels, 1998). Chao (2001) showed that for hybrid products where the country of design, components or assembly may be different from each other, country-of-origin effects are still applicable to its various elements. In their research, the authors extend this conceptualization to the context of offshore outsourcing of customer services. The authors call these services as hybrid services, in which different elements of the same service are performed in different countries.

Based on prior literature in COO area, the authors hypothesized several relationships among an antecedent (home country) and moderator (consumer ethnocentrism) with several dependent variables (service quality, customer satisfaction, brand image, brand loyalty, repeat purchase intentions and complaint behavior). The authors used a survey-based research methodology to test these hypotheses. 100 consumers each were approached at local malls in three countries — United States, United Kingdom and Australia. They completed a questionnaire consisting of scales to measure all the constructs used in this study — customer ethnocentrism (Sharma et. al., 1995), brand image (Aaker, 1996), brand loyalty (Quester & Lim, 2003), service quality (Parasuraman et al., 1988), customer satisfaction (Oliver, 1997), repurchase intentions (Hellier et. al., 2003) and customer complaint behavior (Singh, 1988).

Consumers in all the three countries had lower service quality perceptions and customer satisfaction, greater complaint behavior towards firms using offshore outsourcing. However, the findings on brand image, brand loyalty and repurchase intentions were mixed, with customers in U.S. and Australia showing lower brand image and repurchase intentions in Australia, but only lower brand image in the UK. On the other hand, high ethnocentric customers had distinctly lower perceptions for all the dependent variables compared to low ethnocentrics, thus supporting our hypotheses about the moderating influence of consumer ethnocentrism. The authors also found females and younger customers to be less ethnocentric and less influenced by offshore outsourcing of customer services, compared to older males as reported in prior research. The authors hope that their research would pave the way for a more comprehensive framework and further empirical work in this area because of its high managerial relevance.

*Chapter XVI, authored by Michael Amberg and Martin Wiener, explores IT Offshoring From A German Perspective.*

Increasing competition in globalized markets drives IT offshoring worldwide. In the United States, the relocation of IT activities and processes to low-wage countries like India is already an established business practice. But also in European countries like Germany, IT offshoring is gaining in importance. A number of German major enterprises are currently planning or are already involved in IT offshoring initiatives, while numerous German small and medium enterprises (SMEs) are currently thinking about how to take best advantage of offshoring.

As a result of the growing IT offshoring trend in Germany, the fear of job losses on a grand scale has encountered strong resistance to offshoring in the German public. The announcement by numerous companies to relocate a remarkable share of their jobs to countries in Asia and Eastern Europe intensified these fears even more. For instance, in July 2003, IBM published plans to move a great number of their jobs offshore until 2015. Siemens, which already operates a software development center in Bangalore (India), also plans to expand their offshoring and nearshoring activities.

As a result of this trend, according to estimations by experts, 10,000 highly skilled IT service jobs are jeopardized in Germany alone. Therefore, the discussion about offshoring attracts vast attention, both in the United States and in Germany. In the U.S. election campaign, for instance, IT offshoring was a major topic and triggered a new wave of protectionism. Even in Germany, parts of the political left-wingers encouraged protectionism in an attempt to prevent the relocation of IT service jobs to countries like India or Russia.

In consideration of this development, this chapter examines company- and economy-related drivers and economic effects of the rising trend to IT offshoring in Germany as well as possible responses by German companies and policy makers.

The chapter is structured as follows: To start off, section two gives an overview of the German economy, and compares it with economies of developed and developing countries. In the third section, factors driving the offshoring trend in Germany are presented from a company's and an economy's perspective. The fourth section points out the extent of the current offshoring trend in Germany and describes the German IT offshoring market. The fifth and the sixth section represent the main part of the chapter. While section five addresses possible impacts of IT offshoring in Germany, section six deals with reforms required for turning offshoring to Germany's advantage. Finally, section seven summarizes the key points of the chapter and gives a forecast of future developments in respect of the German IT offshoring market.

*Chapter XVII is a Information Systems/Information Technology Outsourcing in Spain: A Critical Empirical Analysis written by Felix R. Doldán Tié, Paula Luna Huertas, Francisco Jose Martínez López and Carlos Piñeiro Sánchez.*

Outsourcing has been a major issue in literature and managerial practice for the last decade; externalization initiatives spread from complementary, support activities and now lie at the heart of many critical activities. The authors' point of interest is the sourcing of those activities in which company makes an intensive use of IT resources, in the specific case of small and medium-sized enterprises.

The authors have conducted an experimental study to scrutinize the attitude of Spanish firms about the outsourcing of IT-based services and activities. Primary data about sourcing decisions were collected through a questionnaire and in-depth interviews in a random sample of 530 Spanish companies; complementary data about turnover, capital and so forth were compiled from official public records. The results indicate that up to a 50% of Spanish companies is at this time running at least one outsourcing contract in IT-related areas and services, from data processing to Web development or e-shops management.

Some recent experiments found evidence of a negative relationship between outsourcing and business size; one specific goal of the experiment was to evaluate the attitude of small and medium-sized enterprises (SMEs), in order to verify if these companies show any specific pattern in terms of justification and/or evaluation of IT outsourcing projects.

The authors had not found any symptoms of systematic association with size indicators (such as assets value, turnover, or capital), although the data confirm that outsourcing is more frequent (and quantitatively more relevant) among larger companies. Moreover, SMEs show a palpable inclination to outsource some services and activities that larger companies tend to insource, for example, user support, maintenance, or Internet-based services.

This general shape is broken by a group of emergent high-tech, knowledge-intensive companies where most of IT-related activities are performed by internal staff; the main arguments for internalization are, in these cases, the competitive implications of IT/IS and the need to build invisible assets by managing information and promoting collaboration. Most of these companies are relatively small and are equipped with a flat structure, thus the hypothesized link between size, complexity, uncertainty, and outsourcing attitudes must be revised.

These results contradict the common belief that outsourcing is characteristic of big corporations with efficiency problems, and put in question the prevalence of cost economies as the main argument of externalization, particularly in the case of SMEs and the considered IT-based activities.

In fact, SMEs managers pointed out some other arguments, aside from cost savings, when they were asked why the company had decided to outsource IT-activities: management complexity, technology uncertainty, and some operative risks involved in information systems, such as security and disaster recovery; in some cases, these arguments were reported to be more relevant than savings themselves.

Spanish SMEs rely on outsourcing to cover temporary and exceptional processing needs, and to take advantage of expert knowledge when they deal with complex IT projects, for example, development of integrated systems or implementation of EDI applications. The data indicate that the lack of internal expertise and financial stress are critical factors in SME's decision to outsource.

The development and maintenance of Internet-related services, such as Web sites or e-commerce applications, were given special attention in the experimental design; data indicate that these activities are commonly insourced in high-tech and "young-looking" companies. On the contrary, SMEs and some basic industries show an inclination towards outsourcing, because management issues entailed by the Net are interpreted as complex and uncertain.

*Chapter XVIII, written by Arjun K. Pai and Subhajit Basu, deals with the Emerging Legal Challenges in Offshore Outsourcing of IT-Enabled Services.*

A burgeoning outsourcing market for IT-enabled services has outpaced the growth of virtually every other market sector these days. This advancement has led to numerous legal and commercial issues from the perspective of an outsourcing customer. Although this growing mega-trend enables companies to leverage operational efficiency and consolidate costs by taking advantage of the expertise of speciality vendors; outsourcing is not a panacea to cure all business adversities and management problems. This chapter provides insightful information on the impending pressures and challenges on the IT-enabled service industry to minimize operational risks and avoid the common legal pitfalls governing the different aspects of an outsourcing relationship. In essence, this chapter has provided comprehensive guidance on the legal and best practice procedures which are critical components to ensure the long-term success of a company's offshore relationship with its service providers. Under such a blend of streamlined and integrated business framework, these next-generation outsourcing strategies would deliver value through: cost arbitrage, global competitiveness, superior service management and governance.

Offshore outsourcing of non-core business process has rapidly evolved as a ubiquitous organisational phenomenon. However, failure to follow a clear, systematic and effective outsourcing strategy to evaluate threats, uncertainties and numerous imponderables can cause global enterprise businesses major setbacks. The reasons for such setback could be largely due to lack of core competency, careful legal planning and due diligence to operating models associated with an outsourcing initiative.

This chapter has attempted to collate and exemplify the distinct qualifying processes accommodating contractual and intellectual property rights and has provided a worthwhile debate on intricate legal considerations when structuring multi-jurisdictional outsourcing deals.

Importance of legal intervention and due diligence to service agreements is further elevated as, at every phase of an outsourcing arrangement, compliance issues and contractual obligations can affect the success of an enterprise customer and its relationship with their outsourcing service provider.

The authors suggest that an exhaustive qualitative and quantitative industry specific research analysis be conducted in order to better define the principles and standards governing sub-contracting arrangements.

A broader exposure to the strategic management and regulatory framework might provide firms with vantage points from which they could assess and identify new opportunities, evaluate threats and adopt effective risk mitigation strategies. Compliance to security standards and safeguard of information acquisition, analysis and usage should emerge as the mainstream strategy for outsourcing.

The novelty of this chapter lies in the comparative analysis of strategic legal and management framework by weighing the risks and evaluating the threats which would assist the decision making process of firms when selecting an appropriate offshore partner to carry out their IT-development work.

*Does Strategic Outsourcing Undermine the Innovative Capabilities of Organizations? is the 19th chapter of this book, written by Andreas Hoecst and Paul Trott.*

In this chapter the authors argue that firms have responded to the intense pressure from markets and financial operators to reduce asset investments by outsourcing activities. Outsourcing was originally confined to peripheral business functions and mainly motivated by a cost saving logic, but has now developed into a routine strategic management move that affects not only peripheral functions but the heart of the competitive core of organisations. At the same time there is a move from traditional outsourcing with one or a small number of key partners and long-term contracts to strategic outsourcing with multiple partners and short-term contracts. This chapter investigates the innovation-related risks that can arise from strategic outsourcing. It uses the example of information technology/information systems (IT/IS) outsourcing to highlight the increased risks that arise from a move from traditional to strategic outsourcing and discusses some measures that managers can take to attempt to control these risks. The nature of the risk is closely related to the risk of information leakage that arises from collaborative research and technology development between organisations in technology-intensive sectors that has been analysed by Hoecht and Trott (1999).

Strategic outsourcing goes beyond traditional outsourcing in the sense that competitive advantages are being sought through opening up all business functions, including the core competencies which should provide competitive advantage to whoever can provide the perceived best solution, internal or external. In contrast to traditional outsourcing, there are no protective boundaries around core activities in the hope that the organisations can maximise their innovative capacity by being an active part of a networked economy. This means that rather than having exclusive arrangements with one or very few service providers of long periods of time which will be expected to offer tailor-made solutions, strategic sourcing arrangements will be with multiple partners over short periods of time and with very little protection of internal core competency functions against outsiders.

Reliance on outsider providers can be problematic, not only because key area of expertise may be gradually lost to the outsourcing organisation but also because outside providers may not have the desired leading edge expertise over the long term or may (most likely accidentally but possibly even purposefully) spread their expertise among many clients so that it degrades from "best in world" to mere industry standard. The problem of information leakage lies at the heart of this dilemma. Companies want exclusivity in their relationships with their service providers, but consultants who work with many clients are unlikely to be able not to be influenced and not to spread the best practice they acquire when working with different client firms. Detailed legal contracts may offer short-term solutions as they can protect tangible outcomes form specific projects undertaken, but not every innovation related project outcome is tangible and can be clearly defined in legal contracts. Consultants face a dilemma as they are expected to spread cutting-edge level expertise to their respective client firms yet as the same time honour confidentiality commitments. While some may argue that professional ethics, social control (reputation concerns, etc.) and legal instruments are sufficient to contain this risk of information leakage, the authors highlight that with a move from traditional outsourcing to strategic outsourcing, this problem becomes much more acute and needs addressing. The authors put forward a suggestion how at least larger, resourceful organisations can address this problem, namely by employing "boundary spanners" that can make qualified judgements both on the trustworthiness and expertise of service provider consultants. The advantage of this approach is that the employment of "boundary spanners" can mitigate against the risk of losing the absorptive capacity and expertise arising from strategic outsourcing strategies in particular.

*The last chapter of this book, Chapter XX, is the Analysis of a Large-Scale IT Outsourcing "Failure": What Lesson Can We Learn?, written by Ann Rouse and Brian J. Corbitt.*

Much of the research that has been carried out into outsourcing is based on relatively successful case studies. Yet drawing inferences from case studies when those with largely negative outcomes rarely see the light of day represents a significant problem. When negative cases are systematically unrepresented, there is less opportunity to subject theory to scrutiny.

This chapter goes some way towards redressing this trend, by reporting on a large-scale "selective" outsourcing arrangement that has been publicly described as a failure

— the Australian federal government's "whole of government" IT infrastructure outsourcing initiative. This initiative, originally promoted as likely to lead to a billion dollar saving, was abandoned early in 2001, after a damning public report by the Australian auditor general. However, a detailed study of the initiative suggests that the "failure" occurred despite the project adhering to many of the recommended guidelines for successful outsourcing that had been derived from earlier case analysis. The authors conclude that the expectations decision makers had for cost savings from the outsourcing arrangement were naïve and over optimistic, given that extant empirical evidence reveals that substantial savings (over around 10% of the outsourcing contract) are rare for complex services.

The findings have important implications for decision makers confronted with outsourcing choices. The study suggests that the risks of outsourcing are often downplayed, or ignored in the rush to reap expected benefits. The study also suggests that expectations of savings from outsourcing IT are often substantially higher than those that have been empirically confirmed in the field. Decision makers are advised that key assumptions about costs, savings, managerial effort and the effects of outsourcing on operational performance might be incorrect, and to plan for their outsourcing activity accordingly. Key assumptions should be subject to critical analysis, and decision makers should pay particular attention to coordination and transaction costs, as these tend to be overlooked in the business case. These costs will be magnified if "best in breed" multiple-vendor outsourcing is chosen, and if contracts are kept short. Decision makers are also warned of the difficulties they are likely to have at the end of an outsourcing contract if there is not a large and robust pool of alternative vendors willing to bid against the incumbent.

The authors conclude by suggesting that with the growth of new forms of outsourcing such as offshore outsourcing, decision makers should be careful to critically evaluate the promised benefits and to recognize the substantial risks that these benefits do not eventuate.

All the chapters included in this book are original and have been published for the first time. This book covers various aspects of outsourcing and offshoring and the socio-economic impacts, influences and challenges of this phenomenon.

While paying attention to the technical and related issues of outsourcing and offshoring, the focus is on many socio-economic issues and aspects of these activities that other books do not cover. This book aims to provide relevant theoretical frameworks and latest empirical research findings in this area.

The book provides a compilation of some of the latest literature on the subject. The book serves the invaluable purpose of pointing out the socio-economic implications of outsourcing and offshoring in various countries and uses case studies to highlight pertinent points. The relevance of the book to such a topical area of outsourcing and offshoring should be self-evident.

# Acknowledgments

Producing a book is like entering a long-term relationship with many partners, contributors, reviewers, editors and publishers. A collaborative project like this can not exist without enormous support and help. Here we acknowledge all those people who we know have directly or indirectly contributed in shaping this book, from stage one to the published form.

We would like to express our warm note of thanks to professor Mehdi Khosrow-Pour, Senior Editor at Idea Group Publishing, who made this project feasible by planting the seed of inspiration.

We wish to thank all the contributors for their excellent contributions and also for providing constructive reviews to enhance the quality of the book. In spite of having tight schedules, authors always responded promptly and enthusiastically to all our requests. However, Professor Ashima Goyal, Professor Luke Ho, Professor Anthony Atkins, Dr. Parthasarathy Banerjee, Professor Dr. Glauco De Vita, Professor Val Samonis and Professor Jurgis Samuleviciuis need a special mention as their help set the benchmark. Thanks are also due to Professor Ruzic and Professor Alev M. Efendioglu for encouraging us to persist with the project until its successful completion.

The journey on this path over the past two years has been very arduous. Dr. Kehal's wife, Harbans Kaur Kehal, continued to encourage him to complete the work. His children, Harjinder Singh Kehal, Parminder Kaur and Harcharan Singh Kehal, his son-in-law, Dr. Kanwaljit Singh, and his daughters-in-law, Amanda and Paramdeep, played crucial roles in maintaining a cheerful and happy family atmosphere. Dr. Kehal is fortunate to be blessed with fine grandchildren — Sahil, Simrin, Sohan, Pia, Rohin, Cameron, Tej and Josh — and all of them enjoy the fruits of more and more developments, improvements, refinements and the worldwide spread and adoption of information communication technologies (ICTs) in the past centuries and the current $21^{st}$ century, as well as they will share in the future benefits of the ICTs with members of the world population in developed and developing countries. Dr. Kehal takes this opportunity to express sincere thanks and gratitude to his family for their moral support, love, patience and kindness throughout the gestation of this project; without their forbearance, understanding and enthusiasm, it would never have reached fruition.

Varinder P. Singh wishes to express his heartfelt gratitude to his family — his parents, for being the source of great inspiration and immense strength for his accomplishments, and his siblings, Manjinder and Teena, who have been a continuous source of encouragement and unstinting support. Varinder also wishes to acknowledge the understanding and patience of his wife, Dr. Kiran Kaur, during his nearly total absence in the last years as he buried his head into this project. Had it not been for his wife and family, this book would have been merely a dream.

We wish to acknowledge the unselfish help and support provided by friends and well wishers, particularly Dr. Tejpal Singh and Dr. G. S. Sidhu.

Finally, we are deeply indebted to the publishing team at Idea Group Inc., particularly to Jan Travers, Senior Director, and Kristin Roth and Renee Davies, Development Editors, who via their timely e-mails prompted us to always meet the deadlines and keep the project on schedule.

## Chapter I

# Development of Outsourcing Theory and Practice: A Taxonomy of Outsourcing Generations

Glauco De Vita
Oxford Brookes University Business School, UK

Catherine L. Wang
Oxford Brookes University Business School, UK

## Abstract

*This chapter tracks the evolution of outsourcing theory and practice in order to develop a taxonomy of outsourcing generations. Our taxonomy identifies three generations, distinguished according to several definitional criteria: key drivers, outsourcing activities, relational features, critical success factors and performance measurement. Case study evidence consistent with the taxonomy proposed provides support to its efficacy as a valuable analytical platform for the study of outsourcing as a dynamic construct.*

## Introduction

Although outsourcing today is bigger than ever before, and is receiving increasing attention in the management literature, it would be erroneous to think of it as a new phenomenon since sub-contacting practices have been part of the corporate landscape since the industrial revolution. It is equally important to emphasise that the theoretical underpinnings of the make-or-buy decision, framed as it is within the "bigger-is-better" versus "small-is-beautiful" debate (Harrison, 1994; Tucci & Sweo, 1996; Lonsdale & Cox, 2000; Lewin & Johnston, 2000), also have a very long history.

The purpose of this chapter is to trace the evolution of outsourcing theory and practice in order to formulate a taxonomy of outsourcing generations. The chapter begins by exploring the roots of outsourcing theory and by framing its development in the context of the "bigger-is-better" versus "small-is-beautiful" debate. This historical review is then used to identify drivers for, and basic features and outcomes of outsourcing. After a critical evaluation of models aimed at guiding the decision of what should be contracted out, we develop a framework of outsourcing generations articulated across five dimensions (key drivers, outsourced activities, relational features, critical success factors, and performance measurement) and offer case study evidence consistent with the taxonomy proposed.

## Bigger-is-Better vs. Small-is-Beautiful

As early as 1885, in his *Principles of Political Economy*, John Stuart Mill was theorising about the benefits of production on a large vis-à-vis small scale. Drawing from the earlier writings of Adam Smith on the advantages to be accrued from specialisation and the division of labour, Mill argued that "the larger the enterprise, the farther the division of labour may be carried. This is one of the principal causes of large manufactories" (Mill, 1885, p. 81). He further contended that "as a general rule, the expenses of a business do not increase by any means proportionally to the quantity of business" (p. 82) and concluded that "the large system of production is inevitable" (p. 83).

It is upon these theoretical antecedents to the theory of economies of scale that the rationale for the "bigger-is-better" corporate paradigm of the post-war period can be positioned. As theory developed, the arguments in support of the high volume strategy of large, hierarchical organisations mounted. In addition to taking advantage of economies of scale, vertical integration offered opportunities to secure suppliers and distribution channels, horizontal integration allowed access to a wider market, and conglomerate/portfolio diversification provided the potential to benefit from risk spreading and economies of scope.

As organisations of the 1960s and 1970s kept growing by expanding their boundaries, the 1980s witnessed a radical u-turn in the consciousness of academics, management gurus and captains of industry alike, with the key to competitiveness suddenly being looked for in "small size and high value" rather than "large size and high volume".

At the theoretical level, the emergence of transaction costs economics (Coase, 1937) had already highlighted diseconomies of scale as an influencing factor on the size and limits of the firm. The phrase "small-is-beautiful", however, was not coined until 1973, when the homonymous book by Schumacher reached the shelves. Schumacher's controversial study of the structure of western economies of the time openly challenged the doctrine of increased specialisation and the giant corporation. Schumacher emphasised the benefits to be gained from the development of a more efficient and sustainable system of "intermediate technology" to be based on smaller scale production units. In his own words:

*...I was brought up on the theory of the 'economics of scale' – that with industries and firms, just as with nations, there is an irresistible trend, dictated by modern technology, for units to become ever bigger. Now, it is quite true that today there are more large organisations and probably also bigger organisations than ever before in history; but the number of small units is also growing [...] and many of these small units are highly prosperous and provide society with most of the really fruitful new developments.* (Schumacher, 1973, p. 48)

Whilst Schumacher's contribution provided the philosophical platform of the "small-is-beautiful" paradigm, it was Willamson (1975, 1985) who, working along Coasean lines, framed the choice between carrying out activities in-house or placing them under market governance as one to be informed by production, transaction and monitoring costs. Hence, according to the theory, these are the factors which determine the internal and external boundaries of the firm.

Further impetus to the paradigm shift towards a smaller and more agile organisation capable of rapidly altering its cost structures was given by Kanter's (1989) influential book *Giants Learn to Dance*, and shortly after by Tom Peters (see Peters & Waterman, 1982). The best selling prophet of the management revolution made a strong case as to why large size should no longer be viewed as a competitive advantage and argued that, in searching for excellence, business leaders should "stick to their knitting" and focus on core competencies.

Core competence thinking reached full-blown, mainstream status in 1990 when, in their famous article, "The Core Competence of the Corporation", Prahalad and Hamel attempted to put the final nail in the coffin of the portfolio perspective of the large corporation as a viable approach to strategy. They argued that the true sources of competitive advantage are to be found in the management's ability to mould corporate-wide technologies and production skills into competencies that empower business to react swiftly to fast changing market conditions.

The theory of core competence was simple and, perhaps because of this, appealing to the corporate world: if we focus on what we do best, we'll get even better at it. In a climate of recessionary pressures, ever greater competition and underperformance, business leaders paid attention to the new message and this led to a boom of down-scoping, downsizing and outsourcing activities, all aimed at shaping a smaller, "leaner and meaner", more flexible organisation. In addition to cost reductions, the new wisdom called for management's undivided attention on building core competencies, anything distracting from this focus to be seen as the perfect candidate for outsourcing.

## Defining Features, Drivers and Outcomes

The investigation of the development of the outsourcing phenomenon in the context of the "bigger-is-better" versus "small-is-beautiful" debate, allows us to gain a deeper insight into both the defining features of, and drivers for, outsourcing.

At its broadest, outsourcing can be defined as a contractual agreement that entails the procurement of goods and/or services from an external provider. Drawing from our earlier discussion, four additional basic features can be outlined:

- Prior to being sourced from a local (domestic outsourcing) or foreign (offshoring) enterprise, the activity was being carried out in-house;
- Once outsourced, control over the activity resides with the external provider;
- The outsourcing relationship is bound to be characterised by asymmetry of size and power (unequal partnership between a large organisation contracting out an activity to a smaller, specialised provider);
- The activity outsourced to a more efficient provider must be non-core.

The latter feature is of primary importance for a thorough understanding of the rationale underpinning the outsourcing decision but it is also the most controversial. First, although the authors' review of the development of outsourcing has revealed that the need to increase organisational competitiveness by reducing costs and the new strategic focus on core competencies are inextricably linked, previous literature has, by and large, tended to treat cost reductions and strategic shift as distinct drivers (see Winkleman, Dole, Pinkard, & Molloy, 1993; Kakabadse & Kakabadse, 2000; etc.). This, in turn, has meant that the question of the extent to which each of them is singularly both necessary and sufficient to justify the outsourcing choice has never been satisfactorily squared. Second, ambiguity still reigns on how to establish what, and what not, should be seen as core. Is it what we do best? Is it what creates value? Or is it related to the strategic importance of the activity in relation to changing industry requirements?

It should also be kept in mind that concomitant to the need for cost reductions and greater focus, environmental conditions played a significant role in the acceleration of the use of outsourcing over the last two decades. In addition to the growth in new technologies (McLellan & Marcolin, 1994) and the intensification of competitive pressures, both locally and globally (Miles & Snow, 1986), we wish to draw attention to the parallel trends of privatisation, increased product diversification and industry consolidation. By altering the contestability and concentration of industries, these trends have *de facto* made the oligopoly the predominant market structure. The recognition of the interdependence governing the actions and reactions of competitors, which incidentally represents the defining feature of an oligopoly, has in turn led to imitative defensive strategies that have contributed to the proliferation of outsourcing practices.

But how successful has outsourcing really been? That is, to what extent have the smaller and allegedly more flexible organisations realised the expected benefits of cost reductions, greater flexibility, access to specialised knowledge and superior quality? The evidence available is still insufficient to draw conclusive inferences from which to discern a conventional wisdom. But what can be said with a certain degree of confidence is that although outsourcing has helped to reduce increasing investment requirements in rapidly developing new technologies (Carlson, 1989; Harrison, 1994; Kliem, 1999; Quinn, 1999; etc.) most of the other benefits have been highly overestimated. As early as 1993, research by the PA Consulting Group reported that almost 50% of firms had problems of overdependence on their external provider and 40% suffered from cost escalation and lack of supplier flexibility. These findings were corroborated by the PA Consulting Group (1996) follow up survey of one thousand managers worldwide. The survey revealed that mediocre outcomes were widespread and real failure not uncommon. Only 5% of respondents felt that outsourcing had delivered the high gains hoped for. More recently, Jennings' (2002) review of the benefits and problems of outsourcing led him to conclude that "failure to achieve the anticipated cost improvements is a frequently occurring aspect of outsourcing" (p. 26) and that "in the absence of fully developed service level monitoring the development of quality may on occasion be illusory" (p. 27). The latter problem often forces large organisations to regain control of the activity and redevelop it in-house. As reported in a survey by the Facility Management Association (cited in Elliott, 1995) "better quality control" is the primary reason for bringing back activities that had been outsourced.

A different kind of evidence (see, for example, Ruigrok, Pettigrew, Peck, & Whittington, 1999) also indicates that the "bigger-is-better" paradigm was given its last rights far too prematurely. Indeed, although during the 1980s and 1990s poorly performing conglomerates did indeed undergo a painful restructuring process based on refocusing and rationalising their overly diversified portfolios, as suggested by Whittington, Mayer, and Curto (1999), they are still alive and in a good state of health.

## What Should be Outsourced? A Critical Review of Outsourcing Models

The previous discussion unveiled two definitional grey areas of outsourcing: (i) the question of the individual sufficiency of the cost reduction and strategic focus motivations; and (ii) the lack of clarity over what makes an activity 'core'. Given these problems, it is not surprising that many organisations have faced serious difficulties in deciding what, and what not, to outsource.

These ambiguities have also given rise to a plethora of often contradictory models intended to guide the make-or-buy decision. These frameworks can be broadly classified into three groups: matrix-type, factor-based and process-based models.

Matrix-type models are visually powerful and easy to apply but their scope of analysis is inevitably constrained by the two-dimensional structure of tools of this nature. One such model is the "make-buy-ally" (m-b-a) matrix, developed by Bowman and Faulkner (1997). The vertical axis of the m-b-a matrix measures dimensions (low, medium and high) of the strategic significance of an activity to the competitive success of the organisation while the horizontal axis measures the relative competence of the organisation at carrying out that activity vis-à-vis the market leader along the same dimensions. As far as outsourcing is concerned, the model leads to the conclusion that if an activity is perceived to be of low strategic importance, irrespective of how proficient the organisation is at carrying it out in-house, that activity should be contracted out. By making the measurement of efficiency and effectiveness of the organisation's performance in that activity in relation to competitors irrelevant, the m-b-a matrix places the full-weight of the outsourcing decision upon the assessment of the strategic significance of the activity in question. This not only runs counter to transaction cost theory, it also reduces the operational value of the schema to one which assumes that: (i) it is possible to accurately measure strategic significance; and (ii) an activity of currently low strategic importance will not migrate up the vertical axis on the matrix; that is, that today's hygiene factors do not hold tomorrow's key to competitive advantage.

Factor-based models are more eclectic in nature. They attempt to offer a map of all the factors (including risk, technology and supply environment) that ought to be taken into consideration when deciding whether or not to outsource. Examples of such models can be found in Venkatesan (1992), Quinn and Hilmer (1994), McIvor, Mulvenna, and Humphreys (1997) and Jennings (1997, 2002). These and other similar frameworks have undoubtedly enriched our understanding of the role of contextual issues in informing the outsourcing decision. They have also highlighted the importance of recognising the dynamic nature of competitive markets, an approach that calls for "anticipating how those markets may change in the longer-term as a result of product and supply market evolution and technological change" (Jennings, 2002, p. 31). The generality and complexity of factor-based models, however, also represent their main limitation in that such models do not specify the relative importance of the many factors examined, hence failing to provide clear guidelines on how organisations ought to carry out the process of determining what to outsource.

Process-based models aim to fill this gap and, because of this, are more pragmatic in nature. Examples include the four-stage process developed by Probert (1996) and, more recently, the one developed by McIvor (2000). The latter framework is informed by several perspectives (value chain, core competence thinking, supply side influences) and articulated along four sequential stages of decision-making: (i) initial identification of core and non-core activities; (ii) evaluation of relevant value chain activities for benchmarking purposes; (iii) total cost analysis; (iv) relationship analysis for assessing the compatibility of potential suppliers. Evidently, the first stage of this process hinges upon a definition of core activities, which are described as "critical skills that are central to its overall strategy ..[and].. enable a company to differentiate itself from its competitors in the way in which it serves its customers" (McIvor, 2000, p. 30). By McIvor's own admission, however, the model assumes that "in general, all non-core activities will be outsourced" (p. 30), taking us back to the reductionist connotation of the matrix-type models reviewed initially. Interestingly though, the model also introduces the idea that the organisation may wish to consider outsourcing a critical, or core, activity in which it has no competitive advantage. Under this scenario, the fourth stage of McIvor's process guides the organisation toward the development of a partnership-type relationship with the external provider.

## A Taxonomy of Outsourcing Generations

The difficulties encountered thus far in our search for a consensus on the drivers of outsourcing, its defining features, and what should be contracted out, can be explained, at least in part, by the fact that outsourcing practice itself has evolved over time. The changing nature of outsourcing has therefore made the analysis of this moving target rather difficult and often imprecise.

Although the existing literature has already pointed to a shift in the nature of outsourcing, from the procurement of support activities to that of more critical functions, to the authors' knowledge, no formal taxonomy of different waves of outsourcing has yet been developed. In the sub-sections that follow we wish to fill this gap by proposing a detailed taxonomy of outsourcing generations that can help us to shed some light on the ambiguities and contradictions that have characterised the debate on the outsourcing phenomenon.

### *First Generation*

First generation outsourcing refers to contractual arrangements confined to the procurement of non-core competences. Primarily driven by cost or headcount reduction, firms outsource simple back-room functions or peripheral activities, such as payroll processing, security, cleaning, catering and so forth, to a more efficient service provider. The case of Rank Xerox (see below) is the most emblematic example to illustrate facilities management outsourcing, which is why it is often used in the literature (see Houston & Youngs, 1996; Lonsdale & Cox, 2000).

*In 1994 Rank Xerox outsourced the facilities management at its UK technical centre to CBX Ltd. The outsourcing decision was mainly driven by cost saving motivations although improvement in the quality of the workplace was also cited as an objective. The contract was signed for five years, with CBX expected to provide a range of services including planned maintenance, estate management, security and catering. Xerox paid CBX a flat management fee. CBX was responsible for reducing the facilities cost at the centre, for which they received incentives from Xerox, but passed the savings back to Xerox. Xerox assessed the quality of services, and the whole team at CBX was directly responsible to Xerox's business operations manager (single point of contact). In terms of outcomes, CBX reported that the cost savings in the various services varied from 5% to 62%.*

The case of Rank Xerox captures the traditional basic features of outsourcing that were outlined earlier in the chapter:

- Outsourced activities are non-core, and were carried out in-house prior to being outsourced;
- The supplier takes over control of the outsourced activities, and little integration is required — only a single point of responsibility is maintained;
- The two organisations are asymmetric in terms of size and power, leaning favourably towards the outsourcing firm;
- Performance is measured by the extent of cost savings stemming from the outsourced activities.

Despite the positive outcome of the Xerox case, first generation outsourcing is not problem-free: the lack of in-depth understanding of the outsourced activities and the inflexibility of contract terms tend to severely hinder the attainment of cost-cutting objectives. Many outsourcing firms suffer from unbearable hidden costs. Clear stipulation of contract terms and the inclusion of clauses that allow for fine-tuning exercises seem to be essential conditions for achieving the expected benefits.

## *Second Generation*

Since the mid 1980s, a new form of outsourcing practice emerged: firms started to outsource their near-core activities. Lonsdale and Cox (2000) refer to near-core activities as primary supply chain activities. In the automotive manufacturing industry, rapid changes in consumer preferences, shortened product life cycles and the high rate of technical obsolescence have forced firms to reduce costs, improve quality and shorten development time (Fine, 1998). To fully implement new product strategies firms, such as Toyota and Chrysler, outsource new product development, at least in part, to their suppliers (Dutton, 1992; Quinn & Hilmer, 1994).

Second generation outsourcing is also distinguished by a change in the view of how services can be supplied to customers, a change identifiable in the movement to offshoring of services. While in the manufacturing sector it has always been relatively easy to decompose the various processes of production and locate them around the world so as to take full advantage of lower costs, specialist skills and technical know-how, most services cannot be fragmented in this way because they require that production and consumption be co-located. However, the developments in information technology (IT) that have taken place in the last two decades have significantly increased the speed and minimised the cost of communication and thereby, in many cases, reduced the need for co-location between consumers and producers of services. The technical feasibility of offshoring means that some areas of the service sector which had previously been considered non-tradable have now started to face intense international competition. Activities such as data processing and analysis, software design and research and development (R&D) can now, in most instances, be performed the other side of the globe and then exported, often simultaneously, worldwide. This transformation has been further augmented by the birth of new sectors of economic activity. For example, the emergence of the biotech sector, marked by the breakthroughs of genetic engineering and human genomics, has transformed the traditional pharmaceutical industry. Large pharmaceutical companies, such as GlaxoSmithKline, Pfizer and Bayer, now commonly outsource part of their R&D to small, specialist biotech companies (Mc Namara, 2000).

Second generation outsourcing also reflects the industry response to resource limitations in addition to cost saving. It is notable that the cost of remaining up to date in a multitude of supply chain activities has become increasingly expensive. Furthermore, resource limitations have constrained firms from fully developing their competences, particularly in the area where rapid innovation is a key feature (Brown & Eisenhardt, 1995; Kurokawa, 1997; Lowe & Taylor, 1998). To fulfil their developmental needs, firms need to tap into external resources.

Second generation outsourcing is also characterised by some transformation in the area of IT outsourcing. IT was originally considered as a supporting activity, something "thrown over a wall", but its strategic importance has grown over time and it is now generally regarded as a near-core competence. For example, on September 15, 2004, J. P. Morgan Chase & Co., the U.S.'s second-largest bank, announced that it was terminating a seven-year, $5 billion technology-outsourcing deal with IBM, to bring this operation in-house (Hamm, 2004). The underlying rationale was that technology, by boosting reliability and efficiency, was now seen as a strategic activity, crucial to improving services. As illustrated in the case reported below, even for companies that are still true believers in outsourcing, such as General Motors Corp., the integration of IT outsourcing activities with the internal business processes has been addressed as a top priority.

*General Motors Corp. (GM) has radically changed how it deals with its former supplier, EDS, which once handled most of GM's IT needs. To reduce its reliance on EDS and foster greater competition, GM has handed off about a third of its outsourcing to other contractors, such as Accenture. GM's new providers cannot work with another auto company on a similar project, but may use the same IT management processes with any other companies. GM issues standardized contracts with standardized terms and conditions for all suppliers, and evaluates its suppliers and how they work collaboratively on a regular basis. To streamline outsourcing processes, GM ensures that its 13 top tech-services providers adopt the same processes for running computers, software, and networks. Using a matrix management structure, IT is tied to GM's daily business operations: each IT leader reports to the Chief Information Officer (CIO), Ralph Szygenda, as well as to a president of a business unit or the business leader for processes such as manufacturing or product development. Ralph Szygenda leads 2,000 techies who craft the overall strategy, select technologies, and manage its suppliers' managers. IT performance objectives go far beyond just IT: all IT investments are linked to business end goals, such as innovative products, quality, productivity and profitability.* (Accenture, 2004)

The GM case allows us to highlight some distinctive features attributable to second generation outsourcing:

- Outsourced activities are near-core competences and have strategic importance. Cost effectiveness is still a concern, but the driver for outsourcing is shifting towards accessing external expertise or complementary resources and capabilities;
- Enhanced integration is demonstrated. Under most circumstances, the outsourcing and outsourced partners work closely to achieve synergy between their resources and capabilities;
- Outsourcing organisations seek more than one partner, in search of strategic compatibility and in favour of more flexible cooperative relationships, with emphasis weighed towards one outsourcing partner;
- Necessary resources are maintained in the outsourcing firm to manage the outsourced activities. Mutual control over outsourced activities is evidenced;
- A certain level of flexibility is built into outsourcing contracts, allowing for technological evolution and capital contribution;
- Performance measurement shifts from cost saving only to overall business performance, that is, revenue growth, profitability and so forth.

The problems associated with second generation outsourcing are primarily two-fold: First, the standardisation of outsourcing contracts and technological platforms is essential in streamlining the business processes interplayed by multi-suppliers, as demonstrated by the case of GM. Second, outsourcing near-core activities, such as new product development, may place the outsourcing firm in danger of losing its competitive edge due to leakage of technological know-how.

## *Third Generation*

Third generation outsourcing appears to be driven by heated competition in industries where the technological platform — core proprietary elements — is standardised, but novel technological features emerge constantly and rapidly. The competitive edge in such industries lies in firms' ability to respond quickly to customer demand and satisfy, simultaneously, the multiple industry requirements of efficiency, innovation and adaptation. Firms must be capable of undercutting existing competitors, and of providing innovative products or services as well as customised solutions to customers. This has caused fundamental changes in some industries, such as personal computer (PC) making, fashion and so forth, where flexibility and responsiveness have become increasingly important. The demand on time-based competition challenges the traditional argument that 'bigger is better' and that economies of scale are the sole source of competitive advantage. While in the 1980s firms' imperative was to disaggregate its value chains, focus on value-adding activities and outsource the rest to specialised suppliers, entering the 1990s, the advancement of IT prompted organisations to reconsider the activities in their value chain and outsource most, if not all, value chain activities. As a result, many firms have become virtual in terms of both physical location and ownership (Lawton & Michaels, 2001).

A most astonishing phenomenon is that firms have started to outsource activities that are traditionally viewed as core competences. This phenomenon is exemplified by firms such as Cisco Systems, Amazon, and Dell, which have outsourced most of the primary activities in their supply chains. Essentially, firms operate virtual value chains, with their suppliers now seen as partners integrated in their value-adding activities.

In recent years, we have also witnessed the birth of smaller firms in which all functions are outsourced from day one, and in which only the soul of the business is kept in-house (Heywood, 2001). The fashion accessories firm, Topsy Tail, is a case in point. The firm, with revenues of U.S. $80 million, has only three employees and never touches its products through the entire supply chain (Rahman & Bhattachryya, 2002). Outsourcing and virtual integration are the firm's only core competences — the soul of Topsy Tail. It is, of course, early days for making judgements on the rights and wrongs of starting a business on these premises. These new trends, however, prompt serious questions: Has outsourcing gone too far? Can firms really outsource their core competences?

Dynamic capability, the evolutionary version of the resource-based view, provides a theoretical lens for such concerns. The resource-based view argues that at the heart of the firm's competitive advantage is a bundle of firm-specific assets and distinctive capabilities, which effectively deploy these assets, rather than a particular product-market combination chosen for its deployment (Wernerfelt, 1984; Coyne, 1986; Day & Wensley, 1988; Dierickx & Cool, 1989). A firm's core competences — valuable, rare, inimitable and non-substitutable resources and capabilities — and its unique ability to transform such resource advantage to marketplace advantage are sources of competitive advantage (Mahoney & Pandian, 1992; Collis & Montgomery, 1995).

Dynamic capability, built on the above propositions, further emphasises that resources and capabilities are becoming obsolete at an accelerated rate in the competitive marketplace, and firms must constantly reconfigure, renew, upgrade and re-create resources and capabilities (Teece, Pisano & Schuen, 1997; Eisenhardt & Martin, 2000). This indicates that core competences are not obsolete in fast-moving industries, but, with the rapid technological changes, the concept of core competences returns with renewed vigour in the era of outsourcing. Firms need to re-evaluate and re-focus their core competences in the new business context. R&D was once viewed as the lifeblood of pharmaceutical companies, but is now commonly being outsourced, at least in part, to small, specialist firms. Six sigma manufacturing, once developed as a core competence in large companies like HP and Motorola, is now fully adopted by smaller firms. By way of contrast, IT was traditionally considered as a supporting function of firms' operations, and still is, in many firms today. However, the fashion retailer Zara, and the PC maker Dell, have integrated IT as a core competence with a resulting transformation in their business processes.

*Founded in 1984, Dell Inc. has a singular focus on the customer. Dell aims to provide customers with superb value, high quality, relevant technology, customised systems, superior service and support as well as products and services that are easy to buy and use. Dell adopts 'the direct business model' (i.e., direct sales and direct supplier relationships) to provide a more efficient path to the customer, a single point of accountability, a built-to-order system, low-cost and standards-based technology (Dell Inc., 2004). Underlying the direct model and customer focus are Dell's core competences in IT, outsourcing and virtual integration, which together have transformed its business processes. Dell uses IT to effectively integrate business operations — from customer configuration systems to sales and technical support — and to manage its relationships with customers and suppliers (Kraemer et al., 2000). Dell provides an unparalleled information flow from its customers to its suppliers. By fostering IT as a core competence, Dell has achieved real-time, virtual integration. According to Michael Dell, 'virtual integration means you basically stitch together a business with partners that are treated as if they're inside the company. You're sharing information in a real-time fashion' (Magretta, 1998, p. 75). Michael Dell also gave a few tips on outsourcing: (1) maintaining a close relationship with as few supplier partners as possible and keeping them only as long as they are technical and quality leaders; (2) communicating inventory levels and replenishment needs to supplier partners, in real time; and (3) ordering from suppliers only when demand from customers is received.* (Magretta, 1998)

Dell responded to the industry challenge by adopting the direct business model, which in turn accelerated the pace of change in the industry. The velocity of change in the industry has accelerated to the point where only the most flexible organisational structure is able to survive. This is suggestive of a new competitive platform which calls for the need to break away from the restriction of spatial boundaries, and build a new perceptual framework bounded by trust-based, flexible and cooperative relationships. Traditional and hierarchical boundaries are removed to facilitate the sharing of information and knowledge within the firm, and between the firm and its customers and suppliers. Against this backdrop, Dell's experience epitomises essential characteristics of what we see as third generation outsourcing, where outsourcing itself becomes a core competence:

- The industry features standards-based technology, where flexible and responsive customer solutions provide value-added. What makes outsourcing possible is the PC's open architecture — standardised, modular production, and the availability of state-of-the-art suppliers in the industry;
- Virtual integration. The outsourcing firm expands its boundaries, sharing real-time information with closely linked, and focused (outsourced) partners, giving rise to a virtual value chain;
- The standardisation of outsourcing processes provides a common platform for the flexible integration of partners throughout the virtual value chain;
- The outsourcing firm maintains central control of business operations whilst allowing decentralisation of business processes;
- Outsourcing transforms business processes and serves to achieve overall organisational objectives.

*Table 1. A taxonomy of outsourcing generations*

| | **First generation** | **Second generation** | **Third generation** |
|---|---|---|---|
| **Key drivers** | - Efficiency, cost-saving. | - Efficiency;<br>- Focus on core competences;<br>- Sourcing complementary capabilities. | - Efficiency, innovation and adaptation;<br>- Flexible solutions for customers;<br>- Business process transformation. |
| **Outsourced activities** | Peripheral activities. | Near-core activities. | Traditionally defined core activities. |
| **Relational features** | - Little integration;<br>- Single supplier;<br>- Asymmetry of size and power favours the outsourcing firm;<br>- Detachment of the outsourced activities from the outsourcing firm. Only a single point of responsibility is maintained between the outsourcing firm and the supplier. | - Enhanced integration;<br>- Asymmetry of size and power favours the outsourcing firm;<br>- More than one outsourced partner, but still weighed towards one partner;<br>- Necessary resources are maintained in the outsourcing firm to manage the relationship with external providers. | - Virtual integration;<br>- Asymmetry is indeterminate;<br>- Establishing close relationships with several, but focused partners;<br>- The outsourcing firm expands its boundaries, sharing real-time information with outsourcing partners to create a virtual value chain;<br>- Outsourcing as a core competence. |
| **Critical success factors** | - The supplier is more efficient than the outsourcing firm;<br>- Heavy reliance on choosing the right partner in the first place;<br>- Identification of hidden costs, and clear stipulation of cost structure in the original contract. | - Built-in flexibility of contracts allowing for technological evolution and capital contribution;<br>- Standardisation of contracts and technological platforms;<br>- Protection of knowledge from leakage in the outsourcing process. | - Flexible and responsive customer solutions to provide value-added;<br>- Clear definition of core competences;<br>- Standardisation of outsourcing processes;<br>- The outsourcing firm maintains central control of business operations, whilst allowing decentralisation of business processes. |
| **Performance measurement** | Cost saving. | The impact of outsourcing on overall business performance. | Business process transformation and the achievement of overall objectives. |

# Conclusions

The chapter began by investigating the development of outsourcing theory in the context of the "bigger-is-better" versus "small-is-beautiful" debate. This historical review guided the identification of drivers for, and basic features and outcomes of outsourcing. It also helped us to unveil some important grey areas in the study of the outsourcing phenomenon.

Our critical evaluation of the theoretical frameworks aimed at informing the outsourcing decision has also revealed that the unresolved ambiguities and contradictions over the why and how of outsourcing have hindered the ability of these models to provide clear and consistent guidelines on how firms can determine what, and under what conditions, to outsource.

In this chapter we have argued that these theoretical inadequacies are mostly due to the inevitable difficulties associated with the analysis of what we see as a phenomenon in motion, since the very nature of outsourcing has kept changing over time. It seems to us that a coherent analysis of outsourcing requires the recognition that outsourcing practice itself has evolved, redefining itself, and its role, in the context of increasingly competitive markets marked by ever greater pressures of globalisation and technological development.

Our taxonomy (see Table 1 for a full summary) classifies the evolution of outsourcing into three generations, distinguished according to several definitional criteria: key drivers, outsourced activities, relational features, critical success factors, and performance measurement. Case study evidence consistent with the taxonomy proposed provides support to its efficacy as a valuable analytical platform for the study of outsourcing as a dynamic construct.

# References

Accenture. (2004). Why IT means business at General Motors. *Outlook 2004*, 3.

Bowman, C., & Faulkner, D. (1997). *Competitive and corporate strategy*. London: Irwin.

Brown, S. L., & Eisenhardt, K. M. (1995). Product development: Past research, present findings, and future directions. *Academy of Management Review*, *20*, 343-378.

Carlson, B. (1989). Flexibility and the theory of the firm. *International Journal of Industrial Organisation*, *7*, 179-203.

Coase, R. (1937). The nature of the firm. *Economica*, *4*, 386-405.

Collis, D., & Montgomery, C. (1995). Competing on resources: Strategy in the 1990s. *Harvard Business Review*, *73*, 118-128.

Coyne, K. (1986). Sustainable competitive advantage: What it is, what it isn't. *Business Horizons*, *29*, 54-61.

Day, G. S., & Wensley, R. (1988). Assessing advantage: A framework for diagnosing competitive superiority. *Journal of Marketing*, *52*, 1-20.

Dell Inc. (2004). *About Dell*. Retrieved December 10, 2004, from http://www.dell.com

Dierickx, I., & Cool, K. (1989). Asset stock accumulation and sustainability of competitive advantage. *Management Science*, *35*, 1504-1511.

Dutton, B. (1992). U.S. car companies: Changing fast enough? *Manufacturing Systems*, *10*, 12-13.

Eisenhardt, K. M., & Martin, J. A. (2000). Dynamic capabilities: What are they? *Strategic Management Journal*, *21*, 1105-1121.

Elliott, V. (1995). Outsourcing without risk. *Journal of Property Management*, January-February, 40-41.

Fine, C. H. (1998). *Clockspeed: Winning industry control in the age of temporary advantage*. Boston: Perseus Books Group.

Hamm, S. (2004). Is outsourcing on the outs? *Business Week*, October 4.

Harrison, B. T. (1994). *Lean and mean: The changing landscape of corporate power in the age of flexibility*. New York: Basic Books.

Heywood, J. B. (2001). *The outsourcing dilemma: The search for competitiveness*. London: Pearson Education.

Houston, A., & Youngs, G. (1996). Pro-active outsourcing: A strategic partnership: Rank Xerox technical centre. *Facilities*, *14*, 40-47.

Jennings, D. (1997). Strategic guidelines for outsourcing decisions. *The Journal of Strategic Change*, *6*, 85-96.

Jennings, D. (2002). Strategic sourcing: benefits, problems and a contextual model. *Management Decision*, *40*, 26-34.

Kakabadse, N., & Kakabadse, A. (2000). Critical review – Outsourcing: A paradigm shift. *The Journal of Management Development*, *19*, 670-728.

Kanter, R. (1989). *When giants learn to dance*. New York: Simon and Schuster.

Kliem, R. L. (1999). Managing the risks of outsourcing agreements. *Information Systems Management*, Summer, 91-93.

Kraemer, K. L., Dedrick, J., & Yamashiro, S. (2000). Refining and extending the business model with information technology: Dell Computer Corporation. *The Information Society*, *16*, 5-21.

Kurokawa, S. (1997). Make-or-buy decisions in R&D: Small technology based firms in the United States and Japan. *IEEE Transactions on Engineering Management*, *44*, 124-134.

Lawton, T. C., & Michaels, K. P. (2001). Advancing to the virtual value chain: Learning from the Dell model. *The Irish Journal of Management*, *22*, 91-112.

Lewin, J. E., & Johnston, W. J. (2000). The impact of downsizing and restructuring on organisational competitiveness. *CR*, *10*, 45-55.

Lonsdale, C., & Cox, A. (2000). The historical development of outsourcing: The latest fad? *Industrial Management & Data Systems*, *100*, 444-450.

Lowe, J., & Taylor, P. (1998). R&D and technology purchase through license agreements: Complementary strategies and complementary assets. *R&D Management*, *28*, 263-278.

Magretta, J. (1998). The power of virtual integration: An interview with Dell Computer's Michael Dell. *Harvard Business Review*, *76*, 72-83.

Mahoney, J. T., & Pandian, J. R. (1992). The resource-based view within the conversation of strategic management. *Strategic Management Journal*, *13*, 363-380.

McNamara, P. (2000). *Biotechnology industry note: Strategy and performance of some UK biotech independents 1995-1997*. European Case Clearing House Case Study No. 300-071-6.

McIvor, R. T. (2000). A practical framework for understanding the outsourcing process. *Supply Chain Management: An International Journal*, *5*, 22-36.

McIvor, R. T., Mulvenna, M. D., & Humphreys, P. K. (1997). A hybrid knowledge-based system for strategic purchasing. *Expert Systems with Applications*, *12*, 497-512.

McLellan, K., & Marcolin, B. (1994). Information technology outsourcing. *Business Quarterly*, *59*, 95-104.

Miles, R. E., & Snow, C. C. (1986). Network organisations, new concepts and new forms. *California Management Review*, *28*, 62-73.

Mill, J. S. (1885). *Principles of political economy: With some applications to social philosophy*. London: Longmans, Green and Co.

PA Consulting Group. (1993). *IT outsourcing survey*. London: PAGC.

PA Consulting Group. (1996). *Riding the wave of channel substitution: International strategic sourcing survey*. London: PAGC.

Peters, T., & Waterman, R. (1982). *In search of excellence*. New York: Harper & Row.

Prahalad, C. V., & Hamel, G. (1990). The core competence of the corporation. *Harvard Business Review*, May-June, 79-91.

Probert, D. R. (1996). The practical development of a make or buy strategy: The issue of process positioning. *Integrated Manufacturing Systems*, *7*, 44-51.

Quinn, J. B. (1999). Strategic outsourcing: Leveraging knowledge capabilities. *Sloan Management Review*, *40*, 9-22.

Quinn, J. B., & Hilmer, F. G. (1994). Strategic outsourcing. *Sloan Management Review*, *35*, 43-54.

Rahman, Z., & Bhattachryya, S. K. (2002). Virtual organisation: A stratagem. *Singapore Management Review*, *24*, 29-45.

Ruigrok, W., Pettigrew, A., Peck, S., & Whittington, R. (1999). Corporate restructuring and new forms of organising: Evidence from Europe. *Management International Review*, *39*, 41-64.

Schumacher, E. F. (1973). *Small is beautiful: A study of economics as if people mattered.* London: Vintage.

Teece, D. J., Pisano, G., & Schuen, A. (1997). Dynamic capabilities and strategic management. *Strategic Management Journal*, *18*, 509-533.

Tucci, J., & Sweo, R. (1996). Strategic groups: Firm structure, industry diversification, and performance determinants. *American Business Review*, *14*, 73-79.

Venkatesan, R. (1992). Strategic sourcing: To make or not to make. *Harvard Business Review*, *70*, 98-107.

Wernerfelt, B. (1984). A resource-based view of the firm. *Strategic Management Journal*, *5*, 795-815.

Whittington, R., Mayer, M., & Curto, F. (1999). Chandlerism in post-war Europe: Strategic and structural change in post-war Europe, 1950-1993. *Industrial and Corporate Change*, *8*, 519-551.

Williamson, O. E. (1975). *Markets and hierarchies*. New York: Free Press.

Williamson, O. E. (1985). *The economic institutions of capitalism*. New York: Free Press.

Winkleman, M., Dole, D., Pinkard, L., & Molloy, J. (1993). The outsourcing source book. *Journal of Business Strategy*, *14*, 52-56.

# Chapter II

# Making Sense of the Sourcing and Shoring Maze: Various Outsourcing and Offshoring Alternatives

Subrata Chakrabarty
Texas A&M University, USA

## Abstract

*Many terminologies have grown out of the outsourcing and offshoring bandwagon. While the corporate world continues to experience these phenomena, the academic world continues to research the same. An attempt has been made to give an overview of the various outsourcing and offshoring alternatives. We first discuss the basic sourcing strategies (insourcing and outsourcing) and the shoring strategies (onshoring and offshoring). We then move deep and wide into the maze and unravel the multiple alternatives that businesses exercise in order to get the best deal for their information system (IS) needs. Approximately 50 terminologies that are related to this growing maze have been discussed. The literature was scanned for various sourcing alternatives and terminologies. The purpose of this chapter is to compile and elucidate the various facets of domestic and global sourcing of IS needs. The reader will gain holistic perspective of a phenomenon that is continuously changing the way business is carried out globally.*

# Introduction

"*Outsourcing*" and "*offshoring*" are two of the media-friendly terms being bandied about in recent times. However, there are many other aspects to the phenomenon. These terminologies are often confused and misunderstood.

The notion that jobs move out of some economically rich countries due to "*outsourcing*" may not be terminologically correct. For example, in "*onshore-outsourcing*" (or "*domestic-outsourcing*") the jobs have simply been outsourced to a vendor in the same country. The terminologically correct notion is that jobs move out from one country to another country due to "*offshoring.*"

Similarly when programmers think that "*offshoring*" of software development implies that their code will be written by people of a different company, they may not be terminologically correct. In "*offshore-insourcing*" (or "*global-insourcing*"), the task is still performed by the same company, though in a different land.

In brief, work is "*outsourced to vendors*" and "*offshored to another country.*" *Outsourcing* of work is *across organizational borders*, while *offshoring* of work is *across geographical borders.*

A large number of terminologies are already being used, and as the business world explores and experiences new information system (IS) sourcing alternatives, newer terminologies will be coined, and existing terminologies may be subjected to multiple interpretations. This chapter will attempt to elucidate many the existing terminologies.

We broadly define a *client* as anyone in need of services. For the purposes of maintaining clarity, the terms "*client*", "*customer*" and "*buyer*" have been treated synonymously to imply a firm (or even an individual) that is seeking services, from either internal service providers (like the client's own internal department, or a subsidiary) or from external service providers (a vendor/supplier ). The client *owns* any "*client-entity*" such as the client's internal IS department or a subsidiary. In the same vein, the terms "*vendor,*" "*supplier,*" "*third party*", and external "*consultant*" have been treated synonymously to imply an "*external service provider*" or a *non-client entity* whose business is to provide services to the client.

In this chapter, the term "*information system*" (IS) has been assumed to broadly refer to not just *information technology* (IT), but also various types of information systems whose functioning has been influenced by use of IT (e.g., financial, accounting, health care, educational, human resource, customer service, logistics, management and other information systems). This has been done as the concepts in this chapter can be applied to a wide variety of industries and services that gather, process, store, transmit, display, disseminate, and act on information. For example, the term *IS* department when understood in the context of this chapter, can be considered as *any* department that engages in collecting, processing, editing, storing, transmitting and supplying data or information relating to a certain area of application.

# The Basic "Sourcing" Strategies

*Insourcing* and *outsourcing* are the two basic sourcing strategies. Simplistically, it is the choice between either "*walking the path alone*" or "*building on acquaintances along the way*" such that a firm's business interests are best served.

## Insourcing

- *The service provider is a client entity*

Often organizations have their own IS departments or IS subsidiaries from where they *insource* their IS needs. The responsibility and delegation of tasks involved the firm's IS needs are handled internally (*in-house*). Hence, when the service provider to the client is a *client-entity* such as a *subsidiary* or the *internal IS department*, it is known as *insourcing.*

Insourcing has also been interpreted as being part of a *multi-sourcing continuum* having two possible insourcing strategies: (a) the *"OK as is"* strategy where the status quo of insourcing IS activities is considered the best sourcing strategy, and (b) the *"fix and keep in-house"* strategy where insourcing is again considered the best strategy but the internal IS department needs to adopt better practices to become more efficient and effective (Wibbelsman & Maiero, 1994, as cited in Dibbern, Goles, Hirschheim & Jayatilaka, 2004, p. 11).

## Outsourcing

- *The service provider is a non-client entity*

Due to various factors, organizations (clients) often need to *outsource* work to external entities. Hence, when the service provider is a non-client entity, such as a vendor/supplier it is known as *outsourcing. Outsourcing* has been defined in many interesting ways in the literature, which are quoted below, further aid our understanding:

*Outsourcing means selectively turning over to a vendor some or all of the IS functions, ranging from simple data entry to software development and maintenance, data centre operations and full system integration.* (Apte, Sobol, Hanaoka, Shimada, Saarinen, Salmela & Vepsalainen, 1997, p. 289)

*Outsourcing is the contracting of various information systems' sub-functions by user firms to outside information systems vendors.* (Chaudhury, Nam & Rao, 1995, p. 131)

*...we define broadly outsourcing of IS functions as: the organizational decision to turn over part or all of an organization's IS functions to external service provider(s) in order for an organization to be able to achieve its goals.* (Cheon, Grover & Teng, 1995, p. 209)

*Information systems (IS) outsourcing is an increasingly common business practice in which a company contracts all or part of its information systems operations to one or more outside information service suppliers.* (Hu, Saunders & Gebelt, 1997, p. 288)

*The term 'outsourcing', although not specific to IS in that it reflects the use of external agents to perform one or more organizational activities (e.g., purchasing of a good or service), is now in vogue in the IS domain and applies to everything from use of contract programmers to third party facilities management.* (Lacity & Hirschheim, 1993b, p. 2)

*IS outsourcing refers to the third party management of IS assets, people, and or activities required to meet pre-specified performance levels.* (Lacity & Hirschheim, 1995, p. 4)

*We define IT outsourcing as the significant contribution by external vendors in the physical and/or human resources associated with the entire or specific components of the IT infrastructure in the user organization.* (Loh & Venkatraman, 1992, p. 9)

*IT outsourcing ... a decision taken by an organization to contract-out or sell the organizations IT assets, people, and/or activities to a third party vendor, who in return provides the services for a certain time period and monetary fee.* (Willcocks & Kern, 1998, p. 2)

*Table 1. Categorization of sourcing alternatives based on* "Percentages of IS Budget as a Differentiator Between Total and Selective Sourcing Decisions" *(Lacity & Hirschheim, 1995, pp. 4, 223-224; see also Dibbern et al., 2004, p. 10)*

| # | Terminology | **Definition as quoted in literature** (Lacity and Hirschheim, 1995, p. 4, pp. 223-224; see also Dibbern et al., 2004, p. 10) |
|---|---|---|
| 1. | **Total Outsourcing** | "... to refer to those organizations that decided to outsource at least 80% of their IS budgets to third party providers." |
| 2. | **Total Insourcing** | "...refers to those organizations that formally evaluated outsourcing but selected their internal IS departments' bid over external vendor bids, thus keeping over 80% of the IS budget provided by the internal IS department." |
| 3. | **Selective Sourcing** | "...refers to organizations that opted to use third party vendors for certain IS functions which represents between 20 and 60% of the IS budget (typically around 40%) while still retaining a substantial internal IS department." |

*Table 2. Categorization of sourcing alternatives based on* "How Should We Source" Instead of "Should We Outsource" *(Wibbelsman & Maiero, 1994, as cited in Dibbern et al., 2004, p. 11)*

<table>
<tr><th>#</th><th>Terminology</th><th>Definition as quoted in literature (Wibbelsman & Maiero, 1994, as cited in Dibbern et al., 2004, p. 11)</th></tr>
<tr><td>1.</td><td>multi-sourcing (continuum)</td><td>"The multiple sourcing of IS services. More specifically, they see multi-sourcing as a continuum. The end points of their continuum span from 'OK as is' to 'divest completely'."<br><br>Various strategies of the multi-sourcing continuum described in the literature are:<br><br>
<table>
<tr><th>Main Strategy</th><th>Sub-Strategy</th></tr>
<tr><td>insourcing</td><td>"OK as is"</td></tr>
<tr><td></td><td>"fix and keep in-house"</td></tr>
<tr><td>co-sourcing</td><td>"rehabilitation and return"</td></tr>
<tr><td></td><td>"transition assistance"</td></tr>
<tr><td></td><td>"capability development"</td></tr>
<tr><td>outsourcing</td><td>"option to reverse"</td></tr>
<tr><td></td><td>"divest completely"</td></tr>
</table></td></tr>
<tr><td>2.</td><td>(multi-sourcing continuum:)<br>insourcing -> "OK as is" strategy</td><td>"The 'OK as is' point on the continuum relates to the belief that the status quo is the best sourcing strategy; IS activities are insourced."</td></tr>
<tr><td>3.</td><td>(multi-sourcing continuum:)<br>insourcing -> "fix and keep in-house" strategy</td><td>"This strategy believes that insourcing is the best strategy but the internal IS department needs to adopt better practices to become more efficient and effective."</td></tr>
<tr><td>4.</td><td>(multi-sourcing continuum:)<br>co-sourcing -> "rehabilitation and return" strategy</td><td>"...the IS organization is reformed through the assistance of a third party and then kept in-house."</td></tr>
<tr><td>5.</td><td>(multi-sourcing continuum:)<br>co-sourcing -> "transition assistance" strategy</td><td>"...a third party takes on certain IS activities while the internal IS group transitions itself to a new set of skills."</td></tr>
<tr><td>6.</td><td>(multi-sourcing continuum:)<br>co-sourcing -> "capability development" arrangement</td><td>"...a third party takes on either permanently or temporarily IS activities while the IS organization develops new capabilities. This option allows the IS organization to focus on certain core capabilities."</td></tr>
<tr><td>7.</td><td>(multi-sourcing continuum:)<br>outsourcing -> "option to reverse" strategy</td><td>"...hereby IS is outsourced to a third party but there is a specific plan which would allow the function to return in-house without undue hardship at a later time if the management of the company deems this desirable."</td></tr>
<tr><td>8.</td><td>(multi-sourcing continuum:)<br>outsourcing -> "divest completely" strategy</td><td>"...the IS function is outsourced permanently. In such cases, IS is perceived to be a non-core business function best handled by an outsourcer."</td></tr>
</table>

Outsourcing has also been interpreted as being part of a *multi-sourcing continuum* having two possible outsourcing strategies: (a) the *"option to reverse"* strategy where IS functions are outsourced to a vendor but there is a planned roadmap which would allow the functions to return in-house without undue hardship at a later date if desired, and

*Table 3. Categorization of sourcing alternatives based on* How the Client Manages or Utilizes the Suppliers *(Currie & Willcocks, 1998, pp. 122-125)*

| # | Terminology | Definition as quoted in literature (Currie & Willcocks, 1998, pp. 122-125) |
|---|---|---|
| 1. | **Total Outsourcing** | "Total outsourcing is when an organization chooses to outsource as much as 70-80% of its IT facility, usually to a large single supplier. These contracts are usually for between 5 and 10 years." |
| 2. | **Multiple-supplier sourcing** | "…entered into IT sourcing arrangements with a variety of suppliers" |
| 3. | **Joint Venture / Strategic alliance sourcing** | "An organization enters into a joint venture with a supplier on a shared risk/reward basis. This may involve selecting an existing IT supplier or helping to create a new company to which work can be outsourced. Sometimes an organization may take share ownership in an existing IT supplier or vice-versa." |
| 4. | **Insourcing** | "An organization opts to retain a large centralized IT department and insource management and technical capabilities according to the peaks and troughs of IT work. Contractors may be given employment contracts lasting between 3 months and a year, although there are many examples of them staying with an organization for several years." |

(b) the *"divest completely"* strategy where IS functions that are perceived to be non-core business functions and that are thought to be best handled by a vendor are outsourced permanently (Wibbelsman & Maiero, 1994, as cited in Dibbern et al., 2004, p. 11).

## Categorization of Various Sourcing Alternatives in Literature

Let us now understand how some sourcing alternatives are categorized in literature. At this stage, we directly quote the literature, and then proceed in later sections to explain these categorized sourcing alternatives along with many other sourcing alternatives.

As shown in the following table, Lacity and Hirschheim (1995, pp. 4, 223-224) categorized the sourcing alternatives into *total outsourcing, total insourcing* and *selective sourcing*, by using the percentages of IS budget as a differentiator between total and selective sourcing decisions (see Table 1).

Dibbern et al. (2004, p. 11) cited the categorization of sourcing alternatives by Wibbelsman and Maiero (1994) where the focus is on "how should we source" instead of "should be outsource", and the entire sourcing scenario has been treated as a continuum (see Table 2).

Currie and Willcocks (1998) have categorized the sourcing alternatives on how the client manages or utilizes the vendors into *total outsourcing, multiple-supplier sourcing, joint venture/strategic alliance sourcing,* and *insourcing* (see Table 3).

*Table 4. Categorization of outsourcing capturing the range of* Outsourcing Options *(Lacity & Hirschheim, 1993a, pp. 17-18)*

| # | Terminology | **Definition as quoted in literature** (Lacity & Hirschheim, 1993a, pp. 17-18) |
|---|---|---|
| 1. | **Body Shop** | "...management uses outsourcing as a way to meet short-term demand. The most common type of body shop outsourcing is the use of contract programmers/personnel that is managed by company employees." |
| 2. | **Project Management** | "...management outsources for a specific project or portion of IS work." "...the vendor is responsible for managing and completing the work." |
| 3. | **Total outsourcing** | "...the vendor is in total charge of a significant piece of IS work." |

*Table 5. Categorization of outsourcing based on* How the Client Manages or Utilizes the Suppliers *(Millar, 1994, as cited in Lacity & Hirschheim, 1995, pp. 4-5)*

| # | Terminology | **Definition as quoted in literature** (Millar, 1994, as cited in Lacity & Hirschheim, 1995, pp. 4-5) |
|---|---|---|
| 1. | **General outsourcing** | "... encompasses three alternatives: (a) *selective outsourcing* ...(b) *value-added outsourcing* ... or (c) *cooperative outsourcing* ..." |
| 2. | *(General outsourcing:)* **selective outsourcing** | " ...where one particular area of IS activity is chosen to be turned over to a third party, such as data center operations" |
| 3. | *(General outsourcing:)* **value-added outsourcing** | "...where some area of IS activity is turned over to a third party who is thought to be able to provide a level of support or service which adds value to the activity that could not be cost effectively provided by the internal IS group" |
| 4. | *(General outsourcing:)* **cooperative outsourcing** | "...where some targeted IS activity(ies) is (are) jointly performed by a third party provider and the internal IS department" |
| 5. | **Transitional outsourcing** | "...involves the migration from one technological platform to another." |
| 6. | **Business process outsourcing** | "...refers to an outsourcing relationship where a third party provider is responsible for performing an entire business function for the client organization." |
| 7. | **Business benefit contracting** | "...contractual agreement that defines the vendor's contribution to the client in terms of specific benefits to the business and defines the payment the customer will make based upon the vendor's ability to deliver those benefits. The goal is to match actual costs with actual benefits and to share the risks." |

*Table 6. Categorization of outsourcing based on* Number of Clients and Vendors *(Gallivan & Oh, 1999, pp. 1-6; see also Dibbern et al., 2004, pp.12-13)*

| # | Terminology | **Definition as quoted in literature** (Gallivan & Oh, 1999, pp. 1-6; see also Dibbern et al., 2004, pp.12-13) |
|---|---|---|
| 1. | **Dyadic outsourcing arrangement** | "one client, one vendor" "...presume that client firms seeking IT services act independently of each other, while IT vendors do the same. Thus the assumed relationship between client firm and IT vendor has been a simple 'dyadic' one." |
| 2. | **multi-vendor** | "one client, multiple vendors" "A one-to-many relationship indicates that one client uses multiple outsourcing vendors to achieve its objectives, and that division-of-labor is jointly negotiated and understood by all parties to the agreement." |

*Table 6. cont.*

| | | |
|---|---|---|
| 3. | **co-sourcing** | "many clients, one vendor"<br>"A many-to-one alliance where several clients contract with a single IT vendor for services." |
| 4. | **complex outsourcing** | "many clients, many vendors"<br>"...combining multiple clients and multiple vendor firms into a single contract or alliance" |

## Categorization of Outsourcing in Literature

Some of the categorizations of outsourcing terminologies in the literature are quoted. The terms defined in these categorizations, have been explained independently in later sections of this chapter.

Lacity and Hirschheim (1993a) categorized outsourcing into *Body Shop*, *Project Management* and *Total Outsourcing* (see Table 4).

Lacity and Hirschheim (1995, pp. 4-5) have cited the work of Millar (1994), which categorizes outsourcing on the basis of how the client manages or utilizes the suppliers, and have described general, selective, value-added, cooperative, transitional, business process outsourcing and business benefit contracting (see Table 5).

Gallivan and Oh (1999, pp. 1-6), categorized outsourcing on the basis of number of clients and vendors into *dyadic*, *multi-vendor*, *co-sourcing* and *complex outsourcing* (see Table 6).

## The "Shoring" Strategies

As described earlier, the client's service provider can be either internal (its own IS department or a subsidiary) or external (a vendor). In our shrinking world, where exactly is this service provider located?

- **Onshoring:** The service provider is located in the same country as the client. This is also known as **domestic sourcing** or **onshore sourcing**.
- **Nearshoring:** The service provider is located in a country which is geographically close the client's country. Hence, countries which share borders, or are neighbors can be considered as "nearshore" countries. Ireland and Spain may be considered as nearshore for the United Kingdom, whereas Mexico and Canada may be considered as nearshore for U.S. This is also known as *nearshore sourcing.*
- **Offshoring:** The service provider is located in a country which is geographically far away from the client's country. India and China may be considered as "offshore" for both the United Kingdom and U.S This is also known as *offshore-sourcing.*

"Shore" in the words *onshore, nearshore* and *offshore* does not necessarily imply that the respective country has land along the edge of a body of water. It only indicates a different geographical location.

The *geographical distance* is a predominant classifier when comparing between onshore, nearshore and offshore locations. At the same time, the *time zones* of the locations may also be considered. In the IS industry, as communication technology improves, the exact geographical distance is a lesser barrier when compared to the time zones. It may not be wrong if we choose to classify between onshore, nearshore and offshore on the basis of both time zones and geographical distance.

One may do away with the specific term "*nearshoring*," and generally use "*offshoring*" instead. The term "*offshoring*" is often used to broadly imply "*nearshoring*" too. When someone says, that work has been "*offshored*," it may simply imply that work has been sent away from *onshore* (i.e., to *nearshore* or *offshore*). Hence, we can adopt a simpler binary logic of onshore versus offshore, where anything that is not "*onshore*" can be simply called "*offshore*". *Offshoring* may therefore be defined as a scenario where the service provider is located in a country that is different from the client's country; this is also known as "*global sourcing*".

## Basic Combinations of the Shoring and Sourcing Strategies

The shoring strategy may be either an onshore, nearshore or offshore strategy. And the basic sourcing strategy may be either insourcing or outsourcing. As illustrated by Figure 1 (onshore-centric view of sourcing and shoring), the various combinations are onshore-insourcing, onshore-outsourcing, nearshore-insourcing, nearshore-outsourcing, offshore-insourcing and offshore-outsourcing:

### *Domestic Sourcing or Onshore Sourcing or Onshoring Alternatives*

- **Onshore-Insourcing:** Both the client and its subsidiary or IS department that provides the services are located in the same country. This is also termed as **domestic insourcing**.
- **Onshore-Outsourcing:** Both the client and the vendor are located in the same country. This is also termed as "domestic outsourcing". This is also termed as domestic outsourcing.

### *Global Sourcing Alternatives*

- **Nearshore-Insourcing:** The client's subsidiary or IS department that provides the service is located in a country which is geographically close the client's country.

*Figure 1. Sourcing and shoring: Onshore centric view*

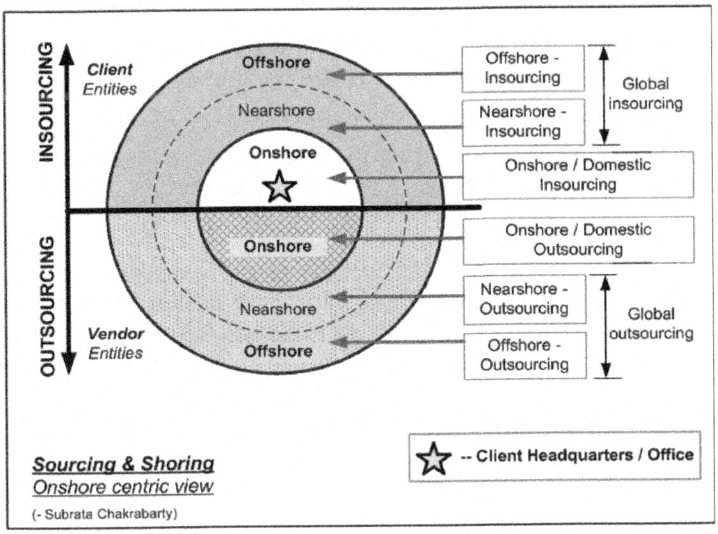


*Figure 2. Sourcing and shoring: Insourcing centric view*

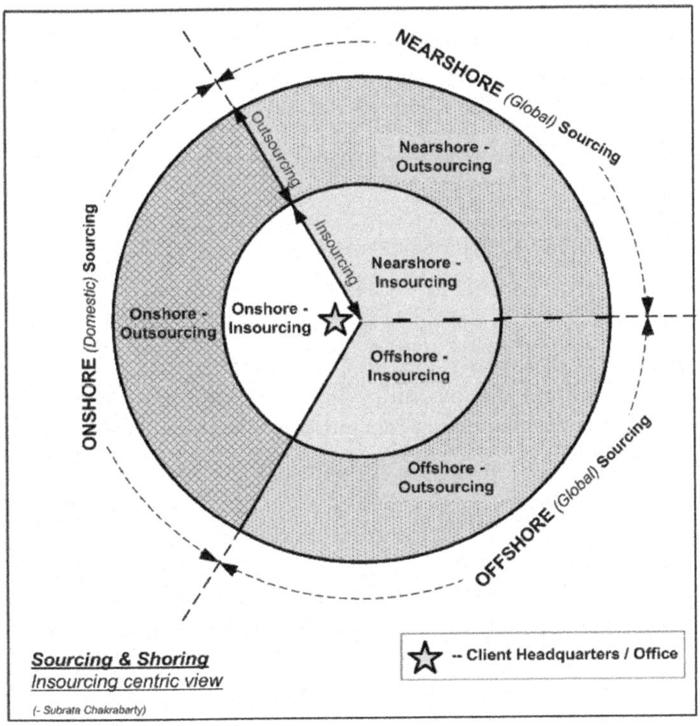

- **Nearshore-Outsourcing:** The vendor is located in a country that is geographically close the client's country.
- **Offshore-Insourcing:** The client's subsidiary or IS department that provides the service is located in a country that is geographically far away from the client's country.
- **Offshore-Outsourcing:** The vendor is located in a country that is geographically far away from the client's country.

Figure 2 illustrates an insourcing-centric view of sourcing and shoring; the various combinations shown are onshore-insourcing, nearshore-insourcing, offshore-insourcing, onshore-oursourcing, nearshore-outsourcing, and offshore-outsourcing.

As discussed earlier, the term "*offshore*" is often used to imply "*nearshore*", too, that is, anything that is not "*onshore*" may simply be called "*offshore*". While the term "*domestic*" relates to "*onshore*", the term "*global*" relates to "*offshore*", where "*off-shore*" encompasses "*nearshore*" too (Dibbern et al., 2004, p. 43). Hence, for the purposes of simplification, one can narrow down the above classification to the following four basic choices, where the earlier *nearshore sourcing* options are now encompassed within the *offshore sourcing* options.

Domestic sourcing or onshore sourcing or onshoring alternatives:

1. onshore-insourcing or domestic-insourcing
2. onshore-outsourcing or domestic-outsourcing

Global sourcing or offshore sourcing or offshoring alternatives:

3. offshore-insourcing or global-insourcing
4. offshore-outsourcing or global-insourcing

Therefore, in **offshore-insourcing**, the subsidiary or IS department (of the client) which provides the service is located in a country different from the client's country; while in **offshore-outsourcing**, the vendor is located in a country different from the client's country.

## Overview of Various Sourcing Alternatives

Let us now gain an understanding of the various sourcing alternatives.

*Table 7. List of sourcing alternatives*

| Terminology | Definitive feature | Basic sourcing strategy: ○ Insourcing ○ Outsourcing ○ Both ○ Any | Shoring strategy focus: ○ Onshore ○ Offshore ○ Anywhere |
|---|---|---|---|
| Application Service Provision / Application Service Providing / Net-sourcing / On-Demand | Accessing remotely hosted IS applications | Outsourcing | Anywhere |
| Backsourcing | Insourcing what was outsourced | Insourcing | Anywhere |
| Benefit based relationships / Business benefit contracting | Linking payments to realization of benefits | Outsourcing | Anywhere |
| Body Shop Outsourcing | Using contract personnel | Outsourcing | Anywhere |
| Business Process Outsourcing | Vendor performs client's entire business processes | Outsourcing | Anywhere |
| Complex sourcing | Multiple clients and multiple vendors in a single contract or alliance | Outsourcing | Anywhere |
| Cooperative Sourcing | Client's internal IS department and the vendor perform IS activity cooperatively | Both | Anywhere |
| Co-sourcing | Client's performance determines vendor's revenue | Outsourcing | Anywhere |
| | Helping the client's IS department mature | | |
| | Multiple clients jointly seek services from vendor | | |
| Creative Contracting | Innovative contracts for better deals | Outsourcing | Anywhere |
| Distributed Consulting | Vendor has teams both at onshore and offshore | Outsourcing | Offshore |
| Dyadic outsourcing arrangement | Independent client dealing with independent vendor | Outsourcing | Anywhere |
| Facilities Management | Vendor maintains the client's assets | Outsourcing | Anywhere |
| Facilities Sharing | Sharing ownership of facilities needed by each | Both | Anywhere |
| General outsourcing | Selective, value-added and cooperative outsourcing | Outsourcing /Both | Anywhere |
| Global Delivery | Large vendor delivering services from various global locations to clients at various global locations | Outsourcing | Offshore |
| Managed Offshore Facilities | Outsourcing the process of setting up facilities for offshore-insourcing | Outsourcing | Offshore |
| Multi-sourcing | One contract with multiple vendors | Outsourcing | Anywhere |
| | multiple sourcing strategies in a continuum | Both | |
| Multi-vendor outsourcing / Multiple-supplier sourcing / Dual sourcing | Client dealing with multiple interdependent vendors | Outsourcing | Anywhere |
| Project Management Outsourcing | Vendor manages a project | Outsourcing | Anywhere |

*Table 7. cont.*

| Terminology | Definitive feature | Basic sourcing strategy:<br>o Insourcing<br>o Outsourcing<br>o Both<br>o Any | Shoring strategy focus:<br>o Onshore<br>o Offshore<br>o Anywhere |
|---|---|---|---|
| Selective / Smart / Right / Flexible / Modular Sourcing | Outsourcing and insourcing optimally | Both | Anywhere |
| Spin-offs | An IS department that now sells to the market | Any | Anywhere |
| Strategic alliances / Partnerships / Joint Ventures / Equity holdings / Strategic sourcing | Sharing risks and rewards | Outsourcing | Anywhere |
| Tactical Outsourcing / Contracting-out / Out-tasking | Outsourcing for rapid solution to problems | Outsourcing | Anywhere |
| Total Insourcing | Insourcing maximum % of IS budget | Insourcing | Anywhere |
| Total Outsourcing / Traditional Outsourcing | Outsourcing maximum % of IS budget | Outsourcing | Anywhere |
| | Vendor having complete charge of significant IS work | | |
| Transformational Outsourcing | Streamlining of client's internal organization alongside outsourcing | Outsourcing | Anywhere |
| Transitional Outsourcing | Outsourcing during a major changeover | Outsourcing | Anywhere |
| Value-added outsourcing | Combined strengths for the market | Both | Anywhere |
| | Vendor adding value to IS activity | Outsourcing | Anywhere |

*Figure 3. Application service providing*

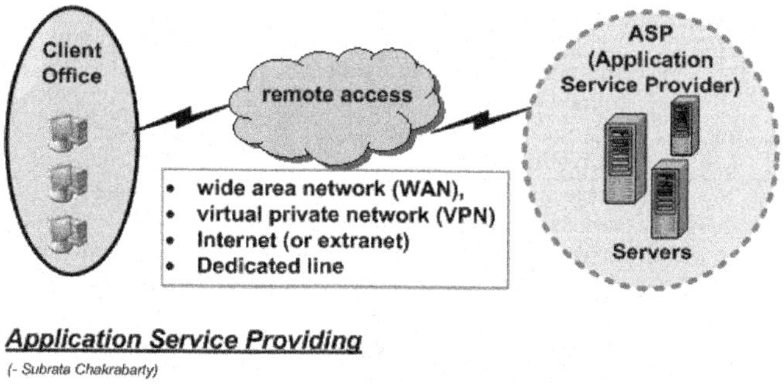


# List of Sourcing Alternatives

The sourcing alternatives that will be eventually discussed are summarized and listed in Table 7. The definitive feature of each term is provided along with information on the possible basic sourcing strategy (insourcing, outsourcing, both or any) and the possible shoring strategy (onshoring, offshoring or simply anywhere).

We will now briefly explain each of the terms listed in the Table 7.

*Figure 4. Backsourcing*

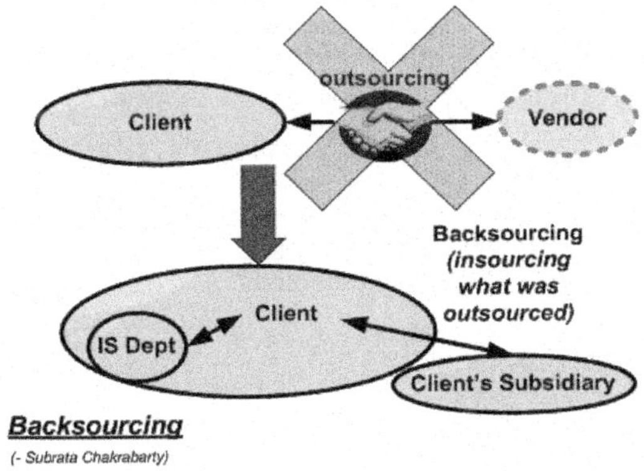


## Application Service Provision / Application Service Providing / Net-Sourcing / On-Demand

- *Accessing remotely hosted IS applications*

An *application service provider* (ASP) is a vendor that provides access to remotely hosted IS-applications over a wide area network (WAN), a virtual private network (VPN), or over the Internet (Susarla, Barua, & Whinston, 2003, p. 103). Bennett and Timbrell (2000, p. 196) define *application service provision* as a form of selective outsourcing where an organization rents generally available packaged software applications and related services. Dewire (2000, p. 14) states that an "*application service provider (ASP) provides a contractual software-based service for hosting, managing, and providing access to an application from a centrally managed facility.*" Furthermore, clients have remote web-access to the applications that are running on the ASP's servers. Figure 3 illustrates a client having remote access to applications on servers hosted and managed by the vendor (ASP), over a wide area network (WAN), virtual private network (VPN), internet/extranet or a dedicated line.

IDC (International Data Corp.) explains the following about ASP (as cited in Dewire, 2000, p. 14):

*An end user accesses an application resident on a server, just as he or she would on a LAN or in the enterprise data center. However, the server resides at the ASP's third-party data center and is reached via a dedicated line or the internet (or extranet). The*

*Figure 5. Benefit-based relationships / business benefit contracting*

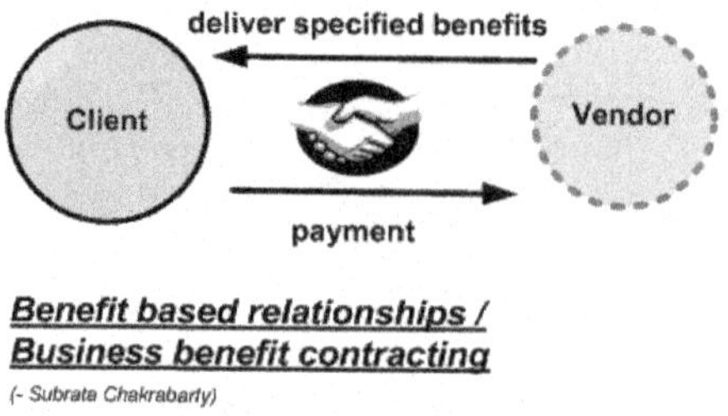


*Figure 6. Body shop outsourcing*

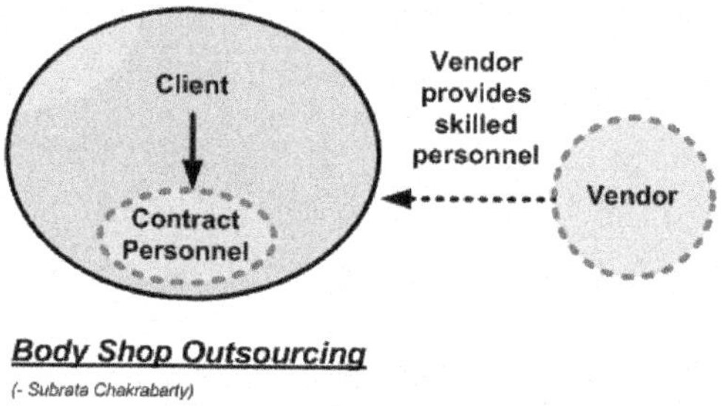


*applications can range from low-end, productivity programs (e.g., word processing) to high-end ERP modules. The service is provided on a subscription basis and can bundle a full range of hosted application services.*

The Application Service Provider Consortium defines an ASP as an organization that "*manages and delivers application capabilities to multiple entities from a data center across a wide area network (WAN)*" (as cited in Susarla et al., 2003, p. 92).

Hence, ASPs purchase/develop/customize, install, and manage software applications at remote locations and host them for clients over the Internet (or maybe over a VPN or Extranet). Various flavors of this kind sourcing have also been termed as "Net-sourcing" (Kern, Lacity & Willcocks, 2002), "on demand" service, "application utilities", "real-time delivery" and "software-as-a-service" (SAAS), all of which encourage the delivery of online and externally managed information systems (Pring & Ambrose, 2004).

## Backsourcing

- *Insourcing what was outsourced*

When the IS functions that had previously been outsourced are brought back in-house, it is known as *backsourcing* (Dibbern et al., 2004, p. 12). *Backsourcing* is the insourcing

*Figure 7. Business process outsourcing*

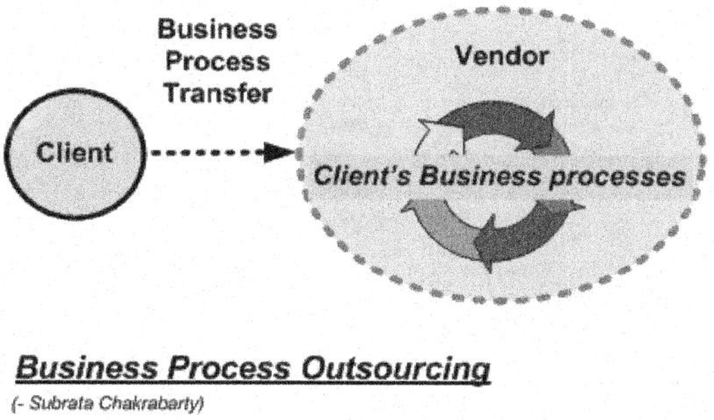


of previously outsourced IS functions. As illustrated by figure 4, the client decides to insource its previously outsourced IS needs from either its own internal IS department or its subsidiary.

## Benefit-Based Relationships / Business Benefit Contracting

- *Linking payments to realization of benefits*

In *benefit-based relationships*, both the parties (customer and external service provider) make an upfront investment in a relationship, and thereafter share both the benefits and the risks (Sparrow, 2003, p. 13). Sparrow (2003, pp. 13-14), has given the example of the UK government's employment service which formed a public-private, benefit-based relationship with EDS to deliver IS services, thus securing business benefits from use of IS, while establishing a payment methodology that links EDS's reward to realizing those benefits. As illustrated by this example, private sector companies invest up-front in developing public sector services with payments based on outcomes or benefits gained from these services.

In *business benefit contracting*, a contractual agreement defines the vendor's contribution to the client in terms of specific benefits to the business and defines the payment the client will make based upon the vendor's ability to deliver those benefits, thereby matching actual costs with actual benefits and sharing the risks (Millar, 1994, as cited in Lacity & Hirschheim, 1995, pp. 4-5). As illustrated in Figure 5, the client makes its payments to the vendor depending on the specific benefits received.

Lacity and Hirschheim (1995), note that though *business benefit contracting* is used often in the marketing of outsourcing services by vendors, it is typically not adopted due to the difficulty associated with measuring benefits. Furthermore, in *business benefit contracting* the vendor's revenue and margin potential is linked to the benchmarks, and therefore it is not surprising that getting an agreement by both parties on the benchmarks proves to be problematic.

*Figure 8. Complex sourcing*

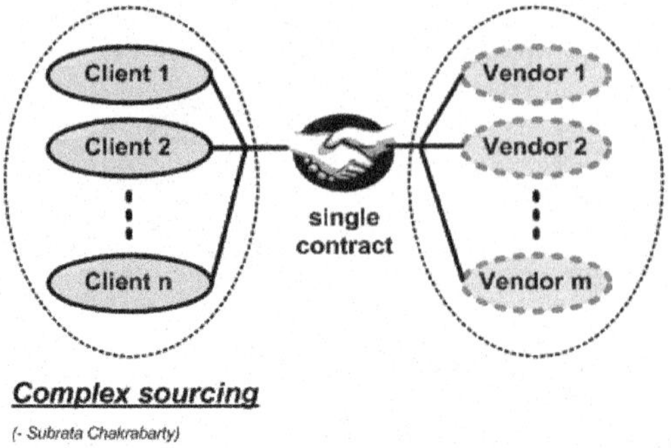


*Figure 9. Cooperative sourcing*

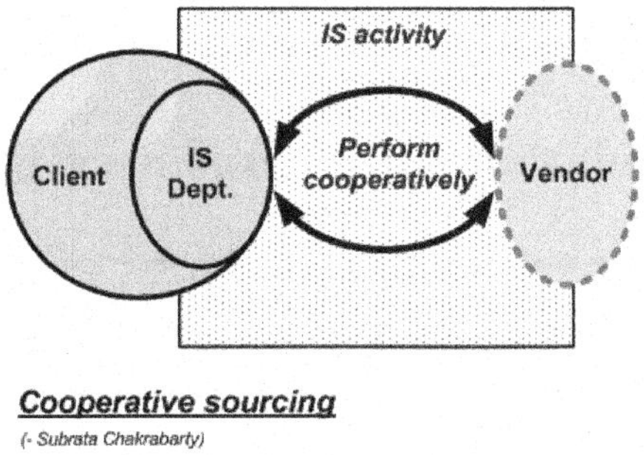


## Body Shop Outsourcing

- *Using contract personnel*

*Body shop outsourcing* is a way for firms to meet short term demands, by the use of contract personnel (such as programmers), who are managed by the employees of the hiring firm (Lacity & Hirschheim, 1993a, pp. 17-18). As illustrated in Figure 6, the client contracts skilled personnel from a vendor; these contract personnel are the vendor's paid employees who work at the client site, under the supervision of the client. The client *shops* for skilled *bodies* from vendors.

## Business Process Outsourcing

- *Vendor performs client's entire business processes*

*Figure 10. Co-sourcing: Client's performance determines vendor's revenue*

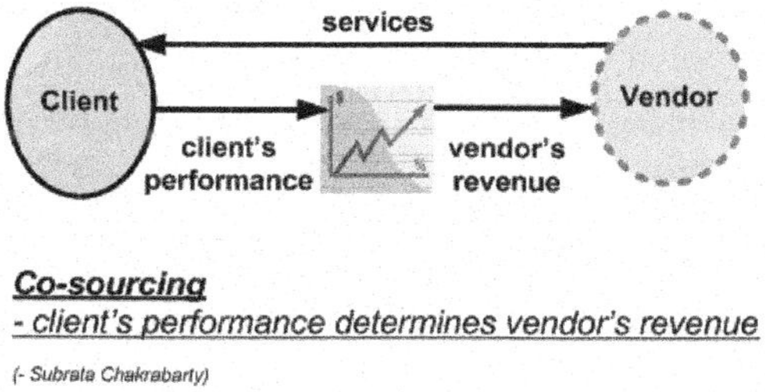


*Business process outsourcing* refers to an outsourcing relationship where a vendor is responsible for performing an entire business function for the client (Millar, 1994, as cited in Lacity & Hirschheim, 1995, pp. 4-5). As shown in Figure 7, the client transfers certain business processes to the vendor, and the vendor site is now the *back office* for the client's outsourced business processes.

In *business process outsourcing*, companies hire external service providers to manage entire business process functions such as hotlines, helpdesks, claims management, call centers, document processing and storage, data management, payroll, financial services (banks and insurance), accounting, auditing, transportation, travel management systems, logistics and various IS services (Millar, 1994, as cited in Lacity & Hirschheim, 1995, pp. 4-5; Sparrow, 2003, p. 11). Vendors provide a range of services spanning all areas of business with the overall aim to improve and allow seamless and consistent levels of customer service.

## Complex Sourcing

- *Multiple clients and multiple vendors in a single contract or alliance*

As illustrated in Figure 8, *complex sourcing* is a many-to-many relationship that involves both multiple clients and vendors in the same outsourcing contract or in an alliance (Gallivan & Oh, 1999, pp. 1-6; see also Dibbern et al., 2004, pp. 12-13). Moreover, this can be interpreted as a combination of both the *multi-vendor* and *co-sourcing* relationships as defined by Gallivan and Oh (1999).

## Cooperative Sourcing

- *Client's internal IS department and the vendor perform IS activity cooperatively*

When a targeted IS function is performed jointly by the client's internal IS department and the vendor, it is known as *cooperative sourcing* (Millar, 1994, as cited in Lacity &

*Figure 11. Co-sourcing: Helping the client's IS department mature*

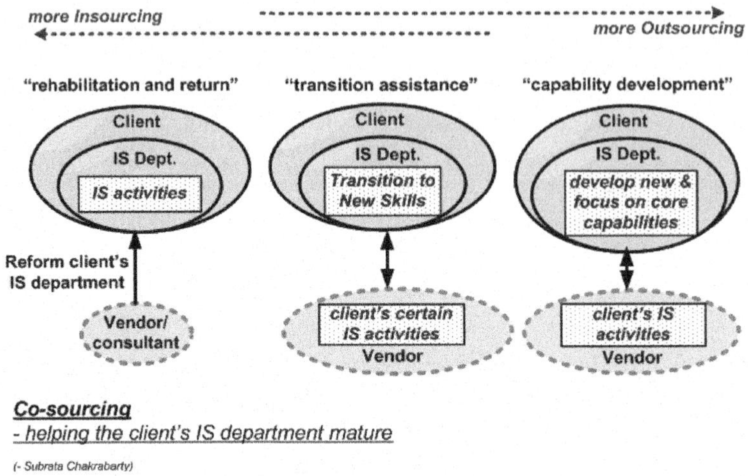


Hirschheim, 1995, pp. 4-5). As shown in the Figure 9, the client's IS department works closely with the vendor as a single team, towards the successful completion of the IS activity.

## Co-Sourcing

- *Client's performance determines vendor's revenue*
- *Helping the client's IS department mature*
- *Multiple clients jointly seek services from vendor*

Three interpretations of the term *co-sourcing* exist. While the first interpretation is based on performance being linked to revenue, the second interpretation is based on the role of the vendor in the growth or maturation of the processes in the client's IS department, and the third interpretation is based on clients jointly seeking IS services.

When the vendor's revenue from the client to which it is providing services is linked to the performance of the client, it is known as *co-sourcing* (Willcocks & Lacity, 1998, pp. 26, 30-31). As shown in Figure 10, the vendor provides services to the client with the underlying contractual expectation that it would positively affect the client's performance; the client evaluates the improvement in its own performance due to the vendor's contribution and pays the vendor proportionately.

As shown in Figure 11, *co-sourcing* has also been interpreted as being part of a *multi-sourcing continuum* having three possible co-sourcing strategies: (a) the "*rehabilitation and return*" strategy where the internal IS department is reformed through the assistance of a vendor or consultant and the IS functions are kept in-house, (b) the

*Figure 12. Co-sourcing: Multiple clients jointly seek services from vendor*

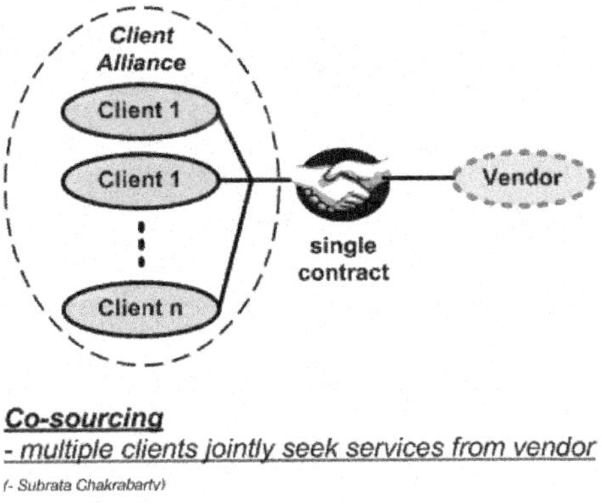


*Figure 13. Creative contracting*

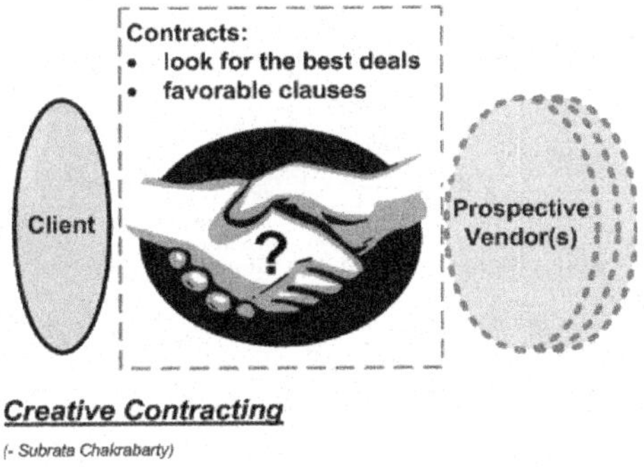


*"transition assistance"* strategy where a vendor takes on certain IS activities while the internal IS department transitions itself to a new set of skills, and (c) the *"capability development"* strategy where the internal IS department develops new capabilities and focuses on certain core capabilities, while a vendor either permanently or temporarily takes on IS activities (Wibbelsman & Maiero, 1994, as cited in Dibbern et al., 2004, p. 11).

Going by this interpretation, *co-sourcing* can be defined as a process where the vendor assists in the growth or maturation of the processes in the client's IS department, as dictated by the needs of the client. The "*transition assistance*" part of *co-sourcing* has also been termed as "*transitional outsourcing*" (Millar, 1994, as cited in Lacity & Hirschheim, 1995, pp. 4-5).

Finally, in another interesting interpretation as shown in Figure 12, *co-sourcing* is defined as a many-to-one relationship where multiple clients form an alliance by pooling their needs and resources, and contract with a single vendor for joint delivery of IS services (Gallivan & Oh, 1999, pp. 1-6; see also Dibbern et al., 2004, pp. 12-13). Furthermore, Gallivan and Oh (1999) state that in addition to IS outsourcing such client

*Figure 14. Distributed consulting*

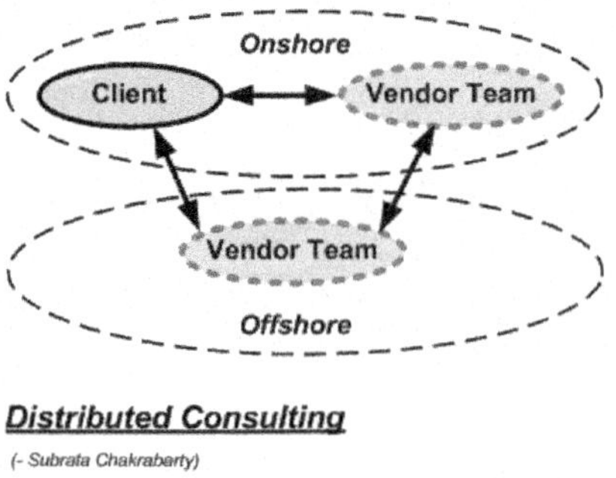


*Figure 15. Dyadic outsourcing arrangement*

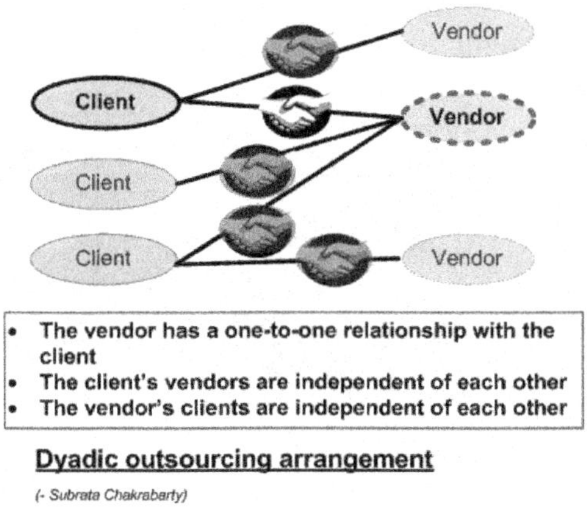


alliances can also be found in business disciplines such as marketing (i.e., co-marketing) and management (i.e., R&D consortia), and have advantages of risk sharing and reduction, increased bargaining power, and buyer economies of scale.

## Creative Contracting

- *Innovative contracts for better deals*

In *creative contracting*, the client is a *tougher shopper* and includes special clauses in the contract in order to satisfy its own needs and get better deals (Willcocks & Lacity, 1998, pp. 26, 32). The client examines various options and is looking for the best deal.

As illustrated in Figure 13, the clients include ingenious and favorable clauses in the contract so that it can get the best deal. Willcocks and Lacity (1998, pp. 32-33), list the following four *creative contracting* practices:

- Inclusion of a customer-written contract with the request for proposal.
- Provide for competitive bidding of services beyond the contract.
- Flexible pricing mechanisms.
- Beginning a long term relationship with a short term contract.

## Distributed Consulting

- *Vendor has teams both at onshore and offshore*

In the case of offshore-outsourcing, there is often a need to have vendor team both at onshore and offshore, where the onshore vendor team coordinates face-to-face with client and the bulk of the outsourced work is carried out by the offshore vendor team, this is known as *distributed consulting* (see Figure 14).

This is a widely accepted practice to ensure effective coordination between onshore-based clients and offshore-based vendors. For example, TCS (http://www.tcs.com), Infosys (http://www.infosys.com), Wipro (http://www.wipro.com) and Satyam (http://www.satyam.com), all large software service providers (primarily based in India), have for long incorporated this concept into what they call the "*global delivery model.*" Kobyashi-Hillary (2004, p. 153) calls this particular concept of having offshore/onshore blends of vendor teams as *distributed consulting.*

## Dyadic Outsourcing Arrangement

- *Independent client dealing with independent vendor*

A *dyadic* outsourcing arrangement assumes a one-to-one relationship between a client and a vendor, the presumption being that the client firms seeking IS services act independently of each other and that the vendor firms providing the IS services act independently of each other (Gallivan & Oh, 1999, pp. 1-6; see also Dibbern et al., 2004, pp. 12-13).

*Figure 16. Facilities management*

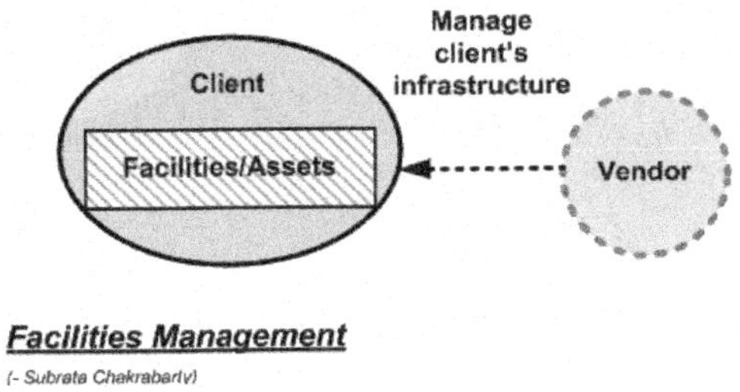

*Figure 17. Facilities sharing*

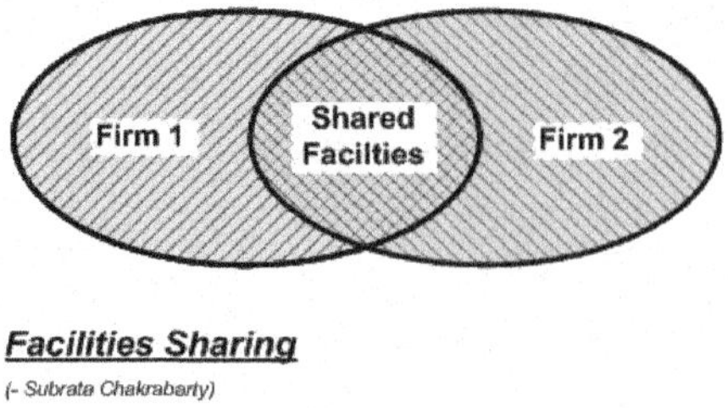


As shown in Figure 15, in *dyadic* outsourcing arrangements a client can engage multiple vendors for various IS functions, however its vendors are independent of each other; similarly, a vendor can provide services to multiple clients, but its clients are independent of each other. There is a one-to-one relationship between each client and each vendor providing services to that client.

## Facilities Management

- *Vendor maintains the client's assets*

In "*facilities management*" outsourcing, the client owns the technology assets but hires a vendor to take over the operational control of these assets (Dibbern et al., 2004, p. 7; Sparrow, 2003, pp. 6-7). As illustrated in Figure 16, the ownership of the technology assets (which may reside at either the client's premises or elsewhere) is not transferred

*Figure 18. Global delivery*

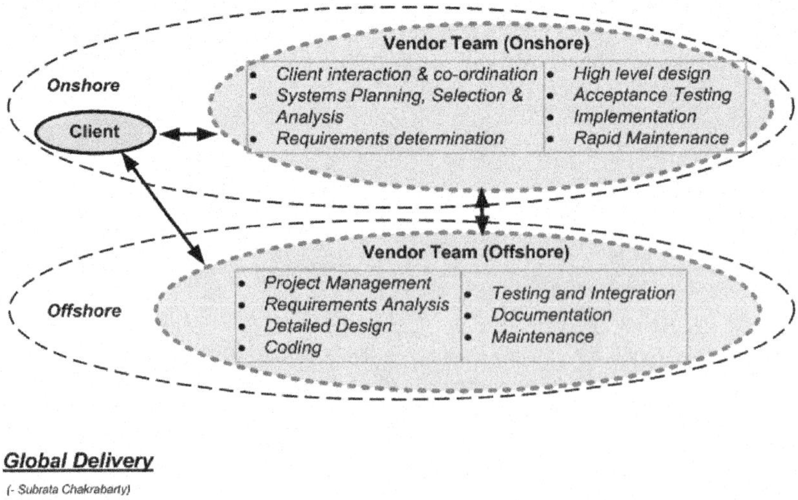

*Figure 19. Managed offshore facilities*

to the vendor. The vendor is expected to offer expertise and also lower the costs of maintaining these technology assets. For example, a vendor may be hired to manage the computer hardware and also regularly upgrade the software needs of the customer more efficiently. The vendor may involve in operational and systems programming tasks (for the technology assets being managed), but not in the development of applications (which are outside the scope of "facilities management").

## Facilities Sharing

- *Sharing ownership of facilities needed by each*

As shown in the Figure 17, in the "*facilities sharing*" form of outsourcing, a firm chooses to share ownership of IS facilities with either a vendor or others in the same industry (Dibbern et. al., 2004, p. 7). This can be prove to be a cost effective approach, where more than one firm chooses to share the ownership of the IS facilities required by each of the firms. The details regarding maintaining operational control over these shared facilities will need to be worked out.

On one hand, a firm may choose to share both the *ownership* and *operational control* of facilities with another firm. On the other hand, a firm may choose to share the *ownership* of the facilities with a vendor, and in addition the vendor is hired by the firm to assume *operational control* over the shared facilities.

## General Outsourcing

- *Selective, value-added and cooperative outsourcing*

*Figure 20. Multi-sourcing continuum*

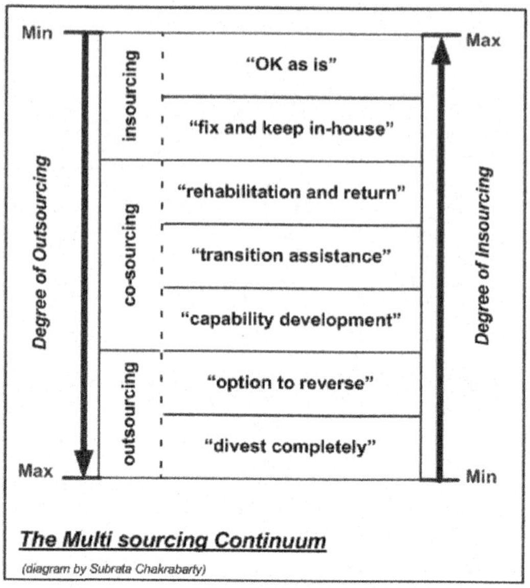


*General outsourcing* encompasses the three alternatives of selective outsourcing, value-added outsourcing, and cooperative outsourcing (Millar, 1994, as cited in Lacity & Hirschheim, 1995, pp. 4-5).

## Global Delivery

- *Large vendor delivering services from various global locations to clients at various global locations*

*Figure 21. Multi-vendor outsourcing*

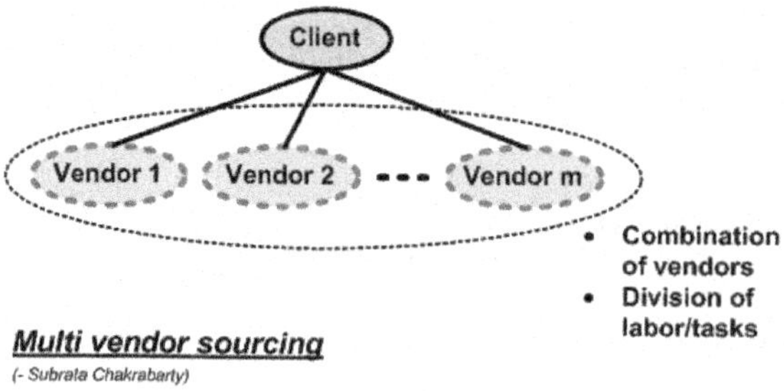

In *global delivery*, a large vendor's IS delivery centers are located worldwide and are comprehensively networked with collaborative systems that allow seamless integration of projects delivered from multiple locations and thereby providing economies of scale and scope (Tata Consultancy Services, n.d.).

The "*global delivery model*" is an offshore-outsourcing model that takes advantage of the global talent pool to give the best value to the client in terms of cost and quality. As illustrated in Figure 18, the work is broken down into logical components, which are then distributed to suitable global locations such that the client gets access to the vendor's global talent and also creates maximum value for the client in terms of cost and quality (Infosys, n.d.). For example, in the case of software production, the onshore vendor team can be involved in client interaction and co-ordination, systems planning and selection, systems analysis, requirements determination, high level design, acceptance testing, implementation, and rapid maintenance support; while the offshore vendor team can be involved in project management, requirements analysis, detailed design, coding, testing and integration, documentation, and maintenance.

## Managed Offshore Facilities

- *Outsourcing the process of setting up facilities for offshore-insourcing*

As illustrated in the Figure 19, in "*managed offshore facilities*", the client *outsources* the process of creating its offshore subsidiary to a vendor; once the offshore facility is up and running, the client can take full ownership and hence carry out its *offshore-insourcing* operations. Also, vendors may be given the task of "*facilities management*" of the client's offshore subsidiary.

*Managed offshore facilities* is a variant of the *Build-Operate-Transfer* model, where the vendor manages the process of creating the offshore facility, and the client has the option of taking full ownership by a specified date (i-Vantage, n.d.; Kobyashi-Hillary, 2004, p. 153). This *outsourcing* alternative has the potential to reduce many hassles for a firm that decides to set up a subsidiary for *offshore-insourcing*.

## Multi-Sourcing

- *One contract with multiple vendors*
- *Multiple sourcing strategies in a continuum*

The term *multi-sourcing* has been interpreted in two ways.

In one interpretation of *multi-sourcing*, the client has one outsourcing contract with multiple suppliers (Willcocks & Lacity, 1998, pp. 26, 29-30). Willcocks and Lacity (1998) note that in multi-sourcing, while the risks of being dependent on a single vendor are reduced, additional time and resources are required to manage multiple vendors. This interpretation of Multi-sourcing has also been termed as "*multi-vendor outsourcing*" by

Gallivan and Oh (1999) and as "*multi-supplier sourcing*" by Currie and Willcocks (1998).

In another interpretation as shown in Figure 20, *multi-sourcing* has been defined as the multiple sourcing of IS services, specifically seen as a continuum, where the end points of the continuum span from "*OK as is*" to "*divest completely*" (Wibbelsman & Maiero, 1994, as cited in Dibbern et al., 2004, p. 11). Furthermore, the various strategies of the *multi-sourcing* continuum have been given as:

(1a) *Insourcing* -> "OK as is"

(1b) *Insourcing* -> "fix and keep in-house"

(2a) *Co-sourcing* -> "rehabilitation and return"

(2b) *Co-sourcing* -> "transition assistance"

(2c) *Co-sourcing* -> "capability development"

(3a) *Outsourcing* -> "option to reverse"

(3b) *Outsourcing* -> "divest completely"

## Multi-Vendor Outsourcing / Multiple-Supplier Sourcing / Dual Sourcing

- *Client dealing with multiple interdependent vendors*

In *multi-vendor* outsourcing a one-to-many relationship exists, indicating that one client uses multiple vendors and that division of labor is jointly negotiated and understood by all parties to the agreement (Gallivan & Oh, 1999, pp. 1-6; see also Dibbern et al., 2004, pp. 12-13).

As shown in figure 21, *multi-vendor* or *multi-supplier* outsourcing arrangements allow a client to engage multiple vendors for various IS functions which are then jointly performed by the multiple vendors through an agreed upon division of labor. This implies that a cooperative and also competitive environment exists between the vendors working together.

In *multiple-supplier* sourcing the client enters into IS sourcing arrangements with a variety of suppliers/vendors (Currie & Willcocks, 1998, pp. 122-123). Currie and Willocks (1998), state the following three advantages of *multiple-supplier* sourcing: (a) the client can safeguard against being dependent upon a single vendor, and prevent a scenario where a single vendor controls all its IS assets, (b) the client with short-term contracts that are and liable for renewal not necessarily with the same vendor (or combination of vendors) encourages competition and innovation, and (c) the client can concentrate on its core business while the suppliers manage and provide IS services.

The identical concepts of *multi-vendor* outsourcing (Gallivan & Oh, 1999, pp. 1-6) and *multiple-supplier sourcing* (Currie & Willcocks, 1998) have also been termed as simply "*multi-sourcing*" by Willcocks and Lacity (1998).

*Figure 22. Selective / smart / right / flexible / modular sourcing*

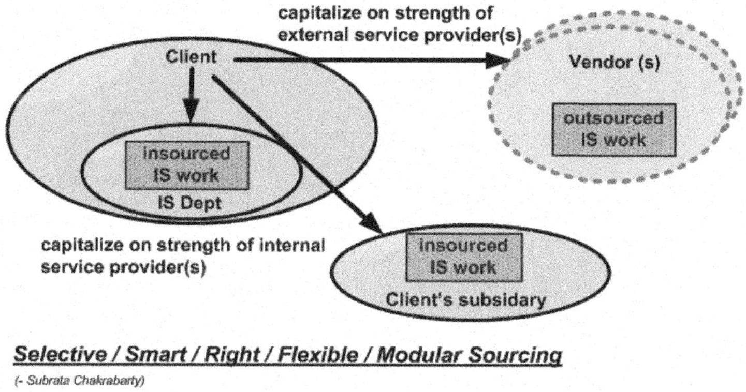


Klotz and Chatterjee (1995, p. 1317) have used the term "*dual sourcing*" to indicate a scenario where a client sources from two vendors, which prevents the client from being held by hostage by a monopolistic vendor over time, and helps the client to derive cost advantages due to the competition between the vendors.

## Project Management Outsourcing

- *Vendor manages a project*

In *project management outsourcing*, the client *outsources* a specific project or portion of the IS work, and the vendor is responsible for managing and completing the work (Lacity & Hirschheim, 1993a, pp. 17-18). Further, project management outsourcing may involve the use of vendors for development of new systems, maintenance of existing systems, providing training, managing networks, and handle disaster recovery.

## Selective / Smart / Right / Flexible / Modular Sourcing

- *Outsourcing and insourcing optimally*

*Selective sourcing* or *smart sourcing* is the practice of outsourcing select IS applications to vendors, while retaining other IS applications in-house (Lacity, Willcocks & Feeny, 1996, pp. 13-14). *Right sourcing, flexible sourcing,* and *modular sourcing* are synonyms of the same.

When one particular area of the client's IS activity is chosen to be turned over to a vendor, it is known as *selective outsourcing* (Millar, 1994, as cited in Lacity & Hirschheim, 1995, pp. 4-5).

*Figure 23. Strategic alliances / partnerships / joint ventures / equity holdings*

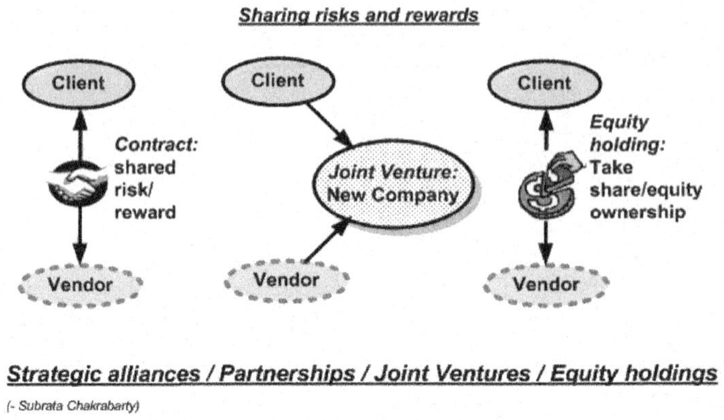


As illustrated in Figure 22, firms often prefer to keep select IS functions in-house based on their own strengths and capabilities, and *outsource* the IS functions which they feel can be better performed by a vendor. This is a flexible and modular form of outsourcing where all the IS functions are broken down into multiple modules, some of which are outsourced and some are retained in-house based on cost analysis, technology and resource needs.

*Selective sourcing*, which eschews the all-or-nothing approach in favor of more flexible, modular outsourcing, is characterized by short-term contracts of less that five years for specific activities, and hence meets the customer's needs while minimizing risks associated with total outsourcing approaches (Lacity et al., 1996, pp. 13-14).

In *selective sourcing*, clients outsource between 20 to 60% of the IS budget to vendors (typically around 40%) while still retaining a substantial internal IS department (Lacity & Hirschheim, 1995, pp. 4, 223-224; see also Dibbern et al., 2004, p. 10). Furthermore, this recommended approach is capitalizes on the respective strengths of both internal and external service providers.

## Spin-Offs

- *An IS department that now sells to the market*

A *spin-off* is an entity, which was originally an internal IS department of a firm, and is now selling its services to the market (Willcocks & Lacity, 1998, pp. 26, 31-32). The parent firm either totally or selectively sources IS functions from the spin-off (Dibbern et al., 2004, p. 12). A spin-off is a *client entity* as long as its ownership control remains with the client, however if the client gives up the ownership control (for example by divesting its majority equity stake) it becomes a *non-client entity*. So a client *insources* from a spin-off that it owns, but *outsources* to a spin-off that it does not own anymore.

## Strategic Alliances / Partnerships / Joint Ventures / Equity Holdings / Strategic Sourcing

- *Sharing risks and rewards*

As shown in the Figure 23, a client enters into a *strategic alliance* or *partnership* with a vendor on a shared risk/reward basis which may involve (a) contracting with a vendor to share risk/rewards, (b) helping to create a new *joint venture* company to which work can be outsourced, or (c) take share/equity holding in each other (Currie & Willcocks, 1998, p. 124; Sparrow, 2003, p. 12; Willcocks & Lacity, 1998, pp. 26, 27-28). Furthermore, by entering into a joint venture a client has greater control of the vendor's activities. Currie and Willcocks (1998) have treated the terms "*joint venture*" and "*strategic alliance*" synonymously.

*Benefit-based relationships* (Sparrow, 2003, p. 13) and *business benefit contracting* (Millar, 1994, as cited in Lacity & Hirschheim, 1995, pp. 4-5) may be considered as methodologies to share risk/reward on the basis of the contractual agreement.

The client and vendor can set up a separate "*joint venture*" organization which has its own management team, and its IS staff can be provided by both the parties, thus enabling the client to gain access to new technical skills and resources, reorganize IS functions and processes and investigate new sources of revenue (Sparrow, 2003, p. 12).

In *equity holding* deals, the client takes an equity position in the vendor, and vendor may also take an equity position in the client (Willcocks & Lacity, 1998, pp. 26, 27-28).

In s*trategic sourcing*, a customer decides in a wider business context on what, when, and how to outsource, and hence aiming to achieve a significant improvement in business performance rather than a short-term cost saving alone; the customer and supplier work towards mutual interests and are willing to share risk and rewards (Sparrow, 2003, p. 8). Ideally, a *partnership*, *joint venture* or *strategic alliance* is best classified as an arrangement for sharing risks and rewards between a client and a vendor. Dibbern et al. (2004, p. 52) interestingly state the following:

*It should be noted that the terms partnership, alliance, and relationship are loosely defined in the outsourcing literature. For example, Grover et al. (1996) suggest a connection between the presence of certain elements of 'partnership' and outsourcing success. However, they go on to note that other researchers (Lacity & Hirschheim, 1993; Fitzgerald & Willcocks, 1994) believe the relationship between an outsourcing vendor and its customer should not be characterized as a partnership unless there is a true sharing of risks and rewards. In another example, Lacity and Willcocks (1998) state that the term "partnership" was commonly used by firms when referring to fee-for-service contracts. The vague and inconsistent use of these terms contributes to the difficulties in comparing results among studies.*

## Tactical Outsourcing / Contracting-Out / Out-Tasking

- *Outsourcing for rapid solution to problems*

*Tactical outsourcing* is adopted to solve a particular need or problem rapidly over a short period of time; it is also known as *contracting-out* or *out-tasking* (Sparrow, 2003, p. 8). When a firm finds itself short of in-house resources to complete a particular task in quick time, the task can be contracted out to competent firms or individuals thereby giving the firm rapid access to new technical skills.

## Total Insourcing

- *Insourcing maximum percentage of IS budget*

In *total insourcing*, though a firm formally evaluates outsourcing options, it finally selects its internal IS departments' bid over vendor bids, thus keeping over 80% of the IS budget in-house (Lacity & Hirschheim, 1995, pp. 4, 223-224; see also Dibbern et al., 2004, p. 10). Furthermore, *total insourcing* can sometimes be a poor IS strategy because it may fail to capitalize on the inherent cost advantages provided by vendors, and may create a political environment of complacency.

## Total Outsourcing / Traditional Outsourcing

- *Outsourcing maximum percentage of IS budget*
- *Vendor having complete charge of significant IS work*

There are two interpretations of *total outsourcing*. One is based on the percentage of IS budget outsourced, and the other is based on the totality of the work or project outsourced.

*Figure 24. Transformational outsourcing*

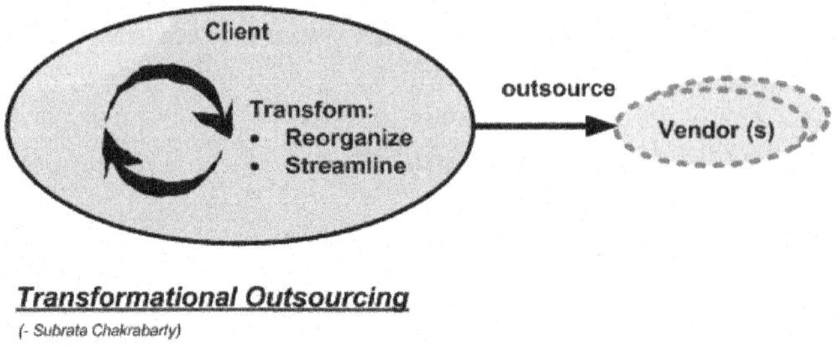

*Figure 25. Transitional outsourcing*

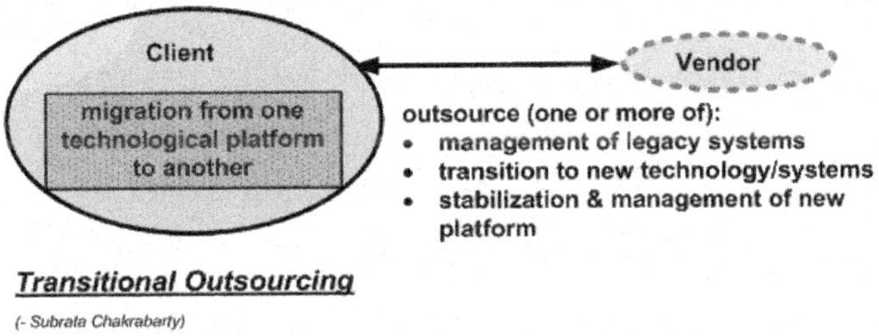


In the first interpretation of *total outsourcing*, clients outsource at least 80% of there IS budgets to vendors (Lacity & Hirschheim, 1995, pp. 4, 223-224; see also Dibbern et al., 2004, p. 10). Furthermore, *total outsourcing* can sometimes be a poor IS strategy because it fails to capitalize on the potential inherent cost advantages of internal IS departments. *Total outsourcing* has also been referred to as *traditional outsourcing* (Dibbern et al., 2004, p. 12).

In the second interpretation of *total outsourcing*, the vendor is in complete charge of a significant piece of IS work, such as entire hardware operations (e.g., data center and/ or telecommunications) and software support (sometimes including applications development) (Lacity & Hirschheim, 1993a, pp. 17-18).

## Transformational Outsourcing

- *Streamlining of client's internal organization alongside outsourcing*

In *transformational outsourcing*, companies transform by comprehensive reorganization and streamlining of its business processes and technology infrastructure and the outsourcing of IS needs, in order to reduce costs and improve services (Sparrow, 2003, p. 10). As shown in Figure 24, a company (client) decides to *transform* by reorganizing and streamlining the way it operates; and a component of such reorganization and streamlining would be outsourcing.

*Figure 26. Value-added outsourcing*

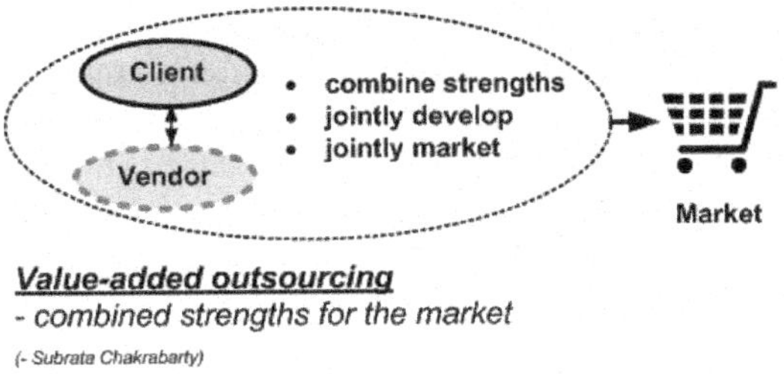

## Transitional Outsourcing

- *Outsourcing during a major changeover*

When companies need to introduce a major transition, such as migration from one technological platform to another involving the outsourcing of one or more of the following three phases: (a) management of the legacy systems, (b) transition to the new technology/systems, and (c) stabilization and management of the new platform, it is known as "*transitional outsourcing*" (Millar, 1994, as cited in Lacity & Hirschheim, 1995, pp. 4-5), which is illustrated in figure 25.

Firms sometimes undertake transitions like infrastructure overhauls and IS consolidation in order to bring in more efficiency, and make use of newer technologies. Conceptually, *transitional outsourcing* has also been addressed as "*transition assistance*" in the *co-sourcing* continuum (Wibbelsman & Maiero, 1994, as cited in Dibbern et al., 2004, p. 11).

## Value-Added Outsourcing

- *Combined strengths for the market*
- *Vendor adding value to IS activity*

There are two interpretations of the term "*value-added outsourcing*". One interprets on the basis of selling jointly developed products and services in the marketplace, and other interprets on the basis of additional value added to a service by the vendor.

In the first interpretation of *value-added outsourcing* that is shown in Figure 26, both the client and the vendor combine their strengths to jointly develop and market new products and services (Willcocks & Lacity, 1998, pp. 26-27). Willcocks and Lacity (1998) argue that because each partner shares revenue from the external sales, the partnership resulting from *value-added outsourcing* is an alliance with shared risks and rewards.

As per the second interpretation, when some area of the client's IS activity which could not be cost effectively provided by the internal IS department, is turned over to a vendor that can provide a level of support or service that adds value to the activity, it is known as *value-added outsourcing* (Millar, 1994, as cited in Lacity & Hirschheim, 1995, pp. 4-5).

# Future Trends

As the reader would gauge after reading this chapter, a large number of terminologies are already being used in the world of IS sourcing. There are two highly noticeable aspects that come to fore. The first is that most of the terminologies in literature deal with the client's perspective (for example, what is best for the client and how the client should handle vendors), and the vendor's perspective is almost absent. The second is that most of the terminologies in literature relate to the insourcing versus outsourcing line of thought and relatively fewer terminologies relate to the lateral phenomenon of offshoring.

A large majority of available literature has analyzed issues from the perspective of the client. The lack of literature giving the vendor perspective implies that this gap may be filled in the future, leading to a greater understanding of the vendor's methodologies. This would imply more terminologies being added with the vendor's perspective in mind (like global delivery).

Though offshoring in the manufacturing and textile industries had taken place a long time back, the offshoring of IS work is a relatively new phenomenon. Most the sourcing alternatives that were discussed in this chapter are conceptually applicable to both onshoring and offshoring. However, due to various advantages (like cost savings, skilled labor pool, etc.) and disadvantages (like communication and coordination problems, etc. ...), the offshore versions of insourcing and outsourcing are quite distinctive from the conventional onshore versions. Hence, there is the possibility of a more onshore versus offshore line of research (for both insourcing and outsourcing).

# Conclusions

This chapter compiled the maze of sourcing alternatives and terminologies that have come into being in recent times. The sheer number of these alternatives justifies the need for this chapter. This pursuit for terminologies and concepts resulted in the understanding of various sorts of insourcing, outsourcing, onshoring and offshoring of business needs and therefore elucidated this behemoth of a phenomenon that is continuously changing the way business is carried out globally.

# References

Apte, U. M., Sobol, M. G., Hanaoka, S., Shimada, T., Saarinen, T., Salmela, T. & Vepsalainen, A. P. J. (1997). IS outsourcing practices in the U.S.A., Japan and Finland: A comparative study. *Journal of Information Technology, 12*, 289-304.

Bennett, C., & Timbrell, G. (2000). Application service providers: Will they succeed? *Information Systems Frontiers, 2*(2), 195-211.

Chakrabarty, S. (2006). The journey to new lands: Utilizing the global IT workforce through offshore-insourcing. In P. Yoong & S. Huff (Ed.), *Managing IT professionals in the Internet age*. Hershey, PA: Idea Group Publishing.

Chaudhury, A., Nam, K., & Rao, H. R. (1995). Management of information systems outsourcing: A bidding perspective. *Journal of Management Information Systems, 12*(2), 131-159.

Cheon, M. J., Grover, V., & Teng, J. T. C. (1995). Theoretical perspectives on the outsourcing of information systems. *Journal of Information Technology*, *10*(4), 209-210.

Currie, W. L. (1998). Using multiple suppliers to mitigate the risk of IT outsourcing at ICI and Wessex Water. *Journal of Information Technology*, *13*(3), 169-180.

Currie, W. L., & Willcocks, L. P. (1998). Analyzing Four Types of IT Sourcing Decisions in the Context of Scale, Client/Supplier Interdependency and Risk Mitigation. *Information Systems Journal*, *8*(2), 119-143.

Dewire, D. T. (2000). Application service providers. *Information Systems Management*, *17*(4), 14-19.

Dibbern, J., Goles, T., Hirschheim, R., & Jayatilaka, B. (2004). Information systems outsourcing: A survey and analysis of the literature. *ACM SIGMIS Database*, *35*(4), 6-102.

Fitzgerald, G., & Willcocks, L. P. (1994). Contracts and partnerships in the outsourcing of IT. *Proceedings of the 15th International Conference on Information Systems,* Vancouver, Canada (pp. 91-98).

Gallivan, M. J., & Oh, W. (1999). Analyzing IT outsourcing relationships as alliances among multiple clients and vendors. *Proceedings of the 32nd Annual International Conference on System Sciences,* Hawaii.

Grover, V., Cheon, M. J., & Teng, J. T. C. (1996). The effect of service quality and partnership on the outsourcing of information systems functions. *Journal of Management Information Systems*, *12*(4), 89-116.

Hirschheim, R. A., & Lacity, M. C. (1998). Reducing information systems costs through insourcing: Experiences from the field. In *Proceedings of the 31st Annual Hawaii International Conference on System Sciences*, Hawaii (pp. 644-653).

Hu, Q., Saunders, C., & Gebelt, M. (1997). Research report: Diffusion of information systems outsourcing: A reevaluation of influence sources. *Information Systems Research*, *8*(3), 288-301.

Infosys. (n.d.). *Global delivery model.* Retrieved January 27, 2005, from http://www.infosys.com/gdm/default.asp

i-Vantage. (n.d.). *Global insourcing services*. Retrieved January 27, 2005, from http://www.i-vantage.com/GlobalInsourcingServices.html

Kern, T., Lacity, M. C., & Willcocks, L. P. (2002). *Netsourcing: Renting business applications and services over a network.* New York: Prentice Hall.

Klotz, D. E., & Chatterjee, K. (1995). Dual sourcing in repeated procurement competitions. *Management Science*, *41*(8), 1317-1327.

Kobyashi-Hillary, M. (2004). *Outsourcing to India: The offshore advantage*. Berlin: Springer-Verlag.

Lacity, M. C., & Hirschheim, R. A. (1993a). Implementing information systems outsourcing: Key issues and experiences of an early adopter. *Journal of General Management, 19*(1), 17-31.

Lacity, M. C., & Hirschheim, R. A. (1993b). *Information systems outsourcing: Myths, metaphors, and realities*. Chichester, UK: Wiley.

Lacity, M. C., & Hirschheim, R. A. (1995). *Beyond the information systems outsourcing bandwagon: The insourcing response*. Chichester, UK: Wiley.

Lacity, M. C., & Willcocks, L. P. (1998). An empirical investigation of information technology sourcing practices: Lessons from experience. *MIS Quarterly, 22*(3), 363-408.

Lacity, M. C., Willcocks, L. P., & Feeny, D. F. (1996). The value of selective IT sourcing. *Sloan Management Review*, *37*(3), 13-25.

Loh, L., & Venkatraman, N. (1992). Determinants of information technology outsourcing: A cross-sectional analysis. *Journal of Management Information Systems*, *9*(1), 7-24.

Pring, B., & Ambrose, C. (2004). Vendors vie for competitive position in ASP market. *Gartner Research* (Publication Date: 3 November 2004, ID Number: G00124388).

Sparrow, E. (2003). *Successful IT outsourcing*. London: Springer-Verlag.

Susarla, A., Barua, A., & Whinston, A. B. (2003). Understanding the service component of application service provision: An empirical analysis of satisfaction with ASP services. *MIS Quarterly*, *27*(1), 91-123.

Tata Consultancy Services. (n.d.). *Flexible global delivery*. Retrieved January 27, 2005, from http://www.tcs.com/investors/BusinessOverview/FlexibleGlobalDelivery.aspx

Tata Consultancy Services. (n.d.). *Our industry practices*. Retrieved January 27, 2005, from http://tcs.com/0_industry_practices/index.htm

Tata Consultancy Services. (n.d.). *Our service practices*. Retrieved January 27, 2005, from http://tcs.com/0_service_practices/index.htm

Willcocks, L., & Lacity, M. (1998). *Strategic sourcing of information systems*. Chichester, UK: Wiley.

Willcocks, L. P., & Kern, T. (1998). IT outsourcing as strategic partnering: The case of the UK inland revenue. *European Journal of Information Systems*, *7*(1), 29-45.

## Note

The author may be contacted at schakrabarty@tamu.edu or chakrabartys@yahoo.com.

## Chapter III

# Global Sourcing: East-West Divide or Synthesis?

Ashima Goyal
Indira Gandhi Institute of Development Research, India

## Abstract

*This chapter shows that ICTs make possible a more inclusive global trade, since now labour intensive components of production can be unbundled and sent where it is cheaper. The new mobility of virtual labour, together with the rise in capital mobility, will lead to a wider diffusion of benefits. ICTs reduce frictions and search costs in labour markets, and allow access to new hitherto excluded segments, whether firms or workers in developing countries or women. The smaller scale of efficient production induces more entry of new firms, thus raising wages and employment more than profits, and benefiting workers. Higher levels of employment and learning-by-doing can, in turn, induce more labour using technological progress and further raise both productivity and wages. Policy that targets education and training of workers and reduces barriers to the entry of new firms can minimize underinvestment and short-run job loss for developed country workers.*

# Introduction

This chapter examines the benefits and costs of global sourcing and how they are distributed over workers and firms, over time and across countries, and the implications for social processes. Internet and communication technologies (ICT) which support global telecommunication networks, have the potential to decrease global inequalities, since technology now allows labour intensive components of production to be unbundled and sent where it is cheaper. But a selective focus on one or other aspect of benefits or costs, or ignoring the short-run nature of the costs compared to the widely diffused long-run gains, can place impediments on global sourcing thus reinforcing old divides and lowering potential benefits.

Since definitions are not yet settled and many words are used, we use the term *global sourcing* to cover *offshoring* or the relocation of business processes, which could be either production or services to a lower cost location, which maybe overseas, and *outsourcing* which is normally used for a third party service provider running a business process. Intermediate or component goods trade, which involves a horizontal splitting of the production process, has formed a major part of international trade in the '90s. Outsourcing of business processes or services is more recent and is affecting the welfare of millions as work migrates across the globe to find the lowest cost supplier.

The basic change that allows global sourcing is that ICTs reduce frictions and search costs for labour and allow market access to geographically separated entrants. Thus it is possible for a worker in one country to be employed in, or do some work for, a firm in another country. Entry costs fall also for new firms. If some component of production is offshored or a component acquired from another firm, ICTs facilitate the greater coordination required. If a service is contracted to a third party, ICTs make this outsourcing feasible, and the third party is part of the process that matches labour to a distant job.

Opportunities improve for one set of workers, but home workers face more competition. These emotive issues of livelihood and relative gains have led to a spate of recent studies. But the effect of easier matching of firms with labour, and the thickening of market opportunities in developing countries, has not received attention. Cost savings are driven by falling cost of coordination due to new technology, and the cumulative productivity increase from improved incentives for education and technology adoption. These will make wage increases in provider nations sustainable.

This perspective is particularly suited to analyze the marriage of ICT and different types of global sourcing and makes a number of contributions. First, it shows why freer trade will increase global equality. This was the conclusion of classical trade theory, but was reversed by new trade theory, and is now reinstated but with some modifications we explore.

Second, the implications of improved matching give lessons for business. These include the importance of investing in new technology and in worker training, both to take advantage of trends that are inevitable if the required policy support is forthcoming, and to contribute to these trends. There are also lessons for workers and policy makers. Technology, competition and education turn out to be the important factors. Under easier entry of firms, the availability of more workers would induce entry of yet more firms, and encourage more adoption of technology, education and training, in virtuous cycles of productivity increase, leading, over time, to large change. If there is free entry of firms, skill upgrading of workers, and policy support, fears of sustained local unemployment due to some jobs going abroad are unfounded. Tax or insurance can cover transitional unemployment. Complementary local jobs will be created as profits and activities expand.

Third, the analysis has implication for expected income distributional changes, over time, across countries, workers and firms. A rise in per worker productivity combined with a fall in the cost of entry of new firms increases the opportunities available for workers. Thus although outsourcing is seen as benefiting firms while workers lose jobs or are offered low-wage jobs, the longer-term trends set in motion are exactly the opposite — they favour workers over firms. Wages rise with productivity for workers under rapid entry of new firms.

Fourth, it shows why easier access to thicker markets and more flexible work conditions will reduce inequalities in power and income by lowering exclusion of developing country workers and firms and of women.

Finally, the analysis helps understand the rapid changes taking place in global sourcing and the expected global trends. It is important for business to understand the forces driving these trends.

After drawing out the effects of global sourcing on the expected benefits from trade we turn to the analysis of improved matching and the effect of easier access to markets of hitherto excluded sections. Since underinvestment is possible, there is a role for policy. We draw together policy recommendations. Finally we show that evidence and emerging trends are consistent with the analysis.

## Background: Issues, Controversies and Problems

What does trade theory imply for the effects of ICT and the global sourcing it has facilitated? Classical trade theory expected a country to export labour intensive goods and import capital intensive goods if it has relatively more of labour supplies compared to capital. Thus populous developing countries would specialize in labour intensive low technology production. Trade would tend to equalize wages between trading countries.

But much of the growth in trade took place between developed countries with similar labour endowments. This came to be known as intra-industry trade, or exchanges of goods within standard industrial classification, and was driven by scale economies due to specialization. It did not involve any reduction in the wage dispersion between the developed and the developing world. In fact, trade increased inequalities, as new trade theory[1] predicted, due to continuing productivity improvements in established clusters. Such inequalities are expected to rise not only in the developing East, which is unable to compete with the technological lead of the developed West, but also in developed countries, between skilled and unskilled labour. On the whole, new trade theories predict an advantage to developed country firms and to skilled workers. But contrasting with this expectation is the decline in global inequality that has occurred due to the trade-linked rise in growth and employment in the populous countries of East Asia, China and now India. Some other mode of analysis is required to understand these trends.

Offshoring or the growth in components trade was the big change of the nineties, accounting for about 30% of exports. Obstfeld and Krugman (2003) call this "pseudo-intraindustry trade" since it was driven not by economies of scale but by comparative advantage from cheap labour, as labour intensive components were sourced from developing countries. Athukorala and Yamashita (2005) point out that over 1992-2003 world component trade grew from $400 to $1000 billion, the annual rate of growth was 3.4% constituting one-fourth of the total increment in trade. The share of developing countries increased from 16 to 35, with rapid growth in Asia.

Although intra industry trade was unable to affect relative wages, component trade is expected to have major effects. Feenstra and Hanson (1995) argue that the offshoring of capital and production to Mexico in the eighties raised the wages of skilled workers in both countries. Skilled U.S. workers benefited from cheaper imports but relative wages and employment of unskilled workers fell. Standard economic analysis suggests lower relative wages should have led industries to substitute towards the low wage cheaper factor, but they actually employed relatively fewer low skilled workers. Technology was favouring skilled workers, making them much more productive. Newer research suggests that while inequality within countries may rise, relative wages maybe equalized between countries. Egger and Pfaffermayr (2004) provide evidence that such equalization has occurred both within and between the EU-15 member countries, but not within some Eastern European countries.

This technology-enabled offshoring has been boosted by outsourcing of services. New technology is magnifying global sourcing and changing its character, steeply reducing transaction costs. Jones and Kierzkowski (2005) suggest that future increasing returns will come not from economies of scale but from fall in the fixed cost of coordinating far flung production units as global production rises. Therefore expansion in trade will include sourcing labour intensive components from developing countries. This splitting or fragmentation of the production chain across countries, will create external economies, and raise productivity for all countries. Each firm's labour demand, at different lowest-cost production locations producing different components, becomes complementary; labour at one location does not substitute for that at another. Ethier (1982) had demonstrated that with this type of specialization factor prices equalize under free trade.

This virtual labour mobility reduces the importance of labour endowments for the pattern of trade in final goods but increases it for component sourcing and local production. New technology makes labour surpluses locally available as inputs for final outputs produced in other lands. Since capital is a produced means of production, the barriers to increasing its supply are reduced, only profitability limits its expansion. Along with near perfect mobility of virtual labour, easier entry of new firms is the key change.

A major implication of the new technology and its embodiment in the current global sourcing wave is the ease in putting together labour and capital to produce a product or a service, anywhere in the world. Falling transaction costs imply more efficiency in the allocation of resources. In these conditions, analysis of the process through which distant labour is matched to new firms offers a useful unexplored framework to understand the new sources of global increasing returns, productivity and trade expansion, in addition to those coming from falling fixed costs of coordination.

The framework has implications for inequality, reversing those of earlier trade theories. It is helpful to differentiate between the impact on inequality between the regions, such as the West and the East, between labour and capital or workers and firms, and between skilled and unskilled workers. After developing the framework in the section below, we will collect potential effects on each type of inequality in the concluding section.

# Insights from Analysis

## Search and Matching

When a firm in one part of the globe can employ a worker in another, the process cannot be analyzed in terms of standard demand and supply because skills and types vary and there are frictions in bringing together or matching a firm and a worker. Since workers differ from each other there is no uniform market determined wage giving their opportunity cost. Returns are not driven to these outside options. A particular pairing, will occur only if it suits requirements, and will yield a match-specific surplus. Since a worker can be matched to a firm anywhere in the globe, firms do not have monopsony power, and workers are not limited to their marginal product. Relative bargaining power decides the distribution of the match surplus.

This search, matching and bargaining framework, with heterogeneous workers and frictions in the labour market, is well suited to analyze distance work. It has been used to analyze the evolution of unemployment in labour markets under macroeconomic shocks, but not to exploring the effects of new technology[2]. We use it to draw out the effects of ICT when opportunities in one region can be matched to searches made by entrants, who could belong to another. Benefits to workers come from the jobs, wages and the distribution of match surplus. Benefits to firms are the difference between price and cost.

We use workers as a generic term, which could stand for service providers, traders, or firms. Outsourcing part of services to another firm or to workers in a distant land is possible only if there is good quality of work. This requires harmonization of standards and relationship specific investment since it is not possible to specify all these details fully in a contract (Grossman & Helpman, 2002). The local firm or worker will have to invest in equipment or training relevant for a particular job. ICT reduces transaction costs in finding and maintaining such a relationship. It facilitates the spread of common standards and improves monitoring, which can compensate to some extent for incompleteness of contracts. By creating more opportunities and making markets thicker, it reduces the degree of specificity of investment or training all of which implies a fall in matching costs.

Workers search for an employment opportunity, and firms enter to create such opportunities. The two are brought together by a matching technology. A firm incurs a cost to acquire the technology and then employs the worker[3]. Opportunities and searches yield a flow of new jobs according to a matching function, which proxies for the complex process of bringing them together. An improvement in technology or a reduction in frictions raises the matching rate. The match must determine a wage, but because labour is heterogeneous and a replacement cannot be found instantly, there is a range of wages between the demand and supply price of labour. Any wage in this range makes each party better off than they would have been without the match.

A rise in the probability of finding a worker and a rise in entry cost raise the firm's outside option and therefore lower its wage offer. A rise in output raises the total available for distribution and therefore raises wages. Improvements in the worker's bargaining position also raise wages. For example, more options become available to workers when the probability of locating a vacancy rises, so that the wage-offer they receive also rises.

The expanding use of ICT raises the efficiency of the matching process and per worker productivity in outsourcing jobs, and reduces the cost of firm entry. All these three factors will raise wages. The match surplus will rise and so will firm's profits initially, but easier entry implies that these will be competed away.

Higher output, productivity, improved matching and scale economies benefit both firms and workers equally, under free entry of firms. Reduction in the cost of entry for employers (technological innovation) and higher employee productivity (training and technology) raise employees' share of the match surplus.

Entry of distant workers facilitated by ICT expands the availability of workers and therefore raises the entry rate of workers. This has permanent scale effects, raising the level of employment or the size of the market. Therefore equilibrium searches and opportunities both rise, which in turn improves matching thus benefiting both firms and workers. The free entry assumption implies that the fall in costs and rise in output will attract more firms and thus benefit workers in the longer-run, since opportunities for workers rise compared to the searches they have to do. Thus although outsourcing is seen as benefiting firms while workers lose jobs or are offered low-wage jobs, the longer-term trends set in motion favour workers over firms.

## Underinvestment

Determining technology and education choice within the framework reinforces the results. But multiple outcomes become possible, and inefficient outcomes can persist. Therefore the impact of policy rises.

Since training and technology raise output and therefore the match surplus and wages, they have a self-reinforcing aspect. The more they are adopted, the higher the returns to adopting them. We have seen that a rise in output has a relatively greater impact on the probability of a worker finding a job and therefore on wages. Both better training and technology would raise output. ICT would increase the workers' own returns from training. Outsourcing expands the set of relatively low-wage workers available to firms and this will encourage the further adoption of technology that makes it possible to utilize them. Modern research has brought out the importance of learning by doing and human capital formation for the innovation process. Acemoglu (1997), for example, points out that productivity growth was relatively lower for the British labour force in the nineteenth century compared to the U.S.. He argues that part of the reason could be that high British unemployment lowered learning by doing since fewer people were working. In contrast, in the U.S. under labour shortage, a larger percentage of the population worked and rapid labour using technological progress occurred.

If there are decreasing returns to scale there is a unique determinate outcome, which maximizes welfare. But putting in realistic features brings in stretches of increasing returns. First, it is highly possible that training could rise with the probability of a successful search, since the expected benefits from education rise. But this has two effects on the entry of firms. It raises wage and therefore lowers firm entry, but it raises the level of workers' training and therefore raises entry. Thus there could be a sharp jump in firm entry after training crosses a threshold, giving rise to multiple stable outcomes[4] at low and at high probability of successful searches. The multiple outcomes imply inefficiencies could exist. There is a possibility of being trapped in a low-level equilibrium steady state, where the level of private investment will be less than socially optimal. A policy-induced boost to ICT could shift the system to the high level equilibrium with optimal investment.

If there is a probability of separation after a match, likely in distant work, multiple outcomes arise again, but for a different reason. In the new random match found after a separation from the old match, there is a probability that technology and training will not occur together. Then private parties may not recover the full returns to their investment, making multiple outcomes and underinvestment possible. If the proportion of the population investing and training approaches one, all will find it profitable to undertake investment but as the proportion approaches zero the private returns to investment fall and can even be negative if the probability of separation is high (for example, close to one). Then all agents investing are a possible outcome, but so is one with no one investing. Crossing a critical diffusion of investment, facilitated by ICT, can lead to sustained improvement.

New technologies and the outsourcing they make possible have the potential to mitigate long entrenched global inequalities. Developing country firms or labour may be excluded from networks or their share in a transaction may be low because of the large networks established firms can leverage. The former's bargaining power in a transaction is low. Developed country firms may use strategic forward-looking behaviour to influence bargaining positions, extract surplus and maintain relative power.

Globalization and the use of ICT make dense networks of interaction possible in many activities. ICT makes it feasible for new entrants to participate in established networks, and thus reduces inequities.

## Mitigating Inequalities and the Extraction of Surplus

Markets are relatively thin in developing regions, and the density of interactions is much higher in developed regions. Then agents in the latter have the power to leverage their networks to extract more of the match surplus. When third parties are involved, developing country agents may even be forced to enter into transactions that give them zero or negative surplus. A simple example[5] can illustrate this process.

Suppose there are two firms in the developed region, one of the two is bigger. We call them the big and the small firm respectively. They have two potential business transactions with each other, the first business plan or strategy gives highest returns to both firms. If one or both of them follow the second strategy returns are lower. In effect, they play a coordination game where if they coordinate on the first strategy, so that both implement business plan one, they earn more.

Next both enter into transactions with a firm from the developing region, which we call the new entrant. But the big firm has the first move. It offers a wage and employment pair to the new entrant for a sub-contracting job. In the next period the latter can accept or reject the take it or leave it offer. In the third period, the other small developed country firm and the new entrant decide on their trade and in the final period the two developed country firms carry out their transaction.

If the new entrant refuses the big firm's offer, then the latter threatens to implement the less remunerative business plan with the small developed country firm unless it boycotts the new entrant. This threat is effective in stopping the small firm from trading with the new entrant if its loss from the reduction in its transaction with the big firm exceeds its gains from trading with the new entrant. The big firm's threat is credible only if its loss on implementing the less profitable business plan with the small firm is less than its potential gain from its trade offer to the new entrant.

Then the outcome is that, the big firm maximizes its profits, giving the new entrant just enough to make it worthwhile for the latter to participate in the transaction. That is, the sum of the new entrant's gains from its transactions with the two other firms must not be negative. The big firm's profits are maximized if its trade offer to the new entrant is such that the sum of the latter's gains from its transactions with the two developed country firms sums to zero. Thus, the payoffs will be such that new entrant will earn zero, the big firm will not only be able to extract the entire surplus from its own transaction with the new entrant, but also will successfully extract all that the new entrant earns from its transaction with the small firm.

Thus the new entrant can be left at its no trade level of profits, and can even make a loss on its transactions with the big developed country firm.

Since the credible threat lies off the equilibrium path it would not be observed in actual play. It is only implicit. The general point is that future trades, including those between sellers and other buyers, matter when there are networks; so that trade between any two parties depends also on their interactions with a third. Then strategic, dynamic effects occur (Farrell & Klemperer, 2002). The big firm is able to extract some of the new entrant's surplus from its interaction with third parties, as long as the big firm has more interactions with these other parties than the new entrant does.

ICT will increase the small firm's profits from transactions with the new entrant and raise it above the loss on its transactions with the big firm, so that the third party would not want to endanger its interaction with the new entrant; the big firm's threat is no longer effective and the surplus extraction fails. As the density of the new entrant's interactions rise, it will have alternatives to both the developed country firms. By making entry of new firms easier it will reduce the hold of the big firm on both the two other firms. The hold arises from its premier position in the network, which will be eroded. The new entrant will improve its exit options and bargaining positions.

The source of the big firm's advantage is partly greater information. It knows more about the markets and other firms. Equivalently the new entrant does not know firms other than the two it is interacting with or finds the transaction costs of contacting them very high. ICT lowers the cost of acquiring information. The Internet[6] lowers these costs but, unlike a monopolistic firm, does not require to be compensated for doing so, partly because adding content advertises other contents, and partly because it is not owned by anyone. The big firm, in contrast, extracts a rent for the information it provides or the trade it allows, and gives the new entrant the least consistent with its participation[7]. Research has discovered, however, that the Internet only benefits those job searchers who are otherwise qualified (Kuhn, 2003); since costs of search are low, the proportion of inadequate candidates who use it is higher. Therefore some independent certification and initial physical contact are also important to enter networks.

Apart from information about trading partners, information on international standards is essential for the developing region to raise the quality of its output sufficiently to access new markets. ICT helps acquire this information also but open standards are essential for these benefits to accrue fully. This issue is explored further when we draw together the conclusions for policy.

## Economic Opportunities for Women

Outsourcing also has important implications for women's work, relative position and participation in the labour force. Just as workers in developing regions have had low bargaining power, women have long been disadvantaged in the labour force because of higher transaction costs of external work and limits on mobility. This has lowered their economic status and power in society and at home.

Women allocate more time[8] to the household, often in a critical period in their career. This lowers their productivity in the external labor market, and by lowering learning-by-doing in remunerative skills, lowers future earnings as well. Perceptions and power magnify the distortions. In these circumstances ICT and the Internet offer great benefits to society and to women. They can reduce this waste of potential human resources since they facilitate flexi-time activity, lower location constraints, and make it feasible for women to maintain and upgrade skills.

A richer menu of better paying jobs become available for women as ITES (IT-enabled services) and outsourcing centres turn to employing part time workers, mainly women, in distance work. Datamatics, an Indian software company, had women as 98% of its 600 home-based workers in 2000. They consciously set out to tap the pool of skilled women who have left their jobs for family reasons. Call centres, finding a high attrition rate among their youthful workers, are turning to older and part-time staff. U.S.-based Lason Inc. offshores integrated data service out of Chennai to Fortune 500 companies. The managing director says they are willing to train anyone who can see and type. Their large talent pool among housewives gives them single digit attrition. Of the workforce in their production shops more than half are housewives. IT experts expect many mid-sized software companies to soon embrace this model (*Times of India*, Oct. 23, 2004). Firms such as Novell and Wipro are using telecommuting to maintain the skills of female staff with young children.

Modernization did not help women as much as it was expected to. The women in development (WID) approach blamed the liberal world-view for identified them only with housework and welfare. Boserup (1970) argued that differences between the sexes arose from differing work experiences, and with professional training, women could be as rational, objective and competitive as men in the external world. Instead the development process had marginalized women, since new resources, experience and opportunities had largely gone to men.

But this emphasis on modernization meant neglecting women's own priorities and biological constraints, thus contributing to a devaluing of "women's work". There are vulnerable points in birth, death, childhood and old age where care and nurture are essential (Kabeer, 1994) for almost everyone. It is beginning to be understood that to succeed development has to be gender aware. Both sexes must change: men contribute more to nurture while women become more active outside the home.

Historical processes were part of the reason technological development could not effectively liberate women. Throughout history, women's status was better when they had a productive and not merely a reproductive role. For millions of years women worked and brought home 60% to 80% of the evening meal and their relative position was almost equal to that of men. But the agricultural revolution made male roles more important than female roles (Fisher, 2003). Esther Boserup (1970) also argues that the colonial period made matters worse in many developing countries. Males were recruited for plantations and so forth, but women were pushed to subsistence production, which kept the supply of male labor cheap. For example, the British colonial administration destroyed the checks and balances that had maintained equality among the sexes in traditional Igbo culture. The latter had assigned women separate resources in female farming systems (Nzegwu, 1994). From being co-partners in pre-colonial landholding arrangements women became dependents in India, as landed property was put exclusively in male hands. Translation of flexible social and customary practice into legal codes made men the dominant legal subject (Oldenburg, 2002), particularly in the patriarchal households of the northern plains. In southern India women sometimes inherited property rights, and had greater independence and autonomy in decision-making and in household tasks. Thus although initially modernization and technological development disadvantaged women, but a technological U-turn may now be possible.

ICT can allow both men and women the freedom to participate in care and nurture while maintaining active professional lives. Being at the technological frontier becomes compatible, for women, with more presence in the household and flexi-time.

The failure of modernization to substantially improve women's position has contributed to a deep ambivalence in women's relation with technology. The women's movement recognizes the importance of the Internet, but fears are expressed that women may be left behind and end up as have-nots. There are arguments both that women have been systematically excluded from technology, which is a source of power, and that the high tech world has been used to exploit them.

It is argued that although ICT can make many other options available for them, such as part-time outsourcing work, entrepreneurship, marketing, and skill upgrading, this may imply a double burden, of home and of outside work. The key to delivering more freedoms and control of their lives for women is either developing a high level of skills with the superior economic status and bargaining power it gives, or the presence of supportive organizations that improve exit options and generate awareness. Women's perceptions of possibilities are also limited and need to be changed. ICT makes more options available; but having the ability to do more does not mean that one has to do more. It means that the choices one makes are better suited to ones skills and therefore more rewarding materially and mentally.

## Solutions and Policy Recommendations

Many policy recommendations follow from the analysis, relating to access, education and training, entry barriers, taxes, subsidies and regulation[9].

As ICT reduces transaction costs, raises the efficiency of the matching process, and facilitates global sourcing, it benefits both firms and workers. The entry of new distant workers increases the scale, improves matching, and again benefits both. With easier entry of firms, the availability of distant workers would induce entry of more firms and expand the level of activity. Therefore encouraging the spread of ICT, access and bandwidth, should be a key policy objective.

Since Western firms obtain the major share of the match surplus and make large transient profits, a low tax on them can be used to help establish a specific welfare fund to upskill and redeploy Western workers that loose jobs temporarily. Firms will factor in some of the losses to workers, but unlike with a ban, will still be able to outsource if cost savings are very high[10]. Subsidizing education and training facilities will also reduce adverse effects on low skill Western workers. De Long (2002) argues that a major reason for the rapid rise in inequality in America in the last decade has been the decline in the quality of primary education and the affordability of secondary education. Here there is clearly a role for government policy.

A rise in the efficiency of the matching process, affects both search and opportunities equally, but a rise in per worker productivity, and fall in the cost of entry of new firms increase opportunities and reduce search by workers. Since they benefit workers relatively more than they benefit firms, the workers get a larger share of the match surplus. Free competitive entry of firms reduces excess profits to zero. Therefore policy that gives a larger weight to technology and training, and ensures competitive entry will tend to reduce inequality between wage and profit earners, within and across countries, over time.

Moreover, the enhanced matching model shows that training and technology have a self-reinforcing aspect. The more they are adopted, the higher the returns to adopting them. Training choice responds positively to a rise in the probability of a match, and to firms' adoption of better technology. Returns to the technology and learning by doing, in turn, improve with training. Since the level of private investment may be less than socially optimal under multiple outcomes, policy to stimulate investment further will raise social welfare. Well-designed public intervention can trigger large changes that would benefit both regions. Any one country imposing a ban on outsourcing would loose out in the benefits from technology and training.

There are strong incentives for training in conditions where opportunities are expanding. Strict quality standards can strengthen these incentives[11]. Such quality standards will make employers more willing to expand education and training facilities to shift workers above the threshold. The availability of labour skills, in turn, can induce firms to adopt new technology in a beneficial feedback cycle.

Participation of girls in IT education lags that of boys. More special women only technical training institutes ranging from engineering colleges to computer training institutes to more basic training centres for ITES type jobs should be set up. Active collaboration from local communities, business and governments, and special initiatives for backward areas and communities would be fruitful (Umrani & Ghadially, 2003).

Eastern workers' bargaining power will improve with their exit options as ICT allows them to participate in distant markets. Better information and deeper networks available to Western firms or individuals, is a source of their advantage, and explains the low share of Eastern workers in the match surplus. ICT has the potential to improve developing region's access to networks but institutional support is required for access to be established. Industry bodies, governments, or international institutions can encourage new specialized networks. ICT lowers the cost of acquiring information both about potential trading partners and about standards of acceptable products. This knowledge is vital for developing regions to access new markets.

Open standards contribute to the above effects[12]. If network effects dominate it pays to expand the market, so far-seeing policies should lock-in the large new populations into the networks, even at the cost of some minor current concessions on openness and market access. Costs of conversion to common standards should be lowered. When conversion costs of standardization are small relative to network effects, all regions gain from accepting common standards (Gandal & Shy, 2001). A. T. Kearney (2004) point out companies need more understanding of new markets in China, India and Eastern Europe from which sourcing activity is slated to increase. The key is greater collaboration with suppliers, which is necessary for adoption of the advanced sourcing techniques required for competitive advantage. These are the processes that lead to technology spillovers and uniform standards.

Open standards enhance competition and innovation as they have in the ICT industry itself. This experience gives valuable lessons, to apply to different kinds of networks. Open standards are especially valuable when they apply to inputs, and where innovation occurs in small steps through a series of contributors. Interoperability can turn competitors into complementors. International patent rights (IPRs) should be limited to facilitate interoperability between competing products. When there are network effects, consumers value compatibility and IPRs by turning the initial choices of a small user group into *de-facto* standards, may confer monopoly rights without any significant innovation. There should be only limited copyright protection for a firm improving an interface. To allow products of different manufacturers to work together in a computer system, reproduction and translation of copyright code is essential (Gandal, 2002).

Network externality destroys small local networks unless compatibility is built in. Small new entrants need to think strategically and combine with those who gain. They must be willing to learn the language before contributing to it, be willing to engage in a range of activities and move slowly up to higher value-added products.

Although standards help specialists who want to compete globally, incompatibility provides local protection. For inefficient firms with large installed bases, incompatibility maybe a strategic choice, in order to deter rivals. Thus markets maybe locked into inefficient standards. It is necessary to enhance the development of public and quasi-public standards development organizations and their speed and conflict resolution capabilities.

Regulation is required, but under network externalities competition policy has to consider dynamic aspects. Firms may have to give concessions initially in order to make a market; the concessions may not be aimed at destroying competition. Policies that improve one's product need to be distinguished from those that block a competitor. Open standards can help prevent the latter. As Farrell and Klemperer (2002) suggest, competition policy should give rivals rights such as reverse engineering that allow them to insist on compatibility, notwithstanding patent rights.

A high rate of new firm entry is essential for the beneficial effects on equality to occur. ICT can reduce barriers to the expansion in size of a firm, and therefore lead to giant firms and reduced entry; but it can also reduce the viable size of a firm thus encouraging entry. Regulation can encourage the latter, and ensure entry and access.

Unions should push for training facilities and easier entry of new firms, rather than try to stop global sourcing. Otherwise they may be able to protect their current members for a short period, but will harm future members, labour elsewhere, and even the future of their current members.

## Future Trends

The analysis aids interpretation of the rapid changes in global sourcing, and therefore indicates future trends, with and without policy intervention. The future will differ in many ways because of offshoring, outsourcing and new technology. The composition of the labour force, by country and gender will change. It will affect global trade and the distribution of current account deficits. We examine evidence on changes in inequality across different categories and time horizons. Since events are very recent we rely on the press and reports from consultancy firms as the major source of information. The trends the evidence brings out are italicized. They are consistent with our analysis.

The media is full of reports of job losses in the developed countries, which is the expected initial impact of global sourcing. There is also a loss of union power — workers lose compared to firms who have more options available. Bronfenbrenner and Luce (2004) collated information on U.S. job losses through online tracking of media reports and corporate research. Since they believe their methodology only captures one-third of all production shifts, they boost their estimates to get a figure of 406,000 jobs lost to India, Mexico, China and other Asian nations by end 2004, compared with 204,000 in 2001, as multinational corporations outsource and shift production overseas.

They report that over January to March 2004, 23,396 of the documented jobs that left the U.S. went to Mexico, 8,283 to China, 3,895 to India, 4,419 to other Asian countries, 5,511 to Latin American countries other than Mexico and 2,933 to other countries. These trends are weakening union power. Unionized jobs accounted for a disproportionate 39% of the U.S. jobs lost. In addition, 29% of the companies shifting production out of the U.S. were unionized.

Other predictions are similar. A high-end projection from Forrester Research predicts a loss of 3.3 million U.S. jobs by 2015, including 1.7 million back-office jobs, or 200,000 jobs annually for the decade starting in 2005. But this is still only a small dent in the American labour market, whose strength is its flexibility (McKinsey Global Institute, 2003). Global Insight (2004) estimates for the Information Technology Association of America (ITAA) that 2% of 10 million U.S. computer-related jobs have been sent abroad and 12% of IT companies have outsourced work.

Firms throughout the developed world are using this opportunity to save costs: if 77% of U.S. multinational companies outsourced financial functions over 2002-04, 72% of European companies have done so. Moreover, 71% of European companies compared to 78% in the U.S. planned to use these services over the next two years[13]. Amicus, the largest British private sector union, quotes the biggest figure of an expected loss of 200,000 UK jobs by 2008. The Confederation of British Industries is worried that 43% of British companies are considering relocating even head office functions to India (Rajghatta, 2004). Norwich Union is Britain's largest life insurer. Its chief executive, Gary Withers reported a saving of 140 million pounds during 2003 due to outsourcing a range of front and back office functions, including call centre posts to India. He announced plans to save a further 130 million pounds within the next three years, through moving 7000 more jobs to India (Times of India, Internet Edition, October 10, 2004). Its rival, Royal and Sun Alliance also announced plans to move 1,100 jobs from Britain to India over the next two years, in order to save more than 10 million pounds a year (Times of India, Internet Edition, October 12, 2004).

Although job losses are in the limelight the second strand is that firms have major gains but it is necessary for them to outsource in order to remain competitive. This competition will ensure that the profits fall in the long-run, and gains accrue to workers through more job creation, and to consumers through cheaper prices.

For example, the Global Insight (2004) study finds that most U.S. industries would gain new jobs in the long run due to offshore IT outsourcing. The study put the total number of such new jobs created in 2003 at 90,264. The projected increase by 2008 was 317,367. Global sourcing was also projected to benefit other U.S. economic indicators. A 2.1% fall in the consumer price index, a 1% rise in GDP and labour productivity, a 0.5% fall in prime interest, a 4.2% rise in real investment and a 0.5% rise in real exports were expected.

Although in the short-run developing countries gain jobs, in this same time horizon firms in developed countries make large profits. McKinsey Global Institute (2003) estimates that one dollar of U.S. job loss creates from $1.45 to $1.47 of global value added out of which the U.S. gets back $1.12 to $1.14 through various channels, including higher exports, while the country receiving the offshoring job gets just 33 cents. A major source of future gain will come from firms concentrating on creativity and more workers focusing on innovation. Dossani and Kenney (2003) write that outsourcing to India saved GE $340 million annually. Similar economics is at work in all developed countries who are outsourcing or offshoring.

Developing countries do gain jobs in the short-run compared to developed, but the short-term gains and losses across the two regions are balanced by the gains of developed country firms. The rise in options available to developing countries is not inequitable because it only reverses existing inequalities. And over the long-term, higher global growth will stimulate growth and jobs in developed countries. That job and productivity gains are already being tabulated in the latter, suggests that the long-term will not be long in coming.

Over the last 10 years, the Indian software industry has grown at annual rates of over 50%. Nasscom (2004) estimates that in 2001-02 it accounted for 2.87% of Indian GDP, 16.5% of its exports, and 500,000 direct jobs. In 2008, it is expected to account for 7% of India's GDP and 30% of its foreign exchange inflows with exports totaling $70-80 billion and own and indirect jobs that employ 4 million people. IT enabled services (ITES) is projected to reach $21-24 billion, or 12% of the world market, and create 1.1 million jobs by 2008. Industry minister Maran in a press interview (Business Standard, Internet Edition, October 2, 2004) put India's software services exports at $12 billion with $38 billion as the expected figure for 2008. At current rates the projections may well be exceeded.

Opportunities in developing countries are not available only for the skilled. Every direct job in software creates 2.5 indirect jobs through supporting service industries such as catering, transport, housing and so forth. In software itself the jobs range from high value added creative work, to more mechanical problem solving by engineers, through outsourcing jobs such as call centres that just require knowledge of English and typing. Jobs created at the low end tend to decrease inequality.

The boom in ICT related jobs in India means that there is an expansion in both the supply of education and the demand for it. Thakore (2002) documents that large firms in ICT are becoming more involved in the provision of primary education because their future depends on trained manpower. The rise in the returns to education means a rise in the demand for education all down the education chain. A major positive spin-off is that returns to literacy will rise, and contribute to its spread, thus decreasing inequality.

We should see technology advance in bursts as large volumes of labour are matched into higher productivity work. A virtuous cycle can occur, as technology develops to use the new volumes of cheaper and skilled workers that become available. The East has the advantage of a large number of youth that can more easily acquire the new skills in demand.

India produces 70,000-85,000 software engineers annually, along with about 45,000 other IT graduates, and there are plans to double the capacity (Kogut & Metiu, 2001). Maran put the figure of IT graduates that enter the labour market every year in India at 120,000 and contrasted it to 5000 in Germany and 25,000 in the U.S. as a major source of India's advantage (Business Standard, Internet Edition, October 2, 2004). The pull factor is not only lower wages but also availability of skilled manpower.

Although higher wages in the home region are one of the drivers of global sourcing, and the latter would cause the wage differential to narrow, it would be a slow process. Skill differentials and higher productivity due to better systems would tend to preserve developed country wage levels, with differentials falling more due to a rise in low end wages. The rise would be sustainable since it would come from rising productivity. A major spin off would be a fall in physical labour migration required, and the tensions that accompany it. The reduction in migration would reduce the downward pressure on unskilled wages in developed countries. As technology advances, over time, wages can rise sooner with outsourcing compared to the standard result that inequality rises before falling with freer trade.

There are already examples of reverse offshoring from developing countries creating jobs in the developed countries. Indian HCL Technologies took over the Belfast-based contact centre Apollo from BT in 2004, and created huge employment opportunities taking the staff strength up to 1,600, and investing about £2 million in infrastructure (Economic Times, Internet edition, January 30, 2005).

The large U.S. trade deficits are a major problem for the global payments system. Will the trends in outsourcing help or hinder adjustment? A number of researchers have documented the Houthakker-Magee asymmetry that the U.S. income elasticity for imports significantly exceeds the foreign income elasticity for U.S. exports. Therefore equal U.S. and world growth will not be sufficient to improve the deficit, and a depreciation of the dollar will be required. But Mann (2004) notes that the asymmetry is reversed for traded services[14]. The U.S. exports relatively more to richer nations that tend to have a higher share of modern service sector output. Outsourcing will lead to a boom in service trade between developing countries and developed countries. Moreover, service sector growth is high in developing areas, which will also boost developed country exports. In the medium-term outsourcing will also expand the service sector through the working of a result in trade theory (Krugman & Obstfeld, 2003) that as the supply of one factor increases relative to the other, production of the good that is less intensive in the more abundant factor has to decrease relatively, to keep factor prices unchanged. The initial relative rise in labor supply implies a rise in labour-intensive service sector output, explaining the larger share of the service sector in modern output growth.

# Conclusions

The analysis attempts to understand the dynamics that drive global sourcing, to discover the key issues beyond selective interpretations and political positions, and identify the policies that can make inevitable change more beneficial for all.

British mill workers had revolted against new technology. If they had been successful, and the industrial revolution had bypassed Britain, what would be the current income levels of British workers? Technology, over time, has raised productivity, wages and living standards for workers. While automation does decrease labour requirement per unit output, the new feature of ICT is that they enable a much smaller scale of efficient production, compared to the earlier factory technologies. Therefore it is easier for new firms to enter, which, over time, tends to raise wages and employment more than profits, thus benefiting workers. Higher aggregate labour absorption and learning-by-doing can, in turn, induce more labour using technological progress and further raise productivity and wages. Policy that targets education and training of workers and reduces barriers to the entry of new firms can minimize short-run costs on one set of workers and maximize aggregate welfare. While start-ups may eventually be absorbed by larger firms, new niches will develop and attract entry.

The ability of ICT to facilitate a horizontal splitting and matching of production processes into the least cost components makes jobs in different locations complements. Wages and productivity rise and converge over time, making standard trade theoretical analysis less relevant.

The implications of our analysis for the three types of inequalities are that there will be more wage equalization between developed and developing countries, but established Western firms will make considerable profits in the short-term. Advantages to new firms and workers from developing countries will only reverse long-entrenched inequalities. Greater prosperity in the East and more intra-firm trade will increase exports from the West and create more jobs there in the medium-run. While capital gains relative to labour in the short-run, the longer-term implications are exactly the opposite. Again skilled labour gains relative to unskilled initially, but the multiplier effects of ITES jobs, the range from low to high end jobs created, and the boost given to education will create gains for unskilled labour in developing countries also. Unskilled labour in developed countries will gain because of a fall in physical migration combined with an expansion of traditional service sector jobs, a large proportion of which are not tradable. These trends will lower social and global tensions.

Countries with the highest per capita incomes are those with open flexible systems and willingness to adopt innovations. Concern about short-term job losses from global sourcing can harm this very willingness to use and advance technology. Potential synthesis and convergence to higher living standards across the globe could then be aborted into a stagnant divide.

## Acknowledgment

I thank an anonymous referee for very useful comments, and T. S. Ananthi for help with the processing.

## References

Acemoglu, D. (1997). Training and innovation in an imperfect labour market. *Review of Economic Studies, 64*, 445-464.

Athukorala, P. C., & Yamashita, N. (2005, February 25). Production fragmentation and trade integration: East Asia in a global context. Paper presented at workshop on "Regional Economic Integration in Asia", Claremont McKenna College, California.

Basu, K. (2000). Prelude to political economy. New York: Oxford University Press.

Boserup, E. (1970). Women's role in economic development. New York: St. Martin's Press.

Bronfenbrenner, K., & Luce, S. (2004). The changing nature of corporate global restructuring: The impact of production shifts on jobs in the U.S., China, and around the globe. Prepared for the *U.S.-China Economic and Security Review Commission.* Retrieved January, 2004, from http://www.uscc.gov/researchpapers/comm_research_archive.htm

Diamond, P. A. (1982). Wage determination and efficiency in search equilibrium. *Review of Economic Studies, 49*, 217-227.

De Long, B. (2002). New U.S. paradigm for the times. *Economic Times*, July 30.

Dossani, R., & Kenney, M. (2003). Went for cost, stayed for quality?: Moving the back office to India? Berkeley Roundtable on the International Economy, working paper 156. Retrieved January, 2004, from http://repositories.cdlib.org/cgi/viewcontent.cgi?article=1020&context=brie

Egger, P., & Pfaffermayr, M. (2004). Two dimensions of convergence: National and international wage adjustment effects of cross-border outsourcing in Europe. *Review of International Economics, 12*(5), 833-843.

Ethier, W. J. (1982). National and international returns to scale in the modern theory of international trade. *American Economic Review, 72*, 950-9.

Farrell, J., & Klemperer, P. (2002). Coordination and lock-in: Competition with switching costs and network effects. Forthcoming in *Handbook of industrial organization, Vol. 3*. Retrieved January, 2004, from http://www.paulklemperer.org

Feenstra R. C., & Hanson, G. H. (1995). Foreign investment, outsourcing and relative wages. NBER working paper 5121.

Fisher, H. (2003, May 24). A century for women? *New Scientist Magazine*, 2396.

Gandal, N. (2002). Compatibility, standardization, and network effects: Some policy implications. *Oxford Review of Economic Policy, 18*, 80-91.

Gandal, N., & Shy, O. (2001). Standardization policy and international trade. *Journal of International Economics, 53*, 363-383.

Global Insight. (2004). The impact of offshore IT and services outsourcing on the U.S. economy and IT industry. Sponsored by the Information Technology Association of America. Retrieved January, 2004, from http://www.itaa.org/eweb/upload/execsum%20final.pdf

Goyal, A. (2005, October-December). New technology and labour markets: Entrants, outsourcing and matching. *Indian Journal of Labour Economics, 48*(4), 853-868.

Goyal, A. (2000, December 10-13). Developing women: How technology can help. Presented at the GDN 2000 Conference, Tokyo, Japan. Retrieved January, 2004, from http://www.gdnet.org/pdf/842_Ashima.pdf and revised version at http://papers.ssrn.com/sol3/papers.cfm?abstract_id=509324

Goyal, A. (2003). Why women lag and why they may lead. *Information for Development*, issue on Can ICT cross the gender barrier?, *3*, 13-21, September-October. Retrieved January, 2004, from http://www.i4donline.net/issue/sept-oct03/women.htm

Goyal, A. (2004). Foreign investment in India: Riding the wave. In H. S. Kehal (Ed.), *Foreign investment in developing countries*. UK: Palgrave Macmillan.

Grossman, G., & Helpman, E. (2002). Outsourcing in a global economy. NBER working paper 8728.

Jones R. W., & Kierzkowski, H. (2005). International trade and agglomeration: An alternative framework. *Journal of Economics, Supplement, 10*, 1-16.

Kabeer, N. (1994). *Reversed realities: Gender hierarchies in development thought.* London: Verso.

Kearny, A. T. (2004). Assessment of excellence in procurement 2004: Can procurement deliver on its promise?

Kletzer, L. G., & Litan, R. E. (2001). *A prescription to relieve worker anxiety*. Policy brief 01-2, Institute for International Economics, February.

Kogut, B., & Metiu, A. (2001). Open-source software development and distributed innovation. *Oxford Review of Economic Policy, 17*(2), 248-262.

Krugman, P. R., & Obstfeld, M. (2003). *International economics: Theory and policy, 6th edition*. Singapore: Pearson Education.

Kuhn, P. J. (2003). The Internet and matching in labour markets. In D. C. Jones (Ed.), *New economy handbook*. San Diego: Academic Press.

Liang, D., Palivos, T., & Wang, P. (1995). Learning, matching, and growth. *Review of Economic Studies, 62*, 115-129.

Mann, C. L. (2004). The U.S. current account, new economy services, and implications for sustainability. *Review of International Economics, 12*(2), 262-276.

Mansell, R. (2001). Digital opportunities and the missing link for developing countries. *Oxford Review of Economic Policy, 17*(2), 282-295.

McKinsey Global Institute. (2003). *Offshoring: Is it a win-win game?* San Francisco: McKinsey Global Institute.

Nasscom. (2004). Reports available at http://www.nasscom.org

Nzegwu, N. (1995). Recovering Igbo traditions: A case for indigenous women's organizations in development. In M. C. Nussbaum and J. Glover (Eds.), *Women, culture, and development: A study of human* capabilities. Oxford: Clarendon Press.

Oldenburg, V. T. (2002). *Dowry murder: The imperial origins of a cultural crime*. New York: Oxford University Press.

Rajghatta, C. (2004). U.S. makes a mountain out of a BPO molehill. *Times of India*, Mumbai Edition, January 18.

Rama, M. (2003). Globalization and the labour market. *The World Bank Research Observer, 18*(2), 159-186.

Thakore, D. (2002). Corporate champions of Indian education. *Education World*, November.

Umrani, F., & Ghadially, R. (2003). Empowering women through ICT education: Facilitating computer adoption. *Gender Technology and Development, 7*(3).

## Endnotes

1 Krugman and Obstfeld (2003) is a good introduction to classical and new trade theories. Rama (2003) surveys empirical work based on new trade theories and documents that wages first fall and then rise with freer trade.

2 The next three sections draw upon and summarize analysis in Goyal (2005).

3 See Goyal (2005) for the explicit specification of the model and derivation of the results. The seminal reference for search and matching models is Diamond, P.A., 1982.

4 Such equilibria are explicitly derived in Liang, Palivos and Wang (1995) and Acemoglu (1997). See Goyal (2005) for an application to the analysis of ICT.

5 Basu (2000), chapter 6, analyses the effect of third party transactions on coercion in the context of interlinked rural markets.

6 Open standards are a key feature to realize these benefits. As Mansell (2001) points out electronic EDI systems allowed established firms to exchange standardized information using proprietary software platforms and create closed networks.

7 To borrow a metaphor from one of India's ancient poets Kabirdas, what does a river loose if a bird takes away a beak-full of water? ICT functions like the river where use barely affects availability.

8 Goyal (2000) demonstrates this formally in a model of household decisions based on a specific technology of production of the household good. The arguments made here follow some evidence presented in that paper and in Goyal (2003).

9 This section is also based on Goyal (2005).

10 Kletzer and Litan (2001) estimate that if companies purchase targeted insurance to cover workers laid-off due to outsourcing and protect their salary it would cost only 4% to 5% of the companies' savings from outsourcing. An interesting example of outsourcing that did not lead to job loss, was when Dabur an Indian Pharma company outsourced its IT and other system maintenance to Accenture, an American company, in 2004. Accenture employed some Dabur employees to do the job.

11 Such quality standards are automatic for traded goods and by demonstration extend to others. NASSCOM (2004) argues that high quality is the reason for India's success in software exports. Mansell (2001), "...producer firms are required to meet new quality, time-to-delivery, or other standards introduced by buyers in the industrialized countries (pp. 290)." Such standards are impossible to achieve with illiterate and subsistence labour.

12 See Goyal (2004) for a discussion of standardization in the context of FDI inflows. These issues are even more relevant in the context of outsourcing. Even though the FDI involved may be small the necessity of harmonizing inputs leads to a rapid standardization.

13 PricewaterhouseCoopers' Management Barometer Survey, reported in the Economic Times, Internet Edition, October 31, 2004.

[14] She collects estimates over the 80s and 90s and estimates a component of services herself. While for goods, the export elasticity is 1.21 compared to an import elasticity of 2.10, for the service component travel with a trade weight of 0.35 the elasticities are reversed 2.18 and 1.22 respectively. For the component "Other Private Services" with a trade weight of 0.44 the respective elasticities she calculates are close, at 2.00 and 2.12 respectively.

# Chapter IV

# Strategies of Outsourcing: From De-Risking to Uncertainty

Parthasarathi Banerjee
NISTADS, India

## Abstract

*This chapter investigates conditions when economic profit can be made from outsourcing. In order to have profit a firm must pursue strategies of cooperation while outsourcing business processes. Strategic interdependence between the client and the provider firms has led us to look into the maneuverability of one structure by the other. The client firm in order to de-risk its business from risks generated by its own structure outsources part of the business. The structure of the outsourced partner, described sometimes as the extended enterprise, together with the structure of its client generate endogenous demand for outsourcing. Structures are the sources of demand here. Boundaries of the two structures become fuzzy, and transactions in intermediate outsourced goods shift the management of coordination between the two firms to a novel platform. Now each firm forms an expectation on what the counterparty expects, and through this the parties evolve norm. Norm based transaction leads to uncertainty and this uncertainty is the source of an entrepreneurial profit. Outsourcing when undertaken strategically thus might lead to a profit solution.*

# Introduction

Outsourcing is not a new concept. Early history of automobiles in the U.S.A. shows prevalence of this practice. Over the decades and in particular following the paradigmatic influence of Chandler's work (1962) businesses grew hierarchically integrating vertically and then horizontally. Large corporations became the norm (Galambos, 1983). A departure from this trend in resorting back to the previously known outsourcing practices albeit taking into account global markets of resources could not therefore be considered entirely novel or outlandish. Commonly held belief attributes resurgence of outsourcing to cost-leadership strategy on cutting costs through sourcing from low wages countries. Another perspective de-emphasizes this low-wage view and insists on globalization of coordination. Little perusal taking cues from Coase (1990) and Richardson (1972) makes us believe that outsourcing is but continuation of the old theme on coordination and on market to structure discourses. With this assertion we might have a smug comfort that outsourcing has been explained once and for all. However, streaks of doubts prevail. Does contemporary outsourcing offer something new, not known from previous accounts? Or, does outsourcing based on information systems (IS) act as a subterranean tremor to unlock and restructure the shibboleth of organizational structure? Possibly the stupid face of outsourcing tells us that this is "just" getting done a job cheaper. The deeper face conceals that through sourcing out one creates an entity outside the structure. These two structures are related through endogenous formation, which necessarily continues to transform structures of both client and provider. This present chapter is about this under-noticed face of outsourcing, and it claims that outsourcing can be utilized for great strategic advantages, unavailable from within the client's organizational structure. The first claim of this chapter is about this novel aspect of coordination, not captured in Richardson (1972). There is another second and more important claim of this chapter. A closer look at the first claim — that a firm outsource to only a handful of provider firms who do not often belong to the same industrial sector or who do not belong to the client's geography albeit who belongs to a close strategic milieu — leads us to the second: outsourcing is analogous to trades in derivatives that is, outsourcing as derivatives of client's risks being traded with a provider firm who undertakes the risk at an agreed cost. Received managerial practice distinguishes between two kinds of risks: operational and financial. A corollary of the second claim leads to a revision of this received wisdom of management. We also assert that there is a third type of risk that we define as structural. Operational and structural risks, we insist, are different. Our theory therefore, has significant practical implication for the practicing manager. This second claim leads us to the other dimension of lean organization. These claims are novel. Together these claims portray certain insights into the organizational black box. A manager in the outsourcing business benefits reading our arguments. Such a manager receives instructions in methods of strategy. As a follow up we can hint at a set of policies that countries dependent on outsourcing might take up. In the following we explicate in greater detail these two aspects of outsourcing.

# Background and Summary

## First Claim

In the corporate world, understanding on strategies of cooperation and outsourcing of business processes has come closer over the years. Rather often, outsourced partner is described as an extension of the client's enterprise. Provider adds values, suggests and offers strategic inputs and the separation between two structures of client and provider appears fuzzy. Much of this inter-dependence appears ex-post. Mutual structural dependence between the business entities largely unplanned ex-ante but begin to happen ex-post. Provider's organizational structure, following the logic of extended enterprise, must correspond in a certain strange manner with the client's organizational structure. These two structures never remained static, however. Early experience in outsourcing had seen spinning off a large corporation into fragments one or few of what provided outsourcing services to the parent. Currently a typical provider has not been spun off from the client (as parent) and core competencies of the two firms are very different. Structurally too they are unlike. These two structures belonging in general to two different countries and two different industrial sectors cannot be fitted together as in a jigsaw puzzle. In order to provide services of outsourcing provider's structure, however, must in some sense grapple with client's structure because what has been outsourced is a business process. The client too in order that solutions can be availed must restructure ex-ante albeit nominally only — because, a previously integral business process has now been handed over to the provider. Client and provider both therefore commence a journey towards a coordinated structural outcome. This latter is the process of finding a fit between two or more structures and is the expression of a demand arising out of structure. This first claim is thus about structural coordination. Previous literature on coordination referred to business coordination. We argue that outsourcing generates a demand for structural coordination, which is unique and different from business coordination. Our departure to structural coordination offers freedom to both provider and client to pursue independent of this outsourcing transaction, business initiatives unique to each. A perfect fit between the two structures cannot be desired lest the two merges together rendering outsourcing vacuous. Necessarily there should remain imbalance and incongruity. The latter always drives the process of coordination endogenously. The demand for outsourcing must look for sources of structural incongruity. As a result contrary to a stable balance between two structures, an unstable balance continues to destabilize all the structures in dynamic interactions. This happens ex-post and this is the source of demand for structural transformation. Unstable bargaining and negotiation between these two entities result into generation of new and novel demands all the more. Increasing returns are experienced and interacting structures are the sources of demand here. Continuation of structural changes ex-post keeps generating new demands on outsourcing relationships. In short, demand for outsourcing gets generated because there are structural mismatches between client and provider. Outsourcing can benefit through structural coordination between two businesses that continually design strategies to remain structurally distinct. The first claim of this chapter is about this structural coordination.

## Second Claim

The client prior to outsourcing has, however, been facing a business risk. The literature on risk has differentiated between two kinds of risks, typically the first is out of business model pursued by a firm, and the second commonly known as "exposure" refers to risks that this firm faces and that arises out of the business environment, such as currency risk or political risk. Received literature has, however, not dealt with factors and systems that cause risk in the firm's business model. Typically a business model refers to the revenue model, the cash flows models and therefore customers and competition of the firm. Such a model strays away from describing the structure of the firm. It is therefore tacitly assumed that a business model is independent of the structure of the firm, or, varieties of structures from vertically integrated to diversified, from large to small or from multi-divisional to multi-dimensional can undertake identical business model. It appears that risk in a business then is independent of the structure of the business. We differ from such an account. In fact our reading of Chandler (1962) informs us that structures are precisely meant for hiding ignorance about the causal chain of risk generation first within a transaction and then within a firm. Risks within transaction, known as transaction cost, are reduced when the two parties to transaction are brought under one firm or one authority. Experience with and theories about agency theory and incentives have shown us how inadequate could be the realm that an authority-manager commands. Junior managers undertake multiple projects, agendas and activities. A small fragment of such large domain the authority can command. As a result, micro-strategic interactions within the structure of firm generate huge and uncontrollable agendas. Necessarily, the information system (IS) or the managerial processes within the firm remain ignorant of most of such agendas. These multiplicities of agendas, projects and activities generate uncertainty owing to ignorance of both the agendas and their causal chains, as well as risks owing to unpredictability of organizational or structural outcome. Conversely, it is structure that both generates and distributes risks of a business within the firm in a manner described as the structure. Or, sites of ignorance's describe a structure. We define structure as negotiated outcome on risk distribution within a firm constrained by the ignorance on systemic and causal chains of risk.

The board of the firm and the operational divisions as well as the managers has differential access to information pertaining to generation and distribution of risks. Risks multiplier effects arising from the systems within the firm and from the interactions of sub-systems are most often not known to the board or the managers. Ignorance of risk multiplications remains hidden behind the divisional or multi-dimensional matrix of the firm. Both cash flow and accounting refer to only value of assets and these cannot refer to risks of assets. As a result, sub-structural such as of a division assets fail to testify to the risk associated with that asset or the risk associated with a system of assets. Ignorance on the risks remains under cover of the structural constituents such as of a division, and therefore, business risks fail to capture this aspect of risk generation.

At this stage of our discussion we might learn from an example — regarding emergence of trade in derivatives. In this trade ownership of assets are not transferred while the risks of assets are traded between two parties. Most contemporary firms have undertaken such trades in derivatives possibly to their advantage. However, in most cases of derivatives risks owing to factors outside business such as currency risks have been covered because quantification of such risks is possible. This has led to a situation where risks pertaining to business structure remain with the firm while most of exposures get transferred at a price. At this stage a firm looks forward to further diminution of risks associated with its undertaking, however, with one constraint that risks in revenue model can possibly be traded while risks associated with structures cannot be traded.

Another example can be drawn from Basel II recommendations about banking. In this case two kinds of risks, operational and financial, have been identified. Basel II believes that increasing equity can cover operational risks. In other words, equity is the sunk-in element of last resort. However, derivatives have taught us that equity and debt are no longer different because equity and debt can be exchanged utilizing derivatives. In other words, operational and financial risks can both ultimately be covered under the same instrument of trade in risks. This operational risk, however, is hostage to the structure. The latter, generating both risks and uncertainty conceals behind the operational risks the more sinister structural risks. Operational risk arises out of known and planned business agenda. Structural risks arise out of mostly unknown causal chains of fuzzily known risks and uncertainties within the structure.

An intermediate solution, which some firms have adopted, pertain to reengineering the structure of the firm in terms of a set of business processes. Each business process cuts across structural formations within the business while referring to a unique revenue/ business model. Therefore to the extent the structure of a firm can be transformed to a set of business processes, part of the risks can be profiled across business processes. However, most often business processes transform a small part of the structure, and more importantly, causal relations between two or more business processes are not known. Hence, even if a firm wishes to mitigate risks through trading of business processes a la derivatives, it would remain limited and possibly would remain peripheral only. Therefore, the popular belief that a firm outsources business process to economize appears unsustainable.

In fact, in typical outsourcing practices firms resort to outsourcing of back office operations (which is not an integrated business process) or therefore of a division or a part of its value chain. In all such cases the structure never outsourced remains in interactions with structures or value-chains or business processes outsourced. Such a firm in order to mitigate risks associated with structure engaged its current structure with the structure of another provider firm, by way of transferring activities, functions or even part-structures at a price. Therefore we can explain outsourcing as a trade in derivatives on risks associated with the client's structure. This appears to be a novel way of looking into business process outsourcing. Limits to outsourcing are again attributable to the structure of the firm. Inability of a firm to possibly locate a source of risk that can be transferred across firms as a trade in derivatives is precisely the factor limiting the rise in outsourcing. Contrarily, the desire to reduce risks endogenous (because structurally determined or influenced) to a business forces a firm to increase its dependence on outsourcing. As a corollary, outsourcing will continue to grow as the derivatives trade has continued to grow.

## Integrating the Two Claims

Structural risks of a business can be partially mitigated through resorting to outsourcing. Very similar to a trade in derivatives, where risk assessor gets privileged access to privileged information internal to the firm alone, in outsourcing too the provider firm comes very close to knowing fairly-deep internal events, micro-strategies and other micro business decisions and information about the client firm. Cases where the outsourcing takes place through arms length transaction it must be understood that the client was in a position to hive off a chunk of structure or a particular business process of low value, and hence such stray cases of auctioning of outsourced businesses can take place. However, in rather large number of cases outsourcing cannot follow this path of arms length. In all these other cases, outsourcing refers to, we would argue, a strategic relation.

The provider firm now having deep access within the structure of client firm enjoys thereby a capability to maneuver. In fact in the absence of strategic intervention by a second structure, the client firm's structure remain static. We have no theory, I suppose, whereby a structure can innovate upon itself. Incentives based structural design (Baron & Besanko, 2001), for example, is dependent on changes in incentives designed by an outsider agency. Such an approach cannot be endogenous. Incentives do not evolve from within the structure. Moreover, any set of incentives becomes effective by denying all other acts not included in that set; and this denial is a stronger signal than what the positive set of incentives can generate. However, incentives-based designing has failed to take into account this aspect of denial. Provider-client inter-structural relations are, however, endogenous to the system of outsourcing business. Provider enjoying deep access can negotiate with client's structure in order that the provider can continue to enjoy increasing business with the client. The client's stakeholders too now under the threat from provider begin negotiation with the structure of provider by demanding close scrutiny of client's decisions and acts. Therefore through an indefinitely repeated game these two interacting structures keep structural risks under check and maneuver each other's structure.

# Elaboration on the Theme

## Generating Demand

Demand for outsourcing is generated within the client's structure because the client wished to de-risk. However, following outsourcing to a provider, the contents of outsourced business changes because of the interaction between the two structures. Demand for outsourcing differs from several other modes of demands. Possibly the most stale type of demand exists a priori and it is generated internally. In another mode of demand this internally generated demand could be influenced, especially through externally influencing the internal sources of generation. This achieved through macroeconomic instruments sustains certain generalized conditions and in that case the generated demand belongs to general types. Demand customization is not achievable through this general mode.

We often, however, fail to appreciate a third mode where the very process of satisfying client's demand generates another new demand. In this last instance management of current demand must in consequence create the future demand. A train of demands could be located in this case. Such a cascade must be based on increasing return or an endogenous satisfaction of demand. This appears to be provocative enough. Management of an endogenous demand rests upon the strategic relations between the interacting structures of provider and client firms. Source of the demand remains in structural incongruity between the two interacting firms and depends on the strategic competence of the provider (as an extended enterprise of the client) to offer innovative solutions regarding structural transformations to the client. The provider firm acts here as agent provocateurs as it were. This chapter argues that this endogenous demand is novel, of recent origin and is evidenced especially in the business of software services provisioning, including in some other modes of business process outsourcing.

The former two types of demand generation believed that a firm organization enjoys definite boundary. Demand can be generated only from within, endogenously, the structure. The latter type of demand evidenced in outsourcing is endogenous to a set of interacting structures. In contemporary language we refer to such relations of dependence as part of fiduciary relations or as part of norm-based relations between multiple structures. A fiduciary relation is contractually incomplete. Therefore, price and quantity exchanged between two structures as part of outsourcing cannot complete transactions and hence fails to clear the market. This type of market failure unlike what Coasian transaction cost (1990) would have implied, does not lead to the integration of two interacting structures. Legally the structures retain separate identities while transactionally these structures never can complete transactions.

## Transaction Incomplete

From a transactions cost perspective the structure of a business is the outcome of negotiations between several producers for reducing the cost of transactions. Journey from multiple firms to one or few vertically integrated or horizontally diversified firms can be explained through transaction cost. The reverse journey must then entail a sudden and unexplained rise in transactions cost, which forces the integrated structure of a firm to splinter away into several once again. The current theory (Williamson, 1985) does not provide an account of dynamics of transaction costs firstly, and secondly how within a firm such costs might rise above the level obtained in the market is also not explained. In order that transaction costs might rise within a firm we must account for a structurally differentiated firm. The structure of a firm, following Chandler (1962) and Simon (1991), is the system and instrument to implement coordination of resources towards achieving a plan. Implementation within a firm cannot be undertaken through contract. Boundary of a firm is then as per this definition drawn by boundary drawn by contracts — within the structure the contracts are ineffectual while all external relations are contractual. In such a case firm-based market can clear the market through completing transactions.

However, all contemporary firms have brought contracts within the firm and the degree of such induction varies. This induction results in weakening of Chandlerian administrative fiat, and brings norms and fiduciary incompleteness within the structure. The result is a situation where incomplete contracts and incomplete administrative fiats co-exist. This co-existence is precisely the source of structural risk. Resolution of structural risk cannot be completed within the boundary of the structure, because firstly the boundary has become fuzzy with the entry of contract within the structure, and secondly because, fiduciary relations encompass a region that is distributed further than the firm's structure.Theory of firm provides the account of firm as a homunculus. Such a monadic firm in fact cannot explain hierarchy. The latter implicitly recognizes that authority is required to plan, coordinate and direct the otherwise conflicting multiple units put together inside the firm (Chandler, 1962). This takes us to knowing a firm's internal organization a la Penrose (1968) and making use of contemporary theories including agency theory we can proceed towards a better account of the diverse and conflicting sub-structures of interests. Further, in case the authority (or the governance) turns out to be weak or in cases where corporate governance fails to mitigate conflicts to ordering a cohesive flow of resources (Lazonick & O'Sullivan, 2000) several market based relations and entities including the strategic alliance partners or the market for corporate control appear to take charge of coordination of firm-internal resources. However, an important question needs to be answered before we can accept this position that corporate governance weakness throws up the firm to the cradle of market.

## Shackle Space

This question relates to the existence of an intermediate layer between the market and a firm — does the firm exchange information with the market or with a zone nearby its structure? Banerjee (2004a) explained this zone, strategically most relevant to the incumbent firm, as the Shackle space. Saha (2004) in commenting upon Banerjee (2004b) refers to the interdependent and inter-firm structural relations as between Toyota as the assembler and large number of satellite firms as suppliers. It has been accepted that these inter-firm exchanges are not market-based; often authors have referred to such exchanges as relational contracts. The purport of relational contract is to portray the above kind of exchanges as non-market but socially embedded. Thickness of social relations, the relational perspective argues, substitutes market by society.

Banerjee (2004a) offers an alternate explanation. His description talks about a Shackle space in between a group of firms. An incumbent firm chooses its strategy depending on both the behaviors and the strategic maneuverability of a set of other firms in its strategy-vicinity. Together these firms constitute a strategic milieu. The incumbent firm in order to earn a profit in the Knightian sense (that is a profit arising out of ignorance or uncertainty) attempts to maneuver firms in this milieu, and the most important instrument that the incumbent could use towards this purpose is the intermediate goods. Incumbent firm chooses to maneuver other firms using intermediate goods and the incumbent achieves thereby an ability to coordinate the expectations of other firms. Expectation of a firm is a function of its structure. Hence, coordination using intermediate goods has the ability to strategically maneuver structures of firms in the strategic milieu.

Information generative intermediate good helps a firm achieve strategic vantage point of sustained competitive advantage. Coordination and capability are thus interdependent and the site of capabilities is also the site of coordination amongst firms. Information-in-expectation is the foundation of innovation that, in all likelihood, is beyond the Schumpeterian technological innovation and supports increase in Knightian or Cantillon profit.

This strategic space between firms where incomplete transactions in intermediate goods take place is named as Shackle space, the private space common to a partial market that brings together internal processes and structures of firms in a strategic milieu through repeated exchanges of intermediate good. A Knightian or Cantillon innovation, different from the Schumpeterian idea, requires the continuous creation and sustenance of Shackle space that is the space created through repeated flows of intermediate good providing a measure of mutual coordination. Norms evolve because there is mutual ignorance, and owing to mutual ignorance contracts cannot be effected or transactions necessarily are rendered incomplete. Business processes outsourced assist information passage across firms and thus outsourcing enables transformation mutually by structures. Norms, however, do not wipe off the differences between firms. Differences between firms depend on differences in strategic knowledge that each possess. This strategic knowledge reflects the capability to influence the processes internal to an incumbent and its partner firms belonging to the same partial market. A provider firm and the client firm possess such strategic knowledge about other. This strategic knowledge is a representation of the expectations and of utilization of information-in-expectation. Expectations depend on the deferment or the delay. Differences across firms are a function of delay. The uniqueness of a firm then does not depend on the resources that it has procured from respective factor markets. This uniqueness would depend on the degree to which an incumbent can utilize strategic knowledge to influence business processes and structure of other firms. Banerjee (2004a) argued that learning, like R&D, is a deferment of consumption. A firm situated in the context of a partial market strategic milieu is expected to follow the deferment characteristic of that market. This deferment acts as a norm. In outsourcing relation one of the two parties in transaction — the provider and the client, would be in a position to lever strategic knowledge about the other party's internal structure. Such a firm is active vis-à-vis the other dormant party. The delay effected by such an active firm needs to follow this norm with the exception that even though the length of the period of deferment remains nearly the same for firms in a partial market, the potential gains of firms do differ. Differences in this potential gain mark out the firm's individuality. Thus not only the client might gain from outsourcing, the provider too could gain. This potential gain is owing to the learning or knowledge-generative dimension of the time-period of deferment.A Knightian innovation is of a different kind requiring the continuous creation of Shackle space. This space cannot be intra-structural or -organizational neither can it be public. It ceases to exist with the flow of intermediate good and expectations on expectations stopped. Shackle space is created through repeated actions. A firm acting as a provider of outsourced business is in fact in search of the envelope of innovation. This receiving firm cannot, through technical or market information, attempt to co-ordinate its own expectations with the expectations of the other firm without having accessed information-in-expectation. This information-in-expectation exists transactionally between the client and the provider because each structure expects on the expectations of the other structure. Organizational integration such as through vertical integration would destroy such a Shackle space and information-in-expectation will cease to be produced. This means that the possibility of Knightian innovation would be lost. In order to reap entrepreneurial profit, firms need to innovate in a partial market Shackle space, while not abstaining from innovations conducted within the structure. Both client and provider firm structures seeking entrepreneurial profit are founded as much externally as are founded internally.

## From De-Risking to Uncertainty

The client firm suffered from risks generated within its structure. The business of de-risking brought this client firm closer to a strategic milieu shared by the provider firm. The client expected the provider to provide solutions to structural risks; and the provider expecting on such expectations of the client entered into the business of transactions in intermediate goods of business processes. Such transactions, however, as we saw above, are incomplete and the two firms get entangled in web of fiduciary or incomplete relations. These relations because of their incompleteness are encumbered with ignorance — an ignorance by the client as to what precisely the provider would provide, or conversely, an ignorance of the provider on the expectations of the client.

Ignorance, Knight (1921) argued, generates uncertainty and uncertainty is the source of profit. The client firm's journey towards minimization of structural risk generated uncertainty, and the client can thus look for profit now. Such an entrepreneurial profit, however, is not owing to reductions in costs of the client. The latter is a pure rent. Profit is generated between the structures in interaction because each structure is ignorant of the other's complete range of expectations. Outsourcing looked at from this perspective can generate novel entrepreneurial profit. The question then is: what to outsource? From whom to outsource and how?

# Conclusions

Outsourcing in the received literature recognized interdependence between providers and clients and this literature discussed strategic leverage through vertical integration in the event co-ordination transactions prove costlier to govern (Azoulay, 2002; Fixler & Siegel, 1999; Wildener & Selto, 1999). This transaction cost approaches based their estimates on differences in factor market prices and on costs of governance.

Our approach considered risks generated within a structure as the cause for a firm to outsource. This took us to inter-firm space where firms transact in intermediate goods of outsourced business. Both the client and the provider firms attempt to coordinate their expectations. Coordination of expectations necessarily generates norms and in the presence of norms, transactional relations between firms are not complete while the interacting firms remain in ignorance or uncertainty. De-risking of structure thus generated a strategic interdependence or inter-maneuverability between client and provider firms. In this uncertainty regarding coordinated outcome a firm can expect to generate an entrepreneurial profit. This profit, described as Knightian or Cantillon in nature, is not because of reduction in cost or risks, which having been achieved throws the incumbent firm in the grips of uncertainty; and the Knightian profit appears because a firm can speculate on uncertain outcome. The lesson then for outsourcing is that an incumbent must choose carefully process to be outsourced, the party supporting outsourcing and the transaction through which the parties can expect on outcomes of outsourcing.

# References

Azoulay, P. (2002). *Outsourcing as commitment to insiders: Evidence from drug development.* Mimeo, Colombia University.

Banerjee, P. (2004a). *The Indian software industry: Business strategy and dynamic coordination.* London: Palgrave-Macmillan.

Banerjee, P. (2004b). Strategies of subversion: Management of demand for software through destabilizing organizational structure of your customer. *Metamorphosis, 2*(1 & 2), 79-91.

Baron, D. P., & Besanko, D. (2001). Strategy, organization and incentives: Global corporate banking at Citibank. *Industrial & Corporate Change, 10*(1), 1-36.

Chandler, A. D. Jr. (1962). *Strategy and structure.* Cambridge, MA: MIT Press.

Coase, R. (1990). The nature of the firm. In O. Williamson (Ed.), *Industrial organization* (pp. 3-22), Aldershot: Edward Elgar.

Fixler, D., & Siegel, D. (1999). Outsourcing and productivity growth in services. *Structural Change and Economic Dynamics, 10*, 177-94.

Galambos, L. (1983, Winter). Technology, political economy, and professionalization: Central themes of the organizational synthesis. *Business History Review, 57*, 471-93.

Knight, F. H. (1921). *Risk, uncertainty, and profit.* Boston: Hart, Schaffner & Marx; Houghton Mifflin. Available at http://www.econlib.org/cgi-bin/printage.pl

Lazonick, W., & O'Sullivan, M. (2000). *Perspectives on corporate governance, innovation, and economic performance.* CGEP, INSEAD, Fontainebleau. Available at http://www.insead.fr/projects/cgep

Penrose, E. (1968). *The theory of the growth of the firm.* Oxford: Basil Blackwell.

Richardson, G. B. (1960). *Information and investment.* Oxford: Oxford University Press.

Richardson, G. B. (1972). The organization of industry. *Economic Journal, 82*, 883-96.

Saha, B. (2004). Subversion or cooperation: Searching for sites of creativity in a world of large organizations. *Metamorphosis, 2*(1 & 2), 92-96.

Shackle, G. L. S. (1972). *Epistemics and economics: A critique of economic doctrine.* Cambridge: Cambridge University Press.

Simon, H. (1991, Spring). Organizations and markets. *Journal of Economic Perspectives, 5*(2), 25-4.

Wildener, S. K., & Selto, F. H. (1999). Management control systems and boundaries of the firm: Why do firms outsource internal auditing activities. *Journal of Management Accounting Research, 11*, 45-73.

Williamson, O. E. (1985). *The economic institutions of capitalism.* New York: Free Press.

## Chapter V

# New Ethics for E-Business Offshore Outsourcing

Fjodor Ruzic
Institute for Informatics, Croatia

## Abstract

*In today's dynamic e-business environment where fast time to market is imperative, where information and telecommunications technology is costly and changing rapidly, and where skilled technical resources are scarce, e-businesses need reliable, high-end outsourcing infrastructure and resources. E-business companies should consider corporate social responsibility and they must work on reducing the pain and stress of disruption in home countries while increasing the socio-economic benefits of these jobs in the receiving country. E-business should develop offshore outsourcing ethics program. It presents the analysis of the nature and the social impact of information technology and the corresponding formulation and justification of policies for the ethical use of technology. These notions are considered in efforts to produce globally acceptable ethics program that would articulate both individual company and global interests in an appropriate way. This chapter examines e-business ethics development, and new standardization efforts toward unified, globally acceptable Code of Ethics. It covers the analysis and discussion on the needs for such instrument and findings on how to reach unified global solution.*

# Introduction

Currently, there is considerable confidence that we are on the edge of an important deepening of the information society. This is the era of ubiquitous computing, in which computer-based devices become so cheap, seamlessly interoperable and easy to use that they will find application across a broad field of everyday activities. The implications of these changes for policies on technology, employment and competitiveness will be profound. The issue of ubiquitous computing also directly raises a series of links to issues of competitiveness and employment. Chips are already embedded into many everyday devices (particularly automobiles and domestic appliances, and increasingly locks, alarms, payment machines, vending machines, cash machines, street furniture, hand tools and smart cards for identification, financial transactions and electronic wallets). In the same time, the production, services and trade become increasingly dispersed over wider area dealing with new goods market and labor market as well. Besides that, the new forms of e-business are aimed toward sharing resources in development, production and sale processes.

At the turn of the millennium, the e-business has become a new environment where new business models are practiced. Web sites are in most a reflection of businesses on the Internet. The three principal keys in doing e-business: honesty, integrity, and trustworthiness crossover directly to the Web site framework and the Internet. This is especially true for the online service providers. Professional service providers have the funds and staff of programmers to do the global Web site right and after all, that is their principal business specialty on a very large scale. However, sad to say, doing Web sites right is not always true for some of these big online providers. In fact, there are many e-business regulatory perspectives, ethical, copyright, and electronic commerce global legal issues at prominence.

The information society with e-business environment in use could form a more sustainable society (Cornford, Gillespie, & Richardson, 1999). It is possible due to the four key streamlines:

- there are potential environmental gains from organizational re-engineering since information technology can be used to lower waste for instance by reducing material usage or more accurate matching of production and delivery levels to realized demand;
- information technology is in its essence a dematerializing technology, and it works through three dimensions: the replacement of traditional control technologies by information technologies; the informational content of physical goods is increasing; the business shifts from trading physical goods to immaterial services. Most of the fastest areas of growth in our economies are in informational services such as software, design, new media and telematic services — all areas that directly depend upon information and communications technologies;
- information technology makes direct substitution effects, especially in transport. There are more substitution possibilities including teleworking and teleshopping.

Teleworking, in particular, holds out a promise of a more efficient use of people's time and the World's resources;

- information technology also provides decision tools for monitoring and controlling the use of the environment and resources over the distance, thus making e-business offshoring and outsourcing more reliable and useful.

The information technology based business, and specially doing business over Internet, is characterized by its openness. The result is that a rich and chaotic wealth of information, images and ideas are being made available on a worldwide basis, to anyone who has the tools and interest to work online. Because of its size, global scale, complexity, openness and dynamism, this chaotic network effectively renders obsolete traditional mechanisms for structuring and controlling informational content. Strains are apparent across a broad range of legal domains: decency laws, privacy protection, security services, intellectual property rules and authentication systems. With extensions of the Web to include more and more people and with ubiquitous computing to connect more and more devices, a large credibility gap could be opened between the scale of the information flows and regulatory tools. This scenario could lead to a loss of trust in the network society. The Internet economic phenomenon is extremely high, and it is currently generating a lot of attention as the fastest growing area of business. We have already seen that it raises serious challenges to existing rules on how to conduct trade, to protect consumer rights, to combat tax avoidance and so on. The intrinsic global nature of the Internet also means that new international conventions on these issues will have to be established and considerable effort is being expended by national and international bodies to adjust legal frameworks to create a coherent system of liabilities and trust. These issues are stimulus for strengthening efforts in the process of new forms of business ethics that could deal with the new challenges.

Information technology systems are important for doing e-business, but will not be by themselves enough to provide an appropriate system of governance for the new era of computing. It is the fact that the e-business is different now — it is played faster and it extends deeper into private lives. Consequently, new rules are needed which will provide a mature framework of governance for the new phase of the information society. There are tremendous challenges involved such as globalization and communications convergence. However, the confidence of people and enterprises will also be needed. This will call for a clear statement of rights and responsibilities in the information age that could build confidence in the global networking. As technology in general, and the Internet in particular, becomes a more important part of how virtually all companies do business, many are finding themselves faced with new ethical dilemmas. These notions urgently ask for new agenda for business ethics. Business ethics is not new. Efforts to apply ethical theories and values to commerce can be found throughout history and in the works of the great philosophers. Until recently, business ethics was largely an academic affair. However, allegations of waste and fraud in the business are increasing and there is need for a solution to the growing problem. The answer is in issuing and enforcing codes of ethics with adequate controls to monitor these codes of ethics and sensitive aspects of business compliance. The particular insight in the e-business outsourcing, as well as offshore outsourcing, is the key of successful and sustained development in all countries and regions where the e-business firms work under globally accepted and harmonized rules and universal code of ethics. The idea of this work is to express why and how the role of the global ethics environment is important to e-business, and what is done to make harmonized and balanced platform for sustained development of e-business offshore outsourcing in all regions around the globe.

## Background on E-Business Outsourcing and Offshoring

In the process of finding definition on outsourcing, it is important to be clear about what is meant by outsourcing. Outsourcing has become a commonly misused term, and much of the apparent disagreement over the merits and risks of outsourcing can be traced to differing definitions. Outsourcing is essentially a *how* term rather than a *what* term. It describes how technology and services are obtained, and not what the services are. Outsourcing could also be defined as a contractual relationship where an external organization takes responsibility for performing all or part of a company's functions. This can involve a partial or complete transfer of staff and/or resources. Outsourcing in broad terms is a transfer of some business functions or components of business processes to an outside contractor. To remain competitive, many companies outsource as a way to reduce costs, increase efficiencies, and refocus critical resources.

Outsourcing is done for various reasons. The driver can be generating cost reductions and downsizing. These factors have been a traditional reason for outsourcing. But, there are others factors such as gaining capabilities that are not available internally, implementing lean programs, streamlining operations, strategically positioning the company, or improving capabilities to gain competitive advantage. Regardless of the reason, outsourcing succeeds when it is well thought out and done properly. All parties involved in outsourcing should consider several key activities during the outsourcing project cycle:

- Defining the reasons for outsourcing
- Evaluating outsourcing business processes versus functions
- Recognizing seller and buyer roles
- Preparing for the risks
- Planning the change

### Information Technology Outsourcing

In a sense, outsourcing is just a name for old practices. Services such as, bureau services, contract programming and project management have long been outsourced. In its present usage, however, outsourcing implies a greater level of handing over ownership and/or managerial control than has hitherto been the case. There are differences between outsourcing and contracting out. Thus, outsourcing is distinguished from the in-house provision of services; and in-house provision means that the people who deliver the information technology goods or services are normally employees of the organization.

Many organizations find keeping up with technical developments in computing and communications very difficult. Operational decisions in regard to the operation of computing and communications are often adversely effected by a lack of in-depth knowledge of the full range of technical options available. This can lead to using inappropriate technology and/or inappropriately using technology. Many e-business organizations have their own information technology departments catering to their software and other information and communications technologies (ICT) enabled services needs, while others go for information technology outsourcing.

It is forecasted that the business process outsourcing segment of total information technology outsourcing will lead the way, with a 30% annual growth rate in the first decade of 21$^{st}$ century. The Internet and intranet management portion of this takes over 80% annually through 2004 and it would be through 2005, largely due to e-business and e-commerce spending. The impending, large-scale adoption of Internet-enabled wireless devices of all types will boost demand for networking upgrades, new services customization, and expanded desktop services outsourcing that includes this new technology and eventually ICT outsourcing. Because "Internet rates of speed" infect rates of technology change within the ICT industry as a whole, clients are increasingly reluctant to undertake independent, in-house migrations to upgraded architectures and applications.

Information technology outsourcing is typically the catalyst driving corporate re-engineering processes to reduce costs, and focus on business strengths. Besides banking, discrete manufacturing and insurance that have traditionally led information technology outsourcing, the fastest-growing sectors in the next few years will be the telecom and utilities industries. Hence the future prospects for information technology outsourcing will be very bright in the coming years.

## E-Business Outsourcing Issues

Outsourcing e-business processes is an obvious choice for most companies within national and international markets. Even for large enterprises, it is not possible to keep up with all the changes influencing e-business management. The lack of trained resources and faster time to market pressure accelerate this evolution. Cost reductions and higher quality results are free bonuses granted by an outsourcing strategy. Consequently, outsourcing technical jobs to other countries has become widely used solution.

Business processes outsourcing often starts with technical information technology outsourcing. The growing complexity of information technology and the difficulty to find and retain trained computer and telecommunications staff are the key elements in the priority given to technical information and telecommunications technology outsourcing.

Technical ICT outsourcing remains a very important decision with many complex aspects. Without an independent trusted ICT consultant with experience in both business management and technology, some outsourcing experiences ended in disasters. In the same time, information technology management in most e-business firms is not the core business function. Successful information technology management requires a fundamental understanding of both business and technology, and a long experience. Thus, in most cases, information technology management outsourcing is solution that is much more flexible and cost effective for most companies doing business electronically and over the network be it on regional, international or global level.

E-business outsourcing services dealing with the ICT services depend on Web-based processes that include several key activities:

- **Web design:** Creating a Web site is more than a simple online business card or catalogue. It is a real e-business tool contributing to corporation's profit and making brand image and position on e-marketplace.
- **Web site marketing and Web promotion:** Without e-marketing and Internet marketing, no e-business strategy can be successful. Creating a Web site presence is a first step in a succession of actions. Web site marketing and Web site promotion should be essential parts of e-business management strategy. The worldwide scale of Internet access and its full time availability are two of the most powerful strengths of a Web site.
- **Search engine optimization:** Many words generate more than a 30 million searches per month. However, search engine optimization is complex. This is why a professional team best executes search engine optimization.
- **Viral marketing and e-mail marketing:** Internet reacts fast, and viral marketing techniques can deploy very effective results in both a massive and quick way to get business message to the market. E-mail marketing is another very effective tool.
- **Web services:** As e-business activity is growing, Web services will become an easy and cost effective way to interact with business partners and customers. Since Web services are technically oriented business tool, they should be professionally set-up.

When e-business processes are planned to be outsourced, it is obvious that ICT outsourcing is involved. E-business firm should consider several outsourcing key categories:

- **Insurance:** The outsourcer should have adequate public liability insurance against loss or liability through injury or damage.
- **Third party suppliers:** The arrangements setting which party will hold and which party will administer the terms of any agreements currently in place between the purchaser and other third party suppliers.

- **Information technology licenses:** Where third parties supply goods and services used to provide outsourced services, the appropriate licenses must be obtained. Any licenses currently held by the purchaser that relates to services being provided may need to be extended to cover the activities of the outsourcer.
- **Ownership of information:** The ownership of data and information needs to be agreed.
- **Contract duration and commencement:** The commencement date of the contract should be decided as early as possible to minimize transition difficulties when service provision is handed from the purchaser to the outsourcer. Given the complex problems that can arise during the handover of information technology services, it may be prudent to include a defined transition period as part of the term of the contract.
- **Service level agreements:** Service level agreements are put in place to define the minimum level of service that must be provided. They are, therefore, the basis for measuring the outsourcer's performance.
- **System access and security:** Access to the purchaser systems by the outsourcer needs to be considered, and an outsourcer may only require system access at certain levels to enable them to perform their service. The level of security measures required to protect the purchaser's system and information from unauthorized access will continue to require rigorous planning, implementation and management. Outsourcing services will bring additional issues of protection, confidentiality and ethics that the parties will need to ensure are documented and agreed with regard to their responsibilities and obligations.
- **Personnel/staff:** Although the issue of personnel is often crucial, it is sometimes overlooked by those involved in outsourcing. People are fundamental to a business and are required to maintain business continuity during the transition period. The arrangements for the retention, redeployment or other options for existing staff must be negotiated. This issue is critical, as the outsourcer will require the institutional knowledge of the purchaser's staff. Business continuity must be maintained during the transition, which requires that the purchaser's staff be kept fully informed where appropriate. Staff may need to be transferred from the payroll of the purchaser to the payroll of the outsourcer and a transition plan should be used to minimize the risk of service disruption and employment-related legal claims. The employment contracts and/or collective agreements under which the purchaser's staff is employed may require negotiations to be held with the relevant staff or their representatives. The early involvement of professional human resource managers and employment law specialists to advise and assist with contractual and privacy issues is critical to any transition to outsourcing. The purchaser may also specify that the outsourcer should hire a certain number of staff and the outsourcer may require a certain number of people for the purpose of acquiring system and corporate knowledge. In these cases, there should be an agreed process for the outsourcer to select, assess and engage the appropriately skilled staff from the purchaser.

- **Intellectual property indemnity:** Each party should generally indemnify the other against claims of intellectual property rights infringement arising from the use of facilities and resources that they supply to the other as part of the outsourcing arrangements.

## E-Business Offshore Outsourcing

E-business topic that has become a key issue in the first decade of 21st century is offshore outsourcing. Many e-business companies that have shipped work to countries like Ukraine, India and Russia have claimed the cost savings and the quality of the output have increased efficiency, productivity and return of investment. However, information technology professionals have noticed that the recent economic stage does not include an increase in jobs. Some are pondering whether a high-tech union should be formed to stop the massive exodus of jobs across the Pacific Ocean.

Offshore development in the information and telecommunications technology (ICT) sector is the term most often used to describe the business of outsourcing software programming and engineering services beyond national boundaries. The three most common justifications for offshore development are cost reduction, internationalization and inadequate supplies of domestic resources. Cost reduction is the traditional reason for offshore development. Low-level tasks such as coding and software testing can be performed in less-developed countries at costs as low as 10% of domestic ones. Software manufacturers seeking international markets and needing to localize their products to specific platforms, languages and cultural requirements often find it most efficient to use offshore development resources in, or near, their target markets. Ireland, Australia and Finland are in the most demand for this type of outsourcing today. Cost savings from these more-developed countries remain available, but are less dramatic. The most attractive sources for offshore development are countries with well developed information technology support infrastructures, favorable demographics and labor costs, competent technical education facilities in national university systems, a well established presence of leading hardware and software platform manufacturers, and a favorable government regulatory environment supporting offshore development activities. However, a number of fundamental drawbacks remain. The largest is a lack of experienced project managers at all levels of the process from top management to junior project managers, resulting in very few domestic companies whose project management and quality control processes are certified according to international standards. Language is another concern, as many major offshore software development locales are primarily English speaking.

The growing shortage of information technology (specially, computer) professionals, especially in the most developed industrial countries, is rapidly becoming the most important reason for offshore development. Business needs are overcoming the biggest barrier against true offshore development, the lack of trust and perception of risk among clients, and now most offshore development is actually taking place offshore. In order to reduce the risk, many clients choose to retain as much control as they can over production. One major method is mandating that at least the project manager for each project remains onsite. This type of onsite/offsite combination of offshore outsourcing is often referred to as the fourth generation outsourcing model. It is offered only by the more progressive offshore companies who have established strong, demonstrable communications infrastructures for this type of project management.

Offshore outsourcing was developing through the initial three generations that made the basis for evolution into new, fourth generation.

The first generation in the evolution of offshore outsourcing is recognized as onsite staff augmentation, where the offshore services originated as a tactical solution for importing high-quality but low cost services in a staff augmentation mode. Offshore professionals were brought onsite and were paid at lower rates. The potential for labor saving was limited because of the need to import high skilled professionals.

The second generation of the offshore outsourcing is known as offshore production with small regional marketing offices near major customers, while sending work offshore. It was more cost effective than first generation offshore model, but limited to less complex engagements where e-business functions did not require extensive project management.

The third generation in the evolution of offshore outsourcing is based on the emerging onsite and offshore models with adding local project management to improve daily coordination and problem resolution with projects sent offshore. Complexity of management is higher than in previous two generations and this model is in use for high complexity systems that require frequent change.

Fourth generation of offshore outsourcing combines the traditional benefits of offshore development with sophisticated program management and in-depth local consulting presence. By contrast, traditional high-end consulting firms emphasize business strategy and reengineering. While many of them also provide systems integration, outsourcing, and in some cases offshore development services, their cost structures are significantly higher. Consequently, fourth generation providers deliver the economies of offshore development and maintenance, plus the ability to manage multiple highly complex projects, while drawing on local or regional talent to help clients refine their technology strategies and execute them. Although contractual relationships and roles will vary by client and engagement, fourth generation outsourcing providers focus on technology execution. Fourth generation offshore outsourcers have the processes and expertise to help advise their clients how to achieve business objectives through technology, and how to execute their technology strategies. Given today's budgetary realities, most internal information technology units cannot afford to retain such expertise internally.

Fourth generation providers maintain core competencies in a wide range of execution-related areas, ranging from program management and portfolio analysis to legacy platform consolidation, e-business integration, and emerging technologies such as Java, .NET, and XML Web services. These capabilities are critical for organizations consolidating multiple overlapping systems in the wake of merger or years of turbulent growth, or for enterprises focused on e-business integration. Complementing internal information technology unit, fourth generation providers furnish the program management competence, technology expertise, and technical resources that internal information technology unit of an e-business firm can no longer afford.

Traditional outsourcing models provide e-businesses firm with a common communications platform, and usually include a personal visit to the outsourcing partner's destination. In the scope of offshore outsourcing, the global delivery model gives the benefit of resolving the issues onshore. As required, e-businesses firm can always verify the necessary resources at the onshore office of the outsourcing partner. The involved parties could document issues collaboratively. Both parties, in real time, can easily and flexibly implement necessary alterations in business processes upon mutual agreement. This might not be possible with a traditional offshore model, where e-business company does not have any point of contact onshore.

Pioneered by Infosys in 1980s, the *Global Delivery (and Service) Model* refers to the philosophy of breaking pieces of work into logical components, and distributing these components geo-locationally, to perform them where it creates the maximum value. The global delivery model is a great value multiplier, and it is driven by the currently highest process and quality standards in the world. Thus, it gets assurance of the best product quality, which cuts down costs of fixing defects and maintenance. Advantages coming out of the continuous improvements keep improving all the key parameters. In the same time, it also gives e-business access to the best global talent increasing the degree of innovation.

Global Delivery Model gives e-business coping with offshore outsourcing extremely high values in:

- **Accountability:** E-business firm contracting outsourcing offshore under global delivery model has a single point of accountability for all project engagements, and all contracted projects are managed through local, on-site personnel, typically through a project management office in near site office.
- **Flexibility:** Outsourcing contractor render service to e-business firm by allocates work across delivery options to support changing e-business requirements.
- **Responsiveness:** Outsourcing contractor supports various levels that can be quickly tailored to any requirement; resources are available when and where needed.

Dealing with information and telecommunications technology in use, these companies generally do not allow their employees to have paper and pens at their desk. They work at terminals that are unable to download information or new software. Any intrusion or infraction is treated as criminal offenses. In that way, these employees are functionally the same as domestic employees for an e-business company, because they sign on to the same server and do all their work in that virtual space. No company data is transmitted or downloaded, minimizing the risk of a security defect. The security e-business has in place for its own firm is the same as for a staff member offshore, and they are under original e-business company rules and regulations.

One of the most critical elements of offshore outsourcing is vendor evaluation process and vendor selection (Rice, 2002). Loss of control (on quality, time lines, etc.) is inherent to offshore outsourcing. Besides, there are concerns about compatibility, business culture and ethics. Clarity is necessary between the outsourcer and the offshore vendor on the following issues:

- Ownership of information
- Security
- Business continuity agreement
- Reporting

Outsourcing contracts are designed to enable customers to receive services from independent contractors. Independent contractors are governed by a variety of laws and legal principles, including taxation, employment, and contract. However, one of the darker areas is the law of conflicts of interest, fiduciary duty and ethics. Both customers and service providers should seek professional advice on such issues during the design, negotiation, delivery and termination of any outsourcing service contract. There are on the scene conflicts of interest, too. A conflict of interest arises when a person owes loyalty to two persons who have conflicting legal or economic interests. Parties entering into services agreements should define the limits of any duties so that unwanted conflicts can be avoided. It is expanded to the term of fiduciary duty. A fiduciary duty is one kind of loyalty. Thus, a fiduciary must put its own personal interests behind, or secondary, to the interests and welfare of its beneficiary. The concept of fiduciary duty arose out of the concept of a trust under English common law, and under civil law in continental Europe and other countries.

When we consider these notions, it is obviously that we are considering business ethics. Ethics principally relates to morality of what well-behaved people do, and sometimes, ethical rules are binding as on regulated professionals, such as lawyers and accountants. Hence, ethical rules are generally not incorporated into contracts, although e-business outsourcing and offshoring urgently need them.

# Ethics Issues in E-Business Offshore Outsourcing

## Background on Ethics

The field of ethics, also called moral philosophy, involves systematizing, defending, and recommending concepts of right and wrong behavior. Philosophers today usually divide ethical theories into three general subject areas: metaethics, normative ethics, and applied ethics: Metaethics investigates where our ethical principles come from, and what they mean. Normative ethics takes on a more practical task, which is to arrive at moral standards that regulate right and wrong conduct and it is a search for an ideal litmus test of proper behavior. Applied ethics involves examining specific controversial issues, such as abortion, infanticide, animal rights, environmental concerns, homosexuality, capital punishment, or nuclear war.

The lines of distinction between metaethics, normative ethics, and applied ethics are often blurry. In recent years, applied ethical issues have been subdivided into convenient groups such as medical ethics, business ethics, environmental ethics, and sexual ethics. Generally speaking, two features are necessary for an issue to be considered an applied ethical issue. First, the issue needs to be controversial in the sense that there are significant groups of people both for and against the issue at hand. The second requirement for an issue to be an applied ethical issue is that it must be a distinctly moral issue. On any given day, the media presents us with an array of sensitive issues such as affirmative action policies, gays in the military, involuntary commitment of the mentally impaired, capitalistic versus socialistic business practices, public versus private health care systems, or energy conservation. Although all of these issues are controversial and have an important impact on society, they are not all moral issues. Some are only issues of social policy.

In theory, resolving particular applied ethical issues should be easy. With the issue of abortion, for example, we would simply determine its morality by consulting our normative principle of choice, such as act-utilitarianism. If a given abortion produces greater benefit than disbenefit, then, according to act-utilitarianism, it would be morally acceptable to have the abortion. Unfortunately, there are perhaps hundreds of rival normative principles from which to choose, many of which yield opposite conclusions. Thus, the stalemate in normative ethics between conflicting theories prevents us from using a single decisive procedure for determining the morality of a specific issue. The usual solution today to this stalemate is to consult several representative normative principles on a given issue and see where the weight of the evidence lies.

## *Normative Principles in Applied Ethics*

Arriving at a short list of representative normative principles is itself a challenging task. The principles selected must not be too narrowly focused, such as a version of act-egoism that might focus only on an action's short-term benefit. People must also see the principles as having merit on both sides of an applied ethical issue. The following principles are the ones most commonly appealed to in applied ethical discussions:

- **Personal benefit:** acknowledge the extent to which an action produces beneficial consequences for the individual in question
- **Social benefit:** acknowledge the extent to which an action produces beneficial consequences for society
- **Principle of benevolence:** help those in need
- **Principle of paternalism:** assist others in pursuing their best interests when they cannot do so themselves

- **Principle of harm:** do not harm others
- **Principle of honesty:** do not deceive others
- **Principle of lawfulness:** do not violate the law
- **Principle of autonomy:** acknowledge a person's freedom over his/her actions or physical body
- **Principle of justice:** acknowledge a person's right to due process, fair compensation for harm done and fair distribution of benefits
- **Principle of rights:** acknowledge a person's rights to life, information, privacy, free expression, and safety

The above principles represent a spectrum of traditional normative principles and are derived from both consequentialist and duty-based approaches. The first two principles, personal benefit and social benefit, are consequentialist since they appeal to the consequences of an action as it affects the individual or society. The remaining principles are duty-based ones. The principles of benevolence, paternalism, harm, honesty, and lawfulness are based on duties we have toward others. The principles of autonomy, justice, and the various rights are based on moral rights.

## *Ethics and Culture*

All cultures have a set of ethical values or rules concerning what is morally right and what is morally wrong (Anscombe, 1981). Through globalization, non-western cultures around the world are being exposed to the values of the west, and on a superficial level at least, appear to be adopting western culture. However, the adoption of the outward signs of western culture such as business dress codes does not necessarily mean that one culture has abandoned its own social, ethical and moral values in favor of those of the other. Indeed, the underlying values of non-western cultures appear to remain intact in the face of exposure to western culture.

Within e-business environment, while there is evidence that the processes of engineering and implementation of information technology systems are being successfully exported to non-western cultures as a consequence of globalization, the adoption of western social and ethical values by these other cultures is another matter. However, the ethical values of the world's cultures remain diverse.

The field of computing is generating new and difficult ethical questions, and the variation in the ethical and social norms across the globe merely adds to the level of complexity in finding answers to these questions. How can issues be answered if the ethical rules are not fixed? How, for example, can an ethical or moral question about the content of a Web site be considered when a hypertext link in that Web page may not only take the user to a different part of that site, but to a site in another part of the world where different ethical values may prevail?

These notions impose the cultural relativism. Cultural relativism recognizes that moral values vary from one society or culture to another, and that no culture's ethics are any better than any other's. This leads to the conclusion that the variations of values between cultures are all equally valid, and the variation between cultures can indeed be significant. Since the Second World War, the technological and economic growth of western nations has lead to the almost universal exposure of other cultures around the globe to western culture. Indeed, the culture of the West is propounded by many in the West to be of universal validity, which can result in a form of ethical imperialism. Although western e-business organizations are beginning to understand the problems associated with effort to universally apply western cultural values, it remains a problem for subsidiaries of western companies operating in the third world. Arguments by non-western cultures against this view of the universal validity of western values by the local cultures have invariably been dismissed in the West, particularly when issues such as royalties for western intellectual property rights and patents are at issue.

A code of ethics developed by an organization will be a consensus of the moral and ethical values of the organization and the individual professionals within that organization (Weston, 1997). Can such a code be applied outside of the culture in which it was developed? Does there need to be some qualification of a code of ethics when it is applied to different cultures? Besides individual country ethics values, there are some fundamental values that cross cultures, and that some activities are wrong no matter where they take place. Therefore, it could be possible to define a set of ethical values that could be applied universally.

As the Net develops, English will cease to be the dominant language, with Chinese, French, German and other languages generating webs within webs. Important for countries where English is only one spoken language is the fact that most of their citizens only speak a single language, while English is the most spoken second language in the world. In other words, as the Web sources develop, non-American surfers, who generally speak two or more languages, will have access to a larger web of services and contents. Enormous differences still remain from country to country. The U.S.-centric pattern wanes only with substantial and sustained infrastructure builds of the sort that has swept Europe, rolled into Asia, announced itself in Latin America, and stalled in most of Africa.

## Applied E-Business Ethics

The field of business ethics examines moral controversies relating to the social responsibilities of capitalist business practices, the moral status of corporate entities, deceptive advertising, insider trading, basic employee rights, job discrimination, affirmative action, drug testing, and whistles blowing. Issues in environmental ethics often overlap with business and medical issues. These include the rights of animals, the morality of animal experimentation, preserving endangered species, pollution control, management of environmental resources, whether ecosystems are entitled to direct moral consideration, and our obligation to future generations.

The massive diffusion of information and telecommunications technology causes radical changes in public and private institutions in general as well as in national and international information and communication policies in particular. This may concern:

- the creation of specialized (regional) knowledge markets
- the development of electronic commerce
- the publication and diffusion of scientific knowledge through the Internet
- the creation of services for public access to the Internet
- the promotion of local cultures in the digital medium
- the participation of individuals and groups in the political (communal, regional, national, international) processes

In the scope of information and telecommunications technology, we are speaking about information ethics. Information ethics as a descriptive theory explores the power structures influencing attitudes towards information and traditions in different cultures and epochs. Information ethics as an emancipatory theory develops criticisms of moral attitudes and traditions in the information field at an individual and collective level. It includes normative aspects. A basis for ethical thinking in the information field that is the basis for e-business ethics as well are the following principles of the Universal Declaration of Human Rights: respect for the dignity of human beings, confidentiality, equality of opportunity, privacy, right to freedom of opinion and expression, right to participate in the cultural life of the community, right to the protection of the moral and material interests concerning any scientific, literary or artistic production.

The literature dealing specifically with the ways in which the Internet affects ethics and moral decision-making in e-business is scarce. Specifically in terms of credibility and verification of information, two of the core issues relating to new media ethics, there seem to be little or no published studies at hand. The one possible definition of ethical issues in e-business environment could be defined as, a set of principles of right conduct — the rules or standards governing the conduct of a person or the conduct of the members of a profession. It also includes the statement that e-business ethics in an organization relates to a corporate culture of values.

Speed, freedom and individual power are thoroughly modern concepts that define the Information Age in which e-business exists. They triangulate to create a new kind of human being particularly adapted to life in the networked society (Borgman, 2000). The result is that e-culture turns the once well-defined areas of social ethics into a huge gray area of individual and situational considerations that require research and reflection to navigate but which provides no time to do so. Among many issues related to applied e-business, ethics is *social responsibility*.

Social responsibility in e-business environment is an organization's obligation to maximize its positive impact on stakeholders and to minimize its negative impact (Deborah, 1991). It includes legal, ethical, economic, and philanthropic dimensions.

- Legal dimension refers to obeying governmental laws and regulations civil law: rights and duties of individuals and organizations criminal law; prohibits specific actions and imposes fines and/or imprisonment as punishment for breaking the law;

- Ethical dimension refers to behaviors and activities that are expected or prohibited by organizational members, the community, and society (not codified into law) standards, norms, or expectations that reflect the concern of major stakeholders;
- Economic responsibilities refer to how resources for the production of goods and services are distributed within the social system;
- Philanthropic dimension refers to business' contributions to society.

In life, the people that we trust the most are those individuals that provide close consultations to us: our spouse, family and friends. Likewise, secure and successful e-commerce business owners are most likely to loan trust to those that qualify, were a good relationship has been built up. This is true for most of the e-business on the Internet. Technically, this important trust relationship is built by the three ethical issues in e-business ethics: honesty, integrity and trustworthiness.

## E-Business Outsourcing Ethics

Issues dealing with ethics in e-business outsourcing refer mostly on legislation, security, information, and business itself.

Legislation, codes and national standards relevant to the workplace include:

- Award and enterprise agreements
- National, state, regional legislative requirements
- Industry codes of practice
- Copyright laws
- Privacy legislation
- Intellectual property, confidentiality requirements
- Legal and regulatory policies affecting e-business

Security issues include:

- Security measures
- Privacy
- Confidentiality
- Information management
- Risk management

- Intellectual property
- Fraud prevention and detection
- Business ethics

Information and development support include:

- Advice on information and communications technology issues and compatibility
- Protocols for electronic data interchange
- Protocols relating to legal or security issues
- Personal identification and password for online access including electronic signature
- Contact person

Ethical issues include:

- Privacy legislation
- Confidentiality of records and information
- Intellectual property
- Fraud prevention and detection
- Trade Practices Act

Changes in technology and business processes can outpace companies' ability to consider their ethical implications or to train employees to deal with them (Brenner, 1992). Most everyone in e-business agrees that questionable ethical moves that compromise customer privacy for short-term marketing gain are bad for business in the long run. Online business is entering a more mature phase, and the issue of who the customer trusts becomes more of a competitive differentiator. Web sites are a reflection of businesses on the Internet. The three principal keys in doing e business: honesty, integrity, and trustworthiness crossover directly to the Web site framework and the Internet. This is especially true for the big online service providers.

The consensus seems to be that offshore outsourcing operations are at higher risk of copyright or intellectual property theft, especially when said operations pertain to software development. The European Union governments and U.S. have a good policy on intellectual property theft and piracy, compared to many other countries. Intellectual property protection laws are strictly implemented in first-world countries. Even Singapore, which accepts outsourcing jobs, has very firm intellectual property policies. This is part of what makes Singapore very attractive to outsourcing entrepreneurs, despite the high cost of labor and infrastructure. Still, it is not enough that the host country's government supports intellectual property efforts. The prime concern of entrepreneurs who seriously consider offshoring is cost efficiency. Many entrepreneurs in the software development field offshore their projects even with the knowledge that intellectual property protection laws are loose in the host country. The support of a host country's government is important in securing intellectual property rights in offshore operations. However, this is not to say that absolutely no software piracy occurs in first-world countries, where government control over intellectual property rights is known to be the strictest and intellectual property violations happen everywhere.

## Development of E-Business Ethics as Ongoing Process

The competitive pressures companies face to reduce costs and increase efficiency, will not decrease anytime soon. The practice of offshoring, therefore, is a business reality, one that companies and their many stakeholders will face and need to manage far into the future. There is the fact that employees, governments, communities, and others are best served not by opposing the offshoring trend, but by campaigning to encourage companies and governments to address the negative impacts and ensure the greatest spread of benefits to those affected.

With all the recent headlines about company misconduct and ethics violations has come a significant, and long overdue, increase in the consideration of ethics among businesses. Companies have quickly penned ethics codes, instituted ethics compliance monitoring programs, or have had high-level corporate officers visibly touting their company's ethics focus in the hope of regaining consumer confidence in a devastated economy. While businesses are fighting for survival in adverse conditions, they need to be looking to the future and building solid foundations upon which to base their future efforts. Even without investing vast financial resources, any company can reap tremendous benefits from considering and initiating an ethics program. In addition to the widely recognized value of improved company image and a smoother, more effective and happier work environment, an ethics program can contribute to a better bottom line, through stronger and more solid client relationships and decreased expenses in a variety of areas.

Attention to business ethics is critical during times of fundamental change (Madsen & Shafritz, 1990). In times of fundamental change, values that were previously taken for granted are now strongly questioned. Many of these values are no longer followed. Consequently, there is no clear moral compass to guide leaders through complex dilemmas about what is right or wrong. Attention to ethics in the workplace sensitizes leaders and staff to how they should act. Perhaps most important, attention to ethics in the workplaces helps ensure that when leaders and managers are struggling in times of crises and confusion, they retain a strong moral compass. Thus, attention to e-business ethics is next step in developing new e-business environment.

Changes in technology and business processes can outpace companies' ability to consider their ethical implications or to train employees to deal with them. Few companies have formal programs to complete of ethics training (Toffler, 1991). It is traditionally been seen as an add-on. Thus, it is needed to bring ethics into e-business context, since e-business raises ethical issues that may have existed before, but not in such clear reality. In large part to address potential information technology-related liabilities, both inside and outside a company, a growing number of businesses have high-level ethics executives or chief privacy officers to enforce company standards. The goal is to raise awareness, to be proactive and preventive rather than punitive. As e-business moves more and more business processes and transactions online, information technology, and the people who manage it, is at the forefront of decisions with ethical implications.

The debate over ethical standards in business is not new. What is new, or at least more apparent than ever, is central role of information technology in some of the most important business-ethic issues of the day: privacy, the ownership of personal data, and the obligations created by extended e-business partnerships. How these controversies affected information technology managers and others involved with technology? What ethical issues, if any, are business executives grappling with in connection with cutting-edge technology? And where do information technology professionals go for guidance on ethically ambiguous situations? Far from self-evident, the answers may be critical to the development of the trust and integrity needed to succeed at and global e-business.

Trust between workers and employers is another key issue putting information technology managers in the middle of ethical decisions. Most companies forbid employees using company computers to access Web sites with material that is pornographic, violent, or hate-related. Most information technology managers and executives agree there needs to be more training in ethics, especially now that information technology has taken a central role in doing business. Indeed, thinking of business and ethics, or information technology and ethics, as opposing forces may be a false dichotomy.

## Standardization of E-Business Ethics at Company's Level: Code of Ethics

An e-business company's ethics code ought to address both general values for which the company stands, and particular principles specific to the daily operations of that particular enterprise. Thus some codes may focus on full disclosure of their own abilities, time estimates, and costs, while others might address safety and/or full acceptance of responsibility for the quality of some product. The key is to generate a code that is tailored to the activities and goals of a particular organization, while simultaneously upholding universal ethical principles. A code of ethics, and thus compliance, must be universal. What is appropriate for the organization as a whole applies to all individuals. An organization's code of ethics must not be waived for selected executives or board members.

Proper use of company and customer property, electronic communication systems, information resources, material, facilities, and equipment is employees' responsibility.

They should use and maintain these assets with the utmost care and respect, guarding against waste and abuse, and never borrow or remove them from company property without management's permission. While these assets are intended to be used for the conduct of business, it is recognized that occasional personal use by employees may occur without adversely affecting the interests of the company. Personal use of company assets must always be in accordance with corporate and company policy.

Companies develop the code of ethics and ethics programs in order to allow employees and stakeholders to understand the values of the business to comply with policies and codes of conduct, and to create the ethical climate of the business (Dean, 1992). Within unethical behaviors found by employees in many firms there are sexual harassment, lying on reports or falsifying records, conflicts of interest, theft, lying to supervisors, discrimination, drug or alcohol abuse, improper accounting procedures, and violation of environmental laws.

The code of ethics is defined as formal statement of what an organization expects in the way of ethical behavior (what behaviors are acceptable or unacceptable), and it reflects senior management's organizational values, rules, and policies. In the process of formulating and implementing a code of ethics in an organization, it is presumed that several steps are considered:

- the code of ethics is distributed internally and externally;
- employees are assisted in understanding entire code of ethics;
- management's role is specified in detail; and
- employees are instructed about their responsibility for understanding and accepting the code of ethics.

The results in code of ethics effectiveness and proper utilization are under the special and professional work that should be supported by an ethics officer (Berenbeim, 1992). Ethics officer primarily job is to coordinate the ethics program with top management, to develop, revise, and disseminate the code of ethics, to develop effective ethics training tools, to establish audit and control systems, and to develop enforcement techniques in order to give some kind of legality to the code of ethics in use. The process of development and implementation of an effective e-business ethics is under the special business function on business conduct. The ethics and business conduct staff manages and administers the code of ethics and e-business conduct program, and should be full-time professionals who have responsibility for program development, including ethics training and revision of the code of ethics. They provide an objective resource available to assist employees in ethical decision making and in addressing allegations of unethical or illegal conduct.

The code of ethics helps employees make ethically sound business decisions and provides an overview of company's issue-resolution process. The code is often based on several key areas including:

- Antitrust and Competition Laws
- Company Assets
- Conflict of Interest and Corporate Opportunities
- Employment Practices and Expectations
- Environmental Responsibility
- Full and Fair Disclosure
- Gifts and Entertainment
- Government Affairs and Reports
- Inside Information and Insider Trading Laws
- Intellectual Property and Confidentiality
- International Business Conduct
- Privacy
- Safety and Health
- Suppliers, Contractors and Customers

## *Ethical and Legal Guidelines*

The legal guidelines under which the firm operates are in the hands of corporation general counsel. When e-business activities are initially undertaken, the general counsel should be consulted for their perspective on proposed methods of collection and sources. Final decisions about the legality of activities are the exclusive purview of the counsel. Ethical guidelines, however, are the realm of various subjects that share duties, obligations and liability where differences in geographical and cultural levels of acceptance for methods vary widely.

Ethical and moral hazard arises in outsourcing for two principal reasons. Businesses do not guard themselves prior to contract against their dependency on that supplier. Separately, they fail to appreciate the power which transfers to the outsource supplier in respect of their own business activities. They can manage and control both of these, to some extent, if they appreciate how and why power transfers after the contract has been signed. In the case of very substantial outsourcing contracts placed by major institutions, there is an increasing dominance. Some refer to it in non-legal terms as a monopoly — by a small number of very large outsourcing organizations controlling a significant share of the outsourcing revenues in that sector. That is a power and dependency that can only be controlled, in the longer term, by legal and, in sectors such as financial services, regulatory intervention. How does dependency on outsourcers arise? There is an increasing trend for organizations to outsource their non-core activities but maintain the conduct of their core activities. Outsourcing organizations, which are matured in the strategic partners, are engaged to conduct the non-core activities. The intentions are broadly to reduce the cost base for these services; maintain and where possible improve the delivery of these services; and to enable the resource savings to be deployed in core activities for the benefit of the company and the shareholders.

Outsourcing transactions have to be analyzed for the changes in power that they bring over the provision of service and the impact that has on the core business. This brings out the nature of the dependency and the power that gives to the supplier. Trust and confidence may be mitigating factors but are only tried and tested as a result of practical operation of the outsourcing agreement incorporating basic ethics standards.

Besides the continually strive in increasing respect and recognition of basic ethical issues, there are several key subjects that most of codes of ethics involve:

- to pursue one's duties with willingness and patience while maintaining the highest degree of professionalism and avoiding all unethical practices;
- to faithfully adhere to and abide by one's company's policies, objectives and guidelines;
- to comply with all applicable laws;
- to accurately disclose all relevant information, including one's identity and organization;
- to fully respect all requests for confidentiality of information; and
- to promote and encourage full compliance with these ethical standards within one's company, with third party contractors, and within the entire profession.

Now many organizations have presented codes and instruments for measuring corporate social and environmental performance. These codes and instruments vary widely in their goals, authors, country of origin, and effectiveness. Each contributes something to the effort to monitor corporate performance and inform corporate stakeholders of a firm's successes and failures. Given this variety, there is an increasing need for cooperation and focusing among the various global organizations that seek to bring transparency, fairness and trust to global business operations.

## *Compliance with Code of Ethics*

In the context of corporate governance, compliance means comply with the law. Ethics is the intent to observe the spirit of the law — it is the expressed intent to do what is right. In the wake of recent corporate scandals, a program that strongly emphasizes both ethics and compliance is good business. In fact, the business case for such a program is compelling. Within U.S. e-business environment, the Sarbanes-Oxley Act of 2002, along with related mandates by the Securities and Exchange Commission and new listing rules instituted by the major stock exchanges, raise the ante for ethical behavior and effective corporate compliance programs. Public companies and their senior executives and board members may be held accountable not only for the financial reporting provisions of the new legislation, but also for the aspects pertaining to ethics and corporate compliance. Conversely, companies and their leadership that are complying both to the letter and with the spirit of the law can achieve substantial benefits.

An interesting landscape is developing ethics and corporate compliance. Public and private policies are being enacted that will force companies and their executives to behave better. However, is compliance with these policies and related legislation enough? In the current e-business outsourcing and offshoring, corporate leaders should extend their efforts and their ethics beyond the propositions of the law. In reality, companies that follow both the letter and the spirit of the law by taking a values-based approach to ethics and compliance will have a distinct advantage in the marketplace. Such an approach requires senior executives to understand clearly the e-business culture and compliance controls that exist at all levels of their organizations. Companies must position ethics and compliance programs as a responsibility of each employee and a respected part of the company culture, not just an obligation. Companies' senior executives and board members must adhere to the code of ethics and compliance policies in the same way that all other employees must. Benefits of this approach include improvements to a company's market performance, brand equity, and shareholder value that is the must for the success on the global market.

Controls are used to safeguard corporate assets and resources, protect the reliability of organizational information and ensure compliance with regulations, laws and contracts — a control helps in:

- limit employee or management opportunism;
- ensuring that board members have access to timely and quality information;
- the ability to anticipate and remedy organizational ;
- minimizing negative situations; and
- uncertainties that need to be hedged.

## *Code of Ethics Compliance Audit*

Code of ethics compliance audit is systematic evaluation of an organization's ethics program and/or performance to determine its effectiveness, and it focuses on the key factors that influence how ethical decisions are made. A critical component of an effective ethics and compliance program is the ability to monitor and audit compliance.

As e-business companies cross geographical and industry boundaries, it is becoming harder to perform this role in the traditional manner. Consequently, e-business companies are increasingly seeking technology solutions to help them identify potential unethical behaviors before the cost becomes too great. There are software tools that are deployed through a worldwide network using search-and-retrieval technology coupled with powerful data and network analysis capabilities. These tools identify and analyze potential indicators of misappropriations and financial statement frauds, as well as preserve the information as evidence for use in court. Employing these sophisticated technological tools, an e-business company is capable in proactively detecting unethical behavior and helps it maintain compliance with its own policies and procedures.

Many e-business firms argue that they do not have the budget or staff to develop, implement and enforce full-scale ethics and compliance policies. This may be true, but it must not be excuse because ethics compliance is the forerunner of e-business outsourcing activities. To develop a solid compliance program, an e-business firm should force several activities as follows:

- **Develop open lines of communication:** For a compliance program to be effective, the most important element is that employees feel comfortable asking questions and reporting possible violations.
- **Identify the risks:** Management must first search out risks that the company faces, so the right factors can be monitored, audited and evaluated. A wide range of potential risks should be considered, including environmental risks, health and safety, money laundering, especially when involved with foreign entities.
- **Establish standards and procedures:** Some fundamental standards and procedures should be included in any organization's compliance program.
- **Designate a compliance official or committee:** Every compliance program must be overseen by an individual or committee that has ultimate accountability.
- **Conduct appropriate training and education:** Every employee in the organization must receive both initial and periodic training to ensure employees fully understand the company's compliance policies.
- **Respond to detected offenses:** When employees violate the company's policies, action must be swift and decisive. Corrective action must be taken, and any corrective action must be documented and communicated to all employees.
- **Enforce disciplinary standards through well-publicized guidelines:** Provide a detailed explanation of the consequences for breaches in conduct. Ensure that compliance officials, managers and employees are comfortable discussing ethical matters openly.

Many e-business organizations are also in possibility to use five-phase approach for assisting them in creating or enhancing an ethics and compliance program.

- **Phase One:** Risk and cultural assessment. Through employee surveys, interviews, and document reviews, culture of ethics and compliance at all levels of the organization is validated with a detailed work plan.
- **Phase Two:** Program design and update. Creation of guideline documents that outline the reporting structures, communications methods, and other key components of the code of ethics and compliance program. This encompasses all aspects of the program, from grass roots policies to structuring board committees that oversee the program.

- **Phase Three:** Policies and procedures development. Development of the detailed policies of the program, including issues of financial reporting, antitrust, conflicts of interest, gifts and entertainment, records accuracy and retention, employment, the environment, global business, fraud, political activities, securities, and sexual harassment, among others.
- **Phase Four:** Communication, training, and implementation. It includes institutionalization of the best policies and procedures that become part of the everyday work of an e-business organization.
- **Phase Five:** Ongoing self-assessment, monitoring, and reporting. The true test of ethics and compliance program comes over time, and techniques such as employee surveys, internal controls, and monitoring and auditing programs, are in use to help achieve sustained success.

Business ethics procedures must be presented at the core of every business decision based on standards of business conduct (Carroll, 1990). Also are included continuous education on ethical decision making with permanent monitoring adherence to laws, company policies and guidelines. The current trend of increasing focus on ethics is a much-needed change, with recent events rightly drawing attention to its importance. If used well, ethics enhancement may not be just another expense for businesses that are already struggling, but the solution that reverses the economic difficulties of late and builds a better way of doing business, and of living in general.

## Globalization of Ethics for E-Business Offshore Outsourcing

Since e-business is considering information and communications technology, technology impact on global scale is undoubtedly vial to all sectors. However, some authors state that far from creating paradise on Earth, technology has instead produced an unsustainable contest for resources. For example, Mander (1992) surveys the major technologies shaping the new world order and new forms of globalization — computers, telecommunications, space exploration, genetic engineering, robotics, and the corporation itself. He warns that they are merging into a global megatechnology, with dire environmental and political results.

One generally expects it to be the responsibility of the host country to set fair standards for wages, working conditions and pollution. However, this does not work well in poor countries. There is an overabundance of potential workers and work sites in poorer nations. Therefore these countries do not have the negotiating power to insist on living wages, humane working conditions and reducing pollution (Sethi, 2003).

The contemporary global digital economy is guided by market competition that brings efficiencies, so to provide better quality goods and services at a lower cost (Negroponte, 1995). Globalization has also brought jobs, investment and new technologies to many poor peoples. However, reports have documented the disparities in income and wealth that develop, as those people and nations who possess resources are able to obtain a greater share of benefits, while those who have little resources or skills fall further behind (World Bank, 2004). Hence, there is a need for effective international acceptable guidelines for the operation of the international digital economy that will take into account current inequities, and thus the interests of all people.

Defining a code of ethics, which would be acceptable to e-business organizations in all cultures, has been said to be an impossible task. However, given that there are some ethical values that can and do cross cultural boundaries, it may be possible to select a set of ethical values and to construct a set of guiding principles that would be acceptable to all societies. Each cultural group would then, in turn, build these principles into a code of ethics appropriate for their cultural values. The set of guiding principles may be universally acceptable, but the detail of their application will likely not be. An allowance for variation must be a component of any code of ethics that aims to be applied and accepted across multiple cultures. Multinational, multicultural e-business organizations may well find it necessary to translate corporate directives and policies for the various cultural groups across their organization based on the ethical values of those cultures just as they now must translate material into the various languages used by their workforce.

Current efforts on international scene is considering the programs that encourage a culture of mutual respect in which everyone understands and values the similarities and differences among employees, customers, communities and other stakeholders. An e-business company with offshore outsourcing must provide equal access to the best jobs in the world for people who are willing to compete, and equal employment opportunity to all employees regardless of age, race, color, national origin, sexual orientation, gender, disability or religion. Besides these global ethics issues, there are nine key ethics issues on the global scene that should be the core for any particular company's code of ethics and for any international agreement or standard:

- **Diversity, Equal Opportunity and Respect in the Workplace:** It is policy to provide all employees with an environment of mutual respect that is free from any form of harassment and discrimination. Harassment and discrimination of any form is not acceptable and will not be tolerated. In some countries, harassment is against the law; in all countries, it is wrong under global ethics standards.
- **Environment, Health and Safety:** Protecting people and the environment is key issue in global standardization for ethics. Health and safety rules and procedures are designed to provide a safe and healthy work environment and meet applicable health and safety laws.
- **Financial Integrity:** All e-business company's accounting records, and reports produced from those records, must be kept and presented according to the laws of each applicable jurisdiction. Moreover, the records must accurately and fairly reflect the e-business company's assets, liabilities, revenues and expenses.
- **Accurate Company Records:** Laws and regulations require e-business company records to accurately reflect the events they represent. Falsifying business records is a serious offense that may result in criminal prosecution, civil action and/or

disciplinary action up to and including termination of employment and close of whole business offshore unit.

- **Conflicts of Interest:** This means that employees, officers, and directors should avoid any investment, interest, association or activity that may cause others to doubt their or the e-business company's fairness or integrity, or that may interfere with their ability to perform job duties objectively and effectively.
- **Obligations to Customers:** Competitors and Regulators. It is consider the commitment to free, fair and open business competition, and is equally committed to competing ethically and in compliance with laws that foster competition in the marketplace. It includes also the freedom in gathering competitive information.
- **Computer Systems and Telecommunication Security Policy:** It is the core issues for an e-business company. The application/data owner and information systems professionals share responsibility for protection of e-business system from misuse — the information is an e-business company's asset and information technology unit of company is responsible for all of its assets including data and information, too.
- **Safeguarding Important Information:** It much relies on protection of confidential information such as trade secrets, proprietary know-how, personnel records, business plans and proposals, capacity and production information, marketing or sales forecasts, client and customer lists, pricing lists or strategies, construction plans, supplier data and so forth.
- **Corporate Social Responsibility:** The continuing development of international codes of conduct and principles governing corporate social responsibility are positive indicators for redefining business accountability for the 21$^{st}$ century.

The basic principles that change e-business offshore outsourcing scenes of today are considering two key issues: the responsibilities of businesses and the economic and social impact of business.

The responsibilities of businesses states that the value of a business to society is the wealth and employment it creates and the marketable products and services it provides to consumers at a reasonable price commensurate with quality. To create such value, a business must maintain its own economic health and viability, but survival is not a sufficient goal. Businesses have a role to play in improving the lives of all their customers, employees, and shareholders by sharing with them the wealth they have created. Suppliers and competitors as well, should expect businesses to honor their obligations in a spirit of honesty and fairness. As responsible citizens of the local, national, regional and global communities in which they operate, businesses share a part in shaping the future of those communities.

The economic and social impact of business is consider the notion that e-businesses established in foreign countries to develop, produce or sell should also contribute to the social advancement of those countries by creating productive employment and helping to raise the purchasing power of their citizens. Businesses also should contribute to human rights, education, welfare, and vitalization of the countries in which they operate.

Businesses should contribute to economic and social development not only in the countries in which they operate, but also in the world community at large, through effective and prudent use of resources, free and fair competition, and emphasis upon innovation in technology, production methods, marketing and communications.

Since the e-business outsourcing and offshoring is actually global scaled, many efforts are in the beginning to promote universal, international system of value assets, dominantly by shaping the form of an international code of ethics. Current works on international scene promote several global ethical issues related to sexual and racial discrimination, human rights, price discrimination, harmful products, pollution, and telecommunications issues.

*The American Institute of Certified Public Accountants* (AICPA) issued a new set of ethics requirements for members who outsource. The new requirements state that AICPA members must inform their clients that the firm will use a third-party service provider when providing professional services to the client. The new rules also clarify that AICPA members are responsible for all work performed by the service provider. Furthermore, AICPA members using third-party service providers are required under the new rules to enter into a contractual agreement with the third-party service provider to maintain the confidentiality of the client's information, and to be reasonably assured that the third-party service provider has appropriate procedures in place to prevent the unauthorized release of confidential client information. New rules are effective for all professional services performed on or after July 1, 2005.

## *Caux Round Table*

Caux Round Table is the example of the efforts to determine universal conceptualization of ethical conduct that should help doing business internationally, and it is of core interest for e-business outsourcing and offshoring. The Caux Round Table is an international network of principled business leaders working to promote a moral capitalism targeting on settings Principles for Business through which principled capitalism can flourish, and sustainable and socially responsible prosperity can become the foundation for a fair, free and transparent global society. At the company level, the Caux Round Table advocates implementation of the principles for business (Caux, 2002) that applies fundamental ethical norms to business decision-making. The Principles have been translated into more than 15 languages, and have been used as benchmarks for firms' codes throughout the world. The Caux principles are aspirational, and they are proposed as a model, starting point and benchmark when executives write or attempt to improve their own firm's code of ethics. The basis for the Principles is the idea that mobility of employment, capital, products and technology is making business increasing global in its transactions and its effects. The principles have credibility because they were written by and have been actively supported by senior business executives from around the world. A more proactive recent focus of the Caux Round Table is to contribute to the alleviation of world poverty and to make it possible for poor nations to share in global prosperity.

To promote better outcomes for globalization, the Caux Round Table is working to raise the level of awareness of senior business leaders, thought leaders and elite opinion around the world about new opportunities to attack global poverty. These include legal and regulatory changes in developing countries that will improve the environment for productive investment of foreign and domestic equity capital. The Caux Round Table is working in alliance with global business leaders, international institutions and policy makers to improve investment environments in selected developing countries by also suggesting certain principles for governments and the adoption of the core standards for transparent management of national financial institutions.

## *United Nations Global Compact with Business*

The Global Compact seeks to advance responsible corporate citizenship so that business can be part of the solution to the challenges of globalization. To achieve these objectives, the Global Compact offers facilitation and engagement through several mechanisms: policy dialogues, learning, local structures, and projects. This in turn helps organizations to redefine their strategies and courses of action so that all people can share the benefits of globalization. The Global Compact is a network. At its core are the Global Compact office and four UN agencies: Office of the High Commissioner for Human Rights, United Nations Environment Program, International Labor Organization and United Nations Development Program. The Global Compact involves all the relevant social actors: governments, who defined the principles on which the initiative is based; companies, whose actions it seeks to influence; labor, in whose hands the concrete process of global production takes place; civil society organizations, representing the wider community of stakeholders; and the United Nations, the world's only truly global political forum, as an authoritative convener and facilitator.

The United Nations Global Compact with business was born when United Nations Secretary General Kofi Annan was invited to give a major address to world business and political leaders at the World Economic Forum in 1999. He warned global business leaders that we have underestimated the fragility of the global economy. People around the world fear and distrust the resulting loss of jobs, trashing the environment and the huge rewards that go to a few, while leaving the vast majority very poor. Annan warned that this could lead to widespread unrest and even civil wars and terrorism. To counter potential civil strife, Annan proposed a global compact for business firms. For firms that sign, the United Nations would on one hand support the open global market and signing business firms on the other hand would pledge to support human rights, worker standards and sustainable environmental practices. The Global Compact is based on the recognition that development and poverty reduction depend on prosperity which can only come from efficient and profitable business. International trade and investment create new employment, raise skill levels and increase local economic activity. At the same time, companies have a duty to manage all aspects of their business in a responsibly and sustainable way.

These universal ideals are specified in ten precise principles under four headings: human rights, labor standards, environment and anti-corruption. The Global Compact's 10 principles (United Nations, 2003) in the areas of human rights, labor, the environment and anti-corruption enjoy universal consensus and are derived from:

- The Universal Declaration of Human Rights
- The International Labor Organization's Declaration on Fundamental Principles and Rights at Work
- The Rio Declaration on Environment and Development
- The United Nations Convention against Corruption

The Global Compact principles by prime categories:

*Human Rights*

- **Principle 1:** Businesses should support and respect the protection of internationally proclaimed human rights; and
- **Principle 2:** Make sure that they are not complicit in human rights abuses.

*Labor Standards*

- **Principle 3:** Businesses should uphold the freedom of association and the effective recognition of the right to collective bargaining;
- **Principle 4:** The elimination of all forms of forced and compulsory labor;
- **Principle 5:** The effective abolition of child labor; and
- **Principle 6:** The elimination of discrimination in respect of employment and occupation.
- **Principle 7:** Businesses should support a precautionary approach to environmental challenges;
- **Principle 8:** Undertake initiatives to promote greater environmental responsibility; and
- **Principle 9:** Encourage the development and diffusion of environmentally friendly technologies

*Anti-Corruption*

- **Principle 10:** Businesses should work against all forms of corruption, including extortion and bribery.

The Global Compact is a symbol of leadership in a complex world. It goes back to basics by focusing on a concise set of fundamental principles for living and working in a global society. Its 10 principles addressing human rights, labor standards and the environment are truly universal — both precise enough to be relevant and general enough so as to avoid cultural conflict. The Global Compact is not a regulatory regime or a code of conduct, but a platform and forward-looking forum for the exchange of good practices in order to achieve actual progress in creating a more prosperous and sustainable world.

## *The Global Reporting Initiative*

The Global Reporting Initiative provides a structure whereby a firm can publicly report on its business activities over three sets of criteria: economic, social and environmental. It currently has more than 500 organizations in 50 countries that participate in doing an annual report on economic, social and environmental issues. It also operates as an environmental reporting mechanism for the United Nations Global Compact and for the Organization for Economic Cooperation and Development (OECD) Guidelines for Multinational Enterprises. The OECD, in cooperation with many intergovernmental and nongovernmental groups, has also developed "A Working Set of Core Indicators for Measuring Global Development Progress". These indicators are straightforward and quite useable measures of economic, social, environmental and general development in the respective countries.

## *ISO Standard on Social Responsibility*

In order to set more precise and more appropriate for all stakeholders around the globe, new standard settlement is needed. It is especially true when e-business offshore outsourcing is in place. Most countries recognized two key issues — the responsibilities of businesses and the economic and social impact of business — as the promoter of new placebo for globally acceptable norm of social responsibility in the era of digital economy. In 2005, the national standards institutes that are members of the International Organization for Standardization (ISO) approved the development of a standard on social responsibility that will provide guidance to organizations on social responsibility (ISO, 2005). The goal is to develop guiding principles with global relevance that will be useful to organizations worldwide in establishing, implementing, maintaining and improving the way they address social responsibility. By reducing environmental damage caused by their operations, and improving the living conditions and health of their workers, organizations have the ability to improve the quality of life for the communities in which they operate. The real challenge for ISO is to design a meaningful standard for organizations which will supplement existing tools and build a bridge between national legislation and international norms on the one hand and recognized voluntary initiatives on social responsibility on the other. ISO is referring to this as a standard on "social responsibility", a somewhat misleadingly narrow term given the fact that the standard is expected to address a broad range of organizational activities including social, labor, and environmental impacts. As ISO develops this new standard over the next three years, it will transform how concepts like "corporate social responsibility" and "the triple bottom line" are defined, measured and reported on. Of equal importance, ISO has established a ground-breaking new approach to stakeholder involvement in its own standards development that could transform the world of standards making and spill over into the broader sphere of global governance. The Goal of the ISO Social Responsibility standard is to encourage organizations around the world to improve their performance on key indicators of sustainable development. This new standard dealing with global social and environmental sustainability is settled as ISO 26000 with publication in 2008 – there is enough time to all interested stakeholders to participate in preparing the final document. ISO is working to make the development of its ISO 26000 standard as representative and inclusive as possible. The three years scheduled project includes six sectors: industry, government, labor unions, consumers, non-governmental organizations, and others (primarily academics and consultants). Each country participating is encouraged to involve a representative from each sector. The new ISO 26000 social responsibility standard provides an unprecedented opportunity for global discussion and widespread involvement to implement the goals of sustainable development at many levels of organizational activity throughout the world. At present, no internationally recognized standard exists to manage organizational ethics, compliance and business conduct programs. The ISO 26000 social responsibility standard could be crucial actor in the process of harmonization and ethical development of e-business offshore outsourcing. It will be mutually compatible with the management system standards ISO 9000 for quality and ISO 14000 for the environment. It will be also a practical way for organizations around the world to integrate e-business ethics into their operations.

## Discussion

Outsourcing infrastructure is crucial to e-business companies' success — if their customers cannot access their application, how good is it, especially when competitors are on the e-market. In today's dynamic e-business environment where fast time to market is imperative, where information and telecommunications technology is costly and changing rapidly, and where skilled technical resources are scarce, e-businesses need reliable, high-end outsourcing infrastructure and resources to ensure that mission-critical applications will be up and running when customers want to do business.

A shift to outsourcing moves employment from the company to its outsourcing vendor, and may move employees as well. The outsourcing vendor virtually is stealing employment from people in the company. Is this ethical? It does not feel like a good thing to do, but our economy is not driven by acts of goodness and mercy. The question remains: Is it ethical? Answering the question is driven by a code of ethics. The overall preference is for a simple code. It can be boiled down to basic ethical injunctions. The benefit of a simple code of ethics is that it gives us a relatively clear measure against which to judge ethical questions. None of the injunctions can be absolute, but they do provide a useful starting point. Codes of ethics are properly silent about competing — that is the accepted driver in global economy. It is ethically acceptable to compete. It may be personally distasteful to enter a competition, and there is nothing ethically wrong with such competition.

Offshore outsourcing vendors are ethically free to compete for business. In many cases, they are effectively importing labor of people who have no right to work in the country. Thanks to the wonders of telecommunications, a telephone can be answered anywhere in the world. What does that do to immigration policies? What are the policy implications for the development of skilled local workers? Technology may be pushing interdependence further than we are prepared to accept. It is not an ethical question, but it is a vitally important question about local values and their appropriate role in the global economy.

Employees working for a company considering outsourcing also face ethical questions. Fundamental to any good code of ethics is a requirement to not put personal interests above those of employer. Employees are obligated to work for the best interests of employer, even when that might not be in their personal best interest. It is not ethical to skew the outcome of outsourcing contract talks just because someone does not want to be a personal part of outsourcing. That may be true in general, but what happens if the benefit of outsourcing to employer is very low, and the cost to employees is very high? Judgment is required about when an employee's interests are so much more important than an employer's interests that the first injunction can be suspended. Many offshore workers are unprotected by their country's trade laws, and job conditions can be less than ideal. It is true that the law in their home countries poorly protects laborers, with some countries not even having an efficient social security, medical and unemployment compensation system. However, this does not change the fact that offshoring creates opportunities for hardworking, skilled laborers to rise above poverty, to seek a better lifestyle than the one they used to struggle with. Actually, offshoring companies are bound to adhere to international rules and regulations preventing them from mistreating their employees, and sending them to work in sweatshop conditions. It is a rabid myth, for example, that a software development team offshore is underpaid, overworked and worse — undereducated. In order to stay competitive, offshore software development companies make it a point to hire only credentialed, skilled programmers, who can keep up with the market demand, minimize risk, and ensure absolute professionalism on the job.

Offshoring e-business, or the shifting of jobs from developed to developing countries, represents a litmus test for corporate social responsibility, too. Viewed through one lens, the practice is irresponsible, as it strips workers in the developed world, where the companies are typically based, of their livelihoods. Viewed through another lens, the practice is the paragon of responsibility when implemented in a fair manner, as it infuses income into emerging economies. This issue of ethical consumerism has captivated thinking in the corporate social responsibility field for some time, and survey after survey demonstrates consumer concern for a range of environmental and social factors in purchasing choices. However, the reality of ethical consumerism is very different. Truly ethical consumers are very rare. Of course, whether consumers buy for ethical reasons or not, companies that claim a reputation for corporate social responsibility must be prepared to defend the ethics of their actions. This means decent working conditions, environmental responsibility, sensitivity to community needs and all the other good practices that make up corporate social responsibility.

Establishing an ethics program, it is not an exact science. It involves the input, interaction, cooperation, decision-making and ongoing commitment of many people. Proper planning is important, but the effectiveness of any company's or organizations' approach will also depend on characteristics that are unique to its culture: the leadership style of the president or chief executive officer and the executive team; the company's or organizations' relationship with its board of directors; and so on. The benefits of developing clear ethics and compliance policies are immeasurable. Managers can have peace of mind knowing that every employee has a detailed understanding of the impact of their actions on the business. Moreover, the business will establish itself as a moral environment concerned about its impact on society. The company's stakeholders, from employees to customers, will have a positive feeling about the firm and confidence in its operations.

Historically, companies have moved activities from one place to another for various reasons, and their mobility has only increased in recent decades. In developing countries, this can encourage mass migration from villages to urban areas, practice development experts generally consider unsustainable. In an era of telecommunications, it is better to move jobs to people than to move people to jobs. Advances in technology and global networking of economies support this trend. Whether jobs move or people move, communities suffer losses. E-business companies with a commitment to corporate social responsibility must work to reduce the pain and stress of disruption in home countries while increasing the socio-economic benefits of these jobs in the receiving country. Both must be done responsibly and to the best of the ability of the company.

E-business should develop outsourcing ethics program. It presents the analysis of the nature and the social impact of information technology and the corresponding formulation and justification of policies for the ethical use of technology. Ethics cover both social as well as personal policies for the ethical use of technology. It is a dynamic and complex field of study, which takes into account, the relationships between facts, conceptualization, policies and values concerning the ever-changing information technology. These notions are considered in efforts to produce globally acceptable ethics program that would articulate both individual company and global interests in an appropriate way. Recent work on international scene is promising and we could expect development of offshore outsourcing activities in accordance with globally accepted rules/codes of ethics — it will be the new age of global e-business ethics.

# References


Anscombe, E. (1981). *Ethics, religion and politics.* Oxford: Blackwell.

Berenbeim, R. E. (1992). The corporate ethics test. *Business and Society Review, 31*(1), 77-80.

Borgman, Ch. L. (2000). *From Gutenberg to the global information infrastructure: Access to information in the networked world.* Cambridge: MIT Press.

Brenner, S. N. (1992). Ethics programs and their dimensions. *Journal of Business Ethics, 11*, 391-399.

Carroll, A. B. (1990). Principles of business ethics: Their role in decision making and in initial consensus. *Management Decision, 28*(8), 21-23.

Caux Round Table. (2002). *Principles for business.* Saint Paul, MN: Caux Round Table Secretariat.

Cornford, J., Gillespie, A., & Richardson, R. (1999). *Regional development in the information society.* Boulder, CO: Rowman and Littlefield.

Dean, P. J. (1992). Making codes of ethics real. *Journal of Business Ethics, 11*, 285-290.

Deborah, B. (1991). Asking for help: A guide to using socially responsible consultants. *Business Ethics Magazine*, *11*, 24-29.

ISO Working Group on Social Responsibility. (2005). ISO 26000 standard on social responsibility guidelines. ISO.

Madsen, P., & Shafritz, J. M. (1990). *Essentials of business ethics*. New York: Penguin Books.

Mander, J. (1992). *In the absence of the sacred*. San Francisco: Sierra Club Books.

Negroponte, N. (1995). *Being digital*. London: Hodder and Stoughton.

Rice, D. (2002). Refining the Zippo test: New trends on personal jurisdiction for Internet activities. In *The Computer & Internet Lawyer*. Prentice Hall Law & Business.

Sethi, S. (2003). *Setting global standards: Guidelines for creating codes of conduct in multinational corporations*. New York: John Wiley & Sons.

Toffler, B. (1991). Doing ethics: An approach to business ethics consulting. *Moral Education Forum*, *16*(4), 14-20.

United Nations. (2003). *The Global Compact: Corporate citizenship in the world economy*. New York: Global Compact Office.

Weston, A. (1997). *A practical companion to ethics*. New York: Oxford University Press.

World Bank. (2004). *World development report 2004: Making services work for poor people*. New York: Oxford University Press.

## Chapter VI

# Information Technology Offshore Outsourcing: A Perspective of Advanced Countries

Smita Gupta
Technology Partners Inc., USA

Narendra S. Chaudhari
Nanyang Technological University, Singapore

## Abstract

*Offshore outsourcing is a term covering a range of information technology (IT) and business services delivered to companies in developed countries by IT personnel based in developing countries. The significant cost savings achieved by the offshore model is the prime factor in its growing acceptance and use. IT software and service outsourcing is becoming a new reality for employers, employees, government and academicians. The widespread use of Internet, standardization of software development methodologies, efficient IT project management techniques, low cost of telecommunications, have provided the necessary thrust for global production of software and services. In this chapter, we analyze the impact of today's offshore outsourcing movement to the United States economy, education, jobs, wages, and social issues. We suggest that offshoring is a viable economic model. It leads to improved productivity, lower inflation and eventually growth in jobs and wages. The*

*U.S. will also see significant numbers of "in-sourced" jobs because of subsidiaries of foreign based companies. Future job growth in different areas of business and skills, require young students and present IT workforce to acquire them with education and training. Federal Reserve chairman Alan Greenspan has also expressed the need to produce highly skilled workers. The loss of jobs of IT workers is the difficult aspect of offshoring. Laid-off workers should be provided assistance to find a new comparable job, both by the U.S. government and companies. In this chapter, we make some recommendations to reduce, minimize and overcome the hardships caused by the IT outsourcing.*

# Introduction

Gartner, a leading industry research firm says in a report (McDougall, 2005) that by 2015 the number of information technology jobs being outsourced from the United States and other developed countries is going to increase to 30%. India, China, Israel, South Africa, Northern Ireland, Southern Ireland, Czech Republic, Poland, Hungary and Russia are popular offshore outsourcing destinations. The IT offshore outsourcing is a global phenomenon. In this chapter, we primarily focus our attention on the exchange of IT activities between the U.S. and India; this allows us to site concrete illustrations for developing our scenario. Amongst America's biggest companies, those using offshore software development include American Express, Aetna U.S. Healthcare, Compaq, General Motors, Home Depot, IBM, Microsoft, Motorola, Shell, Sprint and 3M. GE's technology partnership with India in 1991 was a pioneering step in offshore outsourcing arena. Since then, India has grown its call center, business process outsourcing and software business. In addition, India has welcomed the research and engineering facilities established by the U.S. and multinational corporations like Microsoft and IBM. In the context of offshore IT projects, the comments of global business leaders on India's potential are worth mentioning (NASSCOM). In the inaugural ceremony of John F. Welch Technology Center in Karnataka, India, on September 17, 2000, John F. Welch Jr., GE Chairman & CEO commented, "A truly global company will be one that uses the intellect and resources of every corner of the world. India is a developed country as far as intellectual capital is concerned. The opening of [offshore] development centers marks a new level of commitment by GE in India." When Bill Gates, founder of Microsoft, visited Hyderabad (Microsoft India Development Center) India to mark Microsoft's 25th anniversary on September 27, 2000, he commented, "Three years ago, during my visit to India, the country was emerging as an IT superpower. Today, the country is handling the most sophisticated projects in the world. I am impressed with the talent we have in our India Development Center and the quality of software being developed." Total value of outsourcing to India was U.S.$17.2 billion in 2004, estimated at 44% of the worldwide total. By 2008 the value of work outsourced to India is forecasted to reach 48 billion (Ramadorai & Karnik, 2005).

The significant cost savings achieved by the offshore model is the prime factor in its growing acceptance and use. IT software and service outsourcing is becoming a new reality for employers, employees, government and academicians. The rapid increase in offshore outsourcing of IT software and services has led the U.S. workforce to believe in widespread loss of "white-collar" IT jobs. Offshore developing countries invest considerably high in science, math and engineering education. Large numbers of technically skilled students are graduating from those countries to work on the offshore projects. The widespread use of Internet, standardization of software development methodologies, efficient IT project management techniques, low cost of telecommunications, have provided the necessary thrust for global production of software and services. Global outsourcing provides several other practical benefits as described by Global Insights (2004):

1. the ability of multinational organizations to efficiently stage 24×7 operations;
2. the opportunity to customize products and services to meet local needs; and
3. the means of geographically deploying workers and facilities to succeed in globally dispersed highly competitive markets.

Offshore vendors offer quality methodologies such as SEI-CMM, ISO 9000 and Six-Sigma capabilities that most U.S. organizations lack on an in-house basis (The Economic Times, 2004). According to Thoms (June 2005), 59% of overseas companies are at CMM Level 4 in comparison to 41% of U.S. companies and 83% of overseas companies are CMM Level 5 in comparison of 17% of U.S. companies.

The U.S. government supports offshoring as is evident from the President George W. Bush's chief economic adviser, Gregory N. Manikw's economic report (Manikw, 2004). He has presented offshoring in this perspective: "Offshoring of professional services is a prominent example of a new type of trade. The gains from trade that take place over the internet or telephone lines are no different than the gains from trade in physical goods transported by ship or plane."

IT software and services include software project management services, software support and training, development of software products, which includes software design, development, testing and integration with other systems and sales of packaged/proprietary software. There is wide spectrum of IT jobs to support these services, which need software skills of different levels. There are highly skilled jobs like software analysts, business requirements analysts, software design and software architects, which may not easily be outsourced. Then there are programming and testing jobs, which require medium skills level and are first in line to be outsourced. IT software and service outsourcing is becoming a new reality for employers, employees, government and academicians. IT offshoring is not only limited to industries but state government projects have also been outsourced (Mattera, Woolsey, & Purinton, 2004). The rapid increase in offshore outsourcing of IT software and services has led the U.S. workforce to believe in widespread loss of "white-collar" IT jobs.

In this chapter, we provide a background of the IT offshore outsourcing environment and examine its impacts in a typical advanced country; for the purpose of concrete illustration, we choose the advanced country to be U.S.A, and give an in-depth study of on this topic under the major section in this chapter, titled "Impacts of IT offshoring in the U.S.".

We discuss this impact by examining five related prominent themes. The first theme, "Job projections up to year 2012", discusses the IT employment projection numbers up to year 2012. The second theme, "Jobs and Skills: Trends in Near Future", presents the jobs and skills which are going to remain in demand for coming years. The third theme, "Salaries of IT professionals", discusses the impact of outsourcing on the salaries of IT professionals. The fourth theme examines the role of education in "Outsourcing-education connection". The fifth theme, "Social Impacts", analyzes the impact of outsourcing in social perspective. We then put forward recommendations to minimize offshoring impact for government, companies and IT workers and suggest future trends.

# Background

Offshore outsourcing is not a new industrial practice and is not just being practiced by U.S. businesses. Globalization of the production of computer hardware in the 1990s has lowered the hardware cost significantly. The positive responses of the IT professionals and business to the lowered hardware cost were the key to improved productivity, lower inflation, faster income growth and increased employment, described by Mann (December 2003). The reduced cost of hardware has enabled the industries to use IT software and services extensively. If we can now bring in the reduced cost of IT software and services, businesses are going to flourish further. Less expensive imported software and services will make the whole IT package more attractive to the businesses leading to a second wave of productivity. Authors agree with Mann (Dec. 2003), that this would enable small businesses and other areas of industry to use software and services.

Globalization of IT software and services will and has resulted in reduction of "white-collar" jobs in advanced countries like the U.S. The true magnitude of offshore outsourcing is unknown. Business cycle, declining manufacturing jobs, dollar overvaluation and tech-bubble burst are equally important reasons for the decline of U.S. jobs. In the coming decade however, broader diffusion of IT throughout the economy points to even greater demand for workers with IT skills and proficiency. Over the next decade, the Bureau of Labor Statistics (BLS) projects that job growth to 2012 in occupations requiring IT skills will be more than three times the rate of job growth in the overall economy (Hecker, 2004). We believe that overall IT jobs would continue to grow as IT continues to diffuse in business. There will be new job areas with new demands for IT skilled people. IT workers and U.S. economic growth is also going to be benefited by the operations of U.S. subsidiaries of foreign-headquartered multinational companies through their operations that are "insourcing" American jobs, see executive summary, Slaughter (2004).

The large difference in the salaries of IT professionals in developing countries like India and the U.S. is the major source of cost advantage mentioned by Kumar (2003). Offshoring has a lot of media, newspapers, television and Internet attention also. Moyers (2004) on public broadcasting channel (PBS) has provided the salary comparison of jobs in the U.S. and India. Jobs are even moving from India to even cheaper countries like China, Russia, Vietnam, Philippines, and Malaysia. U.S. IT workers are also seeing their salaries decline.

The viewpoint of the authors is that the IT salaries are now at more competitive levels and the IT jobs of future will have high salaries.

Snell (2004) has expressed in her article on the outsourcing-education connection that faltering education system could eventually prompt employers to look overseas for skilled labor. Developing countries like China, India, Taiwan and South Korea produce large number of graduates in the science and engineering courses, providing a positive factor for the growth of offshore model. In 1990s increasing number of students joined well-established universities in the United States, United Kingdom and France for higher education. Foreign students in the U.S. at master's level in the year 2000, earned 45% of computer science and 38% of engineering degrees awarded (National Science Board, 2004, p. 23). A presentation by Harker (2004) shows that American public education system both at the school, college and university level, is one of the reasons why so many companies are sending job overseas. Federal Reserve chairman Alan Greenspan (2004) has also urged the need to produce highly skilled workers. The authors also agree that the education system in the U.S. especially in the subjects of math and science should undergo improvement.

In many cases and in discussions in this chapter, India is viewed as an important outsourcing destination. The impact of outsourcing is still being understood and measured. For our jobs, skills, salaries discussions, we have used the employment statistics data made available for public use by the U.S. Department of Labor, Bureau of Labor Statistics. For the discussions on education, degrees awarded, we have used the National Science Board, Science & Engineering Indicators - 2004.

# Impacts of IT Offshoring in the U.S.

## Job Projections Up to Year 2012

The biggest impact of outsourcing is on the information technology (IT) jobs in America, (Kalakota & Robinson, 2004). IT offshore outsourcing is a reality that the IT workers in the U.S. are facing. Some people believe that outsourcing is a phase, which will eventually go away. However, we argue that outsourcing is a viable economic model even for a long term. In fact, many companies have already outsourced or are in the process of outsourcing for reduced project costs, which has resulted in widespread layoffs. There is, however, a need for restructuring of jobs for utilizing the skills of IT workers being laid-off from their work. In order to maintain the productivity and maintain the strength of economy, this restructuring of jobs needs to be identified in the context of new business opportunities arising from the globalization of software and IT services. This will, in fact, lead to a strong demand of workers with IT proficiency and skills. The economic and employment projections for 2002-2012 news release (U.S. Bureau of Labor Statistics, 2004) also reflect strong demands in computer-related occupations.

Total employment is projected to increase by 21.3 million jobs over the 2002-12 periods, rising to 165.3 million, according to the latest projections of the BLS in employment outlook: 2002-12 (Hecker, 2004, p. 80). This increase represents about 600,000 more jobs than were added over the previous 10-year period (1991-2002). Employment in professional and related occupations is projected to grow the fastest and to add more workers (6.5 million) than any other major groups (Hecker, 2004, p. 81).

Table 1 shows the employment by major occupational group, 2002 and projected 2012. There are eight occupational subgroups within professional and related occupations. Three occupational subgroups: (1) education, training, and library; (2) healthcare practitioners and technical; and, (3) computer and mathematical, should account for three-quarters of the job growth (Hecker, 2004, p. 81). Computer and mathematical occupations are projected to add 1.1 million jobs, and grow the fastest among the eight subgroups.

It has been predicted that the demand for computer-related occupations should increase. Growth will not be as rapid as during the previous decade; however, as the software industry begins to mature, the routine work is increasingly outsourced overseas. The BLS publication of the factors affecting industry output and employment, 2002-12 (Occupational projections and training data, chapter IV, p. 136) clearly states for Computer systems design and related services "Employment will increase significantly

*Table 1. Employment by major occupational group, 2002 and projected 2012 (Source: U.S. Bureau of Labor Statistics, News Release, USDL 04-148, February 2004)*

| Occupational group | Employment | | | | Change | |
|---|---|---|---|---|---|---|
| | Number in thousands | | Percent distribution | | Number in thousands | Percent |
| | 2002 | 2012 | 2002 | 2012 | | |
| Total, all occupations | 144,014 | 165,319 | 100.0 | 100.0 | 21,305 | 14.8 |
| Management occupations | 10,056 | 11,277 | 7.0 | 6.8 | 1,221 | 12.1 |
| Business & financial operations occupations | 5,445 | 6,606 | 3.8 | 4.0 | 1,162 | 21.3 |
| Professional & related occupations | 27,687 | 34,147 | 19.2 | 20.7 | 6,459 | 23.3 |
| Computer & mathematical occupations | 3,018 | 4,069 | 2.1 | 2.5 | 1,051 | 34.8 |
| Architecture & Engg. Occupations | 2,587 | 2,809 | 1.8 | 1.7 | 222 | 8.6 |
| Life, physical, & social science occup | 1,237 | 1,450 | 0.9 | 0.9 | 212 | 17.2 |
| Community & social services occupations | 2,190 | 2,764 | 1.5 | 1.7 | 574 | 26.2 |
| Legal occupations | 1,168 | 1,357 | 0.8 | 0.8 | 190 | 16.2 |
| Education, training & library occupations | 8,530 | 10,639 | 5.9 | 6.4 | 2,109 | 24.7 |
| Arts, design, entertainment, sports | 2,376 | 2,769 | 1.7 | 1.7 | 393 | 16.5 |
| Healthcare practice & technical occup. | 6,580 | 8,288 | 4.6 | 5.0 | 1,708 | 26.0 |
| Service occupations | 26,569 | 31,905 | 18.5 | 19.3 | 5,336 | 20.1 |
| Healthcare support occupations | 3,310 | 4,452 | 2.3 | 2.7 | 1,143 | 34.5 |
| Protective service occupations | 3,116 | 3,885 | 2.2 | 2.4 | 769 | 24.7 |
| Food prep. and serving related occupations | 10,200 | 11,807 | 7.1 | 7.1 | 1,607 | 15.8 |
| Building, cleaning & maint. occupations | 5,485 | 6,386 | 3.8 | 3.9 | 901 | 16.4 |
| Personal care and service occupations | 4,458 | 5,375 | 3.1 | 3.3 | 917 | 20.6 |
| Sales and related occupations | 15,260 | 17,231 | 10.6 | 10.4 | 1,971 | 12.9 |
| Office and administrative support occup. | 23,851 | 25,464 | 16.6 | 15.4 | 1,613 | 6.8 |
| Farming, fishing, & forestry occupations | 1,072 | 1,107 | 0.7 | 0.7 | 35 | 3.3 |
| Constr., maintenance & repair occupations | 7,292 | 8,388 | 5.1 | 5.1 | 1,096 | 15.0 |
| Installation, maintenance & repair occup. | 5,696 | 6,472 | 4.0 | 3.9 | 776 | 13.6 |
| Production occupations | 11,258 | 11,612 | 7.8 | 7.0 | 354 | 3.2 |
| Transportation & material moving occup. | 9,828 | 11,111 | 6.8 | 6.7 | 1,282 | 13.1 |

*Notes: (1) Numbers in thousands of jobs. (2) Detail may not equal total or 100% due to rounding.*

over the projection period as a result (of productivity). While there should continue to be growth in this industry, it will be tempered by a shift toward outsourcing information technology service job overseas."

Jobs are projected to increase in information-industry primarily in software publishers, data processing and related and Internet-related industries. Self employed computer and mathematical workers are expected to increase by 39.8% (Hecker, 2004, p. 98).

It is clear from the BLS statistics that offshore job movement is a reality and the labor market in the U.S. seems slow but still "white-collar" occupations which are at risk of declining will increase and not decrease. IT professionals who work in computer software industry can very well see that computer and mathematical occupations are going to increase. Software publishing and Internet related industries are also going to have a large number of job opportunities.

Jobs for word processors and typists; stock clerks and order fillers; secretaries, except legal, medical, and executive; telephone operators; postal service mail sorters are declining not just because of offshoring but also because of advances in computer, optical scanning, and voice recognition technologies.

## *Jobs and Skills: Trends in Near Future*

It may come as a surprise to IT professionals, but global outsourcing in the 1990s, by reducing the price of IT hardware, yielded increased investment in IT and more jobs for U.S. workers with IT skills (Mann, 2003, pp. 2-3). Going forward, the global outsourcing of software and IT services will further reduce the price of these products, yielding a further increase in jobs demanding IT knowledge and skills. The problem of global outsourcing is that new IT jobs may not require the same skills or be in the same sectors of the economy. Some of the industry sectors, like health care and education that did not use IT to the fullest extent, may now start using it with decreased cost of software products and services. This would lead to increased employment opportunities for software engineers and managers. Meanwhile, U.S. IT jobs continue to move up the IT skills ladder. Demand increases for workers with the skills needed to design, customize, and utilize IT applications, particularly in the lagging sectors. Even though the programming jobs are reducing but the IT jobs requiring application design and requirements are increasing and are still highly paid (Mann, 2003, p. 9).

Network systems and data communications analysts, computer software engineers, applications; computer software engineers, systems software; computer systems analysts are listed (see Table 2) amongst the fastest growing occupations for 2002-12 (U.S Bureau of Labor Statistics, 2004, p. 5).

The increasing demand for computer-related occupations reflect the rapid advances in computer technology and the continuing developments of new computer applications, including the Internet and intranets. Overall, computer specialists (Standard occupation code [SOC] 15-1000, a component of computer and mathematical occupations, is projected to grow by 35.8%; and computer and information systems managers (SOC 11-3021) — classified within management, business, and financial occupations is projected to grow by 36.1% (Hecker, 2004, pp. 82-83).

*Table 2. Fastest growing occupations, 2002-12 (Source: U.S. Bureau of Labor Statistics, News Release, USDL 04-148, February 2004)*

| 2000 Standard Occupation Classification code and title | Employment (no. of jobs ) (in thousands) | | Change (% distribution) Percent distribution | | Quartile rank by 2002 median annual earnings |
|---|---|---|---|---|---|
| | 2002 | 2012 | 2002 | 2012 | |
| 31-9092 Medical assistants | 365 | 579 | 215 | 59 | 3 |
| 15-1081 Network systems & data communications analysts | 186 | 292 | 106 | 57 | 1 |
| 29-1071 Physician assistants | 63 | 94 | 31 | 49 | 1 |
| 21-1093 Social & human service assistants | 305 | 454 | 149 | 49 | 3 |
| 31-1011 Home health aides | 580 | 859 | 279 | 48 | 4 |
| 29-2071 Medical records & health information technicians | 147 | 216 | 69 | 47 | 3 |
| 31-2022 Physical therapist aides | 37 | 54 | 17 | 46 | 3 |
| 15-1031 Computer software engineers, applications | 394 | 573 | 179 | 46 | 1 |
| 15-1032 Computer software engineers, systems software | 281 | 409 | 128 | 45 | 1 |
| 31-2021 Physical therapist assistants | 50 | 73 | 22 | 45 | 2 |
| 39-9031 Fitness trainers and aerobic instructors | 183 | 264 | 81 | 44 | 3 |
| 15-1061 Database administrators | 110 | 159 | 49 | 44 | 1 |
| 29-2056 Veterinary technologists & technicians | 53 | 76 | 23 | 44 | 3 |
| 47-4041 Hazardous materials removal workers | 38 | 54 | 16 | 43 | 2 |
| 29-2021 Dental hygienists | 148 | 212 | 64 | 43 | 1 |
| 31-2012 Occupational therapists aides | 8 | 12 | 4 | 43 | 3 |
| 31-9091 Dental assistants | 266 | 379 | 113 | 42 | 3 |
| 39-9021 Personal and home care aides | 608 | 854 | 246 | 40 | 4 |
| 25-3021 Self enrichment education teachers | 200 | 281 | 80 | 40 | 2 |
| 15-1051 Computer systems analysts | 468 | 653 | 184 | 39 | 1 |
| 15-1071 Network and computer systems administrators | 251 | 345 | 94 | 37 | 1 |
| 11-3021 Computer and information systems managers | 284 | 387 | 103 | 36 | 1 |

*Notes: (1) Numbers in thousands of jobs. (2) The quartile rankings are by 2002 median earnings. (3) Occupational employment statistics annual earnings data are presented in the following categories: 1=very high ($41,820 and over), 2=high ($27,500 to $41,780), 3=low ($19,710 to $27,380), and 4=very low (up to $19,600). The rankings were based on quartiles using one-fourth of total employment to define each quartile. Earnings are for wage and salary workers. (3) Some occupations in the BLS table have not been included in this table.*

In spite of all the offshoring job loss fears, the U.S. still remains an immensely attractive location for foreign direct investment and "insourcing" by foreign companies. According to the vice chairman of the joint economic committee of the U.S. Congress, Saxton (2004), a major source of job insourcing is inward foreign direct investment. From 1988 to 2003, foreign companies increased their direct investment in their American subsidiaries by 326%. Between 1988 and 2002, majority-owned American subsidiaries of foreign companies created 2.3 million U.S. jobs. In 2002, these subsidiaries employed a total of 5.4 million U.S. workers. Moreover, these jobs are high paying. Exports of services subject to international competition have also created insourcing jobs.

What this means for IT professionals is that even though programming jobs may be moving offshore, there is going to be rise of software jobs which will require higher level software skills of software analysis, design and architecture, requirements gathering and different customer facing roles.

According to Su (2004) regarding the BLS article on U.S. economy projections to 2012: signs of growth, the unemployment rate reached an eight-year high of 6.0% in 2003. However, with the long-term economic growth and job recovery will gradually push the unemployment rate down over the projection period. There is an expected employment rate of 5.2% in 2012.

## *Salaries of IT Professionals*

Offshore outsourcing will also put wage pressure on workers whose jobs are not outsourced. If there is somebody offshore who has the same skills, is capable of doing the same job, then over the longer time frame, as pointed by Thibodeau (2003), the economic forces are inevitable. The significant cost savings of the IT offshore model is the key factor for its continuous growth and acceptance to use. According to Kumar (2003), India has an estimated 85% share of the IT offshore outsourcing market. Kumar has listed three factors as the causes of salary differences in the U.S., U.K. and India (p. 2). They are: (1) effect of exchange rates in converting Indian Rupee (INR) costs to Western currencies; (2) lower cost of living; and, (3) abundant supply of skilled personnel. Out of all these factors exchange rate appreciation is the only factor that can reduce the cost advantage of offshoring.

It is expected that the enormous salary rise that the IT professionals in the U.S. had seen during the technology boom period, will reach to more realistic and competitive levels. When professionals know that their jobs could be outsourced, they are in a difficult position while pressing for higher wages.

Maybe the salaries may not rise to the same levels as during the technology boom period. However, according to BLS projections (U.S. BLS, 2004, p. 5) the industries which are growing fastest in wage and salary employment growth are the ones which are IT-related, and they are: (a) software publishers; (b) management, scientific and technical consulting services; (c) computer systems design and related services; (d) Internet services, data processing, and other information services. For our reference, the industries are listed in Table 3.

*Table 3. Industries with the fastest wage and salary employment growth, 2002-2012 (Source: U.S. Bureau of Labor Statistics, News Release, USDL 04-148, February 2004)*

| Industry description | 2002 NAICS | Thousands of jobs | | Change 2002-12 |
|---|---|---|---|---|
| | | 2002 | 2012 | |
| Software publishers | 5112 | 256.0 | 429.7 | 5.3 |
| Management, scientific, and technical consulting services | 5416 | 731.8 | 1,137.4 | 4.5 |
| Community care facilities for the elderly and residential care facilities, nec | 6233,6239 | 695.3 | 1,077.6 | 4.5 |
| Computer systems design and related services | 5415 | 1,162.7 | 1,797.7 | 4.5 |
| Employment services | 5613 | 3,248.8 | 5,012.3 | 4.4 |
| Individual, family, community, and vocational rehabilitation services | 6241-3 | 1,269.3 | 1,866.6 | 3.9 |
| Ambulatory health care services except offices of health practitioners | 6214-6,6219 | 1,443.6 | 2,113.4 | 3.9 |
| Water, sewage, and other systems | 2213 | 48.5 | 71.0 | 3.9 |
| Internet services, data processing, and other information services | 516, 518, 519 | 528.8 | 773.1 | 3.9 |
| Child day care services | 6244 | 734.2 | 1050.3 | 3.6 |

*Note: (1) nec = not elsewhere classified.*

Even though salaries may not increase as much as during the technology boom period but still we can see clearly that computer and related occupations are still going to be the highly paid.

## *Outsourcing's Education Connection*

Outsourcing has reduced the number jobs in IT, including those on the entry level. As of 1999-2000, academic year the most sought after graduates were those completing degree requirements in a wide variety of information systems based programs. Now, four years later, as pointed out by Pollack (2004), many information systems professionals are unemployed and many others are fearful of losing their well-paid positions to offshore outsourcing initiatives.

Today's offshore outsourcing movement and economic impact has resulted in decreased number of entry-level career opportunities and a decline in interest in information systems education. The dilemma that computer science and information technology educators face deals with employment opportunities for graduating students. The

*Table 4. Education pays (Source: Unemployment rate, 2003 annual average: Bureau of Labor Statistics; earnings, March 2003: Bureau of the Census.)*

| Unemployment rate in 2003 (Percent) | Education attained | Median weekly earnings in 2003 (Dollars) |
|---|---|---|
| 2.1 | Doctoral degree | $1,349 |
| 1.7 | Professional degree | 1,307 |
| 2.9 | Master's degree | 1,064 |
| 3.3 | Bachelor's degree | 900 |
| 4.0 | Associate degree | 672 |
| 5.2 | Some college, no degree | 622 |
| 5.5 | High-school graduate | 554 |
| 8.8 | Some high-school, no diploma | 396 |

graduating students will have fewer entry level opportunities than has traditionally been in the past. We have seen indicators from the intellectuals in general that new skills, education and training will be required to be able to meet the demands of new job areas that will be created (Greenspan, 2004). Students, as well as all of the IT community is interested to get assurance from the educators that, computers and information systems is still a promising job area.

Educators can look at the professional business occupation category (Table 1, p. 8) to validate that it has: promising job growth, industry growth and is highly paid. This will provide assurance to the students to pursue computer related courses as before. It is a well-established fact that workers with higher education get more wages and have good employment prospects (Table 4).

The number of students in the U.S. obtaining engineering degrees in comparison to other countries is far less (Figure 1).

China has the largest number of students graduating with technical and professional degrees, followed by Japan. Doctorate students in science and engineering are vital for science and technology research and development (R&D) projects of any country. From various higher educational institutions in the U.S., foreign students are earning doctorate degrees in large proportions. In 2001 foreign students received: 49.1% of mathematics and computer science doctorate degrees, and 55.8% of engineering doctorates degrees (Figure 2).

Foreign students earning U.S. science and engineering (S&E) doctorates are increasingly planning to stay in the United States after degree receipt (National Science Board, 2004). This is a positive trend for the R&D efforts of the country. In the U.S.A, the foundation of school going children (grade levels K-12) in the math and science subjects is not strong, and it needs urgent attention. We believe that the current slump in IT positions, largely due to economic conditions and offshore outsourcing, will not last

*Figure 1. Engineering degrees awarded in selected countries in 2001 (Source: National Science Board, Science and Engineering Indicators, 2004, Vol. 2, Chapter 2, data table 2-33)*

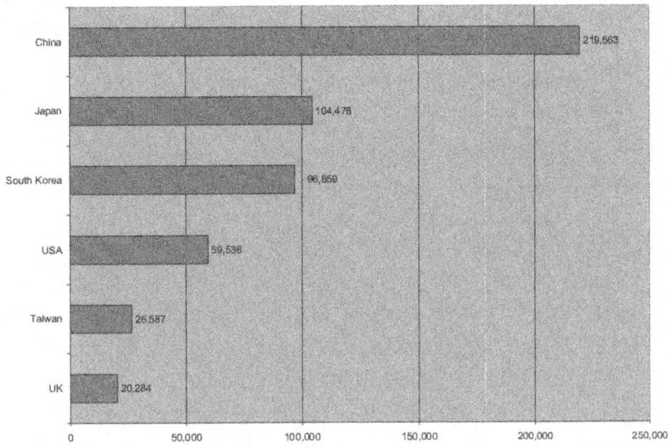


*Figure 2. Doctorate degrees earned at U.S schools, U.S. versus foreign students (Source: National Science Board, Science and Engineering Indicators, 2004, Vol. 2, Chapter 2, data table 2-44)*

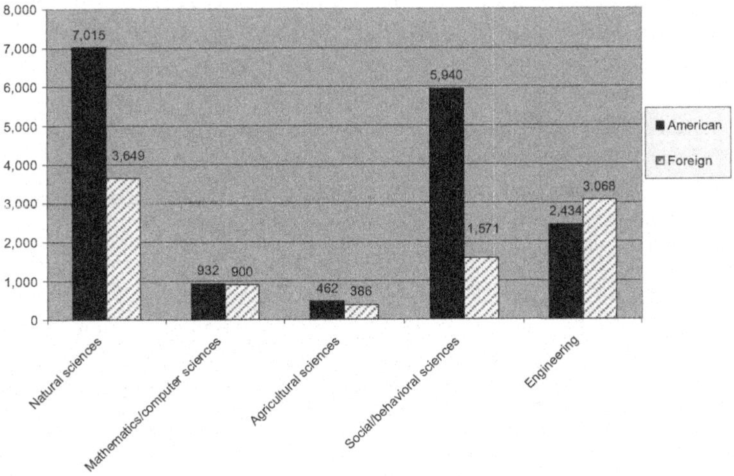

very long. When there are jobs in industries and businesses, we want our students and IT professionals to be equipped with education and skills to fill them. The statistics of BLS clearly suggest that jobs related to IT occupations will continue to grow but the growth will be tempered by outsourcing. Companies are more likely to outsource if they do not find the skills and education level of U.S. students comparable to that of foreign students.

Employment projections for education, training and library occupations are projected to grow faster than the average for all occupations (Table 1). This is favorable for people seeking career in academics. It is expected that the number of adults attending both career and job training schools and self-enrichment classes are going to increase.

## *Social Impacts*

Professionals who have actively been working in the IT industry and have made a reasonably good living out of it are facing several social issues. Jobs and economy are very important for citizens of any nation. There is more visible differentiation in the IT job market between citizens and permanent residents of the U.S. and those working on temporary work visas (Pardon, 2004). The temporary work visa workers are considered as taking away the jobs of the citizens and permanent residents of the country. Being out of work in the U.S. has other consequences apart from no income. Health insurance is a benefit that the companies provide to the workers and their family. Laid-off workers loose health insurance benefits and have to pay out of their savings, abnormally high health insurance premiums until another job is secured. Internet chat rooms and bulletin boards often share IT worker job loss and not being able to find another one with comparable wages and skills. Our personal experience in IT industry indicates growing dissatisfaction amongst the IT workers who had to transfer their knowledge to their foreign counterparts for several months and then in the end being laid off from their current jobs in the companies. *USA Today* had a news story (Armour, 2004) about an IT professional that worked for Boeing before his job was shipped overseas. One of his last assignments was to train his foreign counterpart who would be taking over his job. Some companies are offering another paycheck or better severance if the laid-off employees are willing to participate in the training of foreign workers. Another quality assurance IT professional for a telecommunications company felt trapped that before being laid off she had to train foreign workers (Armour, 2004). IT professionals who are over the age of 50 are facing serious difficulties in securing another job in the event of layoffs.

With privacy regulations like HIPAA and Sarbanes-Oxley gaining a lot of attention in the U.S., there are apprehensions regarding the critical personal and financial data being sent to offshore companies. Some citizens and permanent residents of U.S. are not comfortable with the fact that their social security number, financial history, health history are being sent to overseas companies.

# Recommendations

Offshoring has painful and destabilizing consequences for the hundreds of thousands of workers who find themselves laid off. Government, companies and IT workers, all three parties have to shoulder the responsibility to take appropriate steps to minimize the negative impacts of outsourcing. With our experience of the U.S. IT job market, we would like to make the following recommendations to government, companies and IT workers in order to minimize the impact.

## *Government*

1. It is important that laid-off workers are provided assistance in finding new jobs.
2. There should also be adjustment assistance to the IT workers above certain age hurt by the globalization of IT software and services, on the same lines as trade adjustment assistance aids to the manufacturing sector.
3. There should be training program in place to train the laid-off workers to new labor market skills.
4. Some of these workers may have to change locations to find another job. Relocation assistance should be provided.
5. There should be improved unemployment benefits and health insurance to let the workers recover from laid-off situations.
6. Improving the U.S. education system starting from K-12 to higher education to prepare younger generation for highly skilled jobs. Community colleges and universities should provide more enriching courses as part of continuing education.
7. Higher education has to be made less expensive so that more students are able to pursue higher degrees instead of taking employment after passing high school.
8. Government should encourage immigration of foreign nationals earning high academic degrees so that they stay and work in this country instead of going back to their home countries and working on offshore projects.

## *Companies*

1. The companies that are reaping the benefits of increased revenues because of outsourcing should try to retrain some percentage of employees in new job skills and try to find positions for them in some other sectors of the company.
2. There should be more generous severance and health care package for laid-off employees.
3. Companies before outsourcing should analyze which projects or components of projects are really going to be benefited by outsourcing and outsource accordingly.

### *IT Workers*

There may be policies, regulations and assistance for providing reemployment and relief to displaced workers, each individual who is impacted or may be impacted should also play an active role in protecting their jobs or finding new ones. Yourdon (2004) in his book has given realistic suggestions to face the offshoring tide for individual IT workers, companies engaged in outsourcing and government. Based on these sources, some suggestions are:

1. Find alternative jobs while you still have a job, develop versatile skills which can be applied to other IT areas or in other occupations, start your own business, provide value addition to work you do.
2. Some IT jobs at the moment are somewhat protected from outsourcing like: IT requirements analyst, business process design, architect, IT contract management. Try to position yourself in these areas.
3. IT is a fast-growing and dynamic industry. The key to staying useful in the job market is to continuously learn new skills and technology.
4. IT workers have to continuously strive for improved productivity and creativity.

## Future Trends

Offshoring of IT projects are going to continue. Economic history of America has shown that economy benefits from full and vigorous engagement in global economy. There is a wide disagreement between (a) the arguments of economists who always say that the country will benefit from free and open trade and, (b) the people who are caught in the lay offs as a result of the offshore exposure. History of unemployment figures shows that the unemployment rate has averaged less than 6% since World War II, and the real earnings of the workers have always increased even with outsourcing, irrespective of the factors of trade deficit or trade surplus. The standard of living of people has increased. The older technologies are scrapped to make way for the newer more productive technologies. The workers also migrate with the technologies. Technological advancement is instrumental in shaping the economic process. The population has to be more technologically trained for the new jobs. For the changing skills of the IT jobs, our students and work force has to be better educated to fill up the challenging job positions of high wage and new skills when they arise. Considering all the economic facts, economists' viewpoint and previous business cycles' history, there will be future IT jobs with high salaries, which will require skilled and technically educated professionals.

# Conclusions

Offshore IT software and services outsourcing is a reality for the IT workforce, government and academia. Offshoring is highly debatable as there are so many IT workers displaced from their jobs, while on the other side there are projections of increasing job numbers, growing economy and improved productivity. The economy in the U.S. is going to gain from global outsourcing in the form of more competitive software packages which can be used by large segments of business, more IT and service segment jobs, improved productivity and inflation under control. Education in schools, colleges and universities may see improvements because of the focus on preparing students for highly skilled jobs. It would be unwise to put protectionist legislations in place to prevent the outsourcing movement as it may impede the progress of U.S economy. It is very important for the offshoring companies and government to provide assistance to the American laid-off workers to find another comparable or better job.

# References

Armour, S. (2004, April). Workers asked to train foreign replacements. *USA Today* [online version]. Retrieved June 3, 2005, from http://www.usatoday.com/money/workplace/2004-04-06-replace_x.htm

Bureau of Labor Statistics. (2004). Occupational projections and training data, Bureau of Labor Statistics, chapter IV (2004-05 ed.). [Online]. Retrieved January 15, 2005, from http://www.bls.gov/emp/optd/optd004.pdf

*The Economic Times*. (2004, August). A cut above the rest. Retrieved June 2, 2005, from http://www.nasscom.org/artdisplay.asp?Art_id=3212

Global Insight, Inc. (2004). Executive summary: The comprehensive impact of offshore IT software and services outsourcing on the U.S. economy and the IT industry. Retrieved Jan. 15, 2005, from http://www.itaa.org/itserv/docs/execsumm.pdf

Greenspan, A. (2004, March). Testimony of chairman Alan Greenspan before the committee on education and workforce, U.S. House of Representatives. Retrieved Jan. 15, 2005, from http://www.federalreserve.gov/boarddocs/testimony/2004/20040311/default.htm

Harker, J. V. (2004). Offshore outsourcing in an increasingly competitive and rapidly changing world. Retrieved Jan. 15, 2005, http://www.professionallyspeaking.org/media/Harker.ppt#1

Hecker, D. E. (2004, February). Employment outlook: 2002-12 occupational employment projections to 2012 monthly labor review. Retrieved Jan. 15, 2005, from http://www.bls.gov/opub/mlr/2004/02/art5full.pdf

Kalakota, R., & Robinson, M. (2004, February). Offshore outsourcing: Will your jobs disappear in 2004? Addison Wesley. Retrieved January 15, 2005, from http://www.informit.com/articles/article.asp?p=169548&seqNum=1

Kumar, S. (2003, September). How sustainable is the cost advantage of offshore outsourcing? Retrieved January 15, 2005, from http://www.nasscom.org/download/Cost_Advantage.pdf

Mankiw, N. G. (2004, February). The economic report of the president. Retrieved Jan. 15, 2005, from http://www.gpoaccess.gov/usbudget/fy05/pdf/2004_erp.pdf

Mann, L. C. (2003, December). Globalization of IT services and white collar jobs: The next wave of productivity growth. Institute for International Economics Policy Brief Number PB03-11. Retrieved Jan. 15, 2005, from http://www.iie.com/publications/pb/pb03-11.pdf.

Mattera, P., Woolsey, L., & Purinton, A. (2004, July). Your tax dollars at work...offshore: How foreign outsourcing firms are capturing state government contracts. Retrieved Jan. 15, 2005, from http://www.washtech.org/reports/TaxDollarsAtWork/offshoring_execsum_finalpdf.pdf

McDougall, P. (2005, March). Gartner predicts huge increase in offshore outsourcing by 2015. *Information Week* [online version]. Retrieved June 3, 2005, from http://informationweek.com/story/showArticle.jhtml?articleID=160400498

Moyers, B. (2004, May). NOW PBS politics and economy, America and jobs. Retrieved Jan. 15, 2005, from http://www.pbs.org/now/politics/outsource.html

NASSCOM. (2005). Global business leaders are bullish on India's potential. *Testimonials* [online version]. Retrieved June 2, 2005, from http://www.nasscom.org/artdisplay.asp?cat_id=27

National Science Board. (2004). Science and engineering indicators-2004. Chapter 2 of *Higher education in science and engineering* [online]. Retrieved January 15, 2005, from http://www.nsf.gov/sbe/srs/seind04/pdf/c02.pdf

Pardon, J. (2004, April). Lost your job yet? *Computerworld* [online version]. Retrieved January 15, 2005, from http://www.computerworld.com/careertopics/careers/story/0,10801,92150,00.html

Pollack, T. A. (2004, June). The potential impact of offshore outsourcing on information systems education programs. *Proceedings of the 2004 ASCUE Conference*, June 6-10, 2004, Myrtle Beach, South Carolina. [Online]. Retrieved January 15, 2005, from http://fits.depauw.edu/ascue/Proceedings/2004/p205.pdf

Ramadorai, S., & Karnik, K. (2005, June). *Indian IT-ITES-FY05 results and FY06 forecast.* [Online]. Retrieved June 3, 2005, from http://www.nasscom.org/download/Indian_IT_ITES_%20FY05_Results_FY06_Forecast.pdf

Saxton, J. (2004, October). *Insourcing jobs*. Retrieved January 15, 2005, from http://www.house.gov/jec/imf/insourcingjobs.pdf

Slaughter, M. J. (2004). *Insourcing jobs making the global economy work for America.* Retrieved January 15, 2005, from http://www.ofii.org/insourcing/insourcing_study.pdf

Snell, L. (2004). The outsourcing-education connection: Privatization watch. *Reason Foundation, LA, 28*(4).

Su, B. W. (2004, February). Employment outlook: 2002-12, the U.S. economy to 2012: Signs of growth. *Monthly Labor Review*. [Online version]. Retrieved January 15, 2005, from http://www.bls.gov/opub/mlr/2004/02/art2full.pdf

Thibodeau, P. (2003, April). Outsourcing growth predicted, but impact on the workers may be uneven. *Computerworld* [online version]. Retrieved January 15, 2005, from http://www.computerworld.com/managementtopics/outsourcing/story/0,10801,79906,00.html

Thoms, D. (2005). *How to keep your job*. Retrieved June 2, 2005, from http://www.pragmaticprogrammer.com/talks/HowToKeepYourJob/HTKYJ.html

U.S. Bureau of Labor Statistics. (2004, February). News release USDL 04-148: BLS releases 2002-12 employment projections. Retrieved Jan. 15, 2005, from http://www.bls.gov/news.release/pdf/ecopro.pdf

Yourdon, E. (2004). *Outsource competing in the global productivity race*. Upper Saddle River, NJ: Pearson Education.

# Chapter VII

# Business Process Outsourcing to Emerging Markets: A Knowledge Management Approach to Models and Strategies

Jurgis Samulevičius
Vilnius Gediminas Technical University, Lithuania

Val Samonis
Cornell University, USA and Vilnius University, Canada

## Abstract

*A major phenomenon of globalization, outsourcing is a complex and controversial issue. It occurs when companies contract out activities previously performed in-house or in-country to foreign (usually offshore) companies globally. Couched in the terms of a SWOT analysis and using a modified Harvard-style case study that was subjected to the SWOT analysis, the chapter analyzes business process outsourcing (BPO) to emerging markets, frequently called outsourcing or offshoring in short. The overarching advantage of outsourcing is that it allows a business to focus on core activities as called for by core competence, strategic alliance, and competitive advantage theories of international business. Such a global restructuring of production has been sometimes called the true WMD (weapon of mass destruction) of jobs in the developed world.*

*However, a more balanced approach could borrow the term "creative destruction" from the prominent Austrian economist Josef Schumpeter and emphasize the all-important transformational aspect of outsourcing. A transformational aspect of outsourcing is evidently very important for emerging markets but also for many companies in the developed world; therefore, BPO is sometimes called BTO (business transformational outsourcing).*

*The global digital/knowledge economy offers unprecedented opportunities to produce and sell on a mass scale, reduce costs, and customize to the needs of consumers, all at the same time. Whether you live in a large country such as the U.S. or China, mid-sized country such as Canada or a smaller country such as Lithuania, your potential market is of the same global size. And you can source (netsource) inexpensively wherever you wish. Added to that are immensely increased opportunities to access new knowledge and technologies, driving productivity and living standards further up. BPO to emerging markets is or should be driven by those fundamental reasons having to do with rapid organizational change, reshaping business models to make them viable in the long term, and launching new strategies. This is the essence of transformational outsourcing.*

*In this chapter, BPO is used in the broader, integrated, and comprehensive understanding of changes in the company's business models and strategies but first of all the company's changing core competencies and competitive advantages: partnering with another company to achieve a rapid, substantial, and sustainable improvement in company-level performance. A knowledge management approach is advocated in this research that is to be continued in the future. The chapter concludes that outsourcing is a wave of the future. Postcommunist and other emerging markets countries are well advised to jump to these new opportunities as they represent the best chance yet to realize the "latecomer's advantage" by leapfrogging to technologies and models of doing business which are new for Western countries as well. The chapter analyzes and outlines some of the ways in which contemporary and future business models are deeply transformed by the global digital/knowledge economy. Global outsourcing provides a compelling platform to research the issues of upgrading competitive advantage in developed countries and contract out non-core competencies to emerging markets. Therefore, suggestions for further research are included in the chapter as well.*

## Introduction: What Do We Know About the Nature of Business Process Outsourcing?

Business process outsourcing (BPO) is generally defined as the transfer of the control of the business process to external suppliers. BPO deals with differentiated activities, such as finance and accounting, procurement and supply, customer relations' management, human resources, security and so forth.

BPO implies a more comprehensive — or business process oriented — approach to outsourcing information technology (IT) services, which is the original and narrower term. BPO contracts are seen as being more inclusive, covering a great deal of process redesign work, redeployment and retraining of the people doing the work, and almost always include the information and communication technology (ICT) or information and telecommunication technology (ITT) that enables and supports the business process. The goal is to provide an even greater opportunity for generating innovation, efficiency and speed in reaching markets and, ultimately, shareholder value through this more comprehensive, integrated approach. In this research, BPO is used in this broader, integrated, and strategic sense of changes in the enterprise's management models and strategies but first of all the enterprise's changing core competencies and competitive advantages.

Under the dual pressures of global competition and shareholder expectations, Western companies are driven to reduce operating costs and focus on core competencies. To accomplish this in the global economy, companies are turning to business process outsourcing (BPO), outsourcing or offshoring in short. BPO can be defined as the practice of turning over the operation of an internal business process, like customer care or transaction processing, to a third party service provider. Service providers use their process expertise, human resources, and available technologies to provide the required services. The client company ("client") manages and compensates the service provider by defining measurable performance metrics and then evaluating the service provider's performance using those agreed metrics. Service providers can be located onshore, nearshore or offshore. Companies assessing a service provider usually compare different service provider locations, as differences in culture, business strategies/models, and technical infrastructure affect price and other performance parameters.

Global outsourcing provides a compelling platform to research the issues of upgrading competitive advantage in developed countries and contract out non-core competencies to emerging markets. Such a global restructuring of production has been sometimes called the true WMD (weapon of mass destruction) of jobs in the developed world, especially so in America. However, a more balanced approach could borrow the term "creative destruction" from the famous Austrian economist Josef Schumpeter and emphasize the all-important transformational aspect of outsourcing. A transformational aspect of outsourcing is evidently very important for emerging markets but also for many companies in the developed world. While global executives began outsourcing substantial portions of their operations more than a decade ago to offload activities regarded to be non-core to cut costs and refine their strategies, in modern outsourcing companies are looking around globally for more fundamental reasons — to facilitate rapid organizational change, to launch new strategies, and to reshape business models. In essence, they are engaging in transformational outsourcing, that is partnering with globally scattered companies to achieve rapid, substantial, and sustainable improvements in performance.

According to The McKinsey Institute (Agrawal & Farrell, 2003), on a practical level BPO can be executed through several business models depending on the process and the company's business strategies:

- **Conventional outsourcing:** where a company contracts with a service provider for services over a defined time period.
- **Joint ventures:** where a Western company partners with an offshore company to provide outsourcing services to the Western company and/or third parties.
- **Build operate transfer (BOT):** where a Western company engages with a service provider to establish an offshore facility, hire and train employees, transition the onshore process to the offshore operation and then run the facility and manage the workforce. The Western company then has the option, after a pre-defined time period, to purchase the offshore operation.

In conventional outsourcing and joint venture models, a company may transfer an entire functional area to a service provider on start up (transfer of assets).

## State of Knowledge Assessment: Literature Review and Theoretical Underpinning

There is no established body of literature dedicated to the business process outsourcing (BPO) per se. By 2005, what we have are fragmentary contributions to the understanding of the BPO process that is rapidly changing, evolving, and providing new empirical material. This is due to the novelty of the issue.

However, the proposition of this chapter is that, in deeper essence, the theoretical background of this research is based on the multinational production body of knowledge (Dunning 1996, 1998), especially the international alliance formation literature, foreign direct investment literature, and related contributions.

There exist different theories and models that are relevant to the study of BPO in general. Research on strategic alliances between firms has received increasing attention in the literature during the last decade, reflecting the increasing frequency, diversity, and importance of strategic alliances in regional and/or global business and finance. The main theoretical explanation for why firms form strategic alliances is offered by the transaction cost perspective. According to Williamson (1985, 1991), internalization is the strategy here and it can take different forms.

Two main streams of literature can be identified; one stream is mainly concerned with examining the underlying conditions favoring alliance formation (motivation for alliance formation or intent) (Harrigan, 1985; Teece, 1986; Contractor & Lorange, 1988; Hennart, 1988; Kogut, 1988; Oliver, 1990; Williamson, 1991), the other stream is occupied with investigating alliance outcomes and the impact of alliances on the partner firms (Kogut, 1989; Blodgett, 1992; Dussage & Garette, 1995; Doz, 1996; Mitchell & Singh, 1996; Park

& Russo, 1996; Nakamura, Shaver, & Yeung, 1996). Recently, researchers have begun exploring issues related to alliance dynamics and related knowledge management issues (Singh & Mitchell, 1996; Gulati, 1998; Koza & Lewin, 1998). For more insights, please consult the structured and annotated references section.

## Methodological Approaches

In this chapter, the researchers attempted to approach the subject using statistical and legal/institutional research couched in the SWOT analysis terms as well as using a modified Harvard-style case study that was also subjected to the SWOT analysis. The researchers also attempted to study broader actual empirical/practical processes, as they have been experienced in transition economies such as Lithuania, thus bringing important evidence and empirical insights into the subject of the analysis.

# Background, Trends, Interpretations

By 2005, the debate about outsourcing focused upon its impact on the U.S. and other Western countries' jobs. But it is important to take a broader and longer-term view of what best serves the interests of the U.S. and Western countries in general. The West stands to gain tremendously by promoting a healthy and stable global economy, particularly important and challenging is the integration of emerging markets into the integral global economy. This is something that eluded globalization efforts in the $20^{th}$ century.

No doubt, specific groups of workers in the West might lose out from outsourcing. Emerging markets do pose a competitive threat to some Western companies that stand to lose market shares due primarily to the shortage of their thinking and action about moving to new business models and strategies. But the costs to those specific companies are outweighed by the benefits to Western consumers, a much larger group. In case after case, they enjoyed far lower prices, and often more choice and better goods, after markets were opened to globalization, including BPO. Outsourcing to emerging markets will increase sharply as companies there develop a critical mass of competitive advantages due to restructuring, organizational learning, and organizational change in general. By 2005, skill-intensive Western sectors such as pharmaceuticals and auto parts have not shifted production overseas but are likely to feel the brunt of this next wave of outsourcing. By 2015, manufacturing imports from emerging markets to the United States could increase to more than 50% of total U.S. manufacturing imports, up from 42% in 2002 — a shift worth hundreds of billions of dollars (Agrawal & Farrell, 2003).

The benefits are substantial to emerging markets as well. The price of passenger cars in China, for instance, fell by more than 30% from 1995 to 2001, years when Ford Motor, General Motors, and Honda Motor entered the market. In Mexico, the "everyday low prices" of Wal-Mart stores ended a long history of hefty margins for leading domestic retailers and reined in fast-rising food prices so much that some analysts credit the company with helping to reduce the country's inflation rate. In India, the price of air conditioners, television sets, and washing machines fell by roughly 10% in 2001 alone after foreign companies entered the market. Similarly, prices for cars declined by 8 to 10% a year during the 1990s after the government opened the sector, and the number of models available has now risen from a handful to more than 30. Lower prices have unleashed demand, and India's auto sector has grown by 15% a year.

Outsourcing IT and business processes generates more than $10 billion a year for India and gives employment to half a million of Indian workers. Suppliers to the companies that provide outsourced services employ another half million people. With wages in the sector 50 to 100% higher on average than those for other white-collar occupations, a new middle class of educated workers is being formed. Foreign direct investment played a key role in the creation of these industries: the fast-growing Indian companies that now dominate the global sector got started only after multinational companies pioneered the approach, showed the world that India was a viable outsourcing destination, and trained a critical mass of local employees. Foreign companies continue to provide healthy competition that forces Indian companies to improve their operations continually. They hone the efficiency and productivity of the local industries by bringing in new capital, technology, new business models, and management skills. Equally important, they increase the level of competition, forcing less efficient domestic companies to improve or go out of business (transformational aspect).

BPO is thus held in this chapter to be both very complex and very important to the realization of the benefits of transformation and global integration at both micro and macro levels in emerging market economies and in developed economies. A Schumpeterian "creative destruction" and micro foundations of growth perspective and approach is important in this research, as this approach is more and more relevant to processes in today's global (knowledge) economy. While there are, admittedly, theoretical controversies as to why firms grow (e.g., Romer's new growth theory) and how the growth process works specifically, it is the restructuring and outsourcing processes that shape the impact of corporate behavior and investment on economic performance via capital productivity and new competitive advantage building through technological and organizational innovations, adaptability, Schumpeterian change in general.

As a first stage of a larger research effort, the chapter attempts to contribute to the understanding of the theory and practice of BPO processes as they occur in the direction developed economies-emerging markets, with special reference to Central and Eastern Europe, Lithuania in particular, see the case study below. The authors tried to identify and define key policy areas and measures aimed at improving corporate governance, finance, and competitive advantage building in enterprises with regard to requirements of effective participation in BPO. They also tried to collect other theoretical and empirical evidence pertaining to the impact of the post-communist transformation (esp. privatization, enterprise restructuring, financial sector reform) and new information and communication technologies (ICT) on enterprise strategies/models, with special reference to further restructuring and competitive advantage building via BPO.

# Research Methodology: The Analytical Frame

Given the complex nature of modern research topics, different aspects need to be analyzed and evaluated, not unlike in the biological systems that are very complex by nature. The Strengths-Weaknesses-Opportunities-Threats (SWOT) analysis lends itself very well to the study of such complex living or human-devised systems. The broader explanation and rationales for using the SWOT analysis are as follows.

## SWOT Stands for: Strengths, Weaknesses, Opportunities, Threats

### *Strengths, Predominantly Internal*

Every organization or country has some strengths. In some cases this is obvious; for example, dominant market shares. In other cases, it is a matter of perspective, for instance, a country is small and hence has the ability to move fast using certain strategic moves, like BPO. It is important to note that countries that are in a weak competitive position also have strengths. Whether these strengths are adequate is an issue for analysis.

### *Weaknesses, Predominantly Internal*

Every organization or country also has some weaknesses. In some cases, this is obvious; for example, a stricter regulatory environment. It is important to note that companies or countries that are extremely competent in what they do (that stick to their core competencies) also have weaknesses. How badly these weaknesses will affect them is a matter of analysis.

### *Opportunities, Predominantly External*

All organizations and countries have some opportunities that they can utilize by certain strategic moves. Identifying hidden opportunities is the matter of analysis.

### *Threats, Predominantly External*

No organization or country is immune to threats in the global economy that is characterized by increased competitive pressures. These could be partially internal, such as falling productivity due to outdated technologies, or they could be almost entirely external, such as lower priced international competition.

# Towards a Knowledge Base of Business Process Outsourcing

As stated above, due to the novelty of the topic of business process outsourcing to (and from) emerging markets, especially transition economies, there is no body of dedicated literature. However, the chapter looks for theoretical and empirical clues in some of the broadly relevant Western and Eastern literature, for example, on enterprise restructuring, corporate governance and finance, turnaround management, core competencies, competitive advantage building and so forth. The chapter takes a look at enterprise restructuring in Central and Eastern Europe (with special reference to Lithuania) and argues that the transformation from a state-owned enterprise into a truly capitalist firm involves more than reacting to economic stimuli. Enterprises need access to capital markets to finance investment and they have to acquire new capabilities (esp. identify and define core competencies, "polish" Porter's Diamond, etc.) to be able to grow and compete successfully in Europe and in the global knowledge economy (GKE). In the crucial areas - human resource development, investment capital including new technologies, new models of corporate governance and finance, overall competitive capability building — interaction with Western businesses can make a key contribution to transformations, within the European Union and globally. In general, global outsourcing provides a compelling platform to research the issues of upgrading competitive advantage in developed countries and contract out non-core competencies to emerging markets so that a new and modernized global economic architecture is achieved.

Some broad hypotheses relating to common elements of the restructuring and BPO processes include a shift to flatter, less hierarchical organization structures within Williamson's markets-hierarchies dichotomy and related schemes; the adoption of Western knowledge management and financial/accounting practices, and the introduction of Kornai's hard(er) budget constraints; the evolution of the marketing function and the rationalization of product ranges in light of rapidly changing and increasingly global market needs. Moreover, in the global knowledge economy (GKE), what needs essential redefinition is the enterprise (firm) itself; one obvious point of departure here is the transaction cost theory and the Ronald Coase theorem. Below is a modern take on the Coase theorem relevant changes brought about by the Internet and the global knowledge economy in general (with special reference to emerging markets).

## Why Firms Exist?

Ronald Coase's answer was that, due to a number of impediments (e.g., distance, shortage of information, coordination costs, etc.), it is many times difficult and/or costly to conduct such transactions. Consequently, it is a useful and cost-reducing proposition to "internalize" such transactions within a firm. A "transaction cost" model and strategy of business was born.

## The Internet Revolution

How does the advent of the Internet change business models under the new paradigm of the global digital economy (GDE)?

## The Death of Distance

The geographical distance used to play a very important role in the world economy, for example, expressed operationally in the gravitational models of international trade. Now distance is (almost) dead. Anybody on the Internet can collaborate or do business with any other Web-based individual or business at a small fraction of costs incurred in the pre-Internet era. This is true especially for the service sector but increasingly for the goods sector as well. Consequently, irrespective of whether one operates in small Lithuania or huge China or the U.S., the market is the same: the globe; anybody on the Internet faces a fully global competition, not just local/domestic or regional/international competition.

## The Collapse of Time

The instant interactivity brought about by the Internet is fuelling change. Companies have to accept a strong culture of constant change known as the Schumpeterian "creative destruction" because in a world of instantaneous interactivity and connection there is a big premium on fast response and learning and adapting quickly to clients needs.

## The Undoing of Old Paradigms:

### *The New Nature of Business and Comparative/Competitive Advantage*

The old "bricks and mortal only" model of corporations is dead in a much shorter run than most people are inclined to think. In the global digital village, to paraphrase Marshall McLuhan, every individual or small business can go global and directly compete with any company. At the professional level, there will be fewer traditional 9-to-5 jobs and more outsourcing/contracting with free-agent skilled workers Web-based globally. Competition in the goods and services markets has been brought to new, higher levels, and permanently so.

Developed countries can no longer hide behind politically motivated barriers, physical or other walls to protect themselves from competition from developing countries or emerging markets. Rather than clinging to old models, individuals and corporations in developed and (increasingly) in developing or transition nations need to upgrade their competitive advantages through more education and training. It is far more important to improve human capital (human resources) than it is physical capital (buildings, machines, etc.) or "natural" capital (raw materials, geographical position, etc.).

New information and communication technologies (ICT), especially the Internet (increasingly wireless), bring new opportunities to concentrate on core competencies, specialize and increase trade and investment flows. For these gains to occur, however, what needs essential transformation is the corporation itself.

Corporations need to change the ways they do business; they must become less hierarchical and flatter. Above all, they must be more focused on their core competencies albeit see them dynamically (as constantly changing) and not statically (as, for example, "natural" gateways in trade). Also, they must rely less on their locally available "jack-of-all-trades" workforce and increasingly distribute tasks (outsource or "netsource" them) to other contributors Web-based globally. These new contributors (or teams of contributors) may or may not be full-time employees, but they will generally be equally or better qualified, more willing to learn, and offer greater flexibility, all of which will increase economic efficiency and create new competitive advantages that will become more sustainable.

The above means that corporations need to become much more flexible, amorphous networks of international professionals and knowledge managers working on particular projects. How such corporations should be governed is a new challenge before the managers working in the global knowledge economy. It is postulated in this chapter that a knowledge management (KM) approach should be adopted in trying to solve the above problems. Specifically, three elements of this KM approach are relevant: models and strategies of modern business, human resources, and underlying technologies, especially the Internet technologies.

## Conclusions and Recommendations

Under the dual pressures of global competition and shareholder expectations, Western companies are driven to reduce operating costs and focus on core competencies. To accomplish this in the global economy, companies are turning to business process outsourcing (BPO), outsourcing or offshoring in short. BPO can be defined as the practice of turning over the operation of an internal business process, like customer care or transaction processing, to a third-party service provider. Service providers use their process expertise, human resources, and available technologies to provide the required services. The client company ("client") manages and compensates the service provider by defining measurable performance metrics and then evaluating the service provider's performance using those agreed metrics. Service providers can be located onshore, near-shore or offshore. Companies assessing a service provider usually compare different service provider locations, as differences in culture, business strategies/models, and technical infrastructure affect price and other performance parameters.

Global outsourcing provides a compelling platform to research the issues of upgrading competitive advantage in developed countries and contract out non-core competencies to emerging markets. Such a global restructuring of production has been sometimes called the true WMD (weapon of mass destruction) of jobs in the developed world, especially so in America. However, a more balanced approach could borrow the term "creative destruction" from the famous Austrian economist Josef Schumpeter and emphasize the all-important transformational aspect of outsourcing. A transformational aspect of outsourcing is evidently very important for emerging markets but also for many companies in the developed world. While global executives began outsourcing substantial portions of their operations more than a decade ago to offload activities regarded to be non-core to cut costs and refine their strategies, in modern outsourcing companies are looking around globally for more fundamental reasons — to facilitate rapid organizational change, to launch new strategies, and to reshape business models. In essence, they are engaging in transformational outsourcing, which is partnering with globally scattered companies to achieve rapid, substantial, and sustainable improvements in performance.

Couched in the terms of the SWOT analysis, the chapter concludes that outsourcing is a wave of the future. Outsourcing can create wealth both for the countries that send jobs offshore and for those that receive them.

Outsourcing is a major part or aspect of globalization. No longer can a company stay in its country of origin and remain competitive. Companies are roaming the globe (increasingly digitally) in search of the location(s) that will provide them with the economies of scale that will ensure efficiency with cost reduction and increased productivity. The U.S. economy gains more then $1 in new wealth for every dollar of corporate spending that U.S. companies outsource abroad. The primary objective of outsourcing should be to create added value. Value is added by providing the product at a lower price and maintaining or improving quality.

The U.S. and other Western countries will always have a competitive advantage in something. That something is shifting, however, up the ladder of competitive advantage towards higher value added activities (Americans want higher wages than those in China or India, for example), like research and development as opposed to IT, simple manufacturing or even the main elements of the business process that gets outsourced to emerging markets. In order to get up the ladder of competitive advantage, more Americans will need to upgrade their skills/education. The Internet technologies are making that possible through the lifelong process learning processes, especially online education of executives and other working professionals.

In the last few years, outsourcing has moved from "traditional outsourcing" to the next generation called "strategic outsourcing." Using the strategic outsourcing approach, many companies have reaped the benefits of improved performance, increased access to international markets, access to leading edge technologies, enhanced responsiveness to customer needs, contributed to organizational goals of increased productivity and efficiency, reduced costs, reduced cycle time, and improved quality of the goods and services in their organizations. In today's economy, the outsourcing approach is considered a viable option for achieving the best possible results, that is, in-depth business transformation.

In the future, outsourcing will be an even more effective and globally available model to reduce costs, boost productivity and exports, and increase profits. Thus, outsourcing will continue to be a viable business strategy, and even to the greater extent in the decade to come.

## Business Process Outsourcing: Suggestions For Further Research and Knowledge Building

What is a corporation and how corporations should be structured and governed is a new challenge before the managers working in the global knowledge economy of the 21st century. It is postulated in this chapter that a comprehensive knowledge management (KM) approach should be adopted in trying to solve the above problems. Specifically, three elements of this comprehensive KM approach are most relevant: models and strategies of modern business, human resources, and underlying technologies, especially Internet technologies.

In the crucial areas — human resource development, investment capital including new technologies, new models of corporate governance and finance, overall competitive capability building — interaction with Western businesses can make a key contribution to transformations, within the emerging markets and globally. Global outsourcing provides a compelling platform to research the issues of upgrading competitive advantage in developed countries and contract out non-core competencies to emerging markets. In this context, outsourcing should be studied in connection with mergers and acquisitions (M&A) and foreign direct investment (FDI) as the two engines of global restructuring. Global financial institutions should be more active in research, explanation, and promotion of such a global restructuring. For the insights, please consult the structured and annotated reference section.

There are several promising lines of further research and fruitful approaches to outsourcing. One of them is the cluster method and strategy for modern growth developed at Harvard by Prof. Michael Porter (1990). The cluster method fosters high levels of productivity and innovation and lays out the implications for competitive strategy and economic policy. Economic geography in an era of global competition poses a paradox that is not well understood, needs further research. On one hand, location should no longer be a source of competitive advantage. Open global markets, rapid transportation, and high-speed communications should allow any company to source anything from any place at any time. But on the other hand, claims Prof. Porter, location remains important to competition. The global economic map is characterized by clusters: critical masses in one place of linked industries and institutions — from suppliers to universities to government agencies — that enjoy unusual competitive success in a particular field or fields. Porter explains how clusters affect competition in three broad ways: first, by increasing the productivity of companies based in the area; second, by driving the direction and pace of innovation; and third, by stimulating the formation of new businesses within the cluster. Geographic, cultural, and institutional proximity provides companies with special access, closer relationships, better information, powerful incentives, and other advantages that are difficult to tap from a distance, according to Porter. The more complex, knowledge-based, and dynamic the global economy becomes, the more this is true, claims Porter. Competitive advantage lies in local things - knowledge, relationships, and motivation — that distant rivals cannot replicate very efficiently, Prof. Porter continues. However, the advent of the Internet, knowledge management, and the global knowledge economy seems to be changing that and profoundly affecting the essence of "thinking globally but acting locally".

On top of more theoretical research (e.g., based on new growth theories) and the relevant argumentation advanced, there is a need to critically analyze outsourcing experience from a number of old and new and cases, etc, in such leading countries as China, India, Finland, Poland, U.S., Canada. Case-study type insights need to be presented on specific approaches that worked well within specific institutional/systemic settings called policy environments. Such policy environments (their parameters) are created mainly on the interaction of business, government (various levels), and other elements of a civil society in particular countries or integration groupings. Apparent failures in this regard are to be studied as well. By going deeper into the nature of policy environments (especially incentives they create), we need to refine the discussion on this issue and thereby build the knowledge base. The case study below is such an attempt.

# The Case Study: Lithuania

## Introduction

Full member of NATO and the EU since 2004, Lithuania is offering excellent business opportunities in a stable political, economic and social environment. Lithuania is strategically located in the gateway between the EU and the CIS. Being on a sea and land route, Lithuania is serving as an arterial road between the East and the West, the North and the South. In fact, one of geographical centers of Europe is located just north of Vilnius.

In spite of the heavy burden of the Soviet occupation legacies after regaining its independence in 1990, Lithuania embarked on a path of determined, radical, and sustained reforms aimed at re-establishing democracy and a functioning market economy. It succeeded remarkably and is now regarded Europe's transformation success story.

### *Lithuania in the European Union: Implications for Business Process Outsourcing*

The widening and deepening of the European integration (especially the introduction of the euro) markedly increased competitive pressures, so companies began looking for new, sustainable and dynamic advantages. Given that the continent is aging pretty rapidly and immigration presents a problem for a number of reasons, a shortage of qualified labor is developing that can be best addressed by taking advantage of the digital/knowledge revolution and of the potential of new EU members such as Lithuania. Under these circumstances, a better use of the continent's resources has become critical to winning the competitive game or even survival in the unified Europe and the integrated world.

Large European and multinational corporations (e.g., BT, Buckman Labs, Nokia, Siemens, etc.) are the early adopters of new thinking. They first realized that high initial costs of research, human/intellectual capital costs, etc., are efficiently spread only over longer periods and larger geographical areas. The vision they have, specifically their new-frontier mentality and the ability to develop integrative thinking across functional areas of business, not only at the highest management levels but, what is even more important, at lower management levels resulted in knowledge-sensitive enterprise cultures and the resultant organizational learning regarding new business models and strategies. Also, such issues are pretty high on the EU institutions' agenda (e.g., Lisbon Strategy). The unique European competitive advantage (e.g., compared to the U.S.) is that EU institutions are able to give push and pull to many continent-wide initiatives that fall within the public goods category (e.g., earlier adoption of continent-wide standards for mobiles, knowledge management practices, etc.).

The chief criterion of readiness to become a full member of the EU is the capability to withstand the European competitive pressures. While in the first period lower labor costs do provide certain competitive advantages pretty much across the branches of economic activity, this factor is of rather short duration in the case of Lithuania or other transition economies. Lithuania will need to develop higher added-value market niches that will precisely call upon the Lithuanian capabilities to create an entrepreneurial economy that is integrated continentally and globally. BPO provides such opportunities especially in the context of knowledge and innovation in the European and global business.

Knowledge industries in Lithuania are still not very advanced, compared to global leaders. But some pioneering firms that were created around research institutes do have histories going back a decade or so, esp. those in biotechnology, laser research and so forth. A national political consensus was reached and the national agreement was signed calling for Lithuania to become a knowledge-based economy. Further development of the knowledge economy infrastructure (e.g., better access to high-speed Internet) is needed. That will necessitate a better public sector-private sector collaboration so as to arrive at innovative management models and strategies underpinning the knowledge economy in Lithuania. One such innovative scheme is the Sunrise Valley in Vilnius, deliberately modeled after the Silicon Valley, California. There are other such schemes at different stages of implementation. Among Lithuania's corporate leaders are SICOR Biotech, Fermentas, Alna, Sonex, Omnitel, Bite GSM, Ekspla, Laser Research Institute. They are members of The Knowledge Economy Forum of Lithuania.

The dominant challenge before Lithuania is how to use a considerable theoretical research (e.g., biotech, lasers, semiconductors, game theory) potential of the Lithuanian research institutes, universities, and industry. There is a need to develop a practice-oriented strategy for knowledge-based economy in Lithuania. The theory-practice gap has been something of a problem inherited from the communist period, as are the inter-institutional collaboration shortcomings. One important aspect of that challenge is the interdisciplinary and cross-disciplinary nature of modern business models that mandates integrative thinking and puts a premium on those managers who are able to integrate functional perspectives. Educational institutions in European countries are still somewhat attached to the subject-based teaching/learning; and this problem is therefore more pronounced in Europe than in North America. It could well be that BPO is that vehicle and that frame of mind that can help overcome such shortcomings.

## Business Process Outsourcing: Lithuania's Strengths

### *Availability of Well-Trained, Competitive Labor Force*

The annual number of university graduates per 1000 inhabitants is one of the highest in the region. The cost of labor is among the lowest. The average monthly wage in the manufacturing sector in Lithuania is about one tenth that of industrialized countries, including those in the EU.

### *Attractive Operating and Living Costs, Lifestyle*

Utilities, rent, building, overhead, service and living costs are among the lowest in the EU. Thus, Lithuania has significant cost advantages while offering geographical proximity to the Eastern markets. Lithuania's modern European life style is predicated on its long national and statehood history and a largely unspoiled natural environment.

### *Well Developed Transportation Networks*

The EU Transport Commission designated Lithuania as the region's transport hub, with two out of the 10 priority corridors in Europe intersecting in Lithuania.

A network of European-standard four-lane highways links major industrial centres. By most standards, Lithuania has a well-developed transportation system. Road construction is underway for connecting with the trans-European transportation network. It will be part of the transportation system around the Baltic Sea and a transportation axis linking Russia and the Baltic Sea. The country offers four international airports and an ice-free seaport on the eastern Baltic Sea.

### *Free Economic Zones and Industrial Parks*

Lithuania's Free Economic Zones and Industrial Parks boast excellent infrastructure and trans-shipment facilities, highly qualified labor force, and offer investors very attractive incentives. There is also plenty of industrial land with direct access to ports, railroads, and highways available.

### *World Standard Export Production*

Most foreign businesses invest in Lithuania for export production purposes. Many local producers have already obtained ISO 9000, ISO 14000, GMP and other standards. Lithuanian exports in 2004 were €7.5 billion and growing.

## *Multinational Investor Satisfaction*

Siemens, Telia, Philips, Motorola, Mars/Masterfoods, Sonera, Kraft Food International, Festo, Lancaster Steel, Partec, Kemira, Danisco, SEB, Carlsberg and Marzotto are among the multinationals that have chosen to locate production facilities in Lithuania.

## *Strong FDI Growth*

Foreign investment in Lithuania has been steadily increasing and reached close to Euro 5 billion as of the end of 2004. There are attractive "greenfield" and privatization projects in infrastructure, transport, energy, to name a few sectors.

There are some forward-looking initiatives in Lithuania (e.g., Window to the Future, The Knowledge Economy Forum) that in some ways lead the Central and Eastern Europe. With regard to outsourcing, Outsource2Lithuania is a project worth a closer analysis.

## *Outsource2Lithuania: A Business Process Outsourcing Project*

Outsource2Lithuania is a new project aimed at uniting Lithuania's information technology and telecommunications (ITT) corporations, who are potential exporters of products and/or services within the European and global outsourcing models and strategies. The goal of the Project is for the Lithuanian ITT corporations to take the leading positions among the providers of ITT outsourcing services in Europe and globally. It also seeks to develop Lithuanian ITT products and services, promote exports to international markets, and contribute to the establishment of a positive image of the Lithuanian ITT market. According to Gartner Inc. experts' evaluation, the growth of the Lithuanian ITT outsourcing market reached some 40% over 2003 alone. Lithuania is rated as one of the most attractive providers of this type of service in Eastern Europe.

The project is open for participation by member corporations of the Association Infobalt (grouping Lithuania's ITT and other high-tech companies), pursuing business related to cross-border activities, promotion of exports and so forth. It is expected that up to 40 Lithuanian ITT corporations could be attracted within the first stage of the project, working in such fields as system integration, software development, data center operation, as well as education establishments, marketing organizations, training facilities, etc; thus covering a major part of the entire BPO spectrum. According to the project's policy, any strategic decision on the project's activity shall be taken through a consensus of all the project members. Particular implementation task of the project are to be carried out by the Infobalt staff.

For achievement of the goals of the project, efficient international marketing efforts are to be employed including dissemination of the information on the Web portal, through international exports Web sites, specialized publications, presentation of the Lithuania's ITT potential at various ITT offshore services forums internationally, enticement of potential partners, as well as through relevant governmental institutions and agencies. The participants of the project are offered training courses, including topics like the management of outsourcing, marketing, exports, public relations in international business, participation in business missions and so forth.

Participation in the project is based on a fee. Each corporation willing to participate shall be charged a membership fee assessed in relation to it's sales, ranging from 1000 to 3000 litas (LTL) a year. Membership fees, however, shall by no means be the sole source of funding the project. Additional sources of financing shall be sought to expand the value added by the project.

Each member of the project is offered a Web space for the placement of its corporate information and sales pitch on the portal (www.outsource2Lithuania.com) and on a compact disk to be distributed to potential partners in outsourcing services in Europe and Asia. The information on the undertakings of the participating businesses, their services and products are to be distributed by the Association Infobalt and it's partners including The Lithuanian Development Agency, International Chamber of Commerce, and the Lithuanian Ministry of Foreign Affairs, as well as at international ITT events. Each project member is entitled to use the service mark "Member of the Project: Outsource2Lithuania".

## *BPO to Lithuania: Services*

"Outsource2Lithuania" companies provide a substantial range of enterprise solutions. They help to plan, analyze, design, develop, deploy and sustain solutions in high business impact areas like:

## *B2B*

Business Intelligence, Customer Relationship Management, Enterprise Resource Planning, Document and Content Management, Supply Chain Management, Product Data Management, Enterprise Application Design and Development, Enterprise Application Integration, Enterprise Application Testing;

## *Development Services*

Software Development, Testing, Data Warehousing, Content Delivery Network, Digital Signal Processing, Embedded Software, Engineering Services, Middleware Verification and Validation Services;

## *ICT Infrastructure and Solutions*

Internet Infrastructure, IT Infrastructure Services, Hardware Design, Security Solutions, Storage Area Network, Voice over IP, Wireless Technologies, Broadband, Multimedia;

*Box 1. The SWOT analysis of the Lithuanian ICT and other high tech industry: Summary and outline*

| **STRENGTHS** | **WEAKNESSES** |
|---|---|
| Human resources suitable for innovative activities and knowledge-based production;<br>Healthy economy, growing most rapidly among the CEE (5-6% for 2001-2005);<br>Well-developed high tech & other universities producing over 500 specialists in ICT and other disciplines annually;<br>Other well-trained & low-cost human resources available;<br>Modern telecom infrastructure with a digitalization ratio of 100% and mobile penetration of some 50%;<br>Labor force versatile in English, German, Russian, and Polish;<br>Open economy with rule-based system aligned to the EU & WTO – economic stability;<br>Developed financial institutions & intermediaries;<br>Location between the EU, Nordics, Commonwealth of Independent States (CIS);<br>Capacity to promptly adapt to rapidly changing ICT & knowledge based economy;<br>Full scale privatization accomplished; industry re-structured based on comparative advantages;<br>Institutional support to SME development;<br>Well-developed IT infrastructure across the region;<br>Sound linkages between academia and industry for development of applications;<br>EU and NATO integration to provide large market opportunities for ICT-enabled services. | Manpower adequately skilled but needs re-training on project management and quality management of ICT projects;<br>Slow drafting and implementation strategies of ICT & other high tech;<br>Vague long-term vision for ICT development including action plans or prioritization of funds;<br>Comparatively small market - small investment by MNCs;<br>Foreign economic relations still to be formulated on the basis of national and EU interests;<br>Capital market in the development stage;<br>ICT penetration not sufficient to give a substantial boost to e-commerce and e-business development;<br>Logistics management poor - railway transport system physically inadequate;<br>Public-private partnerships weak & cooperation among economic entities underdeveloped;<br>Insufficient incentives for R&D by business. |
| **OPPORTUNITIES** | **THREATS** |
| Development of labor-intensive sectors like computer science and knowledge-based sectors to serve a larger market of EU and CIS;<br>Availability of structural funds from the EU to provide support to business modernization, employment promotion, improvement in quality of life, etc.;<br>Industrialization processes based on FDI, advanced technology and international management experience to enhance competitiveness and leverage advantages to achieve export-led growth;<br>EU accession to expand sales markets and provide preconditions for foreign trade;<br>Globalization of financial resources will provide alternative possibilities for financing;<br>Use of digital technologies will open wider markets and provide conditions for more efficient cooperation with advanced economies in ICT, BPO, R&D, and other IT-enabled services;<br>Possibility to establish positions in the transport service markets of continental Europe, with logistic centres in Kaunas, Klaipeda and Vilnius;<br>Free movement of IT and high-tech personnel to provide opportunities for application development and onshore software development. | Emigration weakens the intellectual potential of Lithuania;<br>Potential closures of domestic ICT companies due to fierce competition unless they develop sustainable niche markets;<br>Fear of becoming a center of higher cost production because of alignment with the high-cost EU and trade distortions imposed by third countries;<br>Loss of General Preference Systems discounts for exports to North America and Japan;<br>International environmental obligations may lead to higher costs of production;<br>Advanced ICT countries may wrongly see Lithuanians as consumers and not as developers/partners for modern products and services thereby leaving Lithuania out of BPO networks;<br>Lack of coherent vision of the Lithuanian industry;<br>Inconsistent policies and inadequate communications may lead to fragmented growth of IT and other high-tech industry. |

### *ICT-Enabled Services*

Process Support Services, Contact/Call Centers, Sales and Marketing Support.

### *Business Process Outsourcing to Lithuania: A SWOT Analysis*

The World Trade Organization and the International Trade Centre (WTO&ITC, Geneva) team of experts carried out extensive consultations with the Lithuanian Ministry of the Economy, Ministry of Internal Affairs, Ministry of Transport and Communications, Communications Regulatory Authority, Committee on Development of Information Society, Association of Lithuanian Chambers of Commerce, The Lithuanian Development Agency, Infobalt, the Information Technology Centre, the Lithuanian Standards Board, the Internet Service Providers Association, leading ICT companies, leading banks, customs authorities and others. The purpose of these consultations was to assess and help develop a knowledge-based industry in Lithuania and the Baltic region so that it gains a major share of the global ICT marketplace.

The WTO&ITC team compared Lithuania's ICT industry with similar industries of countries in the region. The conclusion was that the industry is developing and expanding its activities across the region. In the EU market, activities related to subcontracting or onshore software application were taking place. Although the Lithuanian ICT industry is relatively small compared to the ICT market of Poland, for example, it has good growth potential driven by niche areas and niche products.

Box 1 shows the results of the WTO & ITC team's and others' research on Lithuania's ICT industry based on analysis of its strengths, weaknesses, opportunities and threats (SWOT).

# References

## International Production Literature: A Theoretical Background of Business Process Outsourcing

Badaracco, J. L. (1991). *The knowledge link.* Boston: Harvard Business School Press.

Balakrishnan, S., & Koza, M. (1993). Information asymmetry, adverse selection and joint ventures, theory and evidence. *Journal of Economic Behavior and Organization, 20*, 99-117.

Beamish, P. W. (1988). *Multinational joint ventures in developing countries.* London: Routledge.

Birkinshaw, J., & Hood, N. (2001). Unleash innovation in foreign subsidiaries. *Harvard Business Review, 79*(3), 131-137.

Blodgett, L. L. (1992). Factors in the instability of international joint ventures: An event history analysis. *Strategic Management Journal, 13*(6), 475-481.

Borys, B., & Jemison, D. B. (1989). Hybrid arrangements as strategic alliances: Theoretical issues in organizational combinations. *Academy of Management Review, 14*(2), 234-249.

Brealey, R. A., & Myers, S. C. (2003). *Principles of corporate finance* (7th ed.). New York: Irwin/McGraw-Hill.

Case: La Société Générale de Belgique. (1994). In R. I. Tricker, *International corporate governance* (pp. 566-568). New York: Prentice Hall.

Chakrabarti, A., & Hauschildt, J., & Sueverkruep, C. (1994). Does it pay to acquire technological firms. *R&D Management, 24*(1), 47-56.

Cohen, W. M., & Levinthal, D. A. (1990). Absorptive capacity: A new perspective on learning and innovation. *Administrative Science Quarterly,* 128-152.

Conner, K. R. (1991). A historical comparison of resource-based theory and five schools of thought within industrial organization economics: Do we have a new theory of the firm? *Journal of Management, 17*, 121-154.

Contractor, F. J., & Lorange, P. (1988). Why should firms cooperate? The strategy and economic basis for cooperative ventures. In F. J. Contractor & P. Lorange (Eds.), *Cooperative strategies in international business* (pp. 3-30). Lexington, MA: Lexington Books.

Doz, Y. L. (1996). The evolution of cooperation in strategic alliances: Initial conditions, or learning processes? *Strategic Management Journal,* Summer Special Issue, *17*, 55-83.

Dunning, J. H. (1996, December). The geographical sources of the competitiveness of firms: Some results of a new survey. *Transnational Corporations, 5*(3), 1-29.

Dunning, J. H. (1998). The eclectic paradigm as an envelope for economic and business theories of MNE activity. Unpublished paper, Graduate School of Management, Rutgers University, Newark, NJ.

Dunning, J. H., & Lundan, S. M. (1998). The geographical sources of competitiveness of multinational enterprises: An economic analysis. *International Business Review, 7*, 132.

Dunning, J. H., &Wymbs, C. (1998). The sourcing of technological advantage by multinational enterprises. Unpublished paper, Graduate School of Management, Rutgers University, Newark, NJ.

Dussauge, P., & Garrette, B. (1995). Determinants of success in international strategic alliances: Evidence from the global aerospace industry. *Journal of International Business Studies, 26*, 505-530.

Dussauge, P., Garrette, B., & Mitchell, W. (2000). Learning from competing partners: Outcomes and durations of scale and link alliances in Europe, North America and Asia. *Strategic Management Journal, 21*, 99-126.

Eisenberg, E. M., & Witten, M.G. (1987). Reconsidering openness in organizational communication. *Academy of Management Review, 12*(3), 418-426.

Erramilli, M. K., & Rao, C. P. (1990). Choice of foreign entry modes by service firms: role of market knowledge. *Management International Review, 30*(2), 141.

Gammelgaard, J. (2000). How foreign subsidiaries develop into integrated competence centres. In J. Larimo & S. Kock, *Recent studies in interorganizational and international business research* (pp. 164-181). Proceedings of the University of Vaasa, Reports 58.

Gammelgaard, J. (2001). Knowledge transfers following acquisition: The impact of prior trust-based relations. *Proceedings of the University of Vaasa, Reports.*

Gassmann, O., & von Zedtwitz, M. (1999). New concepts and trends in international R&D organization. *Research Policy, 28*(2,3), 231-250.

Geringer, J. M. (1988). *Joint venture partner selection: Strategies for developing countries.* New York: Quorum.

Gertsen, M. C., & Soderberg, A. M. (2000). Tales of a trial and triumph. A narratological approach to acquisitions. In C. Cooper & A. Gregory (Eds.), *Advances in mergers and acquisitions* (pp. 239-272). London: JAI Press/Elsevier Science.

Gertsen, M. C., Soderberg, A. M., & Vaara, E. (2000). *Cultural change processes in mergers. A social constructionist perspective.* Working paper no. 38, Department of Intercultural Communication and Management, Copenhagen Business School, Copenhagen.

Gulati, R. (1995). Does familiarity breed trust? The implications of repeated ties for contractual choice in alliances. *Academy of Management Journal, 38*, 85-112.

Gulati, R. (1998). Alliances and networks. *Strategic Management Journal, 19*(4), 293-317.

Gulati, R. (1999). Where do interorganizational networks come from? *American Journal of Sociology, 104*(5), 1439-1493.

Hagedoorn, J., & Sadowski, B. (1999). The transition from strategic technology alliances to mergers and acquisitions: An exploratory study. *Journal of Management Studies,* 36(1), 87-107.

Harrigan, K. R. (1985). *Strategies for joint ventures.* Lexington, MA: Lexington Books.

Hennart, J. F. (1988). A transaction cost theory of equity joint ventures. *Strategic Management Journal, 9*(4), 361-374.

Hennart, J. F., Roehl, T., & Zietlow, D. S. (1999). Trojan horse or workhorse? The evolution of U.S.-Japanese joint ventures in the United States. *Strategic Management Journal, 20*(1), 15-29.

Hill, C. W. L. (2001). *Global business today, 2nd edition.* New York: Irwin/ McGraw-Hill.

Hirsch, S. (1993). The globalization of services and service-intensive goods industries. In Y. Aharoni (Ed.), *Coalitions and competition: The globalization of professional business services* (pp. 66-78). New York and London: Routledge.

Hof, R. D. (1999, October 4). A new era of bright hope and terrible fears. *Business Week,* European edition, 50-57.

Inkpen, A. C., & Dinur, A. (1998). Knowledge management processes and international joint ventures. *Organization Science, 9*(4), 454-468.

Keld, J., & Iwar, U. (2002). *Negotiating partnerships: Increase profits and reduce risks.* London: Pearson Education.

Kogut, B. (1988). Joint ventures: Theoretical and empirical perspectives. *Strategic Management Journal, 9*(4), 319-332.

Kogut, B. (1989). The stability of joint ventures: Reciprocity and competitive rivalry. *Journal of Industrial Economics, 38*, 183-198.

Kogut, B., & Zander, U. (1992). Knowledge of the firm, combinative capabilities, and the replication of technology. *Organization Science, 3*, 383-397.

Koza, M. P., & Lewin, A. Y. (1998). The co-evolution of strategic alliances. *Organizational Science, 9.*

Larsson, R., & Finkelstein, S. (1999). Integrating strategic, organizational and human resource perspectives on mergers and acquisitions: A case survey study of synergy realization. *Organisation Science, 10*(1), 1-26.

Latour, B. (1986). The powers of association. In J. Law (Ed.), *Power, action and belief* (pp. 264-280). London: Routledge and Kegan Paul.

Lei, D., & Slocum, J. W. (1992). Global strategy, competence-building and strategic alliances. *California Management Review, 35*(1), 81-97.

Lindahl, D. P., & Beyers, W. B. (1999, January). The creation of competitive advantage by producer service establishments. *Economic Geography, 75*, 1-20.

Lowendahl, B. P. (1993). Co-operative strategies for professional service firms: Unique opportunities and challenges. In Y. Aharoni Ed.), *Coalitions and competition: The globalization of professional business services* (p. 166). New York and London: Routledge.

March, J. G. (1991). Exploration and exploitation in organizational learning. *Organization Science, 2*, 71-87.

Minshall, T. H. W., & Garnsey, E. W. (1999). Building production competence and enhancing organizational capabilities through acquisition: the case of Mitsubishi Electric. *International Journal of Technology Management, 17*(3), 312-333.

Mitchell, W., & Singh, K. (1996). Survival of businesses using collaborative relationships to commercialize complex goods. *Strategic Management Journal, 17*(3), 169-195.

Morgan G., & Smircich, L. (1980). The case for qualitative research. *Academy of Management Review, 5*(4), 491-500.

Nakamura, M., Shaver, J. M., & Yeung, B. (1996). An empirical investigation of joint venture dynamics: Evidence from U.S.-Japan joint ventures. *International Journal of Industrial Organization, 14*, 521-541.

Napier, N. K., Simmons, G., & Stratton, K. (1989). Communication during a merger: The experience of two banks. *Human Resource Planning, 12*(2), 105-122.

Nohria, N., & Ghoshal, S. (1997). *The differentiated network – Organizing multinational corporations for value creation.* San Francisco: Jossey-Bass Publishers.

Nonaka, I., & Takeuchi, H. (1995). *The knowledge-creating company: How Japanese companies create dynamics of innovation.* New York: Oxford University Press.

Oliver, C. (1990). Determinants of interorganizational relationships: Integration and future directions. *Academy of Management Review, 15*, 241-265.

Park, S. H., & Russo, M. V. (1996). When competition eclipses cooperation: An event history analysis of joint venture failure. *Management Science, 42*, 875-890.

Parkhe, A. (1993). Strategic alliance structuring: A game theoretic and transaction cost examination of inter-firm cooperation. *Academy of Management Journal, 36*, 794-829.

Porter, M. E. (1990). *The competitive advantage of nations.* New York: The Free Press.

Porter, M. E. (1998). *On competition.* Boston: Harvard Business Review Press.

Porter, M. E., & Fuller, M. B. (1986). Coalitions and global strategy. In M. E. Porter (Ed.), *Competition in global industries* (pp. 315-344). Cambridge, MA: Harvard University Press.

Powell, W. W. (1990). Neither market nor hierarchy: Network form of organization. In B. M. Staw & L. L. Cummings (Eds.), *Research in organizational behavior* (pp. 295-336). Greenwich, CT: JAI Press.

Powell, W. W., & DiMaggio, P. J. (1991). *The new institutionalism in organizational analysis.* Chicago: The University of Chicago Press.

Prahalad, C. K., & Hamel, G. (1990, May-June). The core competence of the corporation. *Harvard Business Review.*

Risberg. A. (1999). *Ambiguities thereafter. An interpretive approach to acquisitions.* Malmo: Lund University Press.

Sakakibara, M. (1997). Heterogeneity of firm capabilities and cooperative research and development: An empirical examination of motives. *Strategic Management Journal,* Summer Special Issue, *17*, 143-164.

Schweiger, D. M., & DeNisi, A. S. (1991).Communication with employees following a merger: A longitudinal field experiment. *Academy of Management Journal, 34*(1), 110-135.

Seth, A. (1990).Value creation in acquisitions: A re-examination of performance issues. *Strategic Management Journal, 11*, 99-115.

Seth, A. (2000). Synergy, materialism or hubris? An empirical examination of motives for foreign acquisitions of U.S. firms. *Journal of International Business Studies, 31*(3), 387.

Simonin, B. (1999). Ambiguity and the process of knowledge transfer in strategic alliances. *Strategic Management Journal, 20*, 595-623.

Singh, K., & Mitchell, W. (1996). Precarious collaboration: Business survival after partners shut down or form new partnerships. *Strategic Management Journal,* Summer Special Issue, *17*, 99-115.

Smircich, L. (1983). Concepts of culture and organizational analysis. *Administrative Science Quarterly, 28*(3), 339-358.

Spender, J. C. (1996). Making knowledge the basis of a dynamic theory of the firm. *Strategic Management Journal,* Special Issue, 45-62.

Stalk, G., Evans, P., & Shulman, L. E. (1992, March-April). Competing on capabilities: The new rules of corporate strategy. *Harvard Business Review.*

Stewart, T. A. (1997). *Intellectual capital: The new wealth of organizations.* New York & London: Doubleday/Currency.

Teece, D. J. (1986). Profiting from technological innovation: Implications for integration, collaboration, licensing and public policy. *Research Policy, 15,* 285-305.

Weick, K. (1995). *Sensemaking in organizations.* Thousand Oaks, CA: Sage Publications.

Wernerfelt, B. (1984). A resource-based view of the firm. *Strategic Management Journal, 5*(2), 171-180.

Williamson, O. E. (1985). *The economic institutions of capitalism. Firm, market, relational contracting.* New York: The Free Press.

Williamson, O. E. (1991). Strategizing, economizing, and economic organization. *Strategic Management Journal,* Winter Special Issue, 12, 75-94.

Young, M., & Post, J. E. (1993, Summer). Managing to communicate, communicating to manage: How leading companies communicate with employees. *Organizational Dynamics, 22*(1), 31-43.

## Business Process Outsourcing Literature: Selected Items in Applied Approaches

Agrawal, V., & Farrell, D. (2003). Who wins in offshoring? *The McKinsey Quarterly,* Special Edition: Global Directions.

Arora, A., & Gambardella, A. (2004, June). The globalization of the software industry: Perspectives and opportunities for developed and developing countries. NBER working paper.

Bivens, J. (2004). Globalization of IT hardware did not add $230 billion to U.S. GDP in 2002. Economic Policy Institute Policy memo. Washington, DC: EPI.

Egger, P., & Pfaffermayr, M. (2004, November). Two dimensions of convergence: National and international wage adjustment effects of cross-border outsourcing in Europe. *Review of International Economics, 12*(5), 833-843.

Feenstra, R. C., & Hanson, G. H. (1995, May). Foreign investment, outsourcing and relative wages. NBER working paper.

Grossman, G. M., & Helpman, E. (2002, January). Outsourcing in a global economy. NBER working paper.

Price, L., & Bivens, J. (2004). Perspectives on white-collar offshoring. Economic Policy Institute briefing paper. Washington , DC: EPI.

## General Resources on Outsourcing/Offshoring

Bardhan, A., & Kroll, C. (2004). *The new wave of outsourcing*. Fisher Center for Real Estate & Urban Economics research report. University of California, Berkeley.

Cline, W. (1997). *Trade and income distribution*. Washington, DC: Institute for International Economics.

Gordon, R. J. (2003). *Exploding productivity growth: Context, causes and implications*. Brookings Papers on Economic Activity, Volume 2. Washington, DC: The Brookings Institution.

Mann, C. (2003). *Globalization of IT services and white-collar jobs: The next wave of productivity growth*. Institute of International Economics policy brief. Washington, DC: IIE.

Oliner, S., & Sichel, D. (2002). *Information technology and productivity: Where are we now and where are we going?* Federal Reserve Bank of New York working paper.

## Offshoring/Outsourcing Resources on the Web: Selected Annotated Items

- http://www.techsunite.org/news/techind/offshoring1.cfm

  TechsUnite is an association devoted to connecting IT workers to data critical to their careers. TechsUnite is a project of the Communications Workers of America collaborating with the a range of other partners, supporters, and stakeholders. This page is their stance on offshoring.

- http://www.cwa-union.org/misc/outsourcing.asp

  The CWA outsourcing Web log; it tracks company announcements, news reports, and other breaking stories about outsourcing and offshoring jobs.

- http://www.aflcio.org/aboutaflcio/ecouncil/ec03112004i.cfm

  Statement by the AFL-CIO executive council regarding offshoring.

- http://www.ieeeusa.org/forum/POSITIONS/offshoring.html

  Statement by the Institute of Electrical and Electronics Engineers, the world's largest technical professional society.

- http://www.itaa.org/itserv/docs/execsumm.pdf

  Executive summary of a study commissioned by the Information Technology Association of America (ITAA) from the consulting firm Global Insight.

## Chapter VIII

# Outsourcing Decision-Making: A Review of Strategic Frameworks and Proposal of a Multi-Perspective Approach

Luke Ho
Staffordshire University, UK

Anthony S. Atkins
Staffordshire University, UK

## Abstract

*In recent years, outsourcing deals have increased in number and the strategic importance of the decision-making process has correspondingly increased. This chapter reviews various strategic frameworks that practitioners have attempted to develop for outsourcing decision-making and highlights the differences between proposed theories and current practice. While outsourcing decision-making is multi-faceted in nature, the frameworks reviewed appear to be largely mono-faceted in coverage, which indicates potential inadequacies in existing capabilities. The chapter proposes a framework to address such inadequacies by means of a tri-perspective approach, which extends the decision-making process to take into consideration issues from multiple domains. The proposed framework highlights a wide variety of issues, ranging from the need to maintain internal expertise, to how national legislations can enforce unique constraints on the outsourcing decision-making process. The framework also attempts to provide a multi-perspective approach, which is required of current outsourcing decision-making practices, to enable both quantitative measurements and qualitative articulations.*

## Introduction

Outsourcing, which began as an arrangement of necessity and later a major cost cutting move, has now evolved to become a mainstream management practice in a myriad of industries. Recent years have seen dramatic growth in its use — statistics indicate that outsourcing is now an $180 billion industry (Anderson, 2004) and information technology outsourcing now accounts for over 35% of global information technology spending (Cap Gemini Ernst & Young, 2003).

Outsourcing decision-making is a potentially complex process, which ideally addresses issues within a wide range of domains, such as political (e.g., union pressures), economical (e.g., financial feasibility) and technological (e.g., performance metrics). Managers not only need to critically analyse all aspects of the business, but also need to interact with multiple organisational layers (e.g., strategic, tactical and operational) in order to understand the associated implications.

Like any other business move, there is a degree of risk involved with outsourcing (Aubert, Patry & Rivard, 1998; Earl, 1996). In its 2004 report, the research group Gartner states that as many as 80% of outsourcing deals are unsuccessful and that European businesses wasted $7 billion on poorly managed contracts. This highlights two main issues — the first being the potential complexity of outsourcing decision-making and the second being the financial risks involved.

Recent advances in transmission technology and the deregulation of telecommunication facilities have resulted in the ability for cheaper global communication via voice and data networks (Namasivayam, 2004; Weinstein, 2004). Combined with proliferated access to computing capabilities, this has in turn permitted the vast outsourcing of service-related functions, such as call centres, medical transcription and insurance claims processing. With the emergence of groupware and collaboration tools empowering virtual teamwork, it is anticipated that functions will be increasingly outsourced to best-skilled knowledge workers around the world beyond the traditional boundaries of geography. At present, there are already indications of computer aided tomography (CAT) scans from U.S. hospitals being remotely analysed in Israel and magnetic resonance imaging (MRI) scans from UK hospitals being remotely analysed in Spain.

The prevalent location choices for this offshore outsourcing trend are India and China, primarily due to the potential of exploiting labour cost arbitrage to achieve an overall reduction in operation costs. Emergent markets that are being considered include South Africa and the Philippines. South Africa is noticed for its pool of readily available middle management (particularly suited to call centre operations) while the Philippines is noted for the availability of strong technical skills, a mature infrastructure and its close cultural affinity to U.S. businesses and language.

The increased uptake of outsourcing, particularly in the form of global-sourcing, raises a number of critical and crucial issues for corporate management (Currie, 1995). It is anticipated that framework techniques will play an increasingly important role in the strategic management of outsourcing.

# Background

## Origins and Past Developments

There are conflicting accounts about the origins of outsourcing, but its first documented practice appears to be in the area of information systems (IS) when General Electric Corp. contracted with Arthur Andersen and Univac in 1954 (Klepper & Jones, 1998). Outsourcing has since evolved over time because of different business issues and these developments are summarised in Table 1.

## Recent Developments

It has been indicated that outsourcing is now moving into a third wave, where application service providers (ASPs) offer a unique business model in which software is rented, usually on a per-seat, per-month basis (Currie, 2005). Although often packaged by service providers as a new offering, the per-seat model has seen use as early as 2000, in projects such as the Navy Marine Corps Intranet (NMCI) initiative. With increasingly volatile business environments driving the need for scalability and flexibility, it is anticipated that the uptake of the per-seat model, and hence ASPs, will become commonplace.

*Table 1. Outsourcing issues and forms over time*

| Time | Issue | Forms of Outsourcing |
|---|---|---|
| 1960s | Cost of hardware (expensive mainframes) | Time-sharing (e.g., payroll processing) |
| 1970s | Cost of software development (feasibility of maintaining dedicated in-house team) | Contract programming |
| 1980s | Plummeting cost of computing capability | Reverting to insourcing / in-house retention |
| 1989 | Kodak Eastman mega-deal | Reactionary trigger (sparked bandwagon effect) |
| 1990s | Strategic concerns (competitive advantage and upgrade 3rd GL systems to 4GL) | Onsite facilities management and selective outsourcing |
| 2000s | Transformational concerns (shift to focus solely on core competencies) and market hype | Business process outsourcing and offshore outsourcing |
| 2005 | Trend predictions | Application services providers (ASPs) and rural-sourcing |

There has been an increase in the uptake of the global-sourcing strategy, in which companies acquire services from best-of-breed service providers located anywhere in the world, thus potentially involving a mix of on-shore, near-shore and off-shore locations. This outsourcing strategy, which is sometimes known as "best-sourcing" or "right-shoring", has been spurred on by the recent globalisation effects produced by a combination of forces such as increased bandwidth, reduced telecommunication costs, and increased availability of groupware and collaborative working tools (Friedman, 2004).

The global-sourcing strategy has been recently expanded to include rural-sourcing — an obscure form of outsourcing in which the provision and management of services are transferred to rural regions of the client organisation's home country (e.g., Arkansas in the United States). It has been indicated that Rural-sourcing has the potential to deliver up to 40% cost savings (Frauenheim, 2004) while providing an opportunity for companies to project a positive public image from the concept of retaining jobs onshore and benefiting rural communities in the process. As such, rural-sourcing is anticipated to be an increasingly viable alternative to offshore outsourcing, which has generated considerable negative publicity due to the controversial connotation of job losses to the client country and the potential of long-term adverse effects to its economy (Ho, Atkins & Eardley, 2004).

## The Need for Strategy

Figure 1 illustrates the key reasons for outsourcing as identified by a study in 2004 conducted by PMP Research (Mills, 2004). The two main reasons identified are to reduce operational costs and to improve service levels, both of which are tactical (i.e., short-term) in nature, which hints at the potential lack of strategic considerations in some instances of outsourcing decision-making.

Although there are various advantages associated with outsourcing, there are also risks involved, such as loss of organisational competencies and confidentiality issues. The latter was recently highlighted by a case in the United States involving medical

*Figure 1. Key reasons for outsourcing*

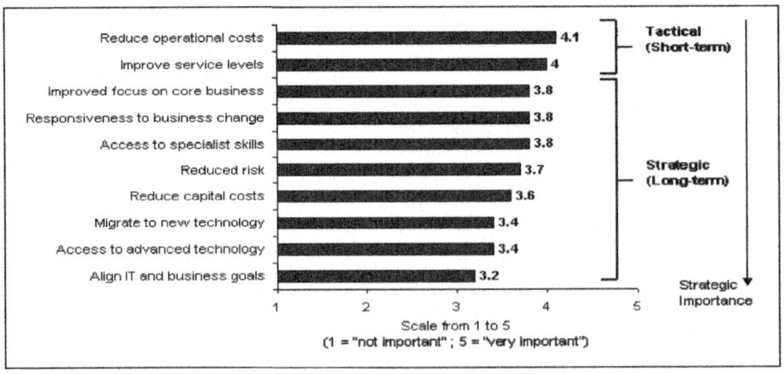

transcription, which is a commonly outsourced process in the healthcare industry. The University of California, San Francisco (UCSF) Medical Centre had been outsourcing for the past 20 years, but unknown to them, part of the work was outsourced by their service provider in Florida. It had been subcontracted to a company in Texas which, without the knowledge of anyone, further subcontracted to a physician in Pakistan (Bagby, 2003). This offshore arrangement went without a hitch for 18 months, until the company in Texas refused to pay the Pakistani physician, who then threatened to post the patient medical histories on the Internet if not given the back pay, thereby infringing privacy and confidentiality laws. Although short of total failure in the sense that the outsourcing arrangement was salvaged following private financial settlement with the Pakistani physician, the potential fiasco illustrates the possible risks of outsourcing.

One of the risks that companies are increasingly concerned about is the potential lack of flexibility in long-term contracts. This was highlighted by the collapse of the Royal Bank of Scotland's (RBoS) 10-year, $1.2 billion mega-deal with IBM, which was indicated to have failed because of its inflexibility to accommodate the business change following the merger of RBoS with Halifax ("Bank bins £700m IBM deal", 2002). Such incidents underscore the need for a strategic perspective to outsourcing decision-making, rather than a tactical perspective that focuses primarily on short-term benefits.

The advent of outsourcing as a mainstream management practice will further underscore this need for a strategic perspective. The term *strategic* points to long-term nature and to the large magnitude of the advantage an organisation seeks to gain over its competitors (Turban, McLean, & Wetherbe, 2002). In order to achieve this advantage, there needs to be strategic management of the outsourcing decision-making process, in which short-term objectives are defined and long-term goals are articulated.

## Strategic Frameworks

A literature review of outsourcing suggests about eight strategic frameworks for outsourcing decision-making, namely:

- Willcocks Frameworks
- Yang-Huang Decision Model
- De Looff Framework
- Perry Matrix Analysis
- Systems Audit Grid
- Cox Methodology
- McIvor Framework
- FORT Framework

# Willcocks Frameworks

The Willcocks Frameworks are a set of empirically-derived frameworks, focused on critical factors, which are designed for use as tools in a variety of outsourcing decision-making processes. The set, suggested by Willcocks, Feeny, and Islei (1997), is comprised of three frameworks which are described as follows:

## *Business Matrix*

The Business Matrix is a framework which allows for analysis of a function's contribution to business operations against its contribution to the company's business positioning. Some literatures suggest that "commodity" functions (traditional examples such as payroll) are suitable candidates for outsourcing while "differentiator" functions should be retained in-house. However, it is important to note that "commodity" and "differentiator" functions may differ for individual companies (Willcocks, Feeny, & Islei, 1997), and thus should be examined in the corresponding business context instead of a generalisation. The Business Matrix provides classification into one of four possible quadrants, namely:

- **Critical Commodity:** Functions classified under this quadrant are critical to business operations but fail to distinguish the business from its competitors. These functions should be subject to a reasoned evaluation against offerings of external service providers to determine its viability for outsourcing. This selection process which determines the "best" service provider, in terms of cost effectiveness and process efficiency, is known as "best-sourcing".
- **Critical Differentiator:** Functions classified under this quadrant are not only critical to business operations, but they also help to distinguish the business from its competitors. These functions should be retained in-house as it protects the company's ability for rapid innovation along with its expertise in the domain. However, in some instances, companies are known to utilise consultants or expert

*Figure 2. Willcocks Frameworks: Business Matrix*

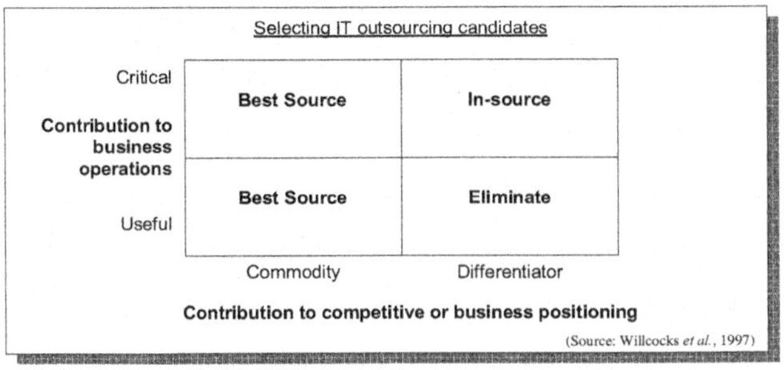

advisors from external service providers to boost or enhance the existing internal capabilities.

- **Useful Commodity:** Functions classified under this quadrant provide incremental benefits to the business, but fail to distinguish it from its competitors. These functions are considered by most literature as prime candidates for outsourcing as they free up valuable internal resources, and hence allow the company to better focus on its core business. In addition, depending on the selection of external service provider, the company may benefit from economies of scale. This selection should be done by "best-sourcing", similar to the case of critical commodities.
- **Useful Differentiator:** Functions classified under this quadrant differentiate the business from its competitor, but in a way that is not critical to business success. In an ideal business setting, such functions are not supposed to exist, but they sometimes do exist in real-world business settings due to the isolation of information technology (IT) functions from business functions which leads to separate agendas, that is, the lack of strategic alignment of IT with business objectives. These functions could be specialist-developed products looking for a business purpose or products which are well in advance of current business needs. These functions should be eliminated, either by outsourcing or mitigation within the portfolio (possibly by development into critical differentiators to be retained in-house).

## *Economic Matrix*

The Economic Matrix is a framework which allows for analysis of a function's in-house economies of scale against the standard of managerial practices. It is commonly assumed that external service providers can reduce the information technology (IT) costs via their inherent economies of scale which the internal IT departments are unable to achieve. Contrary to this, several medium to large companies can still manage to achieve considerable economies of scale, which suggests that the key to external service providers' continued ability to underbid internal IT costs lies only in effective managerial practices which internal IT departments are unable to replicate. The Economic Matrix provides classification into one of four possible quadrants, namely:

*Figure 3. Willcocks Frameworks: Economic Matrix*

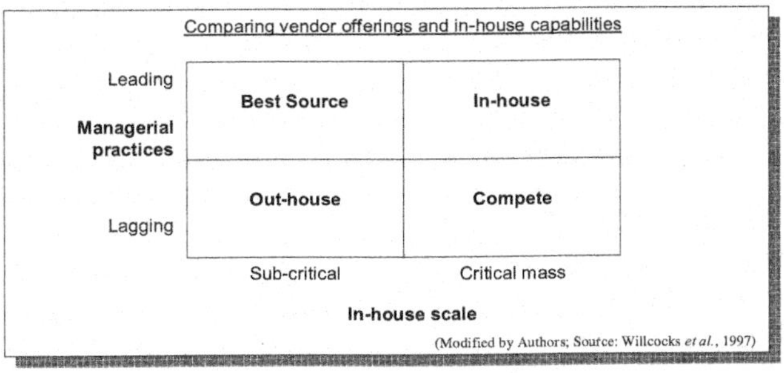

- Leading managerial practices with Sub-critical mass

  Functions classified under this quadrant should be "best-sourced" to explore the possibility of extending economies of scale beyond that of internal capabilities. This is typically initiated by a market test to determine the viability of outsourcing in terms of economic factors.

- Leading managerial practices with critical mass

  Given that economies of scale have reached critical mass, it is unlikely for any external service provider to be able to further reduce costs due to their inherent profit-making nature compared to that of the internal IT departments of just covering costs. As such, functions classified this quadrant are likely to be retained in-house within the company.

- Lagging managerial practices with sub-critical mass

  Given that both managerial practices and economies of scale are of less than favourable standards, there is strong justification for such functions to be outsourced. One possible avenue is to "out-house" which involves total outsourcing as a means of infusion to the business in terms of both financial assets and technical expertise.

- Lagging managerial practices with critical mass

  In such instances, it is suggested that senior management allow internal IT departments to compete against bids submitted by external service providers. Such competition may provide the IT managers with the kind of empowerment required to overcome internal resistance to the use of outsourcing.

## *Technical Matrix*

The Technical Matrix is a framework which allows for analysis of the company's technology maturity against its degree of IT integration. Technology maturity refers to the degree to which the company is familiar with the IT technologies utilised. High technology maturity implies well-established use of familiar technology which facilitates the company's ability to clearly and precisely define their requirements for outsourcing operations. Low technology maturity, on the other hand, implies complications as the company would be unable to evaluate the external service providers' performance accurately without having the corresponding knowledge in the relevant areas. The degree of IT integration refers to the extent to which IT functions are integrated into business processes, such as manufacturing. A low degree of IT integration implies that the IT functions can be easily separated from business processed and handed over to external service providers, which hence facilities the use of outsourcing. The Technical Matrix provides classification into one of four possible quadrants, namely:

- **High degree of integration with low technology maturity:** Functions classified under this quadrant are likely to be outsourced to a preferred supplier, which refers to an external service provider that the company has been dealing with for a

*Figure 4. Willcocks Frameworks: Technical Matrix*

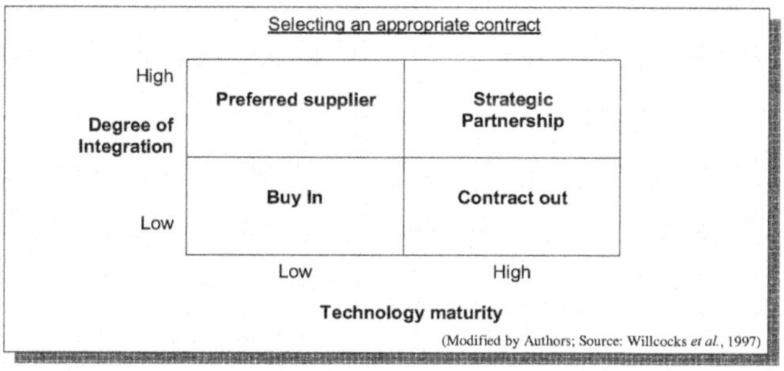


considerable time period and hence has cultivated a certain degree of understanding and mutual trust with. This facilitates a strong business relationship which is necessary given that a high degree of integration implies that the success of the outsourcing operation can directly affect business processes.

- **High degree of integration with high technology maturity:** In such instances, it is suggested that companies engage in strategic partnerships, as the high degree of integration enforces a need for close business relations to ensure the integrity of the integrated IT and business aspects while a high level of technology maturity enables the company to negotiate detailed outsourcing contracts. The use of such strategic partnerships allows companies to engage external service providers in mutual risk sharing.
- **Low degree of integration with low technology maturity:** Given that both degree of integration and technology maturity are of less than favourable standards, it is suggested that company "Buy In", which involves the integration of consultants or/and specialists from external service providers to enhance the capabilities of internally managed functions.
- **Low degree of integration with high technology maturity:** In such instances, it is suggested that companies contract out to external service providers. This is because the low degree of integration implies the ease of separating IT functions from business processes for outsourcing, while the high technology maturity implies that the company has adequate knowledge to negotiate the appropriate contract.

## Yang-Huang Decision Model

The Yang-Huang Decision Model (Yang & Huang, 2000) is a framework which utilises the analytic hierarchy process (AHP) method to aid users in structuring problems related to outsourcing decision-making. The AHP method (Saaty, 1980) addresses how to solve complex multi-criteria decision problems which requires the incorporation of both qualitative and quantitative aspects. It works on the principle that a complex problem can be dealt with by decomposing it into sub-problem within a hierarchy, hence the hierarchical format of the framework. The framework encompasses three phases, which are described as follows:

## *Phase 1: Constructing the Hierarchy*

Figure 5 illustrates the decomposition of a complex outsourcing problem into a series of sub-problems within a hierarchy. In the hierarchy, elements within the highest level, middle levels and lowest levels represent primary objective, secondary objectives and alternatives respectively. The AHP method indicates that the total number of elements within a single level of hierarchy should not exceed seven, as it is difficult for most people to deal with more than seven items simultaneously.

## *Phase 2: Computing the Weight of the Elements at Each Level*

This phase of the framework is comprised of three steps, which are outlined as follows:

- **Step 1: Paired comparison:** The elements within a level of the hierarchy are compared in terms of their importance to the criteria that occupies the level immediately above it. Table 2 illustrates the values used for this comparison, along with their corresponding significance.

  The magnitudes resultant from the paired comparison are then collated into the upper triangle of a square matrix, as illustrated in Table 3, where the main diagonal

*Figure 5. Yang-Huang decision model: Hierarchy analysis (Source: Yang & Huang 2000)*

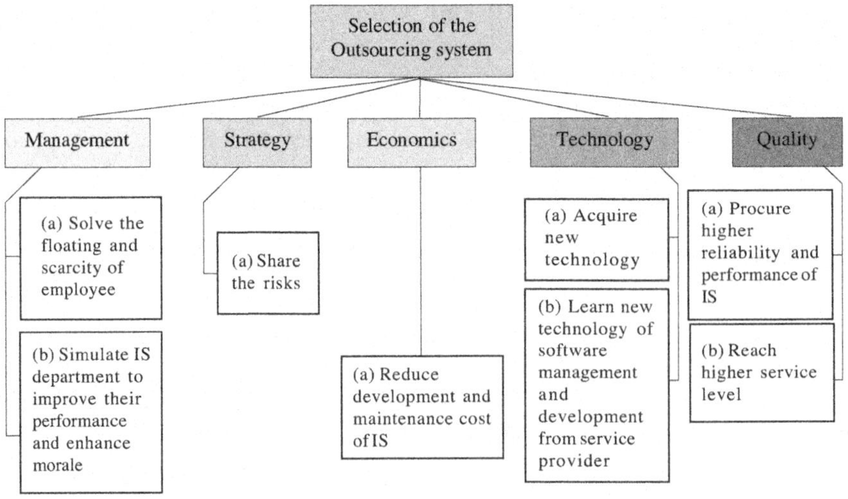

of the matrix must consist of 1s, and the magnitudes of the down triangle is the reciprocals of the corresponding reverse position of the matrix.

- **Step 2: Computing a vector of priorities:** The principal eigenvector is then computed, which becomes the vector of priorities when normalised. This is done using a formula as follows:

$Aw = B_{max} w$ (where $B_{max}$ is the largest eigenvalue of $A$ & $w$ is the eigenvector)

Figure 6 illustrates the corresponding eigenvectors [0.35; 0.32; 0.11; 0.07; 0.15] from the computation, based on the earlier square matrix shown as Table 3. This indicates that the most important factor for outsourcing in this scenario is the management element.

*Table 2. Yang-Huang Decision Model: AHP scale and meaning*

| Intensity of Importance | Definition | Explanation |
|---|---|---|
| 1 | Equal importance | Two activities contribute equally to the objective |
| 3 | Weak importance of one over another | Experience and judgement slightly favour one activity over another |
| 5 | Essential or strong importance | Experience and judgement strongly favour one activity over another |
| 7 | Very strong or demonstrated importance | An activity is favoured very strongly over another; its dominance demonstrated in practice |
| 9 | Absolute importance | The evidence favouring one activity over another is of the highest possible order of affirmation |
| 2,4,6,8 | Intermediate value between adjacent scale values | When a compromise is needed |
| Reciprocals of above non-zero | If activity *i* has one of the above non-zero numbers assigned to it when compared with activity *j*, then *j* has the reciprocal value when compared with *i* | A reasonable assumption |
| Rationales | Intermediate values between adjacent values | When a compromise is needed |

*Table 3. Yang-Huang Decision Model: Square matrix of the first level*

| | Management | Strategy | Economics | Technology | Quality |
|---|---|---|---|---|---|
| Management | **1** | 1 | 4 | 5 | 3 |
| Strategy | 1 | **1** | 2 | 6 | 3 |
| Economics | 1/4 | 1/2 | **1** | 3 | 1 |
| Technology | 1/5 | 1/6 | 1/3 | **1** | 1/2 |
| Quality | 1/3 | 1/3 | 1 | 2 | **1** |

*Figure 6. Yang-Huang Decision Model: Weightage (Source: Yang & Huang, 2000)*

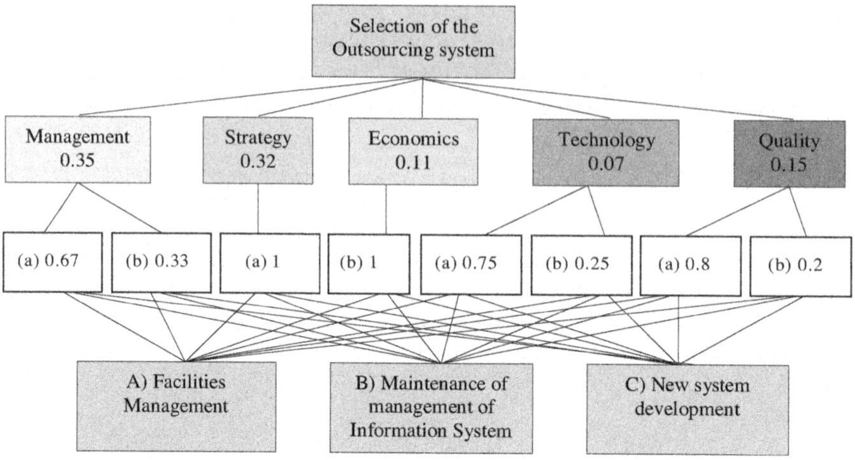


*Table 4. Yang-Huang Decision Model: Absolute measurement*

| **The Total Weight (absolute measurement*)** | | | | | | | |
|---|---|---|---|---|---|---|---|
| Factors and Attributes | Weight | A. Facilities Management | | B. Maintenance of management of Information System | | C. New system development | |
| | | Rank | Weight x Rank | Rank | Weight x Rank | Rank | Weight x Rank |
| M-a | (0.35) x (0.67) | 3.00 | 0.70 | 4.00 | 0.94 | 2.00 | 0.47 |
| M-b | (0.35) x (0.33) | 2.00 | 0.23 | 4.00 | 0.46 | 4.00 | 0.46 |
| S-a | (0.32) x 1 | 1.00 | 0.32 | 3.00 | 0.96 | 5.00 | 1.60 |
| E-a | (0.11) x 1 | 4.00 | 0.44 | 4.00 | 0.44 | 1.00 | 0.11 |
| T-a | (0.07) x (0.75) | 1.00 | 0.05 | 2.00 | 0.11 | 5.00 | 0.26 |
| T-b | (0.07) x (0.25) | 2.00 | 0.04 | 4.00 | 0.07 | 4.00 | 0.07 |
| Q-a | (0.15) x (0.8) | 3.00 | 0.36 | 5.00 | 0.60 | 3.00 | 0.36 |
| Q-b | (0.15) x (0.20) | 4.00 | 0.12 | 4.00 | 0.12 | 2.00 | 0.06 |
| Total | | | 2.26 | | 3.70 | | 3.39 |
| **M: Management; S: Strategy; E: Economics; T: Technology; Q: Quality* | | | | | | | |

- **Step 3: Measuring consistency:** Due to the potential difficulty for decision-makers to maintain consistency in deriving the square matrix, a measure of consistency of the comparisons is required. The framework utilises the consistency ratio (CR) for such a measure, where a factor of 0.1 is considered to be the ideal upper limit. In addition to its use in measuring the consistency of decision-makers, the CR measure can also be used to evaluate the consistency of all the hierarchy (Yang & Huang, 2000).

## *Phase 3: Computing the Weight of Alternatives*

In this phase, the user has a choice between two kinds of evaluation methods, namely absolute measurement and relative measurement, which are outlined as follows:

*Table 5. Yang-Huang Decision Model: Relative measurement*

| **The Total Weight (relative measurement*)** | | | | | | | |
|---|---|---|---|---|---|---|---|
| Factors and Attributes | Weight | A. Facilities Management | | B. Maintenance of management of Information System | | C. New system development | |
| | | Rank | Weight x Rank | Rank | Weight x Rank | Rank | Weight x Rank |
| M-a | (0.35) x (0.67) | 0.42 | 0.10 | 0.45 | 0.11 | 0.13 | 0.03 |
| M-b | (0.35) x (0.33) | 0.23 | 0.03 | 0.32 | 0.04 | 0.45 | 0.05 |
| S-a | (0.32) x 1 | 0.05 | 0.02 | 0.33 | 0.11 | 0.62 | 0.20 |
| E-a | (0.11) x 1 | 0.41 | 0.05 | 0.49 | 0.05 | 0.10 | 0.01 |
| T-a | (0.07) x (0.75) | 0.06 | 0.00 | 0.26 | 0.01 | 0.68 | 0.04 |
| T-b | (0.07) x (0.25) | 0.33 | 0.01 | 0.22 | 0.00 | 0.45 | 0.01 |
| Q-a | (0.15) x (0.8) | 0.21 | 0.03 | 0.54 | 0.06 | 0.25 | 0.03 |
| Q-b | (0.15) x (0.20) | 0.54 | 0.02 | 0.31 | 0.01 | 0.15 | 0.00 |
| Total | | | 0.24 | | 0.39 | | 0.37 |
| **M: Management; S: Strategy; E: Economics; T: Technology; Q: Quality* | | | | | | | |

- Absolute measurement

Absolute measurement involves a measurement unit akin to that of the Likert scale, that is, ranking from 1 to 5 (corresponding to very weak, weak, neutral, good and very good). Table 4 illustrates the evaluation based on the absolute measurement method.

- Relative measurement

Relative measurement involves comparison of importance with corresponding alternatives and computation of the eigenvectors. Table 5 illustrates the evaluation based on the relative measurement method.

In both evaluation methods, the increasing value of the total weight correlates to its priority, that is, a higher total weight implies a higher priority. In this manner, by comparison of total weight, the possible outsourcing options can be prioritised and hence ranked accordingly.

## De Looff Framework

The De Looff framework (De Looff, 1995) is a descriptional framework, targeted at management-level decision-making, which provides for a systematic description of outsourcing options. In the form of a checklist, as illustrated in Figure 7, the framework allows for an outsourcing option to be described by its attributes. It is comprised of four sections, which are outlined as follows:

- **Section 1: Dimensions of the IS function:** The framework advocates that an information systems (IS) function can be described in terms of three dimensions, namely functional IS, analytical IS components and temporal IS activities. The

*Figure 7. De Looff Framework: Descriptional framework for IS outsourcing*

| | | | | | | |
|---|---|---|---|---|---|---|
| **I. Dimensions of the IS function** | | | | | | |
| Information systems | | [] Production IS | [] Personnel IS | [] Land Registry IS | [] Fleet Management IS | Etc. |
| IS components | | [] Hardware | [] Software | [] Data | [] IS Personnel | [] A |
| IS activities | | [] Planning | [] Development | [] Implementation | [] Maintenance | [] B |
| **II. Provider** | | | | | | |
| Owned by client | | [] No | [] Partially | [] Totally | | |
| Dependent on client | | [] No | [] Partially | [] Totally | | |
| **III. Relationship between client and provider** | | | | | | |
| Client's choice of provider | | [] Free | [] Limited | [] None | | |
| Provider's choice of client | | [] Free | [] Limited | [] None | | |
| Spans multiple transactions | | [] No | [] Preferred position | [] Fixed conditions | [] Guaranteed spending | |
| Payment based on | | [] Time and material | [] Fixed fee | [] Work load | [] Benefits to client | |
| Coordination mechanisms | | [] Mutual adjustment | [] Direct supervision | [] Work process | [] Output | [] Skills |
| Resolving disputes | | [] Litigation | [] 3rd party | [] Escalation procedures | [] Common authorities | |
| **IV. Arrangement** | | IS Components | | | | |
| | | Hardware | Software | Data | IS Personnel | Etc. |
| Location | Client | [] | [] | [] | [] | [] |
| | Supplier | [] | [] | [] | [] | [] |
| Ownership / employment | Client | [] | [] | [] | [] | [] |
| | Supplier | [] | [] | [] | [] | [] |
| Exclusiveness | Dedicated | [] | [] | [] | [] | [] |
| | Shared | [] | [] | [] | [] | [] |
| Control | Client | [] | [] | [] | [] | [] |
| | Supplier | [] | [] | [] | [] | [] |

combination of these three dimensions allows a company to determine "what IS activities are performed by which components of what Information Systems", which may be graphically represented by means of a three-dimensional diagram as illustrated in Figure 8.

- **Section 2: Provider:** This section is focused on the description of the degree to which the service provider is owned by the client, along with the degree of

*Figure 8. De Looff Framework: Dimensions of the IS function*

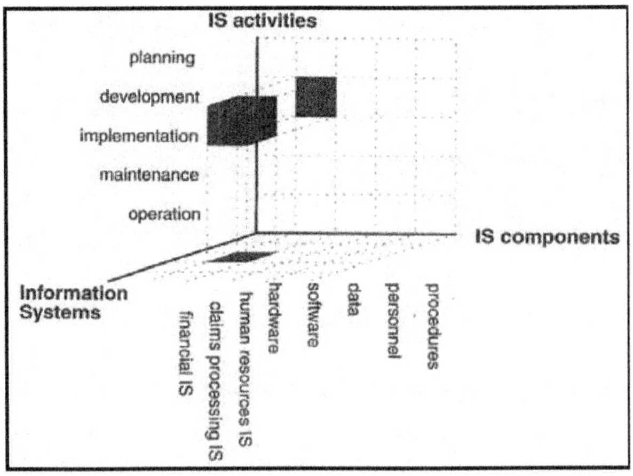

dependence that the provider has the client (e.g., client is a major customer of service provider). This degree is described as no, partially or totally.

- **Section 3: Relationship between client and provider:** This section of the framework provides description of whether the client and service provider are free to choose their business partners, and whether the client-provider relationship spans multiple transactions. Dispute resolution mechanisms (e.g., litigation and third party consultation), along with payment terms and coordination mechanisms, are also covered in this section.
- **Section 4: Arrangement:** This section is focused on the description of the outsourcing option based on location, ownership and control of IS components, along with its exclusiveness of use (i.e., dedicated or shared — whether the service provider is allowed to share its resources over multiple customers).

## Perry Matrix Analysis

The Perry Matrix Analysis (Perry, Stott, & Smallwood, 1993) is a framework based on the concept of unit of competitive advantage (UCA), which is similar to the theory of core competence, for use in decision-making with regards to support work. The framework, as illustrated in Figure 9, takes into account whether the support work is UCA-oriented (i.e., distinguishes the business from its competitor) and whether the support work is value-adding in nature. It provides classification into one of four possible quadrants, namely:

- **Value-added work with proprietary capability:** Work classified under this quadrant enhances the UCA of the business and plays a vital role in differentiating the business from its competitors. The combination of this along with its proprietary nature (i.e., contains secret or unique characteristics) implies that there is strong justification for it to be retained in-house. It is important that companies periodi-

*Figure 9. Perry Matrix Analysis*

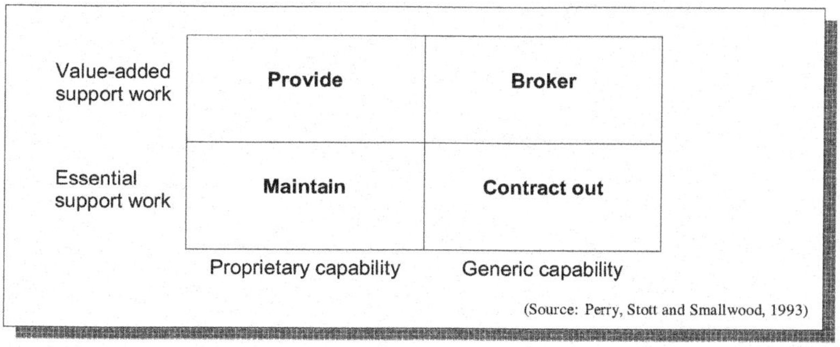

cally develop such work further in order to provide for the best internal capability possible.

- **Value-added work with generic capability:** Work classified under this quadrant enhances the UCA of the business but is not of a proprietary nature. In such instances, it is recommended that companies conduct a through evaluation of the external service provider capabilities and internal capabilities in order to ensure on-going access to best capabilities possible. This approach is similar to that of "best-sourcing."
- **Essential work with proprietary capability:** Although work classified under this quadrant is only of an essential (i.e., non value-added) nature, its proprietary nature implies that the work is unsuitable for outsourcing. Thus, such work should be retained in-house but due diligence must be observed to ensure that the work is well managed in order to achieve cost-effectiveness and meet quality standards.
- **Essential work with generic capability:** Work classified under this quadrant are considered to be prime candidates for contracting out (i.e., outsourcing) as it neither enhances the UCA of the business nor involve proprietary capabilities. It is important that companies conduct performance monitoring of the outsourced work, in order to ensure service compliance by the service provider.

## Systems Audit Grid

The Systems Audit Grid (Earl, 1989) is a framework which enables companies to conduct an audit of their information systems (IS) via analysis of the respective system's business value against its technical quality.

Business value refers to the worth of the system in the business context, which is ideally evaluated by the actual users of the system. An effective measure can be derived by asking three questions:

*Figure 10. Systems Audit Grid*

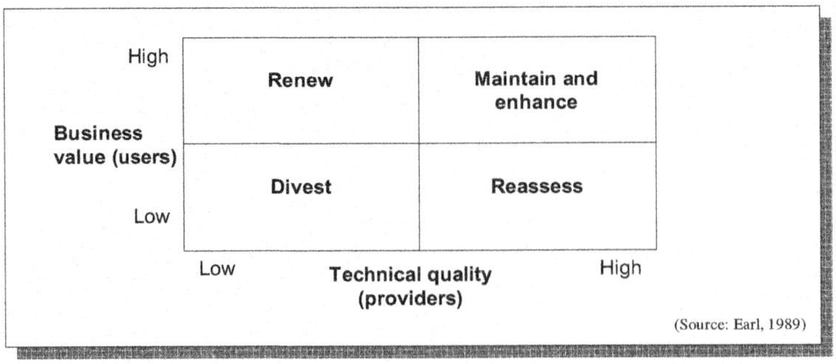

- How much impact does the system have on the business?
- How complex is it to use the system?
- How often is the system used?

Technical quality refers to the technical condition of the system, which is ideally evaluated by specialised staff or the service provider. Similarly, an effective measure can be derived via asking three questions:

- How reliable is the system?
- How easy is the maintenance of the system?
- How cost-efficient is the system?

This allows both the user perspective and the specialist perspective to be taken into account during the analysis, which is important due to the possibility of difference between individual perceptions. Mapping business value against technical quality, the framework provides classification into one of four possible quadrants, namely:

- **High business value with low technical quality:** The combination of high business value and low technical quality implies that the risks of system failure, which can consequently have a significant impact on business operations and management capability. As such, such systems represent potential business exposures, and hence should be considered for renewal to safeguard the business.
- **High business value with high technical quality:** Systems classified under this quadrant are high in both business value and technical quality, and hence should be given top priority for both maintenance and enhancement to sustain the benefits and competitive advantages gained. The failure to adequately maintain such systems can cause them to become severe business exposures.
- **Low business value with low technical quality:** Systems classified under this quadrant may have become obsolete due to changes in the business environment they used to support or were never necessary in the first place (e.g., purchased for political reasons rather than practical reasons). Hence, they are considered prime candidates for diversification (possibly by outsourcing) from the business.
- **Low business value with high technical quality:** The combination of low business value and high technical quality implies that systems classified under this quadrant may be the technicians' products looking for a business application or products which are in advance of current business needs. It is suggested that such systems be reassessed to determine whether they should be eliminated (possibly by outsourcing) or enhanced to value-add to the business.

## Cox Methodology

The Cox Methodology (Cox, 1996) is a framework based on relational competence analysis, which asserts that outsourcing decision-making involves an understanding of asset specificity. This is defined as the relative lack of transferability of assets intended for one use in a given transaction to other uses. The framework operates on the principle that a profitable exchange (i.e., outsourcing arrangement) can be achieved by either economising (i.e., reducing transaction costs) or exploiting unforeseen opportunities for production (i.e., reconfiguring transaction costs). It provides classification into one of three possible categories, namely:

- **Low asset specificity:** Functions classified under this category are considered to be residual competencies, which should be outsourced by means of arm's length contracts (i.e., adversarial leverage) to exploit the capabilities of external service providers.
- **Medium asset specificity:** Functions classified under this category are considered to be complementary competencies, which should be outsourced by means of close external contracts. The client-provider relationship for these range from preferred supplier (in the event where there is "relatively low" medium asset specificity) to strategic supplier alliances (in the event where there is "relatively high" medium asset specificity).
- **High asset specificity:** Functions classified under this category are considered to be core competencies, which should always be controlled by means of internal contracts in order to maintain the company's strategic advantage.

*Figure 11. Cox relational competence analysis methodology*

| **Nature of Asset Specificity and Competence** | **Type of Contractual Relationships** | |
|---|---|---|
| High Asset Specificity (Core Competencies) | Internal Contacts and Incentives | *Variable Boundary of the Firm* |
| *Relatively High* ↕ Medium Asset Specificity (Complimentary Competencies) *Relatively Low* | Strategic Supplier Alliances<br>Network Sourcing<br>Single Sourcing<br>Preferred Suppliers | ↕ |
| Low Asset Specificity (Residual Competencies) | Adversarial Leverage | *Fixed Boundary of the Firm* |

## McIvor Framework

The McIvor Framework (McIvor, 2000) is a framework which addresses the decision-making process by integrating some key theories associated with outsourcing, such as core competency thinking, value chain perspective and supply base influences. It encompasses four stages, which are described as follows:

- **Stage 1: Define the "core" activities of the business.** This stage involves the classification of business activities into the categories of core and non-core. A core activity is defined as an activity which is central to the company in successfully serving the needs of potential customers in the respective market (McIvor, 2000). It is hence perceived by the customer as adding value, and thus considered a major determinant of competitive advantage for the business. The framework assumes all non-core activities, in general, are outsourcing fodder. However, it acknowledges that some non-core activities may have to be retained in-house due to political reasons, such as pressures from trade unions.
- **Stage 2: Evaluate relevant value chain activities.** Having identified the core and non-core activities, the relevant value chain activities are then evaluated. In this stage, each identified core activity is benchmarked against the capabilities of external service providers. The benchmarking provides a structured analysis which

*Figure 12. McIvor Framework*

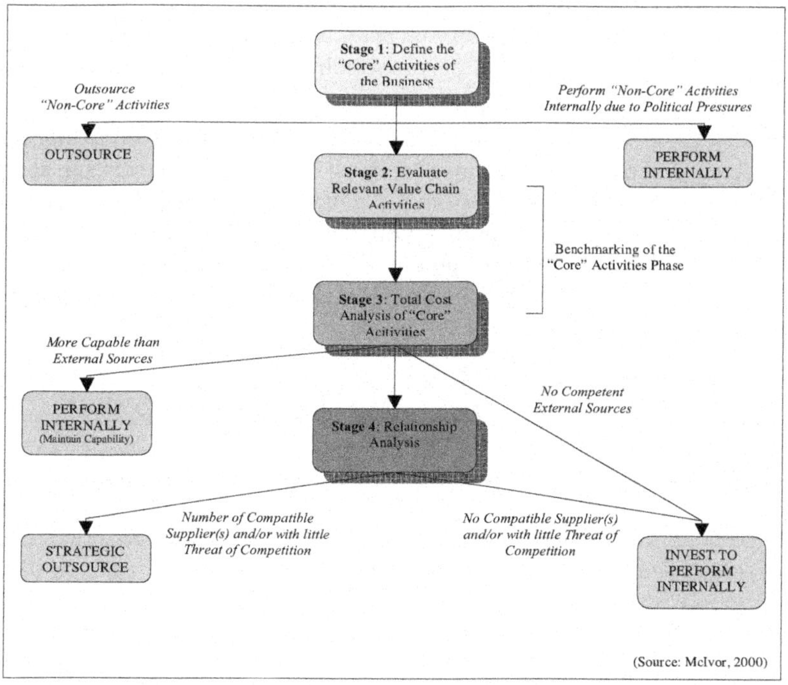

(Source: McIvor, 2000)

enables the business to identify its relative capabilities in the provision of each core activity, as compared to external service provider alternatives. This in turn allows the business to understand the potential impact on its competitive advantage if the respective core activity was to be outsourced.

- **Stage 3: Total cost analysis of "core" activities.** This stage involves a measure of all costs (both actual and potential) involved in the sourcing of the activity from both an internal and external perspective. The framework identifies two types of costs, namely:

  - Cost estimation of performing the activity internally
  - Cost estimation associated with the potential external service providers earlier identified

  It is suggested that activity-based costing (ABC) management systems would be more appropriate for the analysis instead of conventional accounting, which identifies costs according to broad categories such as wages and travel. The total cost analysis allows the business to benchmark its cost position relative to that of external service providers. The combination of this with the earlier benchmarking of capabilities provides the business with an understanding of the current best practices in performing the core activities.

- **Stage 4: Relationship analysis.** Potential client-provider relationship types are examined in this stage. Typical literature assumes that in the outsourcing of a core activity, a partnership type relationship with the external service provider is developed. Contrary to this, McIvor (2000) suggests that the business can instead engage in a buyer-supplier relationship which would enable it to maximise competitive advantage.

  This stage also examines the possibility of future competition from the external service providers. This is because it is possible for the external service provider to establish its own company or spin-off, having acquired the necessary knowledge and skills, to compete directly with the client. After considering these aspects via relationship analysis of the potential external service providers, the business can then filter any external service providers which are deemed to be unsuitable for performing the respective core activities.

## Four Outsourcing Relationship Types (FORT) Framework

The four outsourcing relationship types (FORT) framework (Kishore, Rao, Nam, Rajagopalan, & Chaudhury, 2003) is a framework which allows for analysis of the extent of ownership substitution by outsourcing service providers against the strategic impact of the outsourcing IT and systems (ITS) portfolio. It can be used to depict both static and dynamic types of client-provider relationships, and consequently utilised to examine

*Figure 13. FORT Framework*

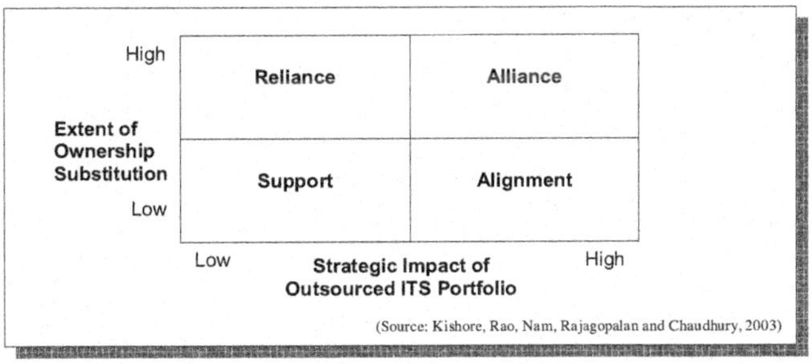


the movement of changing ITS outsourcing relationships over time. The framework provides classification into one of four possible quadrants, namely:

- **High extent of ownership substitution with low strategic impact:** Client-provider relationships classified under this quadrant are of the reliance type. This relationship type requires more commitment to the relationship because a significant part of the company's in-house operations are transferred to external service providers.
- **High extent of ownership substitution with high strategic impact:** Client-provider relationships classified under this quadrant are of the alliance type. These relationships typically grow and build upon previous small, but successful, exchanges between the client and service provider. In such relationships, the company and external service providers work together as strategic partners due to the presence or establishment of common goals.
- **Low extent of ownership substitution with low strategic impact:** Client-provider relationships classified under this quadrant are of the support type. In such relationships, the role of external service providers is limited and hence in-house retention tends to be more prevalent than outsourcing. A support relationship involves low coordination costs, and monitoring the relationship is easy because the extent of substitution by the service providers is low.
- **Low extent of ownership substitution with high strategic impact:** Client-provider relationships classified under this quadrant are of the alignment type, which enables companies to obtain service providers' technical expertise on a project or "on-demand" basis.

## Analysis of Identified Outsourcing Frameworks

In order to evaluate their existing capabilities, the identified outsourcing frameworks were analysed by tabulation against a selection of criteria, which address various factors such as ease of use, the inclusion of financial costing methods and the use of performance benchmarking. These factors, identified by means of focus groups, are briefly outlined as follows:

*Table 6. Comparison of identified outsourcing frameworks*

| | 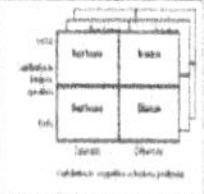 | 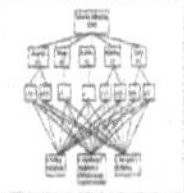 |  | 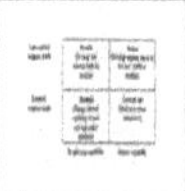 | 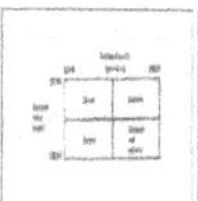 |  | 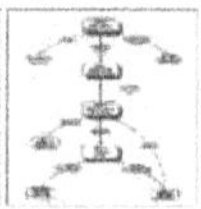 |  |
|---|---|---|---|---|---|---|---|---|
| | Willcocks Frameworks | Yang-Huang Decision Model | De Looff Framework | Perry Matrix Analysis | Systems Audit Grid | Cox Methodology | McIvor Framework | FORT Framework |
| Based on | Matrix Analysis | Score & Weight | Guidelines | Matrix Analysis | Matrix Analysis | Guidelines | Decision Tree | Matrix Analysis |
| Ease of understanding | ✔✔ | ✔ | ✔✔ | ✔✔ | ✔✔ | ✔✔ | ✔✔ | ✔✔ |
| Ease of use | ✔✔ | | ✔✔ | ✔✔ | ✔✔ | ✔✔ | ✔ | ✔✔ |
| Quantitative | | ✔✔ | | | | | ✔ | |
| Qualitative | ✔ | | ✔✔ | ✔ | ✔ | ✔ | | ✔ |
| Financial costing | | | | | | | ✔ | |
| Classification guidelines | | | | | | | | |
| Ranking/Prioritisation | ✔ | ✔✔ | | ✔ | ✔ | ✔ | | ✔ |
| Business dimension | ✔ | ✔ | ✔ | ✔ | ✔ | ✔ | ✔✔ | ✔ |
| Technical dimension | ✔ | ✔ | | | ✔ | | | |
| Organisational dimension | | | ✔ | | | | | |
| Customisation | | ✔✔ | | | | | ✔ | |
| Application guidelines | | ✔✔ | ✔✔ | | | | ✔✔ | |
| Benchmarking | | | | | | | ✔ | |

(Source: Ho *et al.*, 2004)

Legend: ✔ - Partial Coverage; ✔✔ - Full Coverage

- **Concept based on:** This criterion refers to whether the framework is based on an established concept or principle, such as the matrix analysis (i.e., Strategic Grid/ Boston Matrix positioning grid), score and weight technique, and the decision tree model.
- **Ease of understanding:** This criterion relates to the degree of difficulty in learning the framework in theory, that is, whether it is easy to comprehend the theory behind the framework and whether specialised (e.g., matrix calculus) or prior knowledge is required before it can be understood.
- **Ease of use:** This criterion relates to the degree of difficulty in applying the framework in practice, that is, whether specialised training or prior guidance is required before the framework can be utilised by practitioners. Ease of use facilitates quick and easy adoption of a framework by potential users.
- **Quantitative:** This criterion refers to whether the framework includes quantitative measures. The use of quantitative measures minimises variance in perceptions (i.e., absolute numerical values such as 5 and 10 are a more definite measure over relative descriptive properties such as low and high), thus provides for an objective approach in the outsourcing decision-making process.
- **Qualitative:** This criterion refers to whether the framework includes qualitative measures. The use of qualitative measures allows for the provision of a rich description of the various circumstances related to an outsourcing decision. This facilitates better communication in instances where multiple parties are involved in the outsourcing decision-making process.

- **Financial costing:** This criterion refers to whether the framework includes financial costing. More than often, major decisions, particularly board-level ones, such as outsourcing require comprehensive financial justification before approval by management. A framework that incorporates financial costing enables the company to economically justify its decision and benchmark its cost position relative to that of external service provider(s).
- **Classification guidelines:** This criterion refers to whether the framework provides detailed guidelines on the classification of business activities (i.e., functions) into the categories of core and non-core. The lack of classification guidelines may lead to conflicting interpretations if analysis using the same framework was carried out by different parties working independently of each other.
- **Ranking / prioritisation:** This criterion relates to whether the framework provides comparison of importance in the event that multiple outsourcing alternatives are examined in parallel. An ideal framework should provide for a means of ranking which will enable examined alternatives to be prioritised accordingly.
- **Business dimension:** This criterion relates to whether the framework addresses business issues, such as in-house economies of scale, contribution to business positioning (i.e., differentiator or commodity functions) and contribution to business value (i.e., crucial or useful functions).
- **Technical dimension:** This criterion relates to whether the framework addresses technical issues, such as the availability of in-house expertise, degree of IT integration, level of access to specialist IT skills required and technical complexities of migrating to new technology (e.g., upgrading from a partially manual system to a fully electronic enterprise resource planning system).
- **Organisational dimension:** This criterion relates to whether the framework addresses organisational issues, such as hierarchy of authority, client-provider relationship and management mindset (e.g., historical precedent may lead to de facto insourcing).
- **Customisation:** This criterion relates to whether the attributes of the framework can be modified to cater for purpose-specific evaluation, for example, frameworks based on the Strategic Grid/Boston Matrix (SG/BM) positioning grid involve a comparison of two fixed attributes (i.e., dimensions) and hence are not deemed to be able to cater for customisation.
- **Application guidelines:** This criterion refers to whether the framework provides detailed guidelines on its application in practice, for example, systematic steps on how the framework can be applied to a particular outsourcing decision-making scenario.
- **Benchmarking:** This criterion relates to whether the framework includes benchmarking of the organisation's internal performance against that of potential service providers. Benchmarking, although potentially expensive and time-consuming, provides an organisation with detailed information to validate its relative capabilities and hence determine the technical need for outsourcing.

The analysis indicated that most of the frameworks reviewed are based on the use of the Strategic Grid / Boston Matrix (SG/BM) positioning grid, which is a well-established technique (Earl, 1989; Ward and Peppard, 2002). There is clear consensus in literature of its use in business decision-making (Pearlson, 2001; Ward & Peppard, 2002; Laudon & Laudon, 2003) which accounts for SG/BM-based frameworks being intuitive to use for business users.

There appeared to be a lack of quantitative measures in the reviewed frameworks. The use of quantitative measures within an outsourcing decision-making framework is considered to be important as it increases the precision of decision-making by increasing objectivity in the decision-making process (Yang & Huang, 2000). There also appeared to be a lack of financial costing and benchmarking in the reviewed frameworks, which is contradictory as cost savings and service level improvements are commonly identified as the top drivers behind the use of outsourcing. Recent work by McIvor (2000) attempts to include financial costing within a framework, but does not provide examples or procedural guidelines in its application. Financial costing is considered important in a framework approach as it facilitates the ability of the business to benchmark its cost position relative to external service vendors and provides a comprehensive financial justification in the decision-making.

# HABIO Framework

In order to address the identified issues, a new strategic framework was developed, based on the Strategic Triangle concept which is both a well-documented concept and a well-known convention (Frenzel & Frenzel, 2004; Robson, 1997). The Holistic Approach [Business, Information, Organisational] (HABIO) Framework proposes a tri-perspective approach (i.e., organisational perspective, information perspective and business perspective) to assist businesses in the formulation of an effective outsourcing decision. Similar to the Strategic Triangle concept where the corners of the triangle are interlocking, the three perspectives are interrelated, and hence a change in one perspective will require re-evaluation of the other two so that corresponding adjustments can be made as required.

## Organisational Perspective

The organisational perspective includes factors which may have an overriding effect (e.g., outsourcing as a top-down mandate from CxO level) and hence should be considered before the Information Perspective and the Business Perspective. It involves the consideration of organisational issues and political influences which are outlined as follows:

*Figure 14. HABIO Framework*

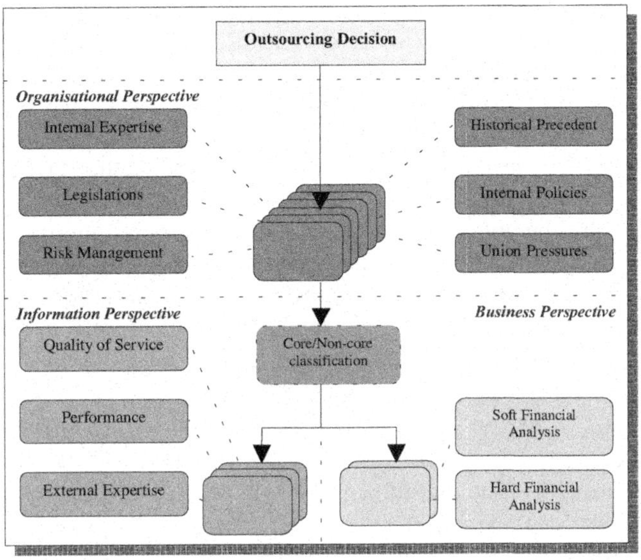


- **Internal Expertise:** One commonly cited risk associated with the use of outsourcing is the loss of internal expertise which increases the level of dependence the organisation has on the external service provider(s). The organisation thus risks being more locked into the service provider(s) and therefore is more vulnerable to business disruptions from service provision failures. As such, in the outsourcing decision-making process, an organisation has to take into account the degree of internal expertise (if any) which it intends to retain to ensure business continuity in the event of complications in the outsourcing arrangement.

  The need to retain internal expertise is particularly crucial in instances where outsourcing have been utilised in military domains. At present, Private Militaries Companies (PMCs) take up 1/3 of the $100 billion budget earmarked for U.S. military operations in the Middle East and are responsible for maintaining 28% of all U.S. weapon systems (Eyal, 2004; Traynor, 2003). This is a particularly worrying figure as PMCs can legally withdraw their employees when faced with danger in a combat zone. Thus, without retaining some degree of internal expertise, the U.S. military may be stranded in a combat zone with complex weapon systems that they no longer have the skill or know-how to operate (Yeoman, 2003).

- **Legislation:** In each country, there are different legislations (e.g., the UK Data Protection Act 1998, Basel II Accord and the U.S. Sarbanes-Oxley Act 2002) that shape the operating environment for organisations and thus national legislations enforce a set of unique constraints on the outsourcing decision-making process.

  An example of national labour legislation that affects the outsourcing decision is the UK Transfer of Undertakings (Protection of Employment) Regulations 1981

(TUPE), which applies where there is a transfer of undertaking from one person to another. The purpose behind the legislation is to provide special protection for employees when the business in which they work is transferred to a new employer. TUPE has recently been expanded in 1998 to include contracting out (i.e., outsourcing), change of contractors (i.e., service providers) and the creation of a franchise (Lorber, 2004). Under the legislation, employees involved in the undertaking automatically continue in their jobs with their existing terms and conditions, thus preserving continuity of employment. In addition, TUPE requires that recognised trade unions and elected employee representatives are informed and consulted about the potential transfer and its corresponding implications. Due to TUPE, the decision-making process for outsourcing within United Kingdom has to take into account additional time required for the consultation period (with trade unions and employee representatives) and potential requirement for staff transfers across the organisations (e.g., from the company to the external service provider).

Another national legislation that affects the outsourcing decision is the UK Data Protection Act 1998 (DPA) which imposes a duty on "data controllers" to comply with eight data protection principles in order to ensure that personal information is handled properly. The eighth principle states that personal data should not be transferred outside the European Economic Area (EEA) unless the country ensures an adequate level of protection for the rights and freedom of data subjects in relation to the processing of personal data, which has particular implications to the use of offshore outsourcing.

- **Historical Precedent:** Historical precedent refers to a procedure or method which is not formally established within an organisation but accepted as the standard because it was widely used and recognised as a historical practice. One example of this is the payroll function being perceived as an aspect that is traditionally outsourced due to its generalisation as a "commodity" function. There is a tendency to utilise banks to manage the payroll function due to their perceived expertise in combining payment systems and hence the expected ability of making timely payments to the company's employees.

- **Internal Policies:** In every human organisation, there are some individuals that have more influence over key decisions than others (Dahl, 1958). A business firm is a political coalition and the executive in the firm is a political broker (March, 1988). The nature of a business organisation endows the management level with higher authority (i.e., political influence) than others in the organisational strata and hence internal policies implemented by the management level tend to take precedent in decision processes.

- **Union Pressures:** One distinct characteristic about the business environment within the United Kingdom is the strength of trade unions as demonstrated by their willingness to utilise strike action (Oates, 2004; Richardson, 2004) and legal action to achieve their objectives. Recent literature have noted that such trade unions have disrupted attempts by a number of companies to outsource work traditionally carried out internally (McIvor, 2000) and union pressure is considered one of the most significant hurdles to overcome among obstacles to effective outsourcing (Healy & Linder, 2004).

- **Risk Management:** This refers to the process of identifying, assessing and controlling risks that may result in financial loss or organisational impact in the outsourcing process. Risk management strategies include risk avoidance, risk abatement (e.g., contingency planning), risk retention, risk transfer (e.g., corporate insurance or indemnification provisions) and risk allocation (e.g., joint venture).

## Information Perspective

The Information Perspective involves the consideration of technical issues which are outlined as follows:

- **Quality of Service:** This refers to the degree to which the service provided is fit for purpose, that is, fitness for intended use. The International Organisation for Standardisation defines three components of quality of use, which are outlined as follows (ISO 9241, 1998):

    - *Effectiveness* relates to whether the service provided fulfils the requirements of its intended users.
    - *Efficiency* relates to whether the service provided allows its intended users to perform their required tasks effectively with a minimum of effort (i.e., without unnecessary effort).
    - *Satisfaction* relates to whether the service provided meets the expectations of its intended users, that is, the intended users are content with the service provision.

- **Performance:** This refers to the standard of measurements which is applied in the evaluation of the activities which are being considered for outsourcing. There exists a myriad of metrics which can be used to track areas such as system response and to measure compliance with set performance standards. Each activity being considered for outsourcing should be benchmarked against the capabilities of all potential service providers of the activity. This will enable the organisation to identify its relative performance for each activity along a number of selected measures (McIvor, 2000). Although the benchmarking process may be time-consuming and expensive, it can provide useful detailed information to validate the relative capabilities of the organisation, and hence determine the need for outsourcing.
- **External Expertise:** This refers to the market availability of the required skill sets, that is, the ability of external service provider(s) to supply the required skill sets at a price considered affordable by the organisation. For example, the organisation may require outsourced services provided by highly specialised medical experts, such as in the field of epilepsy surgery (Malmgren, 2003), which is limited in

availability and hence potentially expensive. This lack of market availability and affordability of the required skill sets can thus constrain the decision-making process for outsourcing.

## Business Perspective

This involves the consideration of business issues related to the outsourcing decision. The outsourcing decision can often be a major determinant of profitability making a significant contribution to the financial health of the company (Yoon & Naadimuthu, 1994), thus financial feasibility is a key consideration in the decision-making process.

There is a need for financial costing to allow the organisation to benchmark its cost position relative to potential service providers (i.e., comparison of costs associated with keeping activities in-house against outsourcing). This allows identification of the disparity between the organisation and potential service providers of the activities (McIvor, 2000) which provides the financial justification required for outsourcing decision-making. Distinction is made between two types of financial costing (namely soft financial analysis and hard financial analysis) which are outlined as follows:

- **Soft Financial Analysis:** Soft financial analysis refers to financial analysis via the use of costing methods that utilise qualitative (i.e., relative) metrics which provide measurement for intangible aspects such as research and development work. It is recommended that the information economics scorecard (IES) method be utilised in the event that soft financial analysis is required in the outsourcing decision-making process. Information economics extends traditional cost benefit appraisal methods to include the assessment of intangible benefits. It utilises an extended form of return on investment (ROI) to assess the potential returns on a candidate project along with the ripple effect of technology change determined from factors such as value linking, value accelerating and innovation valuation (Robson, 1997).
- **Hard Financial Analysis:** Hard financial analysis refers to financial analysis via the use of costing methods that utilise quantitative (i.e., absolute) metrics which provide measurement for tangible aspects such as the product delivery work. It is recommended that the activity-based costing (ABC) method be utilised in the event that hard financial analysis is required in the outsourcing decision-making process. Activity-based costing (ABC), developed by Cooper and Kaplan (1988), is based on the principle that overheads do not just occur, but that they are caused by activities, such as holding products in stores, that "drive" the costs (Atrill & McLaney, 2004). The ABC method provides a means of managing costs, by controlling the activities that drive them, which is considered to have the greatest potential for contributing to cost management, budgeting, control and performance evaluation (Drury, 1998), and hence the method has been increasingly adopted by organisations in recent years.

## Core / Non-Core Classification

The term "core competence" (i.e., segmentation of activities into core and non-core) has been frequently mentioned in connection with the outsourcing decision-making since the work of Prahalad and Hamel (1990). Core competencies are deemed to underpin the ability of the organisation to outperform the competition (McIvor, 2000) and thus convention suggests that they should be defended and nurtured (i.e., kept in-house). However, such convention appears to be designed for a stable and well-defined environment which is far from a live environment where technologies, priorities, finances and demands are more volatile (Healy & Linder, 2004).

Non-core activities have traditionally been labelled as prime candidates for outsourcing (Willocks et al., 1997) but the clear identification of activities by such core / non-core classification remains a challenge as it is subject to an organisation's strategy — which can change quickly (Healy & Linder, 2004). For example, prior to the September 11 incident, U.S. airport security was classified as a non-core activity, but it has since been reclassified and U.S. airport security workers have been correspondingly federalised. Distinguishing between core and non-core activities is a complex task (McIvor, 2000) and to some degree a subjective process. For example, the processing of tax records may be considered by some as a core activity of the UK Inland Revenue and hence its outsourcing mega-deal with the Cap Gemini Ernst & Young consortium (Cullen, 2003) could be deemed as contradicting the convention that core activities should be retained in-house.

Similarly, in terms of classifying other activities, some organisations may perceive that nothing is sacristan and hence everything can be outsourced, while other organisations may perceive it as crucial for core activities to be retained in-house. Hence, the core and non-core classification is a judgement that varies from organisation to organisation and thus is considered to be an optional process within the framework. It is important to include both the business user perspective and technical specialist perspective (Earl, 1989) in decisions, such as the core / non-core classification, as there are often differences between their perceptions. As such, the core / non-core classification process is illustrated in the framework as spanning both the information (i.e., technical) perspective and business (i.e., user) perspective.

## Conclusions

Outsourcing decision-making is a potentially complex process which requires consideration of multiple issues from a wide range of domains such as political, economical and technological. As outsourcing becomes an increasingly mainstream management practice, the role of framework techniques in its decision-making process is anticipated to be increasingly significant. By means of a literature review, eight strategic frameworks for such decision-making were identified — many of which appeared to be based around the well-established Strategic Grid/Boston Matrix (SG/BM) positioning grid technique.

Analysis of the identified frameworks highlighted a lack of quantitative measures, financial costing and performance benchmarking, which is contradictory as cost savings and service level improvements are commonly identified as the top drivers behind the use of outsourcing. This contradiction indicates possible misalignment between existing theoretical frameworks and current practice, which is the motivation behind the development of a new framework.

The developed strategic framework proposes a tri-perspective approach to address the identified issues and to assist organisations in the formulation of an effective outsourcing decision. It extends outsourcing decision-making to take into consideration issues from multiple domains (e.g., financial costing, risk assessment issues and influences from national legislations), thus progressing towards a holistic approach that seeks to address the complex multi-faceted nature of outsourcing decision-making. These issues are denoted by "cards" that compose the framework, which allows components to be modified as appropriate to individual company requirements (akin to adding or removing a card from a deck). Current research is being carried out to develop a method which integrates the evaluative information, both of a quantitative and qualitative nature, gathered from the multi-domain issues to provide an overall collated result within the framework.

## References

Andersen, D. (2004). *Proactive planning: A prerequisite for successful sourcing.* Retrieved November 19, 2004, from http://www.metagroup.com/us/displayArticle.do?oid=49284

Atrill, P., & McLaney, E. (2004). *Accounting and finance for non-specialists* (4th ed.). New York: Prentice Hall.

Aubert, A. B., Patry, M, & Rivard, S. (1998). Assessing the risk of IT outsourcing. In *Proceedings of the 31st Hawaii International Conference on Systems Sciences.*

Bagby, R. (2003). *Data: Navigating the rough waters of offshore data security.* Retrieved November 18, 2004, from http://www.outsourcing-requests.com/center/jsp/requests/print/story.jsp?id=4153

*Bank bins £700m IBM deal.* (2002). Retrieved November 28, 2003, from http://www.computerweekly.com/articles/article.asp?liArticleID=115273&liArticleTypeID=1&liCategoryID=2&liChannelID=16&liFlavourID=1&sSearch=&nPage=1

Cap Gemini Ernst & Young. (2003). *The outsourcing report: Making choices - Insight into successful outsourcing.* Retrieved January 05, 2004, from http://www.cgey.com/outsourcing/media/MakingChoices.pdf

Cooper, R., & Kaplan, R. S. (1998, September/October). Measure costs right: Make the right decisions. *Harvard Business Review,* 96-103.

Cox, A. W. (1996). Relational competence and strategic procurement management: Towards an entrepreneurial and contractual theory of the form. *European Journal of Purchasing and Supply Chain Management, 2*(1), 57-70.

Cullen, D. (2003). *Inland revenue sacks EDS*. Retrieved January 17, 2004, from http://www.theregister.co.uk/content/archive/34454.html

Currie, W. L. (1995). *Management strategy for IT: An international perspective*. Great Britain: Pitman Publishing.

Currie, W. L. (2005). *AIS special interest group on outsourcing*. Retrieved January 18, 2005, from http://disc.brunel.ac.uk/CSIS/sig.html

Dahl, R. A. (1958). A critique of the ruling elite model. *American Political Science Review, 52*(2), 463-469.

De Looff, L. A. (1995). Information systems outsourcing decision-making: A framework, organisational theories and case studies. *Journal of Information Technology,* (10), 281-297.

Drury, C. (1998). *Costing: An introduction* (4th ed.). London: Thomson Business Press.

Earl, M. J. (1989). *Management strategies for information technology*. Upper Saddle River, NJ: Prentice Hall.

Earl, M. J. (1996). The risks of outsourcing IT. *Sloan Management Review, 37*(3), 26-32.

Eyal, J. (2004). *Armies Inc*. Retrieved June 08, 2004, from http://straitstimes.asia1.com.sg/world/story/0,4386,255062,00.html

Frauenheim, E. (2004). *Outsourcing to Arkansas*. Retrieved November 12, 2004, from http://news.com.com/2061-1022-5449083.html?tag=rsspr.5449099

Frenzel, C. W., & Frenzel, J. C. (2004). *Management of information technology* ($4^{th}$ ed.). Canada: Course Technology.

Friedman, T. (2004, March 04). Smaller and smaller. *New York Times*, 29.

Healy, T. J., & Linder, J. C. (2004). *Outsourcing in government: The path to transformation*. Retrieved June 23, 2004, from http://www.accenture.com/xdoc/en/ideas/institute/pdf/outsourcing_in_gov.pdf

Ho, L., Atkins, A., & Eardley, A. (2004). The growth of outsourcing and application of strategic framework techniques. In Z. Irani, S. Alshawi & O. D. Sarikas (Eds.), *CD-ROM Proceedings of the European and Mediterranean Conference on Information Systems (EMCIS) 2004.*

ISO 9241. (1998). Ergonomic requirements for office work with Visual Display Terminals (VDTs).

Kishore, E., Rao, H. R., Nam, R., Rajagopalan, S., & Chaudhury, A. (2003). A relationship perspective on IT outsourcing. *Communications of the ACM, 46*(12), 87-92.

Klepper, R., & Jones, W. (1998). *Outsourcing information technology, systems and services*. Upper Saddle River, NJ: Prentice Hall.

Laudon, K. C., & Laudon, J. P. (2003). *Management information systems: Managing the digital firm* (8th ed.). Upper Saddle River, NJ: Prentice Hall.

Lorber, S. (2004). *TUPE - A brief guide to navigating the maze.* Retrieved June 22, 2004, from http://lawzone.thelawyer.com/cgi-bin/item.cgi?id=110197&d=205&h=207&f=259

Malmgren, K. (2003). *Epilepsy care across Europe and key concerns.* Retrieved June 22, 2004, from http://www.bbriefings.com/pdf/14/lth031_p_MALMGREN.PDF

March, J. G. (1988). The business firm as a political coalition. In J. G. March (Ed.), *Decisions and organisations* (pp. xx-xx). Great Britain: Basil Blackwell.

McIvor, R. (2000). A practical framework for understanding the outsourcing process. *Supply Chain Management: An International Journal, 5*(1), 22-36.

Mills, C. (2004). *Outsourcing - The latest research from the public and private sectors.* Retrieved November 18, 2004, from http://www.conferencepage.com/outsourcing4/downloads/CliffMills.pdf

Namasivayam, S. (2004). Profiting from business process outsourcing. *IT Professional, 6*(1), 12-18.

Oates, J. (2004). *Inverclyde IT staff fight outsource threat.* Retrieved June 3, 2004, from http://www.theregister.co.uk/2004/06/15/inverclyde_strike/

Pearlson, K. (2001). *Managing and using information systems: A strategic approach.* New York: John Wiley & Sons.

Perry, L. T., Stott, R. C., & Smallwood, W. W. (1993). *Real time strategy: Improvising team based planning for a fast-changing world.* New York: John Wiley & Sons.

Prahalad, C. K., & Hamel, G. (1990, July/August). The core competence of the corporation. *Harvard Business Review,* 79-91.

Richardson, T. (2004). *Bradford IT staff vote to strike.* Retrieved June 2, 2004, from http://www.theregister.co.uk/2004/01/21/bradford_it_staff_vote/

Robson, W. (1997). *Strategic management & information systems* (2nd ed.). Great Britain: Pitman Publishing.

Saaty, T. L. (1980). *The analytic hierarchical process.* New York: McGraw-Hill.

Traynor, I. (2003). *The privatisation of war.* Retrieved June 10, 2004, from http://www.guardian.co.uk/international/story/0,3604,1103566,00.html

Turban, E., McLean, E., & Wetherbe, J. (2002). *Information technology for management: Transforming business in the digital economy* (3rd ed.). United States of America: John Wiley & Sons.Ward, J., & Peppard, J. (2002). *Strategic planning for information systems* (3rd ed.). New York: John Wiley & Sons.

Weinstein, L. (2004). Inside risks: Outsourced and out of control. *Communications of the ACM, 47*(2), 120.

Willcocks, L., Feeny, D., & Islei, G. (1997). *Managing IT as a strategic resource.* Berkshire, MA: McGraw-Hill.

Yang, C., & Huang, J. (2000). A decision model for IS outsourcing. *International Journal of Information Management,* (20), 225-239.

Yeoman, B. (2003). *Soldiers of good fortune.* Retrieved June 10, 2004, from http://www.motherjones.com/news/feature/2003/05/ma_365_01.html

## Chapter IX

# Outsourcing and Offshoring: Issues and Impacts on Venture Capital

Alev M. Efendioglu
University of San Francisco, USA

## Abstract

*Recently, outsourcing/offshoring has gained significant exposure in the popular as well as academic publications, with authors arguing the many different facets of the concept and its implications. The ongoing debates have revolved around issues related to cost of operations, benefits for outsourcing countries and countries that are recipients of outsourcing, the types of skills and associated unemployment, the types of industries that are being most effected, and even its political implications. This chapter discusses various issues related to outsourcing/offshoring and presents the findings of a research study (a survey of 364 individuals from 101 San Francisco Bay Area venture capital firms) attempting to validate (or disprove) some of the most widely discussed and presented points of view.*

## Introduction

In September 1989, Jack Welch, then General Electric Co.'s chairman, flew to India hoping to sell products like airplane engines and plastics to the Indian government. During a breakfast meeting with top government advisers, Sam Pitroda, chief technology adviser to the late Indian Premier Rajiv Gandhi, surprised Mr. Welch by saying "We want to sell you software." Mr. Welch, by agreeing to start this business relationship, became the impetus that started India on its way to becoming one of the bastions of outsourcing and sparked a global outsourcing revolution (Solomon & Kranhold, 2005). Since then, this revolution has sparked major debates around the issues of operating cost advantages and country benefits, as well as the possible financial, social, and political ramifications of such industry wide practice, on both countries involved in the process.

Even though Jack Welch may have been the impetus that started the revolution, outsourcing is not an U.S. only phenomenon. It is a process that has been used and continues to be used by most developing countries. A recent survey by N. Aggarwal (2004) shows that 40% of Western Europe's 500 largest companies have already begun moving their service operations abroad. According to Forrester Research, the Cambridge, Mass., consulting and research company, European spending on outsourcing is expected to rise to more than Euro 129 billion (U.S.$156 billion) in 2008 from Euro 82 billion (U.S.$99.16) in 2002, and the number of firms that spend more than 20% of their outsourcing budget abroad will go from 7% in 2004 to 20% in 2008. Never the less, despite the growing interest, European companies still outsource far less than their U.S. counterparts, of which more than 20% will spend over 20% of their outsourcing budget offshore this year (Campoy, 2004). The primary reason for these differences may be the rigid labor laws in Europe that make relocating jobs a long and costly process. For example, while it's relatively easy for companies in the U.S. to fire employees whose jobs they want to outsource, to lay off an employee in Germany, a company first has to justify its decision to the union and then give its worker a notice period of four weeks to seven months.

## Cost Benefits of Outsourcing

To most executives in the U.S. and Europe, offshoring means cheaper wage rates for labor-intensive activities. Discussions of wage rate differentials between Asia, on the one hand, and the U.S. and Europe, on the other, tend to focus on less skilled jobs. However, even in the more skilled jobs the differentials can be compelling as well. In electronics, the wage rate ratio between the U.S. and China for product engineers is about 10:1. For software developers, the ratio between the U.S. and India is about 8:1. These wage rate differentials, undeniably, generate cost savings. However, the really compelling gains come from pairing savings with top-flight skills. While it is true that only a few Asian countries offer enough English-speaking call-center representatives to deal with U.S. customers, many other skills are more abundant in Asia than in the U.S. China, for example, produces 350,000 graduate engineers every year, compared with 90,000 for U.S. engineering schools. According to a recent GAO report, "despite the widespread belief that global sourcing is driven primarily by companies chasing after low-wage workers, 'low-wage' India ranked only eight in 2002 among countries to which the United States sends business, professional and technical service tasks. Ranking ahead of India were Canada, UK, Japan, Germany, France, Mexico and the Netherlands" (*Economic Times*, 2004). Other authors also argue and support the position that, as labor arbitrage opportunities begin to disappear, the primary reason for offshoring is becoming strategic rather than cost (Shah, 2004).

Offshoring is not confined to a few manufacturing industries but rather utilized across many industries, even by non-manufacturing industries trying to decrease their operating or support costs. Biotech industry is one such industry. They have recently awakened to an international climate where firms can get qualified workers for as little as a tenth of the U.S. cost and are on the verge of an offshoring wave of its own, A brief look at the companies in the San Francisco Bay Area turned-up biotech companies that are already testing the offshore waters, among which are Stanford University spin- off SRI International signing an outsourcing deal with a research firm in Shanghai and South San Francisco's Genentech Inc., founder of the biotech industry, manufacturing some supplies of an innovative cancer drug in Spain.

This same trend can also be seen in the financial sector. A recent report by Deloitte Research forecasts that by 2010, the world's 100 largest financial institutions will also move $400 billion of their cost base offshore, saving an average of just under $1.5 billion annually each. The survey forecasts that by 2010 more than 20% of the financial industry's global cost base will have gone offshore (Wu, 2004).

Even though that there are significant cost saving opportunities for Europe (where offshoring is not as prevalent as it is in U.S.), with services costs dropping by 50% to 60%, the cost savings potential seem to have a geographical bias. On one hand, IBM estimates that European companies have so far outsourced less than 8% of the U.S.$19 trillion they spend each year on sales, general, and administrative expenses, and many companies have stated that they can offshore more than one-half of this work (Tyson, 2004). On the other had, according to McKinsey Global Institute, there are significant differences in cost savings by U.S. companies (save U.S.$0.58 of every dollar) versus German companies (save Euro 0.52 for every euro) of corporate spending on jobs they send abroad to India (the largest recipient of latest offshoring activities). When German companies send their offshore work to Eastern Europe (where 59% of their offshoring goes), they save even less. The primary reason for this difference seems to be the cost to coordinate projects across different languages and cultures.

## Country Benefits: Unemployment/Employment

There are contradictory arguments on country benefits (or costs) of offshoring. On one side of the argument are projections about the types of jobs that will be offshored and their negative employment consequences for the outsourcing country. A compelling supportive argument uses the advances in the digital revolution and the dramatic fall in international telecommunications costs as the impetus that provides the opportunity for white-collar jobs — once insulated from global competition — to be offshored to low-wage nations such as India, where labor can be hired for as little as one-tenth its cost in the United States. Among the jobs listed are call-center agents, data processors, medical technicians, and software programmers. According to Forrester Research, an estimated 315,000 U.S. services jobs had been moved overseas by the end of 2003, and by 2015, roughly 3.3 million U.S. business-processing jobs will be performed abroad. However, although this number might seem startlingly large, it is not a significant number when one looks at the total number of 150 million employed workers in United States. Furthermore, in 1999 alone — at the peak of the economic bubble — 15 million workers lost their jobs through mass layoffs as companies restructured their operations (Brainard, 2004).

On the other side of the argument is the contention that the industries that are moving jobs out of the U.S. are the more backward industries and U.S. remains the cheapest place in the world to produce for many of the more advanced industries. Peter Drucker, the well known management professor and consultant, represents this camp. He argues that wage cost is of primary importance today for very few industries, namely ones where labor costs account for more than 20% of the total cost of the product — like textiles, and the proportion of the cost of a typical American product attributable to labor costs are continuing to shrink. Using his consulting experiences with one of the world's biggest auto-parts makers as an example, he states that their internal cost structure show that it is still very much cheaper to produce in this country than to import, because the parts, while labor-intensive, are also very skill-intensive to design and make. He continues to argue that we import twice or three times as many jobs as we export, jobs created by foreign companies coming into the U.S. and as such, we are exporting low-skill, low-paying jobs but are importing high-skill, high-paying jobs (Schlender, 2004).

There are also mutually gained benefits through skilled workers that are brought into U.S. and employed by U.S. firms. At the request of firms mainly located in the Silicon Valley (San Francisco Bay Area where significant number of biotech and IT clusters exist), the H-1B (temporary work permits for professionals) were increased from its original 65,000/year to 190,000/year in 2000. U.S. Citizenship & Immigration Services figures show that by the end of September 2004, there were 46,000 petitions for 2005, making it very likely that the 65,000 cap (the increased cap will expire at the end of 2004) will be met even before the new year (Bernstein, 2004). In one sense, the activities these temporary imported workers undertake can also be considered as offshored work. Part of their earnings continue to support their families in the countries they come from and create wealth for those countries, while creating wealth and contributing to the productivity of the companies that employ them and are located in the U.S.

## Country Benefits: Financial Impacts

There are some figures that support creation of mutual economic benefit for the outsourcing and outsourced countries, presenting a case against offshoring being a zero-sum game. A 2003 study by the McKinsey Global Institute (MGI) showed that offshoring creates wealth for the U.S. as well as for India, the country receiving the jobs.

Their findings show that, for every dollar of corporate spending outsourced to India, the U.S. economy captures more than three-quarters of the benefit and gains as much as $1.14 in return (transfer to India creates around $1.46 in new wealth, with $0.33 going to Indian companies). Unfortunately, for German companies the recaptured wealth is only Euro 0.80 for every euro of corporate spending on service functions moved offshore (Agrawal & Farrell, 2003).

In addition to wealth creation, there are benefits gained from increased exports by the offshoring countries. MGI estimates that for every dollar of U.S. corporate spending that moves to India, U.S. exports there increase by five cents, which partially may explain the significant increase of exports to India (from U.S.) from $3.7 billion in 2000 to $5.0 billion in 2003. For Europe, it is estimated that for every euro of spending on work outsourced to India or Eastern Europe, Germany gains Euro 0.03 from new exports (Bailey & Farrell, 2004).

There are also other benefits, primarily in employment and earnings, for companies and countries that host these outsourcing firms. Outsourcing firms, U.S. and foreign, with operations in India, Eastern Europe and other parts of Asia are seeing a swift increase in business. In India, Wipro, and Indian outsourcing firm, is continuing to hire staff rapidly and it has added more than 5,500 employees in the recent quarter, lifting its total work force to about 37,000. U.S.-based outsourcing companies also are growing. Electronic Data Systems Corp., which is based in Plano, Texas, with operations all over the world, states that its pipeline of potential deals is robust and growing and, last quarter, signed a $1.1 billion outsourcing deal with Bank of America Corp. of Charlotte, N.C. EDS primarily services the bank inside the U.S. (Drucker & Solomon, 2004). India today earns more than $17 billion from corporations worldwide seeking low-cost overseas talent to do everything from write software to collect debts to design semiconductors (Solomon & Kranhold, 2005).

## Other Issues: Political and Regulatory Environments, Security, and Investment Risks

Offshoring is frequently blamed for the agonizingly slow pace of recent job growth in the United States, despite a recovering economy; the response from Congress has been to include in a fiscal 2004 spending bill a provision prohibiting federal agencies from outsourcing some kinds of work to private companies that use workers in foreign countries. Twenty-three states are also considering similar restrictions and 4 have already passed them. An example of one such effort is the proposed state Senate bill in Colorado, which was intended to bar the use of offshore workers to perform services such as call-center operations. It was only shelved because the Senators thought the price tag of $24 million was too high. Nevertheless, this was the second year that Colorado had weighed such legislation before killing it (St. John, 2005; McDougall, 2005). Outsourcing also remains a hot political issue in Europe. Around 30% of the companies polled in a recent survey by Munich-based Roland Berger Strategy Consultants and the U.N. Conference on Trade and Development said they considered public backlash to be a risk to offshoring.

In the U.S. and European countries, in addition to wages (which are direct labor costs), there are employment related costs, such are pension costs, benefits and health-care costs, costs associated with complying with regulations, taxation, and labor relations requirements, that are quickly beginning to be more significant than direct labor costs. Even though we have not come across any studies that have measured these costs, these costs might also encourage offshoring/outsourcing by organizations that have to bear these costs.

There are also identifiable investment risks that companies have to consider as part of their decision to offshore. These risks have been identified and quantified annually since 2000 by Kurtzman, Yago and Phumiwasana (2004). They have studied 50 countries to create a country-by-country ranking (data complied from 70 different sources, 40 of which were directly comparable) of opacity — the degree to which the country lacks clear, accurate, easily discernible and widely accepted practices governing the relationships among businesses, investors, and governments. They have identified and used five items as components of their opacity index: corruption, efficacy of the legal system, deleterious economic policy, inadequate accounting and governance practices, and detrimental regulatory structures. Based on the "opacity rating", they determine the interest rate premium or discount derived from doing business in a given country as compared to the risk of doing business in the U.S. Their system and analysis is intended to create an awareness of the investment risk factors and enable companies to make better portfolio and direct investment decisions regarding where to develop markets, locate productive resources, or find the best outsource partner.

Finally, there are broad security issues that will impact organizations that offshore to countries that have more turbulent environments than the ones one might be used to seeing in the U.S. and Europe. A case in point is the bomb threats against two Indian outsourcing companies, Wipro Technologies and Infosys Technologies, both of which were received during March 2005 (Krishnadas, 2005). Since the largest U.S. target of IT offshoring is India, comprising nearly 25% of the global IT and business process offshoring, for U.S. companies (McKinsey, 2003), these types of threats create environments for interruption and delay of ongoing projects, loss of data, compromised technical know how and personal information, and increase the risk of doing business with companies in such environments.

# Research Study

To shed some light into these differing perspectives on costs and benefits of outsourcing/offshoring, and to identify specific a survey issues for and the concerns of venture capitalists, was sent to 364 individuals (venture capitalists) from 101 San Francisco Bay Area venture capital firms. Of the 364 mailed questionnaires, 53 were returned, of which, 42 were usable. The primary objective of the study was to determine if the issues that are generally associated with offshoring were the same issues for the venture capitalists and to understand the "impact of this business practice on funding decisions by the venture capitalists". The study questionnaire was designed to focus on offshoring's impact on

*Figure 1. Expected cost savings*

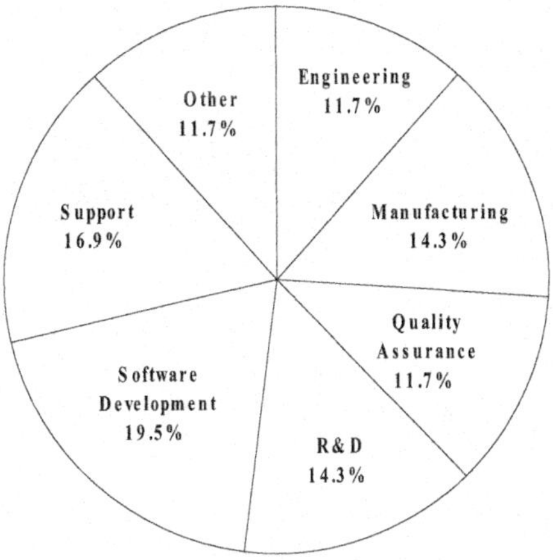


availability of capital for expansion or start-up, impact of potential duplication of effort and loss of centralization of business process on the valuation of a company, impact of the decision to outsource/off-shore on long term shareholder value, impact of outsourcing/offshoring on company's perceived liability exposure, potential risk/cost of noncompliance (Sarbanes-Oxley, etc.) affect financial valuation of outsourcing/offshoring. We also tried to identify the perceptions the study participants' on whether outsourcing programs have generally attained the expected magnitude of improvements in cost bases (managerial and coordination costs versus wage benefits). The secondary objective was to test the validity of some of the claims made through various publications. The study was conducted during December 2004 and January 2005 and the following sections present and discuss the findings as they apply to the general issues related to offshoring, as presented above, and perspectives of venture capitalists on these issues.

# Discussion of Findings

Our survey responses show that offshoring is increasingly an integral strategy for businesses in the U.S. (90.4% of our respondents had funded companies that have used offshoring) and offshoring is seen to provide significant a competitive advantage. When asked the types of off-shored activities, 19.5% of respondents identified "Software Development", 16.9% "Support", 14.3% "R&D", 11.7% "Quality Assurance", 14.3% "Manufacturing", 11.7% "Engineering", and the remaining 11.7% of respondents identified "Other" functions that consisted of responses such as healthcare field trials, data entry, marketing, collection, and consulting.

Study respondents echoed the importance of labor arbitrage but also indicated that the availability of skilled labor is an important factor for sustainability and growth of company operations. In a follow-up discussion, this point was succinctly presented by

*Figure 2. Off-shored activites*

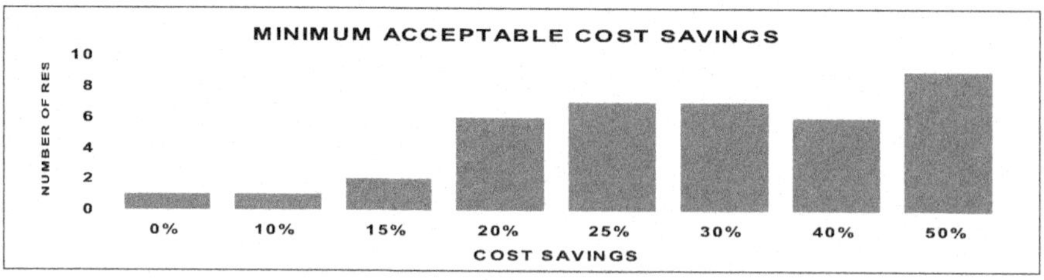


*Figure 3. Acceptable project delays*

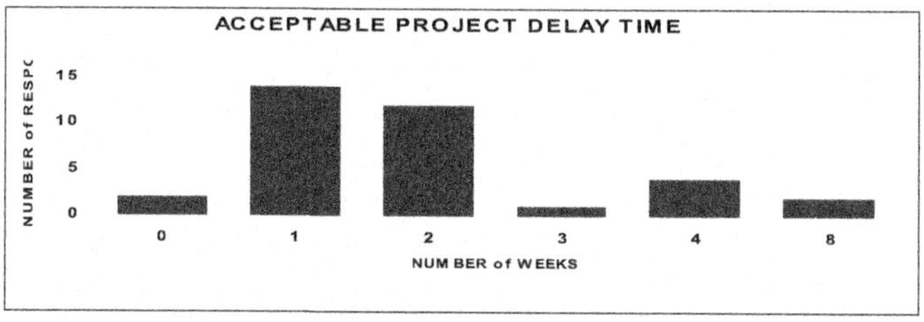


Mr. Ismael Ghalimi (2005), chief strategy officer and co-founder of Intalio, who stated "outsourcing development and quality assurance for a software company is not so much about short-term cost reduction as it is about long-term output scalability". Nevertheless, our study group identified cost savings as the primary benefit of offshoring, and the average of the expected cost savings by our respondents was 31.77%. However, the expectations were not evenly distributed, 51.3% of respondents would accept a minimum 20% to 30% cost savings and 38.5% a minimum of 40% to 50% cost savings. Unfortunately, the survey data did not show how many times these expectations were realized in investments made by survey participants.

Our respondents were not as concerned with a timely and flexible supply chain and nearly 95% expected some time slippage in offshored deliverables. They were willing to tolerate an average of two weeks of project delay time, with 79% willing to tolerate one to two weeks delay and 21% three to eight weeks. Only two respondents identified that they expected no delay (these two respondents had utilized offshoring five times to date).

The study participants had funded companies that primarily offshored to India and China and, based on their experiences, they identified six major areas of concern associated with offshoring which included managerial issues, loss of U.S. jobs, project risk (time loss), intellectual property, regulatory issues, and quality assurance. The most commonly cited managerial issues included communication, coordination, and control. Other areas, such as staff retention, cultural challenges, company culture, labor quality, and trust were also mentioned as areas of concern. While strongly agreeing that cost savings outweighed the specter of unexpected hidden costs, the study respondents indicated a very low

*Figure 4. Acceptable off-shoring investment risk*

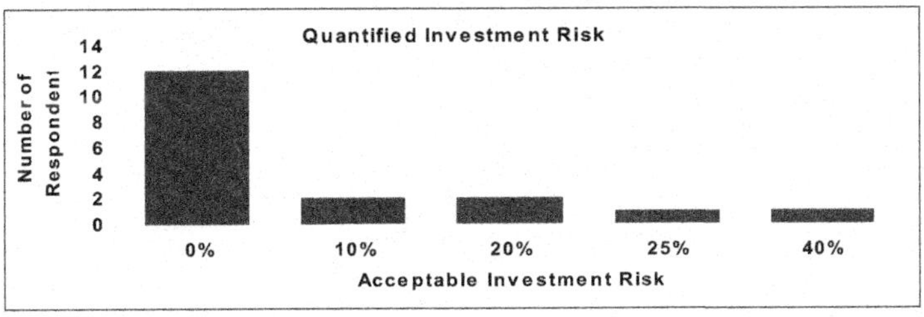


tolerance for added investment risk associated with offshored outsourcing, and they were able to quantify the additional risk premium as 6.94%. This number is comparable to the risk premium calculated using the "Opacity Index — the degree to which the country lacks clear, accurate, easily discernible and widely accepted practices governing the relationships among businesses, investors, and governments" by Kurtzman, Yago and Phumiwasana (2004). These researchers have calculated the "opacity premiums" as 6.09% for India and 6.49% for China, identifying the interest rate premium or discount from doing business in a given country as compared to doing business in the U.S.

However, the majority of our respondents' expectations diverged significantly from the calculated risk premium of the Opacity Index. Unfortunately, all of our respondents did not provide a numeric risk premium and, because our sample size was not large enough, we could not calculate any correlation (or lack of it), between expectations of cost savings and additional acceptable investment risk.

Finally, our findings did not support the perspective that presents causality between increasingly rigid regulatory environments and for increased offshoring, especially for start-ups. 78.5% of our study group responded as neutral or disagreed with the statement "U.S. regulatory compliance was a reason for offshoring."

# Conclusions

As was previously stated, the primary objective of the study was to determine if the issues that are generally associated with offshoring were the same issues for the venture capitalists and to understand the "impact of this business practice on funding decisions by the venture capitalists" and the results of the study present a mixed picture, by supporting some perspectives associated with offshoring, while contradicting other. However, when one looks at the question of possible impact of offshoring on funding and valuation of the offshoring companies, there is no conflict or confusion.

The results of the VC survey reinforced the points of view that argue offshored outsourcing can create a competitive advantage and can yield very significant cost

*Table 1. Summary of questionnaire responses*

| IMPACT OF OFF-SHORING ON INVESTMENT DECISION | AVERAGE | AGREE | NEUTRAL | DISAGREE |
|---|---|---|---|---|
| I would be more inclined to invest in an established firm that utilizes off-shoring. | 2.26 | 22 | 16 | 4 |
| SUPPORT OF OFF-SHORING | | | | |
| Off-shoring can be a competitive advantage. | 1.83 | 36 | 5 | 1 |
| Off-shoring has generally attained the expected magnitude of cost savings. | 2.31 | 31 | 6 | 5 |
| Off-shoring programs have achieved the desired return on investment. | 2.50 | 26 | 11 | 5 |
| The expectation of significant cost savings outweighs the specter of unexpected hidden costs. | 2.19 | 34 | 6 | 2 |
| The financial burden of U.S. regulatory compliance costs is an important reason for off-shoring. | 3.36 | 9 | 14 | 19 |
| AGAINST OF-SHORING | | | | |
| I think off-shoring increases a company's liability exposure. | 3.24 | 5 | 21 | 16 |
| Decentralizing business processes negatively affects valuation. | 3.74 | 2 | 11 | 29 |
| WHERE & WHAT TO OFF-SHORE | | | | |
| Companies should only offshore to countries that company management has cultural ties. | 2.81 | 14 | 14 | 13 |
| Off-shoring is primarily useful for standards based functions. | 2.98 | 13 | 17 | 12 |

*Scale: 1 = Strongly Agree; 2 = Agree; 3 = Neutral; 4 = Disagree; 5 = Strongly Disagree*

*Strongly Agree and Agree responses, and Disagree and Strongly Disagree responses are aggregated for presentation purposes.*

savings for the offshoring company. It also reinforced that there are major, identifiable costs associated with low quality product and information from the offshored company, lost sensitive data and know-how, and investment risk posed by a host of other local environment factors.

Some of the findings were contrary to other claims made through various news programs and prevailing popular beliefs. Our respondents did not see increased government regulations, for example, Sarbanes-Oxley, as a compelling reason for offshoring or thought that a cultural connection to the offshored country was critical.

The results also show that venture capitalists do not view offshoring as a major impediment or negative for funding new or ongoing business enterprises, or see it as having a negative impact on the valuation of the offshoring company or increase its liability exposure. Even though they recognize the practice as an element that increases the "investment risk", this increased risk was not seen as a factor that would eliminate or significantly limit their funding of organizations that utilize offshoring as a business practice. The investment risk premium identified by our respondents (6.944%), who had primarily funded companies that offshored to India and China, was very much in line with the Opacity Index risk premium of 6.09% for India and 6.49% for China, which were calculated by other researchers of offshore investment.

Unfortunately, the claims of cost savings and competitive advantage could not be tested or their validity determined for the venture capitalists (that were part of the study) or the companies utilizing offshoring as a business practice. This requires access to company documents that can provide specifics on the cost of operations, before and after outsourcing, including start-up costs, quality issues, and the communication and managerial costs associated with this new extended enterprise, and we did not have such access. Another aspect of offshored outsourcing that was interesting but could not be identified and modeled was the set of decisions and activities involved in this process. Researching and understanding of these two areas, among others can provide a greater understanding of this concept and enable us, as managers, to deal with some of the critical issues associated with true globalization of business enterprises.

# References

Aggarwal, N. (2004, June 21). Outsourcing takes off in Europe in a major way. *Straits Times*.

Agrawal, V., & Farrell, D. (2003). Who wins in offshoring? *The McKinsey Quarterly*, 2003 Special Edition: Global Directions, 36-41.

Baily, M., & Farrell, D. (2004, July). Exploding the myths of offshoring. *The McKinsey Quarterly*. Retrieved October 22, 2004, from http://www.mckinseyquarterly.com/article_print.aspx?L2=7&L3=10&ar=1453

Bernstein, A. (2004, September 27). Still hungry for foreign hires. *Business Week*. Retrieved September 30, 2004, from http://www.businessweek.com/magazine/content/04_39/c3901020_mz003.htm#ZZZFX9XQ6ZD

Brainard, L. & Litan, R. E. (2004). Offshoring service jobs: Bane or boon and what to do? *The Brookings Institution*, policy brief #132–2004.

Campoy, A. (2004, September 27). Think locally. *Wall Street Journal*, R8.

Drucker, J., & Solomon, J. (2004, October 18). Outsourcing booms, although quietly amid political heat. *Wall Street Journal*, B1.

Ghalimi, I. (2005, March 5). Interview of Ismael Ghalimi of Intalio by Kris Cejka.

India 8th in U.S. outsourcing list. (2004, December 29). *Times News Network*. Retrieved March 9, 2005, from http://economictimes.indiatimes.com/articleshow/974176.cms

Kletzer, L. G. (2001, September). Job loss from imports: Measuring the costs. Institute for International Economics, Washington, DC.

Krishnadas, K. C. (2005, March 15). After Wipro, Infosys now gets bomb threat. Retrieved March 22, 2005, from http://www.outsourcingpipeline.com/news/159900306

Kurtzman, J., Yago, G., & Phumiwasana, T. (2004, October). The global costs of opacity. *MIT Sloan Management Review*. Retrieved February 25, 2005, from http://www.milkeninstitute.org/publications/publications.taf?function=detail&ID=378&cat=Arts

McCarthy, J. C. (2002, November 11). 3.3 million U.S. services jobs to go offshore. *Forrester Brief*.

McDougall, P. (2005). Even in government, dollars And sense prevail on outsourcing. Retrieved March 22, 2005, from http://informationweek.outsourcingpipeline.com

McKinsey & Company. (2003). Globalisation of the ICT sector. In *Information technology outlook 2004* (pp. xx-xx). CITY, STATE: PUBLISHER.

McKinsey Global Institute. (2003, October). New horizons: Multinational company investment in developing economies.

Schlender, B. (2004, January 12). Peter Drucker sets us straight. *Fortune*.

Shah, S. (2004, September 1). India's dwindling IT labor advantage. *Optimize*, 66-71.

Solomon, J., & Kranhold, K. (2005, March 23). In India's outsourcing boom, GE played a starring role. *Wall Street Journal*, A1.

St. John, D. (2005). Offshore outsourcing: Realities and battles. Retrieved February 16, 2005, from http://www.outsourcingpipeline.com/trendwatch/trendwatch.jhtml

Tyson, L. D. (2004, December 6). Offshoring: Pros and cons for Europe. *Business Week*.

Wu, A. (2004, July 6). Looking offshore. *San Francisco Chronicle*, C-1.

Chapter X

# Outsourcing and Offshoring of Finance Activities

Siri Terjesen
Queensland University of Technology, Australia

## Abstract

*This chapter reviews the outsourcing and offshoring of finance activities and the socioeconomic implications for home and host countries. Part one provides an overview of the hierarchy of finance activities in the firm and the phenomenon of outsourcing and offshoring of these activities. The phenomenon is then examined from a firm perspective, highlighting the major drivers, trends and issues using theoretical frameworks and case examples from the author's in-depth interviews with 37 managers at 25 multinational firms. Finally, the socioeconomic issues and implications of offshoring activities are discussed in the context of both home and host countries.*

## Introduction

Globalisation, technology, regulation changes, stakeholder pressures, and firm re-organisations present challenges and opportunities to firm finance functions to improve their contributions to the business. One of these opportunities is the outsourcing and offshoring of finance services. Finance services comprise 10% of the nearly $250 billion worldwide business process outsourcing (BPO) market (Gartner, 2003) and the total number of finance service outsourcing is expected to increase 71% over the next few years (Accenture & EIU, 2004). Firms also offshore these finance activities. A survey of 275 finance executives revealed that 21% send finance and accounting activities offshore (CFO Magazine, 2003). Finance services offshoring is more commonplace among firms based in the U.S. and Europe than those in Asia Pacific. The offshoring of finance activities has important socioeconomic implications for both the home and host countries.

The chapter begins with an introduction to finance activities in the firm. The phenomenon of outsourcing and offshoring of these finance activities is reviewed, paying special attention to the drivers, costs and benefits of outsourcing and offshoring from the firm's perspective. We then review a framework for evaluating location choice based on the author's semi-structured, in-depth interviews with 37 managers at 25 U.S. and European headquartered multinational firms. This research was undertaken jointly by the author, Anne Evison, Julian Birkinshaw and Roy Barden in 2003 and 2004. The managers were identified through the researchers' personal contacts. Respondents' job titles were CEO (2), Finance Director (6), Head of Shared Services (12), Outsource Service Provider (2), Change Director (4) and Other (6). Five customers of shared service operations were also interviewed. The chapter then examines finance services offshoring from the perspective of both the home and host country, exploring the socioeconomic issues. Special attention is paid to two countries with deep involvement in sending and receiving activities abroad: the U.S. and India. The discussion of socioeconomic issues facing home and host countries is based on the expert interviews detailed above, as well as a review of recent government reports, academic research and case studies.

## Finance Activities in the Firm

Finance activities can be seen in terms of a hierarchy of value-added inside the firm. At the top of the hierarchy are strategic finance decisions such as corporate risk management, budgeting and forecasting. The next level includes business partnering activities,

*Figure 1. Finance activities in the firm*

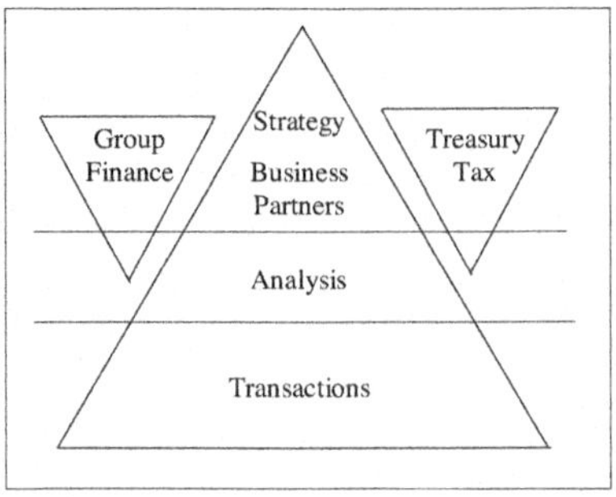

*Figure 2. Evolution of finance transaction processing*

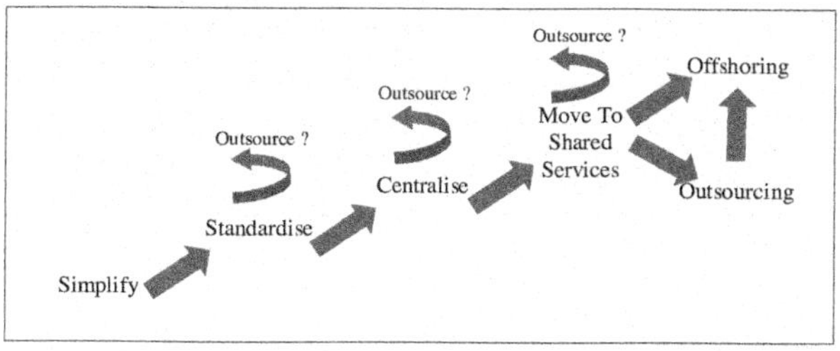


group finance, tax and treasury. Next in the hierarchy are business analysis activities such as managerial accounting and budgeting. Finally, transaction activities include credit, control, payroll, general ledger, accounts payable, and accounts receivable. Figure 1 illustrates the hierarchy of finance activities in the firm.

Strategy, business partnerships, tax and treasury activities at the top of the hierarchy are generally located in in-house at the firm's corporate headquarters. However, new business models of shared services, outsourcing and offshoring are dramatically changing the organisation of finance activities in the rest of the firm. The first step in re-organisation is often the simplification, standardisation and centralisation of transactional and, to a lesser extent, analytical finance activities. Often, a shared service centre (SSC) is established and supporting IT systems are integrated on a single, unified platform. For example, in 1998, London-based supply chain management firm Exel replaced its 13 freight management accounting and administration centres around Europe with one SSC in Dublin. Exel then contracted outsourcer Accenture to provide the service and enable the delivery of future benefits (Accenture & EIU, 2004). This evolution of finance transaction processing from simplification to outsourcing is depicted in Figure 2.

## Outsourcing of Finance Activities

The first finance service activities to be outsourced are generally transactional activities such as payroll, followed by increasingly value-added capabilities. Figure 3 illustrates the evolution of the outsourcing of finance activities.

*Figure 3. Evolution of the outsourcing of finance activities over time*

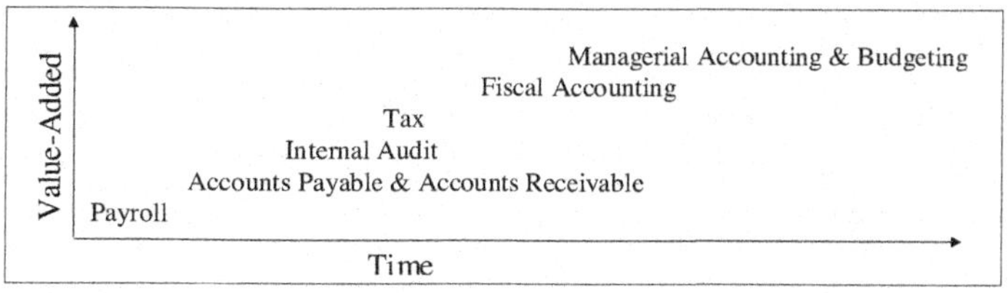

This evolution is reflected in current estimates of finance service outsourcing expenditure: employee payroll (27%), tax compliance and planning (21%), financial systems application support (16%), general and financial accounting (13%), travel and expense processing (12%), accounts receivables and collections (12%), accounts payable and vendor management (9%), financial reporting (7%), management report preparation and analysis (6%), treasury and cash management (4%), financial risk management (3%), budgeting and forecasting (1%) (Accenture & EIU, 2004).

## Offshoring of Finance Activities

Offshoring is the relocation of certain firm activities to foreign "host country" locations. For example, GE Financial Services relocated operations to India several years ago and now has over 12,000 employees in the country (GE Capital, 2005). In the last five years, offshoring has shifted from being a niche to a dominant strategy used by a number of firms, resulting in increased finance services capacity in offshore locations.

# Drivers of Finance Activities Outsourcing and Offshoring

The increasing use of offshoring is part of the never-ending search for efficiency and cost-reduction in large firms. The trend is particularly prevalent in back-office or support activities such as finance and accounting which, by definition, are not as customer-facing as other functions of the business, and are therefore open to being located in lower-cost, non customer-facing locations. Our research (Evison, Birkinshaw, Barden, & Terjesen, 2004) revealed five key drivers of finance activity offshoring. We review these drivers, and then a framework for activity location by activity scope, costs and benefits, and implementation issues.

The five key drivers of outsourcing and offshoring are:

- **Automation:** Routine activities which can be performed without human intervention are automated.
- **Disaggregation:** Activities which were done formally by just one person can be separated into different tasks. For example, an accountant could perform a broad range of tasks, from providing advice to basic bookkeeping. Increasingly, accountants focus on higher-level advisory tasks, and the more routine job tasks are either automated or pushed into a shared service operation.
- **Consolidation:** Similar activities can be combined into a shared service operation. Rather than every operating unit doing its own payroll or accounts payable, these activities can be done far more efficiently in one central location.

- **Commercialisation:** Shared activities can be commercialised, either by making them into a profit centre within the firm, or by spinning them off through an outsourcing arrangement. For example, in 1999, Dairy Farm, a Hong Kong based retailer, established a 50/50 joint venture with Cap Gemini Ernst and Young. The joint venture, OneResource Group, provides accounting services to Dairy Farm and other companies from two SSCs, one in Hong Kong and the other in Guangzhou, China. Of the 200 employees- the same number of employed originally in Dairy Farm's finance and accounting group- just 90 are required for Dairy Farm. The remaining 110 OneResource employees work for other firms in the SSC. Dairy Farm estimates that it has saved 50% of its costs and also minimised capital outlays (Accenture & EIU, 2004).
- **Relocation:** Shared activities can be moved to a carefully-chosen place, typically selected on the basis of cost or availability of employees, but sometimes for particular skills (e.g., language, data entry, analysis). The World Bank's relocation of finance back-office activities from Washington, DC, to India resulted in 15% cost savings and eliminated a backlog of expense forms and accounts payable items. The director of the World Bank's accounting department also describes how the Indian accountants help to improve process, [They] "say 'Why are you are doing this, why don't you think about how we can do the process better?'...You get to clean out the backlog and you also get to reengineer the business" (Knowledge & Wharton, 2002).

We now focus on the aspect of the relocation of outsourced activities and the many options available. The drivers of relocation and commercialisation often go hand-in-hand. The decision to move an activity to its own facility cannot readily be made without also managing that activity in a more commercially-minded way.

## Evaluating Location Options

Our research also revealed two critical dimensions for selecting the location for a support activity. The first is the extent of "codifiability" or the degree to which an activity can be routinised. Highly codifiable activities such as payroll and expense claims lend themselves to automation, and they can also be undertaken by individuals with limited

*Figure 4. Forms of activity interdependence*

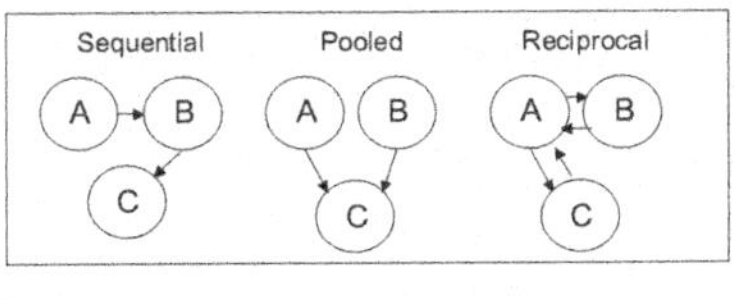

*Figure 5. Framework: Location choices for finance support activities*

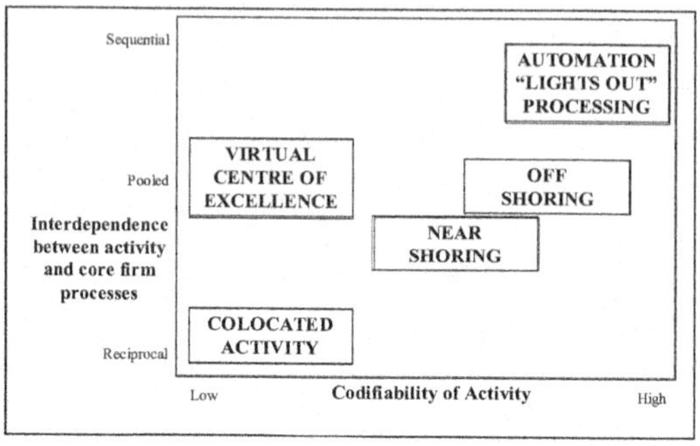


training or skills. Non-codifiable activities such as leasing, treasury, and compensation planning) involve a much higher degree of judgment and experience on the part of the individuals working in the activity. The second dimension is the nature of interdependence between the activity and the firm's core strategic activities. A standard way of framing this location choice is to consider three forms of interdependence (Thompson, 1967): sequential (A is an input to B, which is an input to C), pooled (A and B are inputs to C), and reciprocal (A is an input to B and C, but B and C, in turn, are inputs to A). See Figure 4.

Activities that have only pooled or sequential interdependence with the core can typically be managed on a remote basis, whereas activities involving reciprocal interdependence benefit from co-location. By considering these two dimensions together, it is possible to identify some of the critical differences between the different location options. Five primary options emerged from the research. Each dimension is considered in turn below, and a summary is provided in Figure 5.

## Co-Location

Co-location is necessary for those activities involving a high degree of expertise and significant interaction with the senior executives in the firm. This is a default arrangement because such activities, including business analysis, treasury, and legal, have historically been located at the corporate headquarters. Within these functions there are sub-activities that which shift to other locations, or are automated. For example, Proctor and Gamble outsources accounts payable data entry to Hewlett Packard, but retain other accounts payable processes that interact with their internal customers.

## Virtual Centre of Excellence

Some activities involve a high degree of expertise or professionalism, but there are few benefits from locating the individuals in question together at either the corporate headquarters or a business location. As such, these activities are best managed in what is sometimes called a "virtual centre of excellence". All of the compensation and benefits experts would form part of such a centre, but they would continue to reside in their existing operations, and they would travel between sites and come together for meetings. The virtual centre of excellence requires active management, because the default is for the individuals in question to focus their energies on their local operation. The centre of excellence logic recognises that the expertise in question should be leveraged on a corporate-wide basis, and it provides the resources and the technology to enable this resource sharing.

## Nearshoring

Typically, "'nearshoring" involves a centre or group of centres that perform codified, routine activities for a number of corporate customers. If more than one centre is to be deployed this can be assessed on the basis of quality/cost parameters to take advantage of differences in wages between countries/areas within the region, or alternatively separating activities into different centres, for example, accounts payable in one location, and Human Resources (HR) processing in another. For example, for a business considering a shared service organisation to serve Western and Eastern Europe, this would mean locating the centre(s) within this geographical boundary. Near shoring typically has a higher cost profile than offshoring, but it has several important benefits: lower risk, easier communication with the business, and typically a greater cultural affinity to the core customer groups, which can be particularly valuable in customer-facing entities such as call centres. An example of nearshoring is French chemical manufacturer, Rhodia's relocation of finance and accounting activities to a centre in the lower-cost Czech Republic (Cooper, 2003).

## Offshoring

Offshoring refers primarily to the relocation of activities to emerging economies, such as India, China and the Philippines. The distinction between nearshore and offshore is relevant for European and American firms. For example, European firms typically have medium-cost locations (e.g., Poland, Czech Republic, and Turkey) available that are closer than the big emerging economies of Asia. Offshoring is the preferred option for those activities that are easily routinised, and that offer substantial returns to scale. Enormous amounts of back-office banking work and call centres are done in such locations. Increasingly, firms are experimenting with higher value-added activities. For example, in August 2003, Citigroup and HSBC announced that they would be moving some of their investment bank analyst jobs to India.

*Table 6. Location options and activity scope*

| | Physical Location | Economic Logic | Typical Activities |
|---|---|---|---|
| Co-location | Located with the business being served (including the HQ) | Legal requirements, Proximity to senior executives, Proximity to customers | Partnering, Complex handoffs, Decision support |
| Virtual centre of excellence | Individuals located in existing operations, often traveling extensively | Need to leverage expertise across firm, but without significant economies to scale | Tax planning, Leasing, Compensation & benefits |
| Near Shoring | Inside the geographical region of businesses | Economies of scale, Skills, Expertise, Language and cultural affinity | Regulatory reporting, Specialist call centre activities |
| Off Shoring | Outside the geographic region of businesses | Economies of Scale, Routine activities | Routine call centre activities, Accounts payable |
| Automation 'Lights Out' Processing | None | Process Efficiency and cost reduction | Parts of all the above |

## Automation "Lights Out" Processing

Some activities can be entirely routinised, thereby altogether removing the human component and automating the service. There may, however, be some activities which will have exceptions which require human intervention, such as check processing. At the moment, fully automated or "lights out processing" is a vision rather than a reality. Automation almost always occurs in tandem with one of the other options. For example, an investment bank has recently automated the majority of cash settlement activity to an outsource service provider. However those elements of the process that cannot be automated have been left co-located in the business. The rationale is that the cost to create complex, dynamic system rules would be greater than to retain human intervention. Table 6 summarises these approaches.

# Finance Activities Outsourcing: Costs and Benefits Perceived by Firms

Offshoring makes the business headlines, suggesting that relocation can lead to fantastic cost reductions as well as new skills and expertise. Business benefits, however, are not guaranteed. In the author's interviews, several senior managers reported feeling that 15-20% costs savings of offshoring were not worth the risk. So, how should firms approach the outsourcing and offshoring of finance services?

Earlier chapters have outlined costs and benefits of outsourcing. Here we focus briefly on the key insights specific to costs and benefits of outsourcing finance activities revealed in interviews with 37 executives in 25 multinational firms headquartered in the U.S. and Europe.

## Costs

- **Data disclosure to third parties:** Some managers were reluctant to share finance data with third parties, for fear that this information might somehow reach competitors.
- **Loss of talent:** Managers worried about the loss of in-company finance talent if activities were moved outside the firm.
- **Long time to implement:** Managers noted that outsourcing activities took a long time, particularly if the processes needed to first be simplified, standardised and centralised.
- **New regulation for accountability:** In the U.S., the Sarbanes Oxley legislation requires senior managers to personally attest to the truthful reporting of company accounts. Managers with Sarbanes Oxley requirements said that they were less likely to consider outsourcing of these activities.
- **Lack of flexibility:** A firm's business needs change and the outsourcers may not be prepared to deal with this change.
- **Lack of performance measures:** Performance measures are neither easily developed nor implemented. Many managers expressed a desire to develop service level agreements (SLAs) in the future.
- **Poor performance:** Some managers reported that the third parties did not meet their performance criteria and they considered "in-sourcing" the activities back into the firm.
- **Extra taxes:** Outsourcing can also lead to extra taxes from purchasing from outside the firm. For example, in the UK, most financial institutions exempt their income from the 17.5% value-added tax (VAT), so customers get services free of VAT but then find it difficult to reclaim VAT back on services.

## Benefits

- **Cost savings:** After an initial outlay to establish the centers and contracts, outsourcing arrangements, some managers reported lower labour and transaction charges. The average accountant in the U.S. makes about $41,000 per year. The Indian equivalent earns around $10,000 per year. A financial analyst in the U.S. costs $60 per hour; the Indian equivalent just $10 per hour.
- **Core competency focus:** Outsourcing of transaction activities freed employees and managers from routine tasks and enabled them to focus on core competences and more value-added activities.
- **Leading edge knowledge and track record:** Some managers describe outsource partners as having more detailed knowledge about regulatory and reporting requirements. Managers also reported feeling comfortable with the successful

track record of outsourcing providers in automating high volume, low value activities.

- **Increased transparency:** Managers highlighted the potential for outsourcing to improve transparency and disclosure by distancing the managers who "create" performance from the accountants who measure it.

Costs and benefits are often linked to the implementation and delivery models. Our research also uncovered several implementation issues for firms (Evison et al., 2004).

## Implementation Issues for Firms

Offshore delivery models are primarily constrained by a lack of confidence that the shared service organisation will be able to deliver to existing quality and service levels, although using an outsource service provider usually ameliorates this concern. This is because establishing shared services involves significant change — for both individuals within the back office functions and the businesses themselves. The elements of change are many:

- **Disaggregated Jobs:** Individual jobs often become disaggregated, into (1) tasks that are strategic to the business, (2) tasks that are advisory but can be undertaken remotely, and (3) tasks that are can be automated entirely. Each task typically has a different place in the new organisation.
- **Loss of Control:** Sharing of services means a de facto loss of influence and control over activities that were previously operated directly by the businesses. Not surprisingly, the process of giving up these activities is undertaken with great reluctance.
- **Compromise:** Implementing common systems and processes across the businesses often means that compromises have to be made on the functionality for each specific business.
- **Business Interaction:** Businesses interaction with back office functions has changed. The new approach typically offers a higher level of business discipline, including more self-service technology, higher levels of transparency of cost of service, and "extra services" being charged for separately.

In order to manage this change, most organisations select an implementation path that effectively manages their requirement to achieve cost reduction, whilst managing risk by choosing a location with which they are already familiar, containing scope to a manageable level and bringing the customers into the model in a phased way. Offshoring is usually considered as a second step.

Consider the case of Oracle, the leading database and software company. In January 1998, in response to a need to create a single global brand while also reducing its cost base, Oracle decided to implement a standardised global finance processes and establish a shared services delivery model. It took eight months to agree standardised global processes across sixteen process areas. Through a process of "brown papering" with the best and the brightest resources from the company, these processes were then mapped to the standard Oracle release at the time. Five months of integration testing followed and covered all scenarios, from all parts of the business. Three service centres were subsequently established. The EMEA centre was established in Dublin, and two other regional centres were established in California and Sydney. Forty-two countries were being serviced by the Dublin service centre within four years from programme inception, processing $3.5 billion in revenue, with a peak of almost 400 staff. Some of these activities are now being eliminated through technology or process optimisation and others are being moved to India. There will be 105 service jobs in India by the end of July 2004 and 230 jobs will remain in Dublin. But improvements will not stop there. In the interview, Nicky Sheridan, vice president and managing director of Ireland at Oracle, observed, "You have to keep changing and reinventing. We are always looking to bring in further work to the centre and automate or offshore the most routine work."

Regardless of the back-office strategy selected by the firm, two critical factors are (1) the level of commitment to the initiative from senior executives at country and functional levels, and (2) the overall appetite for change in the organisation. These factors are important in all change projects, but particularly so here, given the number of people who are directly impacted as well as the inherent uncertainty of moving activities overseas. As one interviewee observed, "If senior executives are not spending at least an hour a week on the project, then its not going to be successful. It's tough selling to local country MDs [managing directors] that it's going to be a worse system than before, because they previously had a customised system and process to suit their needs. It's not easy to see the global benefit. If I had my time again, I'd concentrate even more effort and attention to managing the process of change, and getting the active involvement of the top executives."

## Future Trends

While the outsourcing and offshoring of finance and other activities is here to stay, we see changes ahead for the size, scope and location of these activities. The number of firms outsourcing and offshoring finance activities will increase, including new industries and countries. Furthermore, the scope of finance activities offshored will change, expanding up the value chain to include asset management, investment banking, commercial and retail banking. The specific skills demanded in these areas include equity research, and statitical data research and compilation. Finally, the offshore locations will change. Through labour arbitrage and political pressures, BPO in India may move away from the traditional strongholds to more secondary and also tertiary cities. Abroad, other countries will continue to compete for the BPO market. Rising players include Malaysia, Costa Rica, the Phillipines, Russia and China.

Our research suggests scope for more careful thinking about the costs and benefits of outsourcing and offshoring. The challenge is how best to use these alternatives in an integrated way and how to manage them dynamically, according to the evolving needs of the business. While this may not be an exhaustive list, three important trends were identified among some of the more sophisticated firms in the study:

- **Disaggregate:** Activities are divided into constituent parts, with each part done in a different location. Many business process outsourcers now operate on a "layered" model. In one case, the company in question was providing an outsourced Accounts Payable process to a Scandinavian customer. The transaction processing of the invoice and payment activity was carried out in India, and an operation in Poland was used for handling queries from internal customers and external suppliers. The additional costs this entailed were offset by a better quality of service than could currently be achieved in India.
- **Shift:** Activities are relocated between locations according to the shifting demands of the business. Some financial service activities are re-located with the changing demands of management and industry. For example, Guinness and Grand Metropolitan's 1997 merger created Diageo. This new business had an opportunity to take advantage of greater economies of scale within their back office process. The merged service centres were initially located in the UK and Ireland. Subsequently, Diageo migrated its finance and customer service operations, for a number of European markets, from London to Budapest, and onto its global processes and systems, taking advantage of the new business requirements and environment.
- **Monitor:** Costs and benefits of different locations are carefully monitored, and firms remain open to change once the results are clear. This requirements the development and tracking of performance metrics. Thus, cost-benefit analyses prompt both the initial decision to outsource, and subsequent decisions to re-insource or "backsource" these services. This releases the organisation from the outsourcing agreement and enables the organisation retain control over the business. For example, Sears re-insourced finance activities from Andersen Consulting.

We now turn our attention away from the firm and toward the countries where firm activities have been relocated and to where they have been traditionally housed.

## Socioeconomic Issues for Host and Home Countries

To date, much of the research on outsourcing and offshoring has taken the perspective of the multinational firm. Indeed, we followed this approach in the first part of this chapter.

We now turn to the socioeconomic issues faced by both the home and host offshore countries, with specific focus on the impact in two countries with deep involvement in the outsourcing of financial service activities: India and the U.S. We highlight the socioeconomic issues facing each country in terms of economics, education, government and social and cultural realms. We select India as it is expected that by 2008, India's share of IT and back-office activities including finance services will employ four million people, account for 7% of India's GDP and result in a $57B industry. We focus on the U.S. as more than 3 million white-collar jobs worth $136B in wages are forecasted to move from the U.S. to overseas (Kripalani, Engardio, & Hamm, 2003).

## India: Socioeconomic Issues

### *Economy*

The tremendous growth of the BPO sector has stimulated India's economy. This can be seen by evaluating individual, regional and national economic experiences.

- **Job Growth:** The offshoring of BPO in India has created more than 200,000 new jobs, mostly employing the nation's young workforce of 20 to 30 year olds.
- **Multiplier Effect:** BPO employees' spending has helped to grow the economy in what is described as the "multiplier effect of velocity". For example, an employee may spend his or her wages on new clothes, and in turn the clothing retailer invests profits in the business, and so forth. The velocity of this multiplied consumption triggers the economy.
- **Emerging Middle Class:** Currently India's middle class constitutes just 18% of the one billion population. This percentage is believed to increase to 50% over the next 20 years. This rising middle-class will have even more consumer purchasing power.
- **Current Accounts Balance:** Indian companies are paid in foreign currency, usually U.S. dollars, for BPO services but pay wages and other expenses in Indian rupees. This enables a current accounts balance which can facilitate the purchase of certain larger scale investments.
- **Local Knowledge Enhancement:** Through clusters of BPO activities, local Indian firms benefit from network effects. They are able to absorb and apply the financial and accounting expertise used in the offshored operations of multinational firms in their own operations.
- **Concentrated Urban & Regional Growth:** The offsourcing of BPO activities to India is actually limited to a few cities such as Bangalore, a city of 6 million in southern India. Most of the economic growth is experienced in the key cities which are home to the bulk of new BPO services. For example, there are more than 1 million high tech workers in the city of Bangalore. The economic impact is felt much more strongly in urban areas with high literacy and education rates. In tandem, there are more people moving from the countryside into the cities. There is also the growth

of secondary cities such as Mangalore with clusters of outsourcing activities. Still there are many regions in India, such as Kerala, which do not benefit much from the outsourcing. To provide a broader picture, over all in India, there is 45% adult illiteracy and over 72% of the population live in rural communities (UNDP, 1998), though illiteracy is more prevalent in rural communities.

- **Emergent Economic Activity:** The increase in offshoring activities has also stimulated new industries and indigenous entrepreneurship. For example, in large cities with BPO operations, there is now a market for night catering and for keeping stores open during non-traditional hours, shared commuter flats, accent training and transportation to the city and the BPO centres.
- **Catalyst for Change:** The growth of BPO in India has also served as a catalyst for increasing the quality of education and management and attention the environment. Corruption has also been said to have decreased.

## *Education*

- **Formal Education - University Degrees:** Over the past 27 years, there has been a phenomenal 81% increase in the number of Indian students enrolling for commerce-related degrees (Ministry of Human Resource Development, India). Table 7 tracks this enrolment. These numbers are rising steadily, in part due to the establishment of a number of new universities as well as the development of links between Indian universities and those in the U.S. and elsewhere. In 1947, India had just 25 universities and 700 colleges; these numbers are now 216 universities and 8,613 colleges.
- **Bridging Training:** In order to land a job in the fast-growing BPO sector, some Indian students may need to take bridging training courses to satisfy job demands which were not part of university degree studies. This training could take the form of a primer in accountancy and finance for Arts graduates or a special course in advanced and applied finance for Commerce graduates.
- **On the Job Training:** Once they are on the job, Indian BPO employees are obtaining additional skills such as accounting and finance. These jobs are also teaching customer focus and improving workers' skills in educating, coaching and managing others.

*Table 7. India: Graduate degree enrollments*

| Degree type | 1971 | 1981 | 1991 | 1998 | % Increase 1971-1998 |
|---|---|---|---|---|---|
| Arts | 764,387 | 1,016,036 | 1,534,348 | 2,790,889 | 72% |
| Science | 495,285 | 489,415 | 756,896 | 1,142,724 | 57% |
| **Commerce** | **232,404** | **536,217** | **994,532** | **1,202,570** | **81%** |
| Total | 1,492,076 | 447,359 | 3,285,776 | 5,136,183 | 71% |

*Source: Ministry of Human Resource Development*

- **Professional Qualifications Demand:** The rise of financial service activity offshoring to India has resulted in demand for certain qualifications. For example, GE Capital hopes to hire several hundred India-based qualified chartered accountants (GE Capital, 2004). People with accounting skills specialised to the U.S. system are also in demand to meet current and future needs. For example, in 2003, 25,000 U.S. tax returns were prepared in India, but this number was expected to increase over 10-fold to 300,000 in 2004.

## *Government*

- **Initiatives to encourage industry:** The Indian government is keen to continue to develop India's market for offshoring finance and other activities. Government legislation has led to favorable taxes and other business start-up friendly policies for multinationals establishing their own centres in the country and for multinational and Indian third-party providers of outsourcing services. This occurs at both the national level and also the city and regional levels which often compete for new business. The Indian government has engaged in relationship building at company, country and regional levels. One of the major Indian business lobby groups is the Confederation for Indian Industry (CII).
- **Capacity building:** In order to meet new business needs, the Indian government has taken new educational focus in key skill areas for the future such as industry-specific knowledge and new languages. New industry focused curricula are aimed at developing deep skills and requisite environmental knowledge. There is also new training in French, German, Japanese and other languages in order to meet future demands from non Anglo-American countries.
- **Legislation for workers:** The nature of outsourcing work has led to legislative changes for working conditions (to monitor shift work), social security, and health issues (working with computers).

## *Social and Cultural Environment*

- **Westernisation at Work:** At work, Indians may be rewarded for operating within a Western business culture. For example, employees for large multinationals headquartered in the U.S. and UK are encouraged to adapt American or British accents and also to anglicise their names. For example, a call centre worker named Priya may call herself "Polly" on the phone. Furthermore, finance employees must operate according to principles for the companies. Often this can mean developing expertise in American and GAAP guidelines. There are also more Westerners doing business with India although only about 30,000 are estimated to have relocated to India.
- **Consumerism:** In tandem, young Indian finance services employees are using their wages to enjoy greater access to a westernised lifestyle in the form of new clothes, cars, and cell phones.

- **Family Changes:** New jobs and wages enable young people to moving away from home earlier than in the past. India's growing cadre of young BPO employees relocate into shared flats with friends and colleagues.
- **Changing Career Models & Organisational Culture:** Although today's population of talented young workers can enjoy a greater selection of jobs, especially BPO, than their parents experienced, the career model is changing. Individuals no longer expect to work for one firm for the rest of their life. The BPO industry has a very high turnover as the average employee moves to a new company after two or three years. To deal with this hefty attrition rates, some companies have adapted a policy of not hiring an indvidual if they have only been at their previous employer for less than one year or if they held more than three jobs in two years. Companies may also blacklist HR recruitment firms who have a record of poaching candidates.
- **Increase of Women in Private Labour Force:** Approximately half of the new BPO employees are women. Women constitute one of the fastest growing sectors of the private labour force in India. These women may someday reach senior and top management in the private sector, a traditionally male-dominated arena.
- **Shift Work:** Many BPO centres utilise shift work where as many as one-third of the employees regularly work in dark. To accomodate this population, some transportation, stores and clubs have also begun to operate for 24 hours each day.

## United States: Socioeconomic Issues

When firms relocate certain activities offshore, the home country also experiences a set of socioeconomic issues which can be viewed in terms of impacts to the economy, education, social and cultural environment and government.

### *Economy*

- **Jobs Going Offshore:** Only a small number of net job losses (approximately 2%) in the U.S. are actually attributable to offshoring. As highlighted earlier in the chapter, outsourcing and offshoring are not synonymous. A firm may choose to outsource to a third party which is based in the same country. In fact, this relocation

*Table 8. Estimated number of U.S. jobs going offshore*

| Types of Work | 2000 | 2005 | 2010 | 2015 |
|---|---|---|---|---|
| Management | 0 | 37,477 | 117,835 | 288,281 |
| Business | 10,787 | 61,252 | 161,722 | 348,028 |
| Office | 53,987 | 295,034 | 791,034 | 1,659,310 |

*Source: Forrester Research (2004)*

outside of the firm but inside of the country is actually the most common in the U.S. Furthermore, some firms eliminate jobs through automation. Table 8 contains estimates of offshored net job losses in the U.S. over time for management, business and office work in jobs which may contain some finance capabilities.

- **Economic Returns:** For every dollar spent on outsourcing abroad, the U.S. economy is expected to receive $1.12 to $1.14 in return (McKinsey, 2003). This figure is based on the estimated savings to U.S. consumers and investors, import of U.S. goods and services by Indian providers, transfer of profits to the parent company, and the value of the re-deployed U.S. labour.
- **Unionisation:** Some white collar workers have begun to entertain the idea of unionisation, although unions have traditionally been associated with blue colour workers.
- **Possible Deflation:** There is a long-term downward pressure on costs and prices in the U.S. which may lead to deflation.

## *Education*

- **Bridging and On-the-Job Training:** The erosion of jobs has led some American academics decry the need for a knowledge-economy strategy (D'Aveni, 2004), which involves up-skilling the workforce around truly knowledge-intensive activities and industries. New skill training can be an individual initiative or offered through company or government programmes.
- **Formal Degrees:** In tandem, it has been suggested that many American university degrees, including the MBA, are too "generic" and further specialization is needed.

## *Government*

- **Pending Legislative Initiatives**: Just as India's government has sought to increase the number of activities offshored, U.S. city, state and national government initiatives attempt to maintain firm activities at home and relocate offshored activities back home. These initiatives are partly based on fears that further job losses abroad will strap the already underfunded Social Security, Medicare, and workers compensation. At the national level, Representative Bernie Sanders (Vermont) has proposed the Defending American Jobs Act, which limits the amount of federal grants and loans available to companies that replace U.S. employees with foreign workers. At the state level, there are a number of initiatives such as the Keep Jobs in Colorado Act, Opportunity Indiana, and the American Jobs Act of Wisconsin. Several of these efforts have proved successful. For example, in November 2003, the Governor of Indiana was pressurised to withdraw from a $15M outsourcing contract with India-based Tata Consulting Services as it was deemed inappropriate to use state funds to pay for foreign workers.

*Table 9. Socioeconomic issues of finance activity outsourcing in home and host countries*

| Socioeconomic Issue | 'Host' Country: India | 'Home' Country: U.S. |
|---|---|---|
| **Economy** | | |
| Employment Market | Job Growth; Increased number of women in private labour force; New management skills | Loss of low-skill knowledge work; Potential unionisation of skilled work; Net job losses |
| Economic Growth | Emerging middle class; New industry sectors; BPO clusters in key urban and regional areas; Local Knowledge Enhancement; Current Accounts Balance; Multiplier Effect; Catalyst for Change | Economic Returns; Potential for deflation |
| **Education** | | |
| Formal Education | More universities, More commerce degrees | Up-skilling of workforce; Specialised degrees |
| Training | Bridging Training, Professional qualifications; Industry-specific knowledge; Accent and Language training | Bridging Training; On the Job Training; Up-skilling |
| **Government** | | |
| Initiatives | Relationship building; Capacity building by workforce up-skilling | Backlash; capacity building by workforce upskilling |
| Legislature | Favorable Taxes and business start-up policies; Working condition laws | Laws designed to prevent or discourage firm activities from relocating abroad |
| **Social & Cultural Environment** | | |
| Career Models | Shift work; High Turnover; Westernised business practices | Erosion of psychological employment contract; Portable skills |
| Social Environment | Western product consumption; Westernised lifestyle; More women in the private labour force; Earlier moves away from home | Backlash |

## *Social and Cultural Environment*

- **Changing Career Models:** Traditionally, careers have followed an upward, linear progression through one or two firms or consist of stable employment in one profession (Sullivan, 1999). Macroeconomic forces such as globalisation and technology have changed the nature of careers and of the psychological employment contract which was originally seen as exchange of employee loyalty for job security. This contract has further eroded with the pressure of outsourcing and in particular when employees are asked to train individuals from overseas who will take their jobs. A recent study of technology workers found that 20% had trained an individual from overseas or known someone who did. In order to stay employable in this new career model, U.S. workers must focus on developing portable, individual-specific knowledge, skills and competencies.

- **Backlash:** The offshoring of American jobs has generated backlash in the U.S. for a variety of reasons such as consumers' concerns about the security of data abroad and workers who are concerned about losing their jobs. Web sites such as http://www.nojobsforindia.com/ track the movement of U.S. firms' activities abroad and are actively engaged in petitioning governments and companies to retain these activities and jobs in the home country. Consumers have also expressed concerns about the security of their data abroad and a dislike of dealing with foreign call centres.

A summary of socioeconomic issues for home and host countries can be found in Table 9.

## Conclusions

This chapter has examined the phenomenon of the outsourcing and offshoring of finance activities from both firm and country perspectives. We have reviewed our research on the major drivers, costs and benefits and put forward a way of thinking about the location choices facing a firm as it considers how best to manage its back-office finance operations. Offshoring can provide important benefits, but it represents only one of several choices, and it carries with it substantial risks as well. This approach involves taking a disaggregated view of the finance activities in question, and thinking through the locational choice on a task-by-task basis. Once this analysis has been done, the attention can shift to issues of how best to coordinate the tasks across the various locations, and how to ensure an effective implementation process. It should also be noted here in that technology and innovation play a key role in firms' future. Technology will continue to enable the automation and thus elimination of jobs. Technology can also enable communication between groups which are located at a distance in the firm. Through technology, firms will be able to evolve and produce more with less.

Outsourcing and offshoring has profoundly impacted the firm, as well as the country environments. We have illustrated how the increase in offshoring of finance and other activities has led to fundamental changes across in the economy, education, social, cultural and political environment in host and home countries.

## References

Accenture and Economist Intelligence Unit. (2004). Outside upside: Finding focus through finance outsourcing. Report.

Cooper, W. (2003). Case study: Rhodia makes its move. *Outlook Journal.*

D'Aveni, R. A. (2004, June). What should be done about the export of jobs abroad? Academy of Management Online Discussion. Available at http://www.aomonline.org/aom.asp?page_ID=213

Evison, A., Birkinshaw, J., Barden, R., & Terjesen, S. (2004, Autumn). Shifting strategic focus. *European Business Forum*, *19*, 38-42.

Forrester Research. (2004). Near-term growth of offshore accelerating. Report.

Gartner Group. (2003). Outsourcing worldwide: Forecast database.

GE Capital. (2004). Wanted: Indian chartered accountants for GE. Available at http://www.gecapitalindia.com/gecapital/apr2004.htm#2

GE Capital. (2005). Fact sheet: GE Capital India. Available at http://www.gecapitalindia.com/gecapital/factsheet.pdf

Knowledge at Wharton. (2002). The case for, and against, shifting back-office operations overseas. Available at http://knowledge.wharton.upenn.edu/100902_ss1.html

McKinsey. (2003, August). Offshoring: Is it a win-win game? McKinsey Global Institute.

Offshoring: Not everybody's doing it. (2004, June 1). *CFO Magazine*.

Sullivan, S. E. (1999). The changing nature of careers: A review and research agenda. *Journal of Management*, *25*, 457-484.

Thompson, J. D. (1967). *Organizations in action*. New York: McGraw-Hill.

United Nations Development Programme. (1999). Human development index: India.

## Chapter XI

# Open Source and Outsourcing: A Perspective on Software Use and Professional Practices Related to International Outsourcing Activities

Kirk St.Amant
Texas Tech University, USA

## Abstract

*This chapter examines the role of open source software (OSS) in international outsourcing practices that involve the transfer of knowledge work from one nation to another. Included in this examination are discussions of the benefits and the limitations of OSS use in outsourcing. The chapter also presents organization-specific and industry-wide strategies for effective OSS use in outsourcing situations. The chapter then concludes with a discussion of areas of international outsourcing where OSS might have important future applications or effects. The purpose of such an examination is to provide readers with the knowledge and the insights needed to make effective decisions related to the use of OSS in international outsourcing situations.*

# Introduction

International outsourcing now includes the distribution of knowledge-based work to employees in other countries. Much of this work, however, requires the use of software either to perform a task or to provide the technologies that allow clients and outsourcing providers to interact. Conventional "proprietary" software can, however, be prohibitively expensive to outsourcing employees in developing nations.

Open source software (OSS) might offer a solution to this problem, for OSS is often free to use and is relatively easy to modify or to update. Yet open source software also brings with it a new series of problems related to product consistency, user support, and digital piracy. While the relationship between outsourcing and software (particularly OSS) has been known for some time, it has received relatively little attention in terms of social and economic implications both for those who outsource work and for those who perform outsourced work. Knowledge of these issues, however, is essential to understanding both current and future outsourcing practices and the socio-economic development of nations that engage in outsourcing.

The purpose of this chapter is to provide readers with a foundational knowledge of how OSS use could affect international outsourcing practices. After reading the chapter, individuals will understand the relationship between software and outsourcing practices in terms of the opportunities and the limitations it creates for client companies and for outsourcing employees in developing nations. This chapter also presents strategies organizations can employ to use OSS more effectively in international outsourcing situations. The chapter then concludes with an overview of how global computing and OSS use is poised for significant growth and the implications this growth could have for different organizations.

# Background

## The Growth of International Outsourcing

In international outsourcing — or offshoring — situations, companies in one nation transfer the responsibility for completing a task to workers in another country (Bendor-Samuel, 2004). Originally, this transfer of responsibility focused on manufacturing and the production of physical products such as clothing or footwear. The global spread of online media, however, has given rise to a new kind of international outsourcing that involves the export of knowledge-based work. Known as business process outsourcing — or BPO — this practice encompasses everything from computer programming to call center staffing and medical transcription. While such BPO practices have existed on a relatively limited scale to date, they are poised to expand rapidly in the future.

The push to adopt BPO has to do with the perceived benefits related to such practices. Perhaps the most publicized of these benefits is savings related to the cost of skilled labor. Much of today's knowledge work is being outsourced to skilled employees in developing nations — employees who can perform most technical tasks for far less than what counterparts in industrialized nations would charge. For example, gaming developers in Russia earn roughly $100 U.S. a week, while middle managers in mainland China earn roughly $9,000 a year (Weir, 2004; Nussbaum, 2004).

Such wage-based savings, however, are not the only advantage related to offshoring. Rather, proponents of outsourcing note it also offers the benefits of

- **Improved quality of service:** Research indicates overseas outsourcing employees often provide better quality service than "domestic" workers who perform the same jobs (Reuters, July 182004; Farrell, 2004; Hagel, 2004). Certain call centers in the Philippines, for example, take 25% less time to handle incoming calls and receive higher rates of caller satisfaction than do U.S. counterparts (Hagel, 2004).
- **Effective management practices:** Because managers are paid less in developing nations, organizations can easily justify the use of more in-country managers to oversee outsourcing activities (Nussbaum, 2004; Hagel, 2004). This increase means managers have more time to answer employee questions and to provide employee training — factors that contribute to the improved quality of work or service perceived by many consumers (Hagel, 2004; Lewis, 2003; Hagel, 2004).
- **Reduced employee turnover:** Secure employment is often rare in many developing nations, and outsourcing jobs tend to be among the better paying ones. Therefore, outsourcing workers in developing nations tend to stay with employers for longer periods of time (Reuters, July 18, 2004; Farrell & Zainulbhai, 2004). As a result, these long-term employees tend to have more experience performing their jobs while reducing the need for and the cost of new employee training.
- **Reduced production time:** By using online media to distribute work to employees in different nations and time zones, organizations can keep operations going 24 hours a day, seven days a week. Such continual production means that processes and products can be completed more quickly than if done exclusively in one country (Friedman, 1999; Baily & Farrell, 2004; Bierce, 1999; "America's pain," 2003).
- **Increased access to international markets:** In many developing nations, marketplace success is often a matter of knowing someone in that region (Rosenthal, 2001). Companies that provide outsourcing services can provide such an "in," as well as provide advice on how one should proceed with business interactions in a particular nation or region (Rosenthal, 2001).

The manifold benefits of offshoring have prompted many companies to adopt it as a part of their core business strategy. At present, it accounts for $10 billion U.S. in worth and engages the services of some 500,000 workers in India alone (Baily & Farrell, 2004; Rosenthal, 2004b). Moreover, some researchers believe offshoring will grow by 20% a year through 2008, and by 2015, some 3 million business processing jobs will be performed by outsourcing employees (Rosenthal, 2004b; Baily & Farrell, 2004). Some critics expect this number to be much higher and claim at least 5 million international outsourcing jobs will emerge in the next five to 10 years (Garten, 2004).

The perceived benefits of international outsourcing have resulted in such practices spreading to a number of countries and to a variety of industries. French companies, for example, have begun working with French-speaking developing nations such as Senegal and Morocco on a variety of outsourcing projects, and these relationships have met with good results (Reuters, July 18, 2004). Similarly, German firms have begun exploring outsourcing relationships with Easter European nations, while the Netherlands has begun using call centers located in South Africa where Dutch-based Afrikaans is spoken (Farrell, 2004; "Sink or Schwinn," 2004; Baily & Farrell, 2004; Rosenthal, 2004c). Additionally, markets in Spain, combined with the growth in the U.S. Spanish-speaking population, have meant more work is now outsourced to Mexico and to Latin America (Rosenthal, 2004a). Even India, the one time center for international outsourcing, is now outsourcing work to China and to Sri Lanka, where it can be done for less money (Reuters, September 2, 2004).

The majority of BPO practices, however, are reliant on software. Aspects related to software use can thus affect if and how organizations realize the advantages related to the offshoring of knowledge work. For this reason, decision makers in the public and the private sectors need to understand the differences between proprietary and open source software — as well as the limitations and advantages of each — in order to make informed choices related to international outsourcing. Only through such informed decision-making can organizations benefit from the advantages related to offshoring.

# Main Thrust of the Chapter

## Software, Cost, and International Outsourcing Activities

Software is essential to international BPO practices for two key reasons. First, it provides the mechanism for sharing materials and for interacting with others online (e.g., browsers and email systems). Without the software needed to engage with others quickly, easily, and directly via the Internet, many of the cost, time, and quality benefits associated with the international-outsourcing of knowledge work would not exist. Second, production-related software (e.g., Microsoft Word or Adobe Illustrator) is essential to performing most knowledge-based programming, customer support, and IT tasks efficiently and effectively. Again, without the software needed to perform tasks, the time, cost, and quality benefits of international outsourcing cannot be realized.

Unfortunately, the makers of software products have traditionally produced proprietary programs that require individuals to purchase them in order to perform a given activity. The for-profit nature of proprietary software has, however, made it unavailable to large segments of the world's population — particularly in developing nations where high purchase prices are often associated with such materials (Warschauer, 2003). This restriction, in turn, affects online access and thus outsourcing activities in those regions.

One solution to this situation would be for companies to supply prospective international outsourcing providers with free or inexpensive software products that would allow them to participate in outsourcing activities. Such an approach, however, would contribute to a second major software problem — copyright violation. In many developing nations, copyright laws are often weak (if not non-existent) or governments show little interest in enforcing them. As a result, many developing nations have black market businesses that sell pirated versions of software and other electronic goods for very low prices (Balfour, 2005). Such software piracy reduces consumer desire to purchase legitimate and more costly versions of the same product, and thus affects a company's profit margins within that nation. In fact, global software piracy in 2004 accounted for some $33 billion U.S. in lost profits ("One third," 2005). Further compounding this problem is the fact that it is often difficult for companies to track down who is or was producing pirated versions of software products in order to stop that offender. Thus, while the distribution of cheap or free digital materials can help contribute to outsourcing activities, that same strategy can undermine an organization's ability to sell its products abroad. Open source software (OSS) can offer a solution to this situation.

## Open Source Software and International Outsourcing

Software, in essence, is programming code — or source code — that tells a computer's operating system how to perform a certain action (Still, 2004). The source code of Microsoft's software program Word, for example, tells the related operating system how to transfer keystrokes into letters on a page and how to edit or to print that page. In theory, if an individual knows what programming/source code is needed to make a computer perform such activities, then that individual can simply retype that source code into his or her operating system, and the computer will respond as desired — the exact same way the original software would.

Accordingly, if and individual can see how someone else programmed software to work (see the underlying source code), all that person needs to do is copy that programming/source code, and he or she no longer need to buy the related software. Rather, that person can now achieve the same action on his or her own. For this reason, many software companies "close" their source code in order to prevent users from seeing the underling programming that allows the software to work (Still, 2004). In these situations, users need to work through an interface that allows them to activate certain commands indirectly within a software program's underlying source code. Closed software that prevents users from seeing the underlying code is know as proprietary software, for only the creator of that software is allowed to open or to see and to copy or to manipulate the underlying source code.

Open source software is a polar opposite in terms of access to source code/programming. That is, the developer of a piece of software creates it in manner that is "open" and permits any and all users to access, copy, and modify the underlying source that allows software to work (Still, 2004). A classic example of such open source programming is the HTML coding that allows Web pages to be displayed on browsers. The coding of these pages is open for anyone to review and copy; all the user needs to do is view a page's underlying source code by using the "View source" — or related option — in his or her browser.

This openness means individuals do not necessarily need to buy open source software in order to use it. Rather, they can directly access and copy the underlying source code in electronic format, or they can re-code/re-type the programming code and create a free copy of the related software. Such openness also means individuals can alter the underlying source code to make a software program perform different functions. So, in theory, a copy of the underlying source code from one kind of software could be modified into a variety of programs — each of which performs a different task. Updating software, moreover, becomes a matter of copying new/updated code versus purchasing the newest version of a product.

In the case of international outsourcing, OSS can provide individuals with access to affordable software that allows them to work within outsourcing relationships. Moreover, the flexibility permitted by OSS means outsourcing workers could modify the software they use to perform a wide variety of tasks and reduce the need for buying different programs in order to work on different projects. As the software it is produced by the outsourcing employee and not the client, concerns related to copyright and proprietary materials are no longer stumbling blocks to outsourcing relationships. Thus, it is perhaps no surprise that the use of OSS is growing rapidly in many of the world's developing nations ("Open source's," 2003).

## The Problems of Open Source Software in International Outsourcing

While the free and flexible nature of open source software allows it to contribute greatly to international outsourcing situations, OSS also brings with it limitations that could affect the success of BPO relationships. First, because OSS is open for the user to modify as he or she sees fit, it is easy for each individual to use the same programming foundation/source code to develop a different kinds of non-compatible software or other digital products. Such divergence is know as *forking code*, for each programmer can take a different "fork" in the programming "road," and such forking code has long been considered a major problem in OSS use (Still, 2004). These prospects for divergence mean international outsourcing situations are open to a variety of problems related to compatibility. Such problems include

- Employees might generate software or other materials that the related client company cannot use due to compatibility issues.
- Software products might not work as desired or work in unexpected ways/ways not compatible with the client company's intentions.
- Employees working on different parts of the same project might produce component parts that cannot be integrated into the same whole or do not work together correctly or as intended within that same whole due to compatibility issues.
- Addressing compatibility issues either among international work groups or between offshoring workers and clients could take more time and cost more than if the product had been produced domestically.

Thus, the freedom that allows one individual to operate software might also prevent others from making use of digital materials. Additionally, any or all of these factors could contradict the advantages of reduced cost, quicker production time, and increased quality that encourage organizations to use international BPO.

Some OSS companies, such as LINUX, have successfully addressed the problem of forking code through focused oversight processes that govern programming practices (Hamm, 2005). The result has been successful and relatively stable software products that work effectively with other systems. The same kind of management, oversight, and standardization, however, becomes more complicated in an international outsourcing situation where a variety of employees can be working in different nations and different time zones

A second problem involves the kind of technical support available to OSS users — both outsourcing employees and consumers using OSS products. Because no individual or organization really owns an open source software product, there is often no formal or standardized mechanism for providing technical support to OSS users. Rather, technical support often comes in the form of a loose network of OSS programmers/developers who interact informally — and sometimes haphazardly — in online contexts such as chat rooms or listservs (Still, 2004). The idea is that a user who is experiencing software difficulty posts a query to one of these online forums and waits for a member of that forum to read the posting and respond to it.

A major problem in such an informal system is that technical support/answers are not readily available. Rather, individuals who experience "glitches" related to time-sensitive OSS projects could find themselves missing or offsetting deadlines as they wait for some random programmer to respond to a request for help. Unfortunately, such a response could take anywhere from minutes to days depending on who is reading what lists or who is posting when. In the fast-paced environment of global business, such delays could have a major effect on production schedules, profits, and access to international markets. These delays also counteract one of the key benefits of and reasons for using international outsourcing — quicker production times.

Equally problematic is the fact that such support systems are open for anyone to respond to, regardless of a person's technical skills or understanding of the situation (Still, 2004). Thus, the quality of the advice related to such a support system can be haphazard, inconsistent, or even wrong. Moreover, different individuals might offer varying suggestions/solutions to the same situation. Thus, requests for assistance could introduce the similar problem of forking/diverging source code into situations where different individuals encounter problems when working on the same project. As a result of these limitations, materials created using OSS could be incompatible, inconsistent, or even non-functional depending on the kind of "help" one received.

Finally, open source software creates interesting and often unintended problems related to copyright. Most proprietary operating systems (e.g., Microsoft Windows) and proprietary software programs (e.g., Microsoft Windows Media Player) work by opening digital materials loaded into a computer system. That is, Windows Media Player opens the video files on a DVD or the audio files on a CD so that individuals may view or listen to films or music stored on those DVDs or CDs. This approach means the individual is able to access materials while maintaining the copyright related to such items.

Open source software allows users to access the same kinds of files in a very different way. Rather than simply opening files located on a DVD or CD, OSS programs often automatically make a copy of such digital products, store that copy on the hard drive of the user's computer, and then open that copied file so the user can view or can listen to it (Zoellick, 2001). This automatic copying process, known as *ripping*, means that users of OSS materials automatically violate copyright just by trying to access or to use certain digital products. These unauthorized copies are available for anyone with access to the related computer — an important problem in outsourcing situations where more than one employee often uses the same terminal for work. Such ripped copies, moreover, can easily be replicated and sold in black market exchanges — a situation of particular importance as such illegal activities are well established and difficult to monitor in many of the world's premier outsourcing locations (e.g., the People's Republic of China). As a result, the copyright — or piracy — problems OSS could solve in terms of misuse of proprietary software could affect different products should

- The original client company needs to provide outsourcing employees with proprietary digital materials in order to perform certain outsourced tasks.
- The original client company sells OSS products resulting from outsourcing work to different customers who can now use such products to make illegal copies of digital materials.

Thus, the use of OSS in BPO can be a double edged sword. Yet, the use of OSS in international outsourcing is a situation that must be addressed if organizations wish to succeed in the global business environment of the 21st century. For this reason, organizations must find ways to strike a balance between OSS's benefits and detriments in offshoring situations. Such a balance can be established through the development and the use of various organizational and industry-wide practices and policies.

## Strategies for Using OSS Effectively in International Outsourcing

While OSS use in outsourcing creates a complicated situation, these complications can be addressed successfully through approaches that create standards for design and for use. What follows are ten strategies that can create an effective foundation for using OSS in international BPO.

- **Strategy 1: Create a programming standard all outsourcing employees will use when working with OSS.** By creating and sharing standards for how one should program with OSS, organizations that outsource activities can provide overseas workers with guidelines that impose consistency on the programming process. These guidelines would instruct outsourcing OSS users on what programming choices to make during different points in an overall process. Such instructions would help reduce the prospects of forking code and increase compatibility across employees.

Standards should also be created to address the coding of comments — or the bits of verbal explanation that appear within the coding of a program. These comments allow users and clients to know why a particular programming decision was made and to know the effects that decision could have on the operation of the related digital product. By creating standards for when and for how to create such comments, companies that use outsourcing create a built-in mechanism for reviewing materials produced by overseas workers. To make sure that such standards are followed by outsourcing employees, the related client company should suspend all or part of final payment until it has had time to review the final product, and its related comments, in order to confirm standards were followed. While such monitoring could initially slow production, as outsourcing employees become aware of the fact their work is being monitored, they will spend more time adhering to standards. In so doing, these employees will create a better product. Thus, over the long term, the time spent monitoring OSS processes would decrease while the quality of products would increase. The increase in quality resulting from such practices would therefore eventually offset any initial slowdown in production caused by the introduction of monitoring procedures.

- **Strategy 2: Require outsourcing workers to identify themselves as OSS users and require those users to complete organizational training programs in standard OSS practices.** Such identification and training — which can be completely online — would allow organizations to provide outsourcing workers with instruction in how to follow a particular organization's standards for OSS use and coding. It would also allow companies to identify which standards seem most problematic for individuals (via automatically reviewed online tests). Organizations could then provide follow-up online training to help individuals address their particular problem areas related to OSS. Initial expenses dedicated to the development and the delivery of such training can contribute to increased later profits in the form of more efficient, more effective, and more standard uses of OSS by outsourcing employees.
- **Strategy 3: Develop an organizational support mechanism for helping outsourcing OSS users.** To make sure that outsourcing employees using OSS get consistent and accurate answers to technical questions, organizations should develop their own OSS online support lists or Web sites. Such Web sites would be free access, but they would require individuals to enter a username and password (supplied by the organization) to gain access to such resources. Such a measure would cut down on non-employees taking advantage of this resource and thus diverting attention away from the help given to an organization's actual workers.

  This resource would be staffed by employees who have a high degree of proficiency in OSS use, and these "help" persons would be "on call" 24 hours a day to accommodate queries from outsourcing employees in different nations and time zones. These help employees would also be given access to an online database of the kinds of projects being worked on by different outsourcing employees. Help workers could then use this information to determine the prospective problems (and related best solutions) affecting different outsourcing workers. Such help workers would also record all comments and suggestions in a central online database that would cross-reference those suggestions with the names of all outsourcing workers involved in the same project. Such cross-listing would allow other help providers to offer consistent advice (and germane suggestions) to all outsourcing employees working on a project.

- **Strategy 4: Establish a peer-mentoring program for outsourcing workers who use OSS.** The effective use of OSS in a business environment is part understanding programming processes and part understanding the culture and the goals of the organizations using those programs. For this reason, the more outsourcing workers know about an employing organization's culture, goals, and objectives, the more effectively they can use OSS to engage in processes or develop products that address those factors (Clement, 1994; Tan, 2000; Sandholm, 2004). That is, if the outsourcing employee knows how a given OSS product will fit into a company's objectives, that employee will have a better idea of how to program to meet those objectives (Clement, 1994; Tan, 2000; Sandholm, 2004). Similarly, if the outsourcing employee is aware of the importance of copyright and proprietary products to a company, that employee is less likely to make unauthorized copies — either inadvertently or intentionally.

  By pairing outsourcing employees with a peer mentor from the client company, organizations provide such outsourcing employees with someone who can provide an introduction to the organization's culture and its objectives. This mentor could make the outsourcing employee feel more a part of the overall organization. Such a peer could also familiarize outsourcing employees with company standards for OSS use and copyright policy (as well as the consequences for violating such a policy). In so doing, the mentor creates a mechanism for accountability, for the outsourcing employee is no longer a "faceless" worker who exists as a mere payroll number.

  Such a peer mentor should also have a background in OSS so he or she can provide the outsourcing worker with advice on how to best address a particular programming/software situation. The mentor could similarly introduce the outsourcing employee to corporate training materials and support services and review programming work to check its quality. Work with such a peer mentor could be made an essential part of the training process associated with outsourcing workers. The mentor's evaluation of that worker's progress could likewise serve as an important resource when making the decision to continue using a particular outsourcing employee.

- **Strategy 5: Create protocols for sharing or for forwarding work among international outsourcing employees.** In many cases, work that is outsourced to one overseas employee is shared or forwarded to another international outsourcing employee working on the same process (Freedman, 1999). Within such contexts, effective information sharing is essential, for the more time it takes an individual to determine what a predecessor has done and expects that individual to do, the less efficient the international outsourcing process is. For this reason, outsourcing employees need to use a standard mechanism for listing what they have done/how they've used or programmed OSS so colleagues can understand this work.

Outsourcing employees also need to provide standard directions on how the recipient of that information should use OSS to continue with work on that project. By developing standards ways of reporting such information to colleagues, organizations decrease the chances that confusion or a programming inconsistency will occur. These comments should also be shared with/downloaded to a database controlled by the client company. This database can help organizations anticipate or backtrack to locate prospective problems related to OSS use in outsourcing. Such a database should also be accessible to any individuals providing help in such outsourcing situations. The information in this database could allow help providers to better understand and address prospective problems encountered by one of more of the outsourcing employees working on forwarded materials (Strategy 3).

- **Strategy 6: Require all international outsourcing relationships to be long-term contracts.** Many of the disaster stories associated with international outsourcing occurred because of short-term relationships (Goolsby, 2004). In such relationships, neither party feels particularly invested in the long-term success of the other, so the desire to conform to standards or respect copyright is low. Moreover, such short-term relationships often mean that the employment of the outsourcing worker ends just as he or she finally begins to understand and feel comfortable with a client's expectations. By requiring international outsourcing employees who use OSS to contract for longer times, client organizations can retain experienced employees who are accustomed to working according to a company's OSS programming guidelines.

  Such long-term relationships also improve accountability in outsourcing, for outsourcing employees are more likely to conform to programming standards and to respect copyright if they wish to maintain long-term business relations with the client (Atwood, 2004). Thus, long-term contracts enhance accountability in international outsourcing situations. Within such long-term relations, client companies should conduct regular audits of outsourcing employee work to make sure programming and comment guidelines are being followed and that the copyright of materials is respected.

- **Strategy 7: Hire in-house (domestic) employees who are proficient in OSS or train in-house (domestic) employees to be proficient in OSS.** Such employees will be essential to an organization, for they can serve as the peer mentors and the trainers of international outsourcing workers. They can also serve as the individuals who provide online support to outsourcing employees and as the individuals who will audit OSS work in long-term contract situations.

  By having trained OSS employees in house, organizations can rapidly respond to a variety of OSS crisis situations, easily develop new OSS coding practices, and readily share information about new OSS processes. Organizations can also adapt mentoring, training, support, and auditing activities to conform to new computing and business developments. Finally, such in-house employees can help client organizations understand different developments in, successes of, and problems related to OSS when used in an international outsourcing context.

- **Strategy 8: Develop a list of "copyright-friendly" outsourcing locations and refer to this list whenever considering international outsourcing.** To protect materials from piracy, organizations need to make sure they send such materials to nations that will acknowledge and enforce copyright laws and treaties. Such laws and treaties would provide organizations with a method for stopping such piracy if it happens in another nation and provide a method of recourse for curbing sales of and profits made from pirated materials. For these reasons, organizations can benefit from regularly updated listings that overview what international outsourcing destinations offer the best copyright protections. Such listings should include the following information:

    - If a convention or a treaty on copyright protection exists between the nation of the client organization and that of the outsourcing employee; a sample listing of such copyright-based treaties involving the Unites States can be found at www.copyright.gov — the Web site for the U.S. government's Copyright Office
    - What laws a particular nation has to guarantee copyright protection and how enforceable those laws are, for some nations have copyright agreements that are either not enforced or enforced haphazardly (Doyle, 2004; Orr, 2004)
    - How the client organization should file a grievance or petition according to a particular convention or treaty, or according to the laws of a certain nation
    - With which government agencies — both in the client organization's own nation and the outsourcing employee's nation — such a grievance or petition should be filed
    - What actions to expect in response to filing such a grievance and if any losses can be recovered according to international agreements or national laws

  By consulting such a listing in advance of distributing work to overseas outsourcing workers, companies can reduce the risks that copyright violations will occur through restricting the distribution of materials only to employees in nations that provide effective copyright protection.

- **Strategy 9: Develop an industry standard for OSS use.** While an individual corporate standard can address compatibility issues related to one organization, the OSS-based products created by that organization might be used by other companies within an overall industry. At this level, the compatibility of OSS products again becomes an issue. To avoid compatibility problems across overall industries, the members of those industries should work together to develop an industry-wide standard for how to code, record comments, offer help, and record suggested solutions to programming problems. These standards could then be shared via an online database available to all members of a given industry. As computer programming practices are continually evolving, such a site should also have a "recent developments" section in which member organizations share new information and practices, innovations, or responses to previously unconsidered problems. Industry members should also meet regularly (annually or bi-annually) to share experiences and to update the related standards for OSS use in international outsourcing practices.

- **Strategy 10: Establish and maintain an industry-wide database of individuals and organizations that have violated copyright or violated coding standards in international outsourcing relationships.** Several outsourcing experts have noted that the fear of lost employment — and thus lost money — is one of the few ways to force international outsourcing workers to comply with industry standards and procedural (legal) guidelines (Atwood, 2004). The problem with international outsourcing is that an individual might violate the standards or the guidelines of one organization without fear. That is, individuals could think they can simply go to work for a different organization and that new employer would be unaware of an outsourcing worker's past. In this situation, the fear of reprisal through lost income remains low as the international outsourcing employee can easily move on to other clients.

  To counter this practice, organizations within an industry should establish a list of outsourcing offenders who have either failed to conform to OSS programming guidelines or who have used OSS to violate copyright. The idea would be to create an easy-access registry (e.g., a Web site) in which companies could record the names of the outsourcing providers with which they worked.

  Included in such a registry would be a listing of who the violator is, what the nature of the violation was, what the client did in response to this violation, and what results came from this action. Such a registry could help companies avoid working with "disreputable" outsourcing providers as well as offer effective strategies for addressing violations that occur in outsourcing relationships. These industry-wide registries mean that a large number of companies might now avoid "suspect" outsourcing providers and greatly affect their profits by creating a boycott situation. This fear of boycott could be a powerful incentive for outsourcing providers to abide by data processing practices required by client organizations (Atwood, 2004). Such a site should also allow users to provide a synopsis of the effectiveness with which they felt an outsourcing provider performed work.

  For such a registry to be effective and open to the widest range of users, it should be online and allow users to perform internal searches for different outsourcing providers. It should also be updated regularly. Perhaps the best organization to oversee such a registry would be industry oversight bodies or the chamber of commerce or the Better Business Bureau in states where a large number of companies engage in international outsourcing.

  These registries would need to provide users with effective instructions on how to report concerns and locate data on outsourcing providers. They would also need to provide different kinds of information to different companies depending on the size of the company (small business or multinational conglomerate) and the related industry. Such registries could also be made effective by having frequently asked questions (FAQ) sheets or online help functions that facilitate use and provide information on how to address problems related to international outsourcing.

Each of the afore-mentioned strategies is crucial to maintaining consistency and protecting ownership in outsourcing situations involving OSS. This list, however, is by no means comprehensive. Rather, it is a starting point that addresses some of the more fundamental aspects of OSS use in international outsourcing. For this reason, organizations might wish to address new developments in or particular uses of OSS in international outsourcing relationships.

# Future Trends

At present, international OSS use might seem to be a peripheral topic related to a limited number of activities. Certain trends in business practices and international markets, however, indicate that organizations need to explore their OSS practices now, in order to prepare for and effectively address these trends.

## The Projected Demand for Computing and IT Use in International Outsourcing

Among the areas expected to experience the greatest growth in BPO are finance, accounting, and medicine, and all of these areas of growth have one thing in common — data processing that involves computers and information technology. Many managers and bankers in the United States, for example, see international outsourcing as an effective way to address different accounting practices — particularly those related to information technology (IT). This push is in part due to the Sarbanes-Oxley Act of 2002 — section 404 of which requires chief executive officers and chief financial officers of public companies to review their internal controls over financial transactions ("404 tonnes," 2004). The costs and time associated with all of the data crunching related to such activities are massive,[1] and IT could greatly help with the compiling of information and the coordination of related activities. One way to curb costs, maximize time, and focus on computing in processing would be to outsource such activities. After all, the outsourcing of accounting and of IT work is not new and could address a lack of needed and costly domestic employees in both IT and in auditing[2] ("Relocating the back office," 2003). Given the costs related to such activities and the fact that more complex accounting practices are being outsourced, it seems reasonable to expect that some section 404 activities would be prime candidates for international outsourcing.

New U.S. healthcare legislation also seems poised to increase the international outsourcing related to IT work and data processing. The driving force behind this trend is the Health Insurance Portability and Accountability Act (HIPAA), which requires that all of an individual's medical information be placed in electronic format so it can be easily shared via computer systems (Goolsby, 2001b; Goolsby, 2001c). Under HIPAA, print medical records must be processed into a digital format — a task that is time consuming, costly, and monotonous — and maintained via an IT system for sharing such information. The projected result of such processing is massive IT costs for all health care organizations such as hospitals (Goolsby, 2001a; Goolsby, 2001c). These factors make HIPAA-related tasks, such as medical transcription and IT development and oversight, ideal candidates for international outsourcing. They also make the development and the monitoring of related IT systems prime areas for international outsourcing, especially as most healthcare providers are relatively new to such systems and their operations (Goolsby, 2001a; Salkever, 2004; "Sink or Schwinn," 2004). As so much of this financial and medical related work involves computers, it would be safe to assume that some — or many — of the outsourcing employees working on such projects would be using OSS. For this reason, the development of standard OSS practices becomes essential, not only to achieving organizational objectives, but to meeting legal requirements.

## The Value of OSS in International Marketing

OSS also has important implications for how businesses access markets in developing nations. Until quite recently, the majority of individuals within these regions had little or no access to the online environment. That factor of access, however, has changed markedly in recent years, due in large part to a mixture of public and private sector programs designed to increase global Internet use. In China, for example, the number of Internet users grew from 2.1 million in 1999 to a projected 96 million by the end of 2004, and some experts expect this number to balloon to over 200 million users by 2007 ("Wired China," 2000; "China's coming," 2004). In Africa, the United Nations and private companies have undertaken initiatives to increase online access across the continent, and Africa's number of dial-up Internet connections has grown by some 20% in the past two years while the sales of laptop computers remain strong in this part of the world ("Tapping in to Africa," 2000; Kalia, 2001; Reuters, 2002; "Laptop sales," 2004).

In Latin America, Brazil has seen its number of online users grow by 430,000 in recent months, and Global Crossings Ltd. has recently completed a project that uses fiber optics to give, "multinational companies the ability to communicate with Latin America as efficiently as with any other region" ("Active Internet users," 2004; "Tying Latin America together," 2001, p. 9). Additionally, the number of individuals going online in Eastern Europe is expected to climb from 17% to 27% by 2006, and laptop sales in the region remain strong ("IDC research," 2003; "Laptop sales," 2004).

As a result of these developments, companies can now use online media to market goods, supply, and services, and even sell and distribute digital products on an unprecedented scale in the developing world. This concept of scale, moreover, is no small matter, for the poor in many developing nations have a large combined purchasing power. The collective buying power of Rio de Janeiro's poorest residents, for example, is estimated to be some $1.2 billion ("Beyond the digital divide," 2004). The value of such aggregate overseas markets is perhaps the reason that certain companies have started developing online communication technologies that could provide the "less well off" citizens of the world with affordable online access ("Beyond the digital divide," 2004; Kalia, 2001). They have also begun developing inexpensive hubs for online access in nations such as India, Ghana, Brazil, and South Africa (Warschauer, 2003; "Beyond the digital divide," 2004).

Interaction via the Internet and the Web, however, requires the use of software (e.g., a browser) that allows a wide range of individuals to navigate the online environment. For this reason, the only way companies would be able to effectively tap these poorer overseas markets would be through the use of free or inexpensive open source software. If, however, each prospective consumer in developing nations used a different kind of OSS to interact online, then the ability of companies to tap those markets in a mass, and thus a profitable, manner is lost. The development of standards in OSS programming and use provides a mechanism for avoiding such problems. Moreover, by introducing such standards early on and to the more technologically savvy individuals engaged in international outsourcing, organizations can improve the chances that such standards will either "trickle down" or spread throughout an overall region. Thus, the development of international OSS standards has important financial implications that can extend far beyond international outsourcing.

## Conclusions

International outsourcing offers a variety of cost, time, and quality advantages to those organizations that use it effectively. In relation to the international outsourcing of knowledge work, such effectiveness often involves access to and uses of software. While open source software can provide a distinct advantage in international outsourcing situations, such uses of OSS must be guided by both client companies and overall client industries. Fortunately, uses of OSS in international outsourcing are still relatively new. For this reason, organizations have some time to develop the standards, protocols, resources, and relationships essential to effective OSS use in outsourcing contexts. The ideas presented in this chapter provide the reader with a foundation for exploring such developments. By understanding, employing, and building upon these ideas, organizations can improve the success with which they engage in international outsourcing practices both today and in the future.

## References

404 tonnes. (2004, December 16). *The Economist.* Retrieved December 27, 2004, from http://www.economist.com/displaystory.cfm?story_id=3503931

Active Internet users by country, August 2004. (2004, September 22). *ClickZ.* Retrieved October 6, 2004, from http://www.clickz.com/stats/big_picture/geographics/article.php/3410261

Atwood, M. (2004). The art of governance. *Outsourcing Center.* Retrieved December 27, 2004, from http://www.outsourcing-requests.com/center/jsp/requests/print/story.jsp?id=4616

Baily, M. N., & Farrell, D. (2004, July). Exploding the myths of offshoring. *The McKinsey Quarterly.* Retrieved November 11, 2004, from http://www.mckinseyquarterly.com/article_print.aspx?L2=7&L3=10&ar=1453

Balfour, F. (2005, February 7). Fakes! *BusinessWeek Online*. Retrieved May 31, 2005, from http://www.businessweek.com/@@ISYAAIQQjU40VAkA/magazine/content/05_06/b39 19001_mz001.htm

Bendor-Samuel, P. (2004). Lou Dobbs: Here's why you're wrong! *Outsourcing Center*. Retrieved December 20, 2004, from http://www.outsourcing-requests.com/center/jsp/requests/print/story.jsp?id=4565

Beyond the digital divide. (2004, March 13). *The Economist: Technology Quarterly Supplement,* 8.

Byrnes, N. (2005, January 1). Green eyeshades never looked so sexy. *BusinessWeek Online*. Retrieved January 5, 2005, from http://www.businessweek.com/@@na*EhYQQxu80VAkA/magazine/content/05_02/b3915041_mz011.htm

China's coming of age online. (2004, November 16). *eMarketer*. Retrieved November 17, 2004, from http://www.emarketer.com/Article.aspx?1003139&printerFriendly=yes

Clement, R. W. (1994). Culture, leadership, and power: The keys to organizational change. *LookSmart*. Retrieved March 3, 2005, from http://www.findarticle.com/p/articles/mi_m1038/is_n1_v37/ai_149

Doyle, J. F. (2004). Avoiding outsourcing pitfalls. *Outsourcing Center*. Retrieved December 12, 2004, from http://www.outsourcingrequests.com/center/jsp/requests/print/story.jsp?id=4626

Farrell, C. (2004, November 22). Giving thanks for offshoring. *BusinessWeek Online*. Retrieved December 30, 2004, from http://www.businessweek.com/pring/bwdaily/dnflash/nov2004/nf20041122_7377_dbb013

Farrell, D., & Zainulbhai, A. S. (2004). A richer future for India. *The McKinsey Quarterly*. Retrieved August 16, 2004, from http://www.mckinseyquarterly.com/article_page.aspx?ar=1440&L2+7&L3=10&srid=6&g

Friedman, T. L. (1999). *The Lexus and the olive tree*. New York: Farrar, Strass and Giroux.

Garten, J. E. (2004, June 21). Offshoring: You ain't seen nothin' yet. *BusinessWeek Online*. Retrieved December 30, 2004, from http://businessweek.com/print/magazine/content/04_25/b3888024_mz007.htm

Goolsby, K. (2001a). Healthcare's biggest challenge. *Outsourcing Center*. Retrieved December 12, 2004, from http://www.outsourcing-requests.com/center/jsp/requests/print/story.jsp?id=1660

Goolsby, K. (2001b). How to get ready for HIPPA. *Outsourcing Center*. Retrieved December 12, 2004, from http://www.outsourcing-requests.com/center/jsp/requests/print/story.jsp?id=1686

Goolsby, K. (2001c). *Perspectives on HIPPA*. Dallas, TX: Outsourcing Center.

Goolsby, K. (2004). The disgruntled employee: A holistic model addressing behaviors in outsourcing. *Outsourcing Center*. Retrieved May 6, 2005, from http://www.outsourcing-requests.com/center/jsp/requests/print/story.jsp?id=4631

Hagel, J. III. (2004). Offshoring goes on the offensive. *The McKinsey Quarterly*. Retrieved November 1, 2004, from http://www.mckinseyquarterly.com/article_page.aspx?ar=1406&L2=1&L3=106&srid=11

Hamm, S. (2004, September 27). Tech's future. *BusinessWeek,* 82-89.

Hamm, S. (2005, January 31). Linux, Inc. *Businesweek Online.* Retrieved May 2, 2005, from http://www.businessweek.com/@@p3fqe4UQ4k80VAkA/magazine/content/05_05/b3918001_mz001.htm

IDC research: Net usage up in Central and Eastern Europe. (2003, February 19). *NUA Internet Surveys.* Retrieved June 23, 2003, from http://www.nua.com/surveys/index.cgi?f=VS&art_id=905358723&rel=true

Kalia, K. (2001, July/August). Bridging global digital divides. *Silicon Alley Reporter,* 52-54.

Laptop sales continue to climb in third world. (2004, August 20). *eMarketer.* Retrieved October 27, 2004, from http://www.emarketer.com/Article.aspx?1003006&printerFriendly=yes

Lewis, W. W. (2003). Educating global workers. *The McKinsey Quarterly.* Retrieved November 10, 2004, from http://www.mckenseyquarterly.com/article_page.aspx?ar=1357&L2=7&L3=10

Malik, R. (2004, July). The new land of opportunity. *Business 2.0,* 72-79.

Nussbaum, B. (2004, September 20). Is outsourcing becoming outmoded? *BusinessWeek Online.* Retrieved October 11, 2004, from http://www.businessweek.com/print/bwdaaily/dnflash/sep2004/nf20040920_0654.htm?cha

One third of all software in use still pirated, major study finds. (2005, May 18). *IDC.* Retrieved May 31, 2005, from http://www.idc.com/getdoc.jsp?containerId=prUS00150505

Orr, G. R. (2004). What executives are asking about China. *The McKinsey Quarterly.* Retrieved October 6, 2004, from http://www.mckinseyquarterly.com/article_pring.aspx?L2=7&L3=8&ar=1478

Relocating the back office. (2003, December 11). *The Economist.* Retrieved December 20, 2003, from http://www.economist.com/displaystory.cfm?story_id=2282381

Reuters: Internet use increasing in Africa. (2002, October 1). *NUA Internet Surveys.* Retrieved June 25, 2002, from http://www.nua.com/surveys/index.cgi?f=VS&art_id=905358408&rel=true

Reuters. (2004, July 18). France outsources, Senegal calls. *Wired.* Retrieved September 20, 2004, from http://www.wired.com/news/print/0,1294,64262,00.html

Reuters. (2004, September 2). Outsourcing's next big thing – Malaysia? *News.Com.* Retrieved September 7, 2004, from http://news.com.com/2100-1011-5344618.html.

Rosenthal, B. E. (2001). Business risk. *Outsourcing Center.* Retrieved December 21, 2004, from http://www.outsourcing-requests.com/center/jsp/requests/print/story.jsp?id=1685

Rosenthal, B. E. (2004a). How real estate choices affect offshoring decisions. *Outsourcing Center.* Retrieved December 12, 2004, from http://www.outsourcing-requests.com/center/jsp/requests/print/story.jsp?id=4718

Rosenthal, B. E. (2004b). META predicts offshoring will continue to grow at 20 percent clips through 2008. *Outsourcing Center*. Retrieved December 27, 2004, from http://www.outsourcing-requests.com/center/jsp/requests/print/story.jsp?id=4714

Rosenthal, B. E. (2004c). Why the U.S. and UK are calling South African call centers. *Outsourcing Center*. Retrieved December 12, 2004, from http://www.outsourcing-requests.com/center/jsp/requests/print/story.jsp?id=4717

Salkever, A. (2004, July 7). Racing to cure sickly medical security. *BusinessWeek Online*. Retrieved December 30, 2004, from http://www.businessweek.com/print/technology/content/jul2004/tc2004077_9847_tc_171

Sandholm, L. (2004). Strategic responses for customer satisfaction. *Sandholm Associates*. Retrieved March 1, 2005, from http://www.sandholm.se/artiklar/stratrespforcustasais.html

Sink or Schwinn. (2004, November 11). *The Economist*. Retrieved December 6, 2004, from http://www.economist.com/printedition/PrinterFriendly.cfm?Story_ID=3351542

Still, B. (2004). An open source primer. In K. St. Amant & P. Zemliansky (Eds.), *Internet-based workplace communications: Industry and academic applications* (pp. 278-298). Hershey, PA: Information Science Publishing.

Tan, V. S. L. (2000, August 26). Lessons from culture change. *New Straits Times*. Retrieved February 26, 2005, from http://adtimes.nstp.com.my/jobstory/aug26a.htm

Tapping in to Africa. (2000, September 9). *The Economist*, 49.

Tying Latin American together. (2001, Summer). *NYSE Magazine*, 9.

Warschauer, M. (2003). *Technology and social inclusion: Rethinking the digital divide*. Cambridge, MA: MIT Press.

Weir, L. (2004, August 24). Boring game? Outsource it. *Wired*. Retrieved September 20, 2004, from http://www.wired.com/news/print/0,1294,64638,00.html

Wired China. (2000, July 22). *The Economist*, 24-28.

Zoellick, B. (2001). *CyberRegs: A business guide to Web property, privacy, and patents*. Boston: Addison-Wesley Professional.

# Endnotes

1 General Electric, for example, spent some $30 million in extra payments to auditors to review such documents, while J. P. Morgan Chase has 130 full-time employees working on this project, and PriceWaterhouse Coopers has spent some $40 million in training 9,000 U.S. employees to perform these functions (404 tonnes, 2004).

2 There do not appear to be enough trained U.S. auditors available to meet current demands, and as a result, this lack of supply has driven up U.S. auditor pay by some 10-20% (Byrnes, 2005).

## Chapter XII

# Real-Life Case Studies of Offshore Outsourced IS Projects: Analysis of Issues and Socio-Economic Paradigms

Subrata Chakrabarty
Texas A&M University, USA

## Abstract

*The primary purpose of this chapter is to present descriptive real-life case studies of different offshore-outsourced custom software development projects (that the author has actually worked for). The first case study discusses the practical issues in two fixed-term/fixed-price custom software development projects that were offshore-outsourced. The second case study discusses the practical issues in the offshore-outsourcing of a time and materials custom software development project to multiple vendors, which involved simultaneous insourcing, onshore-outsourcing and offshore-outsourcing. Furthermore, the observations and issues from these case studies are analyzed by comparing them with the paradigms of socio-economic theories that have been adopted extensively in the academic IS outsourcing literature (namely the agency theory, transaction cost theory, innovation diffusion theory, social exchange theory, and power-politics theory).*

# Introduction

Companies worldwide are under increasing pressure to cut costs. The price of associated software is often the deciding factor on whether to upgrade to newer and better alternatives.

Every company wants to use the best software — not just to beat the competition, but sometimes to remain in the competition. The lure of low costs and the desire for high software quality has forced companies in advanced economies to look across the horizon.

Case study-1 discusses the issues in two fixed-term/fixed-price custom software development projects that were offshore-outsourced. Case study-2 discusses the issues in the offshore-outsourcing of a time and materials custom software development project to multiple vendors, which involved simultaneous insourcing, onshore-outsourcing and offshore-outsourcing. The two case studies explain two very different approaches to offshore outsourcing of custom software development, and attempt to be of practical significance to managers and software professionals by analyzing the issues involved. The case studies provide insights into the practical and real life strategies adopted by managers to solve issues and problems in offshore-outsourcing and hence will be of value for the readers.

The observations and issues from these case studies are further analyzed by adequately comparing them with the paradigms of socio-economic theories that have been adopted extensively in the literature to study IS outsourcing. To achieve this objective, extensive literature review has been provided both in the introductory sections of this chapter and also in the later sections where the case-studies are related to the theories and paradigms. Hence, an earnest attempt has been made by the author to relate the practical real-life experiences of working in offshore-outsourced projects to the paradigms in the academic literature. This chapter can also be used for instructional purposes for teaching cases in offshore-outsourcing of custom software development projects.

It is assumed that the reader has sufficient knowledge about the fundamental concepts of insourcing, outsourcing and offshoring, and hence before we review the literature for socio economic theories and before we analyze the case studies, we proceed to only briefly describe the reasons behind the growth in offshoring of IS work, and also the primary factors that influence the choice of whether to insource or outsource.

## Discovering New Lands: The Move to Offshore

Overall there is a bright outlook for offshore sourcing of IS functions. Carmel and Agarwal (2002, p. 73), note the following:

*Our assessment is that growth will continue in sourcing IT work offshore for a number of years to come. While the growth rate slowed somewhat in 2001-2002, corporate pressures to reduce costs remained strong. However, putting a figure on the global offshore picture is difficult. Adventis, a research firm, estimates that U.S. firms will spend* *some $7 billion on third-party offshore IT work in 2002. Narrower figures give more guidance: Forrester, a U.S. research firm, found that 44 percent of U.S. firms with more than $1 billion in revenues performed IT activities offshore in 2001, and Forrester estimates that percentage will grow to 67 percent by 2003 (for comparison purposes, a Fortune 1000 firm has $1.2 billion in revenue). Note, though, that these estimates do not include offshore sourcing to wholly owned facilities. Furthermore, offshore sourcing is but a small slice of the global market in IT outsourcing (both domestic and offshore), which is estimated to be more than $100 billion (and again, this figure does not include insourcing).*

In the same vein, Dibbern, Goles, Hirschheim and Jayatilaka (2004, p. 90) note the following:

*Even the popular press (Business Week, 2003; USA Today, 2003) have reported on this issue noting that as much as 50% of IT jobs will be offshored to India and other off- and near-shore destinations in the next 10 years. Such change it is argued is nothing more than the natural progression of first moving blue-collar work (manufacturing, textile production, etc.) overseas followed by white-collar work.*

*Offshore sourcing* of IS will continue to grow for the following reasons:

1. **Modular design of certain IS tasks:** Modular design of certain IS tasks (e.g., software production) aid the offshore sourcing phenomena due to reduced transactions costs (cost of coordinating work activities between two or more parties) and because synchronization, communication, travel, supervision, feedback, and enforcing of contracts are easier (Carmel & Agarwal, 2002, p. 66).
2. **Modern technologies:** The latest technologies allow management and coordination of work across geographic distances (Carmel & Agarwal, 2002, p. 66). The Internet has greatly helped the phenomenon of IS sourcing, by allowing interested parties to easily share information. Communication technologies such as emailing, teleconferencing, videoconferencing and instant-messaging allows better coordination in spite of the geographic distances.
3. **Technical, managerial and quality capabilities:** The technical and managerial capabilities of both offshore vendors and offshore subsidiaries of onshore firms have improved (Carmel & Agarwal, 2002, p. 66). For example, India is reported to have over 150 software development and maintenance firms that have attained the Software Engineering Institute's 'Capability Maturity Model' (SEI CMM) level 4 or level 5 (Dibbern et al., 2004, p. 90).
4. **High cost savings:** Lower cost of offshore outsourcing in comparison to domestic outsourcing (primarily due to lower salary levels of offshore personnel) is a big driver behind offshore outsourcing (Carmel & Agarwal, 2002; Sobol & Apte, 1995; Apte & Mason, 1995, p. 1252).
5. **Skilled labor pool:** There is sizable supply of qualified labor in many offshore destinations like India (Carmel & Agarwal, 2002; Apte & Mason, 1995, p. 1252).

6. **Scalability:** The sizable supply of qualified low-cost personnel allows offshore vendors to have a certain number of personnel in the "*waiting mode*", that is, waiting to be assigned to projects, and are used to quickly ramp-up projects when the need arises. Having a number of personnel in the "*waiting mode*" for being assigned to projects is also known as "*bench strength*," and allows the vendor to respond to client requirements in a very short cycle.
7. **Fastest time to market by working round the clock:** Potentially all 24 hours of the day can be devoted to any task, by globally distributing the work across multiple time zones. This for example can lead to a faster cycle time for software production (Apte & Mason, 1995, p. 1252), allow continuous monitoring of critical IS functions and infrastructure, and allow 24x7 operations (needed for customer service, etc.).
8. **Entry to large markets with high growth potential:** Many of the favorite locations for offshore sourcing like China and India are also large and growing markets. It might be strategically important to establish an early presence in such developing countries which have a higher growth potential than the relatively mature developed countries (Apte & Mason, 1995, p. 1252).

However there are some concerns about offshore sourcing which include problems of communication and coordination, cultural differences, lack of trust, difficulties in arranging visas/work-permits, offshore-unit's lack of domain knowledge, lack of control over quality and schedule, possible violation of intellectual property rights, unclear government attitude towards cross border data flow and trade-in services, inadequate infrastructure in the vendor's home country, and possibility of an unstable economic, political, or social environment (Carmel & Agarwal, 2002, p. 68; Sobol & Apte, 1995, p. 271; Apte & Mason, 1995, pp. 1252-1253).

## The Choice between Insourcing and Outsourcing

Costs (as indicated by relative efficiency in carrying out IS activities) and strategic importance have been the primary drivers behind the decision on whether to insource from an internal IS department or to outsource to a vendor. The *strategic importance* and the *relative efficiency in carrying out an IS activity in-house* determines the choice between insourcing and outsourcing (Apte & Mason, 1995, p. 1258; Dibbern et. al., 2004, p. 33):

- *Insourcing* is the best option when both the *strategic importance* and the *relative efficiency in carrying out the IS activity in-house* are high.
- *Outsourcing* should be preferred when both the *strategic importance* and the *relative efficiency in carrying out the IS activity in-house* are low.
- The option would be to either build a *strategic partnership* or to *invest* in acquiring the necessary capabilities, when the *strategic importance* is high but the *relative efficiency* is low.
- The establishment of a *profit center (subsidiary)* to offer IS functions in the marketplace should be considered when there is *high relative internal efficiency*.

# The Socio-Economic Theories

Since this book deals with the socio-economic perspective, the economic theories and social/organizational theories and the relevant literature will be later used to analyze the case studies. We briefly describe the *economic* theories such as *agency theory* and *transaction cost theory* and also the *social/organizational* theories like *innovation diffusion theory*, *exchange theory*, and *power-politics theory* that have been applied in IS outsourcing literature (Dibbern et al., 2004, pp. 99-102). The adoption of these theories in the relevant IS outsourcing literature, and their linkage with the case studies to be presented, will be adequately dealt with in a later section that comparatively analyzes the practical case-studies with the academic paradigms in literature.

## *Agency Theory*

The *agency theory* or *the theory of ownership structure* considers the firm to be a complex process in which the divergent interests of individuals are brought into equilibrium within a legal framework of contractual relations (Jensen & Meckling, 1976, p. 311). This is illustrated in Figure 1.

Jensen and Meckling (1976, p. 308) define an *agency relationship* as: "a contract under which one or more persons (the *principal(s)*) engage another person (the *agent*) to perform some service on their behalf which involves delegating some decision making authority to the agent," and have further introduced *agency costs* as the sum of *monitoring costs*, *bonding costs* and *residual loss costs* incurred by the *principal*. It is assumed that there is always divergence and conflict of interests between the *principal* and the *agent*, which can be limited by the *principal* by establishing appropriate incentives and by incurring costs. In the IS outsourcing scenario, the principal may be assumed to be the client, while the agent may be assumed to be the vendor.

*Monitoring costs* are incurred by the *principal* to restrict he aberrant behavior of the *agent*, and includes efforts to measure, observe, and control the behavior the agent.

*Figure 1. Agency theory: Principal agent relationship*

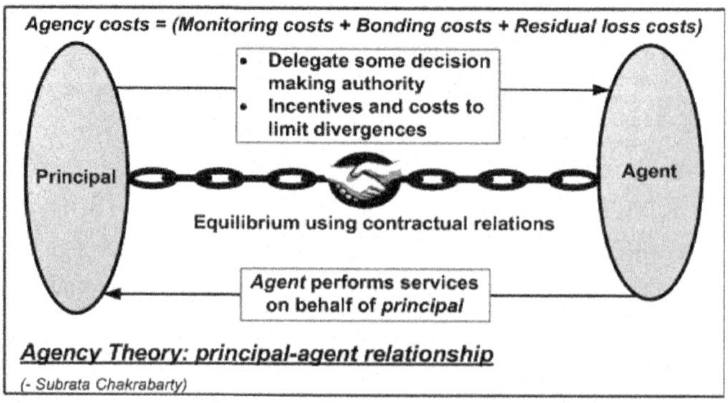

*Figure 2. Transaction cost theory: Analogy*

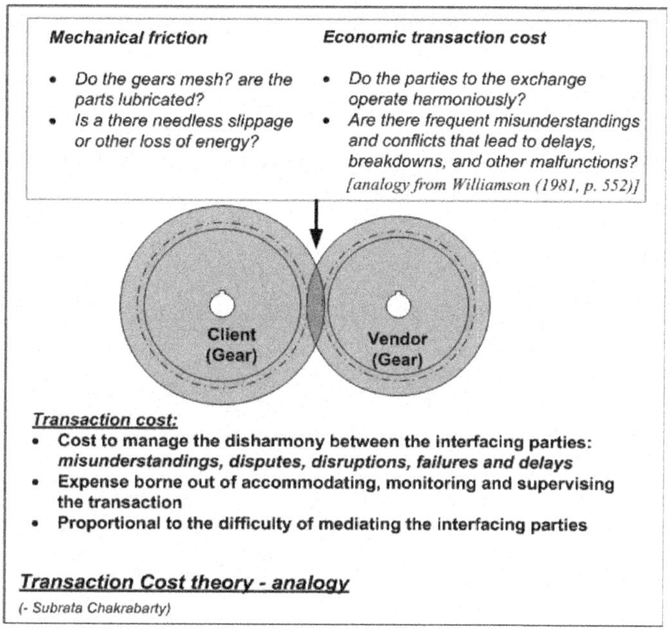


*Bonding costs* are incurred by the *principal* to guarantee that the *agent* will not act in a disadvantageous or harmful way, and in the case that the *agent* does take such aberrant actions the *principal* will be compensated. *Residual loss costs* is the monetary equivalent of the reduction in welfare experienced by the *principal* due to divergence between the *agent's* decisions and those decisions that could have ideally maximized the welfare of the *principal* (Jensen & Meckling, 1976).

## Transaction Cost Theory

When goods or services are transferred across a technologically separable interface such that one activity phase terminates and another begins, a "transaction" is said to have occurred (Williamson, 1981, p. 552). Hence, a transaction involves transfers or exchanges between parties (for example, clients and vendors in an outsourcing relationship) across an interface. A transaction occurs smoothly if the interfacing between the involved parties is trouble free. However, if the parties operate in a non harmonious manner, with misunderstandings, disputes, disruptions, failures and delays, it results in a "*transaction cost*" to manage the disharmony between the interfacing parties. The *transaction cost* is the expense borne out of accommodating, monitoring and supervising the transaction between parties, and is proportional to the difficulty of mediating the interfacing parties.

Williamson (1981, p. 552) gives the analogy of meshing of gears, which certainly helps in the understanding of costs due to "frictions" (see Figure 2) between clients and vendors in an IS outsourcing relationship:

*In mechanical systems we look for frictions: do the gears mesh, are the parts lubricated, is a there needless slippage or other loss of energy? The economic counterpart of friction is transaction cost: do the parties to the exchange operate harmoniously, or are there frequent misunderstandings and conflicts that lead to delays, breakdowns, and other malfunctions?*

## *Innovation Diffusion Theory*

Organizations, countries and various social systems have to often incorporate innovative new technologies or processes. The IS outsourcing process has been considered to be an innovation, which needs to be adopted, and diffused (Loh & Venkatraman, 1992b; Hu, Saunders, & Gebelt, 1997). *Adoption* of *innovations* involves the conscious decision to accept and use such new technologies and processes, and *diffusion* involves the process of spreading them into the social system (Daft, 1978, pp. 195-197; Rogers, 1983, as cited in Dibbern et al., 2004, p. 19). This is illustrated in Figure 3.

## *Social Exchange Theory*

Blau (1964, as cited in Dibbern et al., 2004, p. 19) defined *social exchange* as the *"voluntary actions of individuals that are motivated by the returns they are expected to bring and typically do in fact bring from others"* (see Figure 4). The IS outsourcing relationship can be considered to be a social exchange between clients and vendors.

*Figure 3. Innovation diffusion theory*

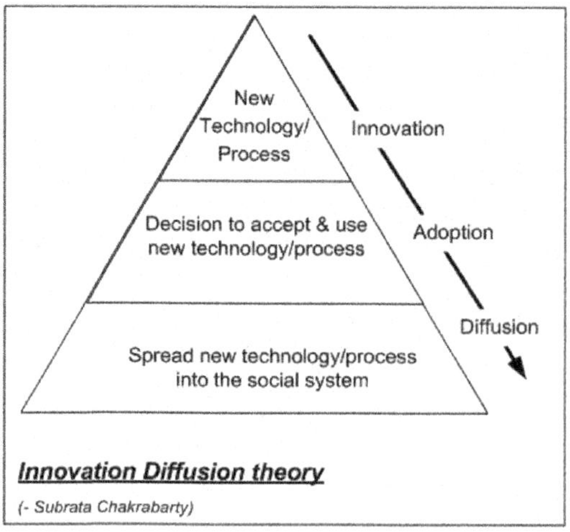

*Figure 4. Exchange theory*

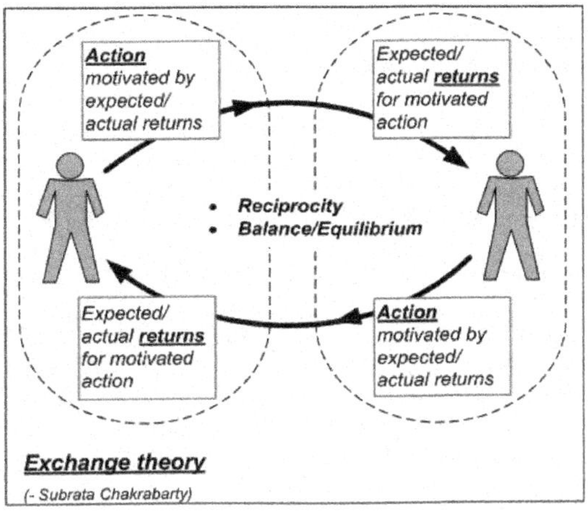


Emerson (1972, as cited in Dibbern et al., 2004, p. 19) noted the following social exchange attributes, which are highly applicable to the outsourcing scenario where the clients and vendors are the parties involved in the social exchange:

- **Reciprocity:** A mutual exchange as a result of the need to reciprocate the benefits received.
- **Balance:** There is an equilibrium or equality in distribution due to mutual dependence between each of the actors in an exchange.
- **Cohesion:** When one or both actors in the exchange run into a conflict involving the exchange.
- **Power:** The amount of monetary influence one can exercise on the other.

## *Power Politics Theory*

Markus (1983, pp. 442) states the following about power and politics:

*Intraorganizational power is an attribute of individuals or subgroups, such as departments, within the organization; it can be defined as the ability to get one's way in the face of opposition or resistance to those desires. There are a number of ways by which an individual or subgroup can come to have power in an organization, including personal characteristics, such as being an expert or being charismatic, but position in the formal structure of the organization often provides greater access to specific power resources and the legitimacy required to use them.*

Organizations have people that wield *power*, that is, they posses a controlling influence and the qualities needed to get things done as per their wishes. The presence of entities with differential *power* in social relations results in *politics*. Exercising *power* often involves maneuvering social relations to gain control and *politics* is the process of exercising *power* in human decision-making. Not surprisingly, power and politics play a big role in IS outsourcing relationships.

# Case Study-1: Offshore Outsourcing of Fixed-Term, Fixed-Price Custom Software Development Projects

This real-life case study gives descriptive accounts of the business scenario, personnel distribution and project life-cycle for two custom software development projects that were offshore-outsourced by a client.

(Though this is a real life case, the actual names of the firms and projects have been replaced with fictitious names.)

## Business Scenario, Relationship Issues and Strategies

### *The Stakeholders*

*'Vendor'* is a large India based CMM level-5 software service provider. '*Old-Client*' was a small UK based telecommunications company. '*New-Client'* is a relatively larger telecommunications company based in both UK and U.S.A. that acquired *'Old-Client'*.

### *The Information Systems to be Custom Developed*

'*Vendor,*' had developed a "sales and commission management" software system for '*Old-Client*' in *Year-1*, which was very well received by *'Old-Client'* and an excellent relationship was established between the two.

'*New-Client*' later acquired *'Old-Client'* and other companies, and had therefore ended up with diverse software systems from different companies (see Figure 5).

'*New-Client*' decided to consolidate its various customer care related IS applications. Parts of the initiative were two projects - (1) *CRM-Europe:* a new Customer Relationship Management (CRM) software system needed for their Europe operations and (2) *CRM-NA:* a new CRM software system needed for their North America (NA) operations.

Each of the CRM systems were designed to replace the current legacy systems and to provide a Web-based front-end for call centers having customers in Europe and North America respectively. For each continent, the respective CRM system would be used to maintain customer data, track all customer interactions and provide a standard look and feel.

The guiding principles were data consolidation and application consolidation. To provide users with rapid access to better quality data, efforts were made to consolidate multiple data sources into one database. Interfaces were developed for the few other databases that had to remain independent and could not be consolidated (for example, it was decided to keep the billing database independent of the consolidation program). The CRM software would call these interfaces to read/write data from/to these few remaining independent databases. Similarly, to give users access a reliable one-stop application, the multiple legacy applications would be replaced the CRM application software.

Each of the new CRM systems were deployed in a three-tier architecture where data was stored on the database server, the application containing business logic was stored and run on the application server, and access to information was provided from an user-interface (Internet browser) that runs on desktop machine.

*Figure 5. Case study-1: Offshore outsourcing - Business scenario*

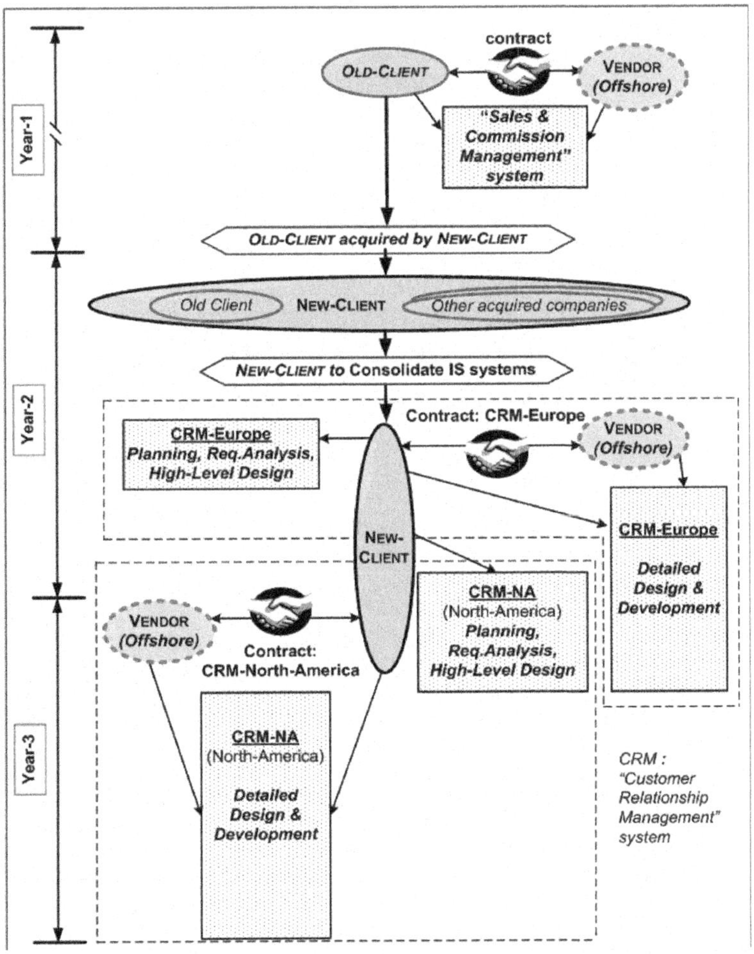

## *The Contractual Negotiations and Relationship Building Issues*

After going through a bidding process, '*Vendor* signed a contract with *New-Client* to develop the new *CRM-Europe* software system. The fact that '*Vendor* had done a good job for '*Old-Client*' was one of the positive factors that helped *Vendor* bag the deal. This new relationship between '*Vendor*' and '*New-Client*' was not always comfortable primarily due to the very strict deadline for project completion, and the client's inexperience with offshore-outsourcing. The project was however delivered within budget and in time by cutting down on a few difficult but relatively unimportant functionalities (reducing scope of the project), and went *live* into production during the early part of *Year-3* (see Figure 5).

For the contract for *CRM-NA*, there were extensive negotiations between '*New-Client*' and '*Vendor*'. The '*New-Client*' contended that the new *CRM-NA* system should be cheaper since the '*Vendor*' could re-use much of the code already developed for the *CRM-Europe* system that had similar business functionality, and similar look and feel. However, the '*Vendor*' contended that though the overall look and feel of the user interface was similar, the database schema was drastically different and larger, the number of validations and error checks were much higher, the number of interfaces were greater, and the business functionality was much more complicated for the proposed *CRM-NA* project. '*Vendor*' further added that though a lot of helpful domain knowledge was gained from the Europe scenario, there is no valid case for re-use of code due to the mentioned factors. The deal was finally signed at price higher than that of *CRM-Europe*,

*Figure 6. Case study-1: Offshore outsourcing: Personnel distribution*

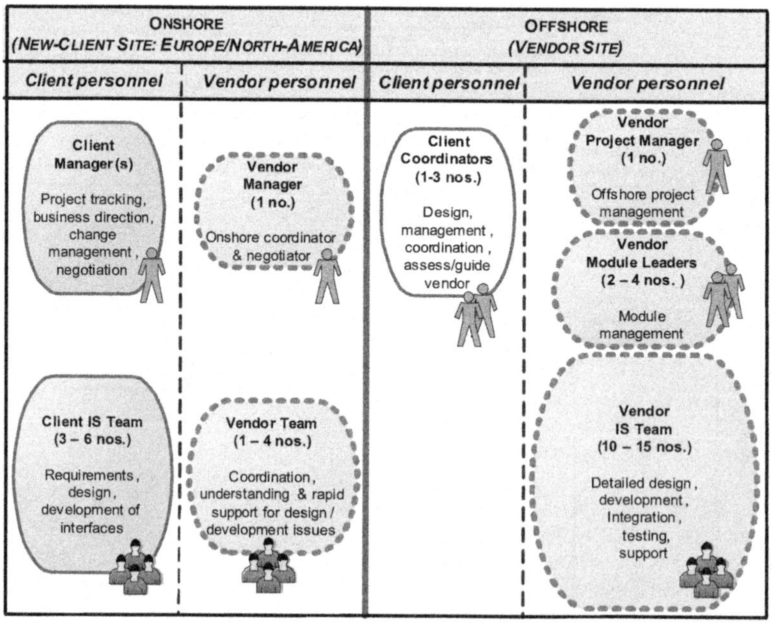

but it was much lower than what the vendor had estimated for *CRM-NA*. On a mutually positive note, '*New-Client*' offered a more realistic deadline for project completion, when compared to the stringent *CRM-Europe* deadline.

This second project executed by '*Vendor*' for the North American operations of '*New-Client*', was a more complicated system with a different database schema. Both '*Vendor*' and '*New-Client*' had learned their lessons from their experience and this time the mutual relationship was very comfortable. The project was delivered well within budget and in time, with additional innovative functionalities that made *'New-Client'* very happy with the performance of '*Vendor*'.

All the contracts signed by '*Vendor*' were of the "*fixed-term, fixed-price*" (Currie, 1996, pp. 232-234) kind, where the deadlines were set, and the price for the entire project was fixed. However if there was a change in the scope of the project (change in design/ requirements) then the vendor could charge additionally for it in proportion to the additional effort required.

From the client's point of view, an advantage of "*fixed-price, fixed-term*" contract is that the cost is known and agreed even before the project starts. However, the disadvantage is that the project can get tied down to the contracted price and any change, for whatever reason, may require a time-consuming negotiation with the vendor where every change can increase the time & money required to complete the project. All such changes are formalized in a written "*Change Order*" or "*Change Request*" document.

## Personnel Distribution Issues and Strategies

The personnel distribution for both *CRM-Europe* and *CRM-NA* projects were similar. The total number of personnel required for *CRM-NA* was only slightly higher than that for *CRM-Europe*, and we consider both these projects in unison (see Figure 6).

### *Personnel Distribution at Client Site*

At the *client site (onshore)*, vendor personnel are present to coordinate effectively with the client personnel. The *client managers* track projects, give direction to future business strategies, negotiate, and handle both technological and organizational change management. In the context of the CRM projects, the *client's IS Team*, that is, the client's internal IS department gather and structure requirements, design systems, and develop interfaces. The *onshore vendor manager* is the principal coordinator and negotiator. The *onshore vendor team* takes pains to understand the client needs, communicates the client needs to offshore, and provides rapid support for design & development issues.

### *Personnel Distribution at Vendor Site*

At the offshore vendor site, the *project manager* has *module leaders* reporting to him. The offshored project is broken down into smaller manageable modules and each module is managed by a *module leader*. The *vendor's IS team* is similarly distributed within each of these modules, where they take care of tasks like low-level (detailed) design, development, integration, testing and post deployment support. The project *manager* and *module leaders* coordinate with the client and vendor personnel at onshore and offshore, to make sure that the project is right on track.

### *Personnel Interaction and Movement*

Sometimes the client may decide to send its *coordinators* (who are generally mid-level managers) to the vendor's offshore site for a few weeks or even months. This is different from the usual client visits to offshore that last only a few days. The *client coordinators* spend time discussing the high-level design with the vendor personnel, keep track of the project progress, and proactively assess and guide the vendor to ensure smooth project execution. Sending such *client coordinators* to offshore for weeks and even months are actually rare. However in this scenario, the *client coordinators* were more than willing to come & stay at offshore, since the offshore country also happened to be their country of birth.

## Project Life-Cycle Issues and Strategies

Though the project life-cycle for both the *CRM-Europe* and *CRM-NA* projects were similar, the outcomes were different. The *CRM-Europe* project was successful in terms of meeting the budget and time, however it was a failure in terms of keeping the client happy and matching their non-budget & non-cost expectations. The *CRM-NA* project was not just successful in terms of cost of time; it also delighted the customers with its smooth execution, value additions to the software and the overall feeling of bonhomie. We will first discuss the similar aspects of the both the project life-cycles and then discuss the intricate differentiating factors between the two projects.

### *Requirements Analysis and Design*

'*New-Client*' always tried to complete the requirement analysis, architecture design, database design and high level application design before engaging '*Vendor*'. If done properly, this an excellent practice since it shows that the client is sure of what it wants.

The life-cycles for the projects executed are shown in Figure 7. As soon as the vendor enters the project, it sends its personnel to the client site (onshore) to understand the requirements and design, and if anything is found undoable then they are encouraged to negotiate and offer alternative solutions. Design documents are also sent offshore, where the *offshore vendor personnel* study them in depth, and ask for clarifications to the vendor personnel at onshore, who in turn discuss the same with the client personnel if needed.

Once the *offshore vendor team* has significant comprehension of the requirements, architecture, database design, and high level application design, it starts to work on the low-level (detailed) design documents that delve deep into the design and sometimes even go to the extent of specifying the programming logic to be adopted.

*Figure 7. Case study 1: Offshore outsourcing - Project life-cycle*

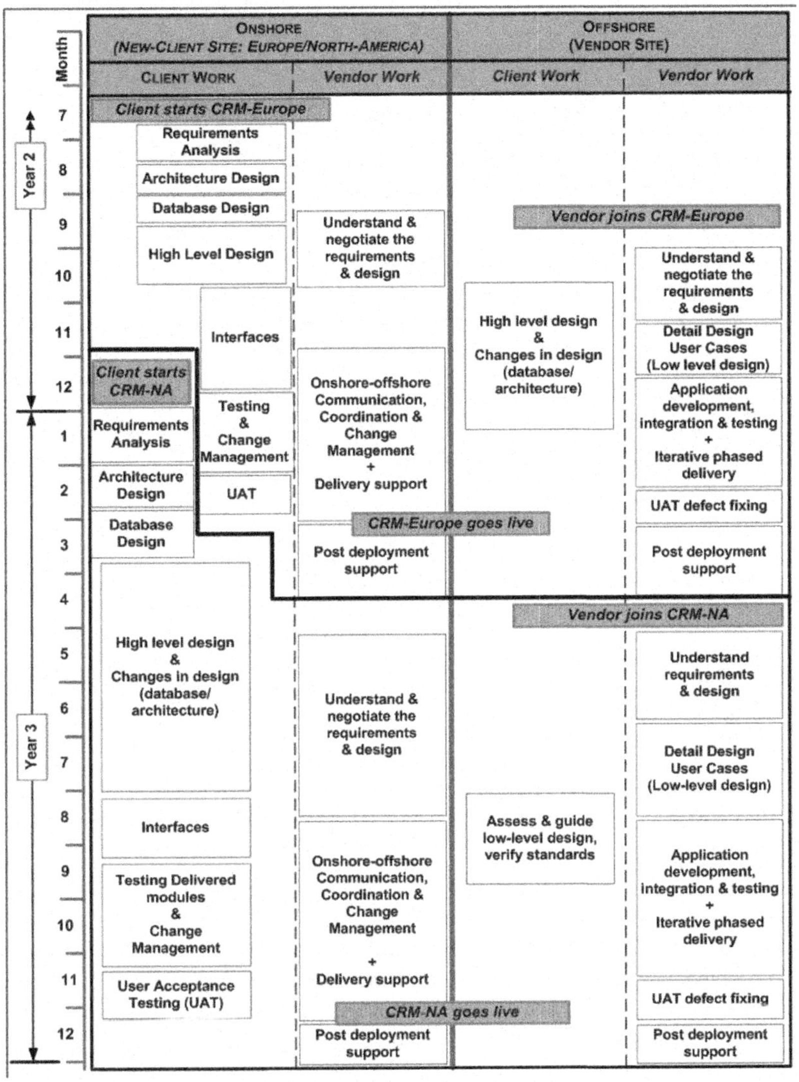


Meanwhile, the *client's IS team* works on the interfaces that will be used by the application to be developed by the vendor, and this involves the design, development, testing and documentation of the interfaces. These interfaces will be used by the CRM software to read from and write into various other databases used by the client's multiple systems, and also to send commands to various network devices. Around this time, *client coordinators* may go to the offshore vendor site, to discuss the design, assess and guide the *offshore vendor personnel*.

*Figure 8. Case study-1: Offshore outsourcing - iterative delivery*

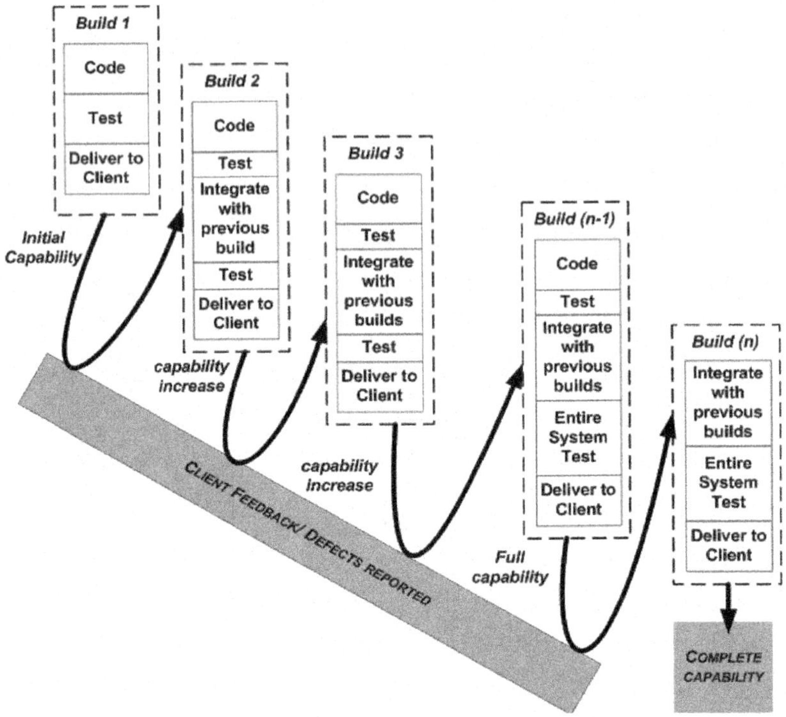


## *Programming, Integration, Testing and Delivery*

After the low-level design has been completed, the *vendor* starts the process of programming, integrating and testing. The vendor delivers the system to client in an iterative fashion that comprises of intermediate phased deliveries or *iterations;* that is the system is segmented into "*builds*" and each *build* is delivered in a phased iterative manner (see Figure 8). This way the client can continually test and give feedback on the system being developed, and also keep track of the project progress. This also allows the client's IS team that was developing interfaces for the CRM system to test the effectiveness of their interfaces. Delivering important system functionalities in early iterations is an effective risk management strategy by the vendor. Hence, instead of having just one final delivery of completed code, the delivery of tested code is made iteratively to the client. Each such iterative delivery of code activates some significant aspect of the software being developed, which can now be tested by the client.

Once the vendor finishes coding and testing the entire application, it is delivered to the client for user acceptance testing (UAT), where the prospective users of the system test it and report defects and desired changes. Once the vendor addresses all the issues reported during UAT, the application is ready to go live into production. After the deployment of the system, vendor teams at both onshore and offshore, work on the real time problems being reported by the users.

## Successful vs. Very Successful: A Comparative Analysis of Issues

As we know, the CRM-NA project was more successful CRM-Europe in terms of the extent to which it pleased the customers with its smooth execution, value additions to the software and the overall feeling of bonhomie. The reasons for these are intricate, and are not apparent on the surface of these two projects.

### *Maturity of Relationship Over Time*

The *CRM-Europe* project started off with the client's considerable mistrust & apprehensions about offshore-outsourcing, primarily borne out of their inexperience in handling such scenarios. '*New Client*' was motivated to go for offshore outsourcing primarily because of its sudden need for high quality skills to develop the system at a low cost, and was inspired by the good experience of '*Old-Client*'; however, the mistrust & apprehensions existed. After the *CRM-Europe* project achieved its budgeted cost and time goals, the client became more comfortable with the process of offshore-outsourcing, which in turn had a positive affect on the execution of *CRM-NA*.

### *Defining the Project Scope and Requirements*

The scope of *CRM-Europe* project was not well defined. The requirements could be interpreted many ways. Often, a seemly innocuous requirement had more hidden requirements within. The client's interpretation of the desired need was often a flashy complicated one, while that of the vendor was a simple easy-to-code one. The client found it difficult to state what it exactly wanted, and the vendor in its efforts keep the client happy often accepted such vague requests without protest. However, when matters reached a stage where the vendor could no longer accommodate such requests without incurring substantial extra costs, resultant negotiations got messy. The client would negotiate based on its flashy (costly) interpretation of a requirement, while the vendor would negotiate based on its easy-to-code interpretation of a requirement. Another problem was that the *seed data* provided by the client to test the system being developed were of a different format in comparison to the *actual confidential data* used by the client. This led to the system functioning erratically in a real time testing environment. Comparatively, the scope of *CRM-NA* project was well defined with fewer hidden requirements. For the *CRM-NA* project, the vendor insisted for a more formal and documented protocol to negotiate *change requests* and possible multiple interpretations of requirements, and also requested the client for prototypes, extensive data models, and quality seed data at the earliest possible stage of the life-cycle.

### *Verification of Requirements and Design*

In *CRM-Europe*, the vendor would blindly assume the client's requirements and design to be perfect and carry on with the development only to discover flaws at a much later stage. But in *CRM-NA* the vendor would spend considerable time early on (before coding) to find possible flaws the client's requirements and design. This approach of searching for flaws in the client's design at an early stage, led to a relatively risk free execution of the project.

## Lessons Learned and Trends

Both the offshore-outsourced projects were successful, and the degree of delight associated with the success increased with greater experience, maturity and better management from both the client and the vendor. In "*fixed-term, fixed-price*" projects, where the deadlines, the price and the scope for the entire project is fixed, it is important to use maximum rigor in defining and verifying the requirements and design. All procedures and processes need to well planned and executed with the cooperation of all stakeholders.

The "*fixed-term, fixed-price*" offshore-outsourcing of projects is a preferred option when the client is very sure of its costs estimates, schedule estimates, and project requirements and can effectively document the same in its contract and project requirement/design documents. As the software project cost and schedule estimation methodologies and tools improve, and as software architects gain more experience with confidently defining and documenting project requirements, the usage of "*fixed-term, fixed-price*" contracts for offshore outsourcing may increase.

# Case Study-2: Offshore Outsourcing of Custom Software Development to Multiple Vendors Under Time and Materials Contract

This real-life case study gives a descriptive account of the business scenario, personnel distribution and project life-cycle of a custom software development project that involved simultaneous insourcing, onshore-outsourcing and offshore-outsourcing.

(Though this is a real life case, the actual names of the firms and projects have been replaced with fictitious names.)

## Business Scenario, Relationship Issues And Strategies

### *The Stakeholders*

'*Client*' is one of Europe's leading providers of telecommunications services. Its principal activities include local, national and international telecommunications services, broadband and Internet products and services.

*Vendor-1* is a very large offshore (India) based CMM level-5 service provider. As stated earlier, it started off with an onshore role & now also has a very significant offshore role. *Vendor-2* is an onshore (Europe) based service provider and also a product seller. In fact, all the vendors use *Vendor-2's* network management software tools/products. *Vendor-3* is a small onshore (Europe) based service provider. *Vendor-4* is a joint venture between the '*Client*' (in Europe) and an offshore partner (in India); however, their role in this project is purely onshore. All teams work both cooperatively and competitively for the project as one large unit.

### *Relationship Building Between 'Client' and 'Vendor-1', and the IS Projects*

The business scenario is illustrated in Figure 9. *'Client'* started its engagement with *Vendor-1* with two projects: *NMS (Network Management software System)* and *VVT (Verification, Validation and Testing)*.

*Figure 9. Case study-2: Offshore outsourcing - Business scenario*

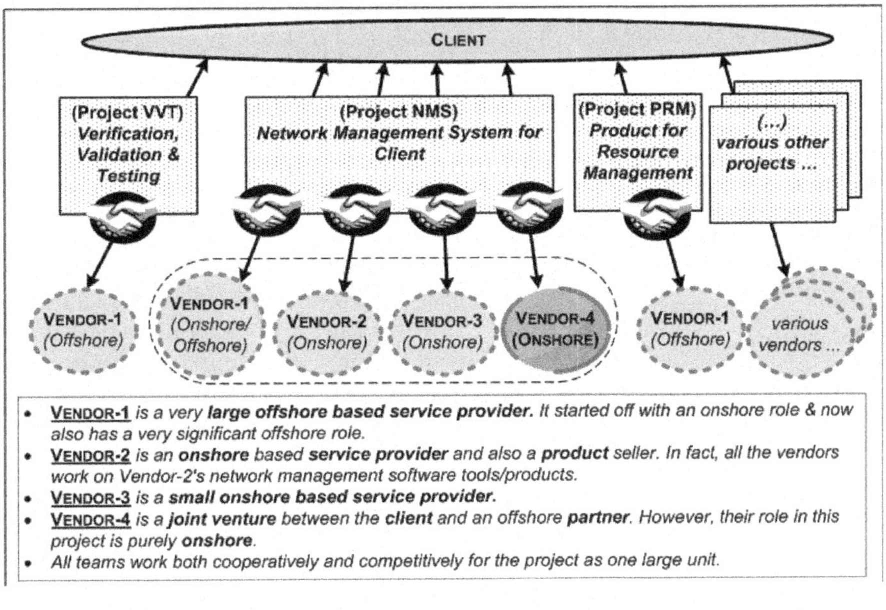

*NMS* was an ongoing evolutionary project where *Vendor-1* was the new entrant, while the three other vendors (*Vendor-2, Vendor-3* and *Vendor-4*) were already working for the same project. The *NMS* project had started and the first version had gone live into production around three years before *Vendor-1* entered the project at onshore. '*VVT*' was a new project with *Vendor-1* as the sole vendor, and it involved the verification, validation and testing of the various software technologies & applications being developed by the client.

The first project to be offshored by the client to *Vendor-1* was *VVT*, and expectations were high as future business deals were at stake. Despite tough times, the *VVT* project led the way in enhancing the "offshoring" image of *Vendor-1*, and gave the client the confidence to try *Vendor-1's* offshore capabilities even further. For *NMS, Vendor-1* initially started the engagement by sending six of its software professionals to the onshore client-site, and soon the client's positive experience in offshoring *VVT* project gave it the confidence to try offshoring of NMS project, too.

*Vendor-1* was the only team in the *NMS* project that grew, and also increased its work portfolio to include various levels of development, design and testing. In a matter of nine months the total number of offshore *Vendor-1* personnel for *NMS* increased from 0 to 25, while the total number of onshore vendor personnel (inclusive of all vendors) remained stagnant. For the *NMS* project, the total number of offshore personnel was now greater than the total number onshore personnel.

Encouraged by the offshoring experience with *Vendor-1*, the client then decided to try offshore-outsourcing of some of its product development work too. *PRM*, a *Product for Resource Management* that was conceptualized by the client was offshore-outsourced. *Vendor-1* will carry out development work at offshore over the next three years to productize *PRM* for the client. The client will give the necessary domain knowledge, requirements and design to the vendor. The client will then sell it to the market, by capitalizing on its own esteemed standing in the telecom industry. Vendor-1 has created an enhanced visual experience of the *PRM* prototype and also worked on redesigning the PRM database.

In this case study we will concentrate on *NMS* project, which is an interesting case of simultaneous insourcing, onshore-outsourcing and offshore-outsourcing.

## *Contractual Specifications*

All the contracts signed by the client for the *NMS* project were of the "*time and materials*" (Currie, 1996, pp. 232-234) kind, where the project is seen as a continuum and is open to change, with the payments being made at pre-specified time intervals on the basis of the amount of vendor resources being used by the client. For example, the vendor bills the client for each of its software professionals on the project on an hourly basis, irrespective of the scope of the project work.

From the client's point of view, an advantage of a "*time and materials*" contract is that the task details can be worked out as the project progresses, and unforeseen changes are an expected part of the process. However, since the final costs are proportional to the utilization of vendor resources by the client, there is very little opportunity for the client to negotiate a bargain or a package deal.

## Personnel Distribution Issues And Strategies

### *Reporting Structure at Onshore and Offshore*

As shown in Figure 10, the vendor teams at onshore report directly to the client manager. Also, *Vendor-1*'s offshore project manager leads the team at offshore and directly reports to the onshore client manager(s).

### *Cooperation and Communication Issues within Vendors*

There is a significant challenge here for *Vendor-1*, who is a new entrant in the NMS project. The *Vendor-1* personnel have to work with other established competitors like *Vendor-2, Vendor-3* and *Vendor-4*; all fighting for the same piece of cake, and all working together in a team! *Vendor-2* & *Vendor-4* personnel are onshore based vendors and consider the *offshoring* trend to be a serious threat to their own growth. As discussed earlier, *Vendor1's* offshore team was the only team in the NMS project that grew, while all the other vendor team sizes remained stagnant. There is also a concern that at some point the vendor team sizes at onshore may actually be reduced, and both existing & new work may be sent offshore to take advantage of the availability of low-cost-high-quality skills. Hence consciously or unconsciously other vendors are often non-cooperative towards *Vendor-1*.

*Figure 10. Case study-2: Offshore outsourcing - Personnel distribution*

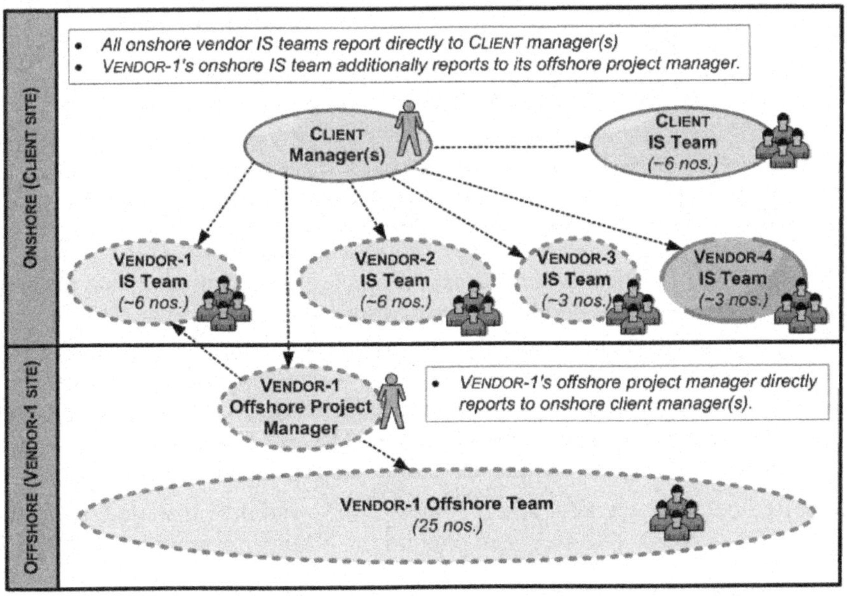

### *Issues with the Client's Multiple-Vendor Sourcing Strategy — Introducing Competitiveness*

In fact, the client induces such competitive spirit among the vendors as a shrewd tactic. By inducing such competition among vendors, the client manages to derive maximum effort and dedication out of the vendors, who all want to prove themselves as the best to get more business from the client. Also, this strategy of having multiple vendors working together for a project prevents the client from being overly dependent on any one vendor. However such competition can also have negative consequences. The competitive atmosphere among vendors motivates them to sometimes be selfish and non-cooperative. The vendor personnel may not always act with the best interests of the project in mind. There is often a desire to show the other vendors in bad light, while trying to gain maximum self credit for at every conceivable opportunity. This causes serious teamwork issues within the NMS project unit, and client management often steps in to douse the fire, and tries to make the competition among the vendors more positive than negative, for example, the client appraises a vendor's performance on its cooperative attitude and teamwork skills. Vendor-1 on the other hand, is trying to gain maximum cooperation from other vendors by simply being highly polite, highly cooperative and professional, and has been quite successful at it.

## Project Life-Cycle Issues and Strategies

### *Issues with the NMS Project*

Large systems like NMS have a long lifetime. The telecom industry is changing fast with newer technologies being adopted at a rapid pace. The NMS system must evolve continually to meet the changing requirements. The NMS system has been changing dramatically during its lifetime in response to the rapidly changing telecom environment, and hence the latest evolution of the NMS system has little resemblance to its first version.

### *The Evolutionary Approach to Custom Software Development*

As shown in Figure 11, the *market* and *user* needs are first evaluated, and the possible "increments" that need to be added to the software are estimated. The requirements for the increments/enhancements are analyzed, engineered, validated and then structured into small *modules* or *work packages*. Each such *module* or *work package* can be considered as small a mini-project that needs to be designed, have its design verified, developed, tested and finally integrated into the NMS. The NMS with the latest module integrated is now verified, validated, and tested, and defects (if any) are reported.

Each reported defect is tracked, and the latest NMS system is installed only after the defects have been fixed. The users can operate the NMS system with the new features

*Figure 11. Case study-2: Offshore outsourcing - Project life-cycle*

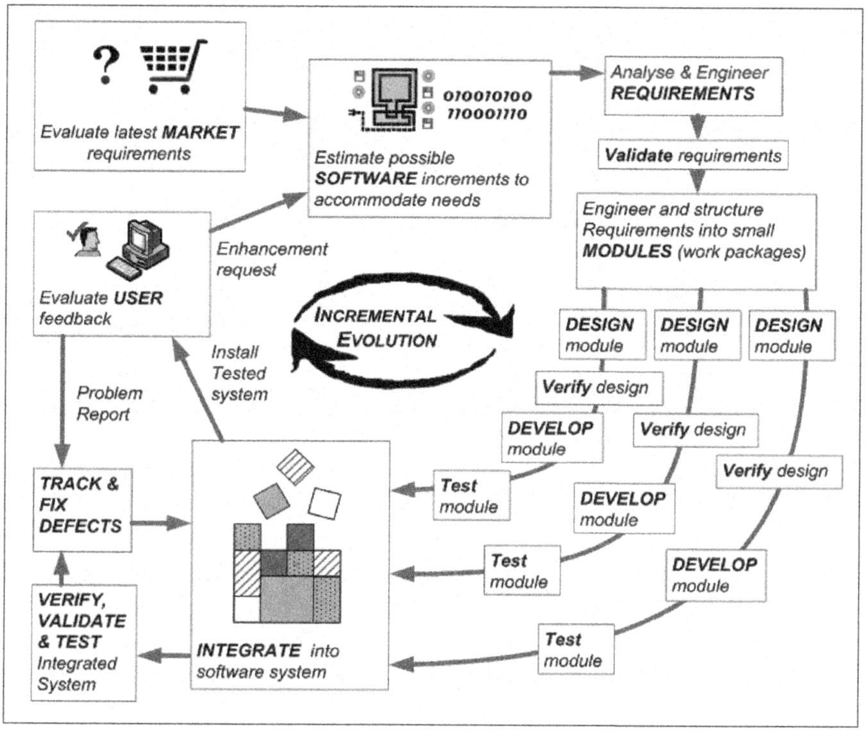


(i.e., the modules), and report any problem back to the testing team, or request further enhancements.

## Lessons Learned and Trends

Companies sometimes form relationships with multiple vendors as a risk mitigation measure (Chaudhury et al., 1995; Cross, 1995). The client has taken up the challenge outsourcing to multiple vendors, inducing competition among the vendors, encouraging cooperation amongst competing vendors, and not being too dependent on any particular vendor. They have been successful at it.

Also, as a new entrant, Vendor-1 convinced the client of the possible low-cost-high-quality advantages of offshoring by its good performances and hence managed to turn the tide in its favor.

The "*time and materials*" contracts combined with the incremental-evolutionary model of offshore-outsourcing custom software development projects is a preferred option when the client is not very sure of its costs estimates, schedule estimates, or project requirements. The client has the liberty to change the requirements, cost estimates, schedule estimates as and when the market or the users demand a change, and implement them in the evolving software system as modularized increments. In a volatile business and technology environment where market, customer and end-user needs are unstable and can changeable, the time and materials contracts combined with incremental-evolutionary model of software development are a feasible offshore-outsourcing option.

# Comparative Analysis of Issues in Case Studies with Socio-Economic Paradigms in Literature

## Offshore-Outsourcing is a Feasible Alternative

As explained in the earlier section "discovering new lands — the move to offshore," offshore outsourcing does have many advantages despite the many hurdles it faces. The real life case studies (the CRM-Europe/NA and NMS projects) highlighted that despite various difficulties, offshore outsourcing does work. In both the cases, various problems had to be overcome by the vendor:

- Communication, coordination and cultural issues were sorted out, and these improved over time
- Degree of mutual trust increased over time, especially since the vendor was able to prove its worth to the client
- Though the vendor was initially a bit weak in client specific business knowledge, with the support of the client the vendor was able to quickly to grasp and gather new knowledge

The client also took various initiatives and derived various advantages from offshore-outsourcing in each of the cases:

- By breaking up the bigger tasks into modular chunks, the client was able to distribute and allocate work better. The client also had the flexibility to scale up or scale down the project personnel size depending on the demands of the project, since the vendor could provide manpower on demand.
- Coordination and cooperation were aided by better use of modern communication technologies. It was also accepted that even the best communication technologies cannot beat the effectiveness of direct face-to-face communication, and hence executives from either the client of vendor firms traveled to their respective counterpart's sites when needed.
- The client got access to a highly skilled workforce at low cost.

Let us now compare the issues and observations from each of the case studies with those in the literature. Combinations of both economic and social/organizational theories have been used in IS outsourcing literature (Dibbern et al., 2004, pp. 99-102).

Gallivan and Oh (1999) had analyzed the economic, strategic, and organizational issues involved in IT outsourcing for four classes of outsourcing relationships: (1) simple outsourcing relationships (one client, one vendor), (2) multi-vendor relationships (one client, many vendors), (3) co-sourcing relationships (many-clients, one-vendor), and (4) complex relationships (many clients, many vendors). The first case study in this chapter that studied the CRM-NA and CRM-Europe projects dealt with simple outsourcing relationships (one client, one vendor), while the second case study that studied the NMS project involved the a multi-vendor relationship (one client, many vendors). As highlighted by these case studies, each of the offshore outsourcing arrangements were very contextual in nature and the nature of implementation varied to a great degree depending on the context. Hence, both client and vendor managers should delve deep into their own individual contexts and carry out extensive planning and preparation before taking up offshore-outsourcing initiatives (Gallivan & Oh, 1999).

Hancox and Hackney (1999) employed four conceptual frameworks of: (1) core competencies, (2) agency theory, (3) transaction cost economics and (4) partnerships, to assess IT outsourcing arrangements in the public and private sectors, and suggested that high transaction costs were a dampener on outsourcing initiatives, and that private firms were more open to outsourcing than public organizations. The case studies in this chapter of course focused on private firms, who were more open to outsourcing risks and were effective in risk management. In the CRM-Europe/NA and NMS projects presented in this chapter, the private enterprises prevented potential conflicts by negotiating resolutions, were committed to derive the beneficial fruits of offshore-outsourcing, and were mutually accountable and responsible. However, the transaction costs and agency costs are dampeners on most outsourcing relationships (Hancox & Hackney, 1999), and this held true for the CRM-Europe/NA and NMS projects too, though the benefits seemed to have overshadowed the numerous difficulties and issues faced.

It would be beneficial to analyze the IS outsourcing literature which have adopted the *economic* theories such as the *agency theory* and the *transaction cost theory,* and the *social/organizational* theories like the *innovation diffusion theory*, *exchange theory*, and the *power-politics theory* (Dibbern et al., 2004, pp. 99-102), and compare and contrast them with the issues highlighted in the case-studies presented in this chapter.

## Agency Theory

### *The Agency Theory and the Case Studies*

When viewed from the perspective of the agency theory, and as highlighted in the case studies, the outsourcing relationship may be considered to be a complex process in which the divergent interests of the clients and vendors are brought into equilibrium within the framework of contractual relations (Jensen & Meckling, 1976, p. 311). CRM-Europe/NA projects involved *"fixed-term, fixed-price"* (Currie, 1996, pp. 232-234) contracts, while the NMS project involved the *"time and materials"* (Currie, 1996, pp. 232-234) contract.

These contracts suited the individual contextual scenarios of each of the projects. In the NMS project the task details had to be worked out as the project progressed, and changes and evolution in the system being developed was a necessity. Whereas, in the CRM-Europe/NA projects, major changes in the scope (that is changes in design/requirements) were not expected, the deadlines were set, and the price for the entire project was fixed.

The client-vendor relationships in the CRM-Europe/NA and NMS projects behave like *agency relationships*, where the client can be assumed to be the *principal* that engages the vendor (assumed to be the *agent*) to perform some service, and where the *agency costs* (which is a summation of the *monitoring costs*, *bonding costs* and *residual loss costs*) is incurred by the client (Jensen & Meckling, 1976, pp. 308-310).

## *Comparative Analysis of Issues in Case Studies with Paradigms in IS Outsourcing Literature*

The agency theory has been successfully adopted to understand IS outsourcing (Dibbern et al., 2004, pp. 99-102). In a conceptual paper, Sharma (1997) presented a framework outlining four types of restraints on potential opportunistic behavior of professional agents: (1) self-control, (2) community control, (3) bureaucratic control, and (4) client control, and suggested that the vendors at times are the more powerful ones in the relationship with clients. In the NMS project, the client certainly had upper hand by cleverly manipulating the competitiveness within multiple vendors. In the CRM-Europe/NA too, the client had an upper hand on account of it being the buyer of the vendor's services and its promises of future business contracts. The vendors in both cases were smart and experienced enough to deal with clients; however, they were never the more powerful ones in the relationship. Hence, though Sharma (1997) believes that vendors at times are the more powerful ones in the relationship, in the case studies in this chapter the clients remain the most powerful.

Sridhar and Balachandran (1997) in a mathematical paper, distinguished an internal employee from an outside vendor on four different informational dimensions: (1) an outside vendor is assumed to be informed of the task environment less often than an internal employee, (2) the principal observes the information set of the internal employee more frequently than that of the outside vendor, (3) the principal is able to control the flow of certain production related information to an internal employee better than to an outside vendor, and (4) the principal may share the details of the outside vendor's contract with the internal employee but not vice-versa. It was further noted that the agency costs and intensity of information required for project execution had a negative impact on the client's willingness to outsource. All the four informational dimensions and the observations of Sridhar and Balachandran (1997) hold true for the CRM-Europe/NA and NMS projects.

Wang, Barron and Seidmann (1997) analyzed the nature of custom software development agreements that can be reached between the user and developers, compared the valued of using internal and external developers, and suggested the inability to measure or predict costs can hamper outsourcing initiatives. In the CRM-Europe/NA projects the costs could be predicted and measured, and hence the "fixed-term, fixed-price" contract was successfully adopted. However, as opposed to the analysis of Wang et al. (1997), the inability to accurately measure or predict costs did not hamper the outsourcing initiatives for the NMS project. The client simply adopted the *"time and materials"* contract for the NMS project which allowed the project task and cost details to be worked out as the project progressed.

Chalos and Sung (1998) presented an agency model in which outsourcing dominates insourcing, where it was argued that a firm outsources to improve managerial incentives resulting from anticipated reduction in overall costs, and to reduce the number of tasks that an overloaded manager executes; however, this approach often ignored the possibility of increase in communication and coordination overheads after outsourcing. The analysis of Chalos and Sung (1998) hold true for the CRM-Europe/NA and NMS projects, where though the big responsibility of executing the large projects were transferred from the client managers to the vendor managers, the client had to still spend time and effort coordinating and communicating with the respective vendor.

## Transaction Cost Theory

### *The Transaction Cost Theory and the Case Studies*

Adopting a transaction cost theory to an outsourcing relationship, involves the realization that clients and vendors "interface" with each other. It is across this assumed interface that services are delivered by the vendor to the client in the projects CRM-Europe/NA and NMS. In other words, "transactions," exchanges or transfers between the clients and vendors occur across this interface.

As highlighted by the case studies, the interfacing between the clients and vendors needs to be well planned and executed in order to harmonious. Otherwise, the frictions (misunderstandings, disputes, disruptions, failures and delays) may result in dampening the outsourcing relationship, which would lead to a *"transaction cost"* needed to accommodate, monitor and supervise the transactions (Williamson, 1981).

### *Comparative Analysis of Issues in Case Studies with Paradigms in IS Outsourcing Literature*

The transaction cost theory has been applied to IS outsourcing by various researchers (Dibbern et al., 2004, pp. 99-102). Jurison (1995) developed a model derived from the two streams of transaction cost theory and modern financial theory, and aimed to assist in the insourcing versus outsourcing decisions (for a particular IS function and in the comparison of competing vendor proposals). They suggested that outsourcing is a "risk" that may lead to a client's loss of control over its resources and also difficulties in monitoring the vendor. Loh and Venkatraman (1995) performed an empirical study to show that technical/business benefits from outsourcing favor outsourcing initiatives, while risks due to loss of control over outsourced work, opportunism, and inability to control vendors negatively affect outsourcing initiatives. Aubert, Rivard and Patry (1996) used the transaction cost approach to investigate the influence of asset specificity and measurement problems on the choice of outsourced activities, and on the terms/ management of the contract. Heisekanen, Newman and Similä (1996) used a process model approach to observe contract negotiations and to explain the forms and evolution of relations between the involved parties; they suggested that the vendor's capability to understand the client's business needs would help in making the relationship more productive. Ang and Straub (1998) simultaneously examined the constructs of production cost, transaction cost, and financial slack to understand what influences the outsourcing decision and concluded a client's large asset size and high transaction costs in an outsourcing relationship can hamper outsourcing initiatives. Duncan (1998) adopted a resource-based view to examine outsourcing contracts and risk, and believed that a loss of control and access over resources, and the threat of knowledge loss hampered possibilities of outsourcing. Loh (1994) constructed and tested an integrated governance model of IT outsourcing in the cost domains of bargaining costs, influence costs, management costs, and decision information costs and concluded that while possible financial benefits and need for access to skills encouraged outsourcing, there were risks of poor vendor behavior/control and difficulties in resolving contracts. Cheon, Grover, and Teng (1995) synthesized four theoretical models (resource based theory, resource dependence theory, transaction cost theory and agency theory) to develop a contingency model, and indicated that agency and transaction costs hampered outsourcing while a client's need for access to greater IS skills and resources encouraged outsourcing. Poppo and Zenger (1998) suggested the integration of transaction cost, knowledge-based, and measurement reasoning for make-or-buy decisions in information services and believed that the need for IS skills encouraged outsourcing, though highly client specific assets/knowledge/resources, uncertainty over technologies, and problems in measurability discouraged outsourcing. The observations from the CRM-Europe/NA and NMS project case studies presented in this chapter seem to be agreeable to the above theories about what promotes outsourcing and what doesn't.

Nelson, Richmond and Seidmann (1996) used field data to support the contention that the two dimensions of software acquisition, that is, custom versus package and insource versus outsource are interrelated at several levels. The CRM-Europe/NA and NMS projects highlight that when project tasks can be modularized, common custom-software development can certainly be outsourced to offshore-based vendors.

Nam, Rajagopalan, Rao, and Chaudhury (1996) explored the impact of organizational, environmental and economic factors on two dimensions of outsourcing decisions: (1) initial outsourcing decision, and (2) intention to continue the relationships, and concluded that the vendor's need for client specific knowledge and resources hampered outsourcing, while the heterogeneity of IS functions and the strategic importance encouraged outsourcing. This is true for the CRM-Europe/NA and NMS projects, where the client modularized the bigger tasks into smaller ones, thereby increasing heterogeneity for more effective outsourcing. Further, the lure of future business contracts was a major motivator for the vendor during both the projects. Also, vendor's partial lack of client specific knowledge might have hindered the initial CRM-Europe project, however, with increased experience, maturity and knowledge the CRM-NA project was more successful.

## Innovation Diffusion Theory

### *The Innovation Diffusion Theory and the Case Studies*

Growth in offshore outsourcing of IS work is a recent phenomena (Carmel & Agarwal, 2002), and this phenomena may be considered to be an organizational or administrative "innovation" process, that is now being adopted and practiced by various clients and vendors. In both the CRM-Europe/NA and NMS projects, *the adoption* of the offshore-outsourcing *innovation* involved the conscious decision by the clients and the vendors to accept and use new processes, and *diffuse* these process their relationship and respective organizations (Daft, 1978, pp. 195-197).

### *Comparative Analysis of Issues in Case Studies with Paradigms in IS Outsourcing Literature*

The usage of the innovation diffusion theory in IS outsourcing literature led to an interesting clash between the research results of Loh and Venkatraman (1992b) and Hu et al. (1997). Loh and Venkatraman (1992b) treated "IT outsourcing as an administrative innovation," and explored the sources of influence in the adoption of this innovation. Using diffusion modeling Loh and Venkatraman (1992b) showed that the adoption of IT outsourcing is motivated more by internal influence (such as communication with peers and managers of other organizations) than external influence (such as the media). Hu et al. (1997) in a repeat of the Loh and Venkatraman (1992b) study tested four diffusion models: internal influence, external influence, and two mixed influence models, and found no support for the conclusions of the Loh and Venkatraman (1992b) on the primacy of internal influence. The study by Hu et al. (1997) instead suggested that the mixed combination of both internal and external influence helped in the adoption and diffusion of outsourcing, and rejected the primacy of any one (internal or external) source of influence. After assessing these two research studies, one might be tempted to consider the answer to the problem of "primacy of sources of influence in the adoption of the outsourcing innovation" to be inconclusive. The same holds true for the case studies presented in this chapter.

# Social Exchange Theory

## *The Social Exchange Theory and the Case Studies*

The CRM-Europe/NA and NMS projects involved clients and vendors whose actions were motivated by the returns they expected, and their exchanges were mutually reciprocated and balanced, though power-play was evident (with the client exerting its monetary influence and decision making rights over the vendor). The social exchange theory can hence be aptly used to study offshore-outsourcing relationships.

## *Comparative Analysis of Issues in Case Studies with Paradigms in IS Outsourcing Literature*

Klepper (1995) and Kern (1997) adopted the social exchange theory for understanding IS outsourcing (Dibbern et al., 2004, pp. 99-102). Klepper (1995) selected the Dwyer, Schurr and Oh (1987) model of partnership development, and applied it on two case studies of IS partnership development to conclude that vendor characteristics and relationship attributes (such as communications, procedures, expectations, and balance of power) influenced outsourcing. Kern (1997) developed a model that is based on exchange theory and contract law, and that captures both the outsourcing relationship's contractual, social, and economic characteristics, and additional elements that have relevance in practice. It was concluded that various exchange characteristics (services/products, information, and financial) and relationship characteristics (vendor behavior and communication) influence the outsourcing process. The observations from the CRM-Europe/NA and NMS project case studies are congenial to the above propositions by Klepper (1995) and Kern (1997).

# Power Politics Theory

## *The Power Politics Theory and the Case Studies*

The offshore-outsourcing relationships described in the CRM-Europe/NA and NMS projects had client organizations which wielded considerable *power*, and they possessed a controlling influence over the project and the vendor and wanted to get things done as per their wishes. At the same time, the vendors in both cases were large CMM level-5 software services firms, the managers of which had considerable experience in dealing with (both cooperative and uncooperative) clients from all around the world. This differential *power* in the outsourcing relationship resulted in *politics,* where both the clients and the vendors tried to maneuver and gain control over their respective projects (Markus, 1983).

## *Comparative Analysis of Issues in Case Studies with Paradigms in IS Outsourcing Literature*

The power-politics theory was adopted by Willcocks and Kern (1998) to explore IS outsourcing in the context of a case study, three critical dimensions: what is outsourced, the contract, and the relationship dimension. The observations from the CRM-Europe/NA and NMS project case studies are conformable to the conclusions of the Willcocks and Kern (1998) study, which states that various relationship characteristics (services/products, information, staff, asset and financial exchanges; vendor behavior, communication, trust, cooperation, flexibility and social/personal relations) influence the outsourcing process.

Lee and Kim (1999) used both the social exchange theory and the power politics theory, proposed a conceptual theoretical framework for outsourcing partnership based on a social rather than an economic perspective, examined the impact of partnership quality on outsourcing success, and established the importance of relationship characteristics (such as commitment, trust, business understanding, and risk sharing) in outsourcing. The conclusions of the Lee and Kim (1999) study about importance of relationship characteristics are again concordant with the observations from the case studies in this chapter.

# Future Trends

Offshore outsourcing is taking the benefits and risks of outsourcing to its extremes. With offshore outsourcing one can reach out the best skills at the lowest costs. At the same time the intensity of the outsourcing risks like challenges in coordination, communication and control are being tested to the maximum due to the distance and cultural divergences.

Many vendor companies in India like TCS (http://www.tcs.com), Infosys (http://www.infosys.com), Wipro (http://www.wipro.com), and Satyam (http://www.satyam.com) seem to have made an art out of providing offshore-outsourcing services, and are hence giving a tough fight to the traditional bigwigs like EDS (http://www.eds.com) and Accenture (http://www.accenture.com). In recognition of the offshoring trend, EDS and Accenture have also set up base in countries like India to take advantage of its low-cost and highly skilled professionals.

Successes are being realized not just in offshore-outsourcing, but also offshore-insourcing. *NewScientist*, a premier science and technology magazine did a cover story on India titled "India: The next knowledge superpower", and one article named "India special: The silicon subcontinent" (Cohen, D., 2005) states the following:

*Some of the biggest names in IT are heading towards Bangalore once more, and this time round its not cheap labour they are looking for. They are hunting down the brightest, most inventive minds in India to populate a swathe of cutting-edge research facilities. The work being done in these labs rivals any in the U.S. and Europe.*

The article goes on to list companies like Hewlett-Packard, Texas Instruments, General Electric, Google, Microsoft, and IBM that have set up research labs in India to take advantage of its skilled professionals.

They come for the cost, and stay for the quality.

## Conclusions

"They come for the cost, and stay for the quality" seems to be an apt summary for the offshoring and outsourcing trend that is not only growing but also maturing. Offshoring and outsourcing is truly about delivering software that's value for money.

The case studies provided insights into the practical and real life strategies adopted by managers to solve issues and problems in offshore-outsourcing. This chapter summarized the usage of socio-economic theories to understand outsourcing of IS, and focused on providing and analyzing the issues in the two very different and descriptive real-life case studies that have the common thread of offshore-outsourcing of custom software development . Most of the paradigms in literature resulting from the adoption of socio-economic theories for IS outsourcing research concurred with the observations in the case studies.

## References

Accenture. (n.d.). *Services*. Retrieved January 27, 2005, from http://www.accenture.com/xd/xd.asp?it=enweb&xd=services\services_home.xml

Ang, S., & Straub, D. W. (1998). Production and transaction economies and IS outsourcing: A study of the U.S. banking industry. *MIS Quarterly*, *22*(4), 535-552.

Apte, U. M., & Mason, R. O. (1995). Global disaggregation of information-intensive services. *Management Science, 41*(7), 1250-1262.

Aubert, B. A., Dussault, S., Patry, M., & Rivard, S. (1999). Managing the risk of IT outsourcing. *Proceedings of the 32nd Annual Hawaii International Conference on System Sciences*, 7.

Aubert, B. A., Patry, M., & Rivard, S. (1998). Assessing the risk of IT outsourcing. *Proceedings of the 31st Annual Hawaii International Conference on System Sciences*, 685-691.

Aubert, B. A., Rivard, S., & Patry, M. (1996). A transaction cost approach to outsourcing behavior: Some empirical evidence. *Information & Management*, *30*(2), 51-64.

Carmel, E., & Agarwal, R. (2002). The maturation of offshore sourcing of information technology work. *MIS Quarterly Executive*, *1*(2), 65-78.

Chakrabarty, S. (in press). The journey to new lands: Utilizing the Global IT workforce through offshore-insourcing. In P. Yoong & S. Huff (Eds.), *Managing IT professionals in the Internet age*. Hershey, PA: Idea Group Publishing.

Chalos, P., & Sung, J. (1998). Outsourcing decisions and managerial incentives. *Decision Sciences*, *29*(4), 901-919.

Chaudhury, A., Nam, K., & Rao, H. R. (1995). Management of information systems outsourcing: A bidding perspective. *Journal of Management Information Systems, 12*(2), 131-159.

Cheon, M. J., Grover, V., & Teng, J. T. C. (1995). Theoretical perspectives on the outsourcing of information systems. *Journal of Information Technology*, *10*(4), 209-210.

Cohen, D. (2005, February 19). India special: The silicon subcontinent. *NewScientist*. Retrieved February 20, 2005, from http://www.newscientist.com/special/india/

Currie, W. L. (1996). Outsourcing in the private and public sectors: An unpredictable IT strategy. *European Journal of Information Systems*, *4*(4), 226-236.

Currie, W. L. (1998). Using multiple suppliers to mitigate the risk of IT outsourcing at ICI and Wessex Water. *Journal of Information Technology*, *13*(3), 169-180.

Currie, W. L., & Willcocks, L. P. (1998). Analyzing four types of IT sourcing decisions in the context of scale, client/supplier interdependency and risk mitigation. *Information Systems Journal*, *8*(2), 119-143.

Daft, R. L. (1978). A dual-core model of organizational innovation. *Academy of Management Journal*, *21*(2), 193-210.

Dibbern, J., Goles, T., Hirschheim, R., & Jayatilaka, B. (2004). Information systems outsourcing: A survey and analysis of the literature. *ACM SIGMIS Database*, *35*(4), 6-102.

Duncan, N. B. (1998). Beyond opportunism: A resource-based view of outsourcing risk. *Proceedings of the 31st Annual Hawaii International Conference on System Sciences*, 675-684.

Earl, M. J. (1996). The risks of outsourcing IT. *Sloan Management Review*, *37*(3), 26-32.

EDS. (n.d.). *Industries index*. Retrieved January 27, 2005, from http://www.eds.com/industries/index/

EDS. (n.d.). *Services index*. Retrieved January 27, 2005, from http://www.eds.com/services/index/

Gallivan, M. J., & Oh, W. (1999). Analyzing IT outsourcing relationships as alliances among multiple clients and vendors. *Proceedings of the 32nd Annual International Conference on System Sciences, Hawaii*.

Grover, V., Cheon, M. J., & Teng, J. T. C. (1996). The effect of service quality and partnership on the outsourcing of information systems functions. *Journal of Management Information Systems*, *12*(4), 89-116.

Halarnkar, S. (2004, December 04). Bangalore crumbling. *The Indian Express*. Retrieved February 10, 2005, from http://www.indianexpress.com/full_story.php?content_id=60231

Hancox, M., & Hackney, R. (1999). Information technology outsourcing: Conceptualizing practice in the public and private sector. *Proceedings of the 32nd Annual Hawaii International Conference on System Sciences.*

Heiskanen, A., Newman, M., & Similä, J. (1996). Software contracting: A process model approach. *Proceedings of the 17th International Conference on Information Systems*, 51-62.

Hu, Q., Saunders, C., & Gebelt, M. (1997). Research report: Diffusion of information systems outsourcing: A reevaluation of influence sources. *Information Systems Research*, *8*(3), 288-301.

Infosys. (n.d.). *Industries*. Retrieved January 27, 2005, from http://www.infosys.com

Infosys. (n.d.). *Quick facts*. Retrieved February 10, 2005, from http://www.infosys.com/about/quick_facts.asp

Infosys. (n.d.). *Services listing*. Retrieved January 27, 2005, from http://www.infosys.com/services/default.asp

Jensen, M. C., & Meckling, W. H. (1976). Theory of the firm: Managerial behavior, agency costs and ownership structure. *Journal of Financial Economics*, *3*(4), 305-360.

Jurison, J. (1995). The role of risk and return in information technology outsourcing decisions. *Journal of Information Technology*, *10*, 239-247.

Kern, T. (1997). The Gestalt of an information technology outsourcing relationship: An exploratory analysis. *Proceedings of the 18th International Conference on Information Systems, Atlanta, Georgia.*

Klepper, R. (1995). The management of partnering development in I/S outsourcing. *Journal of Information Technology*, *10*, 249-258.

Lacity, M. C., & Willcocks, L. P. (1995). Interpreting information technology sourcing decisions from a transaction cost perspective: Findings and critique. *Accounting, Management and Information Technologies*, *5*(3/4), 203-244.

Lee, J.-N., & Kim, Y.-G. (1999). Effect of partnership quality on IS outsourcing success: Conceptual framework and empirical validation. *Journal of Management Information Systems*, *15*(4), 29-61.

Loh, L. (1994). An organizational-economic blueprint for information technology outsourcing: Concepts and evidence. *Proceedings of the 15th International Conference on Information Systems, Vancouver, Canada*, 73-89.

Loh, L., & Venkatraman, N. (1992). Diffusion of information technology outsourcing: Influence sources and the Kodak effect. *Information Systems Research*, *3*(4), 334-358.

Loh, L., & Venkatraman, N. (1995). An empirical study of information technology outsourcing: Benefits, risks, and performance implications. *Proceedings of the 16th International Conference on Information Systems, Amsterdam, The Netherlands*, 277-288.

Markus, M. L. (1983). Power, politics, and MIS implementation. *Communications of the ACM, 26*(6), 430-444.

Markus, M. L., & Robey, D. (1988). Information technology and organizational change: Causal structure in theory and research. *Management Science*, *34*(5), 583-598.

Michell, V., & Fitzgerald, G. (1997). The IT outsourcing market-place: Vendors and their selection. *Journal of Information Technology*, *12*, 223-237.

Nam, K., Rajagopalan, S., Rao, H. R., & Chaudhury, A. (1996). A two-level investigation of information systems outsourcing. *Communications of the ACM*, *39*(7), 36-44.

Nelson, P., Richmond, W., & Seidmann, A. (1996). Two dimensions of software acquisition. *Communications of the ACM*, *39*(7), 29-35.

Parasuraman, A., Zeithaml, V. A., & Berry, L. L. (1988). SERVQUAL: A multiple-item scale for measuring consumer perceptions of service quality. *Journal of Retailing*, *64*(1), 12-40.

Poppo, L., & Zenger, T. (1998). Testing alternative theories of the firm: Transaction cost, knowledge-based, and measurement explanations for make-or-buy decisions in information services. *Strategic Management Journal*, *19*, 853-877.

Sharma, A. (1997). Professional as agent: Knowledge asymmetry in agency exchange. *Academy of Management Review*, *22*(3), 758-798.

Sobol, M. G., & Apte, U. M. (1995). Domestic and global outsourcing practices of America's most effective IS users. *Journal of Information Technology*, *10*, 269-280.

Sridhar, S. S., & Balachandran, B. V. (1997). Incomplete information, task assignment, and managerial control systems. *Management Science*, *43*(6), 764-778.

Wang, E. T. G., Barron, T., & Seidmann, A. (1997). Contracting structures for custom software development: The impacts of informational rents and uncertainty on internal development and outsourcing. *Management Science*, *43*(12), 1726-1744.

Willcocks, L., & Lacity, M. (1998). *Strategic sourcing of information systems*. Chichester: Wiley.

Willcocks, L. P., & Kern, T. (1998). IT outsourcing as strategic partnering: The case of the UK inland revenue. *European Journal of Information Systems*, *7*(1), 29-45.

Williamson, O. E. (1981). The economics of organization: The transaction cost approach. *American Journal of Sociology*, *87*(3), 548-577.

Wipro. (n.d.). *IT services*. Retrieved January 27, 2005, from http://wipro.com/itservices/services.htm.

# Note

The author may be contacted at schakrabarty@tamu.edu or chakrabartys@yahoo.com.

# Chapter XIII

# Growth of Outsourced IT-Enabled Services in India: A Systems Dynamics Approach

Varadharajan Sridhar
Management Development Institute, India

Sangeeta S. Bharadwaj
Management Development Institute, India

## Abstract

*IT-enabled services (ITES) in India have registered tremendous growth in recent years. Availability of English speaking trained manpower and low wages are some of the factors that have contributed to the growth of ITES sector in India. However, recent political movements against outsourcing, quality concerns of the clients, and data theft have had negative effects retarding the growth of this sector. In this chapter we review all the techno-economic factors that positively and negatively affect the growth of the ITES sector. An exhaustive literature survey is done to elicit these factors. We develop a generic causal model indicating the relationships between the various factors and the growth of ITES revenue. We discuss the factors of advantages and disadvantages India has in this sector. We draw some broad conclusions as to how the stakeholders such as policy making bodies and the industry associations can use this model to study the effects of these factors on the growth of the industry.*

# Introduction

The world is in the middle of the third era of globalization. The first and second eras introduced cross border trade and manufacturing respectively. The third era of globalization is offshore outsourcing of services. This era armed with tremendous advances in information and communication technology (ICT), allows services to be provided from remote locations, across national borders. This promises to revolutionize service operations by radically reducing costs and improving service standards.

Outsourcing is defined as the procurement of goods and services from sources that are external to the organization. IT-enabled services (ITES) outsourcing refers to business operations services delivered over telecom networks or the Internet (NASSCOM, 2001). ICT network is used as a tool and enabler to provide these services. Most of these processes tend to be human intensive. Due to human intensive nature, these processes and services are traditionally outsourced to countries where the labor costs are lower and from where the services could be delivered remotely without sacrificing quality and efficiency. Examples of ITES include telemarketing/pre-sales, customer care, technical support, and back office operations. ITES in specific vertical areas of business include medical transcription, digital content development/animation, and legal database possessing. IT enabled services typically include the following (NASSCOM, 2001):

1. Functions and services provided from a country different from the one where end products are delivered.
2. Services are delivered over communication networks.
3. The services are either externally contracted (outsourced) or provided by a remote subsidiary of the same company (out located).

Business process outsourcing (BPO) is defined as the movement of business processes from inside the organization to external services providers. Gartner (2003) describes BPO as "the delegation of one or more IT-intensive business processes to an external provider that, in turn owns, administers and manages the selected processes based on defined and measurable performance metrics." With the global telecommunication infrastructure now well established and consistently reliable, BPO initiatives often include shifting work to international providers at offshore locations. Thus countries such as India, China, Mexico, Ireland, Philippines and Vietnam have emerged as top destinations on the BPO map for offshore locations.

India controls 44% of the global offshore outsourcing market for IT services and IT-enabled services (ITES) with revenues of US$17.2 billion in the year ended March 2005. As many as 400 of the Fortune 500 companies now either have their own centers in India or outsource to Indian technology firms. India's market share is projected to expand to 51% by March 2008, when annual revenues are expected to touch US$48 billion, out of global outsourcing spending of US$96 billion. At the end of March 2005, India's outsourcing industry employed 1.05 million programmers and other skilled workers, while giving indirect employment to 2.5 million people in support services such as transport

*Figure 1. Growth of Indian IT and IT enabled services (Source www.nasscom.org)*

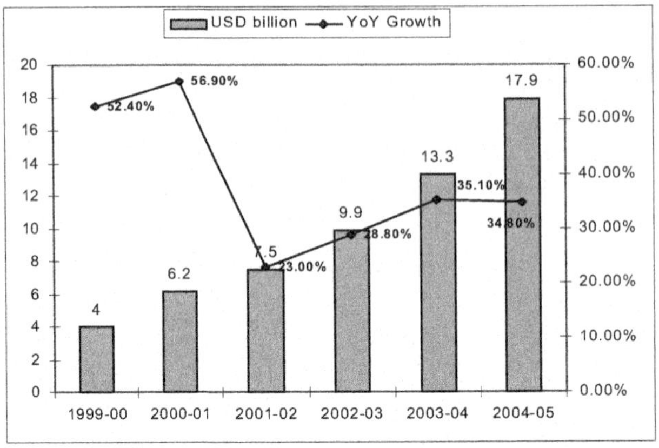


*Figure 2. Growth of Indian IT enabled services Exports (Source www.nasscom.org)*

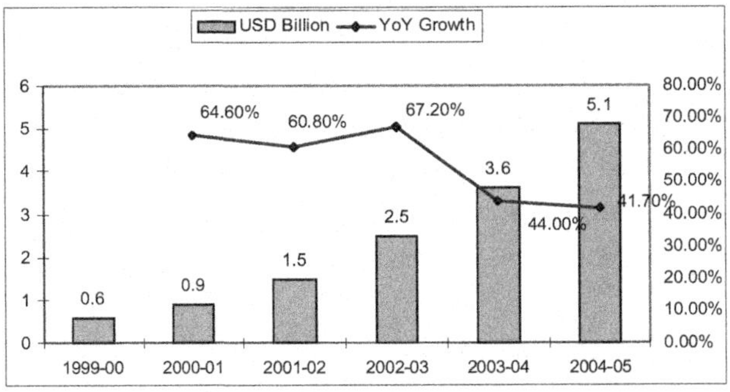


and catering. It took 20 years for the Indian IT services industry to grow to $3 billion while the same was achieved by the ITES industry in less than three years. Growth of Indian IT and IT enabled services exports is shown in Figure 1. Figure 2 shows growth of only ITES exports revenue over the last 5 years.

Starting with medical transcriptions in late '90s, Indian ITES industry has increased the portfolio of offerings. Table 1 gives the breakup of revenue and employment in the various verticals in ITES-BPO exports from 2002-2005.

Customer care and call centers still contribute to a major share of revenue and employment. However, there are niche areas in payment services, finance, and content development in which growth is expected in the near future.

In this chapter we address the following issues:

*Table 1. ITES growth by service lines (Source: www.nasscom.org)*

| | 2002-2003 | | 2003-2004 | | 2004-2005 | |
|---|---|---|---|---|---|---|
| | No. of Employees | Revenues (in US $ million) | Employees | Revenues | Employees | Revenues |
| Customer Care | 66,400 | 830 | 96,000 | 1,200 | 122,000 | 1,500 |
| Payment services | 12,000 | 230 | 21,000 | 430 | 30,000 | 620 |
| Finance | 25,500 | 540 | 41,000 | 835 | 64,000 | 1300 |
| Administration | 26,000 | 325 | 40,000 | 540 | 57,000 | 840 |
| HR | 2,100 | 45 | 4,500 | 75 | 10,000 | 165 |
| Content Development | 48,000 | 510 | 51,000 | 550 | 65,000 | 670 |
| **Total** | 180,000 | 2480 | 253,500 | 3,630 | 348,000 | 5095 |

1. Determine various techno-economic factors that affect positively and negatively the growth of the ITES industry.
2. Build a generic causal model that captures various interactions between these factors and growth of the industry which can be useful to various stakeholders such as the service providers and the government for formulating policies and strategies to augment growth of this sector.
3. Illustrate the causal relationships with specific references to Indian ITES sector and outline factors of advantages and disadvantages India has in this sector.

Though our intention is to build a general model of growth for the ITES industry, it can be used for sensitivity analysis of the various factors and their effect on growth. Note that, given the data limitations of this rapidly evolving industry, we embark upon a qualitative rather than a quantitative approach in explaining the effect of various factors on the growth of the ITES industry.

In the next section, we briefly review trends in the areas of IT and ITES outsourcing. Then we build a generic causal model of growth of the ITES sector and explain the causal relationships between various techno-economic factors and growth of the industry. We then discuss the factors of advantages and disadvantages of offshore outsourcing to India. In the penultimate section, calibration issues and usefulness of the model to various stakeholders are discussed. We conclude with limitations of the modeling approach and highlight future research directions.

## Trends in IT Services Outsourcing

Quinn and Hilmer (1994) suggested that by strategically outsourcing and emphasizing companies' core competencies, managers can leverage their core companies' skills and resources in four ways. First, they maximize return on internal resources. Second, well-developed core competencies provide formidable barriers against future and present competition. Third, greatest leverage is the full utilization of external supplier's investments, innovations and specialized professional capabilities. Fourth, this joint strategy decreases risk, shortens cycle times, lowers investment, and creates better responsiveness to customer needs.

In a related work, Murray and Kotabe (1999) have shown a negative relationship between asset specificity and internal sourcing of supplementary services. The result suggests that unlike product sourcing strategy where asset specificity and internal sourcing are positively related, supplementary services tend to be sourced externally to reduce fixed investment and increase operational flexibility. This would enable the service firm to excel on its core competency. The argument of focusing on core competency cited by researchers (Benson & Ieronimo, 1996; Lacity, Willcocks, & Feeny, 1996; McFarlan & Nolan, 1995; Pralahad & Hamel, 1990; Willcocks, Fitzgerald, & Fenny, 1995), favors outsourcing peripheral activities that the market can perform more cost-effectively. Outsourcing services in ITES fall in this domain. In a qualitative research, Pinnington and Woolcock (1995) have found that the drivers for IT outsourcing were cost control and reduction, focusing on core competencies, access to new expertise and technologies and improved flexibility.

IT outsourcing originated from the professional services and facility management services in the financial and operational support areas during the 1960s and 1970s. In the 1960s, the use of external vendors was confined to time sharing or processing services. In 1963, Electronic Data System signed an agreement with Blue Cross of Pennsylvania for the handling of its data processing services (Dibbern, Goles, Hircheim, & Jayatilaka, 2004). This was the first time when a large business had turned over its entire data processing department to a third party. Since computers were large and expensive, most companies relied on service bureaus. Companies used time-sharing to obtain processing time. The 1970s marked the beginning of the standard application package concept. Increasing demand for IT applications combined with inadequate supply of IT personnel forced companies to utilize contract programmers for system development.

In 1989, when Kodak announced outsourcing data center operations to IBM, telecommunication services to the Digital Equipment Corporation, and PC support to Business Land, it created quite a stir in the IT industry. Never before had such a well-known organization, where IS was considered to be strategic asset, turned it over to third party providers (Applegate & Montealegre, 1991). Kodak appears to have legitimized outsourcing, creating what is known as "The Kodak Effect." A number of high profile multi-billion dollar "mega-deals" were signed increasing the awareness of outsourcing. As outsourcing grew in popularity, debate shifted from whether or not to outsource to how much to outsource (Lacity & Hirschheim, 1993). Concerns during this stage of outsourcing evolution included whether outsourcing should be total or selective, service or asset, long or short term, involve single or multiple vendors.

Through out 1990s, the focus of companies was on outsourcing where an IT company took over the IT services related work of the client company, performed it onsite or offsite in the same country. Large companies in the U.S. first began outsourcing non-core IT services to large companies domestically, preferring to have these services provided securely and reliably from outside, rather that building up in house expertise. Outsourcing work mainly included software application development and maintenance. Large corporations in the United States and Europe have progressively built and acquired or partnered with delivery companies in developing countries. This phenomenon is called as offshore outsourcing and describes outsourcing beyond the shores of client country. U.S. companies expanded off-shoring through partnership, acquisitions and local subsidiaries. Thus they followed a less risky and more strategic approach of alliances by keeping the control with them. Their sourcing strategy more closely resembled the "insourcing" strategy of traditional offshore investments for global manufacturing. This was also the beginning of outsourcing of ITES and business process outsourcing.

## Causal Model of Growth of ITES Industry

There are different approaches to representing dynamic processes such as the growth of ITES industry, each with its own strengths and weaknesses. We propose to use the well-known finite difference equation methodology of system dynamics (SD) (Forrester, 1961) to develop a model of the mechanics of growth of the ITES industry. SD has been used successfully to study process structure in a wide variety of application areas (Sterman, 2001) including online service provision (Dutta, 2001), Internet diffusion (Dutta & Roy, 2001), congestion effects in Internet services (Kim, Juhn, & Ha, 1997), competitive behavior in duopoly markets (Sice, Mosekilde, Moscardini, & Lawler, 2000), growth of cellular mobile services (Dutta & Sridhar, 2003), and growth of basic telecom services (Jain & Sridhar, 2003).

The basic construct of an SD model is the feedback loop. A feedback loop is simply a closed sequence of cause-effect relationships. Developing an SD model of system behavior consists essentially of identifying the feedback loop structure of the system and validating it by comparing the model behavior to actual observed behavior. By simulating the SD models, it is possible to study 'what-if' scenarios.

The causal model shown in Figure 3 illustrates the factors that affect ITES industry growth, highlighting the existence of all major cause-and-effect links, indicating the direction (cause -> effect) of each linkage relationship. The relationship is positive (or negative) if a change in the causal factor produces a change in the same (or opposite) direction in ITES growth. A closed sequence of causal links represents a causal loop. There are a number of factors that affect positively the growth of ITES sector in India. We start with wages.

- **Wages:** Neoclassical economics regards any business organization as a production unit motivated by profit maximization. Williamson (1981) argues that a firm justifies sourcing options based on production economies. In the context of IT and ITES, a firm will choose to outsource or in-source based on the comparative costs of internalizing IT versus the price it has to pay vendors for the IT services (Saarinen & Vepasalainen, 1994). The propensity to outsource exists due to reduction in production cost as cited by Lacity and Wilcocks (1998), Loh and

*Figure 3. Causal Model of ITES Growth*

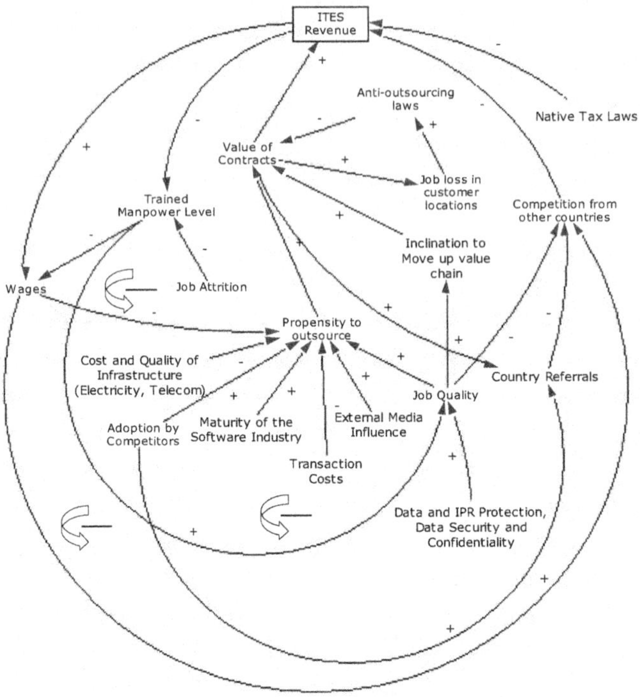


Venkatraman (1992a), McFarlan and Nolan (1995). Although the reports in press and media tend to inflate the potential savings (Lacity & Hirschheim, 1993), the comparative cost advantages offered by vendors is a major factor in outsourcing IT services (Ang & Straub, 1998). Loh and Venkatraman (1992b) have empirically supported a positive relationship between IT cost structure and outsourcing. Thus the key compelling force driving the companies to outsource is savings due to reduction in direct wage costs. Thus lower wages in offshore locations has a positive effect on the propensity of the firm to outsource.

- **Transaction Costs:** Williamson's (1975) transaction cost theory (TCT) provides a useful second point for research, investigation and discussion of the IT and ITES outsourcing phenomenon. TCT assumes that companies make outsourcing decision based on an economic rationale. TCT is obviously relevant as IT specifically addresses outsourcing decisions in regards to producing a good or service internally or externally (Lacity & Hirschheim, 1993). Companies incur extra cost when sourcing externally. Hence transaction costs should be considered when making decision about outsourcing as transaction cost becomes significant when outsourcing globally. Transaction costs refer to the effort, time, and costs incurred in searching, creating, negotiating, monitoring and enforcing a service contract between buyers and suppliers (Mahoney, 1992). Transaction costs can erode comparative advantages in production costs of vendors. However Ang and Straub (1998) have shown that both production cost and transaction costs are important in decision while outsourcing. However, production costs are the overwhelming dominant factor, about six times as large as that of transaction costs. Considerable reduction in production cost with only marginal increase in transaction cost increases propensity to outsource.

- **Trained Manpower Level:** Though the dominant factor driving the global/offshore movement of IT outsourcing is cost-effectiveness, supply-side factors such as the availability of world class talent is also an important driver. When a firm lacks the IS skills to perform particular IS tasks it might choose to outsource. The supply side factors include availability of trained professional manpower, size of the countries workforce, and language skills. Availability of huge technical manpower at off-shore locations reduces market wages. Offshore services are identical to those they replace, and at times better, since offshore workers, enjoying higher-than-usual wages tend to be motivated. However, higher attrition rate has an impact on wages as the companies have to provide better wages and amenities to keep the workforce. As ITES operations grow and mature, employees of remote operations, armed with information about global job opportunities and compensation levels, may eventually bid up the price of their skills, reducing the cost advantage that companies currently enjoy (Sharma, Sood, & Vollenweider, 2000). As wages increase, country's competitiveness as preferred outsourcing location decreases as indicated in the causal loop diagram.
- **Job Quality:** Customers of outsourcing contracts have become particular about the quality of services rendered. The success of IT outsourcing is related to the service quality (Grover, Cheon, & Teng, 1996). Trained manpower improves the quality of services rendered. With improvement in quality, propensity to outsource also increases. Improvement in quality also encourages the outsourcing contractors to move up the value chain, this increasing the value of contracts. However, rising attrition rates results in new hires taking the place of experienced workers. This leads to certain erosion in quality of service levels. For example, Lehman Brothers and Dell discontinued part of their ITES outsourcing jobs in India and moved them back to the U.S. due to quality related problems.
- **Adoption by Competitors:** Firms see success of outsourcing contracts of competitors and imitate. Described as "jump on the bandwagon" (Lacity & Hirschheim, 1993) or "Kodak Effect" (Loh & Venkatraman, 1992a), such imitating behavior results in more companies going for outsourcing. Loh and Venkatraman (1992b) used diffusion modeling, in which there are two basic types of influences (internal and external) that drive the adoption of an innovation by members of a social system. They found evidence for internal sources of influence (outsourcing behavior of other firms) being better predictors for the observed distribution of outsourcing events than external sources (mass media reports and vendor sales figures) or mixed sources of influence (both external and internal). The internal influence model is structurally equivalent to the imitation model of Mahajan and Peterson (1985) which states that impetus for diffusion is an emulation of prior adopters by potential adopters. Organization that have hitherto maintained their ITES function in house, make their sourcing choice based on other organizations

that have already outsourced. The imitation effect has a positive effect on the competitors to adopt outsourcing and is appropriately indicated in Figure 3. Adoption by competitors increases the number of referrals of the outsourcing contractor's country and hence increases the country's competitiveness in attracting outsourcing contracts. For example, GE Capital and American Express were pioneers in establishing their captive ITES centers in India. This resulted in market access and customer referrals to other ITES companies in India.

- **Cost and Quality of Infrastructure (Telecom, Electricity):** When human asset specificity is not important, other factors dominate the propensity to outsource. Resource dependence theory states all organizations are dependent on some elements of their external environment to varying degrees due to control these external environment have on the resources. The controls include other supporting infrastructure such as telecom and electricity. These factors if improved in the offshore location can have a positive impact on firms to outsource either directly or through an improved quality of services rendered as indicated in the causal loop diagram.
- **Data and Intellectual Property Protection (IPR), Data Security and Confidentiality:** Data protection plays a critical role in the ITES industry for maintaining confidentiality of the data handled. Customers demand data security certifications and compliance for various services. Examples include Gramm Leach Bliley Act for financial services, Health Insurance Portability and Accountability Act of 1996 (HIPAA) for the healthcare industry (Gurbaxani, 2004). Organizations that outsource critical processes require the ITES companies to be certified to international data security regulations. Most of the ITES companies are often required by clients to get BS7799 or IS17799 certification for data protection and privacy. Certifications improve the credibility of the industry and hence have positive effect on the growth of the industry. Along with data protection, disaster recovery systems and security services are also required for certain ITES segments. As contractors improve information security infrastructure and intellectual property protection, and hence quality of services, firms are willing to outsource relatively high value added activities such as infrastructure maintenance and security services.
- **Maturity of the Software Industry:** Maturity of the software industry has a positive impact on firms to outsource ITES. Customers prefer to outsource to contractors accredited with process quality certifications such as CMM, CMMI, and eSCM. Contractors who have been providing IT services can use these referrals to get new contracts in the ITES segment.
- **External Media Influence:** External media influence positive or negative also has a corresponding effect on inclination of firms to outsource. Gurubaxani (1990) has highlighted that several external institutions (e.g., government, international agencies, media, and educational institutions) are critical in shaping the international diffusion of IT. Gurubaxani (1990) discovered that the diffusion of BITNET followed an S-curve, or more specifically, a logistic curve. The impetus for its diffusion was a combination of coverage by media and the early adoption by highly visible research universities.

- **Anti Outsourcing Laws:** Companies weigh the advantages and disadvantages of outsourcing and decide in favor or against the outsourcing options. This in turn increases/ decreases the value of outsourcing contracts. However, with increase in size of contracts, outsourcing countries experience job losses in certain sectors, which then lead to the formulation of policies against outsourcing. Managing potential labor disputes back home when a company decides to transfer jobs to a remote location such as India is proving to be a thorny issue (Sharma et al., 2000). Recent political backlash against outsourcing is an example. The recently approved U.S. Omnibus Spending Bill is an example and this has resulted in closures of some of the ITES outsourcing contracts, especially in India.
- **Competition from Other Countries:** There is competition amongst countries with similar capabilities of providing services in securing ITES outsourcing contracts. Global sourcing of services happen as firms want to exploit not only their competitive (firm specific) advantage but also comparative advantage (location specific) advantages (Dunning, 1988). Firm specific advantages are utilized through the ownership aspect of sourcing (internal versus external sourcing), and location specific advantages are exploited through the location aspects of sourcing (domestic or foreign and for ITES sector onshore, nearshore or offshore location).

In the causal model, there are three negative feedback loops. The positive loops increase the ITES revenue to the contractor country while negative loops retard it.

## Advantage and Disadvantages of Offshoring ITES To India

As discussed earlier, one of the basic reasons for offshore outsourcing is the high price of running certain processes on shore for which there exists cost-effective solutions. To keep these processes onshore, companies must hire expensive talent and devote management time. This prevents the company from focusing on its core competency.

*Table 2. Comparing cost structures in the U.S. and India (Source: NASSCOM 2005)*

| **Cost Element*** | US | | INDIA | | **Savings** |
|---|---|---|---|---|---|
| USD/FTE**/Year | Value | Share | Value | Share | On US Cost base |
| Personnel Cost | 42,927 | 73.3% | 6,348 | 48.4% | 85% |
| IT/Telecom Costs | 2,400 | 4.1% | 3,770 | 28.7% | -57% |
| Office Facility Cost | 3,700 | 6.3% | 1,991 | 15.2% | 46% |
| Other General & administration Expenses | 9,571 | 16.3% | 1,012 | 7.7% | 89% |
| **Total Cost** | 58,598 | 100% | 13,121 | 100% | 78% |

** Blended rate for voice and non-voice operations, **FTE:Full Time Employee*

However, when the same process is outsourced, vendors can offer specialized quality services that are impossible to duplicate internally by the client company. India has become a hub for offshore outsourcing of ITES and BPO because of the following advantages.

- **Lower Wages:** Cost of running ITES and BPO operations in India is very low compared to countries like U.S., UK and other European Countries. The most important reason for this is that the labor costs are low. In India, wages for highly skilled professionals in accounting, engineering, and languages (mainly English but also French and German) are lower than they are in developed economies (Table 2 gives comparison of cost structures in U.S. and India). In repetitive processes such as call centre operations, wages account for 70% of the costs in the U.S. while the same account for just 48% in India. Lower wages reduces the production costs of back office operations. Though employee costs in India are increasing at 10-15% annually, they are still very low compared to other countries.
- **Rapidly Growing Pool of Knowledge Professionals:** There is a shortage of skilled manpower in developed countries. On the other hand, NASSCOM (2005) indicates that India's large stock of technically talent, and English-speaking manpower, continue to be the chief driver of the Indian IT/ITES industry. India produces 3.1 million graduates every year and all of them speak good English, a necessary condition for executing ITES outsourcing contracts from English speaking countries. Median age of professional working in the IT sector in India is 27.5 years. The number of IT, ITES and BPO professionals employed in India was estimated to have grown by around 150,000 during 2004-05 alone. Over 81% of software professionals in India had a graduate or a higher degree (NASSCOM, 2005). 13% of the software professionals are professional degree holders in Engineering, accounting, finance and computer applications. 62% of this Indian technical workforce has more than four years of work experience. The ITES-BPO sector hired around 400 personnel every working day of the year (NASSCOM, 2005).

However, as the industry grows, the available technical manpower pool decreases. For example, the National Association of Software and Services Companies (NASSCOM) in India has identified an imminent manpower gap of more than half a million people or roughly 23% of the industry's requirements for ITES by 2009 ("Philippines catching up", March 9, 2004). The study also indicates that at the current growth in human resources from education institutions the supply will not keep up with demand, unless the government takes initiatives in promoting more training institutes in this sector.

The attrition rate in the industry is also very high due to poor working conditions (e.g., night-time shifts) and relatively lower wages. The attrition levels in ITES have increased to 30-40% per annum in 2002-2003 from 10-15% in 2000-2001 ("Manpower gap", March 14, 2004). Some companies have started entering in to non-poaching contract agreements to stem attrition levels. Another factor inducing attrition in this sector is the limited career paths available in this industry to talented workforce. Some companies in India have started providing career advancement programs that includes tying up with educational institutes to offer graduate programs to their employees. Due to these additional

*Figure 4. Growth of Indian IT industry (Source: www.nasscom.org)*

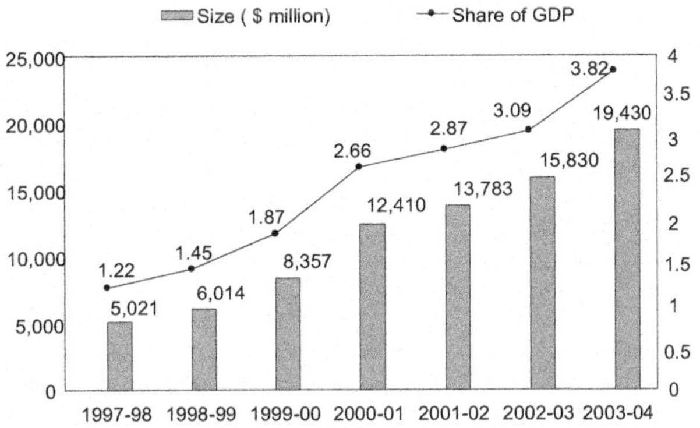


overheads, cost per employee to the company has increased from $200 per month in 2000-2001 to $330 in 2002-2003, resulting in decrease in company operating profit margin from 30-40% down to 17-25%.

- **Maturity of the Software Industry:** Indian IT industry over the last 20 years has perfected the art of global delivery models. Today India's IT industry generates revenue of more than $19 billion. Software and services export continues to grow annually at around 30% and has reached $15.9 billion. Figure 4 illustrates growth of Indian IT industry.

The delivery models for software export have seen a significant shift from onsite to offshore in the past five years. Portion of offshore revenue has increased from 34% in 1999-2000 to 59%. There is a corresponding decrease in onsite revenue from 57% to 41%. Improved infrastructure, especially telecom and the global delivery models perfected by large Indian software companies are the reasons for this shift. Coordination and communication problems in offshore development have been mitigated due to excellent processes and tools for software configuration management and project management adopted by Indian software companies. As of January 2005, India has 85 companies at SEI CMM Level 5 assessment (NASSCOM, 2005), one of the highest in the world. The maturity of the software industry has a positive impact on the growth of ITES services. Some ITES providers in India are using cheap and skilled local programmers to develop their own software instead of purchasing more expensive branded products from the global software giants. American Express, for instance, hired programmers to write software to reconcile accounts, and the software now reconciles over three-quarters of them, or more than half a million every day. The company, which paid only $5,000 to develop this solution, estimates that licensing more sophisticated database software would have cost several million dollars (Agrawal, Farrell, & Remes, 2003). The IT skills of the local labor force reduces operational cost and in turn attracts outsourcing. In fact the big IT companies in India have ITES subsidiaries to compliment their business activities.

- **Job Quality:** Quinn and Hilmer (1994) pointed out the greatest leverage of outsourcing is the full utilization of external suppliers' investments, innovations, and specialized professional capabilities that would be positively expensive or even impossible to duplicate internally. In line with this, the Indian vendors have been expanding their service offerings, thus deepening customers' offshore engagements. When a client company outsourcers a non-core function to outside contractor, it does so to only those companies who have competency in that process. Better process quality leads to improvement in quality of the outsourced business function. The IT and ITES companies in India are the foremost in adopting process quality certifications such as Six Sigma, CMM, CMMI, and eSCM. These vendors are thus able to make improvements in processes and have the capability to implement quality world-class processes. Their processes go through frequent mandatory audits by independent bodies. Improvement in processes by vendors leads to better quality of deliverables.

India with access to a ready pool of huge technical manpower can quickly ramp up activities leading to faster delivery of products and services. Carmel (1998) indicates how time zone differences lead to near 24-hour software development. The large time difference, especially with the U.S., enables faster development cycles and quicker time-to-market of products and services when outsourced to India.

- **Ability to Move up the Value Chain:** Outsourced ITES services in India have also moved up the value chain recently. Starting with medical transcriptions and simple call centre operations, ITES sector in India now handles complicated back office operations for financial, legal, insurance, telecom and other domain knowledge specific industry segments. Though the transition has been slow, Indian ITES industry is moving from simple processes and commodity services to transformational services that involve complex processes and core business functions. This in turn has increased the quality of projects, earning more revenue per man-hour and hence the overall growth of the sector. However, *Economic Times* ("Philippines catching up", March 9, 2004) points out that more complex processes requiring specialized knowledge and expert judgment to fulfill customer requests will increase to just about 10% of offshore ITES activities by 2006.
- **Competition from other countries:** India emerges at the top by a wide margin among the 25 countries in Kearney's "Offshore Location Attractiveness Index" ("The world's top", 2004) which employs 39 criteria to rank the locations. China is ranked second, followed by Malaysia and the Czech Republic. The 30 criteria are organized under three broad categories with varying weights: cost (40%), people

skills and availability (30%) and business environment (30%). Each category is further divided into sub-groups. The "cost" category has three components: total compensation of employees, cost of infrastructure and tax and regulatory costs. The "people skills and availability" category has four sub-groups: overall experience and skills in IT and telecommunication, availability of labor and the size of country's work force, education level of the workforce including language skills and test scores, and the attrition rate in the country's ITES industry. The "business environment" category covers a country's economic and political environment, its infrastructure in telecommunication and IT, cultural adaptability and the security of intellectual property. The study further states that countries such as India and China, with large populations, offer an abundance of educated workers. On the other end of the spectrum, small and highly developed economies like Singapore, New Zealand and Ireland offer excellent infrastructure, education system and business friendly and low risk environment. China trails India in ITES/BPO experience and qualifications. India on other hand has extended a significant lead through its continuing cost advantage and its market maturity. Also dramatic reduction in telecommunication cost in recent years, favorable tax rates and increasing competitive infrastructure costs have helped India maintain its overall cost advantage.

However, both China and India score poorly for political and economic risk and weak infrastructure. The Indian government recognizes IT is a part of government's national agenda and all policies are formulated to achieve maximum benefit to this industry. The liberalization and deregulation initiatives taken by the Indian government in IT and telecommunications are aimed at supporting growth in the IT, ITES and BPO segments. The reforms have reduced licensing requirements and made foreign technology accessible. Customs duty on most of IT and telecom products have been reduced to zero. The reforms have also reduced restrictions on investment and made the process of investment easier. Recently the Indian government increased Foreign Direct Investment limits from 49% to 74% in telecom.

However, India has the following disadvantages.

- **Higher Cost and Lower Quality of Telecom, Electricity and Road Infrastructure:** For ITES sector to grow, the other supporting infrastructure such as electricity and telecom are essential. However, telecom bandwidth prices and electricity tariffs are typically higher in low-wage countries. Telecom, electricity and road infrastructure in India is not at par with those in developed countries and/or in other offshore destinations such as Singapore, Malaysia, Thailand and Philippines. Reduction in price of services especially international long distance voice and data services, deployment of high-capacity international submarine cable networks, and improved quality of telecom services in the outsourcing partner countries has a positive impact on the client towards outsourcing decisions.

Relevant telecom facilities are an important prerequisite for the success of the software industry. In India, Telecom which forms the backbone for ITES has been a public utility service, owned by the government. Until 1985, resource deployment in telecom sector was only around 2% to 3% of the national plan outlay. Telecom prices, especially International Long Distance charges were kept very high to cross subsidize basic services. With no access to any other sources of funds, there was a limited growth in telecom sector. There was about 2.277 million waiting for basic telecom services in 1995 (ITU, 2003). Quality of telecom services was not up to mark. India had the highest fault density of 195.60 per 100 lines in 1995 (ITU, 2003). However with the liberalization policies of the government, currently there is perfect competition in international services. The prices of international calls have come down by as much as five times in the last five years. The mobile subscribers in India have been growing at a compounded annual rate of more than 75%. In a recent review of tariff by the International Telecommunications Union (ITU), cellular telephony tariff is the lowest in India at $16 per month for a 300-minute basket while the same costs $96 in Mexico. After private players were allowed to provide service, the international bandwidth availability has considerably improved. One of the private operators has completed an undersea cable network of 3,200 kms from India to Singapore, capable of carrying up to 8.4 terabits/sec, one of the largest in the world. The country also has now connectivity through international submarine cable operators such as FLAG, SEA-WE-ME-3, SEA-WE-ME-4 networks interconnecting India to rest of the world. Prices of International Private Leased Lines which are used by ITES and BPO companies for their connectivity to client sites has been reduced by 50% recently. Though the Indian government has taken steps to ensure that telecom remains a priority area, telecom infrastructure in the country is still not comparable to world standards. As indicated in Table 2, telecom contributes to about 29% of the telecom costs in India while the same accounts for just about 4% in the U.S. and hence affects negatively the propensity of companies to outsource to India. One way to off-set this high infrastructure cost is to use these as intensively as possible (Agrawal et al., 2003). The time difference between the U.S. and India facilitates round-the-clock shifts which improves the utilization of capital and hence reduces the total operating costs.

It is estimated that high electricity tariffs and the need for power backups makes the cost of doing business in India about eight times costlier. This tends to reduce the propensity to outsource. Recent steps by the Indian government to privatize the distribution of power to bring in greater efficiencies and customer centricity in the market, will improve electricity and power infrastructure in India.

Roads are in poor condition in India when compared to developed countries. The density of roads in 1999 was 2,561 kms when compared to 14,172 kms per million populations for the U.S. Only 20% of the paved roads are in good condition in India compared to the U.S., UK, Italy and other developed countries where more than 85% of paved roads are in good condition. This deters transporting of personnel to the ITES company locations, especially during nights. In fact, the economic losses due to poor condition of roads are expected to be around INR 200-300 billion a year in India.

- **Poor Data and IPR Protection, Data Security and Confidentiality:** Some of the problems faced off-late by Indian outsourcing firms include security breaches, error-prone software programs and service complaints. Many outsourcing firms in India have started using fraud detection software that monitors instant messaging and locks data from being printed or downloaded. Applicants for jobs are screened and personal and background checks are conducted before being inducted in to the company.

India's Information Technology Act 2000 (MLJC, 2000) includes laws and policies for data security. It also specifies a broad framework for the development of public key infrastructure (PKI) for the conduct of e-business. The act has sections that deal with digital signatures, and the regulation of certifying authorities. However, the act lags behind in coping up with the recent technology advances relating to security intrusions and attacks. Professional bodies such as NASSCOM are working closely with ITES companies to create an information security culture within organizations. NASSCOM is also working with the government on making amendments to the various clauses specified in IT Act 2000 in tune with the technology advances (NASSCOM, 2005).

- **Political Climate:** Though India boasts of the largest democracy in the world, over the last decade its political environment has seen unprecedented changes. Instead of a single party running the largest democracy, currently it is run by coalition parties. When the government is run by a consortium, it becomes very difficult to implement policies without the consent of all the parties. Uncertain political climate leads to ambiguity in policy making and its implementation.

## Calibration and Use of Model for Sensitivity Analysis

The cause-effect model shown in Figure 3 can be translated in to a stock-and-flow system dynamics model using SD software such as ithink (2003), or Vensim (2002). Once the model is constructed, it has to be validated. Validation of the system dynamics models is the process of establishing confidence in the soundness and usefulness of a model. Validation begins as the model builders accumulate confidence that a model behaves plausibly and generates problem symptoms seen in the real system. It has been stressed by the researchers that there is nothing like absolute validity of the model and only by testing the system dynamics models against a diversity of empirical evidences, one develops more confidence in the model withstanding these tests.

We plan to validate the feedback model described in Figure 3 using data on ITES industry revenue for the past seven to eight years. Once the model parameters are adjusted to generate simulated data that fits within reasonable tolerance with the real data, what-if and sensitivity analysis can be done on various model parameters to see their effect on the growth of the sector.

The objective of this modeling exercise is not to predict the exact growth numbers. It is to highlight which of the positive/ negative factors to be incremented/ decremented and by how much so that the positive loops dominate to provide sustainable growth of the industry. This will be of much use to IT policy makers, the government, and the service providers. We illustrate below the use of the SD model for various stakeholders through examples:

1. Average wages and administrative expenses of ITES employees is on the increase in India. The labor cost arbitrage is weakening. At the same time, telecom bandwidth prices continue to decline. Recently, the regulator Telecom Regulatory Authority of India reduced International Private Leased Line service tariff by as much as 50%. Decrease in telecom prices enhances the cost arbitrage. The degree of such effects are important for the government and policy makers to decide on (a) pricing plan for telecom services and (b) investment in ITES training institutes to increase labor supply for ITES industry thus reduces the wage levels or a combination of both.
2. ITES companies can increase manpower in basic operations such as call centers to increase their revenue. On the other hand, even with low number of skilled employees the companies can move up the value chain by doing quality work in the areas of knowledge process outsourcing (KPO). It is reported that high-end knowledge process outsourcing could be worth $15.5 billion by 2005. However, given the inherent risk in high-end activities, most of ITES companies in India want to have their legs in both low end call centers and high end KPO. The optimal portfolio mix of low value and KPO activities the service providers should strive to yield maximum revenue can be answered by the SD simulation model.
3. The low-end call centre industry is facing competition from countries such as Vietnam and Philippines. Using SD model, service providers will be able to see the effect of competition from the other countries and choose an appropriate competitive strategy (such as improving the quality of service offerings or increasing country referrals).

## Limitations and Future Research Directions

In this research work we have highlighted the various techno economic factors that affect ITES industry and their causal relationship with the growth of the ITES sector. We plan to use system dynamics methodology (Forrester, 1961) to simulate the causal model we have developed in this chapter. Since the basic construct of a system dynamics model is the feedback loop, insights into cause-effect mechanisms of the growth can be obtained as a by-product of model structure. Limitations of the SD model including its deterministic nature, plausible non-optimal solutions, difficulties in calibration and validation, difficulty in specifying relationships between variables have been well documented by Jain (2004). It has to be noted that ITES industry in India started evolving only in late '90s. Data availability is limited for any empirical work. Hence continuous simulation approaches such as system dynamics methodology are better suited for analyzing the effect of various growth factors of this sector. The model when calibrated using available data on ITES revenue can be of use to various stakeholders such as policy makers and industry professionals. Sensitivity analysis on different model parameters will provide insights in to the mechanics of the growth of the industry. Policies can be formulated to nurture the factors that have positive effect and mitigate the factors that affect negatively the growth of the industry. The model can be used to estimate future growth projections and hence will be a valuable tool for investors and policy makers.

# References


Agrawal, V., Farrell, D., & Remes, J. (2003). Offshoring and beyond. *The McKinsey Quarterly, 4.*

Ang, S., & Straub, D. W. (1998). Production and transaction economies and IS outsourcing: A study of the U.S. banking industry. *MIS Quarterly*, 535-552.

Applegate, L., & Montealegre, R. (1991). *Eastman Kodak organization: Managing information system through strategic alliances.* Harvard Business School, Case #9-192-030, Boston.

Benson, J., & Ieronimo, N. (1996). Outsourcing decisions: Evidence from Australian-based enterprises. *International Labor Review, 135*(1), 59-73.

Carmel, E. (1998). *Global software teams.* Upper Saddle River, NJ: Prentice Hall.

Dibbern, J., Goles, T., Hircheim, R., & Jayatilaka, B. (2004). Information systems outsourcing: A survey and analysis of the literature. *The Database for Advances in Information System, 35*(4), 6-102.

Dunning, J. H. (1988, Spring). The eclectic paradigm of international production: A restatement and some possible extensions. *Journal of International Business Studies*, 1-31.

Dutta, A. (2001). Business planning for network services: A systems thinking approach. *Information Systems Research, 12*(3), 260-283.

Dutta, A., & Roy, R. (2003). Assessing the growth of the Internet: A sociotechnical approach. *Communications of The ACM, 46*(2), 66-71.

Dutta, A., & Sridhar, V. (2003). Modeling growth of cellular services in India: A systems dynamics approach. *Proceedings of the Hawaii International Conference on System Sciences (HICSS-36),* Big Island of Hawaii, January 6-9.

Forrester, J. W. (1961). *Industrial dynamics.* Cambridge, MA: MIT Press.

Gartner. (2003). *The economics of IT services and outsourcing in Europe.* Retrieved on March 18, 2004, from http://www3.gartner.com

Grover, V., Cheon, M. J., & Teng , J. T. C. (1996). The effects of service quality and partnership on the outsourcing of information systems functions. *Journal of Management Information System, 12*(4), 89-116.

Gurubaxani V. (1990). Diffusion in computing networks: The case of BITNET. *Communications of the ACM, 33*, 65-75.

Gurbaxani, P. (2004, April). One critical factor. *Voice & Data, 10*(10).

International Telecommunications Union (ITU). (2003). *Yearbook of statistics.* Geneva, Switzerland: ITU.

iThink. (2003). ithink analyst software version 7.0.3 for Windows. High Performance Systems, Inc.

Jain, P. (2004). *Techno-economic modeling of basic telecommunication services: A system dynamics approach.* Ph.D. thesis, Indian Institute of Management, Lucknow, India.

Jain, P., & Sridhar, V. (2003). Analysis of competition and market structure of basic telecommunication services in India. *Communications & Strategies*, Special issue on ICT Market Dynamics and Market Development in Asia, *52*, 4th Quarter, 271-293.

Kim, D., Juhn, J., & Ha, W. (1997). Dynamic modeling of competitive online services in Korea. *System Dynamics, IX*(2), 1-23.

Lacity, M. C., & Hirschheim, R. (1993). *Information systems outsourcing: Myths, metaphors and reality.* New York: John Wiley & Sons.

Lacity, M. C., & Willcocks, L. P. (1998). An empirical investigation of information technology sourcing practices: Lessons from experience. *MIS Quarterly, 22*(3), 363-408.

Lacity, M. C., Willcocks, L. P., & Feeny, D. F. (1996). The value of selective IT outsourcing. *Sloan Management Review, 37*, 13-25.

Loh, L., & Venkatraman, N. (1992a). Diffusion of information technology outsourcing: Influence sources and the Kodak effect. *Information Systems Research, 3*, 334-58.

Loh, L., & Venkatraman, N. (1992b). Determinants of IT outsourcing: A cross-sectional analysis. *Journal of Management Information Systems, 9*, 7-24.

Mahajan. V., & Peterson, R. (1985). *Models for innovation diffusion.* Beverly Hills, CA: Sage Publications.

Mahoney, J. T. (1992). Organizational economics within the conversation of strategic management. *Advances in Strategic Management, 8*, 103-156.

Manpower gap may cripple BPO industry by 2009, finds survey. (2004, March 14). *Economic Times.*

McFarlan, F. W., & Nolan, R. L. (1995). How to manage an IT outsourcing alliance. *Sloan Management Review, 36*, 9-22.

Ministry of Law, Justice and Company Affairs (MLJC),Government of India. (2000). The Information Technology Act 2000.

Murray, J. Y., & Kotabe, M. (1999). Sourcing strategies of U.S. companies: A modified transaction – Cost analysis. *Strategic Management Journal, 20*, 791-809.

NASSCOM. (2001). NASSCOM's directory: IT-enabled service providers.

NASSCOM. (2005). Strategic Review 2005:The IT Industry in India.

Philippines catching up with India in BPO race. (2004, March 9). *Economic Times.*

Pinnington, A., & Woolcock, P. (1995). How far is IS/IT outsourcing enabling new organizational structure and competences? *International Journal of Information Management, 15*(5), 353-365.

Pralahad, C. K., & Hamel, G. (1990). The core competence of the corporation. *Harvard Business Review, 68*(3), 79-91.

Quinn , J. B., & Hilmer, F. G. (1994, Summer). Strategic outsourcing. *Sloan Management Review*, 43-55.

Saarinen, T., & Vepsalainen, A. P. J. (1994). Procurement strategies for information systems. *Journal of Management Information Systems, 11*(2), 187-208

Sharma, S., Sood, R., & Vollenweider, M. (2000). Globalizing services. *The McKinsey Quarterly, 4.*

Sice, P., Mosekilde, E., Moscardini, A., & Lawler, K. (2000). Using system dynamics to analyze interactions in duopoly competition. *System Dynamics Review, 16*(2), 113-133.

Sterman J. D. (2001). System dynamics modeling: Tools for learning in a complex world. *California Management Review, 43*(4), 8-25.

Vensim. (2002). Vensim PLE 32 version 4.2a, The Ventana simulation environment. Ventana Systems, Inc.

Willcocks, L. P., Fitzgerald, G., & Fenny, D. (1995). Outsourcing IT: The strategic implications. *Long Range Planning, 28*(5), 59-70.

Williamson, O. (1975). *Markets and hierarchies: Analysis and antitrust implications.* New York: The Free Press.

Williamson, O. E. (1981). The modern corporation: Origin, evolution, attributes. *Journal of Economics Literature, 19*, 1537-1568.

The world's top offshoring locations. (2004, May 19). *Business Standard.*

# Chapter XIV

# An Overview of Service Level Agreements

Nicholas B. Beaumont
Monash University, Australia

## Abstract

*This chapter notes and explains the increasing use of outsourcing and service level agreements (SLAs); proposes and describes an outsourcing methodology emphasising the role of SLAs; stresses SLAs' importance to insourcing and outsourcing relationships; proposes a taxonomy of service attributes, and recommends a hierarchical methodology for constructing SLAs. Evidence from interviews and examination of extant SLAs suggests that well-designed SLAs contribute to fruitful relationships between business partners. The proposed methodology and taxonomy will simplify and shorten the time-consuming tasks of writing and negotiating SLAs that are complete, consistent and satisfy business objectives. SLAs have not received academic attention proportionate to their commercial importance. Recommendations to practitioners and for further research are given, In particular, research ascertaining whether SLAs are used effectively and seeking better expression of business requirements in an SLA is appropriate.*

# An Overview of Service Level Agreements

A service level agreement (SLA) is a contract defining services that a vendor will provide to a client. Service level management (SLM) pertains to managing and monitoring a business relationship defined by an SLA. The SLA is best perceived as a hierarchy of service level clauses (SLC) supplemented by other information (see *The Contract*). Each SLC defines an element of the services provided by a vendor for a client, performance targets, the way in which the vendor's performance will be measured, penalties or bonuses for under or over-performance, and the client's obligations.

An SLA is fundamental to an outsourcing relationship. When a business process such as an information technology application, payroll, catering, security, provision of labour, call centre services, delivery, or a professional service such as accounting or legal advice is outsourced (i.e., provided by a separate business entity), the parties should formalise the arrangement by signing a contract for the supply of services (Sturm, Morris, & Jander, 2000, pp. 53-56)

When one department of a firm (e.g., information technology, the mail room, or human resources) provides services for another, there is often no written agreement. Many organisations have instituted "insourcing": the formalisation of a supplier-customer relationship between two departments. SLAs are used to define the services provided and performance criteria but have no legal status in this context (Sturm, Morris, & Jander, 2000, pp. 56-57).

A primary data source for this chapter was five interviews with senior managers of outsourcing vendors operating in Australia and three interviews with senior client executives responsible for outsourced services. Secondary sources were numerous informal conversations with vendor executives, client executives and consultants involved in outsourcing and a survey of outsourcing practice in Australia (Beaumont & Sohal, 2004). Evidence for the size and growth of the global outsourcing market and the use of SLAs was obtained from industry reports.

The most frequently outsourced processes are information technology (IT) applications and this chapter uses many examples from IT. However, the principles espoused apply to all forms of outsourcing. In this chapter we define terms pertaining to outsourcing and service level agreements (SLAs); summarise the scanty literature; give reasons for using outsourcing and SLAs and summarise evidence of their increasing use. We define outsourcing and the outsourcing cycle while emphasizing the role of SLA in outsourcing; describe the structure of an SLA and give a taxonomy of services attributes. We give a non-trivial example of an SLA illustrating the practical problems of writing and negotiating an SLA; summarise the current state of play; describe some outstanding research problems; make some recommendations to practitioners; and venture some forecasts of likely use of outsourcing and SLAs.

## Definitions

Here we define terms used throughout this chapter.

- **Outsourcing:** "The act of transferring some of a company's recurring internal activities and decision rights to outside providers as set forth in a contract" (Greaver, 1999, p. 3). Some disasters have brought outsourcing into disrepute and arrangements have been relabeled **technology services partnerships** or **managed services contracts**. Variants of outsourcing include:

    - *Out-tasking*: The vendor provides resources (computer time or labour) and does work precisely defined by the client (Strassmann, 1997).
    - *Insourcing*: Formalisation of the supply relationship between two departments of the same organisation.
    - *Backsourcing or repatriation*: Taking work that had been outsourced back in-house.
    - *Co-sourcing*: Used instead of *outsourcing* to emphasise that the outsourcing arrangement is based on cooperation (or "partnering") between the parties. The term *partnering* is often used to signify a highly co-operative arrangement but most countries' laws recognise only written contracts (not "a spirit of cooperation") and "de facto" relationships.
    - *Strategic outsourcing*: Outsourcing considered in strategic context (Quinn & Hilmer, 1994). An arrangement attractive on purely cost grounds might be rejected because it reduced the client's ability to react to a changing environment or entailed unhealthy dependence on the vendor.

- **Client and Vendor:** The organisations respectively obtaining and supplying services through an outsourcing agreement.
- **Outsourcing Cycle**: The stages of an outsourcing project: Identification a need; Definition of project objectives; Choice of vendor; Negotiation of a Service Level Agreement; Implementation; Performance monitoring, Incremental modification of the agreement; and Renewal or cancellation of the agreement.
- **Service Level Agreement (SLA):** A contract defining the services to be provided by a vendor and service levels; procedures for measuring performance; payments and penalties and procedures for renegotiation. SLAs are "formally negotiated agreements that enable IT organisations [and vendors of other services] and their customers to collaboratively identify, discuss and manage... service expectations" (Karten, 2004).
- **Service Level Management (SLM):** The management of an outsourcing relationship.

# The Literature

There are several books and manuals offering guidance on SLAs to potential practitioners, many containing SLA templates (Table 1). The academic literature, summarised in Table 2, is quite slight given industry's interest in SLAs; most journal articles pertain to applications of SLA. As far as is known, there are no academic surveys attempting to ascertain SLA use. Some examples of SLAs can be found on the World Wide Web (Table 3).

Buco, Chang, Luan, Ward, Wolf, and Yu (2004) conceptualise service level management in the context of computer networks. Ludwig, Keller, Dan, and King (2003) and Kellor and Ludwig (2003) propose a new computer language based on XML that formalises expression of SLAs pertaining to networks. These three papers propose that a complex set of services can be optimally expressed as a hierarchy of services and that definitions of services, service level targets, algorithms for obtaining compound measures of performance, and penalties or bonuses be logically associated with each node of the network. Different but analogous clauses of a SLA can be advantageously expressed in common form but differentiated using parameters.

*Table 1. Practitioner references to SLAs*

| Book or Report | Application area |
|---|---|
| (Hiles, 1993; Karten, 1998; KPMG, 1998; Management Advisory Services and Publications Consulting Group 2001) | General |
| Pantry and Griffiths (2001) | Library services |
| Hiles (2002) | Electronic commerce |
| (Lee & Ben-Natan, 2002; Verma, 1999) | Computer networks |
| (Hensher, Stopher, & Bullock, 2003) | Bus services |
| (Lewis, 1999) | Enterprise networks |

*Table 2. Research articles pertaining to SLAs*

| Article | Topic |
|---|---|
| (Bhoj, Singhal, & Chutani;, 2001; Blacharski, 2000; Gavi, 1999), (Beck & Allegretti, 1999) | Networks |
| (Coombs & Evans, 2000) | Central support services |
| (Chen, Lin, & Lee, 2002) | Measurement of service levels at hospitals |
| (Ekanayaka, Currie, & Seltsikas, 2002) | A framework for assessing potential vendors |
| (Hensher et al., 2003) | Developing measures of vendor performance |
| (Owens, 1983) | Supply chains |
| (Slaight, 1999) | Telecommunications |
| (Smith, 1995) | Business continuity planning |
| (Parish, 1997) | SLAs and TQM |
| (Dib, Freer, & Gray, 1998) | SLAs struck between departments |
| (Larson & Halldorsson, 2002) | The role of SLAs in delivering IT services to departments. |

*Table 3. Examples of service level agreements*

| |
|---|
| IT services for an education system [4] |
| Provision of pharmaceuticals [5] |
| Help desk services [6] |
| Bibliographic services [7] |
| Internet services [8] |

## Reasons for Using Outsourcing

SLAs are documents that formally define insourcing and outsourcing agreements and growth in their incidence is presumably caused by the growth in insourcing and outsourcing. There are theoretical reasons for outsourcing's growth and empirical evidence for such growth. Empirical evidence of growth in SLA usage is scarce and knowledge of such growth must be inferred from the growth in outsourcing.

A compelling reason for increased use of outsourcing is that information and communications technology (ICT), manifest especially in the World Wide Web, has allowed data to be transmitted amongst organisations with high fidelity, high speed, and negligible marginal costs that are independent of distance. Internal departments (such as payroll departments) running common business processes have lost their natural monopolies; external organisations can compete with them especially if they can exploit expertise or economies of scale. Outsourcing work to countries with low labour costs (offshoring) has obvious attractions. Outsourcing has become an acceptable, even fashionable, management technique, especially amongst governments. Formalising internal relationships by writing insourcing agreements (which allows benchmarking departments against potential external suppliers and clarification of cost structures) is also popular.

The most important of up to 20 reasons for outsourcing's popularity include:

- **Reduced costs and improved service quality**. These may be derived from economies of scale (e.g., running a payroll application for many clients), lower labour costs and/or the vendor's expertise and experience.
- **Risk avoidance:** Purchasing services at a fixed cost per transaction lessens financial risk.
- **"Sticking to the knitting."** Outsourcing non-core activities allows the client to exploit its expertise without distraction (but how do you define "core" activities (Quinn & Hilmer, 1994),
- The mere threat of outsourcing may engender scrutiny and improved efficiency of internal operations. Managers sometimes resort to outsourcing because of dissatisfaction with or inability to understand how an internal operation (most commonly IT) works.

- Governments especially may welcome the opportunity to benchmark internal operations against other organisations.

Outsourcing has some potential disadvantages such as: loss of distinctive competencies, compromised confidentiality, problems of transferring activities to the vendor, ascertainment of relevant costs, a lack of a "cultural fit" between the parties and the lack of flexibility inherent in signing, for example, a three-year contract. More detailed analyses of the advantages and disadvantages of outsourcing are given in Quinn and Hilmer (1994), Beaumont and Costa (2002), Beaumont and Sohal (2004), and Strassmann (1997). Strassmann takes an iconoclastic view, arguing that heavy use of outsourcing is a harbinger of corporate collapse.

## Reasons for Using SLAs

Sturm, Morris and Jander (2000, pp. 16-18) give six reasons for using SLAs in the context of outsourcing or insourcing information technology (IT). The four most important are:

- **Educative:** During negotiations, the client is forced to consider cost-benefit playoffs instead of treating a resource such as IT as a "magic pudding" that delivers constantly improving services at no extra cost to the client.

  A proposal to outsource often provokes scrutiny of the extant operation. Inconspicuous functions such as the mailroom or procurement may be run by habit rather than reflecting changing business requirements and/or exploiting new technology. Organisations are sometimes embarrassed to find long-standing inefficiencies, for example, that FedEx could deliver internal mail cheaper and quicker than one company's own mailroom (Quinn & Hilmer, 1994).
- **Efficient allocation:** SLA methodologies force organisations to recognise that IT resources especially are scarce and that "whole of organisation" decisions about how those resources are used must be made.

  The SLA methodology forces precise definition and justification of service requirements and the way in which the vendor's performance will be measured.

A compelling reason for using SLAs is that they are prerequisites to vendors obtaining and retaining client respect. When asked to develop a new system or deliver accurate, timely, and relevant reports; the stereotypical response from an IT department was not to guarantee performance but to promise to do its best ("all care, no responsibility"). This failure to commit meant that the IT department never earned respect from the rest of the organisation.

An essential aspect of professional behavior is making commitments (expressable as an SLA) and either fulfilling them or enduring the consequences of failure. A professional relationship with the rest of the organisation implies that service departments will be better able to market their services internally. SLAs with internal clients imply that service departments will have an assured income stream and be better able to engage in medium term planning.

### *Incidence and Importance of SLAs*

The increased use of SLAs can be inferred from the size and growth of the outsourcing market (every outsourcing relationship should be defined by an SLA) and from some consultants' surveys. The data on the outsourcing market exclude insourcing arrangements and thereby underestimates SLA use.

## Growth of Outsourcing

The outsourcing market's size and growth are difficult to estimate; practitioners have no intrinsic interest in providing accurate data and there are definitional problems. Is it really outsourcing if the IT department becomes a wholly owned subsidiary (but is otherwise unchanged) and a new system of transfer pricing is imposed? There are few publicly available authoritative sources on outsourcing use (some consultants' reports are available only at high prices). The following information suggests that global outsourcing is growing at about 10-20% pa, but growth rates may be volatile and differ amongst sectors and regions.

*Worldwide spending on business process outsourcing (BPO) services totaled approximately $405 billion in 2003, a growth of about 8% over 2002. According to a new report from IDC, this market (comprising 9 business functions of human resources, procurement, finance and accounting, customer care, logistics, engineering/R&D, sales and marketing, facilities operations and management, and training) will increase to $682.5 billion in 2008, with a compound annual growth rate (CAGR) of 11% [1].*

*Offshore outsourcing is just one small part of a $US5 trillion global outsourcing market. This market is growing by more than 15% pa, and the offshore component is certainly among the fastest growing. We are at the earliest stages of a fundamental transformation from regional economies to a single, integrated global economy. Just*

*Table 4. Forecast growth of offshoring (Gartner)*

| Forecasts in $USbn | 2001 | 2005 | 2008 |
|---|---|---|---|
| Total Business Process Outsourcing Market | 127 | 234 | 310 |
| Percentage Offshored to Countries | 5% | 15% | 20% |
| Offshored BPO Market | 6.4 | 35.1 | 62.0 |
| India ITES Exports | 1.5 | 9.5 | 21 |

*Table 5. Predicted growth in the global BPO market (IDC)*

| Source | Actual US$B 2001 | Forecasts $USB 2004 | 2005 | CAGR 2000-2005 | Notes |
|---|---|---|---|---|---|
| Gartner | 91 | 157 | 181 | 14.7 | Excludes logistics and manufacturing outsourcing. |
| IDC | 109 | 177 | 202 | 13.1 | Includes transaction processing. |

*as companies now compete globally, workers need to realise that they, too, are competing globally [2].*

Table 4 and Table 5 give Gartner and IDC's estimates and forecasts of the global Business Process Outsourcing (BPO) market [3].

## Direct Evidence of Increased SLA Use

One consultant's survey (Oblicore, 2004) gives some evidence of increased use of SLAs (respondents indicated a 10-20% increase in the number of SLAs they used). 61% of 320 respondents had SLAs with suppliers, 56% with customers and 46% had internal SLAs. "The importance of SLAs is demonstrated by their rising popularity. The research firm Cahners In-Stat Group... reports that the use of SLAs rose 25% among Fortune 1000 companies during 1999, and the market for service level management products is expected to reach U.S. $280M in worldwide revenue by the end of 2000" (Sturm et al., 2000, p. 14).

# The Outsourcing Context

## Vendor-Client Relationships

SLAs express commercial relationships between organisations or departments. In theory, the relationship between a client and vendor can be positioned on the spectrum ranging from an arm's-length, black-letter relationship (exemplified by a business process such as payroll in which requirements can be unambiguously specified and performance is easily measured), to one requiring intense day-to-day co-operation between the parties' staffs to improve a business process. The latter kind of relationship, exemplified by the development of an elaborate new computer system, is sometimes described as partnering.

For a different research project, the author interviewed several senior Australian executives of outsourcing vendors. All interviewees strongly opined that the vendors regard partnerships with their clients as the only plausible alternative. The first contract with a client is a "license to sell"; by demonstrating efficiency and commitment the vendor is well-placed to tender for other business processes. More mundanely, failure to demonstrate efficiency and commitment results in termination of the relationship.

It may be very difficult for a client to express in writing every aspect of a service that was provided internally and to anticipate the effects of changes in the client's business or technology. A contract spelling out every detail and allowing for any conceivable change would be inordinately long, at bottom; in some circumstances, the client may have to trust the vendor: relying on the vendor's professionalism and desire to preserve its marketplace reputation.

This trust may be misplaced. Each party's commitment to the agreement depends on the benefits experienced and on direct and indirect costs of continuation versus premature termination. If the vendor has underestimated its costs when tendering, it may be unable to resist pressure to reduce costs by exploiting loopholes in the contract. If premature termination of an agreement would be expensive for either party, that party must construct a watertight agreement.

An outsourcing relationship is symbiotic, simultaneously reflecting elements of co-operation and competition. Each party constantly assesses the short and long-term benefits of continuing the relationship, and of using tactics such as observing the letter rather than the spirit of the agreement, making concessions in order to improve prospects of expanding the operation's scope, and/or threatening to terminate the agreement in order to extract concessions.

## Negotiating and Implementing an SLA

Negotiating and implementing an SLA for a significant business operation is a complex task. Managers with no relevant experience especially are advised to prepare carefully and, if possible, choose a first project that is not crucial to the organisation and/or is an internal agreement. Negotiating, writing, maintaining, and monitoring an SLA takes place in the context of the *outsourcing cycle*. We describe the outsourcing cycle emphasising aspects relevant to SLAs. The SLA will be drafted in stage 2, negotiated in stage 4, modified in stages 7 and 8, and used to monitor vendor performance in stage 6. The eight stages of the outsourcing cycle are:

1. Identify a process to outsource.
2. Define the outsourcing project's objectives and prepare for negotiations.
3. Choose a vendor.
4. Negotiate a contract.
5. Implement the agreement. Transferring the process may be disruptive.
6. Monitor vendor performance.
7. Incrementally modify the agreement as technology or business requirements change.
8. Renew/cancel the arrangement.

## *Identify a Process to Outsource*

There are many different ways of identifying a candidate process for outsourcing (see *Reasons for Using Outsourcing*). It is possible that no potential vendor has appropriate expertise. Some IT systems are vital to the organisation, complex, have been developed over many years by people who have retired, and are imperfectly documented. Management may not take the risk of transferring them to an outside vendor.

## *Define the Outsourcing Project's Objectives and Prepare for Negotiations*

What benefits are being sought by outsourcing a payroll application? Reduced processing costs? More options for employees? Fewer processing errors? More relevant and detailed managerial reports of labour costs? Better compliance with legal requirements? What reports detailing labour costs will be required? Presumably, line managers will require detailed reports and senior managers will require summary reports. How quickly must reports be made available to managers and will the reports be online or paper? What information will be provided on pay slips and what services will be provided to employees? For example, can pays be split between two bank accounts and how many deductions will be allowed? The project scope must be very clearly defined. Is the system for hourly staff, salaried staff, and/or staff paid by commission? Will it incorporate expenses claims? Many organisations have separate, confidential arrangements for very senior staff, are these to be included? What interfaces with other accounting and performance systems will be provided?

The need to ascertain extant costs and service quality (provided internally or by an incumbent vendor) prior to negotiating with a new vendor is obvious. Some inconspicuous services such as printing, security, long-running information systems, and the mailroom may not have kept pace with changing business requirements or exploited new technology. One department may informally provide important but undocumented services to other departments. Some questions users should be asked if, for example, outsourcing the mailroom's services is proposed are:

- Which of the mailroom's services are you currently using?
- Are you familiar with all the services the mailroom provides?
- Are there other services that the mailroom should provide or are there services that you never use?
- How quickly, frequently, and accurately is mail delivered? Are there other aspects of the mailroom's performance that are relevant to your operation?
- Could some functions such maintaining customers' names and addresses be transferred to the mailroom?

- Has your use of the mailroom's services been affected by new technology, for example e-mail and fax?
- Do you know how much the mailroom charges you for its services? If so, are you getting value for money? Is the charging mechanism appropriate?
- What aspects of the mailroom's services could be changed or improved? Are there new services that the mailroom could appropriately provide?

It may be appropriate to consult business partners (especially key customers) if they may be affected by the change.

This exercise, although sometimes embarrassing, often results in beneficial change that obviates the need to outsource. One of the review's outputs is a set of objectives pertaining to costs and performance standards that will help determine the negotiating team's goals. It is essential to sell the project to senior management and thereby retain their support during sometime difficult and protracted negotiations.

## *Choose a Vendor*

The usual methods including public tender, tenders restricted to known suppliers, an invitation to a trusted supplier, or spinning off the task to a group of former employees. For large tasks, a shortlist of vendors is appropriate. Consultation with a potential vendor's clients may be illuminating.

## *Negotiate a Contract*

Before entering negotiations the client team (representing functions materially affected by the transition) should agree on cost and service level targets. The nature of negotiations depends on the tasks to be outsourced. If (as in the case of payroll) the process to be outsourced is a common business process and well understood by a specialist vendor, and most of the performance criteria can be objectively measured; negotiations should be relatively straightforward. If the whole of a complex information technology function unique to the client is being outsourced and some of the criteria such as user-friendliness and quality of training can only be assessed subjectively, then negotiations will be more difficult. Agreed definitions of terms and ways in which service levels are measured facilitate negotiation.

Ideally, the goal is a long-term, symbiotic relationship in which the vendor's expertise contributes to sustained reduction of costs and improvements in services. The client enjoys direct benefits and the vendor may benefit from increases in volumes and taking over other of the client's business processes. However, a vendor simply wanting resources (usually labour or computer time) for a well-defined task (not vendor expertise) will seek the lowest possible price consistent with acceptable service levels.

It is unwise for the client to specify inflexibly the services that are required and/or unrealistic performance standards. Insisting that a computer system be working 99.999%

of the time may be unnecessary for back office operations, unrealistic, and absurdly expensive. The vendor will usually have expertise (in part drawn from its experience with other clients) that the client should exploit. In a fruitful relationship, the client exploits the vendor's specialist knowledge and experience to modify business processes and drive down costs. A professional but cordial relationship is desirable; forcing the vendor to accept unrealistically low prices will engender resentment and parties resorting to the letter rather than the spirit of the agreement.

The parties must agree on payments. Simplest is a fee for each transaction but variants such a fixed annual fee (subject to a maximum number of transactions) and a fixed plus variable fee are possible. A fixed annual fee transfers financial risk from the client to the vendor.

Agreements always include definitions of services that the vendor will provide and penalties (possibly bonuses) for falling below (or exceeding) agreed service levels. These definitions will uses service attributes described in *A Taxonomy of Service Attributes* below. If the attributes are quantifiable, negotiation on service levels will be fairly straightforward albeit vigorous. When intangible attributes such as hospital staff empathy, courtesy and appearance of delivery staff, systems' "user friendliness", and meals' palatability are important; negotiations will be more difficult.

The measurement of performance criteria will require additional procedures and costs. For computer systems and call centres there are myriad systems (Sturm et al., 2000) that can automatically measure attributes such as up time and response times and produce a variety of reports. For other systems, the operators delivering the service must enter source data, for example, FedEx drivers enter delivery details on line. All performance data should be auditable.

Penalties are usually constructed to increase more than linearly with deficiencies in service. If a computer system fails twice in one month, the penalty will be more than twice the penalty for failing once in a month. Performance criteria and penalties usually include measurements of global and particular aspects of service. Thus, an IT vendor could incur a penalty for one application failing for one day although aggregated measures of service exceeded 99% for the month. It is usually assumed that the vendor's performance and unit costs should improve during the contract.

## *Implement the Agreement*

Transferring the process may be potentially disruptive. The vendor's preferred procedures, computer systems and forms may replace those familiar to the client's employees. The SLA may dictate the transfer of some of the client's staff to the vendor's employ. The rights of these staff must be defined in the contract. Other displaced staff may be transferred to other departments or terminated. Conventional wisdom dictates that management should be "up front" and inform employees who may be affected as fully and as early as possible.

### *Monitor Vendor Performance*

As stated, parameters, reports, and methods pertaining to measuring the vendor's performance and calculating penalties should be negotiated and agreed. The client may forego penalties if the vendor is obviously dedicated and efficient.

### *Incrementally Modify the Agreement*

The SLA should contain clauses stating how disagreements will be resolved or escalated; defining periodic reviews of the relationship at the "coalface", middle, and top management levels; how changes to the relationship will be negotiated, and defining renewal or termination procedures.

Few business procedures are static; firms constantly introduce new products, clients, and methods that may require modification of SLAs. Prudent vendors advise clients how to exploit improving technology to reduce costs and improve services, and share the benefits of improving technology with them.

## Analysis of Services

It is convenient to analyse and specify the services to be outsourced hierarchically. The units of analysis are a service (S), a user group (UG) and a service element (SE) (defined in Table 6). The hierarchical approach should be used flexibly; it may be appropriate, in the context of airline baggage handling, to classify baggage services by customer type (First class, business class, frequent flier etc). It might be more fruitful to initially classify luggage as cabin or checked, then by customer type. Hierarchically structured requirements minimise repetition of SLA text.

*Table 6. Service analysis definitions*

| Term | Definition | Example |
|---|---|---|
| Service | A service being provided | Provision of meals to hospital patients |
| User group | A group of clients with homogenous needs | Patients can be classified as short-term, long-term, vegetarian, those needing help with meals, those requiring soft food, and (for completeness) patients who are fasting. In practice, combinations such as long-term vegetarian patients would have to be considered. |
| Service element | An element of the service | The service might be broken down into provision of breakfast, lunch and dinner. Each of these would be a service element. It might be necessary to define more finely the service by expressing the provision of each meal in terms of more elementary service elements: One possible division would be serving the meal, helping the patient eat when necessary, and clearing up afterwards. The breakdown is not unique; in other contexts it might be useful to express a meal as a set of courses. |

Direct services are the useful outputs of the outsourced application and are exemplified by deposits into employees' bank accounts and managerial reports on labour costs. Indirect services are those used to measure vendor performance and calculate vendor payments and penalties. They are exemplified by reports on network performance; time taken to deliver goods, the number of deliveries to wrong addresses; and transaction volumes.

# The Contract

The bulk of the contract will comprise service level clauses (SLCs). An SLC pertains to one service used by one homogeneous group of users (a user group). Repetition is avoided by specifying either (1) one service applicable, with minor differences, to different user groups or (2) a group of services that are applied to one or several user groups. The differences in services amongst groups are conveniently expressed in terms of parameters.

For example, if payroll preparation is outsourced, the contract will include SLCs pertaining to employees' pay slips, depositing money in employees' bank accounts, and providing managerial reports. A parameter might be used to differentiate groups of employees is paid weekly or fortnightly or to differentiate hourly and salaried staff.

## Header

The header information in most contracts will comprise: Identification of the parties to the agreement; the term of the agreement; scope and exclusions; limitations; arrangements for periodic reviews and procedures for resolving disagreements; and procedures for negotiating modification of the contract in the light of new ideas, advances in technology and/or changes in the client's business.

## Service Level Clauses

The bulk of the contract comprises service level clauses that define, for each user group/ service element combination:

- **The service provided.** If the agreement pertains to delivery to households, aspects such as: the place at which goods are to be loaded; the way in which they are to be packaged; allowed times of delivery; the delivery information to be provided by the client; procedures to be followed if delivery cannot be made; and appearance and politeness of delivery staff must be agreed.

- **Client obligations.** The client typically agrees to provide details of new employees or hours worked data by the agreed time and in an agreed format, without this data the vendor will be unable to provide payroll services by the promised times.
- **The payment per service** (if applicable).
- **Performance targets and methods of measuring performance:** For a service such as the maintenance of an in-house computer network, a complex set of measurements and targets representing aspects of performance and overall performance will be required (Buco et al., 2004). Typically, data on network performance (e.g., response times, down time, security violations) and load will be collected, stored and reported for each hour, each location and each function; and aggregate measures of performance will be calculated and reported. There will be a corresponding set of performance targets. The required data can come from digital and other sources such as timesheets. The client should be able to obtain an independent audit of performance reports (Sturm et al., 2000, p. 71). A "stretch" as well as a normal target may be specified.
- **Computation of penalties and/or bonuses:** The agreement must specify how penalties and/or bonuses are calculated. Typically, the calculation incorporates targets and formulae pertaining to several performance measures; and penalties increase more than linearly with underperformance. Formulae can incorporate binary elements (a penalty applies if availability is less than 99%); linear elements (the penalty is proportional to non-availability) or non-linear elements (penalties increase with the square of underperformance) (Buco et al., 2004, Table 1). Achieving stretch targets may earn a bonus.
- **Other clauses** pertaining, for example, to security and privacy may be required.

Writing these detailed clauses is laborious but necessary and beneficial especially if critical processes are transferred to other organisations. The exercise is also beneficial in insourcing arrangements because it makes each party's obligations explicit.

## A Taxonomy of Service Attributes

This section describes service attributes used to assess the quality of services. Their relevance varies amongst different kinds of services and customers.

### Accessibility

A service is accessible if, assuming that it is working perfectly and to schedule, it is usable by customers. Access to an automatic teller machine (ATM) may be restricted because there is no ATM within a reasonable distance; an ATM operates for limited hours; not knowing English precludes use; or an ATM is not usable by the wheelchair-bound. A service encumbered by an excessive number of controls may not be accessible, for example, to occasional users who have forgotten passwords. Accessibility differs from availability in that it is predictable and its parameters (hours, locations, etc.) express organisational policies.

## Availability

Availability is the fraction of the scheduled up time that the service is actually working. An ATM scheduled to work from 6am to midnight but is down for 30 minutes has availability 97.2%. In a complex system such as an in-house computer network, the calculations of availability is multidimensional; at a given time it may be working at some locations, some applications may be malfunctioning, some databases or email addresses may not be accessible or the response time may be so slow as to preclude use. Several measures are combined to give an aggregate measure of availability.

## Performance

Performance criteria vary with the kind of service. Criteria for computer networks, delivery services, HR functions and building security are very different. It is important to consider the variance as well as means of performance measures. An apparently satisfactory average response time may conceal a small number of clients suffering long waits.

### *Time*

Criteria pertaining to time include:

- **Response:** How long does it take for the server to acknowledge a request for service? This sometimes trivial component of the total time required to complete a service can be psychologically important (consider dialing 911 or 000). Long waits for call centre service imply that a customer is unimportant. Long response times may discourage use of a computer system and be tantamount to unavailability.
- **Queuing:** Queuing time is either the time between acknowledgement of a request and service beginning, or the gap between the scheduled and actual start of service. Lengthy queues at ticketing counters, supermarket checkouts, doctors' surgeries, intersections and ATMs lessen service quality. Some queues, for example, of machines waiting for repair or documents accumulating in in-trays are not visible but still detract from service levels.
- **Performance:** The time taken to perform the service once started. Some services are not performed immediately on request but are regularly scheduled. Delivery to a suburb may be scheduled each second day, and computer systems generating reports may be run overnight.

- **Turnaround:** The turnaround time is the time between requesting work and the work being performed and delivered. It is the sum of response, queuing, performance and delivery times.

### *Competence*

The vendor's competence is manifestly important but may have difficult to measure components. For example:

- When a repair is performed it may be impossible to determine whether the repaired item will continue working for several years or fail prematurely.
- A recruitment agency presents a shortlist of three candidates; it is difficult to compare the shortlist's quality with the pool of potential candidates. Has the shortlisting process wrongly eliminated (or failed to eliminate) some applicants?
- Is a computer system "user-friendly"?
- A critical dimension of competence is accuracy: Was tax calculated accurately? Were the goods ordered correctly packaged and delivered to the right address? Did a doctor diagnose correctly?

## Capacity and Flexibility

The number of transactions per hour a network or call centre can manage per hour; the number of patients that seen per hour; or the number of deliveries that can be made each day may be relevant. The vendor may have enough capacity to meet normal demand but not enough to cope with peaks caused by marketing campaigns or Christmas orders.

Flexibility is the vendor's ability to customise services and to cope with exceptional cases. Although a recruitment agent and client may have agreed on a standardised methodology of filling staff vacancies, the detail will differ amongst vacancies to be filled. The parties may acknowledge that it would be extremely tedious to specify in advance every possible job description and agree to rely on the vendor's expertise. This implies that some aspects of service cannot be definitively expressed in legally binding terms and that the client must rely on the vendor's commitment and professional competence. Most organisations have products or customers whose importance warrants special treatment.

## Security and Privacy

Some service attributes pertain to privacy (especially of customer and employee data); preservation of the client's physical and intellectual property; prevention of damage caused by attacks from viruses, hacking, and other kinds of criminal activity; and disaster recovery. A small organisation's difficulty in creating and maintaining an IT disaster recovery plan might a compelling reason for outsourcing.

## Empathy and Ambience

Empathy or ambience may be important, especially for some personal services. The empathy of medical staff or waiters may be an important aspect of the service.

Intangible attributes are (by definition) difficult to measure unambiguously. Customer surveys attempting to measure satisfaction are often used but may not be reliable: response rates are usually low, some people believe that critical comments will result in staff being dismissed; others, complaining of being "surveyed out", may return facetious responses. It may be better for managers to "manage by walking around". By visiting a delivery depot, hospital ward or helpdesk a manager may be able to observe that staff are neatly dressed and sense that staff are positive and cheerful when answering inquiries.

## Status and Prestige

Some services such as flying first class may confer status and/or prestige. The SLA may compel the vendor to preserve distinctions, for example, between first class and tourist class meals.

# Example: Supply of Patients' Meals

We illustrate the concepts and issues with a practical problem. A hospital, perhaps dissatisfied with current internal arrangements or deciding to "stick to the knitting", decides to outsource the supply of patients' meals. There are many aspects of meals and their delivery to patients that were informally or implicitly agreed with the internal supplier but must now be negotiated with a vendor. Prior to negotiating, hospital managers decide the following attributes are critical:

- Cost.
- Times at which meals are served.
- Nutritional and calorific value.
- Palatability.
- Choice and variety at each meal and over a period: It is desirable for patients to have a choice of breakfasts but, even if there is no choice at an individual breakfast, patients should have a variety of breakfasts over a week.

- Service quality: Are meals to be served on paper plates with plastic cutlery or on china with cloth serviettes?
- Temperature: how hot does an ostensibly hot meal have to be when served?
- Food texture: Some patients cannot manage normal food.

Each criterion's importance varies amongst kinds of patient: for example, nutritional value and variety are less important for short-term patients. Hospitals have to provide different diets for diabetic, renal, aged, cardiac, and surgical patients; they may choose to include meals for staff in the contract; and some patients require vegetarian, hallal, or kosher food. Meals will vary with the seasons and special menus may be provided, for example, Christmas day. The SLA will certainly reflect laws pertaining to safe preparation, storage and handling of food.

The parties must negotiate definitions of terms such as nutritional value and palatability; the way in which they are to be measured; performance targets; and penalties. Some attributes can be measured objectively, for others (palatability and variety) the negotiators may have to rely on patient surveys, agreed menus, or expert opinion. Negotiations will be complicated by having to agree on the resources each party will provide, for example: Will hospital or vendor staff serve meals? Will the vendor be able to use hospital facilities to park vehicles, transfer food from containers to trays, heat meals and dispose of rubbish? The parties must negotiate price regimes and volumes. There might be a flat annual fee for serving up to 1,000 meals per day or a fee per meal.

Initially, the requirements can be expressed as a natural hierarchy (Figure 1). However, this simple hierarchy must be changed because some attributes pertain not to individual meals but to the set of all meals or all breakfasts served in a week. The nutritional value of a single meal is unimportant; what matters is the nutritional value of a week's meals. Similarly, the variety of breakfasts is not an attribute of a single breakfast but of a week's breakfasts. Therefore, the simple hierarchy of Figure 1 must be modified as shown in Figure 2. Figure 2 shows, for one class of patient, a more elaborate hierarchy of service

*Figure 1. A hierarchy of user groups and service elements*

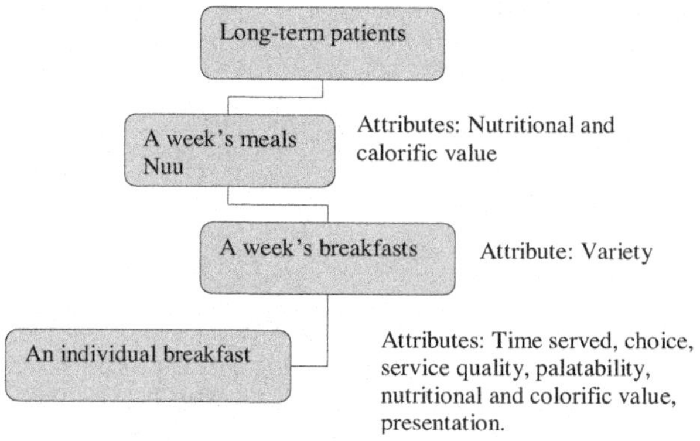

*Figure 2. A hierarchy of service elements and attributes*

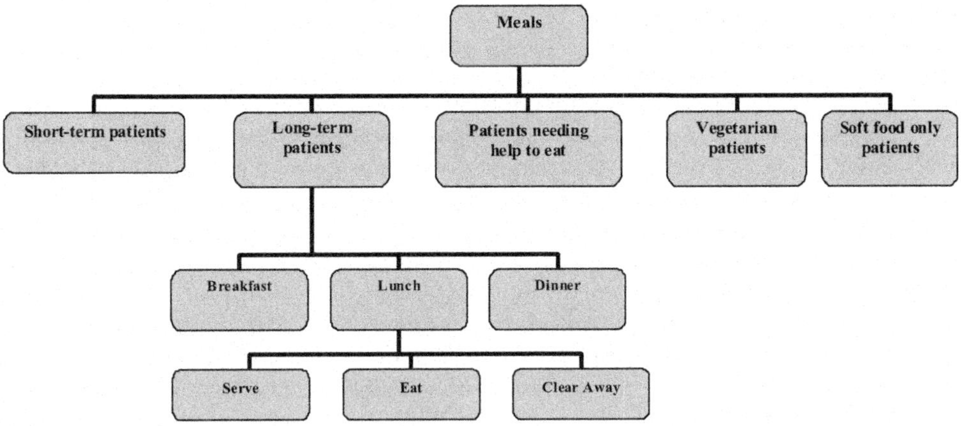


elements and their attributes. At the node "A week's breakfasts" the parties must negotiate a definition of the attribute "variety"; how it will be measured, target levels, and penalties or bonuses for under or overachievement.

The advantage of recognising hierarchies is that the volume of documentation can be reduced by parameterisation. The service level clauses for each kind of meal should have the same form, but different values of parameters should be inserted to express, for example, requirements pertaining to the different times at which each meal is served, and the required calorific value and nutritional value of a meal or set of meals.

# Conclusions

Academic interest in service level agreements has lagged their growing use in industry. Outsourcing and insourcing have become widely used business techniques, primarily because they can reduce costs and improve service quality by giving clients access to expertise and economies of scale. Well-defined objectives and a good working relationship between vendor and client are essential to fruitful outsourcing. Service level agreements help clients precisely define their requirements, assist negotiations between the parties, express the agreements reached, and provide a mechanism for changing the agreement and monitoring the vendor's performance. Their commercial importance and business interest in them suggests that they merit more academic attention.

Despite their importance to business, the academic community appears to have little organised knowledge of business use of outsourcing, insourcing and especially service level agreements. Outstanding research issues include:

- Ascertaining the incidence and success (or failure) of outsourcing arrangements and the effect of service level agreements on outsourcing agreements' success or failure. The assumption that well written SLA's can augment outsourcing's benefits needs to be tested.
- Negotiating, implementing, monitoring and renegotiating an SLA are complex processes requiring considerable amounts of managerial time. Researchers should examine these processes and suggest methodologies that would make these processes efficient and effective. Our interviews suggest that euphoria on signature is sometimes followed by disillusion when the parties (especially when the anticipated benefits do not appear) interpret clauses differently or ignore the 'spirit of the agreement'. A problem that has recurred in Australia is that the able executives who negotiated an agreement move on once the agreement is signed. Less able executives, not privy to the tacit agreements and/or assumptions of their predecessors, take over the operation often taking a literal view of the agreement that reduces the value of the relationship. This may deepen the frequently experienced post-signature disillusionment and accentuate a breakdown of the relationship.
- Outsourcing arrangements vary from those in which the requirements and performance are straightforwardly defined (a payroll system) to those in which requirements are difficult to express and performance is difficult to measure (an elaborate new computer system). In the latter case, maybe impossible to reduce the whole of the relationship to contractual form, an element of trust or different contractual form such as a joint venture is required.
- A possible, even likely, development is that all organisations will outsource their non-core processes, and make money by focusing on a small set of core competences (Evans & Wurster, 2000). This has implications for industry structure (a network of smaller, more focused, organizations will emerge) and competition. Strassmann (1997) eloquently argues that it is foolish for any but the largest organisations to retain their own IT departments whose work is essential reinventing wheels. He suggests that internal IT departments' difficulty in keeping up with demand and obtaining and retaining competent staff will force almost all organisations to outsource IT, treating it as a utility like water or electricity. A few huge IT firms will fulfill organisations' largely standardized IT requirements by supplying and running software modules each of which satisfies a business requirement. Perhaps packages such as SAP are precursors.

# References

Beaumont, N. B., & Costa, C. (2002). Information technology outsourcing in Australia. *Information Resources Management Journal, 15*(3), 14-31.

Beaumont, N. B., & Sohal, A. (2004). Outsourcing in Australia. *International Journal of Operations and Production Management, 24*(7), 688-700.

Beck, J., & Allegretti, B. (1999). SLAs defined: Meeting response time service level agreements in an integrated, multi-protocol network. *Enterprise Systems Journal, 14*(3), 40-44.

Bhoj, P., Singhal, S., & Chutani;, S. (2001). SLA management in federated units. *Computer Networks, 35*(1), 5-24.

Blacharski, D. (2000). The changing face of service level agreements. *Network Magazine, 15*(2), 94-97.

Buco, M. J., Chang, R. N., Luan, L. Z., Ward, C., Wolf, J. L., & Yu, P. S. (2004). Utility computing SLA management based upon business objectives. *IBM Systems Journal, 43*(1), 159-178.

Chen, M.-S., Lin, C., & Lee, C.-C. (2002). Developing a method for measuring the service level of general hospitals with consulting stations. *International Journal of Management, 19*(3), 439-444.

Coombs, H., & Evans, A. (2000). Managing central support services through service level agreements. *The Government Accountants Journal, 49*(1), 54-59.

Dib, N., Freer, J., & Gray, C. (1998). Service-level agreements at the Huddersfield NHS Trust. *International Journal of Healthcare Quality Assurance, 11*(3), 96.

Ekanayaka, Y., Currie, W. L., & Seltsikas, P. (2002). Delivering enterprise resource planning systems through application service providers. *Logistics Information Management, 15*(3), 192-203.

Evans, P., & Wurster, T. S. (2000). *Blown to bits : How the new economics of information transforms strategy*. Boston: Harvard Business School Press.

Gavi, L. (1999). Service level management for IP networks. *British Telecommunications Engineering, 18*(Part 2, Special Issue SI), 106-109.

Greaver, M. F. (1999). *Strategic outsourcing: A structured approach to outsourcing decisions and initiative*. New York: Amacom.

Hensher, D. A., Stopher, P., & Bullock, P. (2003). Service quality — Developing a service quality index in the provision of commercial bus contracts. *Transportation Research: Part A, 37*(6), 499.

Hiles, A. (1993). *Service level agreements: Measuring cost and quality in service relationships* (1st ed.). London & New York: Chapman & Hall.

Hiles, A. (2002). *E-business service level agreements: Strategies for service providers, e-commerce and outsourcing*. Brookfield, CT: The Rothstein Catalog on Service Level Books.

Karten, N. (1998). *How to establish service level agreements*. Randolph, MA: Naomi Karten.

Karten, N. (2004). With service level agreements, less is more. *Information Systems Management, 21*(4), 43-44.

Kellor, A., & Ludwig, H. (2003). The WSLA framework: Specifying and monitoring service level agreements for Web services. *Journal of Network and Systems Management, 11*(1), 57-81.

KPMG. (1998). *Guide to service level agreements*. KPMG.

Larson, P. D., & Halldorsson, A. (2002). What is SCM? And, where is it? *Journal of Supply Chain Management, 38*(4), 36-44.

Lee, J. J., & Ben-Natan, R. (2002). *Integrating service level agreements: Optimizing your OSS for SLA delivery*. Indianapolis, IN: Wiley Pub.

Lewis, E. (1999). Using the risk-remedy method to evaluate outsourcing tenders. *Journal of Information Technology, 14*(2), 203-211.

Ludwig, H., Keller, A., Dan, A., & King, R. (2003). A service level agreement language for dynamic electronics services. *Electronic Commerce Research, 3*(1-2), 43-59.

Management Advisory Services & Publications Consulting Group. (2001). *How to prepare service level agreements (SLAs) for application service provisioning (ASP) - Checklists and guidelines*. Wellesley Hills, MA: Management Advisory Services & Publications.

Oblicore. (2004). *Best practices and trends in service level management and IT outsourcing compliance monitoring*. Oblicore.

Owens, T. W. (1983). Service level management at the distributor level. *Production and Inventory Management, 24*(Second Quarter), 71.

Pantry, S., & Griffiths, P. (2001). *The complete guide to planning and implementing service level agreements* (2nd ed.). London: Library Association.

Parish, R. J. (1997). Service level agreements as a contributor to TQM goals. *Logistics Information Management (Current title: Journal of Enterprise Information Management), 10*(6), 284.

Quinn, J. B., & Hilmer, F. G. (1994). Strategic outsourcing. *Sloan Management Review, 35*(4), 43-55.

Slaight, T. H. (1999). Stategic sourcing: Not a "squeeze your vendors" process. *Telecommunications, 33*(3), 59-62.

Smith, A. (1995). What's the big idea? *Management Auckland, 42*(2).

Strassmann, P. A. (1997). *The squandered computer: Evaluating the business alignment of information technologies*. New Canaan, CT: Information Economics.

Sturm, R., Morris, W., & Jander, M. (2000). *Foundations of service level management*. Indianapolis, IN: SAMS.

Verma, D. (1999). *Supporting service level agreements on IP networks*. Indianapolis, IN: Macmillan Technical Pub.

# Endnotes

1 http://www.in-sourced.com/article/articleprint/1705/-1/1/ (accessed 11 May 2004)

2 www.ecommercetimes.com/perl/story/32114.html (accessed 11 May 2004)

[3] www.it-careernet.com/itc/OS/globalmarket.htm (accessed 11 May 2004)

[4] www.mau.ac.uk/slas/ukerna/2003-04/sla.htm

[5] http://www.druginfozone.org/Record%20Viewing/viewRecord.aspx?id=531627

[6] itd.utc.edu/sla/fac_saindex.shtml

[7] www.bibliocentre.ca/ServiceLevelAgreement3.html

[8] mkruse.netexpress.net/sla/

## Chapter XV

# Understanding Consumer Reactions to Offshore Outsourcing of Customer Services

Piyush Sharma
Nanyang Business School, Singapore

Rajiv Mathur
Percom Limited, India

Abhinav Dhawan
team4U Outsourced Staffing Services, India

## Abstract

*Offshore outsourcing is a fast-growing aspect of the world economy today and it has drawn attention from policy makers as well as public at large in many developed countries. However, there is hardly any research on how outsourcing of customer services may influence individual consumers, their perceptions, attitudes and behaviors. In this chapter, the authors first review the extant literature in the country-of-origin and services marketing areas to highlight key concepts and theories relevant to this area. Next, they show how offshore outsourcing of customer services may influence consumer perceptions about service quality, brand image and brand loyalty on one hand and impact customer satisfaction, complaint behavior and repurchase intentions on the other. The role of several relevant demographic and psychographic variables is also discussed. Finally, the findings from a survey-based study among customers in three developed countries (U.S., UK and Australia) are reported along with a discussion of managerial implications and future research directions in this area.*

# Introduction

## Background

Outsourcing is a fast-growing aspect of the world economy with worldwide spending on outsourcing estimated to cross $6 trillion by the end of 2005 (Corbett, 2002). Forrester Research estimates that by 2015, 3.3 million jobs accounting for $136 billion in wages will move offshore to countries such as India, China and Russia (McCartney, 2003). According to latest estimates by Gartner, IT outsourcing global revenue alone was predicted to grow from $184 billion in 2003 to over $256 billion in 2008 (Blackmore, DeSouza, Young, Goodness, & Silliman, 2005) and IDC estimates business process outsourcing (BPO) in Europe to grow from $43 to $72 billion Euros between 2002 and 2005. Clearly these are very large numbers and companies around the world seem to be relentlessly pursuing outsourcing to benefit the end customers by reducing cost and improving productivity.

However, existing research on offshore outsourcing is primarily focused on the labor and ethical issues of outsourcing and effects of strategic outsourcing decisions on organizations with hardly any attention on how it may influence individual customers (Clott, 2004). Similarly, critics of outsourcing have so far focused on the changing employment patterns, globalization of the labor force, and its effects on individual employees and organizations with little consideration to the end-customers. On the other hand, based on their experience in recent years organizations have already become more cautious about outsourcing and conscious of the need to protect their reputation, brand image, core skills and property rights (Reilly, 1997). Some of the emerging potential downsides of outsourcing include dilution of company's image, lower customer satisfaction, reduced brand loyalty and an increase in customer complaints due to real or perceived concerns about cultural differences, lower service standards and loss of privacy (Cornell, 2004; "AxaAbbey", 2004; "Back office", 2001; Kennedy, 2002; Roy, 2003).

## Consumers and Offshore Outsourcing

In a recent customer survey by American Banker/Gallup (2004) it was found that two-thirds (71%) of the respondents were aware of offshore outsourcing to lower-cost countries. Among those aware, a whopping 78% held an unfavorable opinion about it and more than 80% said they would feel better if outsourcing did not take away American jobs and only less than half would feel better if it made American companies more competitive in the global marketplace (51%) or if it improved American companies' profits (46%). However, besides these general surveys, there is very little research that could specifically help organizations understand the effects of offshore outsourcing of customer service on individual customers, their perceptions, attitudes and behavior.

On the other hand, there is a large body of knowledge in the area of country-of-origin (COO) phenomenon which demonstrates that customers have distinctly different perceptions and attitudes about foreign products and services (Gronroos, 1999; Javalgi, Cutler, & Winans, 2001; Javalgi, Griffith, & White, 2003; Kotabe, Murray, & Javalgi, 1998; Lovelock, 1999; Nicoulaud, 1989; Ruyter, Birgelen, & Wetzels, 1998). Specifically, it is shown that products and services from less-developed countries are evaluated unfavorably by customers in developed countries due to negative perceptions about their quality. In the context of offshore outsourcing of customer services, it is shown that some customers may not want to speak to a customer care representative from a particular country (Briggs, 2005) and some of them believe that continuing outsourcing of call centres abroad will diminish customer satisfaction (Hayward, 2004). However, there is little research in consumer behavior or marketing literature about the socio-psychological process underlying these customer perceptions.

In this chapter we address this important gap in existing research by combining learning from existing literature in the COO and services marketing areas to this emerging field. Specifically, we address the following questions in this chapter:

1. Are customers aware of offshore outsourcing of customer services in general?
2. Are they aware of offshore outsourcing of customer services in their own day-to-day lives?
3. How do they perceive offshore outsourcing of services in general?
4. How do they evaluate their own experiences with offshore outsourcing of customer services?
5. How does offshore outsourcing of customer services influence brand image, brand loyalty, customer satisfaction, customer complaint behavior and repeat purchase intentions?

# Background

## What is Offshore Outsourcing?

Outsourcing is a contractual agreement between the customer and one or more suppliers to provide services or processes that the customer is currently providing internally (Fan, 2000). In other words, outsourcing occurs when an organization transfers some of its tasks to an outside supplier (Siems & Ratner, 2003). The benefits of outsourcing are well-known: (1) reduce cost, (2) improve quality, service and delivery, (3) improve organizational focus, (4) increase flexibility and (5) facilitate change. Numerous studies portray the strategic benefits of offshore outsourcing for firms as a means to reduce costs, improve asset efficiency, and increase profits (Quinn, 1997).

However, in recent years organizations have become more cautious about moving towards outsourcing and conscious of the need to protect their reputation, brand image, core skills and property rights (Reilly, 1997). According to Kennedy companies risk *losing potential customers* for the parent brand due to poor customer relationship management by outsourced sub-contractors. Similarly, companies in UK have been warned of a possible customer backlash if they continue to offshore jobs to lower-cost economies, as further domestic job cuts will undoubtedly harm their *corporate image* ("Axa/Abbey", 2004). Suppliers of outsourced services also play a key role in influencing outsiders' opinions of the organization (Trapp, 1999).

Dell Computers returned its business help desk from India to North America last year because of an *increase in complaints* from its customers about the Indian employees' perceived heavy reliance on scripted answers and lack of expertise required for solving complex computer problems (Cornell, 2004). Moreover, due to concerns that Indian call centers may have distinctly *lower service standards* than the British ones, many "exported" jobs deal with simple customer account queries and the more complex enquires are serviced in UK ("Axa/Abbey", 2004). Some American medical-transcription firms even refuse to outsource work to India due to *concerns about privacy of information*, despite potential savings of up to 50% ("Back office", 2001). There are also concerns about how many American medical and financial services firms are shifting information-processing work to low-wage countries that lack tough privacy laws, leaving the most sensitive details of the lives of millions of their customers *vulnerable to lax security and in the hands of malicious identity thieves* (Swartz, 2004a, 2004b).

## COO, Customer Ethnocentrism and Offshore Outsourcing

Customer ethnocentrism represents a preference for domestic products on the basis of nationalistic feelings and ethnocentric customers are shown to be reluctant to buy foreign products, because of a sense of loyalty towards their home country (Shimp, 1984; Shimp & Sharma, 1987). Customer ethnocentric tendencies can also lead to negative attitudes towards foreign products in general and researchers have identified several antecedents and moderating factors of customer ethnocentricity in the product-sector (Sharma, Shimp & Shin, 1995). These include four social-psychological antecedents: "openness to foreign cultures," "patriotism", "conservatism", and "collectivism/individualism" together with four demographic factors: "age", "gender", "education" and "income" along with two moderating factors: "perceived necessity of the product" and "perceived economic threat of foreign competition".

Ruyter et al. (1998) extended this theory to the services sector and using an empirical study with Dutch customers, they confirmed the generalizability of the ethnocentric model and provided evidence of the fact that COO effects do play a role in customers choice behaviour towards international services. They were also able to replicate Sharma et al.'s (1995) findings with respect to all social-psychological antecedents. Other researchers have explored the influence of customer patriotism, conservatism and ethnocentrism (Ali-Sulaiti & Baker, 1998; Gronroos, 1999; Kaynak, Kucukemiroglu, &

Kara, 1994). On the other hand, offshore outsourcing in the manufacturing industry has been acknowledged by COO researchers in the form of hybrid products, that is, products which may be designed in one country, whose components may be produced in another country and which may be assembled in yet another country (Chao, 1993b, 2001; Han & Terpstra, 1988; Tse & Lee, 1993). Using Osgood and Tannenbaum's (1955) congruency principle these researchers argue that there is a congruency among the different COO elements which influences customer attitudes towards a hybrid product. This has led COO researchers to conceptualize it as a multidimensional construct and incorporate its various dimensions in their research e.g. uni-national versus bi-national products (Han & Terpstra, 1988), country of components versus assembly (Tse & Lee, 1993), country of design versus assembly (Sauer, Young, & Unnava, 1991) country of assembly versus parts versus design (Chao, 1993a, 2001) and multiple COO facets as a result of global outsourcing (Li, Murray, & Scott, 2000).

Using a similar approach, we argue that offshore outsourcing of customer services has converted many conventional services into hybrid forms wherein various components of many services are now performed in different countries. For example, in healthcare services doctors in the U.S. examine their patients physically and record their observations into their dictaphones. Next, these recordings are digitized and uploaded into the servers of medical transcription companies based in Indian cities like Bangalore and Gurgaon where skilled operators decipher these and complete the documentation such as patient records and billing. Similarly, call center operators based in another country like Philippines or Singapore may handle queries from these patients. Researchers have also shown that customers are increasingly becoming aware of such practices followed by more and more businesses that they deal with every day and hence, it is important to study how this awareness would influence their perceptions, attitudes and behavior towards these businesses (Brown & Chin, 2004).

## Conceptual Framework

Prior research in COO area has linked it with several psychographic variables including consumer ethnocentrism, patriotism, conservatism and openness to foreign cultures on one hand and demographic variables such as age, gender, education, occupation, country of birth, residence and citizenship (Ali-Sulaiti & Baker, 1998; Sharma et al., 1995). Specifically, it is shown that highly ethnocentric, patriotic, conservative and less open to foreign cultures consumers are more likely to have negative perceptions about imported products and services. Similarly, older, female, less educated, blue-collar workers and consumers who are born and brought up in developed countries are shown to be more ethnocentric.

Based on these findings in prior literature, we argue that all these demographic variables would also act as antecedents of consumer perceptions about businesses and brands that use offshore outsourcing of customer services. Moreover, we suggest that all the above psychographic variables may not have a direct effect but a moderating influence on consumer perceptions about service quality, customer satisfaction, brand image,

*Figure 1. Conceptual framework*

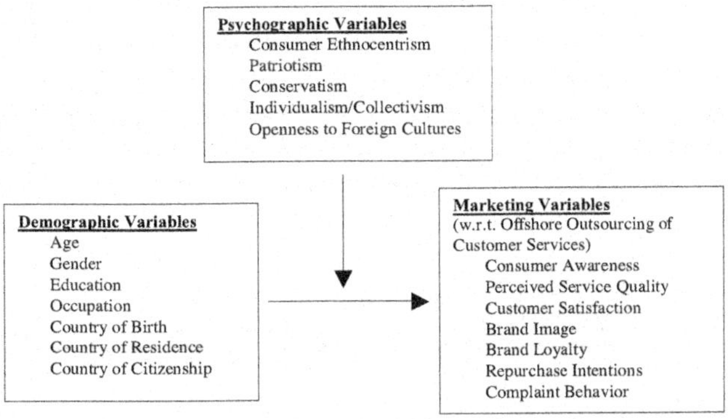


brand loyalty, repeat purchase intentions and complaint behavior. Next we discuss how two of these variables (i.e., home country and consumer ethnocentrism) influence different aspects of consumer perceptions, attitudes and behavior.

## Service Quality Perceptions

Many services which used to be performed within one country or indeed just one city are now performed in two or more countries around the world. This has resulted in an interaction between the customers and service providers from two different cultural and socio-economic backgrounds especially in contact-based services (Clark, Rajaratnam, & Smith, 1996). Managing these interactions has never been an easy task because close cultural relationships within a society and the way various services are offered in that society make it extremely difficult to market services internationally (Dahringer, 1991). In fact, even within one's own country perceived nationality of a service provider may be more important to the customers than the supplementary or extra services offered by the provider as seen in the study of national stereotype effects on the selection of professional healthcare service providers (Harrison-Walker, 1995). To summarize these findings, customer ethnocentric tendencies do affect customer evaluation of services that are perceived to be foreign or provided by foreigners and generally this effect is negative if the COO of these service providers is less developed compared to the home country.

## Customer Satisfaction

Service Quality consists of customer perceptions of the goodness-of-service provided to them (Cronin Jr. & Taylor, 1992; Parasuraman, Zeithaml, & Berry, 1988) and customer satisfaction is conceptualized as an affect-laden fulfillment response to service received (Oliver, 1997). As such, the cognitive perception of service quality logically precedes the affective judgment of satisfaction and therefore, perceptions of service quality are shown to be an antecedent of customer satisfaction (Brown & Chin, 2004). Hayward (2004) suggests that continuing outsourcing of call centres abroad will diminish customer satisfaction, because it is associated with relatively lower levels of service quality. Hence, offshore outsourcing of customer services may lead to lower customer satisfaction for some consumers because they may perceive a decline in the quality of service they received from overseas service representatives.

## Repurchase Intentions

Customer satisfaction is directly and positively related to repurchase intentions because satisfied customers are more likely to want to experience the same satisfactory experience again and again (Anderson & Sullivan, 1993; Brown & Chin, 2004; Butcher, Sparks, & O'Callaghan, 2001; Cronin Jr. & Taylor, 1992; Hellier, Geursen, Carr, & Rickard, 2003). Therefore, it is likely that customers who have negative perceptions about firms that use offshore outsourcing of customer services, may not like to continue purchasing that firm's products or services. In other words, offshore outsourcing may lead to a decline in repeat purchase intentions for some consumers because they may not like to deal with offshore service representatives or perceive the quality of their service to be distinctly lower compared to local staff of the same company in their home country.

## Brand Image

Researchers have shown customers' perceptions about product quality to be positively associated with their perceptions of brand image (Steenkamp, 1990). Similarly, service quality is shown to be closely related to brand image across a wide range of industries such as hospitality (Francese & Renaghan, 1990), auto insurance and copy service (Arora & Stoner, 1996), life insurance (Hill, 1996), travel and tourism (Gilbert & Hewlett, 2003) and cruise lines (Ahmed, Johnson, Ling, Fong, & Hui, 2002). Similarly, customer satisfaction has been positively associated with brand image (Mayer, Bowen, & Moulton, 2003; Palacio, Meneses, & Perez, 2002; Selnes, 1993). Therefore, the customer perceptions about service quality and their level of satisfaction with offshore outsourced customer services would influence their perceptions about brand image. In other words, offshore outsourcing of customer services by companies may lead to erosion in their brand image in the minds of those consumers who have negative perceptions about the quality of service offered by the overseas service representatives.

## Brand Loyalty

Service quality is positively associated with customer loyalty although this relationship appears to be stronger at the company level rather than at the interpersonal level (Wong

& Sohal, 2003). Similarly, it is found that service quality is positively associated with emotional satisfaction, which is positively associated with both customer loyalty and relationship quality (Wong, 2004). Several studies have found a strong positive association between customer satisfaction and brand loyalty across several service categories such as telecommunications (Kim, Park, & Jeong, 2004), financial services (Chernatony, Harris, & Christodoulides, 2004) and travel (McCaskey & Symes, 2004). Hence, offshore outsourcing of customer services would influence customers' brand loyalty through its association with their perceptions about service quality and their level of customer satisfaction.

## Complaint Behavior

It is fairly well-established in extant literature that customer lack of satisfaction often triggers the process of complaining and this effect is stronger in case of services compared to products (Bearden & Teel, 1983; Crié, 2003; Gronhaug & Gilly, 1991; Singh & Pandya, 1991; Singh & Wilkes, 1996). Based on this, it is argued that offshore outsourcing of customer services would influence customers' complaint behavior because of its strong association with their level of satisfaction and perceived quality of service. In other words, some customers when faced with a dissatisfactory service experience, are more likely to complain if this service encounter involved an offshore service representative rather than a local one in their home country.

# Empirical Findings

To test the impact of offshore outsourcing on customer perceptions, a survey was conducted in three developed countries namely, United States (U.S.), United Kingdom (UK) and Australia with 100 customers each, resulting in a total sample size of 300. Graduate students were used to approach shoppers at local malls in these countries and recruited to participate in the survey. The survey questionnaire consisted of the following well-established scales with a Likert-type seven-point response format, to measure all the constructs used in this study: Customer Ethnocentrism (Sharma et al., 1995), Brand Image (Aaker, 1996), Brand Loyalty (Quester & Lim, 2003), Service Quality (Parasuraman et al., 1988), Customer Satisfaction (Oliver, 1997), Repurchase Intentions (Hellier et al., 2003), Customer Complaint Behavior Scale (Singh, 1988). The questionnaire had three parts. First, the customers were asked to rate one of their existing service providers (e.g., bank, insurance company, health care provider, mobile phone service provider, etc.) using these scales. Next, they were asked if they were aware of offshore outsourcing of customer services and asked to complete the same scales again assuming if the same provider were to outsource its customer services to some offshore locations in a less-developed Asian country (e.g., India, Philippines or Thailand). Finally, they were asked to complete the customer ethnocentrism scale and their demographics such as gender and age were also recorded.

We conducted exploratory factor analysis and reliability tests on all the scales used and found high factor loadings on the expected factors (> 0.60) and high Cronbach's alpha values for all the scales (> 0.70). Next we used ANOVA to compare the average scores for all these scales across the two conditions, that is, offshore outsourcing (yes or no). Thereafter, each participant was classified as low (N=196, M=3.7) and high (N=104, M=4.9) on their customer ethnocentrism scores using a median split. There was no significant difference in average consumer ethnocentrism scores across the three countries. Finally, the average scores for each scale were compared across low and high ethnocentric groups for each country. All the results are summarized in Table 1 and 2.

As seen from Table 1, customers in all the three developed countries have distinctly less favorable perceptions about service quality, lower customer satisfaction and greater complaint behavior towards firms which use offshore outsourcing of customer services. However, the findings on brand image, brand loyalty and repurchase intentions were mixed, with customers in U.S. and Australia showing lower brand image, those in Australia showing lower repurchase intentions and those in UK showing a less favorable brand image for companies using offshore outsourcing.

On the other hand, as seen in Table 2 we found high ethnocentric customers were found to have distinctly lower perceptions about service quality, customer satisfaction, repurchase intentions, brand image and brand loyalty along with greater complaint behavior, towards companies using offshore outsourcing of customer services (with the sole exception of brand loyalty among American consumers). We also compared the

*Table 1. Mean comparison – Offshore outsourcing (ANOVA)*

| | United States | | United Kingdom | | Australia | | Overall | |
|---|---|---|---|---|---|---|---|---|
| | No | Yes | No | Yes | No | Yes | No | Yes |
| Service Quality | 5.6 | 4.5 [a] | 4.8 | 4.2 [b] | 6.0 | 4.9 [a] | 5.5 | 4.5 [a] |
| Customer Satisfaction | 5.4 | 4.7 [b] | 4.5 | 4.0 [c] | 5.8 | 5.0 [b] | 5.2 | 4.6 [b] |
| Repurchase Intention | 4.9 | 4.8 | 5.1 | 4.8 | 5.9 | 5.2 [b] | 5.3 | 4.9 [c] |
| Brand Image | 4.5 | 4.2 [c] | 5.5 | 5.2 | 5.5 | 4.5 [a] | 5.2 | 4.6 [c] |
| Brand Loyalty | 4.3 | 4.1 | 5.7 | 5.1 [b] | 6.3 | 5.9 | 5.4 | 5.0 [c] |
| Complaint Behavior | 4.9 | 5.7 [b] | 5.7 | 6.2 [c] | 4.0 | 4.7 [b] | 4.9 | 5.5 [b] |

*Table 2. Mean comparison – Customer ethnocentrism (ANOVA)*

| | United States | | United Kingdom | | Australia | | Overall | |
|---|---|---|---|---|---|---|---|---|
| | Low (69) | High (31) | Low (62) | High (38) | Low (65) | High (35) | Low (104) | High (196) |
| Service Quality | 4.9 | 3.7 [a] | 3.5 | 4.6 [a] | 4.0 | 5.4 [a] | 4.1 | 4.6 [b] |
| Customer Satisfaction | 5.2 | 3.6 [a] | 3.2 | 4.5 [a] | 4.4 | 5.3 [a] | 4.3 | 4.5 |
| Repurchase Intention | 4.9 | 4.6 [c] | 4.3 | 5.1 [b] | 4.8 | 5.4 [a] | 4.7 | 5.0 [c] |
| Brand Image | 4.3 | 3.9 [c] | 4.5 | 5.6 [a] | 4.1 | 4.7 [a] | 4.3 | 4.7 [c] |
| Brand Loyalty | 4.1 | 4.0 | 4.6 | 5.4 [b] | 5.2 | 6.3 [a] | 4.6 | 5.2 [b] |
| Complaint Behavior | 5.4 | 6.3 [a] | 6.6 | 6.0 [b] | 5.1 | 4.2 [a] | 5.7 | 5.5 |

various scores across gender and different age-groups. As in prior literature, females and younger customers were found to be less ethnocentric and less influenced by offshore outsourcing, compared to older males.

Overall, with this study we were able to demonstrate that consumer awareness of offshore outsourcing to less developed countries by companies does have a negative influence on the perceptions, attitudes and behaviors of customers in developed countries. These influences are strongest on service quality, customer satisfaction and complaint behavior, probably because these are a direct consequence of inter-personal interaction with service providers in offshore locations. On the other hand, these influences are less strong on brand image, brand loyalty and repurchase intentions, probably because there are other factors that have a greater influence on these, for example, involvement, perceived need and high exit barriers.

## Conclusions

In this chapter, we discuss the implications of offshore outsourcing for consumer behavior in general and its influence on consumer perceptions, attitudes and behaviors in particular. We first reviewed extant literature in the international and services marketing areas and then combined learnings from these two, to first conceptualize offshore outsourcing of customer services as a "hybrid service" and then develop a new conceptual framework. We also described a survey-based study undertaken in three developed countries (U.S., UK and Australia), which was used to test our hypotheses based on this new conceptual framework.

It is expected that this line of research would make managers more sensitive to the need to understand the challenges in managing the relationships between customers and their offshore service providers, and also draw more academic researchers to this emerging research area. The findings of similar studies may also suggest possible areas for improvement in a wide range of operational and strategic areas in the management of international services organizations, for example, human resources management, operations management, joint-venture and partner alliances management. Organizations with a high reliance on offshore outsourcing of customer services would be well-advised to draw up specific action plans to incorporate these learnings into their recruitment, training and retention programs, operations manuals, telesales scripts and other related materials for their offshore service representatives. Moreover, they may also need to develop customer education programs targeting those customers who are likely to have negative perceptions about the quality of service delivered by offshore service representatives. Such programs may be delivered through mass-media campaigns as well as specifically targeted direct marketing efforts and should attempt to convince the customers about the benefits of offshore outsourcing to them in terms of lower prices for services offered to them. Services organizations may even need to adjust their loyalty management or rewards programs for their regular customers to make sure that they are able to retain them.

Moreover, it would also be very useful to extend this line of research to the business-to- business (B2B) context because that area contributes to a significant proportion of the overall offshore outsourcing business. On one hand, the service standards expected by buyers of professional services could be much more stringent compared to individual consumers whereas on the other hand the exit-barriers in the buyer-seller relationship in this context could also be much stronger because of the money involved and other contractual obligations. Moreover, the awareness of the COO of offshore service providers and perceptions about their service quality could also be much stronger in the B2B context. Therefore, future researchers in this area could try to explore these relationships in the B2B context as well, besides validating and replicating these findings in business-to-consumer (B2C) context.

Finally, future researchers may expand upon our study in many ways. We measured the customer behaviors such as repeat purchase and complaint behavior only indirectly, that is, in terms of behavioral intentions. Future researchers may attempt a more direct measure for more robust results by looking at consumer panel data to track repeat purchase and complaint patterns. Similarly, due to operational limitations we did not measure customer reactions to offshore outsourcing to specific target countries but future research into this may provide some useful insights into this phenomenon.

# References

Aaker, D. A. (1996, May). Measuring brand equity across products and markets. *California Management Review, 31*, 191-201.

Ahmed, Z. U., Johnson, J. P., Ling, C. P., Fong, T. W., & Hui, A. K. (2002). Country-of-origin and brand effects on consumers' evaluations of cruise lines. *International Marketing Review, 19*(2/3), 279-302.

Ali-Sulaiti, K. I., & Baker, M. J. (1998). Country of origin effects: A literature review. *Marketing Intelligence & Planning, 16*(3), 150-199.

American Banker, & Gallup. (2004). *What Americans think about overseas outsourcing*: American Banker/Gallup.

Anderson, E. W., & Sullivan, M. W. (1993). The antecedents and consequences of customer satisfaction for firms. *Marketing Science, 12*(2), 125-143.

Arora, R., & Stoner, C. (1996). The effect of perceived service quality and name familiarity on the service selection decision. *The Journal of Services Marketing, 10*(1), 22.

Axa/Abbey: A passage to India. (2004). *Data-Monitor, 3*(3), 16-17.

Back office to the world. (2001). *Economist, 359*(8220), 59-61.

Bearden, W. O., & Teel, J. E. (1983). Selected determinants of consumer satisfaction and complaint reports. *Journal of Consumer Research, 20*(1), 21-28.

Blackmore, D., DeSouza, R., Young, A., Goodness, E., & Silliman, R. (2005). *Forecast: IT outsourcing, worldwide, 2002-2008 (update).* Gartner.

Briggs, B. (2005). Offshore outsourcing poses risks. *Health Data Management, 13*(2), 68-78.

Brown, S. P., & Chin, W. W. (2004). Satisfying and retaining customers through independent service representatives. *Decision Sciences, 35*(3), 527-550.

Butcher, K., Sparks, B., & O'Callaghan, F. (2001). Evaluative and relational influences on service loyalty. *International Journal of Service Industry Management, 12*(4), 310-327.

Chao, P. (1993a). Partitioning country of origin effects. *Journal of International Business Studies, 24*(2), 291-306.

Chao, P. (1993b). Partitioning country-of-origin effects: Consumer evaluations of a hybrid product. *Journal of International Business Studies, 24*(2), 291-306.

Chao, P. (2001). The moderating effects of country of assembly, country of parts, and country of design on hybrid product evaluations. *Journal of Advertising, 30*(4), 67-81.

Chernatony, L. d., Harris, F. J., & Christodoulides, G. (2004). Developing a brand performance measure for financial services brands. *The Service Industries Journal, 24*(2), 15.

Clark, T., Rajaratnam, D., & Smith, T. (1996). Toward a theory of international services: marketing insights in a world of nations. *Journal of International Marketing, 4*(2), 9-28.

Clott, C. B. (2004). Perspectives on global outsourcing and the changing nature of work. *Business and Society Review, 109*(2), 153-170.

Corbett, M. F. (2002, July 15). Outsourcing's next wave. *Fortune.*

Cornell, C. (2004). Offshore options: Outsourcing operations to overseas providers can save you money or cause you pain. The choice is yours. *Profit, 23*(4), 87-88.

Crié, D. (2003). Consumers' complaint behaviour. Taxonomy, typology and determinants: Towards a unified ontology. *Database Marketing & Customer Strategy Management, 11*(1), 60-79.

Cronin Jr., J. J., & Taylor, S. A. (1992). Measuring service quality: A reexamination and extension. *Journal of Marketing, 56,* 55-68.

Dahringer, L. D. (1991). Marketing services internationally: barriers and management strategies. *Journal of Services Marketing, 5*(3), 5-17.

Fan, Y. (2000). Strategic outsourcing: Evidence from British companies. *Marketing Intelligence & Planning, 18*(4), 213.

Francese, P. A., & Renaghan, L. M. (1990). Data-base marketing: Building customer profiles. *Cornell Hotel and Restaurant Administration Quarterly, 31*(1), 60-63.

Gilbert, D., & Hewlett, J. (2003). A method for the assessment of relative brand strength: A UK tour operator example. *The Service Industries Journal, 23*(2), 166.

Gronhaug, K., & Gilly, M. C. (1991). A transaction cost approach to consumer dissatisfaction and complaint actions. *Journal of Economic Psychology, 12*(1), 156-183.

Gronroos, C. (1999). Internationalization strategies for services. *Journal of Services Marketing, 13*(4/5), 290-297.

Han, C. M., & Terpstra, V. (1988, Summer). Country-of-origin effects for uni-national and bi-national products. *Journal of International Business Studies, 19*, 235-255.

Harrison-Walker, L. J. (1995). The relative effects of national stereotype and advertising information on the selection of a service provider. *Journal of Services Marketing, 9*(1), 47-59.

Hayward, M. (2004, September). I showed them the future and they ignored it. *Management Today*, 68-69.

Hellier, P. K., Geursen, G. M., Carr, R. A., & Rickard, J. A. (2003). Customer repurchase intention: A general structural equation model. *European Journal of Marketing, 37*(11/12), 1762-1800.

Hill, J. (1996). Keeping customers loyal at Liverpool Victoria Friendly Society. *Managing Service Quality, 6*(4), 27-31.

Javalgi, R. G., Cutler, B., & Winans, W. A. (2001). At your service! Does country of origin research apply? *Journal of Services Marketing, 15*(6/7), 565-582.

Javalgi, R. G., Griffith, D. A., & White, D. S. (2003). An empirical examination of factors influencing the internationalization of service firms. *Journal of Services Marketing, 17*(2/3), 185-201.

Kaynak, E., Kucukemiroglu, O., & Kara, A. (1994). Consumer perceptions of airlines: A correspondence analysis approach in an airline industry. *Management International Review, 34*(3), 235-254.

Kennedy, C. (2002). Name and shame: If you outsource, beware. Your brand may be in tatters through appalling customer service - and you may never know it. *Director, 56*(5), 23.

Kim, M.-K., Park, M.-C., & Jeong, D.-H. (2004). The effects of customer satisfaction and switching barrier on customer loyalty in Korean mobile telecommunication services. *Telecommunications Policy, 28*(2), 145.

Kotabe, M., Murray, J. Y., & Javalgi, R. G. (1998). Global sourcing of services and market performance: an empirical evaluation. *Journal of International Marketing, 6*(4), 10-31.

Li, Z. G., Murray, L. W., & Scott, D. (2000). Global sourcing, multiple country-of-origin facets, and consumer reactions. *Journal of Business Research, 47*, 121-133.

Lovelock, C. H. (1999). Developing marketing strategies for transactional service operations. *Journal of Services Marketing, 13*(4/5), 278-289.

Mayer, K. J., Bowen, J. T., & Moulton, M. R. (2003). A proposed model of the descriptors of service process. *The Journal of Services Marketing, 17*(6/7), 621.

McCartney, L. (2003, Spring). A shore thing. *CFO-IT Magazine*, 60-63.

McCaskey, D., & Symes, S. (2004). Travel Inn: Everything you want for a good night's sleep - 100 percent satisfaction guarantee or your money back. *International Journal of Contemporary Hospitality Management, 16*(3), 167.

Nicoulaud, B. (1989). Problems and strategies in the international marketing of services. *European Journal of Marketing, 23*(6), 55-66.

Oliver, R. L. (1997). *Satisfaction: A behavioral perspective on the consumer*. New York: McGraw-Hill.

Osgood, C. E., & Tannenbaum, P. H. (1955). The principle of congruity in the prediction of attitude change. *Psychological Review, 62*(1), 42-55.

Palacio, A. B., Meneses, G. D., & Perez, P. J. (2002). The configuration of the university image and its relationship with the satisfaction of students. *Journal of Educational Administration, 40*(4/5), 486-505.

Parasuraman, A., Zeithaml, V. A., & Berry, L. L. (1988). SERVQUAL: A multiple-item scale for measuring consumer perceptions of service quality. *Journal of Retailing, 64*, 12-37.

Quester, P., & Lim, A. L. (2003). Product involvement/brand loyalty: Is there a link? *Journal of Product & Brand Management, 12*(1), 22-38.

Quinn, J. B. (1997). *Innovation explosion: Using intellect and software to revolutionize growth strategies*. New York: Free Press.

Reilly, P. (1997). Outsourcing: employers becoming cautious. *Management Services, 41*(6), 9-11.

Roy, M. (2003, November 7). Outsourced call centres damage long-term effort. *Precision Marketing*, 14.

Ruyter, K. d., Birgelen, M. v., & Wetzels, M. (1998). Consumer ethnocentrism in international services marketing. *International Business Review, 7*, 185-202.

Sauer, P. L., Young, M. A., & Unnava, H. R. (1991). An experimental investigation of the processes behind the country-of-origin effects. *Journal of International Consumer Marketing, 3*(2), 29-59.

Selnes, F. (1993). An examination of the effect of product performance on brand reputation, satisfaction and loyalty. *European Journal of Marketing, 27*(9), 19-35.

Sharma, S., Shimp, T. A., & Shin, J. (1995). Consumer ethnocentrism: A test of antecedents and moderators. *Journal of the Academy of Marketing Science, 23*(1), 26-37.

Shimp, T. A. (1984). Consumer ethnocentrism: The concept and a preliminary empirical test. *Advances in Consumer Research, 11*, 285-290.

Shimp, T. A., & Sharma, S. (1987, August). Consumer ethnocentrism: Construction and validation of the CETSCALE. *Journal of Consumer Research, 24*, 280-289.

Siems, T. F., & Ratner, A. S. (2003, November/December). Do what you do best, outsource the rest. *Southwest Economy*.

Singh, J. (1988, January). Consumer complaint intentions and behavior: Definitional and taxonomical issues. *Journal of Marketing, 52*, 93-107.

Singh, J., & Pandya, S. (1991). Exploring the effects of consumers' dissatisfaction level on complaint behaviours. *European Journal of Marketing, 25*(9), 7-21.

Singh, J., & Wilkes, R. E. (1996). When consumers complain: A path analysis of the key antecedents of consumer complaint response estimates. *Journal of the Academy of Marketing Science, 24*(4), 350-365.

Steenkamp, J.-B. E. M. (1990). Conceptual model of the quality perception process. *Journal of Business Research, 21*(4), 309-333.

Swartz, N. (2004a). Much more than jobs being outsourced. *Information Management Journal, 38*(3), 3.

Swartz, N. (2004b). Offshoring privacy. *Information Management Journal, 38*(5), 24-26.

Trapp, R. (1999, July/August). Blunder boss. *The British Journal of Administrative Management*, 12-16.

Tse, D. K., & Lee, W.-N. (1993). Removing negative country images: Effects of decomposition, branding and product experience. *Journal of International Marketing, 1*(1), 57-75.

Wong, A. (2004). The role of emotional satisfaction in service encounters. *Managing Service Quality, 14*(5), 365.

Wong, A., & Sohal, A. (2003). Service quality and customer loyalty perspectives on two levels of retail relationships. *The Journal of Services Marketing, 17*(4/5), 495-511.

# Chapter XVI

# IT Offshoring: A German Perspective

Michael Amberg
University of Erlangen, Germany

Martin Wiener
University of Erlangen, Germany

## Abstract

*Increasing competition in globalized markets drives IT offshoring worldwide. In the United States, the relocation of IT activities and processes to low-wage countries like India is already an established business practice, resulting in their leading position in the field of IT offshoring. However, at present, offshoring is gaining increasing recognition in European countries like Germany. A number of German major enterprises are already involved in or are planning offshoring initiatives, while numerous small and medium enterprises (SMEs) are currently considering how best to take advantage of offshoring. In consideration of this development, the following chapter examines company- and economy-related drivers and economic effects of the rising trend to IT offshoring in Germany as well as possible responses by German companies and policy makers.*

# Introduction

Excellent skills and sufficient capacities in low-wage countries (e.g., India), along with an increasing cost pressure due to global competition, have fortified the business trend to IT offshoring. U.S. companies, for instance, have outsourced IT projects to low-wage-countries since the late '80s. Nowadays, in the United States, it is automatically assumed during large bid invitations that a service provider achieves its cost advantage, at least partially, by the use of offshore resources.

At present, established business practices from overseas are finding growing recognition in Europe. According to Farrell (2004a), 40% of Western Europe's 500 largest companies have already begun moving IT service jobs abroad. In Germany, more and more companies have reported on offshoring services in the past months. As an example, German companies' spending on research and development in foreign countries averaged out at 23 billion euros per year between 1995 and 1999, which jumped to approximately 35 billion euros per year in 2000, thereby showing a rising tendency (Mertens, 2004).

As a result of the growing IT offshoring trend in Germany, the fear of job losses on a grand scale has encountered strong resistance to offshoring in the German public. The announcement by numerous companies to relocate a remarkable share of their jobs to countries in Asia and Eastern Europe intensified these fears even more. For instance, in July 2003, IBM published plans to move a great number of their jobs offshore until 2015. Siemens, which already operates a software development center in Bangalore (India), also plans to expand their offshoring and nearshoring activities (Boes & Schwemmle, 2004).

According to Boes and Schwemmle (2004), 10,000 highly skilled IT service jobs are jeopardized by offshoring in Germany alone. Therefore, the discussion about offshoring attracts vast attention, both in the United States and in Germany. In the U.S. election campaign, for instance, IT offshoring was a major topic and triggered a new wave of protectionism. Even in Germany, parts of the political left-wingers encouraged protectionism in an attempt to prevent the relocation of IT service jobs to countries like India or Russia (Schaaf, 2004).

The current debate about IT offshoring invokes emotional responses in Germany. According to Schaaf (2004), the public perception of IT offshoring and the real facts about offshoring strongly diverge from one another.

Before possible impacts of IT offshoring on the German economy can be discussed in the following, a common understanding of the term "*offshoring*" has to be assured. According to Schaaf (2004), IT offshoring refers to the relocation of IT activities and processes to foreign countries, mainly low-wage countries. The different types of IT offshoring are illustrated in Figure 1. In many cases, offshoring projects are performed by external service providers ("*offshore outsourcing*"). However, in some instances, offshoring services can also be rendered by subsidiaries, joint ventures or strategic alliances ("*captive offshore outsourcing*").

The following section examines the economic effects of IT offshoring in Germany and possible responses by German companies and policy makers. To start off, section two

*Figure 1. Types of IT offshoring (Schaaf, 2004)*

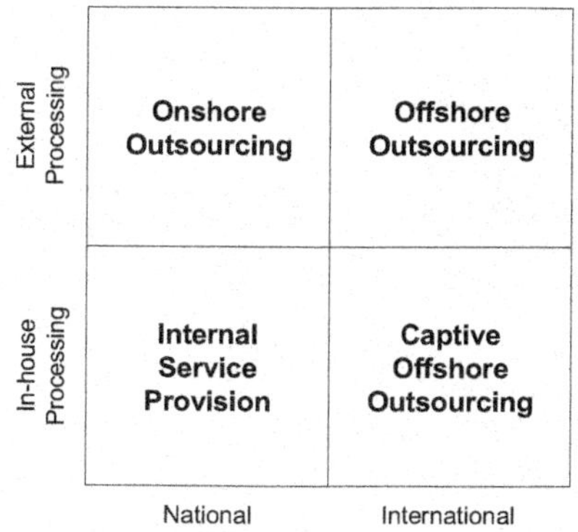


gives an overview of the German economy, and compares it with economies of developed and developing countries. In the third section, factors driving the offshoring trend in Germany are presented from a company's and an economy's perspective. The fourth section points out the extent of the current offshoring trend in Germany and describes the German IT offshoring market. The fifth and the sixth section represent the main part of this article while section five addresses possible impacts of IT offshoring in Germany, section six deals with reforms required for turning offshoring to Germany's advantage. Finally, section seven summarizes the key points of the chapter and gives a forecast of future developments in respect of the German IT offshoring market.

# Overview of the German Economy

The following section aims to provide a brief overview of the German economy. In this context, key aspects are Germany's demography, labor market, and foreign trade. In addition to this basic information about Germany, the German economy is compared with economies of other developed (U.S.) as well as developing countries (India) in terms of future economic growth.

## Basic Data on German Economy

In comparison to other countries' populations, the German population is quite matured in average. According to the Federal Office for Statistics (see Figure 2), fewer than 26% of Germans belong to the so called MTV generation (under the age of 25). In India, for instance, 53% of the population falls in this category (Kalakota & Robinson, 2004).

*Figure 2. Age distribution among the German population*

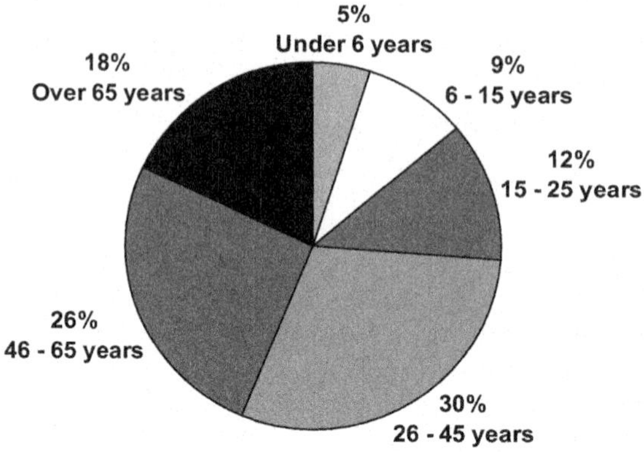


Source: (Federal Office for Statistics, 2003)

Due to an aging population and declining birth rates, Germany faces a drastic decline in workforce. While the elderly population will grow by five million over the next 15 years, Germany's workforce will decrease by two million in the same timeframe (Farrell, 2004a). Associated with the decline in workforce, the funding of the German pension scheme, which is based on an inter-generation contract, is at risk.

In Germany, within the past decades, the service sector gained remarkable importance (see Table 1). For example, in 2001, 68.9% of all German employees worked in the service sector, and only 28.6% were employed in manufacturing. By comparison, in 1991, the share of manufacturing jobs still accounted for 36.7% of the German labor market (in the first half of the 1970s even more than 50% of German employees worked in manufacturing). Proportional to the growth in German service jobs, the share of the whole sector in gross value added increased to 69.9% in 2001. In contrast, the share of manufacturing in gross value added decreased from 35.1% in 1991 to 28.8% in 2001 (Federal Ministry of Economic Affairs and Employment, 2005).

*Table 1. Employment distribution in Germany*

| | 1996 | 1997 | 1998 | 1999 | 2000 | 2001 | 2002 | 2003 |
|---|---|---|---|---|---|---|---|---|
| *Working Population (in thousands)* | | | | | | | | |
| Overall | 37.270 | 37.208 | 37.616 | 38.071 | 38.748 | 38.911 | 38.671 | 38.246 |
| *Classified by Selective Industries (in thousands)* | | | | | | | | |
| Manufacturing | 11.871 | 11.585 | 11.498 | 11.333 | 11.283 | 11.115 | 10.765 | 10.418 |
| Services | 24.391 | 24.632 | 25.124 | 25.765 | 26.501 | 26.844 | 26.967 | 26.900 |

Source: (Federal Office for Statistics, 2003)

*Figure 3. Number of employees within the German IT industry (Broß, 2005)*

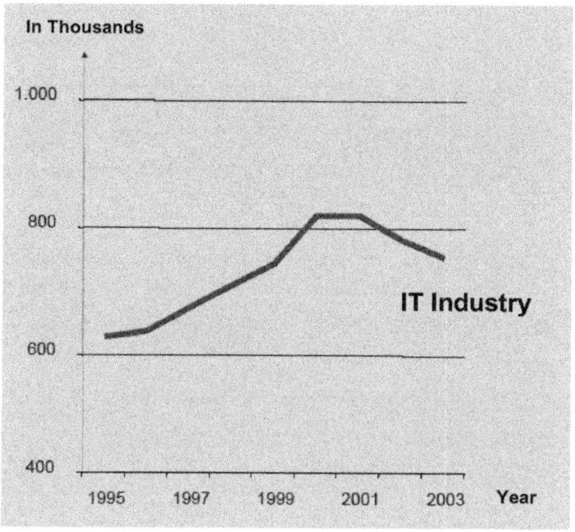


However, within the German service sector, the IT industry only accounts for a small part of the entire industry (compare Figure 3).

According to the German Department for Foreign Affairs (2005), Germany's share in world trade aggregates to 10.5%. In 2003, Germany even surpassed the United States in matters of international trade, making Germany the "export world champion." Between the years 1991 and 2003, Germany's trade surplus in foreign trades increased from 11 billion euros to around 130 billion euros, demonstrating the competitiveness of German companies within this timeframe.

With reference to imports and exports, Germany's most important trading partner is France, followed by the Netherlands and the United States (in terms of imports), and the United States and the United Kingdom (in terms of exports). However, in addition to international trade with developed countries, Germany also cultivates commercial relationships with several developing countries (especially China).

## Comparison to Other Economies

According to recent research by Bergheim (2005), concerning future centers of economic growth, Germany polls badly with a projected average annual growth rate in real GDP of only 1.5% between 2006 and 2020 (see Figure 4).

In contrast to Germany (ranking 27th on the diagram), India, with an annual growth rate in real GDP of 5.5%, is expected to grow faster than any other country worldwide during the considered timeframe. This growth rate means a doubling of the economy's output in only 13 years, making India the world's third largest economy behind the United States and China at the end of this decade. A strong growth of population by 1.6% per year, and

*Figure 4. Annual growth rate in real GDP between 2006 and 2020 (Bergheim, 2005)*

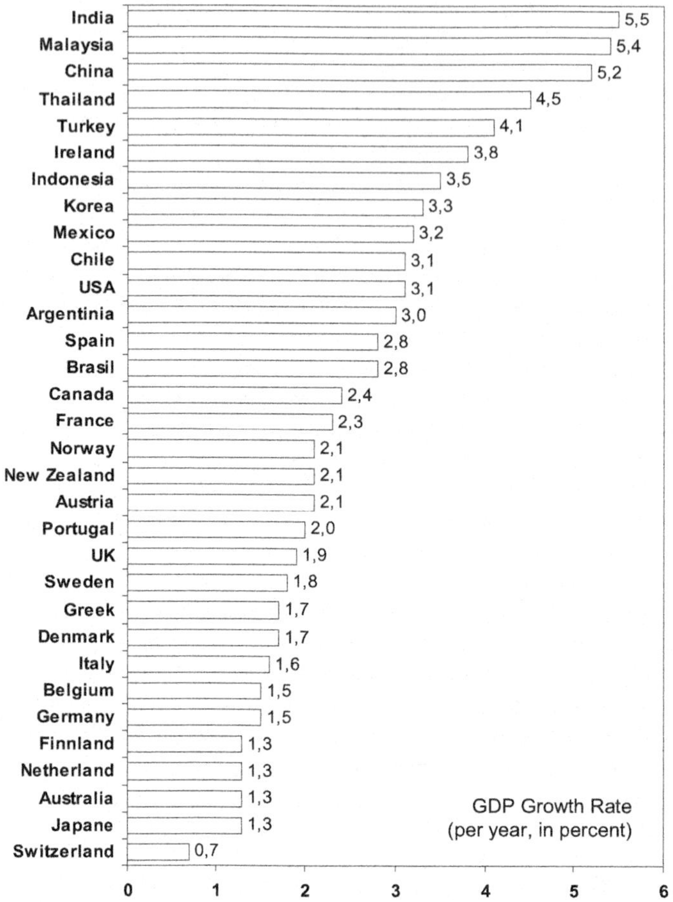


a remarkable growth in GDP per capita by 3.9% contribute to this development. At this rate, the GDP per capita will double in 18 years. However, even in 2020, India's GDP per capita will be the second lowest among the country group considered within the study (Bergheim, 2005).

As demonstrated by the U.S., economies with a high base level in GDP per capita can also achieve a strong economic growth. With a projected annual growth rate in real GDP of 3%, the U.S. rank second behind India. However, the U.S. is still predicted to remain as the worldwide leader in respect of its real GDP (total and per capita) in 2020 (Bergheim, 2005).

# Drivers of IT Offshoring in Germany

The growing trend to IT offshoring in Germany is likely to continue. According to Broß (2005), the German IT offshoring is projected to double within the next three years. The factors driving this development can be viewed from different perspectives. In this context, it should be differentiated between a German company's perspective on the one hand, and the perspective of the German economy, on the other hand.

## German Company's Perspective

From the perspective of a German company, there is a variety of economic, technological, and regulatory factors supporting the step abroad.

**Economic Factors:** In the majority of cases, lower labor costs in developing countries such as India, Russia, and so forth are the main reason for shifting service jobs abroad. Although, the costs of land and other resources may also be much cheaper in these countries, the considerably lower labor costs (see Figure 5) is perceived by companies as the primary advantage about offshoring (Garner & Schwartz, 2004). In addition, the employer's contribution to health insurance, pension fund, and so forth, is likely to be much higher in Germany.

It should be noted that the true difference in labor costs cannot be calculated by just subtracting the labor costs in typical offshoring countries like India from the labor costs in Germany. Due to the high average levels of productivity in developed countries like Germany, the difference in labor costs per unit of output may be much smaller than

*Figure 5. Comparison of average labor costs in the IT industry (Schaaf, 2004)*

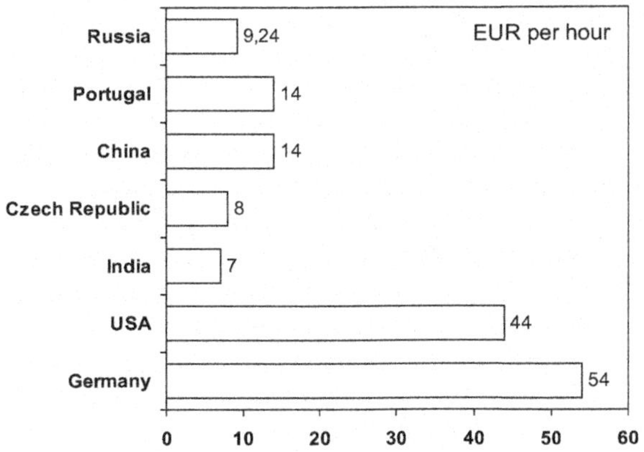

expected. According to Garner and Schwartz (2004), the high average productivity by employees in developed countries like the U.S. or Germany can be justified by the availability of advanced technologies and the large amounts of capital per worker in these countries. Such capital comprises both physical capital (e.g., computers), and human capital (e.g., knowledge). Besides high average productivity, potential cost savings may be further reduced by additional costs for the coordination of the offshoring project. In this context, first of all, the great distance between the offshoring partners can lead to unexpected costs (Amberg & Wiener, 2004).

Still, due to much lower labor costs in typical offshoring countries such as India, many services can be produced at lower cost there. Hence, labor-intensive service activities, such as routine programming, are ideal candidates for going offshore. The relocation of these activities to countries with lower labor costs is also consistent with economists' theory of international trade. According to this theory, countries with a relative large share of unskilled labor within their workforce should concentrate on labor-intensive jobs, whereas, countries with a relative large share of skilled labor (e.g., Germany) should concentrate on capital-intensive jobs (Garner & Schwartz, 2004).

The growing interest in relocating more complex tasks (e.g., offshoring of complete business processes) shows that some developing countries are gradually catching up in terms of skills and level of education. Resulting from national education programs, especially in areas such as programming and mathematics, one can observe a significant increase in skill sets in these countries. However, it is doubtful that a similar development in other kinds of skill sets (e.g., project management) can be reached by such formal programs.

**Technological factors:** The differences in labor costs between developed and developing countries is nothing new, therefore, the trend to IT offshoring must also be triggered by other factors. In this context, especially the huge progress in computer and telecommunication technologies facilitates the relocation abroad. These developments allow companies to locate service activities in foreign countries in much the same way manufacturers outsourced production activities in the past (Garner & Schwartz, 2004).

As a result of technological advances, sharp declines in communication costs could be noticed. Besides remarkable drops in long-distance telephone costs, particularly the increasing usage of the Internet as a communication media (e.g., e-mail, voice-over-IP) makes long distances between the contractual partners appear less of an issue. However, regular meetings cannot be substituted by any technology and, due to the immense distance, cause non-negligible costs.

By lowering communication costs, new information and communication technologies like fiber optic cables, personal computers, and the Internet encouraged vertical specialization in the service sector. In the past, most services had to be produced close to the customer. Nowadays, particularly labor-intensive activities which run in the back-office can be produced almost everywhere. However, more critical services, such as complete IT-related business processes, are already target of offshoring initiatives. It seems like only IT services which require direct customer contact and management functions are excluded from offshoring (Garner & Schwartz, 2004).

Freund and Weinhold (2002) support the hypothesis that the diffusion of new technologies fortifies the international trade of IT services. According to their research, an increasing number of Internet users correlates positively with the growth rate of a country's international service trade. They find that a 10% increase of a country's Internet penetration results in an average 1.7 percentage point increase in service exports and an average 1.1 percentage point increase in service imports.

**Regulatory factors:** A third factor, driving the IT offshoring trend, is the deregulation of the service industries and trade liberalization by both developed and some developing countries in the 1990s. Due to their economic importance and political sensitivity, many service industries (e.g., financial services, transportation, and telecommunications) have been heavily regulated (Garner & Schwartz, 2004). For example, Germany had limited foreign ownership in telecommunications and had closed its postal services to foreign entry. At that time, many German companies criticized that, among other things, regulated and often overpriced telecommunication firms raise their production costs, resulting in a competitive disadvantage in world markets for them. As a result, over the last decade, Germany has begun to deregulate and liberalize its domestic service industries, leading to an increase in competitive pressure.

As developed countries like Germany begin to deregulate and liberalize international service trade, developing countries have considered incentives to attract investors and customers from West-European and North-American countries. For example, the Indian government built a national taskforce for IT in May 1998, which developed a long-term strategy for transforming India into a leading IT offshoring destination. According to IT consultancy TransCrit (2005), as a part of India's strategy, the Indian government provides the following forms of tax relief to foreign companies:

- Complete relief of value-added tax
- Complete relief of federal income tax for profits on exports[1]
- Complete relief of tax for joint ventures (limited to 10 years)

Besides tax relief, the government heavily supports education and the development of IT skills. As a result of the governmental support in India, the software and service market in this country grew by 37% in 2001 and numerous global fortune 100 firms operate joint ventures there as strategic investments (TransCrit, 2005).

In summary, it can be said that cost reduction remains the main driver for IT offshoring from a German company's perspective. According to Eichelmann, Fredriksson, Sauvant and Schneidereit (2004), other important factors include the quality of staff as well as local services.

## German Economy's Perspective

According to Kalakota and Robinson (2004), among other factors, especially the following are key factors which drive offshoring from the perspective of the German economy:

- Globalization
- Evolution
- Deflation
- Demographics
- Competition

The factors mentioned above will be described in more detail in the following.

- **Globalization:** First of all, the transition to an "offshore economy" is heavily driven by the Internet-enabled globalization. The development of new technologies, particularly the Internet, and the rapid technological progress in telecommunications, associated with a drastic decline in telecommunication costs, reduced the importance of international borders. Nowadays, IT projects, which could previously only be performed onsite, can now be distributed to international locations due to technological advance, and the new peculiarities of IT services (Schaaf, 2004).

  German companies like Puma are already pushing the concept of international division of labor to new limits. Puma outsources most of its production and back-office processes to national and international companies, which enables them to concentrate on what they do best: marketing of their products.
- **Evolution:** IT offshoring can be seen as a steady evolution. In the past, work was done where the production factors were physically located. At present, production factors can be moved across international borders to wherever they are most productive (Fruhan, 2004).

  The evolution in manufacturing shows that it is very difficult for countries with high relative wages (e.g., Germany or the U.S.) to compete with labor-abundant countries (e.g., China or India) in the labor-intensive manufacturing industry. For the service industry, a similar development is expected. With an interlinked global economy and reduced international trade barriers, the physical location of a company is no longer a primary concern.
- **Deflation:** As a consequence of global competition, customer demands are mounting (faster, cheaper, better). To counteract decreasing prices, companies are forced to cut costs and improve service quality by adopting the offshore model. Especially SMEs in Germany are heavily affected by this development. In some cases, these companies even have to sell services below production costs in order to be competitive, termed by Kalakota and Robinson (2004) as the "Wal-Mart syndrome": Due to huge purchasing volumes, Wal-Mart is able to operate with very small margins, continuously reducing market prices. Competitors are forced to either keep up with these prices or exit the market.

- **Demographics:** Another factor, driving the offshoring trend, is the aging population and the declining birth rates in developed countries such as Germany. Despite immigration, the average age is on the rise in these countries as baby boomers enter their 50s or 60s. In contrast, according to Kalakota and Robinson (2004), 53% of the Indian population belongs to the so called MTV generation (under the age of 25).

  According to Farrell (2004a), especially Germany faces a drastic decline in workforce because of an aging population. While the elderly population will grow by five million over the next 15 years, Germany's workforce will decrease by two million in the same timeframe. Preparing for this demographic shift, Germany will have no other choice but to raise the productivity of the remaining workforce dramatically, for example, by relocating commodity activities and processes to offshore destinations.

- **Competition:** In connection with global IT service markets and mounting customer demands, worldwide competition increases and reshapes the service provider landscape. Initially, during the IT boom of the late 1990s, German companies and IT service providers did not pay much attention to low-cost providers in developing countries. However, as the economy cooled at the beginning of the 21st century, the market shifted. Customers tried to cut IT costs by cooperating with offshore providers and traditional players were caught with high-cost workforces and overcapacity.

  Consequently, traditional service providers have taken drastic actions in order to remain competitive in the global IT service market. For example, Accenture has tripled its workforce in India since 2001, and plans to employ 10.000 people there by the end of 2005. But not only IT service providers expanded their activities to developing countries. In an attempt to assure their competitiveness on global markets, German companies like Siemens responded to the growing competition by building subsidiaries in developing countries such as Hungary, India, and other countries.

## IT Offshoring in Germany

Due to the difficult economic situation in Germany, the challenges for IT departments of German firms have never been bigger. IT directors must address the problem of conflicting interests: On the one hand, the CEO expects them to get by with a massive reduced IT budget; on the other hand, they have to satisfy the increasing user demands on integration, availability, security, and so forth. In many cases, the existing structures in companies' internal IT departments could not solve this conflict. Therefore, several companies have cut off their IT departments, taking them on the market as independent subsidiaries (e.g., Lufthansa Systems, T-Systems), or have started to cooperate with international and offshore IT providers. As a result, nowadays, local IT service providers (including these newly formed subsidiaries) must compete with internationally operating outsourcing providers like IBM Global Solutions or Accenture, and with, for instance, Indian IT providers like Tata Consultancy Services, Infosys Technologies Ltd. or Wipro

Technologies for outsourcing deals with German companies (Buchta, Linß, Röder, & Ziegler, 2004).

## IT Offshoring Trend

Since the end of the 1990s, outsourcing of non-core company functions has gained increasing popularity in Europe (BITKOM, 2005; Eichelmann et al., 2004). At the beginning, IT infrastructure and IT development in particular were targeted by numerous outsourcing initiatives. Later on, even labor-intensive business processes were considered for outsourcing. Nowadays, with the opening of low-wage countries in Eastern Europe and Asia, outsourcing reaches a new dimension: offshoring.

Especially for internationally operating offshore providers (e.g., IBM, Accenture), the offshoring trend promises considerable growth prospects. These service providers enter local IT markets, putting the local IT service providers under immense pressure. In the United States, approximately 20% of companies' IT budgets are invested in offshore destinations (especially India). The huge differences in labor costs between developing and developed countries in connection with the increasing global competition fortified this trend in the U.S., and also attracted German companies to IT offshoring (Buchta et al., 2004).

Against the background of a total cost savings potential of 2 billion euros per year in Germany (estimated by consulting agency AT Kearney), international offshore providers expect annual growth rates of more than 20% in the German market. As a result, a great number of jobs at German IT service providers and companies' internal IT departments are put at risk. At the moment, a lot of companies in Germany are still adapting their IT organization and processes to the requirements of IT offshoring projects; thereby, granting jobs at risk a kind of grace period. In addition to that, according to Buchta et al., (2004), a third of all German employers have never considered IT offshoring up to now due to strategical or political reasons. However, potential cost savings of more than 30% accelerate the adoption process.

As already mentioned in the previous chapter, huge differences in labor costs between developed countries like Germany and developing countries like India, Russia, and so forth, and the enormous potential of highly skilled IT workers in these countries, fortify the IT offshoring trend in Germany. From a German company's perspective, due to a cultural similarity and an adequate knowledge of the German language, especially IT service providers in Eastern European countries (e.g., Russia, Ukraine, Poland, Czech Republic) are of particular interest.

In contrast to Germany, IT offshoring is already a common business practice in Anglo-American countries. For example, in the U.S., about 20% of companies' total IT budgets is invested in low-wage countries (especially India). Like other non English-speaking countries, Germany is currently trying to catch up. In this context, primarily the cultural and linguistical differences complicate the cooperation of German companies with the predominantly English-speaking offshore providers. As a result, only one third of German companies which cooperate with an offshoring partner could realize cost savings of more than 30%. By comparison, half of all international companies involved in IT offshoring projects realized cost savings of more than 30%. According to Buchta et al. (2004), possible reasons are:

- **High vertical integration in German firms:** In German companies, internal IT departments often cover the complete range of services from software development to IT operations. Therefore, many a time, external service providers are only included sporadically, explaining the low outsourcing rate in Germany compared with the United States and the United Kingdom. As a result, German firms lack experience with relocating IT services and managing these services over a larger distance.
- **Small number of existing relationships with local IT service providers:** German companies are used to fast and direct communication processes with their IT service providers. Due to long lasting partnerships, the small number of local service partners is familiar with the specific characteristics of their customers. In contrast to offshore service providers, which need detailed project specifications, these providers only require a general description of the project. In the case of offshoring, this approach would probably lead to additional expenses.
- **Cultural and linguistical differences with Indian IT service providers:** A lot of German companies followed the Indian mainstream, resulting in additional problems due to cultural and linguistical differences. In Germany, the word offshoring is often used as a synonym for outsourcing to India. As a result, alternative destinations in Eastern Europe are not often considered. But especially, when cooperating with an Indian service provider, German companies face cultural and linguistical problems which U.S. and UK companies do not have to fear, the latter at least not to this extent.

In summary, compared with other international companies' offshore activities, German firms are approximately three years behind. However, according to Buchta et al. (2004), especially German large-scale enterprises will have no other choice but to develop offshoring strategies in the near future. They estimate that the total cost savings potential for German firms amounts to more than 2 billion euros.

## IT Offshoring Market

In comparison to the United States, the German IT offshoring market is still very small. Nevertheless, experts from Deutsche Bank Research project a doubling of the market size for Germany until 2008 (see Figure 6).

In Germany, three major types of offshore providers can be distinguished. According to Buchta et al. (2004), these are:

- **Offshore subsidiaries, joint ventures or strategic alliances:** Especially large-scale enterprises have built or acquired IT subsidiaries in low-wage countries.

*Figure 6. Size of the German IT offshoring market*

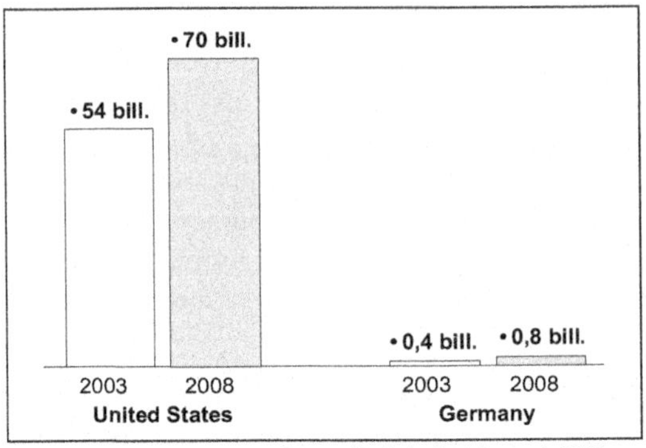


Source: (Deutsche Bank Research, 2004)

Another possibility is to cooperate with IT service providers in these countries by means of joint ventures or strategic alliances. By choosing one of these options, companies can take advantage of the benefits offshoring has to offer (e.g., reduced labor costs, access to a highly skilled workforce, etc.), and minimize the risks associated with relocating IT projects abroad. An example is Munich-based Siemens which possesses IT subsidiaries in Hungary, India and other developing countries.

- **International IT service providers:** Companies like IBM, Accenture or EDS have already established offices in countries like India. Due to their strong competitive position in global markets, these providers do not have to fear the competition with classical offshore providers. They use their global network for performing IT services at the most suitable location.
- **Classical offshore IT service providers:** Offshore providers like NIIT Technologies have tried to enter the German service market to strengthen their competitive position in Europe. In this context, however, offshore providers realized that many German companies had difficulties with relocating IT services directly to countries like India. Therefore, numerous offshore providers established offices or acquired IT service providers in Germany (e.g., Mannheim-based AD Solutions was acquired by NIIT Technologies) in an attempt to penetrate the German market.

Especially in the financial services sector (AT Kearney, 2003), and in the IT industry (Buchta et al., 2004; Allweyer, Besthorn, & Schaaf, 2004), offshoring of IT services can already be referred to as an established business practice (see Figure 7). Furthermore, a similar trend to offshoring is already apparent in the automotive industry (Boes & Schwemmle, 2004).

## IT Offshoring Service Landscape

According to Eichelmann et al. (2004), representatives of European companies consider the full range of IT services, from front office to back office, as suitable for offshoring. Services such as finance, accounting, IT support, human resource and other back office services are already involved in about 60% of all current or planned offshoring projects. But, in reference to their research, a third of the European companies interviewed also mentions front office services as potential offshoring candidates. However, in many cases, this is not feasible for German companies due to the language barrier.

According to Schaaf (2004), from the perspective of a German bank, especially the following IT activities and processes are affected by IT offshoring initiatives (ordered by offshoring likeliness[2]):

1. Application development
2. Coding
3. Application maintenance
4. Help desk
5. Call center
6. IT infrastructure
7. Data center
8. Network management
9. Web hosting

*Figure 7. IT offshoring market shares by industries (Schaaf, 2004)*

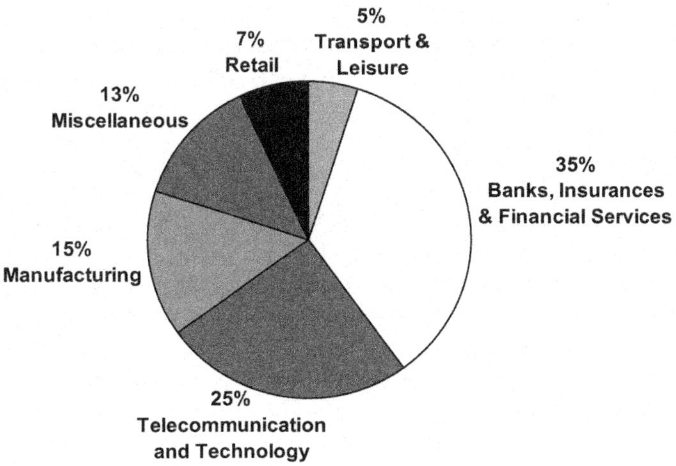

10. Server management
11. R&D
12. System architecture
13. Network and data security
14. Integration of IT and business processes

It should be noted that the above list of potential offshoring candidates is illustrative rather than comprehensive. In addition, the order of the candidates may differ between companies and industries.

# Impacts On German Economy

Considering possible effects of IT offshoring on the German economy, the first part of this section will consider the following impact categories in more detail:

- Competition
- Employment
- Standard of living

In the second part of the section, the potential impacts on the German economy will be compared with those facing the U.S. economy.

## Competition

Against the background of the increasing competition from international and offshore IT providers, domestic providers have to consider the issue of their role in the German IT service market in the future. However, according to Buchta et al. (2004), when asking this question, affected companies often cannot comment on this topic. At the most, these companies try to broaden their service offering by buying in offshore services. But with higher administrative costs and missing know-how in supervising IT offshoring projects, German IT providers often cannot keep up with international competitors.

As already mentioned, at present, many offshore providers face problems with entering the German IT service market. Domestic providers could take advantage of this development by acting as intermediaries between German customers and offshore contractors. German providers, not using this opportunity, are likely to be pushed into niches by international competition, resulting in a further consolidation of the German IT service market (Buchta et al., 2004).

In summary, small and medium-sized IT service providers, which employ the majority of German IT workers, can only anticipate a massive decline in employment by developing the required skills for being competitive in global markets or by concentrating on a small range of specific activities.

According to Buchta et al. (2004), for self-employed persons or freelancers (some 75.000 jobholders which represents 20% of German IT workers), the threat through IT offshoring is less dramatic. As IT offshoring initiatives must exceed a critical project volume, a market niche exists for these workers. Especially in case of smaller tasks, many companies use self-employed workers or freelancers as a flexible and cheap tool for balancing shortages in resources.

## Employment

The loss of service jobs in Germany caused by offshoring is difficult to measure. The Federal Office for Statistics provides comprehensive data on international export and import in services; however, no official data on service jobs moving abroad. It is also difficult to derive the impact of IT offshoring on the number of German service jobs from data on total services employment in Germany. It is a given fact that the service sector in general has taken much longer to recover from the global recession in 2001 than from previous recessions. Many critics trace this back to IT offshoring (Garner & Schwartz, 2004).

Even though, there is no official data, several consulting agencies and research institutes have provided estimates of job losses in the German IT service sector:

- For German-speaking countries, consulting agency AT Kearney forecasts the relocation of 100.000 IT jobs in the financial sector to low-wage countries like India (Deloitte & Touche, 2003).
- The same consulting agency predicts a quadruplication of offshoring activities by German firms within the next three years, resulting in a loss of 130.000 jobs (Buchta et al., 2004).
- By comparison, DB Research, the research institute of the Deutsche Bank, estimates that 50.000 IT service jobs will be shifted offshore until 2008 (Schaaf, 2004).
- According to Frost & Sullivan, more than 825.000 IT jobs worldwide have been relocated to offshore destinations in 2004. For Germany, this estimate means that domestic companies have transferred IT jobs amounting to US$48.2 billion to foreign countries within the last year (Computerwoche Online, 2004).

In this context, it has to be mentioned that many of these estimates are only based on incomplete data. According to Schaaf (2004), reasons are inaccurate reports to the Federal Office for Statistics by many German firms, an insufficient classification of services, especially by emerging countries like India, and the different types of IT offshoring (federal agencies categorize *offshore outsourcing* as international trade, whereas *captive offshore outsourcing* is referred to as foreign investment).

Irrespective of the correct number of IT jobs relocated abroad, there will be jobs that are more likely to go offshore than others. According to Garner and Schwartz (2004), especially service jobs with the following characteristics are at risk through IT offshoring:

- **Labor-intensive:** Due to cheaper labor costs in countries like India or Russia, service jobs in which labor accounts for a relatively large share of production costs are more likely to be offshored.
- **Information-based:** Recent progress in information technology and telecommunications reduced the costs and increased the feasibility of producing IT services at any location worldwide.
- **Codifiable:** Service jobs which can be described by a set of instructions (e.g., standardized or well-documented activities), and, therefore, require less experience or training, can be performed more easily at a remote location.
- **High-transparency:** Service jobs dealing with information that is easy to measure or verify are often potential offshoring candidates.

In terms of impact of IT offshoring on employment in Germany, it should be differentiated between long-term and short-term effects.

**Long-term effects:** Economic theory assumes that international trade will not reduce national employment in the long run; in fact, international specialization could even have positive long-run effects (Garner & Schwartz, 2004). For instance, according to economist David Ricardo, free trade produces shared gains for all nations. Even though, it has to be questioned if the assumptions on which Ricardo's theory is based are still valid in the information age.

In the long run, real GDP is determined by a nation's productive resources (e.g., size of labor force, amount of physical capital, and technology). If a nation is not using its resources effectively, wages and prices will redirect these resources in order to maximize their use, although, the redirection may take a long time as wages and prices change slowly (Garner & Schwartz, 2004).

Besides the effects mentioned above, offshoring may create a growing demand for German products in emerging countries like India or China, and, therefore, may open new export markets for German companies. According to Bergheim (2005), these countries belong to the biggest centers of growth worldwide in the near future. Purushothaman and Wilson (2003) even project that China will have the world's largest economy by 2050, with India close behind, ranking third.

As China's and India's per capita income rise, spending on foreign products and services will increase, creating new demand for German exports. Among other industries, especially German automakers like BMW, DaimlerChrysler, and Volkswagen could benefit from growing wealth in these countries. But also German service providers should benefit from this development.

**Short-term effects:** Although offshoring in the service sector will probably not reduce German employment in the long run, offshoring may have a drastic short-term impact on employment in Germany. The reemployment of displaced service workers could be particularly challenging. Against the background of the inflexible labor market in Germany, it will be difficult to find equivalent jobs for laid-off service workers.

In addition, job losses due to offshoring are more likely to be permanent in the sense that retrenched workers are unlikely to get an offer for a similar position within their company. However, in contrast to the U.S., where people are more flexible and more amenable to new jobs, many people in Germany are reluctant to move to another state or country to accept a job or to switch occupations in order to find new employment.

Research on displaced manufacturing workers by Kletzer (2001) shows that reemployment prospects heavily depend on the individual worker's characteristics. Generally, young and more educated workers experienced fewer problems with finding a new job compared to older, less educated workers. These workers were unemployed longer, and, if reemployed, often faced considerable earnings losses (sometimes exceeding 30%).

Nevertheless, the reemployment prospects of displaced service workers should be relatively good compared with displaced manufacturing workers, due to the fact that these workers tend to be young and better educated. This conclusion is also consistent with Kletzer's (2001) research: Laid-off manufacturing workers faced earnings losses averaging 12% upon reemployment. In comparison, laid-off service workers only had earnings losses of fewer than 4% in their new jobs.

In addition to good reemployment prospects of displaced service workers, even in the United States, where the relocation of IT service jobs to India is already a common

*Figure 8. U.S. job losses due to IT offshoring (Farrell, 2004a)*

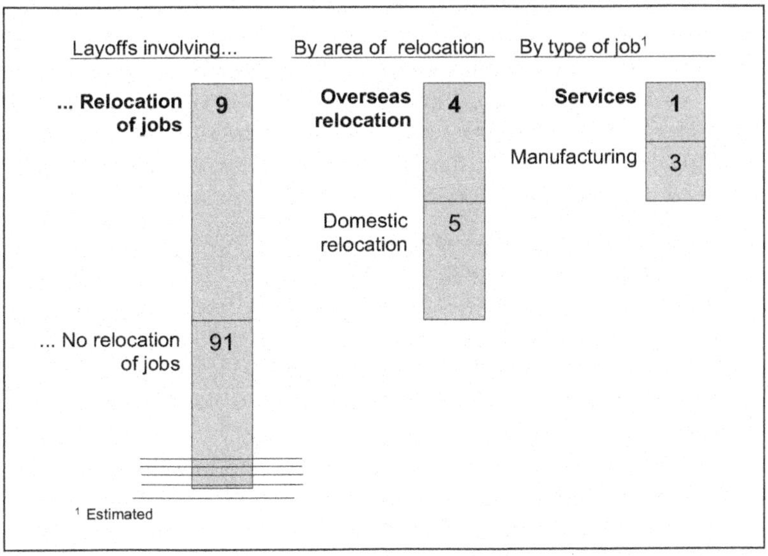

business practice, offshored service jobs accounted for only 1% of job losses in the first quarter of 2004. According to Farrell (2004a), even if manufacturing jobs are included, offshoring accounted for only 4% of all layoffs (see Figure 8).

Although the figures presented above apply to the U.S. labor market, it is unlikely that the corresponding figures for the German market exceed the ones in the U.S. Especially by taking into consideration that offshoring in Germany is still in its infancy stages, it can be assumed that, compared with U.S. job losses, the number of layoffs in the German service sector involving offshoring is comparatively smaller.

## Standard of Living

A major concern about IT offshoring is its impact on the German standard of living. Even though, economic theory suggests that an international trade of services is likely to raise the average real per capita income in developed countries like Germany, many citizens fear a loss in salary due to the relocation of service jobs (Garner & Schwartz, 2004). In theory, it is assumed that IT offshoring will lower costs of some services to consumers because it reduces companies' production costs. However, this is only true if firms pass on their cost savings to consumers. But what happens if companies use their cost savings for further investments in developing countries, instead of passing them on to consumers? In such instances, German citizens will not benefit from service-sector offshoring; in fact, their standard of living will be heavily put at risk.

Beyond controversy, a positive effect of IT offshoring is that increased international trade in services will raise German productivity growth in the long run. International specialization shifts resources from sectors where German workers are comparatively less efficient to sectors where they are comparatively more efficient. In addition, global competition puts pressure on German firms, forcing them to raise their productivity by developing new technologies, improving their management techniques, and so forth (Garner & Schwartz, 2004). According to Edwards (1998), in general, more open economies tend to demonstrate faster growth in productivity.

Moreover, offshoring may facilitate greater IT investment in the future. In the manufacturing sector, offshoring has helped drive down costs of high technology goods (e.g., desktop computers, cell phones, etc.) and accelerated the adoption of new technologies (Garner & Schwartz, 2004). A similar development may be expected in the IT service sector, and, according to Mann (2003), is already under way.

Despite the positive effects of offshoring mentioned before, economists have long realized that the standard of living of some workers and their families is heavily jeopardized by international free trade in services. Even if average real per capita income increases as a result of the growing offshoring trend, there will be many German workers who will not benefit from this trend (Garner & Schwartz, 2004). As always in real life, there will be winners and losers. The only question is whether the number of winners or the number of losers will dominate?

In summary, IT offshoring in Germany may cause temporary dislocation of jobs, but in the long run, domestic employment should not be lowered permanently, In addition, international trade in services may raise the average German standard of living in the long run, although, it is likely that IT offshoring will make the nation's income distribution less equal. However, it should be noted that these forecasts are based on the assumption that the German labor market will adapt to the new circumstances and will react more flexible in the future.

## Comparison to U.S. Economy

In August 2003, Diana Farrell, the director of the McKinsey Global Institute (MGI), published an analysis of the economic impacts (both direct and indirect) of IT offshoring activities from the United States to India. In terms of direct benefits for U.S. investors, Farrell (2004a) considered the following aspects:

- Cost savings
- New revenues
- Repatriated earnings

In addition to direct benefits, Farrell (2004a) considered the economic value from redeploying workers who lost their jobs due to IT offshoring as indirect benefits.

Due to a recent survey which showed that 40% of Western Europe's 500 largest companies have already begun relocating service jobs abroad, a similar analysis was conducted for Germany in July 2004. Within this study, Farrell (2004a) points out that, in comparison to the United States, Germany benefits less in every category, and, as a result, loses EUR 0.20 for every euro spent on IT offshoring. In contrast, the United States gains US$0.12 to 0.14 for every dollar of corporate spending on IT services moved offshore (see Figure 9).

- **Cost savings:** In the United States, a company's cost savings through offshoring IT services, which were originally performed by domestic service providers, average out at 58%. In Germany however, first of all, due to a bigger language barrier and the resulting additional expenses for project coordination, according to Farrell (2004a) companies can reduce their service costs by only 48% in average.
- **New revenues:** The generation of new revenues holds more benefits for the U.S. economy than for the German economy. In this context, the U.S. benefits from exports of goods and services by U.S. companies like Dell, Hewlett Packard, Oracle, and Microsoft to India. The MGI estimates that for every dollar which is invested in India, U.S. exports increase by U.S. $0.05. Contrary to U.S. companies, German companies do not play a major role in terms of exports to developing countries in Asia or Eastern Europe. Therefore, MGI estimates that Germany only gains EUR 0.03 from new exports.
- **Repatriated earnings:** Indian IT service providers, fully or partly owned by U.S. companies, are responsible for 30% of the revenues of the Indian IT service industry. Consequently, additional US$0.04 of every dollar spent on offshoring

*Figure 9. Benefits of German and U.S. corporate spending on IT offshoring (Farrell, 2004a)*

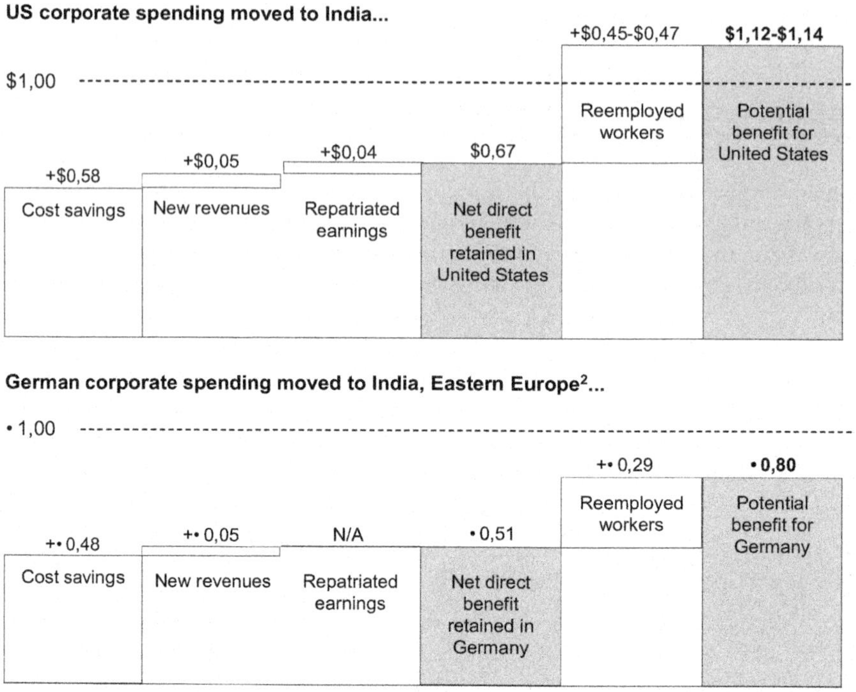


[1] For United States, estimate based on historical reemployment and wage levels; for Germany, estimate based on turn-over in unemployment claims.

[2] Of German corporate spending move offshore, ~ 60% goes to Eastern Europe, ~40% to India.

returns to the U.S. Unlike U.S. companies, the number of German companies which possess IT subsidiaries in India or Eastern Europe is negligible. Thus, Germany misses out on repatriated profits.

- **Reemployed workers:** Even at the current reemployment rate, the U.S. economy gains an additional US$0.45 to 0.47 of economic value for every dollar of corporate spending on IT offshoring. The MGI believes that this is a conservative estimation, since white-collar service workers, as already mentioned at the beginning of the chapter, are more likely to be reemployed than non-service workers.

In contrast to the United States, Germany currently has more than 5 million unemployed workers (Federal Employment Office, February 2, 2005). This unemployment figure is the highest since the end of the Second World War. In addition to that, job growth is very low, making it difficult for German workers who lose their jobs due to offshoring to find new ones. MGI estimates the reemployment rate for service workers to be as low as 40%. Consequently, the German economy only gains EUR 0.29 of economic output for every euro of German companies' investments offshore. As already mentioned before, in this case, Germany would lose EUR 0.20 for every euro offshored. However, according to

Farrell (2004a), if Germany could only raise its reemployment rate to U.S. level, Germany would already gain EUR 0.05 for every euro offshored.

In addition to the quantitative direct and indirect benefits mentioned above, Farrell (2004a) also considered the **added flexibility**, resulting from offshoring service jobs, as a qualitative benefit. In this single category, German companies gain more than their U.S. counterparts: By moving service jobs offshore (or nearshore), German companies can take advantage of foreign labor, giving them more flexibility for responding to market changes and experimenting with new ideas.

The analysis conducted by the MGI impressively illustrates potential impacts of IT offshoring on the U.S. and the German economy. However, critics challenge the correctness of these analyses and the underlying assumptions. A point of criticism is that Farrell's model is based on the benefits of free trade which had been premised on David Ricardo's theory of comparative advantage. As Ricardo said that free trade would benefit all nations, he assumed that the location-specific factors of production cannot be easily transferred over international borders. But in the information age, factors of production can be relocated to wherever they are most productive (at our present situation, usually to countries with low labor costs). In this case, there will be no shared gains: Some countries lose; others win (Fruhan, 2004).

## Required Reforms in Germany

To turn offshoring to its advantage, German policy makers must create new momentum in the local economy. According to Farrell (2004a), since 1993, economic growth in Germany has averaged 1.4% a year, only little more than half of the European average and far below the U.S. growth rate of 3.3%. By spurring economic growth in Germany, policy makers should pay attention to the following fields:

- Politics
- Education and research
- Labor and product markets

The mentioned fields will be examined in more detail in the following paragraphs.

## Politics

In terms of international service trade, German policy makers should behave proactively. Especially in the areas of macroeconomics, trade, and immigration as well as state and local policies, support by political leaders is necessary.

- **Macroeconomic policy:** Facing heavy competition from developing countries like India, maintaining service jobs in Germany is mainly a matter of macroeconomic policies. Monetary and fiscal policies influence the demand for goods and services, and exchange rate adjustments alter the competitiveness of German products relative to those produced abroad. However, in this context, according to Garner and Schwartz (2004), it is crucial that the application of the political instruments available is implemented with the overall economy in mind.

Particularly, the rapid structural change in Germany — including the increasing trend to IT offshoring — makes it more difficult for policy makers to find the proper settings for monetary and fiscal policy instruments. Silvia (2003) reinforces this hypothesis by arguing that past statistical correlations between real GDP growth and employment growth are no longer valid due to globalization.

- **Trade policy:** Throughout the German public, more and more citizens are calling for a restriction on service imports. However, economists discourage from protectionism as an instrument against relocation of German service jobs. As already seen in other industries, protectionism can also have negative effects. For example, safeguards for the German steel industry caused a net loss of jobs because of layoffs in steel-consuming industries. The same phenomenon could be observed in the U.S. steel industry. Therefore, when domestic industries are not competitive in global markets and are unlikely to regain their international competitiveness, policy makers should support the reallocation of labor and capital to domestic industries with a stronger position in global markets (Garner & Schwartz, 2004).

  As discussed in other developed countries like the U.S. and the UK, German policy makers should think about introducing a wage insurance program for displaced service workers. For example, Kletzer and Litan (2001) propose a wage insurance which reimburses eligible workers for a fraction of their earnings losses. As a restriction, only reemployed workers could make use of this insurance, providing stronger incentives for displaced service workers to accept a new job (Garner & Schwartz, 2004). However, according to Schaaf (2004), Kletzer's and Litan's proposal only differs marginally from classical unemployment insurance, and, like any other insurance of this kind, holds the danger of interfering with the market.

  International trade negotiations represent another area where further action by German policy makers is necessary. In this context, on the one hand, foreign trade barriers should be reduced, and, on the other hand, the intellectual property of German companies should be protected. The abolishment of trade restrictions gives competitive German service companies access to foreign markets. In order to assure the competitiveness of these companies, adequate protection for their copyrights, patents, and other intellectual property have to be in place.

- **Immigration policy:** A major concern in connection with immigration is that foreign students and workers acquire skills and business contacts in developed countries like Germany which may be used in favor of offshoring later on. Immigrants return to their home countries after some years and work for a company there (Garner & Schwartz, 2004). In this case, developing countries benefit from the return of highly skilled workers, whereas, developed countries like Germany, where these workers acquired their knowledge, may experience loss in two ways. Firstly, when skilled workers return to their home countries, secondly, when these workers get employed by foreign competitors.

Even though, foreign workers in the service industry may transfer know-how back to their home countries, it should not be disregarded that German companies also heavily benefit from skilled immigrants. For example, some years ago, when software engineers were in short supply in Germany, the German government reacted by handing out "green cards" to Indian IT specialists. Against this background, policy makers must assure that highly skilled workers from other countries are not barred from working in Germany. These workers are needed to run innovative service companies (Garner & Schwartz, 2004).

Another negative aspect of temporary immigration is that it may put downward pressure on the wage level of service jobs in Germany. In the U.S., according to Garner and Schwartz (2004), temporary immigration held down the wages of skilled U.S. workers in the late 1990s. This could be similar for Germany in the near future.

- **State and local policies:** IT offshoring also raises issues for policy makers on state- and local-levels. In some cases, state and local governments offer large incentives in order to attract specific industries to their area. This strategy is often associated with a considerable uncertainty. It is almost impossible to predict which industries will prosper and which will not. For example, a recently attracted call center might be relocated abroad after a short period of time, or might have its workforce substituted by speech recognition software (Garner & Schwartz, 2004).

  As a result, numerous economists advise against focusing on specific industries. From their point of view, state and local governments should concentrate on providing basic services, education, and an infrastructure which is not restricted to a small number of industries, but rather can be used by a wide variety of industries.

## Education and Research

To sustain Germany's position in global competition, policy makers must ensure that German companies have access to a highly educated talent pool. Besides a modern

*Figure 10. Number of graduates in natural sciences per year (Broß, 2005)*

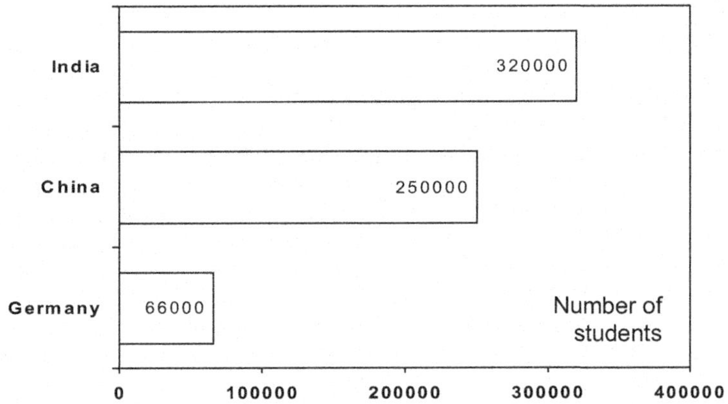

educational system, the existence of an innovative research environment is essential for a nation's competitiveness in international markets (Garner & Schwartz, 2004).

In the majority of cases, economic growth has come from innovative ideas, reflecting a nation's human capital, not from material input. Therefore, the competitive advantage of developed countries like Germany or the United States is based largely on the educational level of their workforce (Garner & Schwartz, 2004). For a long time, Germany was world-famous for its excellent educational system. Nowadays, Germany faces huge problems: Recent studies (e.g., PISA 2003[3]) showed that German students are only on average in comparison to other international students from all over the world. At the moment, Germany still benefits from its highly skilled workforce educated in the past. But what will happen if these workers retire and the current student generation must step into their shoes? Will Germany succeed in keeping its position in global competition? Many economists negate this question, and ask for immediate action by the German government.

Particularly, against the background of companies from developing countries moving into higher value-added jobs, German firms can only remain competitive by creating innovative goods and services. These products could be exported to growing foreign markets like China or India.

According to Buchta et al., (2004), as a precondition for innovative ideas, the content of teaching at German universities should be scrutinized and adapted to the new requirements, resulting from the international division of labor. As an example, educational programs in computer science at German universities are still focused on contents which will not be sought after in Germany in the near future. By relocating labor-intensive tasks to locations with lower labor costs, especially German companies' demand for project and information managers will increase. In connection with these jobs, major skills are:

- Project management
- Software development (especially within early stages: requirement analysis, specification, etc.)
- Communication
- IT strategy
- IT planning

Representatives of German universities have indicated that, at present, the mentioned skills do not make up a main focus in many universities' computer science curriculum. Historically, teachings concentrate on mathematical and technical topics. But especially in these domains, according to university professors, it will be difficult for German students to keep up with international competition from developing countries like India or China where a great number of students graduate every year (compare Figure 10) and where mathematical and technical education is heavily emphasized.

As a result, alongside their studies, German graduates in computer science should try to acquire additional qualifications in related areas like business management and related fields. In global IT service markets, doing this could become a crucial factor for having a better job prospects later on (Buchta et al., 2004).

## *Labor and Product Markets*

As a precondition for spurring growth, German policy makers must react to the inflexible labor market and rethink regulations that constrain competition and innovation. Although Agenda 2010[4] is a good start, according to Farrell (2004a), not all of the country's problems are addressed by this program:

- **Hiring and firing workers remains difficult.** In Germany, hiring and firing workers still causes huge problems because of the required approval from worker representatives. As a result, in many cases, German companies have to wait six months or longer to hire new workers. In the meantime, these companies often have to rely on temporary ones, resulting in higher costs and extensive paperwork. According to Farrell (2004a), in the case of a German-based multinational company, a round of layoffs took two weeks in the U.S., four weeks in the UK, and three months in Germany. Against this background, companies are sensitive to hiring new workers in Germany.
- **High wage level contributes to a sluggish growth in jobs.** Even though, the German government does not define a minimum wage, the German welfare system causes a similar effect. As a result, many low-paid jobs are not economically feasible which reduces the total employment in Germany. For instance, proportionately, U.S. retailing employs 30% more people than German retailing does. In addition, these people also work more hours on average. In an attempt to trigger growth in jobs, the German government introduced so called "minijobs"[5]. However, recent research found that these jobs have mainly substituted full-time jobs rather than spurred growth.

German companies have already reacted to the problems concerning the labor market. For instance, Siemens negotiated a contract with IG Metall, Germany's largest union, for two plants in which they put an end to the 35-hour week and the 13$^{th}$ month of pay (Farrell, 2004a).

Besides reforming the labor market, in an effort to tap the full potential that IT offshoring has to offer, German policy makers must address the inappropriate product market regulations. According to Farrell (2004a), especially the following market restrictions interfere with competition and innovation in Germany:

- Price regulations
- Zoning laws

- Subsidies
- Restrictions on operating hours

And so forth.

Germany's regulations on labor and product markets were designed for achieving social objectives. However, according to Farrell (2004a), in the past two decades, a key issue has become clear: Mixing up social and economical aspects has negative effects on employment and economic growth. Therefore, Farrell recommends decoupling these policies: Spurring economic growth in Germany in order to finance the country's welfare system.

## Conclusions

Although the German IT offshoring market is still relative small to the total German employment, offshoring is likely to increase in the future as especially labor-intensive IT services can be produced more cheaply in low-wage countries like India or Russia. This development was primarily enabled by reduced telecommunication costs, and technological advances (e.g., the Internet).

Currently, it is still unknown whether German companies have any other alternative but to follow the offshore trend in the near future. Companies, which choose to forego purchasing services in low-wage countries, may no longer be competitive in terms of price and quality. Therefore, the inclusion of offshore services could turn out to be an essential requirement for becoming a successful player in a globalized market.

According to an empirical study by Eichelmann et al. (2004), European countries generally benefit from this growing trend to IT offshoring, even though negative influences have to be taken into account. In respect of their research, potential positive effects on the German economy are:

- Increased competitiveness
- Lower prices
- Repatriated earnings
- Increased market share of service exports

And so forth.

These benefits have to be confronted with potential negative effects on the German economy:

- Increased dependence on imports
- Job losses
- Downward pressure on wage levels

And so forth.

In summary, Schaaf (2004) predicts positive effects on the German economy through IT offshoring. Although, offshoring will displace some workers, who may also experience lasting economic losses, it is not likely that offshoring will lower Germany's employment in the long run. In fact, IT offshoring has the potential to improve the average standard of living by moving displaced workers into more sophisticated jobs and by protecting existing jobs.

However, in order to benefit from IT offshoring, decisive structural reforms should be launched in Germany. In this context, appropriate actions by Germany's political leaders are necessary (Schaaf, 2004). Positive long term effects can be expected if German policy makers succeed in changing the structural conditions responsible for Germany's inability to create new jobs. Possible measures for this include: Reforming the educational system, improving the flexibility of the labor market, loosening product market regulations, and re-focusing on innovation (Buchta et al., 2004). Additionally, policy makers should ease the movement of resources from industries that are losing to international competition towards industries which are gaining (Garner & Schwartz, 2004).

Finally, it has to be emphasized that IT offshoring is more than a temporary fashion, but rather a result of global restructuring (Farrell, 2004b). Therefore, according to Boes (2004), it does not make sense to consider offshoring apart from other current developments. In fact, it must be seen as a part of the worldwide restructuring process which is currently taking part.

This process will create new challenges for employers, employees, policy makers, and so forth, in Germany (Boes & Schwemmle, 2004). Nevertheless, according to Farrell (2004a), IT offshoring should be viewed as an important opportunity for the German nation, and not as an economic threat. By offshoring, new wealth could be created for Germany. However, as a precondition for such a development, Germany's political leaders must take the right actions in order to prepare Germany for a globalized economy. Countries like the United States are already prepared, now it is Germany's turn to catch up.

## References

Allweyer, T., Besthorn, T., & Schaaf, J. (2004). *IT outsourcing: Zwischen Hungerkur und nouvelle cuisine*. Retrieved February 4, 2005, from http://www.dbresearch.de/PROD/DBR_INTERNET_DE-PROD/PROD0000000000073793.pdf

Amberg, M., & Wiener, M. (2004). *Wirtschaftliche aspekte des IT offshoring (Arbeitspapier Nr. 6/2004)*. Retrieved December 14, 2005, from http://www.wi3.uni-erlangen.de/forschung/ITOffshoring/arbeitspapiere/2004/AP6_Wirtsc haftliche AspekteITOffshoring_2004_WienerMartin_abstract.pdf

AT Kearney. (2003). *Offshoring financial services – Auf dem weg zum globalen geschäftsmodell.* Unpublished paper, AT Kearney.

Bergheim, S. (2005). *Globale wachstumszentren 2020. Formel-G für 34 Volkswirtschaften.* Retrieved January 22, 2005, from http://www.dbresearch.de/PROD/DBR_INTERNET_DE-PROD/PROD0000000000183205.pdf

Boes, A. (2004). *Industrialisierung und internationalisierung von IT-dienstleistungen (Arbeitspapier 7 des Projekts ARB-IT2).* Retrieved January 10, 2005, from http://www.arb-it2.de/docs/Boes2004_Arbeitspapier7.pdf

Boes, A., & Schwemmle, M. (2004). *Herausforderung offshoring. Internationalisierung und auslagerung von IT-dienstleistungen.* Düsseldorf: Hans-Böckler-Stiftung.

Broß, P. (2005, February). Herausforderungen an unternehmen und politik – Chancen und risiken aus politischer sicht für offshoring. Speech delivered at the conference, "Chancen und Risiken von Software-Offshoring", Munich, Germany.

Buchta, D., Linß, H., Röder, H., & Ziegler, R. (2004). *IT-offshoring und implikationen für den standort Deutschland.* Unpublished paper, AT Kearney.

Computerwoche Online. (2004). *Studie: Verlagerung von IT-arbeitsplätzen nimmt zu.* Retrieved January 27, 2005, from http://www.computerwoche.de/index.cfm?pageid=254&artid=68747&type=detail&kw=Offshoring&rc=73

Deloitte & Touche. (2003). *Outsourcing und offshoring mit indischen IT-unternehmen – Die IT-welt im wandel.* Unpublished paper, Deloitte & Touche.

Department for Foreign Affairs. (2005). *Außenhandel.* Retrieved February 19, 2005, from http://www.tatsachen-ueber-deutschland.de/203.0.html

Edwards, S. (1998, March). Openness, productivity, and growth: What do we really know? *Economic Journal.*

Eichelmann, T., Fredriksson, T., Sauvant, K. P., & Schneidereit, F. (2004). *Service offshoring takes off in Europe – In search of improved competitiveness.* Retrieved December 4, 2005, from http://www.rolandberger.com/press/en/media/releases/RB_Service_offshoring_20040616.pdf

Farrell, D. (2004a). *Can Germany win from offshoring?* Unpublished paper, McKinsey & Company.

Farrell, D. (2004b, December). Beyond offshoring: Assess your company's global potential. *Harvard Business Review*, 82-90.

Federal Ministry of Economic Affairs and Employment. (2005). *Industrie- versus dienstleistungsgesellschaft.* Retrieved February 19, 2005, from http://www.bmwa.bund.de/Navigation/unternehmer,did=8352.html

Freund, C., & Weinhold, D. (2002, May). The Internet and international trade in services. *American Economic Review.*

Fruhan, W. E. Jr. (2004). *Offshoring at Global Information Systems, Inc.* Case study, Harvard Business School.

Garner, C. A., & Schwartz, T. (2004). Offshoring in the service sector: Economic impact and policy issues. *Economic Review (Federal Reserve Bank of Kansas City), 89* (3), 7-29.

Kalakota, R., & Robinson, M. (2004). *Offshore outsourcing. Business models, ROI and best practices*. Alpharetta, GA: Mivar Press.

Kletzer, L. G. (2001). *Measuring the costs of trade-related job loss*. Retrieved February 19, 2005, from http://www.iie.com/publications/papers/kletzer0701.htm

Kletzer, L. G., & Litan, R. E. (2001, February). A prescription to relieve worker anxiety. Institute for International Economics, Policy Brief, No. 01-2.

Mann, C. L. (2003, December). Globalization of IT services and white collar jobs: The next wave of productivity growth. Institute for International Economics, International Economics Policy Briefs, No. PB03-11.

Mertens, P. (2004). Diskussionsrunde zum thema "Auswanderung der informatik/wirtschaftsinformatik aus Deutschland". *Wirtschaftsinformatik, 46*(5), 414-418.

Purushothaman, R., & Wilson, D. (2003). *Dreaming with BRICs: The path to 2050*. Retrieved February 19, 2005, from http://www.gs.com/insight/research/reports/99.pdf

Schaaf, J. (2004). *Offshoring: Globalisierungswelle erfasst dienstleistungen*. Retrieved January 7, 2005, from http://www.dbresearch.de/PROD/DBR_INTERNET_DE-PROD/PROD0000000000178654.pdf.

Silvia, J. E. (2003). Growth without jobs? A new style of economic recovery in the new economy. *Wachovia Economic Watch*.

TransCrit. (2005). *Offshore IT-länder: Indien*. Retrieved February 12, 2005, from http://www.transcrit.com/de/offshore/centers/india.html.

# Endnotes

1 This tax relief is temporary and, actually, only valid to 2005 (TransCrit, 2005).

2 Services which are more likely to be offshored rank first.

3 The Program for International Student Assessment (PISA) is an internationally standardized assessment that was jointly developed by participating countries and administered to 15-year-olds in schools. The survey was implemented in 41 countries in the second assessment in 2003.

4 Agenda 2010 is a multi-level program introduced by the German government for the purpose of reforming the German welfare system and the German labor market.

5 *Minijobs* are part-time jobs that pay EUR 400 to 800 (Farrell, 2004a).

## Chapter XVII

# Information Systems/ Information Technology Outsourcing in Spain: A Critical Empirical Analysis[1]

Felix R. Doldán Tié, University of A Coruña, Spain

Paula Luna Huertas, University of Sevilla, Spain

Francisco Jose Martínez López, University of Huelva, Spain

Carlos Piñeiro Sánchez, University of A Coruña, Spain

## Abstract

*The practice of information systems/information technology (IS/IT) outsourcing is a major issue which has received much attention, as shown by the extensive literature on the topic. However, most works on outsourcing have focused on theoretical topics, and there are but a few empirical, quantitative studies. This chapter presents an empirical study of IS/IT outsourcing in Spain, which has been conducted along the lines of prior research carried out in different countries, and which focuses on the types, functions and targets of outsourcing contracts. We also attempt to examine the influence that this practice may have on the organizations' management structure. A survey carried out on 530 Spanish firms has shown that 50% of Spanish large firms have outsourced part of their IS/IT, whereas outsourcing is practiced by 20% of medium-sized enterprises. Finally, it has been observed that the most frequently outsourced activities in Spain are hosting and Internet-related services.*

# State of the Art: Theoretical Framework For IS/IT Outsourcing

The practice of information systems/information technology (IS/IT) outsourcing is a major issue which has received much attention in both the managerial and the academic spheres, as shown by the extensive literature on the topic. Following Eastman Kodak's IS/IT outsourcing decisions in 1989[2], the outsourcing market grew at an annual rate of 15%, until it expanded to more than $40,000 million in the 1990s. Outsourcing is practised, or at least considered as a medium-term option, by half of the firms whose annual turnover is equal to or more than $5 million[3], which contradicts the common belief that outsourcing is characteristic of big corporations with efficiency problems.

Traditionally, it has been argued that outsourcing helps firms reduce costs, since the external provider benefits from economies of scale and from its own experience. This advantage is even greater in the case of IS, which are frequently defined as an intrinsically cost burden activity, full of management problems and with a dubious contribution to businesses[4].

Outsourcing of IT-related activities has been indeed the area of greater expansion in the last few years, and that with the best expectations in the medium term. In a first stage, organizations outsourced complementary functions such as consulting, training or maintenance until, in a second stage, they also outsourced corporative mainframes and end-user support. More recently, outsourcing practices have expanded in two new trends: the requirements derived from electronic businesses — network management, creation and maintenance of Web sites and management of electronic shops — and the ASP (application service provider) sector, which is expected to generate a business volume of $7,000 million in 2004 (Young, 2000). Similarly, according to IDC consulting, IT outsourcing is expected to reach $177.2 billion in 2004 (Lingblom, 2002). According to Burkhart (2003), in a near future the trend will move from IT outsourcing to a combination of business processes and outsourcing.

There are nevertheless some issues clouding this brilliant panorama. There is evidence to question the magnitude and even the existence of cost saving[5], and it has become obvious that certain crucial aspects should be carefully considered: the quality of the service, the benefits offered by the outsourcing project, its strategic implications[6], and the risk derived from transferring an activity that is critical for business performance. Moreover, outsourcing has become more complex with the emergence of new contractual types that — as in the case of pay-per-use — attempt to meet the demands of an increasingly competitive market.

## Information Services Organization Models

According to Wibbelsman and Maiero (1994), the main decision that the organization must take is not whether or not an activity should be outsourced, but rather determining *the most suitable outsourcing project* according to the cost of the internal service, the economic value of the external offer, and the costs of co-ordination or agency.

We agree with Hsu, Chiu, and Hsu, (2004) that, in order to predict IS outsourcing success, a number of factors must be taken into account, such as the combinations of internal and external activities, different degrees of responsibility transfer, material resources, management capacity, and different levels of centralization.

IS were originally configured as rigidly centralized structures so as to exploit the economies of scale propounded by Grosch's Law[7], which have been proved erroneous thanks to the improvement in the cost/performance ratio of IT and to the recognition of their limitations from the point of view of decision support and business processes.

Facing an ever-increasing competency, organizations adopted the re-engineering projects marketed by consulting firms: the organization should adapt and optimize its structure to the new economic environment in order to control the growth of costs and ensure its competitiveness. These notions gave rise to such phenomena as *downsizing*, *rightsizing*, and a wide range of projects that attempted to simplify organizational structures and to transfer those functions and activities that are alien to the business core[8].

In the case of IT, re-structuring projects were fostered by the managers' frustration of being unable to justify the profitability of IT investments, since the arguments supporting business benefits were weak and the cost of IS implementation was high. Very often, organizations developed outsourcing projects so as to make the role of IS clear — or to get rid of an apparently insoluble management problem[9].

From a financial point of view, outsourcing represents the last link in a chain of techniques intended to clarify and justify the economic value of information services, known as IS cost recovery, or chargeback techniques (Figure 1); the organization can make use of outsourcing (or other similar practices) to clarify the total cost derived from information functions and to assess their contribution to the business objectives. However, as we will see below, these techniques do not eliminate the uncertainty inherent in medium and long-term forecasting and, moreover, they introduce a clear bias towards cost economics at the expense of other management factors[10]. Lacity and Willcocks (1998, 2001) argue that outsourcing acts as a catalyst to improve the quality of the assessment of the IS and its services.

*Figure 1. Internal service assessment techniques*

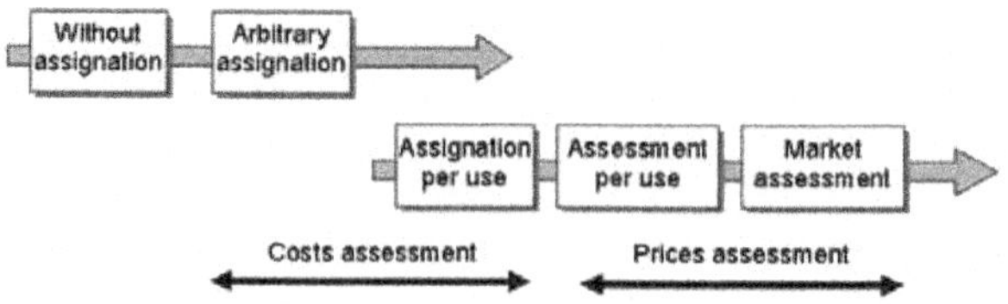

## *Outsourcing Models*

According to Lacity and Hirschheim (1995), organizations can procure a given service in three generic ways: by internally providing the service (insourcing), by contracting an external provider to perform certain activities (selective outsourcing)[11], or by transferring the service to the external provider (total outsourcing), sometimes including the organization's material and/or human resources. Total outsourcing has been defined as a specific instance of selective outsourcing in which the contract implies transferring at least 80% of the total cost of the service.

A special case is that in which the organization outsources just the execution of a specific project, for example, the development of an application or the management of disasters. Lacity and Hirschheim (1993a) call this practice *Project Management*, and they also distinguish those contracts with which the organization intends to meet sporadic needs (*Body Shop*). Lacity and Willcocks (1998) add some other interesting outsourcing types, which they call "emerging sourcing arrangements":

- **Multi-sourcing**, in which the service is provided by multiple co-ordinated and specialized providers.
- **Co-sourcing**, where the remuneration perceived by the external provider is indexed to certain parameters expressing the quality of the service; this model is equivalent to that which Millar (1994) calls *Business benefit contracting* (Table 1).
- **Spin-offs**, where the internal IS department splits off the organization and turns into a business unit[12].
- **Creative contracting**, which encompasses those practices intended to personalize services, functionalities, and operative conditions to the client's specific requirements.

*Table 1. Outsourcing types (Millar, 1994)*

| | | |
|---|---|---|
| **General outsourcing** | *Selective outsourcing* | The target of outsourcing is limited according to economic efficiency and competitive relevance criteria |
| | *Value added outsourcing* | Based on the hypothesis that the external provider will be able to supply a specific value which cannot be obtained internally, for example, better quality of adaptation capacity |
| | *Co-operative outsourcing* | Responsibility for outsourced functions is shared by the internal service and the external provider |
| **Specific outsourcing types** | *Transactional outsourcing* | All or part of the activities related to the transition from one computer system to another are carried out by the external provider |
| | *Business process outsourcing* | The external provider is responsible for the provision of a function or information activity |
| | *Business benefit contracting* | Maintenance of the external service, and its retribution, depend on certain parameters expressing its quality. |

The most limited type of outsourcing consists in contracting material resources in order to meet certain specific, exceptional information management requirements[13]: the vendor provides technical resources such as processing capacity or printing resources (and maybe some human resources too), but responsibility for the activity lies exclusively on the organization. The advantages of this outsourcing model are, first, that the organization has access to material resources whose internal maintenance would be unfeasible, and second, the cost savings as compared to other alternatives of temporary contracting as, for example, renting[14]. Providers share the same infrastructure with several clients, and for this reason they are called *timeshare vendors*.

The organization may contract the performance of a function or an information service to an external provider, for example, accounting or payroll management; in this case, the external vendor supplies both the material resources and the service itself — which in the case discussed in the above paragraph was kept within the organization. This is a limited type of outsourcing called *selective outsourcing* (Payton & Handfield, 2003), in which the organization keeps control of major information services[15] and only transfers those functions with a satisfactory competitive risk/cost saving ratio.

Selective outsourcing has been traditionally identified with transactional or management functions but, according to Lacity, Willcocks, and Feeny (1996), the only criterion to determine the strategic character of functions is their relatedness to the company's competitive basis. The main problem with this type of outsourcing is the individualized evaluation of the performance of every service or function of the system, which requires the application of portfolio management techniques. Millar (1994) calls this *business process outsourcing*, and points out that this alternative is considered by a great number of organizations, including public government, banking, insurance companies, and logistic companies.

A step forward towards outsourcing is represented by facilities management (FM) contracts, which transfer the management of infrastructures to the external vendor. The external provider's degree of involvement in the system may vary depending on the terms of the contract, which usually includes explicit points about the quality, nature and duration of the service[16]; this flexibility is particularly attractive for the outsourcer when there are doubts about the IS area, or when the organization wishes to transfer the management risk.

The most "radical" model of outsourcing is that in which the organization contracts the entire information service to an external vendor; this is not a very frequent practice because it has evident competitive risks. Our own findings show that only a very limited segment of micro-companies, with a notable internal simplicity, choose these contractual types.

It can be concluded that FM — in its different varieties — is the most suitable outsourcing model for relatively stable business types in which the services have been established some time before and the information needs are well defined; the main problems lie in R+D development and management, particularly in the control of technological innovation, placed in between (external) service management and (internal) control of technological platforms.

## Arguments for Outsourcing Projects

Organizations' IS have been a recurrent target for outsourcing projects because of their impact on the cost structure: IT represents a substantial proportion of production costs, and the magnitude of IT investments has direct effects on the financial structure – particularly, on indebtedness and leverage. Additionally, IT investments are usually difficult to justify from a financial point of view, thus the external offer in general, and FM contracts in particular, are an attractive alternative because they simultaneously ensure the provision of the service and transfer the responsibility for IT management to the external provider.

In the context of IS, outsourcing offers some potential benefits[17]:

- It represents an opportunity for optimizing the cost structure, and improving business performance[18]. These advantages are particularly relevant for small businesses, which have difficulty in designing economies of scale. Lacity and Hirschheim (1995) and Ang and Straub (1998) found evidence of a negative relationship between outsourcing and business size, which was later corroborated by Ang and Straub (2002).
- Outsourcing may help re-establishing financial balance, improving leverage and reducing financial distress.
- It may reveal the company's intangibles, and turn them to liquidity[19]. The application of accounting criteria prevents intangible assets (or invisible assets; Itami, 1991) from being included in balances and financial statements; an outsourcing contract implies taking these assets into account and transforming them into liquidity (McFarlan & Nolan, 1995, p. 13).
- It can introduce a change in management perspective. The IS, which has long been regarded as a *service* or *investment centre*, is gradually being managed as a *profit centre* which has to prove its efficiency and its contribution to businesses. The most common outsourcing criterion is that of systematic comparison to the market offer (Dibbern & Heinzl, 2002)[20].
- Outsourcing helps evaluate the company's IS. The decision to outsource implies assessing the IS's relative efficiency and its contribution to the success of the business[21] – two issues that managers tend to avoid because of their apparent complexity.
- Finally, outsourcing favours the development of a model of competence between the internal function and the market. Lacity et al. (1996, p. 16) describe how the operative inertia of the internal service may become an obstacle for its efficiency; the threat of outsourcing may soften the resistance to introduce operative or strategic changes in the system[22].

## *Cost Economics*

According to the neoclassical argument, an organization is a production system ruled by criteria of maximizing profits, and which produces goods or supplies services to the extent to which it can act with greater efficiency than other mechanisms (Williamson, 1981); hence it follows that the organization will transfer those services in which it has disadvantages in terms of costs, thus the decision to outsource will be taken in accordance with the comparative advantages of insourcing in terms of operational and co-ordination costs[23].

The dominant argument for outsourcing projects is indeed the saving of labour, real estate, and equipment costs[24]: the most common hypothesis is that outsourcing helps lightening the cost structure and that it causes a more satisfactory behaviour of financial leverage. This hypothesis is supported by empirical evidence, particularly when there are internal inefficiencies[25] and the assets are not specific (Ang & Straub, 2002)[26]; however, there is some controversy over the economies' intensity. Lacity and Hirschheim (1993a) found that saving is often overvalued because of an excess of optimism on the part of external vendors and, sometimes, because of the managers' desire to justify the transaction of a function that is complex and little attractive in terms of management. The work of Beaumont and Costa (2002), based on a wide sample of Australian firms, suggests that, generally, savings are less significant than expected, and that sometimes the total cost of the service is higher than estimated.

Lacity et al. (1996) also observed irregular behaviours in the cost structure when the service is transferred to an external provider; similarly, Hirschheim and Lacity (2000) point out that the internal service may be as efficient as — or even more efficient than — external offers, thanks in part to its awareness of the company's actual problems.

The existence of idiosyncratic elements, particularly of the specificities of human resources, seems to be a relevant argument in favour of insourcing, a factor that can be examined in the light of Itami and Roehl's (1990) characterization of experience and know how as invisible assets. There are also certain cost factors that are not made explicit in the external provider's commercial offer and that, very often, are not taken into account by the company (Barthelemy, 2001), namely, the efforts made in the search and evaluation of offers, the inefficiencies during the process of transaction to the new model, monitoring the quality of the service, and re-assuming the function once the contract expires[27].

The internal service's efficiency depends on business size, which in turn determines the possibility to exploit economies of scale, the access to qualified personnel, and the intensity of financial restriction (a topic that will be dealt with below); it could be hypothesized that there is an inverse relationship between business size and outsourcing, but this factor does not establish differences in the tendency towards outsourcing, but rather in the types of outsourcing contracts: big companies tend to demand facilities management contracts, whereas SMEs prefer selective outsourcing practices (Lacity & Hirschheim, 1995; Lacity & Willcocks, 1998), which are intended to supply the skills or professional competences lacking in the internal service (Ang & Straub, 2002).

Cost savings attributed to outsourcing could be illusory, partly due to the vendor's effort to present an attractive offer[28], but also to the contract itself: outsourcing contracts usually stipulate a fixed cost that is revised annually according to a representative price index — but, actually, the value of many facilities and resources, and even labour costs, are constantly decreasing. Therefore, the estimation of costs carried out by the external provider could be excessively generous for the vendor's interests, and hence financially prejudicial for the organization; additionally, it seems obvious that the external provider will attempt to maximize *his* own benefit, so the services he provides could be those with the lowest possible quality.

Another relevant aspect in the sphere of cost economics is that of transaction costs, a concept that is related to the effort, time, and burdens involved in designing, negotiating, supervising, and enforcing a contract between the company and the vendor (Coase, 1937)[29]. From this perspective, outsourcing is an attractive alternative when, even if transaction costs originated by the transfer are taken into account, insourcing is anti-economic; on the contrary, the organization may opt for insourcing if *transactional diseconomies* invalidate the benefits in production costs (Bakos & Brynjolfsson, 1993).

## *Financial Issues*

Historically, organizations have used their surpluses basically to finance their growth, particularly to create their IT infrastructures, rather than share profits among the stakeholders (Jensen, 1989). In the '70s and early '80s, the baking, transport and distribution sectors, and part of the industry applied their financial slack to the development of transactional infrastructures which, besides being convenient for businesses, conferred an image of dynamism and originality on executives; the success of certain operations — *American Airlines*, *American Hospital Supply*, etc. — also contributed to the creation of internalized services.

Capital restrictions have caused the emergence of some growing outsourcing practices, such as pay-per-use (the use of computer facilities and infrastructures): offices, computer equipments, Internet services, backup services, etc.

However, it seems reasonable to expect that, in periods of capital restriction, organizations may feel compelled to reduce the size of those functions that do not form part of the business core — among them, the IS — so as to lighten the cost structure and preserve the financial balance. One of the main features of outsourcing is precisely that it allows for transforming the uncertainty characteristic of an IS into the certainty of a fixed cost contractually stipulated; even when the external offer does not show evidence of comparative efficiencies, the expectation of stabilizing costs and suppressing uncertainty may be enough to justify outsourcing.

Hirschheim and Lacity (2000) found that a number of organizations adopted massive outsourcing decisions as a consequence of different kinds of financial imbalance; notice that downsizing, rightsizing and outsourcing decisions, especially when they involve the transfer of facilities or infrastructures, imply cash flow for the client[30].

### *Further Arguments*

The work of Lacity and Willcocks (1998), later supported by further evidence (Lacity & Willcocks, 2003), offers some interesting findings about the reasons which have justified outsourcing of activities related to the IS; apart from the already mentioned cost saving, especially in IT (which, according to Lacity and Hirschheim (1993) ranges between 10% and 50%), companies give a number of reasons: the desire to attain professional skills, experience and other resources which are not available in internal services (59%), concentrating on the business core (31%), altering the cost structure, by transforming fixed burdens into variable burdens (31%), demonstrating the relevance and contribution of the internal service (30%), and even the eagerness to follow the outsourcing trend for no specific reason (38%). Similar results are presented in Choudhury and Sabherwal (2003).

### *The Risks of IS/IT Outsourcing*

IS/IT outsourcing as a management strategy has not only advantages, but also certain disadvantages or possible risks, some of which have been mentioned in the paragraphs above. The first of those risks is related to data security and confidentiality (Collins & Millen, 1995).

Another noticeable risk is hidden costs, that is, not specified in the contract or added by the vendor as additional services. Willcocks and Currie (1997) point out that hidden costs were the greatest risk of outsourcing. The same conclusion is drawn by Hendry (1995), who also detected hidden costs, especially in the long term.

Other risk factors are the client's loss of flexibility (Clark, Zmud, & McCray, 1995; Earl, 1996) and of control, particularly in long-term contracts. Khalfan and Gough (2002) also mention the lack of experience in outsourcing and the loss of the ability to innovate.

During the last several years, a critical movement against IS/IT outsourcing has emerged. Forrester Consulting (2003) has found evidence that 60% of U.S. big companies show considerable reluctance to support this practice, particularly in the most critical functions, despite the fact that outsourcing is actually practised by most of them. Additionally, certain economic and political sectors do not trust such countries as India, China or Brazil when they consider IS/IT outsourcing.

## An Empirical Study of IS/IT Outsourcing In Spain

The Spanish IT outsourcing market has grown steadily over the last years; industry turnover has increased at a 20% annual rate from 2001, and is expected to rise as SMEs and the Public Administration undertake outsourcing arrangements. Spain is an attractive location for offshoring, given the growing number of Spanish-speakers in the U.S.A. and the increasing demand of teleservices in Latin America. At the same time, Spanish and Latin American companies are potential clients for American outsourcing services providers.

However we know very little about the actual outcomes of offshoring projects; some firm-level studies have been conducted among companies from the U.S. and some European countries (e.g., Germany and France) but our view about the current situation of IT outsourcing in Spain is still incomplete.

The research presented in this chapter has been conducted along the same lines of other empirical investigations of IS outsourcing carried out in different countries, for example, Australia (Hurley & Schaumann, 1997; Beaumont & Costa, 2002); Kuwait (Khalfan & Gough, 2002); France and Germany (Barthelemy & Geyer, 2001) and the United States (Collins & Millen, 1995). The attempt is to obtain information about the current situation of IS/IT outsourcing in Spanish firms[31]. With this purpose, we have conducted a number of surveys, whose technical details will be described in the following paragraphs.

Three different groups of companies took part in this study, which finished in 2002. The first group (OUTSOURCING-E) is composed of 395 Spanish firms from all sectors with an annual turnover of more than $1.45 million, chosen by means of random sampling[32]. The second group (OUTSOURCING-G) is formed by 91 large Spanish firms; these are major Spanish organizations because of their turnover, or they are one of the first five in their respective sectors. They were selected with random sampling directed by an expert criterion. Finally, we have analyzed a specific sector for which IS outsourcing is particularly relevant: the banking sector. Forty-four banks (one out of every five Spanish firms) have been surveyed, after being selected by means of directed random sampling.

In all cases, the relevant information has been gathered by means of a questionnaire aimed at organizing and structuring the data so as to allow for their automatic processing. However, we have also held personal interviews with managers and CIOs in order to clarify some responses or to obtain additional comments on topics of special interest. This was the case of some specific outsourcing areas, such as computer security; personal interviews also granted us access to concrete references about contractual arrangements that managers would never express in a questionnaire because of their confidential nature. Meetings also revealed that SMEs' attitude about outsourcing has substantially changed during the last decade; this evolution is more palpable in innovative high-tech SMEs, new-founded companies, and professionally — managed organizations. Family and individual enterprises companies, as well as SMEs focused to local markets, tend to perceive outsourcing as a costly, complex and unsuitable option.

The technical features of the surveys are shown in Tables 2, 3 and 4.

## The Firms Surveyed

OUTSOURCING-E includes companies from all Spanish regions; Catalonia, Madrid and Valencia were those from which the largest number of responses was obtained. This is not surprising because these are the Spanish regions with the highest degrees of economic activity and concentration of industries.

*Table 2. Outsourcing-E*

| | |
|---|---|
| Universe | Spanish firms |
| Target population | Spanish firms with an annual turnover of more than $1,45 million |
| Frame | Database "España 25.000" |
| Sample error | +/- 0.05 |
| Confidence level | 95.5% |
| Hypothesis | Z=2 and P=Q=0.5 |
| Sample size | 395 firms |
| Sampling method | Random sampling |
| Surveying method | Questionnaire sent by post, e-mail, telephone, fax, or personal interview |

*Table 3. Outsourcing-G*

| | |
|---|---|
| Universe | Large Spanish firms |
| Target population | Spanish firms among the first five in their sector, plus those with the highest turnover |
| Frame | Expert sampling per target population from the database "España 25.000" |
| Sample error | +/- 0.1 |
| Confidence level | 95.5% |
| Hypothesis | Z=2 and P=Q=0.5 |
| Sample size | 91 firms |
| Sampling method | Random sampling |
| Surveying method | Questionnaire sent by post, e-mail, telephone, fax, or personal interview |

*Table 4. Outsourcing-F*

| | |
|---|---|
| Universe | Spanish banks |
| Target population | Spanish banks registered in the Bank of Spain |
| Frame | Spanish banks, savings banks and credit unions |
| Sample error | Since the number of organizations is small, one out of every five was taken |
| Sample size | 44 firms |
| Sampling method | Random sampling |
| Surveying method | Questionnaire sent by post, e-mail, telephone, fax, or personal interview |

Because the largest Spanish companies are located in Madrid and Catalonia, these two regions represent three quarters of the sample OUTSOURCING-G[33]. Concentration of industries is particularly relevant in the case of Madrid, a region where the biggest firms have been traditionally established for geographical and political reasons.

The wide range of activities represented in OUTSOURCING-E allows our research to cover almost all economic sectors[34]; Table 6 lists the distribution of companies across sectors in OUTSOURCING-E and OUTSOURCING-G.

Since the sample includes companies of different sizes, we used data such as turnover, number of workers and funds to classify them in four groups[35]: micro-, small, medium-sized and big enterprises. As regards OUTSOURCING-E, the average turnover is $21.78 million, and the average number of employees is 110, although it should be kept in mind that the sample is extraordinarily wide and diverse. Table 7 shows that the Spanish business sector is primarily composed of small and medium-sized enterprises (SMEs)[36] and that the group of large firms, despite its economic relevance, is numerically inferior.

The sample OUTSOURCING-G is composed exclusively of big-sized companies, which are those with more than 250 workers and a high turnover. We have surveyed a large part of all Spanish big firms; the sample contains 91 companies (see Table 5) although, if the

*Table 5. Distribution of responses across geographical areas (Outsourcing-E and Outsourcing-G)*

| | OUTSOURCING-E | | OUTSOURCING-G | |
|---|---|---|---|---|
| AREA | Frequency | % | Frequency | % |
| Centre | 135 | 34.18% | 34 | 59.34% |
| East | 181 | 45.82% | 25 | 27.47% |
| North | 35 | 8.86% | 4 | 4.40% |
| South | 44 | 11.14% | 8 | 8.79% |
| Total | 395 | 100.00% | 91 | 100.00% |

*Table 6. Distribution of firms across sectors*

| | OUTSOURCING-E | | OUTSOURCING-G | |
|---|---|---|---|---|
| **Sector** | **Frequency** | **%** | **Frequency** | **%** |
| Food | 47 | 11.90% | 7 | 7.69% |
| Construction | 20 | 5.06% | 6 | 6.59% |
| Distribution | 107 | 27.09% | 13 | 14.29% |
| Heavy industry | 18 | 4.56% | 7 | 7.69% |
| Chemicals | 31 | 7.85% | 10 | 10.99% |
| Textile industry | 10 | 2.53% | 2 | 2.20% |
| Services | 81 | 20.51% | 23 | 25.27% |
| IT services | 22 | 5.57% | 8 | 8.79% |
| Basic industry | 59 | 14.94% | 15 | 16.48% |
| **Total** | **395** | **100.00%** | **91** | **100.00%** |

*Table 7. Business size: Outsourcing-E*

| Business type | Frequency | Percentage | Accumulated percentage |
|---|---|---|---|
| Micro-enterprises | 24 | 6.1% | 6.1% |
| Small enterprises | 181 | 45.8% | 51.9% |
| Medium-sized enterprises | 154 | 39.0% | 90.9% |
| Big enterprises | 36 | 9.1% | 100% |
| **Total** | **395** | **100%** | |

*Figure 2. Scope of the firms surveyed*

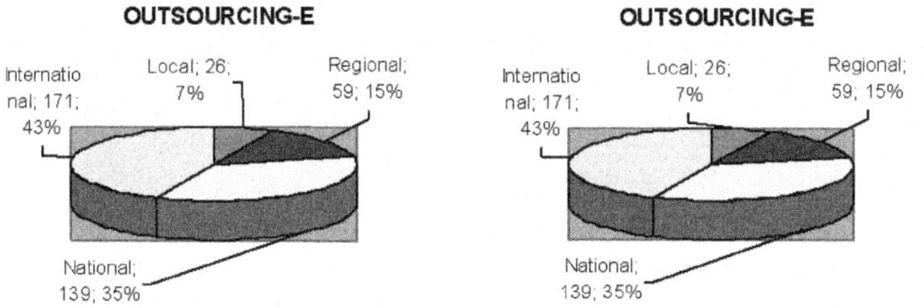


number of employees is solely considered, 12 of them (13.2%) could be classified as medium-sized enterprises. The remaining 86.8% is formed by big corporative, national but mainly international, firms.

Finally, the companies that form part of the sample are national and international; as regards OUTSOURCING-E (a representative sample of Spanish businesses), 43% of them are national companies, whereas 35% are international. Additionally, there is a significant number of regional firms.

OUTSOURCING-G is predominantly composed of international companies (two-thirds of the total); regional or local businesses are poorly represented, which must be attributed to the size of the enterprises included in this sample.

To sum up, it has been shown that the samples analyzed are sufficiently representative of Spain's economy, since they include all Spanish regions, business sizes, economic sectors and business scopes.

## IS/IT Outsourcing in Spanish Firms

Prior research on IS/IT outsourcing has repeatedly shown that this is a growing phenomenon. Our own results, which will be detailed in the present section, are consistent with this idea.

*Figure 3. Proportion of firms that outsource their IS/IT*

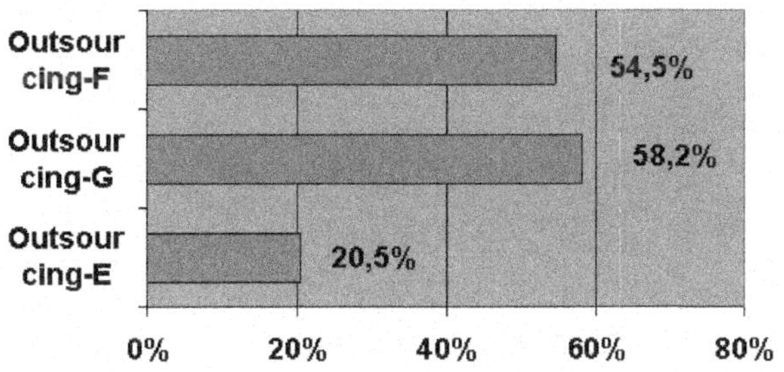


Our data show that 20% of Spanish firms have outsourced part of the activities, functions or tasks of their IS/IT; this proportion is substantially greater in the sample OUTSOURCING-G, composed of large companies, and also in the banking sector, where outsourcing is practised by 54% of firms. Notice that the results point to the existence of outsourcing decisions, but they do not reflect the scope, financial magnitude or importance of these decisions. For this reason, we have carried out a qualitative analysis of IS/IT outsourcing, by examining which types of activities are outsourced and their relevance for the organization.

## Outsourced Activities and Functions

Our results regarding the types of outsourced IS/IT activities are similar to those obtained in studies carried out in other countries (Teng, Cheon, & Grover, 1995; Beaumont & Costa, 2002). Thus, the results derived from the general sample (OUTSOURCING-E) show that the most frequent outsourcing operations are software development (19.59%) and maintenance in different modes: software maintenance (15.46%), hardware maintenance (9.28%) and entire maintenance (15.46%). The development and support of networks is also significant (8.25%), although one of the most interesting findings has to do with Internet services: 8.25% of firms outsources part or all of the activities involved in the creation and maintenance of Web sites; the average percentage of Spanish companies present in the Internet is slightly higher than 60%, thus the proportion of Spanish firms that have outsourced the management of their corporative sites does not reach 15% of the total. This result contradicts the relevance granted by authors such as Young (2000) to this outsourcing practice, and can be explained by the relatively backward situation of Spanish companies with regards to Internet access, as compared with other European countries or the United States[37].

The second group of outsourced activities is formed by management IT support services and payroll management and processing, a traditional outsourcing target that is currently practised by 5% of Spanish companies.

The outsourcing of accounting and other economic-financial management functions is comparatively less frequent (2%), due in part to the fact that it implies the transfer of

*Figure 4. Types of outsourced activities (Outsourcing-E)*

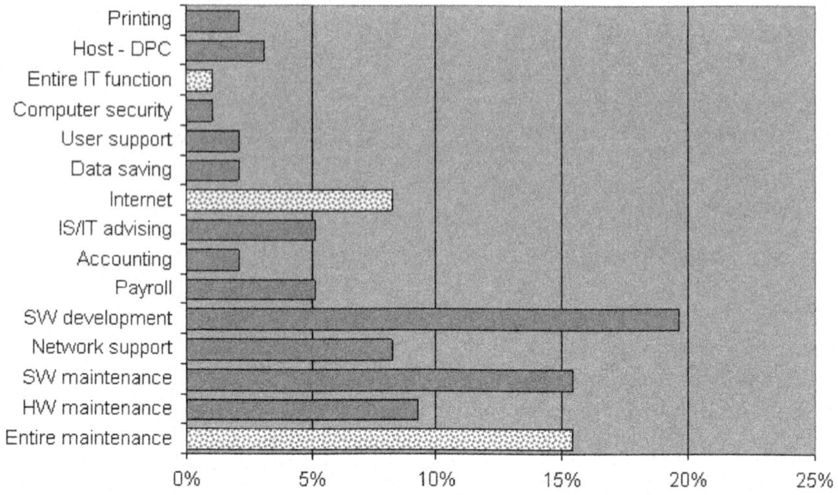


confidential information to the supplier; nevertheless, companies do outsource essentially transactional activities, which do not affect the business core, such as the input of data related to operations in those cases in which the firm does not have a system that allows for direct input into the management information system (2.06%).

The third group of outsourced activities involves subcontracting equipments that host corporative databases. These systems have substituted data processing centres (DPCs) in a wide range of firms, part of which have chosen to outsource the management of these infrastructures by means of facilities management (FM) contracts. The outsourcing of the entire system is less frequent, because of the strategic risks this practice implies.

Other outsourced activities are user support services (2.06%), which are usually contracted together with telemarketing services and telephone sale. In Spain, the vendors of these services are very often the result of spin-off operations, that is, business units that become independent corporations. Spin-off practices are basically motivated by the existence of cost savings, which result from altering the legal framework applicable to salaries and working conditions[38]. It has also been observed that, following spin-off, contracting corporations *rotate* outsourcing contracts with different suppliers so that the employees' length of service disappears and the cost of the provision of the service is reduced, something that would be impossible if the service were supplied internally. This is not, therefore, a multi-sourcing practice but rather a selective strategy that attempts to induce competitiveness between different suppliers — although it causes serious disturbances in the market.

In 2% of cases, the firms have contracted external suppliers to procure massive printing services for advertising campaigns, leaflet distribution or similar activities which involve

*Figure 5. Outsourced activities (OUTSOURCING-G)*

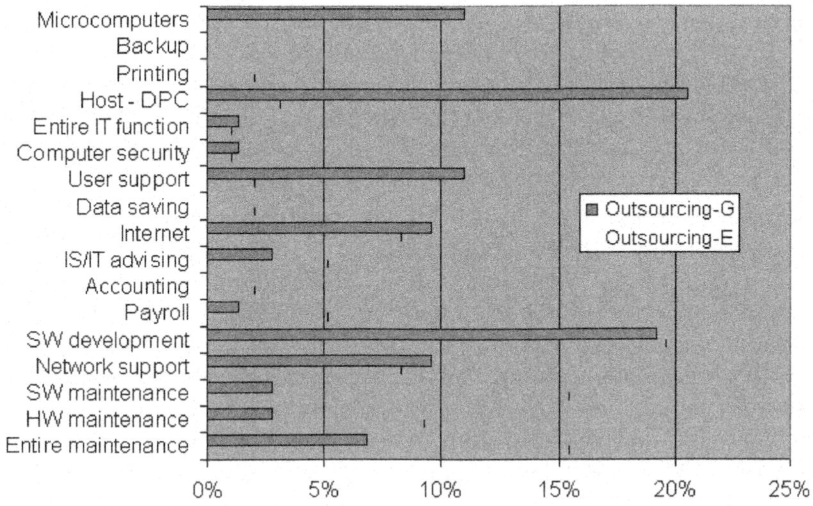


the occasional but intensive use of equipments whose internal maintenance would be economically unfeasible; these contracts are of the same type as the Body Shop deal described by Lacity and Hirschheim (1993a), that is, *ad hoc* contracts intended to meet sporadic needs — although in some cases the contractual relationship with the supplier is kept because the printing needs are recurrent.

Finally, 1% of firms (1.4% of large firms) have outsourced all the IT activities, functions and processes by means of FM contracts or massive outsourcing contracts.

## Outsourcing Strategies in Large Firms

IS/IT outsourcing has traditionally been considered a characteristic practice of large companies, although it has been shown that outsourcing is practised by firms of every size in all sectors. However, big businesses do constitute a special case. The results obtained from the sample of large firms (OUTSOURCING-G) are summarized in Figure 5 below, together with the general results of OUTSOURCING-E.

Rather unexpectedly, the most frequently outsourced activity is the massive processing of data in DPC, or the latest host-based resources management, which amounts to 20% of large firms – a phenomenon that would have seemed impossible 20 years ago. The proportion is substantially greater than that observed in the general sample (3.09%), which is explained by the different IS architectures of large and small companies: small companies are organized around systems (such as peer to peer networks) that are suitable for basically local activities in which a relatively small number of people and departments are involved; on the contrary, corporative systems must face massive data processing needs, what justifies specializing the service.

The second group of frequently outsourced activities is software development, which is transferred to the market in approximately 20% of cases. Outsourcing adopts two models: purchase of standard software, or the external development of software tailored to the specific needs of the firm[39]. Our data do not suggest that large companies behave in a peculiar way towards software development outsourcing, since the rate at which they practise this type of outsourcing is similar to the average[40].

The evolution of IS from the organization's DPC to client-vendor architectures has caused a growing interest in microcomputers, PC networks, and the use of decision support systems (DSS and GDSS). In terms of physical equipments, organizations seem to be focusing their efforts on microcomputing, an activity that is frequently outsourced in large firms (11%) because of its high cost. This result suggests that organizations are concentrating on information resources management (IRM). On the contrary, SMEs often develop this activity internally, because their systems are substantially smaller and simpler both in physical and logistic terms — the physical and logic standardization of PCs is obviously a key factor in facilitating insourcing.

Another outsourced activity is user support, more often practised in the sample of big firms (11%) than in the general sample (5.15%); the information centre is usually converted to a business unit or an independent company in an attempt to evaluate its efficiency by comparing the costs of the internal and external provision of the service.

Other outsourced activities are network support (9.6%) and the development and maintenance of the corporative site and related services (9.6%), sometimes including e-commerce. The rate of outsourcing of this type of activities is higher in the largest firms,

*Figure 6. Outsourced activities in the banking sector (Outsourcing-F)*

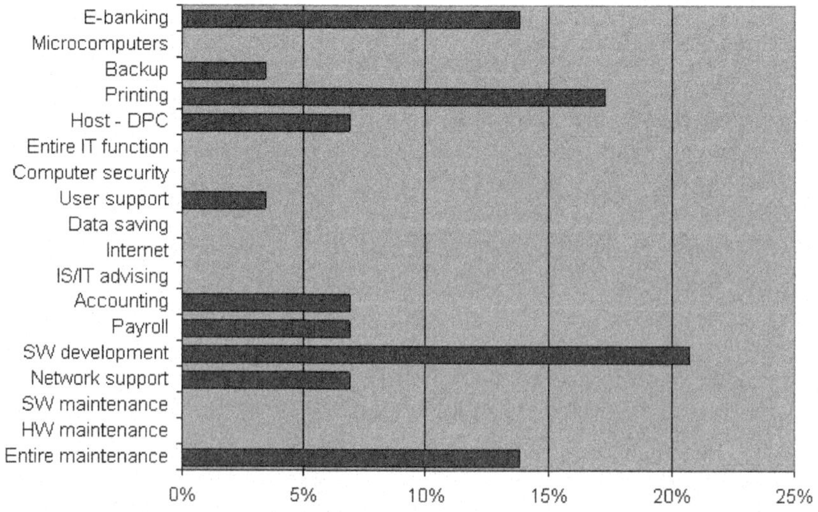

which nevertheless do not often transfer maintenance and advising services. None of the medium-sized and big firms surveyed had outsourced accounting, what establishes a clear difference between these enterprises and SMEs and points to the relevance of the accounting IS for management and decision-making.

All the practices described so far are limited, selective outsourcing decisions, in which the company transfers only certain activities because of strictly economic motivations, that is, cost saving. However, there is a small group of organizations that have signed massive outsourcing contracts involving all IT activities, processes and functions. This group accounts for approximately 1.4% of large firms — a proportion that is clearly higher than that observed in the general sample[41].

As regards outsourcing in the banking sector, more than half of the banks surveyed carry out outsourcing operations. As in the general sample, the most frequently outsourced activity is software development (21%), followed by printing (17.2%); not only are documents for the bank's clients printed, but also documents with information from corporative databases, so as to minimize the consequences of a serious computing error.

The functions related to e-banking are also outsourced (13.8%), as well as the maintenance of equipments, software and telematic services (13.8%), in this case by means of *ad hoc* contracts involving the entire transfer of this function to one or more vendors. Finance companies often outsource or even share the equipments that constitute the core of transactional and tele-processing systems, so as to reduce management costs.

The outsourcing of payroll management and accounting reaches 7%; backup copying is another outsourced activity, which is frequently carried out with geographically distant computers so as to allow for online performance of management systems and transactional applications.

Finance corporations keep the internal performance of activities such as data saving, which is carried out within their own tele-processing networks, and other functions that are considered as essential from a managerial and/or competitive point of view, namely, system security and IT advising: protecting the confidentiality of corporative data and of the clients' transactional data is a basic requirement for the banking business. Additionally, with the advent of e-commerce and e-banking, innovation has become a key competitive factor for the banking sector; as a consequence, these activities have been insourced.

To sum up, our data show that an interesting phenomenon has taken place with relation to IS/IT outsourcing, since this practice was initially presented as a suitable option for small firms which could not face the high costs derived from the ever-changing computer equipments and programs. On the contrary, large firms are precisely those which practise outsourcing more frequently.

## An Outlook on Offshoring in Spain

Outsourcing has come along with increasing worries about the effect of subcontracting over employment, more specifically about possible changes in the regional distribution of labour. Offshoring is the term coined to express the devolution of internal activities, through outsourcing arrangements, into several countries or economic areas, in order to exploit their comparative advantages in terms of cost, skills, and/or infrastructures.

In a wide perspective, cross-border trade in business services should lead to a more efficient global division of labour and to improvements in productivity[42]; nevertheless offshoring has given rise to increasing concerns about job stability in the industrial countries[43], and to reservations among companies because it might entail a drop in the quality of subcontracted services. Social pressures and political resistance might cause a protectionist reaction in developed countries.

This geographical redistribution can be interpreted as a natural consequence of the dynamics of the market system — many developed countries are shifting their manufacturing activities to developing economies, such as China, to lower production costs — and an outcome of the flexibility allowed by information and communications technologies (ICT)[44].

Offshoring usually requires also a certain degree of *cultural* match; for example, the Philippines have been selected by many American companies for outsourcing financial services (e.g., Procter and Gamble, or Citibank) because a large number of Filipino accountants are trained in U.S. accounting standards.

The potential impact of the vanishing of geographical boundaries is particularly evident in the case of the Spanish-speakers community: American companies can take benefit from the availability of skilled Spanish-speakers to offer different teleservices in the Spanish and Latin America markets[45]; Spanish-speakers in the U.S. are also a very attractive market niche both for European and American companies, given the sustained rise of their net income.

However, Spanish companies primarily rely on IT services providers located in the European Union (EU), that is, domestic IT providers. This is due to the relative newness of IT outsourcing in Spain — out interviews revealed that companies primarily trust in local providers because they offer higher *apparent* reliance; we have also verified that large and focused outsourcing contracts are usually signed with local subsidiaries of large American and European IT services providers[46]. These arrangements can be viewed as an atypical form of offshoring where IT services are *locally* sourced by a *foreign* supplier.

## *A Case Study*

Only one of the companies in the sample significantly relies on offshored IT services. This firm is the leading telecommunication services provider in Spain, and it is among the ten major European telecos (in advance, PC); a decade ago, telemarketing services were branched out and turned into a subsidiary company (in advance, SC), in order to lessen personnel costs.

SC was the unique provider of telemarketing services for its parent company for several years, but the increasing competition led PC to adopt a free market strategy for outsourced services. SC has implemented several measures to remain competitive; one of the elements of the new strategy was to create two new telemarketing platforms in Morocco (Tanger & Casablanca), and discharge about 20% of the staff in Spain. The company estimated a saving of 50% of total labour costs, and a huge cash flow as a result of the transfer of facilities and buildings in Spain.

However, why Morocco? For the last five decades, the Spanish government has been supporting 10 "Spanish Institutions" in Morocco. Apart from acting as promoters of the Spahish culture, these institutions offer several educational services exclusively in Spanish — they are, in fact, high schools. Therefore, we can found many Spanish-speaking people in several cities in Morocco, such as Casablanca or Tanger. Moreover, the government of Morocco offered the company several financial advantages, including tax deductions and public grants.

The initiative has not been completely successful due to several reasons. The opposition of trade unions and the Spanish government was hard, because offshoring had a very relevant impact on employment — dismissal of about 4,000 workers in several Spanish cities.

However, the "critical failure factor" was the cultural gap between Spanish clients and teleoperators in Morocco; regardless their ability to speak Spanish, teleoperators were frequently unable to understand some of the issues raised from Spain not only because Spanish clients used some colloquial or unusual expressions, but also because their lifestyle and their environment were radically different.

In broad terms, clients and teleoperators did not share a common view of the problems, therefore the whole system failed and the company was compelled to disclose and cancel its offshoring arrangement by 2004. Now, the platforms in Tanger and Casablanca carry out back-office services and offer focused telemarketing activities in Morocco, Tunisia, and other African countries. The company also offers several telemarketing services in Latin America, through a network of subsidiary firms; cultural match has been taken into consideration, and most clients are served from local platforms.

This case offers some interesting insights about the rationale of offshoring, and the hindrances of the adoption process. Even if we skip over the (likely) future increase of income and wages in the less-developed countries, social and political resistance to change in industrial countries might hinder the adoption of offshoring. Cultural mismatches are also relevant, because they may erode confidence and lead to reluctance or even client dismissal.

# Critical Analysis

The leading motivation for IS/IT outsourcing is cost reduction, although there are other secondary motivations such as the ability to innovate, the reduction of technologic risks, business process restructuring (BPR) or the access to professional expertise and competence. A particularly clear case is that of Web sites and services, which give rise to problems that managers consider complex and difficult to understand. The outsourcing of these activities is generally justified by the complexity of Web technology — especially, when it is compared with traditional management systems — and by professional shortage in the internal IS department. These factors have originated a business niche for firms that specialize in Internet management services (hosting, e-commerce, mobile work, etc.) whose turnover was more than $50,000 million in 2003[47].

However, there seems to be a certain tendency towards using outsourcing as a strategic instrument — rather than a management option aiming at cost saving — in an attempt to maintain or modify the organization's competitive scope; this evolution is clearly observed in the case of e-commerce and in Internet-based banking services.

Some issues especially relevant for large organizations are those related to contingency plans in computing disasters; the crisis of September 11, which intensified hackers' attacks on corporative systems[48] and multiplied the number of viruses in the Internet, brought these recurring problems to the foreground. In general, firms perform security-related functions internally — backup, network security, access to resources, etc. — although major banking corporations contract backup copying to external providers in order to benefit from cost savings derived from massive data processing.

Our results are notably more modest than those obtained in studies carried out in other geographical areas such as Australia, Canada, Europe or the United States[49]; while Hurley and Schaumann (1997) reported the insourcing of 57% of data centre operations in Australia, in Spain this rate increases to 80% of large firms. Similarly, outsourcing of network services is considerably lower in Spain than in Australia (6.9% vs. 50%).

The crisis of digital economy and repeated accounting and finance frauds (WorldCom, Enron, ...) have brought radical changes in the organizations' outsourcing strategies and, more importantly, in the assessment of outsourcing projects: organizations demand external providers with accredited financial stability, potential longevity, experience and reliability[50]. Additionally, benchmarking is increasingly being used to compare insourcing with outsourcing and to assess the economic suitableness of external offers, and there is a growing demand for pay-per-use services and adaptable infrastructures, which facilitate adapting the service to the client's specific needs at any given moment.

# Conclusions

Our results show that 20% of Spanish firms have outsourced part of their IS, and that IS/IT outsourcing is practised by 50% of Spain's large companies and banks. From the point of view of transaction costs, the motivations of large companies for IS/IT outsourcing are the economic advantages obtained thanks to the external procurement of services and functions which are poorly specific in material and human terms.

The main outsourced activities are software development — a function in which the absence of specificities originates an obvious economic advantage — and the maintenance of IS technical resources, both by means of entire transfer contracts and *ad hoc* contracts involving computer applications, equipments, and network infrastructure.

Other frequently outsourced activities are those related to the Internet, an emerging area whose importance increases when the firms decide to implement sites for e-commerce or even when the objective is just to develop a non-transactional corporative site.

The tendency towards outsourcing Internet-based resources is particularly interesting because, from the point of view of resources theory, organizations are supposed to be reluctant to transfer any activity with competitive implications. Besides the strategic relevance of the new models of Internet-based businesses and organizations, a topic beyond the scope of our research, it can be observed that the transfer has frequently been granted to external companies established *ad hoc* by the outsourcer; in other words, the vendor is an independent organization but most of its stakes are held by the outsourcer. Thus, this may be considered a special type of insourcing.

As regards small and medium-sized enterprises, the outsourcing of Internet services is a consequence of the lack of internal human resources, and of the technologic challenges and the risks underlying this type of activities.

The lack of human resources also explains the increasing rate at which the organizations choose external advising services to assist them in issues of computing technology and information resources management. This practice does not seem to depend on business size, but there are obvious differences in the types of advising — basically technological and operational for SMEs, and corporative and strategic for larger firms. A similar practice is that of outsourced user-related services, that is, information centres.

In a fourth group, we have classified diverse transactional activities such as payroll management, accounting, data saving, computer security or massive printing; these contracts are motivated by the absence of specificities and/or strategic implications that could invalidate the cost advantages offered by external providers, who in turn benefit from economies of scale.

Host-type equipments which hold corporative databases are also often outsourced, but in this case it is difficult to distinguish between outsourcing contracts and other contractual types based on financial renting or leasing.

A small proportion of firms have transferred the management of information resources, or they even have outsourced the entire IT, that is, all IT functions, tasks and activities. Our empirical data show that these massive outsourcing projects are developed by large firms; however, our findings do not allow us to conclude that the observed relation is systematic or statistically consistent.

IS/IT outsourcing is indeed being practised by large firms, where DPCs and mainframes are increasingly being outsourced; this strategy, together with software development, suggests that large firms are directing their efforts towards procuring microcomputers. However, we observe again that intranet- and PC-related activities are often outsourced, which points to the fact that organizations are focusing on the management of information resources. This is even more obvious in the banking sector.

Some emerging areas are those related to the design and management of Web sites and e-commerce systems, as well as the use of equipments through pay-per-use contracts, what is known as office outsourcing.

# References


Ang, S., & Straub, D. W. (1998). Production and transaction economies and IS outsourcing: A study of the U.S. banking industry. *MIS Quarterly, 22*(4), 535-552.

Ang, S., & Straub, D. W. (2000). The economics of IS outsourcing. In R. Hirschheim, A. Heinzl & J. Dibbern (Eds.), *Information systems outsourcing. Enduring themes, emergent patterns and future directions* (pp. 47-73). New York: Springer-Verlag.

Antonucci, Y. L., Lordi, F. C., & Tucker, J. J. (1998). The pros and cons of IT outsourcing. *Journal of Accountancy, 185*(6), 26-31.

Aubert, B. A, Rivard, S., & Patry, M. (1996). A transaction cost approach to outsourcing behavior: Some empirical evidence. *Information & Management, 30*(2), 51-65.

Bakos, J. Y., & Brynjolfsson, E. (1993). Information technology incentives and the optimal number of suppliers. *Journal of Management Information Systems, 10*(2), 37-53.

Barthelemy, J. (2001, Spring). The hidden costs of IT outsourcing. *MIT Sloan Management Review,* 60-69.

Barthelemy, J., & Geyer, D. (2001). IT outsourcing: Evidence from France and Germany. *European Management Journal, 19*(2), 195-202.

Beaumont, N., & Costa, C. (2002). Information technology outsourcing in Australia. *Information Resources Management Journal, 15*(3), 14-31.

Burkhart, L. A. (2003). The IT outsourcing question. *Public Utilities Fortnightly, 141*(1), 26.

Chen, Q., & Lin, B. (1998). Global outsourcing and its managerial implications. *Human Systems Management, 17*(2), 109-114.

Chin, T. L. (1997). Outsourcing. Health care organizations are considering strategic goals in making outsourcing decisions. *Health Data Management, 5*, 69-77.

Choudhury, V., & Sabherwal, R. (2003). Portfolios of control in outsourced software development projects. *Information Systems Research, 14*(3), 291-314.

Clark, T., Zmud, R., & McCray, G. (1995). The outsourcing of information services: Transforming the nature of business in the information industry. *Journal of Information Technology, 10*, 221-237.

Claver, E., & González, R. (1999). Análisis descriptivo del outsourcing de los sistemas de información. *Esic Market, 103*, 141-154.

Claver, E., González, R., & Llopis, J. (2000). An analysis of research in information systems 1981-1997. *Information & Management, 37*, 181-195.

Coase, R. (1937). The nature of the firm. *Econometrics, 4*, 386-405.

Collins, J. S., & Millen, R. A. (1995). Information systems outsourcing by large American industrial firms: Choices and impacts. *Information Resources Management Journal, 8*(1), 5-13.

Di Romualdo, A., & Gurbaxani, V. (1998). Strategic intent for IT outsourcing. Sloan *Management Review, 39*(4), 67-80.

Dibbern, J., & Heinzl, A. (2002). Outsourcing of information systems in small and medium sized enterprises: A test of multi-theoretical causal model. In R. Hirschheim, A. Heinzl & J. Dibbern (Eds.), *Information systems outsourcing. Enduring themes, emergent patterns and future directions* (pp. 77-99). Berlin: Springer-Verlag.

Earl, M. J. (1996, Spring). The risks of outsourcing IT. *Sloan Management Review*, 26-32.

Feeny, D., Willcocks, L., & Lacity, M. (2003). *Business process outsourcing: The promise of the enterprise partnership model.* Templeton Executive Briefing, Templeton College, Oxford University.

Forrester Research. (2003). Outsourcing offshore. Retrieved February 3, 2004, from http://www.idg.es

Friedberg A., & Yarberry, W. (1991, August). Audit rights in an outsourcing environment. *Internal Auditor*, 53-59.

GAO. (1992). Depository institutions: Contracting practices with data processing services. Report to the Congressional committees. United Stated General Accounting Office GOA/GGD, 92-19.

Graham, M. E., & Meuse, D. (1997). The technology of benefits outsourcing: Helping employees help themselves. *Benefits Quarterly, 13*(1), 28-31.

Greaver, M. F. (1998). Strategic outsourcing. New York: AMACOM.

Grover, V. (1998). IS investment priorities in contemporary organizations. Association for computing machinery. *Communications of the ACM, 41*(2), 40-49.

Grover, V., Cheon, M. J., & Teng, J. T. C. (1994). A descriptive study on the outsourcing of information systems functions. *Information & Management, 27*(1), 33-45.

Grover, V., Cheon, M. J., & Teng, J. T. C. (1996). The effect of service quality and partnership on the outsourcing of information systems functions. *Journal of Management Information Systems, 12*(4), 89-117.

Grover, V., Teng, J., Segars, A. H., & Fiedler, K. (1998). The influence of information technology diffusion and business process change on perceived productivity: The IS executive's perspective. *Information & Management, 34*(3), 141-159.

Harris, A., Giunipero, L. C., & Hult, G. T. (1998). Impact of organizational and contract flexibility on outsourcing contracts. *Industrial Marketing Management, 27*(5), 373-384.

Helppie, R. D. (1998). Bring in the ringer! Should your organization consider outsourcing IT? *Healthcare Informatics: The Business Magazine for Information and Communication Systems, 15*(2), 161-168.

Hendry, J. (1995). Culture, community, and the networks: The hidden cost of outsourcing. *European Management Journal, 13*(2).

Hindle, J., Willcocks, L., Feeny, D., & Lacity, M. (2003). Value-added outsourcing at Lloyd's and BAE Systems. *Knowledge Management, 6*(4), 28-31.

Hirschheim, R., & Lacity, M. C. (2000). The myths and realities of information technology outsourcing. *Communications of the ACM, 43*(2), 99-107.

Hirschheim, R., Heinzl, A., & Dibbern, J. (Eds.). (2002). *Information systems outsourcing. Enduring themes, emergent patterns and future directions*. New York: Springer-Verlag.

Hsu, C., Chiu, C., & Hsu, P. (2004) Predicting information systems outsourcing success using a hierarchical design of case-based reasoning. *Expert Systems with Applications, 26*(3), 435-441.

Hurley, M., & Schaumann, F. (1997). KPMG survey: The IT outsourcing decision. *Information Management and Computer Security, 5*(4), 126-132.

Itami, H., & Roehl, T. (1991). *Mobilizing invisible assets*. Cambridge, MA: Harvard University Press.

Jensen, M. C. (1989). Eclipse of the public corporation. *Harvard Business Review, 89*(5), 61-75.

Khalfan, A., & Gough, T. G. (2002). Comparative analysis between the public and private sectors on the IS/IT outsourcing practices in a developing country: A field study. *Logistics Information Management, 15*(3), 212-222.

Lacity, M. C., & Hirschheim, R. (1993, Fall). The information systems outsourcing bandwagon. *Sloan Management Review*, 73-86.

Lacity, M. C., & Hirschheim, R. (1993a). *Information systems outsourcing: Myths, metaphors, and realities*. New York: Wiley.

Lacity, M. C., & Hirschheim, R. (1995). *Beyond the information systems outsourcing bandwagon: The insourcing response*. New York: Wiley.

Lacity, M. C., & Hirschheim, Y. (1994). *Information systems outsourcing: Myths, metaphors and realities*. Chichester: John Wiley & Sons.

Lacity, M. C., & Willcocks, L. (1998). An empirical investigation on information technology sourcing practices: Lessons from experience. *Management Information Systems Quarterly, 22*(3), 363-408.

Lacity, M. C., & Willcocks, L. (2001). *Global information technology outsourcing*. Chichester: Wiley.

Lacity, M. C., & Willcocks, L. (2003). Information technology sourcing reflections. *Wirtschaftsinformatik*, Special Issue on Outsourcing, *45*(2), 115-125.

Lacity, M. C., Willcocks, L. P., & Feeny, D. E. (1996, Spring). The value of selective IT sourcing. *Sloan Management Review*, 13-25.

Lee, J. N. (2001). The impact of knowledge sharing, organizational capability and partnership quality on IS outsourcing success. *Information & Management, 38*(5), 323-335.

Lee, J. N., & Kim, S. (1992). The relationship between procedural formalization in MIS development and MIS success: A contingent analysis. *Information & Management, 22*(2), 89-112.

Lee, J. N., & Kim, S. (2001). An integrated approach for interdependent information system project selection. *International Journal of Project Management, 19*(2), 111-118.

Lee, J. N., & Kim, Y. G. (1997). Information systems outsourcing strategies for affiliated firms of the Korean conglomerate groups. *The Journal of Strategic Information Systems, 6*(3), 203-229.

Lee, J. N., & Kim, Y. G. (1999). Effect of partnership quality on IS outsourcing: Conceptual framework and empirical validation. *Journal of Management Information Systems, 15*(4), 29-62.

Lincoln, T. (1988). Retrospective appraisal of IT using SESAME. In X. Bjorn-Andersen & G. Davis, *Information systems assessment: Issues and challenges* (pp. 299-312). Amsterdam: North Holland.

Lincoln, T., & Shorrock, D. (1990). Cost justifying current use of information technology. In T. Lincoln, *Managing information systems for profit* (pp. 309-330). Chichester: Wiley.

Lingblom, M. (2002, June). Outsourcing firms in India: Time to move on. *CRN*, 33.

Loh, L., & Venkatraman, N. (1992). Determinants of information technology outsourcing: A cross-sectional analysis. *Journal of Management Information Systems, 9*(1), 7-25.

Looff, L. A. (1997). *Information systems outsourcing decision making: A managerial approach.* Hershey, PA: Idea Group.

Lopes De Sa Silva, E. (1997). *Análisis del impacto de la tecnología en los sistemas de informacion en la banca portuguesa.* Ph.D. dissertation. Universidad de A Coruña, Spain.

Mayhew, C., & Quinlan, M. (1999). The effects of outsourcing on occupational health and safety: A comparative study of factory-based workers and outworkers in the Australian clothing industry. *International Journal of Health Services: Planning, Administration, Evaluation, 29*(1), 83-107.

McFarlan, F. W., & Nolan, R. L. (1995, Winter). How to manage and IT outsourcing alliance. *Sloan Management Review*, 9-23.

Millar, V. (1994). Outsourcing trends. *Proceedings of the Outsourcing, Cosourcing and Insourcing Conference,* University of California.

Mylott, T. R. (1995). *Computer outsourcing: Managing the transfer of information systems*. Englewood Cliffs, NJ: Prentice Hall.

Ngwenyama, O. K., & Bryson, N. (1999). Making the information systems outsourcing decision: A transaction cost approach to analyzing outsourcing decision problems. *European Journal of Operational Research, 115*(2), 351-367.

OECD. (2001, June). Knowledge, work organization, and economic growth, directorate for education, employment, labor and social affairs, employment, labor and social affairs committee. Labor Market and Social Policy Occasional Paper 50.

The Outsourcing Institute. (1998). Source of current and potential outsourcing end-users. Available at http://www.outsourcing.com

Payton, F., & Handfield, R. (2003). Data warehousing implementation and outsourcing challenges: An action research project with Solectron. CAIS 12.

Ripin, K. M., & Sayles, L. R. (1999). *Insider strategies for outsourcing information systems: Building productive partnerships, avoiding seductive traps*. Oxford: Oxford University Press.

Sabherwal, R. (2003). The evolution of coordination in outsourced software development projects: A comparison of client and vendor perspectives. *Information and Organization, 13*, 153-202.

Sacristán Navarro, M. A. (1996). *Evaluación del outsourcing como opción estratégica en el proceso de transformación de las entidades financieras*. Ph.D. dissertation. Universidad Complutense de Madrid, Spain.

Sacristán Navarro, M. A. (1998). Análisis empírico sobre el uso del outsourcing de la función informática por el sector bancario español. *Carande Revista de Ciencias Sociales y Jurídicas, 2*, 371-387.

Slaughter, S., & Ang, S. (1996). Employment outsourcing. *Communications of the ACM, 39*(7), 47-54.

Smith, M. A., Mitra, S., & Narasimhan, S. (1998). Information systems outsourcing: A study of pre-event firm characteristics. *Journal of Management Information Systems, 15*(2), 61-93.

Teng, J. T. C., Cheon, M. J., & Grover, V. (1995). Decisions to outsource information systems functions: Testing a strategy-theoretic discrepancy model. *Decision Sciences, 26*(1), 75-103.

Wibbelsman D., & Maiero, T. (1994). Cosourcing. *Proceedings of the Outsourcing, Cosourcing and Insourcing Conference,* University of California – Berkeley.

Willcocks, L., & Choi, C. J. (1995). Co-operative partnership and "total" IT outsourcing: From contractual obligation to strategic alliance? *European Management Journal, 13*(1), 67-78.

Willcocks, L., & Currie, W. (1997). Contracting-out information technology in the public sector context: Research and critique. *Journal of the Australian and New Zealand Academy of Management, 2*(2), 34-49.

Willcocks, L., Hindle, J., Feeny, D., & Lacity, M. C. (2003). Knowledge in outsourcing - The missed business opportunity. *Knowledge Management, 7*(2).

Willcocks, L., Lacity, M. C., & Fitzgerald, G. (1995). Information technology outsourcing in Europe and the U.S.A.: Assessment issues. *International Journal of Information Management, 15*(5), 333-351.

Williamson, O. E. (1981, December). The modern corporation: Origin, evolution, attributes. *Journal of Economic Literature, 19*, 1537-1568.

Williamson, O. E. (1990). Transaction cost economics. In R. Schmalensee & R. D. Willig (Eds.), *Handbook of industrial organization* (pp. 135-182). Amsterdam.

Yang, C., & Huang, J. B. (2000). A decision model for IS outsourcing. *International Journal of Information Management, 20*(3), 225-239.

Yates, R. (1997). Virtual network management through outsourcing. *Healthcare Informatics: The Business Magazine for Information and Communication Systems, 14*(2), 122-124.

Young, A. (2000). The future of outsourcing: Thriving or surviving? Dataquest Service Trends 2000. Gartner Group report.

Zerrenner, W. C. (1999). A plan of action. Why outsourcing must be included in the IT strategy. *Healthcare Informatics: The Business Magazine for Information and Communication Systems, 16*(9), 95-98.

# Endnotes

1 The authors wish to thank Mª Isabel Fijo León (University Pablo de Olavide, Sevilla, Spain) for revising the final version of the text in English.

2 In the late 1970s, Electronic Data Systems (EDS) signed contracts with Frito-Lay and General Motors; however, the outsourcing market started growing in the 1980s with the deals Continental Airlines, First City Bank and Enron awarded EDS. The IBM-Kodak deal is particularly relevant because, apart from inaugurating the age of *megadeals*, it provided the first financial support for outsourcing.

3 Source: Outsourcing Institute.

4 The pressures towards outsourcing can be felt in all areas of activity. Lacity and Hirschheim (1993) observed that the managers who were more reluctant to outsourcing projects had to face conflictive situations when the internal systems could not demonstrate their contribution to businesses.

5 See, for example, Lacity and Hirschheim (1993b); Lacity et al. (1996); Hirschheim and Lacity (2000); Beaumont and Costa (2002).

6 Di Romualdo and Gurbaxani (1998); Greaever (1998); Zerrenner (1999). Collaboration between client and vendor, and the concept of strategic alliance, have also been largely debated (Willcocks and Choi, 1995; Sacristan, 1996; Sabherwal, 2003; Ripin, 1999; Lopes, 1997; Grover et al., 1996; Feeny & Lacity, 2003). Pre-implementation tasks, such as project design, have been identified as critical for success (see Lee & Kim, 1992).

7 This principle established that computer power increases as the square of the cost.

8 Rightsizing is the process of choosing an *adequate* dimension for IS/IT infrastructure. Downsizing expresses the migration of IS from mainframe to minicomputer or PC-based platforms; downsizing is the *organizational* consequence of our *technical* ability to develop smaller and more distributable hardware and software infrastructures.

9 One paramount research concern has been the analysis of the outsourcing decision process. See Loh and Venkatraman (1992), Lacity and Hirschheim (1994), Smith et. al. (1998), Yang and Juang (2000), and Lee and Kim (2001).

10 For example, the choice between renting and outsourcing can be stated in terms of cost-volume-benefit analysis, according to the system's break-even point; for a given period of time, the efficiency of renting often grows according to the use given to the equipment, although the weight of fixed costs — licences, infrastruc-

ture, salaries — may incline the decision towards outsourcing; however, this view tends to configure the IS as a cost centre rather than a profit centre, and relegates business requirements and opportunities to the background.

[11] One specific case is value-added outsourcing, described by Millar (1994). See Hindle et al. (2003).

[12] One special situation is that of outsourcing within conglomerates and financial groups. See Lee and Kim (1997).

[13] These "exceptional" requirements were relatively common during the first years of computer processing, but they have gradually disappeared with the improvement of the cost/benefit rate of equipments; for this reason, the market offer has concentrated in specialized business niches, such as the management of disasters, commercial mailing, computer-assisted design (CAD), supercomputing, or telematic services in technologic parks.

[14] The cost of renting is inversely proportional to the duration of the contract: A factor that should be considered is the cost of software licenses, which can be practically impossible to bear if the needs for information management are exceptional; depending on the contractual conditions, outsourcing can offer unbeatable economic advantages.

[15] One of the most common current practices is the physical and logical maintenance of personal computers and their peripheral components (*peer to peer*), an expensive but little compromising practice in terms of competitiveness; some other emerging trends are the management of disasters and the provision of network services, such as the development and maintenance of Web sites.

[16] In some cases, the facilities are kept under the company's control or, at least, they are purchased in accordance to the organization's directions.

[17] General issues on IS/IT outsourcing have been extensively described. See for example Grover et al. (1994), Mylott (1995), Graham and Meuse (1997), Looff (1997), Antonucci et. al. (1998), Grover (1998), or Lacity and Willcocks (2001).

[18] See Grover et. al. (1998).

[19] See Lee (2001) and Willcocks et. al. (2003).

[20] Dibbern *et al.* (2002) summarize the arguments for outsourcing projects in seven theoretical trends: 1) transaction cost theory, the dominant reference theory; 2) resource-based theory; 3) agency theory; 4) power theory; 5) resource-dependence theory; 6) institutional theory; and 7) innovation diffusion theory. The dominant argument is that, even when transaction costs are generated, the external provision of a service can be more efficient than the internal service and can contribute to improve the company's financial structure. The links between transaction costs and outsourcing have been extensively studied (see Aubert et al., 1996; Ngwenyama and Bryson, 1999).

[21] The method is similar to that used in the SESAME technique for evaluating IS technical projects (Lincoln, 1988; Lincoln & Shorrock, 1990).

[22] According to the Outsourcing Institute (1998), the reasons for outsourcing are, firstly, the desire to reduce and control operative costs; secondly, the focus on the

business core, the access to professional skills and competences, and the liberation of financial resources; finally, the third group of reasons is related to corporative re-structuring: accelerating BPR benefits, disengaging from a complex, difficult to manage function, or sharing risks.

23 The argument lies on the relationship between cost efficiency and competitiveness, which is a common principle in the literature on strategy: the company must produce goods or supply services at the lowest possible cost because, in this way, it favours the businesses' economic performance and it creates a solid financial basis to increase competitiveness and ensure survival in the long term.

24 Lacity and Willcocks (1998, p. 369) found that 80% of the companies that had outsourced all or part of their functions had done so in the hope of attaining costs economies. Ang and Straub (1998) found that cost saving is one of the main reasons for outsourcing in the U.S.A. banking, in spite of the fact that transaction costs are generated.

25 Friedberg and Yarberry (1991) point out that internal data processing centres often present inefficiencies that represent between 10% and 30% of their costs.

26 Williamson (1990) defines specificity as the extent to which the market cannot create a replica of the asset with the ability to generate value added.

27 See Harris et al. (1998).

28 A key factor for outsourcing success is the external vendor's reliability (Lee & Kim, 1999).

29 The theories of Ronald Coase (1937) are very relevant for outsourcing; he might be termed a prophet of what is happening with business management in the early 21$^{st}$ century.

30 This argument is supported by the conclusions of the General Accounting Office about outsourcing in the banking sector (GAO, 1992).

31 Some previous works have rendered a basic, but incomplete, vision of outsourcing in Spain. See Claver (1999), Claver et al. (2000), Sacristan (1996, 1998).

32 Some activities, such as health, are missing in our work because they are dominantly developed by *public* institutions in Spain; even though, health care organizations (and workers' safety implications) have been analyzed in detail in outsourcing literature (see, for example, Chen & Lin, 1998; Chin, 1997; Helppie, 1998; Mayhew & Quinlan, 1999; Yates, 1997).

33 Barcelona represents 19.8% of the sample.

34 Except public government, although we have surveyed some private companies whose capital is mostly public.

35 The companies have been classified according to the following criteria: the group "micro-enterprises" is composed of businesses with less than 10 employees; "small enterprises", those with 10-50 workers; "medium-sized enterprises", those with 50-250 workers; and "big enterprises", more than 250 employees. Turnover and funds have been used to assign certain companies to a specific group when the number of workers did not allow for direct classification.

36 The concept of SME has been criticized because it often encompasses micro-enterprises; for this reason, we have deliberately distinguished micro-enterprises from SMEs.

37 80% of firms with 10 or more employees have access to the Internet, however, only half of them is present in the Internet with at least a Web page (Source: *Instituto Nacional de Estadística de España*; www.ine.es).

38 See Slaughter and Ang (1996).

39 Notice that the interest here does not lie on the degree to which software is standardized, but on whether or not software development is outsourced.

40 Nevertheless, it is true that SMEs tend to use standard software for a number of reasons: limited financial resources, lack of internal professionals, limited processing volume, etc.

41 More specifically, it is 40% higher.

42 These improvements have been rated in a 20%.

43 According to OECD, 75% of the Spanish workers are worried about the future of their companies; 30% of the workers of outperforming and profitable Spanish companies feel uncertainties about the stability of their jobs (OECD, 2001, p. 26).These percentages are quite different in the U.S.A. (57% and 42%).

44 India has emerged as a relevant software manufacturer because of the high mathematical skills of graduated professionals but, also, because remote activities can be effectively controlled and coordinated by means of ICT. According to IMF data, the exports of "business services" grew a 43% in India during the second half of the '90s; 20% or the Fortune 500 companies outsource software development activities to India.

45 AOL Time Warner has created a call-center in Mexico to support its Spanish-speaking clients; the company claims this decision has yielded savings of 25-40%..

46 Some of the companies included in our sample are IT providers. Very few of them are currently offering offshoring services outside the European Union (in the U.S.A. and Latin America) because, as it has been said, they are local subsidiaries of international providers.

47 Source: Forrester Research (www.forrester.com).

48 A detailed statistic report of these attacks can be found in the Computer Crime and Security Survey of the FBI and the Computer Security Institute (www.gocsi.gov).

49 See Willcocks et. al. (1995), for a comparison of Europe and U.S.A. companies, in terms of outsourcing strategies.

50 Thus, outsourcing contracts include guarantees and rights previous and subsequent to possible bankruptcy; they limit subcontracting without previous notice, and the client can keep control of hardware, software and data in the event of bankruptcy.

## Chapter XVIII

# Emerging Legal Challenges in Offshore Outsourcing of IT-Enabled Services

Arjun K. Pai, Queen's University Belfast, Northern Ireland

Subhajit Basu, Queen's University Belfast, Northern Ireland

## Abstract

*This chapter provides insightful information on the key drivers of offshore outsourcing and highlights the emerging legal challenges for the IT-enabled service industry. This chapter has attempted to collate and exemplify the distinct qualifying processes in the offshore outsourcing landscape exploring and accentuating their legal and management implications where appropriate. Issues relating to risk assessment, selection of service providers, service level agreements, data protection and privacy, intellectual property rights, termination of contract and post-contract governance strategies have been discussed in detail. The primary intention of this chapter is to provide a broader exposure to the compliance management principles and regulatory frameworks which might provide outsourcing firms with vantage points to assess and adopt effective risk mitigation strategies when structuring multi-jurisdictional outsourcing deals.*

# Introduction

Outsourcing is defined by Griffiths (2001) as "the strategic use of external resources to perform activities traditionally handled by internal staff and resources". In its widest sense outsourcing is a strategy by which an organisation contracts out, usually on a long-term basis, non-core business functions to specialized and efficient service providers, which allows the organisation to refocus their scarce finance and technology resources on creative and value-added services. In the 21st century this phenomenon has created a wide range of scenarios that has particularly characterized the growth and evolution of the IT-enabled service industry.

The META Group Inc. predicts that 80% of organisations will outsource at least one information technology function by 2005 (IT facts, 2004). But, the Outsourcing Pricing Guide report warns that 70% of that group will drive a harder bargain when they renew those outsourcing deals, cutting both the scope and duration of the contract. The META Group (IT facts, 2004) also predicts that the offshore outsourcing market will continue to grow nearly 20% annually through 2008, despite the less-than-favourable light in which it is held in some political quarters, and by 2009, the average enterprise will outsource 60% of application work offshore. META Group also found that application development and maintenance constitutes approximately 30% of the average annual budget for any typical IT organisation and sending work offshore reduces that expense by 30%-60% (IT facts, 2004).

It has been reported in *Financial Times* that the British insurance company, Prudential, had planned to save $26.2m through the creation of 1,000 customer-service jobs in India (*Financial Times*, 2004). The pharmaceutical giant GlaxoSmithKline had decided to outsource a significant portion of their global IT operations offshore with expected budget savings of around 35% a year (Vnuet, 2002). General Electric saved about $350m per year through the 18,000 offshore employees in India (*Business Standard*, 2003). Studies suggest that the U.S. banking industry alone saved as much as $8 billion in the last four years due to outsourcing and estimates on future gains (until 2009) for the overall U.S. industry to be $390 billion, with $138 billion in annual cost savings for the world's top 100 financial institutions (*Business Standard*, 2003). British Telecom, Prudential, British Airways, Citibank, Accenture, HSBC, Standard Chartered and P&O Nedllyod's outsourcing contracts has helped push UK's foreign investments to £5 billion. The current outsourcing revenue estimated at $11.36 billion per year could push upwards to an estimated $27.06 billion by 2006 (*Hindustan Times*, 2003).

So why do some firms spend a greater portion of their IT budget on IT outsourcing? Is this a long-term trend or a short-term obsession? From an organisational context, outsourcing is fuelled largely by cost cutting imperatives coupled with improved budgetary control, refreshing technology and a wish to concentrate on the core functions of the company. Moreover, offshore outsourcing has evolved into an increasingly strategic solution for solving long-term business problems and freeing resources to refocus on core activities.

## Global Outsourcing Market

Offshore business process outsourcing (BPO) has become synonymous with globalisation and corporate strategy wherein companies are realising the strategic role it can play in maintaining global competitiveness and market dominance. The BPO segment of North America represented 57% of the total BPO market worldwide in 2003 — with market figures of $69 billion (Gartner Research, 2004). Further, Gartner analysts say that after several years of double-digit growth, delays in contract signings and lower negotiated rates for large BPO deals have led to moderate growth in 2003 and 2004 (Xicom, 2004b). The western European BPO market has grown by 10.9% in 2003, to $27 billion, according to Gartner Research Inc. (Xicom, 2004b). In Europe, outsourcing of financial services are widely used, however, other industries are growing in respect for different types of BPO. Customer interaction for demand-management BPO is proving popular in the utilities and telecommunications sectors. Supply-management BPO is gaining popularity in local governments, and enterprise services are growing in telecommunications for human resources, finance and accounting. The Asia Pacific BPO market has grown by 7.8% in 2003, to US$8.7 billion, and it is predicated to achieve double-digit growth in the next few years (Xicom, 2004b). META Group found that nearly all Asia Pacific IT organisations will outsource at least one mission-critical technology operation by 2005. McKinsey's research found that Australia and New Zealand are the most mature economies in terms of acceptance of BPO services, followed by Singapore. In most other countries there is almost no history of outsourcing other than product support, education and training and some application development. The Indian market is largely export oriented with exports of IT services and BPO services far outstripping the domestic market size, which is still largely immature. BPO markets in China, Taiwan and Malaysia have a large contract-manufacturing base, but outsourcing of other business processes has yet to take off in a big way in these countries.

The Tower Group estimates that the top 15 global financial institutions will increase IT spending on vendor-direct offshore outsourcing by 34% annually — representing an increase from $1.6 billion in 2004 to $3.89 billion in 2008 (CRM Today, April 2004). Offshore business process outsourcing services - which, unlike application development, typically require the transfer of personal data — grew 38% in FY'03 to just under $2 billion (Gartner Research, March 2004). Global spending on major outsourcing projects — in which a customer hires an outside company to design, implement and run a computer network or other IT endeavour — rose 44% from 2002 to $119 billion in 2003 (Datamonitor PLC, January 2004). Software transfers and technology outsourcing of high-importance business functions, has always been a problem from the point of functional outsourcing. The reasoning being that, virtually no company has distinctly defined the scale for degree of outsourcing of operations in software licensing, which apparently is one of largest source of revenue for companies. Table 1 gives the financial projections of the world-wide outsourcing market for IT-enabled services.

*Table 1. Worldwide IT-enabled services (ITES) BPO market*

| Worldwide ITES BPO spending by region 2002-2006 | | | |
|---|---|---|---|
| Region | 2002 | 2006 | 2002-2006 CAGR (%) |
| Americas | $484,732 | $647,427 | 7.5 |
| EMEA | $171,303 | $237,390 | 8.5 |
| Asia Pacific | $117,622 | $194,228 | 13.0 |
| Worldwide | $773,657 | $1,079,054 | 8.6 |

# Adopting Offshore Outsourcing: An Insight into the Key Drivers

The global market for outsourcing has continued to grow, largely fuelled by the rise in offshore BPO deals. The persistent fears of an economic depression have, as it seems, little effect in general on the outsourcing agenda, partly because outsourcing serves a valid purpose during a recessionary period, when the central focus shifts from core strategic acquisitions of specialist services to more obvious emphasis on sharing strategies that ensure tangible and sustainable results.

## Strategic Imperatives: Competitive Advantage

The evolving dynamics in IT outsourcing has seen the paradigm shift in terms of the type of business functions that are being outsourced. Although, the quest for cost optimisation and quality of service inspired initial forays into offshore outsourcing; companies are now using offshore delivery to achieve significant improvements in their operating efficiency and business performance — transforming outsourcing from a tactical and technical point solution to a long-term business strategy for creating and defending competitive advantage (Robinson & Kalakota, 2004). Organisations are reassessing their strategic outlook about what constitutes the core and non-core aspects of their business and capitalising on strong synergies in governance values and emerging compliance management solutions.

A recent survey found that two thirds of large corporations are now engaged in outsourcing to some extent (*Hindustan Times*, 2003). The total value of major IT services outsourcing contracts throughout the world in 2003/2004 was $119 billion, up 44% on the previous year (Anderson & Strathern Solicitors, June 2004). Intel® and Apple® two of the world's leading manufacturer's of computer, networking and communications products have resorted to 'turnkey contract manufacturing' with their entire manufacturing process being outsourced to overseas manufacturers. This has given these chip manufacturing technology giants the leverage to allocate their assets on future marketing campaigns and branding strategies.

## Economic Imperatives: Consolidated Growth

So what are the drivers of outsourcing that are creating real value? The growth in the use of offshore services has illustrated that its benefits are no longer just about price — they can include service quality improvements, scalability, better risk management and the freeing up of internal resources to focus on core value-adding activities (Pai & Basu, 2005b).

- **Financial restrain and budget planning:** As business pressures continue to evolve, enterprises are confronting a common dilemma; control the expansion of IT budgets, while taking full advantage of the advancements in technology. Often, the search for more efficient ways to run the business ends up increasing the reliance on underlying complex systems and processes. At the same time, every business faces continuous improvement pressures. Technology is increasing the number and quality of the choices available to your customers and competitors. Continuous technology investment is essential and its associated costs must be closely managed.
- **Turn fixed costs into variable costs:** Key commercial drivers for companies involved in outsourcing are employee related costs and their associated overhead. These costs are relatively fixed, regardless of product or service demand. This can be very costly during sluggish sales periods or in times of economic upheaval. Outsourcing turns these fixed costs into variable costs, as the BPO providers have greater economies of scale and thus can price for variable demand.
- **Reduced investments in assets:** Cash infusion into internal resources management and acceleration of product reengineering can benefit from outsourcing. Making strategic investment in the state-of-the-art technology and training, employee skills development, and transformational programs. Outsourcing effectively transfers ongoing investments in infrastructural development to the provider.
- **Building stakeholder's value:** Increased competition within organisations for operational capital funds has driven the rise in outsourcing contracts. Deciding where to invest these funds is onc of the most important decisions that the senior management makes. It is often hard to justify non-core capital investments when areas more directly related to producing a product or providing a service compete for the same money. Outsourcing can reduce the need to invest capital funds in non-core business functions. Instead of acquiring the resources through capital expenditures, they are contracted for on an "as used" operational expense basis. Outsourcing can significantly improve financial prudence of the firm by eliminating the need to show return on equity from capital investments in non-core areas.

## Sustainability and Divergence: Business Continuity and Resilience

A major constraint in effective policy formulation for government and industry is the lack of understanding of how regulatory regimes and business strategy can reconcile competing private and public interests. There is limited knowledge of how to arbitrate competing private interests in sustainable development programs, especially when the market competition objectives involve individual businesses. The evolving policy debate suggests that interest groups may not have a clear understanding of what their interests actually are, let alone how best to serve them. In addition, management through decentralised access to information has resulted in differences and conflicts in domestic and international trade, requiring dispute settlement in various cases. As a result, by adopting sustainable business practices, companies can refocus their effort in business contingency planning and can gain a competitive edge, increase their market share and boost shareholders value. Offshore service providers have refined their approach to customer relationship management, commercial management and service delivery to become highly professional organisations delivering a full range of consulting services, software applications development, IT infrastructure management, help desks and business processing outsourcing.

# Offshoring Marketplace: India and Beyond

India has emerged as "the world's back-office" (Raysman & Brown, 2003), with its wage arbitrage, highly educated and English speaking labour force. It has been estimated that the outsourcing market in India for IT-enabled services (ITES) will reach $16.94 billion by 2008 (Reuters, 2002). The Indian domestic market has seen the revival with 17% growth in 2003 after sliding down to the lowest growth rate of 6% in 2002 for the last 15 years. This growth has been attributed to a strong global economic recovery and the spurt in the BPO industry for IT-enabled services from the U.S. and Europe.

Maturity of the marketplace, precedent, rapid developments in telecommunications and infrastructure, new offshoring destinations and so forth have catalysed the growth of the ITES-BPO industry world over. India has offered a strong value proposition among all other developing countries in recent years. IT-enabled service hubs have spurted in India for the following reasons:

- **Highly skilled labour:** It's true that only a few of the Asian developing economies have fluent English speaking call centre representative to cater for U.S. and European customers, but these countries have many other skills in abundance compared to the U.S. and the European countries.

- **Wage differentials:** India has invested heavily in technical education and can provide a ready supply of highly qualified people at relatively low cost. India produces close to 200,000 qualified IT graduate engineers every year compared to the 90,000 from U.S. engineering schools. Many of these engineering graduates in India are employed with call centres for troubleshooting and providing technical support at salaries that are dramatically lower compared to the pay scales in the U.S. The average monthly salary in India is $400-700 compared to $2,700-2,800 in the U.S. (Xicom, 2004a).

In the outsourcing field, China is the biggest challenge in the future and the largest threat to India as it is expected to become the fourth largest economy in the world overtaking UK. With the largest population and fastest economic growth, China has at least two strengths in the global outsourcing marketplace: manufacturing and IT. The main advantages of China is its lower manpower costs which is about 15% less than an equally qualified Indian together with relatively low real estate and power costs in comparison to India. This business preposition can be very attractive to companies from developed companies mainly U.S. and Europe. But the main disadvantages of China for IT-outsourcing services where India supersedes is:

- **Lack of a good IT-service quality record in software:** India has an excellent image in terms as a quality supplier mostly due to its track record of better quality software than China.
- **Low English speaking population:** This is the biggest drawback of China with only a very small proportion of the population capable of speaking fluent English.
- **Less mature BPO market:** The Indian business processes are much more mature with highly skilled operations base. China has only recently entered into BPO service industry.

The Philippines has also emerged as promising destination with the manpower costs 60%-80% lower as compared to UK and U.S. But the country has a significant shortage of skilled manpower mainly due to the small population as compared to India and China. Philippines currently is getting business from nearly 70 overseas companies employing more than 12,000 people, with revenue earning of US$250 million (Xicom, 2004a). The main advantage of Philippines is its large scale technical training programs that the government has initiated through policies by which the skills can be provided to a larger population and an improved telecom and office infrastructure. But the main disadvantages of Philippines where India takes over are:

- **Not having a record of high quality:** India has consistently delivered very high quality services in the IT and software arena and has built a very high worldwide reputation.

- **Political instability:** Philippines has had frequent elections which make it difficult for companies to outsource as there is lack of uniformity of policies with changes in the government.
- **Lack of disaster recovery facilities or multi-location facilities:** After the WTC bombing terrorism has become a very important issue for the companies in particular and they want that the BPO providers should have multi-location facilities which can be used in case of any terrorist attack.
- **Small scale BPO activities project stunted growth:** The largest call centre in Philippines is that of AOL which employs around 800 people. The size of the Philippines BPO industry was only $150 million, whereas India's BPO industry was at $1.8 billion (Xicom, 2004a).

Ireland and Israel have been the front runners in the BPO industry and started much earlier than India. Thus these countries have built good brand equity particularly in U.S. Both Ireland and Israel have a very conducive regulatory framework and are known for excellent quality standards. Both countries strategically pursued outsourcing services and have been investing heavily in telecom infrastructure, education, health-services and entrepreneurial skills development which are unparallel in the world. Ireland and Israel are actually one of the biggest exporters of software services in the world today. But both Ireland and Israel suffer from a very big disadvantage of lack of a large human resource pool and companies here are forced to outsource work to countries like India,

*Table 2. SWOT analysis of India as an IT-outsourcing destination*

| **Strengths** | **Weakness (Challenges)** |
|---|---|
| • Solid history in software development<br>• English proficiency<br>• Government support<br>• Cost advantage<br>• Strong tertiary education<br>• Process quality focus<br>• Skilled workforce<br>• Expertise in new technologies<br>• Entrepreneurship<br>• Reasonable technical innovations<br>• Reverse brain drain | • Positioning & brand management<br>• Infrastructure<br>• Cultural differences<br>• Sales & marketing<br>• Leverage expertise for higher-value education<br>• Business process experience<br>• Distance from U.S.<br>• Fear/Uncertainty from neighbours<br>• Legal system<br>• Poor globalization skills |
| **Opportunities** | **Threats** |
| • Creation of global brands<br>• BPO & call centre offerings<br>• Expansion of existing relationships<br>• Chinese domestic & export market<br>• Leverage relationships in west to access APAC/middle east markets<br>• Indian domestic market growth | • Internal competition for resources<br>• Over-promise / under-deliver<br>• Regional geopolitical uncertainty<br>• Rising labour costs<br>• Competition from other countries<br>• Government blocking reform/deals<br>• Corruption/piracy/trust |

Taiwan and China. Moreover, Ireland and Israel have been competitively very poorly placed compared with India and China in terms of manpower costs.

Another advantage that most Indian IT sourcing companies have an edge over the rest of the countries is that they operate at Carnegie Mellon Software Engineering Institute Capability Maturity Model (SEI-CMM) level five (Hagel, 2004) — the highest degree of quality expertise of the IT-service, whereas most internal IT departments in the U.S. operate at level two or level three. For instance, in 2004 at least 20 Indian companies were assessed at CMM level five, whereas, China does not yet have a single company above CMM level three (Hagel, 2004). Table 2 gives the SWOT (Strengths, Weakness, Opportunities and Threats) analysis of India as an IT-outsourcing destination (Xicom, 2004a).

## Emerging Legal Challenges: Evolving Priorities and Concerns

It is sometimes easy to get carried away to assume that outsourcing is the panacea to cure all business adversities. Conversely, an outsourcing arrangement can be in dire straits if careful attention is not paid to due diligence strategies, legislative and regulatory procedures. Naturally, any organisation considering offshore outsourcing of IT-enabled services as an option will need to consider the legal implications of the distinct processes and will have to be aware of the judicial system of the outsourced country if the process fails to work satisfactorily. Key issues inherent to outsourcing arrangements are loss of control and multi-faceted differences between the customer and its service providers. Particularly, risks are infinitely higher when the outsourced work is being undertaken in a different time zone or in a different jurisdiction — especially if the outsourcing partner has in possession the software and data of the outsourcing company. As a result, the importance of legal issues is further elevated as, at every phase of an outsourcing agreement, compliance issues and contractual obligations can affect the success of the enterprise customer and its relationship with its service providers. Further, as enterprises continue to adopt varying operating models for outsourcing agreements, they must be in a position to evaluate and weigh the strategic and tactical objectives and priorities primarily involving four key factors, which includes: cost savings, service quality/ delivery, level of control/governance and risk tolerance. Some common legal issues which require special attention are outlined:

- Choosing a governing law for the cross-border contract, and establishing which regulatory laws apply in case of infringement or breach of contract.
- Resolving software licences and usage permission of proprietary support tools.
- Considering data protection and security delegations.
- Establishing the effect of any mandatory local laws which may prejudice the relationship or impact on later litigation.

- Making sure that all IP rights and trade secrets are protected so that they are not violated in the foreign country.
- Covering for the insolvency, winding-up and change of control of the supplier.

In addition to the legal issues mentioned above, there are some purely practical issues like language barriers, geopolitical instability, loss of management control; and accountability problems, which also need to be considered during the decision making process. Hence, as a matter of commercial practicality, clauses in a contract with an overseas company are completely worthless unless there is a mechanism for enforcing the contract in a way which actually works quickly and effectively. In jurisdictions where no reciprocal legal arrangements exist, or where it is unrealistic to expect genuine cooperation from the foreign legal system, the only sensible approach would be to build-in practical measures in the contract itself as discussed later in this section, which do not necessarily require the intervention of the legal process.

In this section, as an example of offshored vendor services marketplace we have focussed our discussion on the Indian IT outsourcing industry in some of our case studies. Further, we have attempted to provide a comprehensive checklist of legal issues along with insightful guidance on coping with emerging challenges in doing business beyond the borders of Europe and U.S., although broader expertise in these areas is desirable in planning and executing international outsourcing transactions.

## Business Risks in Offshoring: Assessment and Evaluation

Offshoring brings with it the risk of losing access to business knowledge and intellectual capital. The senior management of an organisation has the responsibility for understanding the risks associated with outsourcing arrangements for information technology services and ensuring that effective risk management and risk mitigation practices are in place. As part of this responsibility, the management should assess how the outsourcing arrangement will support the institution's objectives and strategic plans and how the service provider's relationship will be managed. Without an effective risk assessment phase, outsourcing technology services may be inconsistent with the organisation's strategic plans, sometimes making it too costly for the company, due to unforeseen future risks.

Outsourcing of information, transaction processing and settlement activities involves risks that are similar to the risks that arise when these functions are performed internally. Risks include threat to security, availability and integrity of system and resources, confidentiality of information, and regulatory compliance (Ramer, 2004). In addition, the nature of the service provided, such as bill payment, fund transfer, or emerging electronic services, may result in entities performing transactions on behalf of the institution, such as collection or disbursement of funds that can increase the levels of credit, liquidity, transaction, and reputation risks. Organisations should consider additional risk management controls when services involve the use of the Internet. The broad geographic reach, ease of access, and anonymity of the Internet require close attention to maintaining secure systems, through intrusion detection and customer authentication, verification, and authorisation. Institutions should also understand that the potential risks introduced are a function of a system's structure, design and controls and not necessarily the volume of activity. An outsourcing risk assessment and mitigation exercise should be able to:

- Assess the strategic goals, objectives, and business needs of the organisation.
- Identify the importance and criticality of the services required by the organisation.
- Adopt due diligence strategies in selection of service providers.
- Define scope of service agreements, with a detailed description of the services and the level to which these services are to be provided.
- Provide operations control, performance reviews and reporting quality of the processes.
- Define clearly the service provider's contractual and compliance obligations.
- Incorporate contingency plans, including availability of alternative service providers, costs and resources required to switch service providers.
- Seek ongoing risk assessments in an outsourcing arrangement to evaluate consistency of performance with the strategic objectives of the organisation.
- Build regulatory requirements and guidance on quality standards for the business lines affected.

In addition to the above mentioned risks the other major concerns to firms involved in the outsourcing race is evaluation of the geopolitical scenario and the risks assessment exercises. Problems such as unstable governments, anti-west sentiments, currency devaluation and political unrest could dramatically affect the ability to outsource key business operations that rely on long-standing government support and policies for the development of their IT infrastructure and industry.

## Selection of Service Provider: Due Diligence Strategies

Once the organisation has completed the risk assessment, the management should evaluate the potential service providers to determine their ability, both operationally and financially, to meet the institution's needs. It would be very beneficial to review the service provider's due diligence process for any of its significant supporting agents (i.e., subcontractors, support vendors, and other parties). A survey of outsourcing companies showed that, 74% felt that IP protection, security; business continuity & disaster recovery process was critical while considering an IT offshore vendor (Kulkarni, 2004). Hence, the management should convey the organisation's needs, objectives, and necessary controls to the potential service provider (Tompkins, 2003). Depending on the services being outsourced and the level of in-house expertise, institutions should consider whether to hire or consult with qualified independent sources. These sources include consultants, user groups, and trade associations that are familiar with products and services offered by third parties. Ultimately, the depth of due diligence will vary depending on the scope and importance of the outsourced services as well as the risk to the institution from these services. Hence it becomes significantly more important for any organisation to seek legal advice before committing to obligations in the contract that could alter the risk profile of the deal. Due diligence strategies for short listing the potential IT-service provider will usually include:

- Conducting a through audit of the service provider's financial position, experience and ability to provide the necessary services and supporting technology for the institution's current and anticipated needs.
- Contacting references and user groups to learn about the service provider's reputation and performance.
- Identifying areas where the organisation would have to supplement the service provider's expertise to fully manage risk in case of failure to meet standards in the contract.
- Evaluating the service provider's knowledge to adhere and comply with standards, policies and procedures relating to internal controls and facilities management.
- Assessing the service provider's security precautions, including, when appropriate, firewalls, encryption, and customer identity authentication, to protect the institution's resources.
- Determining the service provider's ability to detect and respond to intrusions and service disruptions.
- Evaluating the service provider's use of sub-contractors, third party proprietary tools and software licences that would be used to support the outsourced operations.

## Structuring Offshore Agreements: Contractual Provisions

Contrary to popular belief that outsourcing is in the nature of partnership and strategic alliances (Huff, 1991), Lacity and Hirschheim (1993) have exposed this as an "outsourcing myth". Outsourcing vendors do not share the same profit motives as their outsourcing customers. A tight contract is the only mechanism to ensure that expectations of the outsourcing customer are met. Outsourcing services researched by Lacity and Hirschheim (1993) argued that the contract is the key issue to a successful outsourcing relationship. Research on offshore outsourcing contractual issues tends to be mostly theoretical and very limited in scope. For example, Whang (1992) analysed software development contracts using a game theory model incorporating information and incentive issues but conceded that the model, though mathematically neat, would have very limited practical applicability. Richmond and Seidman (1991) also analysed software development contracts but used a transaction cost modelling framework instead. There is relatively little literature available on the systematic and practical treatment of issues relating to outsourcing contracts particularly in relation to IT. Lacity and Hirschheim (1993) seminal work represents a major step in that direction, offering important lessons learnt in contract negotiation.

Software development outsourcing organisations have also emphasised the need to have a robust escrow agreement in place in the contract. An escrow agreement provides for licensee access to the source code and other deposited material in certain limited circumstances such as insolvency of the supplier or where the supplier materially breaches its obligations in relation to maintenance and support. Clearly, a poorly drafted escrow agreement can create more problems than it avoids, particularly where release events and scope of rights of the user upon release are drafted in vague terms. Deposit materials generally include a number of copies of source code, manuals and maintenance tools, names and contact details of key technical personnel and compilation instructions. Certain escrow agents provide a sophisticated service which includes, authentication and verification of source code and its flexibility in relation to the type of escrow agreement to be used, for example facilitating multiple licensees.

Outsourcing contracts fall into many different types, depending on the level of internalisation of human resources and technical resources chosen. Loh and Venkatraman (1991) have identified many alternative types of which three are particularly popular. These types of contracts relate to complete outsourcing, facility management outsourcing, and systems integration outsourcing respectively. Complete outsourcing involves the transfer of the entire IT function of a company, together with existing assets (such as equipment and software) and personnel, from the outsourcing company to the outsourcing vendor. This represents one extreme of the outsourcing spectrum where the whole function of a company is treated as a marketable commodity. Contracts for this type of outsourcing are usually voluminous and complicated, involving a whole range of assets and related legal issues, and are usually long term (i.e., 5 to 10 years) in nature. The outsourcing vendor in this case assumes all the risks and responsibilities of providing the outsourcing customer with its function on a long term basis. The degree of internalisation of human and technical resources is very low for outsourcing of this type.

Facility management involves the outsourcing vendor providing the human resources necessary to operate and manage the outsourcing customer's equipment and software. Facility management outsourcing was particularly popular in the late 1980s when there was an acute shortage of competent IT staff necessary to manage and operate data centres. For facility management outsourcing, the internalisation of technical resources is high while there is a low internalisation of human resources. Systems integration outsourcing usually involves the contracting of a single outsourcing vendor whose role is to manage the installation and operation of the outsourcing company's multi-vendor heterogeneous IT systems in such a way that these systems are integrated and can link with IT systems in other organisations. As the trend in adopting open systems standards (OSS) is gathering momentum and interconnectivity among different organisational IT systems is turning into a key issue, this type of outsourcing is becoming increasingly popular. The level of internalisation of human and technical resources is medium for this type of outsourcing.

Other types of outsourcing include maintenance contracts, installation/procurement contracts, rental contracts, applications development contracts, and time-sharing contracts. However, more recently, contracts for education and training, telecommunication and networking management, and support for end-user computing are also becoming popular as companies move towards down-sizing and distributed computing. Common to most types of outsourcing contracts is the passing of one or more IT management and/or operational responsibilities from an in-house IT department to an outsourcing vendor bound by a contract. Outsourcing contracts involve complicated business and legal issues and are fraught with risks for both the outsourcing customer and the outsourcing vendor. As pointed out by Lacity and Hirschheim (1993), outsourcing vendors and outsourcing customers are not partners because their profit motives are not shared. An outsourcing customer cannot expect the outsourcing vendor to act in the best interests of the customer in situations where a conflict of interest arises. The written outsourcing contract is therefore the most important instrument for defining the rights, liabilities and expectations of both parties which guides the behaviours of both parties concerned. Thus, it is important for management to have some understanding of the complicated business and legal issues involved in IT outsourcing and have some awareness of how these issues should be addressed in the contracts concerned. An outsourcing contract often includes a collection of related agreements covering a variety of issues including service level agreements, intellectual property rights, privacy liability and dispute resolution mechanism (Pai & Basu, 2005a).

## Scope of Services Levels and Agreements

Once the process of selecting the service provider and negotiating the terms of transfer of the function to that supplier have been completed, the long term relationships is then governed by the service delivery or service level agreements (SLA). The SLA defines the boundaries of the project in terms of the functions and services that the service provider will give to its client, the volume of work that will be accepted and delivered, and acceptance criteria for responsiveness and the quality of deliverables (Hayes, 2004). This agreement is likely to be in place for as long period and it has two main functions:

- To set out clearly the parties obligation to each other.
- To allow the parties to evolve service provision over time and to end the relationship rationally.

Hence a well-defined and well-crafted SLA correctly sets expectations for both sides of the relationship and provides targets for accurately measuring performance to those objectives. Allied to the SLA a few of the outsourcing customers have introduced in their contractual schedule key performance indicators (KPI) to cover them for financial loss when service level thresholds are not met. Under this system, a failure to achieve a service level would trigger a service level credit. Service credits are refunds of portions of the service provider's charges paid by the service provider to the retailer upon the service provider's failure to achieve a service level (Klein & Wolsk, 2004). They are designed to incent the service provider to perform, and not to fully compensate the retailer for its losses. Service levels are generally ineffective unless the service provider is required to pay a service credit upon its failure to meet a service levels. However, service credits are a first line remedy available to customers in circumstances of a supplier's failure to achieve KPIs or the agreed service level. Generally, service credits are calculated by reference to a reduction in service fees, to reflect non-delivery of services, rather than a method of customer compensation for loss or damage suffered as a result of non-delivery of services. Clearly, without service credits, the retailer has no effective mechanism to manage the service provider. Use of service levels and service-level credit structures developed to improve vendor performance and client satisfaction in outsourcing transactions can help keep the parties interests aligned and incent the service provider to provide high quality and timely services. Also when setting up a SLA to control and manage the factors described above, there are many possible metrics from a service level credit system arrangement standpoint. The simplest way to approach these metrics is to group them into categories, decide which ones in a given category works best for the particular project, and then construct the desired metrics. The key factors can be managed through four major categories of SLA metrics:

- **Maturity, Capability and Volume:** Maturity of the service provider coupled with capability metrics along the lines of volume of work delivered are typically the key sizing determinants of an outsourcing project, specifying the exact level of effort to be provided by the service provider within the scope of the project. Any effort expended outside of this scope will usually be separately calculated, or will require renegotiation of the terms of the SLA. Broadly defined as the number of units of a work product or the number of deliverables produced per unit of time and volume of work metrics should be specified for every major deliverable cited in the SLA. Projects that are billed on a time and materials basis may discuss volume in terms of number of resources, while a fixed price project will generally specify volume of deliverables.
- **Standards and Quality Scorecard:** Measuring the quality indicators are perhaps the most diverse of all of the SLA metrics. Enhancing information and process quality covers a wide range of work products, deliverables and requirements and seek to measure the conformance of those elements to certain specifications or standards. When deliverables fail to meet the acceptance criteria in the specifications or standards, quality problems arise (Hayes, 2004). Briefly, these metrics include:
    - *Standards compliance practice*: Internal standards for application source code, documentation, reports and other tangible deliverables, including number of enhancement tasks passing standard reviews, number of documented programs, and so forth.
    - *Sustained enhancement of technical quality*: Measurements of the operational excellence is dictated by the technical quality of application solution, which normally is developed by commercial tools that look at items such as program size, degree of structure, degree of complexity and coding defects.

- *Service availability*: The time frame for which the services have been delivered by the outsourced contractor, ranging from online application availability to delivery of reports by a specified time-of-day.
- *Service satisfaction*: Describes the client's level of satisfaction with the perceived level of service provided by the outsourcer, and captured for each major function through internal and/or external surveys. Ideally, these surveys are conducted periodically by a neutral third party. Although subjective, they are a good double-check on the validity of the other SLA metrics.

- **Delivery & Responsiveness:** Delivery metrics measure the response time that an outsourcer takes to handle a client request. They are usually the most important ones from the client's perspective, and figure heavily in its perception of the quality of service provided by the outsourcer. Responsiveness to requests often motivates business areas to seek outsourcing in the first place. Some of metrics usually included in SLAs are:

    - *Time-to-implement & market*: This SLA metric measure the elapsed time from the original receipt of a request until the time when it is completely resolved. Sample metrics include time to consummate an enhancement, time to resolve production and maintenance obstacles, and so forth.
    - *Time-to-acknowledge*: The metric measure how responsive the outsourcer is by focusing on when a request is acknowledged, and accessibility of status information. Sample metrics include time to acknowledge support calls in contact centres and programmer response time to production line crunches.

- **Efficiency:** Efficiency metrics measure the engagement's effectiveness at providing services at a feasible charge. The cost metrics, while important, miss the relationship between volume of work and effectiveness of its delivery. Examples of efficiency metrics include:

    - *Cost/effort efficiency*: This efficiency indicator is typically tied to an index that is based upon cost per unit effort, and is used to register cost reductions in regard to increase in productivity. Sample metrics include number of programs supported per person, cost per support call, and so forth.
    - *Resource utilization*: The resource utilization metric empirically tracks the service load affecting each staff member in relation to the wise utilization of the in-house resources. Engagements that incorporate a charge primarily on a time and materials basis should also include metrics on staff utilization to measure the effectiveness of staff deployment in order to encourage the outsourcer to make staff reductions as efficiency is gained. Sample metrics include percentage of time spent on support, training and percentage utilization, and so forth.

- *Overhaul & rework levels*: Although rework metrics and overhaul are also quality measures, they can be applied on a percentage basis to measure the effectiveness of implementing quality improvements. These metrics track the percentage of work products that returned to a previous step for additional work, correction or completion. They track wasted effort and help to measure the quality of a process and its efficiency.

## Data Protection and Security

Outsourcing of critical information services can pose new challenges to business organisations in regard to data privacy risks and the complexity of managing these risks. European Union businesses that increasingly ship their business functions — credit card processing services, financial audits and sensitive medical data transcription have come under a legal obligation to have an agreement in place to deal with the third party's compliance to the 1995 European Union (EU) directive relating to data protection (ECCD, 1995). Along the same lines of EU's data protection directive the UK's Data Protection Act of 1998 (DPA, 1998), contains a number of restrictions on the transfer of sensitive personal information by a data processor in the UK to a country or territory outside of the European Economic Area (EEA). It provides that such a transfer to third-party countries may not take place unless there are adequate norms governing the data privacy and practice in those particular territories. Moreover, there are a number of exceptions to this general prohibition on the transmission of data outside the EEA. As a result, European companies and manufacturers need to ensure that overseas vendors are contractually tied to specific conditions regarding how data is transmitted, accessed, used, stored and shared. Those challenges include compliance monitoring, enforcement of data protection laws, audits and access regulations.

The U.S. historically favoured self-regulation for privacy protection, and until recently, there were not many privacy laws to support and protect an outsourcing transaction. However, due to increasing pressure from consumer protection groups, legislations that address privacy issues and data protection have been effectively incorporated. In 1999, the U.S. Congress enacted the Gramm-Leach-Bliley Act, which governs personal financial information; the Health Insurance Portability and Accountability Act (HIPAA), which covers health and medical information; and the Children's Online Privacy Protection Act (COPPA), which governs information collected online from children under the age of 13 (Raysman & Brown, 2003).

As mentioned earlier, we have focussed our study here on the data protection and privacy legislation in India, to better understand the complexities of its legal reign. Currently, the Indian legal regime does not have specific legislation for privacy and data protection, although, the Indian government has been considering the idea of enacting a detailed law on data protection soon. It was in 1998 that the National Task Force (NTF) on IT and Software Development had submitted an "IT Action Plan" to the prime minister of India calling for the creation of a "National Policy on Information Security, Privacy and Data Protection Act for handling of computerized data". The IT task force examined the UK's Data Protection Act as a model and recommended several cyber laws including ones on privacy and encryption (NFT, 1998). The lack of Internet penetration in India means the pressure for implementation of such a law is definitely coming from the demands of outsourcing rather than from any concern for privacy. The Constitution of India does not expressly recognise the right to privacy (COI, 1949). However, the Supreme Court of India first recognised in 1964 that there is a right of privacy implicit in the Indian Constitution under Article 21 of the Constitution, which states, "No person shall be deprived of his life or personal liberty except according to procedure established by law" (Jain, 1997). However, Indian courts have interpreted the right to privacy as an unarticulated fundamental right against an action by the state. Though the Information Technology Act, 2000 addresses the issue of protecting privacy rights, it only protects privacy rights from government action. It is unclear whether such protection would be extended to private actions. The lack of adequate privacy protection in India may act as a disincentive for companies in the EU and U.S. to outsource business processes to Indian companies. However, India is expected shortly to enact legislation addressing the issues of privacy and data protection.

It is necessary for an Indian company to be aware of the legislation in its customer's country, as it could have an impact on the service provider. It may be difficult for Indian companies to keep abreast of the latest legislation in foreign jurisdictions that would have an impact on the services that the Indian company provides to a foreign company. Hence, an obligation may be imposed on the customer to update the service provider on the foreign laws and the amendments to which the service provider must adhere. If the service provider does not comply with these laws, an indemnity obligation may be imposed on them. As our business environment becomes increasingly global, and the value of personal data increases, issues of data transfer, and particularly cross-border transfer, will need to be considered seriously by organisations. Certainly, companies should take various steps to ensure that they minimize the risks of unauthorized access to sensitive personal information. Understanding the impact of privacy laws on one's business is the first step. Businesses should appoint a privacy team that will lead them through the assessment, planning, communication, and eventual compliance steps. For example, an appropriate team might include representatives from the following areas: HR, legal, marketing, communications, technology, finance, and corporate strategy. Corporations such as IBM, Microsoft, and AT&T have appointed "Chief Privacy Officers" and privacy teams to lead the effort in helping those businesses meet privacy compliance requirements.

## Intellectual Property: Sharing and Safeguarding Proprietary Information

Protection of the customer's intellectual property (IP) and trade secrets is another significant concern in negotiating outsourcing transactions. In any outsourcing agreement, there could be several IP issues involved, such as the licensing or assignment of copyrights, trademarks, and patents, and so forth. The issues concerning IP would largely depend on whether the IP is licensed by the service provider or the customer, or developed by the service provider. IP laws and enforcement vary considerably around the world, and one of the primary concerns of outsourcing clients is that they retain ownership of their IP and gain appropriate ownership of the deliverables of an outsourcing arrangement (Fernandez, Kemeny, & Bastani, 2003). For example, when an outside vendor is hired to perform information processing services, the vendor will often require access to the customer's IP or IP that the customer has licensed from third parties in order to perform services under the agreement. With respect to customer-owned intellectual property, such as software, the customer will typically grant a limited license to the vendor to use the intellectual property for the term of the outsourcing agreement or until conversion to an agreed upon vendor system. The agreement should provide that the vendor may only use the customer's intellectual property on the customer's behalf. Additionally, the agreement should contain adequate confidentiality provisions.

The major differences in the intellectual property rights of a vendor's country can significantly affect the expectations of an outsourcing relationship. Certain IP protections, such as software and business method patents, may be harder to obtain in the UK than the U.S., while other protections such as copyright for factual databases, may be easier to obtain in the UK. Such disparate treatments of IP in other countries may well affect the value propositions of rights generated through outsourcing arrangements and the extent to which parties may strive to contractually obtain such rights. An issue worth exploring from an outsourcing standpoint is whether the IP laws of the vendor's country can be overridden by the contractual agreement. The local outsourcing council on commerce and industry is in the best position to explore the intricacies of foreign IP laws that may impact an outsourcing transaction.

Patent and trademark legalities have always been expensive and time consuming issues of an outsourcing transaction. Tight contracts and measures might prevent an undesirable situation in which disagreement arises over ownership of valuable patents and IPs. Legal systems in outsourced countries may be very different, thus creating additional time and costs to protect you and fight any legal disputes that may arise. Third-party intellectual property may raise more complicated issues (Evans & Smith, 2002). The customer should first examine the licensing agreements under which it has licensed the intellectual property, in order to ascertain whether there are any restrictions on use, limitations on transfers or assignments, or confidentiality provisions. The customer should also make the outsourcing vendor aware of the terms of such third-party license agreements, when contracting to vendors the use of their IP. If the customer opts to license the IP to the outsourcing vendor, and if this includes any fees associated with assigning the license of such IP to the vendor, the outsourcing agreement should specify which party must pay the fees. The customer should also be aware of the vendor's IP. For example, if the vendor uses its own software to perform data processing services, the customer should be aware of its rights over the software, in the event that the agreement is terminated. The customer should also ask the vendor to place the use of vendor source code and commercial tools in the escrow, in order to maintain its right to use the software, in the event of the vendor's bankruptcy (Raysman & Brown, 1998).

Under the doctrine of "nationality" or "territoriality" U.S. copyright, patent and trademark laws do not directly apply beyond U.S. borders (Rosenberg, 2001). Defining intellectual property rights and protecting them, is largely within the control of the jurisdiction in which the rights are asserted and infringement occurs. Thus, subject to international agreements, the IP rights of a U.S. or UK national in a foreign country are determined by the law of that country detailed in the (Paris Convention, Art. 3). This situation presents at least two important sets of IP concerns in the present context. First, the outsourcing customer must examine the legal environment of the country in which outsourced tasks will be performed to determine how the country's law defines and protects intellectual property rights that are important to the customer. Second, and less obviously, the customer must consider how foreign law may affect the customer's IP ownership even within the home country. This follows from the territoriality of IP law that, if a software outsourcing customer's pre-existing materials or newly developed software are copied, decompiled or otherwise used abroad in a manner contrary to the customer's interest, the customer's only or principle remedy may be to try to enforce, in the country in which infringement occurs, such rights as the customer has under the law of that country (Philips, 2002).

Enforcement issues relating to IP rights in India are well publicised. According to preliminary estimates from the business software alliance, trade losses to U.S. software companies from software piracy in India in 2003 were approximately $229.5 million (IIPA, 2004). The International Intellectual Property Alliance (IIPA) reports that "corporate end user piracy (unauthorised use of business software in a business setting) is endemic in major Indian companies" (IIPA, 2002). Despite the reported high levels of wilful copyright infringement in business settings, since enactment of India's copyright law, "there have been no criminal convictions for software piracy" (IIPA, 2002, p. 126). One possible explanation, according to IIPA, is that copyright cases in India "can take up to 12 years to complete" (IIPA, 2002, p. 127). Civil cases are also reportedly "long" and "drawn out" because of an "under-resourced and bureaucratic judicial system" (IIPA, 2002, p. 136). There are also substantive law concerns. India along side the UK and U.S. is a member of the Berne Convention. IIPA has stated that amendments to India's Copyright Act implemented in 1995 "resulted in one in of the most modern copyright laws in any country" (IIPA, 2002, pp.138). Computer programs are expressly protected by copyright in India (IIPA, 2002, pp.138). Under amendments that took effect in 2000, however, India created new "fair dealing" or fair use rights for software. Specially, newly added section 52(1) (ab)-52(1) (ad) of India's Copyright Act provide that copyright in computer program is not infringed by:

- The doing of any act necessary to obtain information essential for operating interoperability of an independently created computer programme with other programmes by a lawful possessor of a computer programme, provided that such information is not otherwise readily available.
- The observation, study or test of functioning of the computer programme in order to determine the ideas and principles which underlie any elements of the programme while performing such acts necessary for which the computer programme was supplied.
- The making of copies or adoption of computer programme from a personally legally obtained copy for non-commercial personal use.

However section 52(1) (ab)-(ad) have not yet been subjected to definitive judicial scrutiny. The only case which directly deals with the issue is a 2004 judgment of the Delhi High Court in *Microsoft Corporation v. Debasish Seal*, which, although decided two decades after the amendment of the Copyright Act to include computer software, surprisingly dilates on whether or not software in magnetic or electronic form is a literary work. Microsoft had moved the court for an injunction restraining the defendant from reproducing and selling Microsoft Office 2000 Professional and Microsoft Office XP for approximately US$7. Microsoft had registered copyrights with respect to Microsoft Office 2000 Professional in India. The defendant failed to provide any evidence disputing Microsoft's claim that he sold pirated copies of the software to an investigator hired by it. The Delhi High Court began its analysis by raising the question of whether copyright protection could be extended to cover computer programs which generally exist merely in magnetic or electronic form although, when a computer program is converted and transferred to a piece of paper, it would definitely enjoy the protection of copyright like any other literary work. Notably, the court failed to cite the relevant sections of the Copyright Act. It if had, it would have noticed that there is no statutory restriction which limits copyright protection to a computer program only if it is written on paper. Fortunately, the Court nevertheless concluded that computer software is protected by copyright as a literary work whether it is written on paper or appears in magnetic or electronic form. Observing that the defendant had also infringed the registered Microsoft trademark of the plaintiff which appears on the computer screen when the pirated software is used, the Court granted a permanent injunction against the defendant. The Microsoft case involved both registered copyrights and trademarks. However, it is important to note that registration of intellectual property rights in India can take up to six years due to bureaucratic delays. Therefore, in order to prevail in an infringement action, it is important to apply for copyright and trademark registrations well before transferring any sensitive code to any persons in India.

## Limitations and Exclusion of Liability

As with all commercial contracts, service providers would seek to clarify the scope of their legal obligations and liability for incidental and consequential damage resulting from their service to their clients business within the terms of the contract. This may include the use of detailed contractual provisions, together with detailed exclusion warranty provisions. These warranties may contain clauses and invariably include exclusion of statutory and common law implied terms, as legally permissible, hence limiting the amount of liability that can be incurred by the service provider. The Supply of Goods and Services Act 1982 (SOGA, 1982) requires that the supplier of a service to carry it out with reasonable care and skill and, unless agreed to the contrary, within a reasonable time and make no more than a reasonable charge. Exclusion of certain forms of statutory implied terms and conditions in relation to the sale of goods and supply of services is permitted, some being permitted on an absolute basis and some on the basis of a "fair and reasonable test". However, normally a breach of an implied term under SOGA/1982 Act would entitle the injured party to terminate the contract, whereas breach of an implied term, which is stated to be a warranty, will generally enable the injured party to claim for damages only. But, the distinctions between the implied terms and warranties are not entirely clear cut. In the *Salvage Association versus CAP Financial Services case* (Taylor, 2004) the English court considered consequential loss exclusion in the context of a contract for computer software in 1988. The Salvage Association had engaged CAP to create and implement a software accounting system. But the finished system was riddled with over 600 errors and had to be scrapped in 1989 after repeated attempts to modify it failed to produce a usable version. The judge found that as a matter of fact the CAP was not able to perform the contract because it lacked access to relevant skills and experience and consequently, the system that CAP has produced was not fit for intended purpose. The central legal point in this case concerned the application of the Unfair Contracts Term Act 1977 (UCTA, 1977), but it also provided a guide to the classification of losses under an exclusion clause differentiating between direct and indirect losses, which reads as follows:

*CAP Financial Services will not be liable for any indirect or consequential losses, damage, injury, cost or expenses of any kind whatsoever including economic loss, such as loss of production, loss of profits or of contracts...* (Taylor, 2004)

The court held that this clause was enforceable, but the clause and the case tumbled due to the English law's narrow definition of indirect and consequential loss. The court held that, because the other kinds of loss referred to were said to be examples of indirect and consequential loss and not separately listed, the clause was ineffective in excluding direct economic loss. The court therefore held that these losses were and direct and recoverable (in addition to the principal claim of wasted expenditure); (a) payments to a third party bureau facility (b) wasted computer stationary (c) payments to consultants (d) payments for testing.

Almost invariably the exclusion and limitations of liability provisions will be one of the final provisions to be agreed during contract negotiations of an offshoring deal. The provisions and warranties are of great importance to both parties in events of serious difficulties arising under the contract. Limitation and exclusion of liability provisions in IT-outsourcing contracts tend to be structured involving the following components:

- Distinction between liability for direct loss or damage, loss or damage to tangible property and other forms of direct loss or damage. This distinction reflects, first, the availability of large sums of insurance in relation to loss and, secondly, the high value of loss or damage to tangible property.
- Separate limitations of liability figures may be agreed, or uncapped liability agreed, in relation to certain specific forms of loss or damage, which could include fraud, breach of confidentiality obligations, breach of IPR obligations and breach of statutory obligations.
- The contractual limitations of liability provisions may also include indemnity protection by one party to another in relation to certain heads of loss or damage, which from the customer's perspective, might include IPR infringement, breach of

confidentiality obligations, data loss or damage, virus infection, and breach of statutory obligations.

- The contractual limitation of liability provision may be stated to apply on a per event or in aggregate basis. Alternatively, they may be calculated on a per year or other recurring basis. From the customer's perspective per event liability levels may be preferable, while the service provider may seek to limit its liability in aggregate over the contract term, for the purpose of quantifying contractual risks.
- The relationship between the service credit regime in relation to supplier delay in implementation of contractual services and failures to achieve the contractual service levels/ KPIs, and the contractual limitations of liability provisions should be clarified.
- The contract should deal with exclusion of indirect consequential loss or damage, which is generally agreed to both parties and applicable to both parties. What can be contentious is the reference to specific leads of loss or damage, such as loss of profits, and whether these are excluded on an *ab initio* basis, or if rather they are indirect or consequential.

It is very important to tie together all contractual limitations and exclusion of liability provisions in order to avoid uncertainty or ambiguity within the contract.

## Exit Strategy and Termination of Contract

The ability to terminate and method of termination is a key element in any offshoring negotiation. The vendor will want to terminate for clause relatively quickly if payment is not being made on time. In any substantial outsourcing arrangement, cash flow is of key concern to the vendor so that the vendor can meet its payroll, equipment and administrative expenses. Usually, the client does not have any difficulty with this concept. The more seriously negotiated termination provision is termination for convenience. The client will want to have the ability to terminate the outsourcing arrangement without having to go through a lengthy process of declaring and proving a vendor to be in default. Additionally, a client will want to have a termination for convenience clause in the event of an acquisition after which another system is implemented. Sometimes, there is a reverse termination of sorts in the case where an acquiring company prefers the processing systems of the acquired company. Under those circumstances, the acquiring company may want to terminate for convenience so that it can move its processing to the acquired company's more favourable systems. The three main scenarios that the parties engaged in an outsourcing relationship can find themselves in:

- The contract is approaching its end and the user wants to re-tender to decide whether to renew the contract or change suppliers.
- The contract is being terminated at its end with a possibility of change of suppliers, to the transfer of service operations back in-house.

- The contract is being terminated for breach, with a consequent change of suppliers, to the transfer of services back in-house.

Let us consider the first condition of change in service provider or supplier. Assume that neither party is in breach nor even if the customer is satisfied with the services, it is likely that the customer will want to go through a re-tendering process even if the aim is only to renegotiate the existing contract. If the customer allows an existing contract to roll on, it is likely to benefit from the competitive edge offered by other potential service providers, in terms of quality and range of services. Even though it is quite obvious that vendors will not want a termination in the initial phase of the contract for convenience right (Raysman & Brown, 1998); it is during those years that the vendor is being reimbursed for the initial substantial outlays in equipment, real estate and other costs in the start-up phase of the arrangement. Thus the termination for convenience right might not be effective until after the first or second year of an agreement.

In the second condition of change of supplier can have two scenarios — the contract is being terminated for breach or one party has exercised a right to terminate at the end of the agreed term. The latter is relatively straightforward; it is termination for other reason which requires further consideration. The issue of termination of contract for breach could have a number of reasons, which includes that outsourcer must assess and comprehend the legislative, judicial, law enforcement and administrative capacity of the outsourced contractor's country. It requires that the outsourcer have a legal right to call off the contract for non-performance and identifiable breaches in the contractual agreement. Outsourcing transactions should also consider the other infrastructure strategies, such as mergers and acquisitions, divestitures, spin-offs, split-offs, strategic alliances and other special situations.

## Comprehensive Due Diligence Strategies for Reducing Outsourcing Risks

It is absolutely critical that appropriate policies and procedures on privacy, data processing and service level agreements be developed by any organisation handling identifiable and non-identifiable individual-level data, which provides the most zealous protection for legitimate public interests. The debate does not rest with developing policies and procedures, and benchmarking them against risk metrics; the entire organisation needs to understand them and be trained to enforce and implement them (Tompkins, 2003). The keys to success in global sourcing would depend on the best practices and due diligence strategies employed (Pai & Basu, 2005b) by organisation's to reap the benefits from their outsourcing effort:

- **Strategic planning and assessment:** A structured approach for identifying and evaluating the potential candidates for offshore outsourcing, and prioritising their relative benefits would reinforce the mainstream decision making process of enterprises. Outlining a long-term view for offshoring initiatives will avoid long learning curves and minimize redundant efforts in development and deployment of high-quality IT services. Focusing mainly on the labour wage differentials and cost arbitrage sourcing strategies might have an impact on the functional areas of the business in particular performance monitoring and efficiency in resource utilization.

- **Due diligence to operating models and selection of service providers:** The level of due diligence required, and the types of issues to address during supplier selection are substantially different. It's important to review the service provider's core business competencies, credibility, dependability and sustainability which are essential in maximizing returns from an offshoring initiative. Always ask your service provider hard questions and assess the risk associated with your operations. For example, does the service provider have a disaster recovery plan? What are the network security policies? Can the provider sustain a development operation? How will service levels and quality be assessed? And so forth.
- **Risk mitigation:** The outsourcing strategy for risk mitigation prescribes that it is important not to leave too much to change in offshore deals. The long-term success of the initiative is directly related to the level of planning for risk, and the commensurate governance structure set in place. Having a well-considered risk management document that measures the probability of each type of risk and the impact on the enterprise will be critical in determining the ultimately success of the offshore initiative. The risk management framework will also define which risks need to be managed, which can be transferred, and which can be simply ignored.
- **Post-contract governance:** Streamline a strong governance structure, seeded with location expertise for quality of service assessment and risk mitigation. Having a well-defined strategic post-contract monitoring model is imperative in developing a "proactive" monitoring and management process. Push hard on continuous improvement initiatives and give your organisation the leverage to renegotiate price reductions or quality enhancements as the market changes over the term of the agreement.
- **Knowledge acquisition:** The bargain to realise cost savings and meet the value proposition often posses the danger of being information rich but knowledge poor putting your business continuity at risk. Vendor selection based on geographic cost arbitrage for example could be one of the several elements of a knowledge process outsourcing's (KPO) value proposition. Another element would entail; despite the contract, the service provider could fail to manage your critical risks in a crisis. So what do we need here is a crisis and contingency management plan to face undesirable outcome. Changes to your business continuity plans and invocation procedures need to be communicated properly if operational integrity is to be upheld for a stable and secure partnership with your service provider.
- **Compliance risks:** Effective SLAs are extremely important to assure effective outsourcing engagements. The metrics used to measure and manage performance to SLA commitments are the heart of a successful agreement and are a critical long-

term success factor. Lack of experience in the use and implementation of performance metrics causes problems for many organisations as they attempt to formulate their SLA strategies and set the metrics needed to support those strategies.

- **Conflict & litigation resolution:** Conflict resolution and contract negotiation is the process through which two or more parties arrive at mutually acceptable terms and conditions of exchange for items they own or control. Conflict arises between two parties when there is a deadlock between them over the aforesaid terms and conditions. Negotiation acts as an effective tool towards conflict resolution. A good management practice will be to have short-term focus on quality assessment. This can lead to increasing the number of contract renegotiations aimed at achieving cost reductions. Additionally, increasing competition between service providers is expected to intensify and may lead to a lowering of contract prices. The three primary market pressures faced by service providers are the need to acquire new revenue, the need to retain or grow market share against competitors, and the need to avoid "buying into" deals that are only focused on cost reduction (Tramacere, 2004).
- **Contract termination & exit strategy:** The outsourcing firm must assess and comprehend the judicial, law enforcement and administrative capacity of the service provider's country. Be prepared for renegotiations of IT infrastructure deals by planning for changes in the service delivery methodology as technology matures and new business needs emerge. Ensure that you have a legal right to call off the contract for non-performance and identifiable breaches in the contractual agreement. Speculate alternatives to outsourcing transaction and other infrastructural strategies, such as mergers and acquisitions, divestitures, spin-offs, split-offs, bankruptcy reorganisation, strategic alliances, joint ventures, with a possibility to take the operations back in-house.

## Conclusions

In a global economy based on specialised skilled services, navigating and surviving the rough waters of offshore outsourcing has become synonymous to corporate strategy of many global business enterprises. Virtually everyone outsources some function in order to be able to devote scarce resources to their own unique core skills and products (Bierce & Kenerson, 2005). If properly conceived and implemented, offshore outsourcing can fuel revenue growth, enhance service quality, operational effectiveness, and enable organisations to better manage their intangible assets and redefine their market.

To adapt a truism, from a business outsourcing context; it becomes imperative that if one cannot evaluate and assess the vital role that enforcement policies and compliance management processes play, one should not be outsourcing. In other words, using outsourcing as a panacea to all organisational adversities will only compound the existing problem. In essence, it is extremely important that the enterprise business outsourcing houses falling under the EU and U.S. embargo statues restructure their regulative practices in order to enable a smooth transition towards a sustainable business establishment. Additionally, outsourcing would deliver greater control, efficiency and cost reductions which allow organisations to refocus their scarce finance and technology resources on creative and value-added services such as business strategy and execution, new opportunity identification, business interpretation and continuity planning. It is also required that adequate measures should be introduced in order to safeguard interest and proprietary information of the customer's business through protection of their IP. Clearly, such a strategic and structured approach requires substantially more emphasis on due diligence to selection of service providers, contractual enforceability and compliance monitoring, but in return should pay great rewards in a long haul. Finally, the way forward would be to move from precarious and unwarranted region specific legislations and enforcement to a blend of multi-jurisdictional legal framework coupled with stringent informational security and procedural recommendations that are mutually acceptable to the outsourcing customer, service providers, local government and consumers.

# References

Bierce, B., & Kenerson, P. C. (2005). Insights on effective outsourcing. Available at Outsourcing Law Global, LLC, at http://www.outsourcing-law.com/economics.htm

Business Standard. (2003, April 16). U.S. firms saved $8 bn via local outsourcing. *Business Standard*.

COI. (1949). Constitution of India, November 1949. Retrieved December 23, 2004, from http://www.alfa.nic.in/const/a1.html

Cravotta, N. (2004, September 2). Offshore outsourcing: Now boarding – A trip to China may just be the ticket to take your design to reality. *Electrical Design News*.

DPA. (1998). Data Protection Act 1998, Chapter 29, London. Available at http://www.hmso.gov.uk/acts/acts1998/

ECCD. (1995, October 24). European Communities Commission Directive 95/46 EC of the European Parliament.

Evans, P. C., & Smith, R. B. (2002, March). Intellectual property rights in collaborations. *BioPartnering*.

Fernandez, D., Kemeny, D., & Bastani, B. (2003). Intellectual property strategies in security and privacy. Fernandez & Associates, LLP.

Griths, D. (2001). The theory and practice of outsourcing. In the *Proceedings of the Society for Technical Communications*. Available at http://www.beethovan.org/Outsource/Outsourcing.pdf

Hagel, J. (2004). Offshoring goes on the offensive. *The McKinsey Quarterly*, (2), 23.

Hayes, I. S. (2004). Metrics for IT outsourcing service level agreements. Report by Clarity Consulting.

Huff, S. L. (1991, Spring). Outsourcing of information services. *Business Quarterly*, 62-65.

India fears impact of bid to curb jobs exports. (2004, June 4). *Financial Times*.

International Intellectual Property Alliance (IIPA). (2002). India in 2002 Special 301 report on global copyright protection and enforcement 128 (app. C). Available at http://www.iipa.com

International Intellectual Property Alliance (IIPA) USTR. (2004). Special 301 on intellectual property IIPA's 2003 estimated trade losses due to copyright piracy (in millions of U.S. dollars) and piracy levels in-country. Available at http://www.iipa.com/pressreleases/2004_May3_Sp_301_plus_chart-rev.pdf at pp.8

IT facts Web page. (2004). Retrieved January 3, 2005, from http://www.itfacts.biz/index.php?id=P1371

Jain., R. C. (1997, July). Kharak Singh versus State of UP, 1 SCR 332, 1964. National Human Rights Commission, India, Indian Supreme Court on Right to Privacy.

Klein, A., & Wolsk, J. (2004). Outsourcing service levels in POS maintenance transactions. Available at http://www.executivetechnology.com/ViewSOFull.cfm?SOID=133

Kulkarni, J. (2004). Best practices in IP protection when off-shoring. Available at http://www.noa.co.uk/features.http://www.noa.co.uk/features/featuresKeyToneoppc.html

Lacity, M., & Hirschheim, R. (1993). The information systems outsourcing bandwagon. *Sloan Management Review, 35*(1), 73-86.

Loh, L., & Venkatraman, N. (1991). *Outsourcing as a mechanism of information technology governance: A test of alternative diffusion models.* Working paper no. BPS3271-91, Massachusetts Institute of Technology, Alfred P. Sloan School of Management, Cambridge, MA.

NTF. (1998, June 9). National Task Force on IT & SD. Basic background report available at http://it-taskforce.nic.in/it-taskforce/bg.htm

Pai, A., & Basu, S. (2005a, April). *Offshore outsourcing – Weighing the risks of data protection and security*. 20th Annual British and Irish, Legal Education and Technology Conference, BILETA Belfast, Northern Ireland.

Pai, A., & Basu, S. (2005b). Offshore technology outsourcing: Overview of management and legal issues. *International Journal of Business Process Management* (accepted for publication).

Paris Convention for the Protection of Industrial Property, International Bureau of WIPO. (n.d.). Retrieved from http://www.wipo.int/treaties/en/ip/paris/trtdocs_wo020.html#P19_137

Phillips, D. E. (2002, September). Selected legal issues in international software outsourcing. *The Licensing Journal*, 13-19.

Ramer, R. (2004). The security challenges of offshore development. The SANS (SysAdmin, Audit, Network, Security) Institute.

Raysman, R., & Brown, P. (1998, April). Key issues in technology outsourcing agreements. *New York Law Journal*. Available at http://www.brownraysman.com

Raysman, R., & Brown, P. (2003, March). Offshore outsourcing means careful legal planning. *New York Law Journal, 229*(46).

Reuters. (2002, January 1). India becoming world's back office.

Richmond, W. B., & Seidman, A. (1991). *Outsourcing and contractual issues in the systems development life*. Working paper. William E. Simon Graduate School of Business Administration, University of Rochester, NY.

Robinson, M., & Kalakota, R. (2004). Offshore outsourcing: Next wave. *E-Business Strategies, Inc.*, 5.

Rosenberg, P. D. (2001). *Patent law fundaments* (2nd edition). West Group.

SOGA. (1982). The Supply of Goods and Services Act 1982. Consumer and Competition Policy, Department of Trade and Industry, UK.

Taylor, A. (2004). *Excluding consequential or indirect losses in software and outsourcing contracts governed by English law*. Retrieved January 17, 2005, from http://www.mayerbrownrowe.com/Outsourcing/publications/article.asp?id=1835&nid=1853&fl.pdf

Tompkins, J. (2003). *Outsourcing: Solution or setback?* Available at http://www.tompkinsinc.com/publications/competitive_edge/articles/04-04-Outsourcing.asp

Tramacere, G. (2004, June). The future of infrastructure outsourcing in western Europe. Gartner Research Inc.

UK's outsourcing revenue to touch $27 bn in 3 years. (2003). *Hindustan Times*. Retrieved December 29, 2003, from http://www.hindustantimes.com/news/6771_504972,004300190004.htm

Unfair Contracts Term Act (UCTA). (1977). Fact sheets on the exclusion clauses in contracts. Available at http://www.dti.gov.uk/ccp/topics1/facts/unfairact1977.htm

Vnuet. (2002). GlaxoSmithKline considers outsourcing deal. Retrieved December 12, 2002, from http://www.vnuet.com

Whang, S. (1992). Contracting for software development. *Management Science, 38*(2), 307-324.

Xicom. (2004a). Business process outsourcing – Advantage India. Retrieved November 5, 2004, from http://www.xicom.biz/research.html

Xicom. (2004b). Business process outsourcing (BPO) market growth. Retrieved November 6, 2004, from http://www.xicom.biz/bpo_market_growth.html

# Chapter XIX

# Does Strategic Outsourcing Undermine the Innovative Capability of Organizations

A. Hoecht, University of Portsmouth, UK

P. Trott, University of Portsmouth, UK

## Abstract

*In this chapter we argue that firms have responded to the intense pressure from markets and financial operators to reduce asset investments by outsourcing activities. Outsourcing was originally confined to peripheral business functions and mainly motivated by a cost saving logic, but has now developed into a routine strategic management move that affects not only peripheral functions but the heart of the competitive core of organisations. At the same time there is a move from traditional outsourcing with one or a small number of key partners and long-term contracts to strategic outsourcing with multiple partners and short-term contracts. This chapter investigates the innovation-related risks that can arise from strategic outsourcing. It uses the example of Information technology/Information Systems (IT/IS) outsourcing to highlight the increased risks that arise from a move from traditional to strategic outsourcing and discusses some measures that managers can take to attempt to control these risks. The nature of the risk is closely related to the risk of information leakage that arises from collaborative research and technology development between organisations in technology-intensive sectors that has been analysed by Hoecht and Trott (1999).*

# Introduction

Firms have responded to the intense pressure from markets and financial operators to reduce asset investments by outsourcing activities. And just like "downsizing" and "delayering", outsourcing has become one of the staple diets in the strategic management field in last decade and it has recently received much public attention for its impact on national employment in the media as outsourcing does not longer stop at national borders (*Financial Times*, 2004). Meanwhile, the academic and professional literature on outsourcing has matured and overcome its original euphoria stage. Some of the risks associated with large-scale outsourcing, in particular where non-peripheral business processes are concerned, are now increasingly discussed in the literature. These risks include the choice of the right supplier or service provider, their ability to deliver the desired "best in world" expertise or service in the long run and the risk of losing one's core competencies to the service provider.

Despite the rather mixed record of large-scale long-term total outsourcing deals with single suppliers in particular in the IT/IS industry (Lacity & Willcocks, 1998), such contracts are still entered into in significant numbers. The academic literature has identified a number of expected gains that companies can derive from outsourcing. They range from the reduction of operational costs (Lacity & Hirschheim, 1993) and the ability to transform fixed costs into variable costs (Alexander & Young, 1996), to the ability to focus on core competencies (Quinn & Hilmer, 1994) while having access to the industry-leading external competencies and expertise (Kakabadse & Kakabadse, 2002). There is, however, also an emerging literature that highlights the weaknesses and risks associated with large-scale outsourcing arrangements, in particular where non-peripheral business functions are concerned. Alexander and Young (1996) highlight the risk of becoming dependent on a supplier, Barthelemy (2001) draws our attention to the hidden costs of outsourcing and authors such as Doig, Ritter, Speckhals, and Woolson (2001) and Quinn and Hilmer (1994) identify the possibility of a loss of vital know-how in particular with respect to core competencies as a major risk factor in outsourcing. There is also the problem of selecting the most suited supplier/service provider and their longer-term ability to offer the capabilities that are needed in particular in business environments with rapid technology change (Earl, 1996). Table 1 offers an overview of the main risks identified in the literature.

We will discuss innovation-related risks in the next section and we will explain how outsourcing can create an innovation dilemma that very much resembles the risk of information leakage in collaborative research and technology development. In this chapter we wish to draw attention to another strategic risk of outsourcing that so far has received limited attention in the literature (see Table 1). This risk is closely related to the

*Table 1. Main risks identified in the literature*

| | Main negative outcomes | Main references |
|---|---|---|
| 1 | Dependence on the supplier | Alexander and Young (1996); Aubert et al. (1998) |
| 2 | Hidden costs | Earl (1996); Alexander and Young (1996); Aubert et al. (1998); Lacity and Hirschheim (1993); Barthelemy (2001) |
| 3 | Loss of competencies | Bettis et al. (1992); Martisons (1993); Quinn and Hilmer (1994); Khosrowpour et al (1995); Alexander and Young (1996); Aubert et al. (1998); Doig et al. (2001) |
| 4 | Service provider's lack of necessary capabilities | Earl (1996); Aubert et al. (1998); Kaplan (2002) |
| 5 | Social risk | Lacity and Hirschheim (1993); Barthelemy and Geyer (2000) |
| 6 | Inefficient management | Wang and Regan (2003); Lynch (2002) |

more general issue of information leakage that arises when business organisations collaborate in order to gain access to knowledge and expertise that they cannot develop on their own. Hoecht and Trott (1999) have demonstrated that there is trade-off between access to cutting-edge knowledge via collaborative research and technology development in knowledge-intensive industries and the risk of losing commercially sensitive knowledge to competitors. This risk, they argue, cannot be controlled by traditional management approaches and legal contracting alone, but requires the operation of social control and in particular the development of trust to be contained. We will then explain why this innovation dilemma is much more prominent in the new world of strategic outsourcing where companies have short-term relationships with multiple partners than in traditional large-scale long-term single provider relationships. A number of potential management solutions for tackling this problem are discussed at the end of this chapter.

## Why Outsourcing May Hinder Innovation: Lessons from the Innovation Management Literature

The management of innovation is a large and diverse body of literature. It recognises that while there is much complexity and uncertainty in managing innovation and new product development much is known. There is considerable agreement on many of the factors that contribute to success and the activities and processes that need to be undertaken if innovation is to occur. Over the past 50 years there have been numerous studies of innovation attempting to understand not only the factors necessary for it to occur, but how they influence the process and when and where they are required and in what order. Table 2 captures some of the key studies that have influenced our understanding.

At the corporate level, a number of research paradigms have attempted to explain the international difference in technological development and innovation. Neo-classical economic theorists believe market structure, competition pressure, local supply of skills together with openness of communication are the most important factors (Stoneman,

*Table 2. Key studies of innovation management*

| | Study | Date | Focus |
|---|---|---|---|
| 1 | Carter & Williams | 1957 | Industry & technical progress |
| 2 | Project Hindsight- TRACES, (Isensen) | 1968 | Historical reviews of U.S. government funded defence industry |
| 3 | Wealth from knowledge (Langrish et al.) | 1972 | Queens Awards for technical innovation |
| 4 | Project Sappho (Rothwell, 1974) | 1974 | Success & failure factors in chemical industry |
| 5 | Minnesota Studies (Van de Ven) | 1989 | 14 case studies of innovations |
| 6 | Rothwell | 1992 | 25 yr review of studies |
| 7 | Sources of innovation (Wheelwright & Clark) | 1992 | Different levels of user involvement |
| 8 | MIT studies (Utterback) | 1994 | 5 major industry-level cases |
| 9 | Project NEWPROD (Cooper) | 1999 | Longitudinal survey of success & failure in new products |
| 10 | Radical innovation (Leifer) | 2000 | Review of mature businesses |

1983; Geroski, 1995; Ansoff, 1965; Porter, 1980, 1985, 1990). However, this approach has not been able to fully explain the dynamics of innovation processes and the role played by firms and other institutions (Patel & Pavitt, 1984; Lundvall, 1988). In terms of firm specific characteristics that are required for firms to become more innovative much has been written about this (Quinn, 1991; Kanter, 1998; Wolfe, 1994). There is also significant amount of literature on the strategic dimension of competition (Porter, 1980; Pavitt, 1984; de Woot, 1990). Many writers on innovation consider it mainly as a process that needs careful management (Souder, 1987; Trott, 2005; Twiss, 1992; Tidd, Bessant, & Pavitt, 2001), while others view innovation more as a cognitive and behavioural phenomenon (Van de Ven, 1989; Madique, 1988). Despite their differences, most of these writers seem to accept that innovation is a phenomenon that can be subjected to human control and is considerably affected by human interaction. We also know that individuals create knowledge[1] through collaborating with others in groups/teams in an organisational context; helping individuals to achieve their full potential and contribute new knowledge is a critical management issue which has also received considerable attention in the literature (Tidd, 2000; Nonaka, 1991; Nonaka & Takeuchi, 1995; Polyani, 1966).

The studies in Table 2 have contributed to the accepted view that a firm's ability to successfully develop innovative new products is not only the result of public and private investments in tangibles and intangibles by individual elements in the economy, but that it is also strongly influenced by the character and intensity of the interactions between the elements of the system. This position is strongly advocated in the literature on "National Innovation Systems" (Freeman, 1982; Lundvall, 1992; Nelson, 1993). In this view, innovation and technological development in particular depend increasingly on the ability to utilise new knowledge produced elsewhere and to combine this with knowledge already available in the economy and its actors. The capacity to absorb new knowledge, to transfer and diffuse knowledge and the ability to learn through interaction are crucial success factors in innovation (e.g., Cohen & Levinthal, 1989; Chesborough, 2003). New and commercially useful knowledge is not only the result of the conscious action of creative individuals. It is also the outcome of the interaction and learning processes among various actors in innovation systems, that is, producers, users, suppliers, public authorities, and scientific institutions, which David and Foray (1995) have coined the "knowledge distribution power" of the innovation system. Indeed, Rothwell (1992) put forward the idea of a fifth-generation model of innovation management, based on inter-company networking facilitated by IT systems. More recently, the term network has become widely used. The need for connectivity and the complexity of the interactions it entails therefore emerges as a major factor influencing the management of innovation.

Given the significance of the beneficial effect of effect of inter-firm collaboration and the role of networks for innovation and organisational learning (Hamel, 1991), it is necessary to explore this concept in more detail. March (1991) distinguishes between exploration and exploitation in organisational learning. He argues that there are major differences between experimentation with new alternatives (exploration) and the refinement of existing technologies and organisational competencies (exploitation). The latter can be conceived as a close relative of the keep in house-or outsource decision, where collaboration arises from an unwillingness to go-alone and a strong preference for risk-limitation will always be prevalent. On the other hand, explorative knowledge creation relies on much more "openness" and a dedicated participation in research communities, firms, universities, research laboratories, suppliers and customers (Powell, 1990). What is required here is a much more intimate form of collaboration where both parties are contributing, rather than the handing over of responsibility of an activity, which is often associated with the outsourcing decision. Furthermore, Powell at al (1996) argue that the locus of explorative innovations is to be found in networks of inter-organisational relationships and that a firm's success crucially depends on its "centrality-position" in such networks and the experience gained in managing its networks. They argue that internal capability and external collaboration rather than being substitutes are complementary:

*Internal capability is indispensable in evaluating research done outside, while external collaboration provides access to news and resources that cannot be generated internally.... A network serves as a locus of innovation because it provides timely access to knowledge and resources that are otherwise unavailable, while also testing internal expertise and learning capabilities.*

In their empirical study of the network behaviour of biotechnology firms operating in the human therapeutics and diagnostics field (1960-94) they found strong support for their hypothesis that a firm's centrality in network relationships and its incrementally acquired experience in managing network ties is a strong predictor for its growth and economic success. Network experience, it appears, should be considered as an incremental learning process both in terms of the management of collaborative ties and in terms of the actual technical learning of biotechnology innovations (Powell, Koput, & Smith-Doerr, 1996). The decision to outsource an activity includes the inherent risk of forgoing a firm's centrality of participation in valuable networks.

The development of network models of innovation has helped to illustrate further the prominence now given to internal and external interactions (networks) within the innovation process. All these knowledge flows contribute to the wealth of knowledge held by the organisation (Woolgar, Vaux, Gomes, Ezingeard, & Grieve, 1998; Rothwell, 1992; Major & Cordey-Hayes, 2003). Recognising this, capturing and utilising it to develop successful new products is the difficult management process of innovation. Here then lies the potential problem for firms if key activities are outsourced: whether at the very least the firm risks disrupting the knowledge flows to the organisation and more worryingly for senior managers is whether it will isolate a firm from valuable networks.

Furthermore, the inability to retain a company's competitive core will not only endanger its future competitiveness, but can also create a serious risk of dependency on outside providers. A crucial question is whether the desired access to "best in industry" capabilities are sufficient to sustain its competitive advantage in particular where the provider serves "many masters" and the particular expertise ceases to be unique and becomes best-practice industry standard. While there is no shortage of advice in the literature on how to manage the risk of dependency from outside providers and suppliers in general (see, for instance, Currie & Willcocks, 1998, who suggest multi vendor approaches and shorter term contracts for handling large-scale long-term total outsourcing contracts with IT/IS providers), the specific problem that access to world-leading expertise via outsourcing may well be compromised by the "levelling-out" of unique advantages when leading service providers spread their world-leading expertise to several clients has not received much attention.

As a consequence of the problem of "levelling out" of leading edge expertise, the innovation impact of outsourcing is not limited to the issue of core competencies and the need of companies to retain at least the absorptive capacity to exploit innovations that have been developed by outside service providers. There is also the problematic assumption that service providers are always able to infuse best practice into the company. In a traditional outsourcing relationship, a long-term commitment is entered into that "locks" a company to a service provider for the length of the service contract. The ability to infuse best industry practice may not only depend on the relative competence of the provider, but the service providers may also be restricted in their ability to pass on best practices by confidentiality agreement with previous and other current clients. A significant dilemma emerges: Individual firms have a reasoned case against competitors gaining the fruits of their investment and innovation efforts, while at the same time the majority of companies choose outsourcing not least in the hope of gaining such advantages from other firms. This dilemma is mainly left to the service providers and the individual consultants they employ to resolve. It is, however, a very important issue from an organisational innovation perspective. We will see below that this issue becomes even more pressing when companies and industries move away from traditional long-term outsourcing relationships with single service providers to strategic outsourcing, that is, to much more open, short-term relationships with multiple suppliers involving all business processes.

## *Knowledge Management and Information Systems*

In looking at ways for sharing knowledge, transforming individual knowledge into collective, organisational knowledge the field of artificial intelligence (AI) can help deliver the knowledge management systems for organisations. The development of knowledge management systems (KMS) demands that knowledge be obtained, shared and regulated by individuals and knowledge-sharing organizational systems, such as knowledge repositories. People-Finder systems, a type of knowledge repository, attempt to manage knowledge by pointing to experts possessing specific knowledge within an organization. Becerra-Fernandez (2000) has shown how such systems have been implemented at several organizations such as Hewlett-Packard, National Security Agency and Microsoft and how artificial intelligence in the development of People-Finder KMS and automating the process of profile maintenance is used. Inevitably any I.T. Knowledge management system designed to facilitate the storage and distribution of codified knowledge is likely to affect the distribution of power within organizations. Gray (2001) argues that the implementation and use of such knowledge repositories have a dramatic effect on power and control within an organisation. The use of knowledge repositories by employees who are net re-users of knowledge-based work products is expected to increase the extent to which these employees are interchangeable while reducing the level of skill they need to carry out their work. For employees who are net contributors to knowledge-based work products, the use of knowledge repositories produces the opposite effect. When managers choose to capitalize on these effects to increase their control, employees in the former group may find their power position eroded over time (Gray, 2001).

# Outsourcing and Risks of Information Leakage

We have argued above that from an innovation perspective, the reliance on outside providers can be problematic, not only because key areas of expertise may be gradually lost to the outsourcing organisation but also because outside providers may not have the desired leading edge expertise over the long-term (Earl, 1996) or may spread their expertise among many clients so that it degrades from "best in world" to mere industry standard. The problem of information leakage lies at the heart of this dilemma. Companies want exclusivity in their relationship with their service providers, but consultants who work with many clients are unlikely to be able not be influenced and not to spread the best practice that they acquire when working with many client firms. Detailed legal contracts may offer short-term solutions as they can protect tangible outcomes from specific projects undertaken, but not every innovation related project outcome is tangible and can be clearly defined in legal contracts. And consultants are clearly expected to work at the cutting edge of their professional expertise for all of their clients.

Hoecht and Trott (1999) have developed a conceptual framework that links organizations' collaborative research and technology development strategies with the risk of knowledge loss and information leakage. In the collaborative research and technology development context, the risk of information leakage is only one of the risks which organisations face in collaborative ventures. This risk has to be balanced against the risk of missing out on the potential benefits from (relatively) free information exchange both inside and outside the organisation. There is a fundamental trade-off in that companies need to be open to free information exchange in order to benefit from collaboration with other organisations but pay a certain prize in that this openness automatically increases the risk of commercially sensitive knowledge being either accidentally or purposefully leaked to potential competitors.

Hoecht and Trott (1999) found that firms have a constrained choice between a number of strategies: They may be able to rely on internal development with their own manpower (we define this as an *introspective strategy*), they may opt for a complementary *acquisitive* strategy and purchase technology or hire expert staff, they may concentrate on a dyadic *co-operative* strategy (joint venture, co-operative projects) or may choose to risk being involved in research networks (*extrovert strategy*). This conceptual framework has been developed for the analysis of collaborative research and technology development between firms, but it can be used as a starting point for conceptualising outsourcing decisions.

Outsourcing should be considered as an "outward-looking" strategy as the outsourced activities are no longer dealt with within the "information boundary" of the firm. Outsourcing entails a considerable degree of openness and hence carries a high exposure to the risk of information leakage. The inherent risk of information leakage should be considered greater than in cooperative strategies (strategic alliances and joint ventures) as outsourcing firms are increasingly more dependent on their service provider as time progresses and may loose internal expertise.

Table 3 lists organisational strategies on an inward-looking/ outward-looking axis and their respective risks of information leakage (type of risk and source of risk) as well as the principal types of control that organisations have in dealing with this risk.

## Strategic Outsourcing and the Innovation Dilemma

Strategic outsourcing goes beyond traditional outsourcing in the sense that competitive advantages are being sought through opening up all business functions, including the

*Table 3. Information leakage risks*

| Strategic Orientation | Strategy | Level of info leakage risk | Key control means | Degree of control | Main source of risk |
|---|---|---|---|---|---|
| Inward-looking | **Internal "to make"** | low | Bureaucratic control | High | Own employees |
| | **Acquisitive "to buy"** | low | Bureaucratic and legal control | Medium-high | Employees |
| | **Cooperative (Joint ventures)** | medium | Legal control, trust | Medium | Employees and links of partner |
| | **Cooperative (Strategic alliance)** | Medium-high | Legal control, trust | Medium-low | Employees and links of partner |
| Outward-looking | **External "to outsource"** | Principally high (but depends on core competencies and nature of industry) | Social control: reputation concerns, professional ethics and trust | Low | Service provider staff and consultants |

core competencies which should provide competitive advantage to whoever can provide the perceived best solution, internal or external (Quelin & Duhamel, 2003). In contrast to traditional outsourcing, there are no protective boundaries around core activities in the hope that the organisations can maximise their innovative capacity by being an active part of a networked economy. This means that rather than having exclusive arrangements with one or very few service providers of long periods of time which will be expected to offer tailor-made solutions, strategic sourcing arrangements will be with multiple partners over short periods of time and with very little protection of internal core competency functions against outsiders (Gartner Group Strategic Analysis Report, May 2001).

There is a certain paradox inherent in this approach: a very high level of trust is required for such relationships as the risks involved are substantial while at the same time the conditions for building trust are undermined by a shorter-term orientation with less commitment compared to traditional outsourcing relationships. The risks are significantly higher than with traditional outsourcing: Not only is the risk of leakage of commercially sensitive information significantly increased when firm cooperate with multiple partners, but also the very core of the competitive advantage in terms of knowledge, expertise and capabilities will be made dependant on outsiders. There is a danger that the organisations pursuing strategic sourcing may even loose the absorptive capacity required to recognise and exploit new opportunities by themselves.

We have argued above that reliance on outsider providers can be problematic, not only because key area of expertise may be gradually lost to the outsourcing organisation but also because outside providers may not have the desired leading edge expertise over the long term (Earl, 1996) or may spread their expertise among many clients so that it degrades from "best in world" to mere industry standard. The problem of information leakage lies at the heart of this dilemma. Companies want exclusivity in their relationships with their service providers, but consultants who work with many clients are unlikely to be able not to be influenced and not to spread the best practice they acquire when working with different client firms. Detailed legal contracts may offer short-term solutions as they can protect tangible outcomes form specific projects undertaken, but not every innovation related project outcome is tangible and can be clearly defined in legal contracts. And consultants are clearly expected to work at the cutting edge of their professional expertise for all of their clients.

In a networked economy, there is hardly any choice for a firm but to have close relationships with more than one service provider. If an industry develops closer networked links among constituent firms and if every single service provider firm entertains more and shorter-term relationships with competing buyer firms, then "information boundaries" are opened up and long-term relationship commitments are reduced. By entertaining more than one relationship with external service providers itself, the individual buyer firm would still have less certainty than before in its exclusive relationships, but at least it would also have the chance to benefit from the more widely shared industry best practice, spread among its competitors by the service providers. The effect might be a levelling out of core skill advantages within the industry, benefiting the industry overall, but eroding the competitive advantage of some of its members. From the point of view of the individual firm then, the question is how it can maintain a commitment to secrecy and confidentiality from multiple service provider firms while sharing in the benefits of best practice in the industry.

If we believe that social control is a powerful enough instrument to ascertain ethical behaviour of consultants working for multiple clients, that is, that they will refrain from purposeful betrayal, then the problem of information leakage is limited to cases of accidental disclosure. One could argue that this is the prize of "openness" in an increasingly networked economy and recommend companies to employ "good practice" safeguards against accidental disclosure. The question is, however, whether we believe that the social control instruments that we have discussed above (such as self-regulation according to internalised norms of professional behaviour and reputation concerns) are powerful enough to prevent purposeful betrayal acts. One could argue that business consultants, unlike academic researchers who work in a close-knit scientific community, whose work is collaborative by nature and whose social standing crucially depends on mutual trust, are considerably less governed by network-based social control. Scientific networks can, after all, be expected to have much stronger malfeasance detection and sanctioning abilities as scientific research results are constantly peer-reviewed. Business consultants, on the other hand, are working for rival firms and have no established professional bodies (beyond their respective subject discipline affiliation) that are able and willing to effectively self-regulate the "business" behaviour of their members. In a strategic outsourcing context where legal means are of limited effectiveness and conditions for building trust are significantly worse than in traditional outsourcing relationships, companies may wish to retain the ability to control the behaviour of service provider consultants by employing boundary spanning experts of their own. This will not only improve the social control of service provider consultants, but also help to contain the problem of absorptive capability loss we have discussed above. The task of these individuals, who have to be highly regarded experts in their field, would be to act as boundary spanners between scientific research, the service providing consultancy firms and their respective buyer firm. Their job would entail the definition and demarcation of high-risk areas within their home organisations and the selection and supervision of those "externals" that would be granted access to the business functions and processes identified as high risk. As external service providers can easily be made to specify the individuals assigned to specific tasks as part of the tendering process specification and as part of the final contract, the boundary spanner's judgement on the competence as well as trustworthiness of the specified individuals could be used as a device to control the risk of secrecy betrayal. As a consequence, it would be very much in the career interest of the staff of external service providers to keep and earn the trust of the boundary spanners of their main client firms as this would become a key selection criterion for the award of future contracts to their firms. For this system to work, some minimum level of exchange of information among boundary spanners of large buyers would be required. It would be, after all, in the collective interest of buyers to limit the risk of betrayal and therefore to expel unreliable individuals from the circle of consultants with access to high risk areas in their clients' organisations. Whether this collective interest would prevail or the short-term benefits derivable from acts of betrayal would prove to be too tempting is very much a question of the character of the network of boundary spanners in question.

Even if the likelihood of purposeful betrayal by service provider staff can be limited with such a boundary spanner approach, there remains the risk of accidental disclosure and the contribution it can make to the potential loss of sources of competitive advantage to the industry. We do not believe that consultants would normally have a strong desire to betray their clients for short-term personal gain and realise that they may be overburdened with responsibilities beyond their control. After all, it is difficult to maintain client confidentiality and disseminate "best in world" practice at the same time. A key purpose of this chapter is to highlight the innovation-related and competitive risk of outsourcing core business functions and to highlight that these risks are significantly increased when companies move form traditional outsourcing to strategic outsourcing.

# Conclusions

Innovative capability of the firm is largely dependent on cumulative knowledge built up over many years of experience. Contrary to the model used by economists, innovative ability cannot be simply bought and sold. Hence, the need to remind senior managers of the unwitting harm that may be inflicted on the ability of the organisation to survive in the long term if its core competencies are slowly eroded through outsourcing. This chapter has put forward a different conceptual approach for how companies can view the role of outsourcing and its impact on innovative capability. We need to look again at what delivers long-term success as opposed to short-term gains. A different conceptual approach is required. Managers should not be obsessed with cutting costs in a vain effort to compete with developing countries. They should be concentrating on utilising their organisational knowledge bases to develop new products for the future (sometimes referred to as "high added-value products"). Senior managers need to reconsider their strategies to ensure they have activities in place that will facilitate creativity and ultimately realise new products in the future. This of course has to be achieved against a backcloth of fierce pressures to reduce costs and ensure the business remains competitive in the immediate term.

The outsourcing literature has moved on from its early enthusiasm to a more realistic assessment of the benefits, costs and also risks arising form outsourcing. While there is a widespread agreement that peripheral business functions are prime candidates for outsourcing, the literature is much more divided when it comes to outsourcing decisions concerning key business functions that are part of or closely connected to the competitive core of organisations. In this chapter, we draw attention to a particular outsourcing risk that has not yet been adequately addressed in the literature, namely information leakage arising from acts of accidental disclosure or even purposeful betrayal by consultants that work for several client firms at the same time.

Our preliminary findings from ongoing research (see Hoecht & Trott, 2005) reveals a need to counsel caution to general managers: Unless strong social ties and trust in consultants are reliably established, outsourcing should be limited to situations where no unique competence is involved as the risk of industry diffusion via imitation is high and the level of control to protect the competency is limited due to the nature of outsourcing relationship. If the protection of a unique competency is of paramount importance, less outward-looking strategies should be chosen.

We have shown that consultants face a dilemma as they are expected to spread cutting edge level expertise to their respective client firms yet as the same time honour confidentiality commitments. While some may argue that professional ethics, social control (reputation concerns etc.) and legal instruments are sufficient to contain this risk of information leakage, we have highlighted that with a move from traditional outsourcing to strategic outsourcing, this problem becomes much more acute and needs addressing. We have also put forward a suggestion how at least larger, resourceful organisations can address this problem, namely by employing "boundary spanners" that can make qualified judgements both on the trustworthiness and expertise of service provider consultants. The advantage of this approach is also that the employment of "boundary spanners" can mitigate against the risk of losing the absorptive capacity and expertise arising from strategic outsourcing strategies in particular.

## References


Alexander, M., & Young, D. (1996). Outsourcing: Where's the value? *Long Range Planning, 29*(5), 728-730.

Ansoff, H. I. (1965). The firm of the future. *Harvard Business Review*, *43*(5), 162-178.

Aubert, B. A., Patry, M., & Rivard, S. (1998, May). *Assessing the risk of IT outsourcing.* Working paper, 98s-16, Cirano, Montreal.

Barthelemy, J. (2001). The hidden costs of IT outsourcing. *Sloan Management Review, 42*(3), 60-69.

Barthelemy, J., & Geyer, D. (2000). IT outsourcing: Findings from an empirical survey in France and Germany. *European Management Journal, 19*(2), 195-202.

Becerra-Fernandez, I. (2000). Role of artificial intelligence technologies in the implementation of People-Finder knowledge management systems. *Knowledge-Based Systems, 13*(5), 315-320.

Bettis, R., Bradley, S., & Hamel, G. (1992). Outsourcing and industrial decline. *Academy of Management Executive, 6*(1), 7-22.

Carter, C. F., & Williams, B. R. (1957, March). The characteristics of technically progressive firms. *Journal of Industrial Economics*, 87-104.

Chesborough, H. (2003). *Open innovation: The new imperative for creating and profiting from technology.* Boston: Harvard Business School Press.

Cohen, W., & Levinthal, D. (1989). Innovation and learning: The two faces of R&D. *The Economic Journal*, *99*, 569-596.

Cooper, R. (1999). The invisible success factors in product innovation. *Journal of Product Innovation Management*, *16*(2), 115-133.

Currie, W. L., & Willcocks, L. P. (1998). Analysing four types of IT sourcing decisions in the context of scale, client/supplier interdependency and risk mitigation. *Information Systems Journa*l, *8*(2), 119-1434.

David, P. A., & Foray, D. (1995). Accessing and expanding the science and technology knowledge base. *STI-Review, 16*, 13-68.

de Woot, P. (1990). *High technology Europe: Strategic issues for global competition.* Oxford: Basil Blackwell.

Doig, S. J., Ritter, R. C., Speckhals, K., & Woolson, D. (2001). Has outsourcing gone too far? *McKinsey Quarterly, 4*, 24-37.

Earl, M. (1996, Spring). The risks of outsourcing IT. *Sloan Management Review*, 26-32.

*Financial Times*. (2004, November 29). Lex column: Equity research.

Freeman, C. (1982). *The economics of industrial innovation* (2nd edition). London: Frances Pinter.

Gartner Inc. (2001, May). Strategic analysis report.

Geroski, P. (1995). Markets for technology: Knowledge, innovation and appropriability. In P. Stoneman (Ed.), *Handbook of the economics of innovation and technical change*. London: Basil Blackwell.

Gray, P. H. (2001, November). The impact of knowledge repositories on power and control in the workplace. *Information Technology & People, 14*(4), 368-384.

Hamel, G. (1991). Competition for competence and interpartner learning within international strategic alliances. *Strategic Management Journal, 12*, 83-103.

Hoecht, A., & Trott, P. (1999). Trust, risk and control in the management of collaborative technology development. *International Journal of Innovation Management, 3*(1), 257-270.

Hoecht, A., & Trott, P. (2005). Innovation risks of outsourcing. *Technovation*, (forthcoming).

Isenson, R. (1968). *Technology in retrospect and critical events in science (Project Traces)*. Chicago: Illinois Institute of Technology/National Science Foundation.

Kakabadse, A., & Kakabadse, N. (2002). Trends in outsourcing. *European Management Journal, 20*(2), 189-198.

Kanter, R. M. (1998). When a thousand flowers bloom: Structural, collective, and social conditions for innovation in organisation. *Research in Organisational Behaviour, 10*, 169-211.

Kaplan, J. (2002). Partners in outsourcing. *Network World 19*(11), 41.

Katz, R. (1997). *The human side of managing technological innovation*. New York: Oxford University Press.

Khosrowpour, M., Subramanian, G., & Gunterman, J. (1995). Outsourcing organizational benefits and potential problems. In M. Khosrowpour (Ed.), *Managing information technology investments with outsourcing* (pp. 244-268). Hershey, PA: Idea Group.

Lacity, M., & Hirschheim, R. (1993). *Information systems outsourcing: Myths, metaphors and realities.* Chichester: John Wiley.

Lacity, M., & Willcocks, L. (1998). An empirical investigation of information technology sourcing practices: Lessons from experience. *MIS Quarterly, 22*(3), 363-408.

Langrish, J., Gibbons, M., Evans, W. G., & Jevons, F. R. (1972). *Wealth from knowledge.* London: Macmillan.

Leifer R., Colarelli O'Connor, G., Peters, L. S., Rice, M., Veryzer, R. W., McDermott, C. M. (2000). *Radical innovation.* Boston: Harvard Business School Press.

Lundvall, B. A. (1988). Innovation as an interactive process: From user producer interaction to the national system of innovation. In Dosi, G., Freeman, C., Nelson, R., Silverberg, G., & Soete, L., (Eds.), *Technical change and economic theory* (pp. 349-369). London ; New York: Pinter Publishers.

Lundvall, B. A. (1992). Introduction to national systems of innovation. In B. A. Lundvall (Ed.), *National systems of innovation* (pp. 1-22). London: Pinter.

Madique, M. A. (1988). Entrepreneurs, champions and technological development. In M. L. Tushman & W. L. Moore (Eds.), *Readings in the management of innovation* (2nd edition) (pp. 565-584). New York: Harper Business.

Major, E., & Cordey-Hayes, M. (2003). Encouraging innovation in small firms through externally generated knowledge. In L. Shavinina (Ed.), *International handbook on innovation* (pp. 667-679). Oxford: Elsevier.

March, J. G. (1991). Exploration and exploitation in organizational learning. *Organization Science, 2*, 71-87.

Martinsons, M. (1993). Outsourcing information systems: A strategic partnership with risks. *Long Range Planning, 26*(3), 18-25.

Nelson, R. R. (Ed.). (1993). *National systems of innovation: A comparative study*. Oxford: Oxford University Press.

Nonaka, I., & Takeuchi, H. (1995). *The knowledge-creating company*. Oxford: Oxford University Press.

Nonaka, I. (1991, November/December). *The knowledge creating company. Harvard Business Review, 69*, 96-104.

Patel, P., & Pavitt, K. (1994). The continuing widespread (and neglected) importance of improvements in mechanical technologies. *Research Policy, 23*, 533-545.

Pavitt, K. (1984). Patterns of technological change: Towards a taxonomy and a theory. *Research Policy, 13*(6), 343-373.

Polyani, M. (1966). *The tacit dimension*. London: Routledge & Kegan.

Porter, M. (1980). *Competitive strategy: Techniques for analysing industries and competitors*. New York: The Free Press.

Porter, M. (1985). *Competitive advantage*. New York: The Free Press.

Porter, M. (1990). *Competitive advantage of nations*. New York: Macmillan.

Powell, W., Koput, K., & Smith-Doerr, L. (1996). Interorganizational collaboration and the locus of innovation: Networks of learning in biotechnology. *Administrative Science Quarterly, 41*(1), 116-146.

Powell, W. W. (1990). Neither market nor hierarchy: Network forms of organisations. *Research in Organisational Behaviour, 12*, 295-336.

Quelin, B., & Duhamel, F. (2003). Bringing together strategic outsourcing and corporate strategy: Outsourcing motives and risks. *European Management Journal, 21*(5), 647-661.

Quinn, J., & Hilmer, F. (1994, Summer). Strategic outsourcing. *Sloan Management Review*, 43-55.

Quinn, J. B. (1991). Managing innovation: Controlled chaos. In H. Mintzberg & J. B. Quinn (Eds.), *The strategy process: Concepts, contexts & cases* (2nd edition) (pp. 746-758). Englewood Cliffs, NJ: Prentice Hall.

Rothwell, R. (1992). Successful industrial innovation: Critical success factors for the 1990s. *R&D Management*, *22*(2), 221-239.

Rothwell, R., Freeman, C., Horlsey, A., Jervis, V. T. P., Robertson, A. B., & Townsend, J. (1974). SAPPHO updated: Project SAPPHO phase II. *Research Policy*, *3*, 258–91.

Souder, W. E. (1987). *Managing new product innovations*. Lexington, MA: Lexington Books.

Stoneman, P. (1983). *The economic analysis of technological change*. Cambridge: Cambridge University Press.

Tidd, J. (2000). *From knowledge management to strategic competence: Measuring technological, market and organisational innovation*. London: Imperial College Press.

Tidd, J., Bessant, J., & Pavitt, K. (2001). Managing innovation. Chichester: Wiley.

Trott, P. (2005). *Managing innovation and new product development* (3rd edition). London: Prentice Hall.

Twiss, B. (1992). *Managing technological innovation* (4th edition). London: Pitman.

Utterback, J. (1994). *Mastering the dynamics of innovation*. Boston: Harvard Business School Press.

Van de Ven, A. H. (1989). Central problems in the management of innovation. In M. L. Tushman & W. L. Moore (Eds.), *Readings in the management of innovation* (2nd edition, pp. 103-122). New York: Harper Business.

Wang, C., & Regan, A. C. (2003). Risks and reduction measures in logistics outsourcing, TRB Annual Meeting.

Wheelwright, S., & Clark, K. (1992). *Revolutionising product development*. New York: Free Press.

Willcocks, L., & Lacity, M. (1999). IT outsourcing in insurance services: Risk, creative contracting and business advantage. *Information Systems Journal, 9*, 163-180.

Wolfe, R. A. (1994). Organisational innovation: Review and critique and suggested research directions. *Journal of Management Studies*, *31*(3), 405-31.

Woolgar, S., Vaux, J., Gomes, P., Ezingeard, J-N., & Grieve, R. (1998). Knowledge and the speed of transfer and imitation of organisational capabilities: An empirical test. *Organisation Science*, *6*(1), 76-92.

## Endnote

[1] Knowledge is defined here as the learning and theoretical or practical understanding of a subject, task or process.

## Chapter XX

# Analysis of a Large-Scale IT Outsourcing "Failure": What Lessons Can We Learn?

Anne C. Rouse, Deakin University, Australia

Brian J. Corbitt, Shinawatra University, Thailand

## Abstract

*Much of the research that has been carried out into outsourcing is based on relatively successful case studies. Yet drawing inferences from case studies when those with largely negative outcomes rarely see the light of day represents a significant problem. When negative cases are systematically unrepresented, there is less opportunity to subject theory to scrutiny. This chapter goes some way towards redressing this trend, by reporting on a large scale "selective" outsourcing arrangement that has been publicly described as a failure — the Australian Federal Government's "whole of government" IT infrastructure outsourcing initiative. This initiative, originally promoted as likely to lead to a billion dollar saving, was abandoned early in 2001, after a damning public report by the Australian Auditor General. However, a detailed study of the initiative suggests that the "failure" occurred despite the project adhering to many of the recommended guidelines for successful outsourcing that had been derived from earlier case analysis. The findings have important implications for decision makers confronted with outsourcing choices. The study suggests that the risks of outsourcing are often downplayed, or ignored in the rush to reap the expected benefits. The study also suggests that expectations of savings from outsourcing IT are often substantially higher than those that have been empirically confirmed in the field. Decision makers are advised that key assumptions about costs, savings, managerial effort, and the effects of outsourcing on operational performance might be incorrect, and to plan for their outsourcing activity accordingly. They should pay particular attention to coordination and transaction costs, as these tend to be overlooked in the business case. These costs will be magnified if "best in breed" multiple-vendor outsourcing is chosen, and if contracts are kept short. Decision-makers are also warned of the difficulties they are likely to have at the end of an outsourcing contract if there is not a large and robust pool of alternative vendors willing to bid against the incumbent.*

## Introduction

This chapter describes the outcomes of a decision by the Australian Federal Government to outsource the provision of supposedly low-risk, IT (information technology) infrastructure services. The government initiative was an attempt to save up to $1 billion (AU) dollars. The decision caused substantial controversy within Australia, and therefore a large body of public documentation became available to researchers. This documentation, supplemented by anonymous interviews with key players, provided a unique opportunity to explore a "failed" outsourcing case study.

Most large-scale outsourcing arrangements are treated as highly confidential by all players, because both the purchaser and vendor do not wish potential competitors to have information about costings, and because outsourcing announcements tend to have positive impacts on share prices (Loh & Venkatraman, 1992). Any public announcement that the anticipated benefits of outsourcing were *not* achieved would lead to depressed share prices. In the circumstances, it is not surprising then that few announcements of this nature are made by commercial organizations. Consequently, the trade literature is saturated with positive announcements of attractive benefits that outsourcing is *expected* to bring, but very little evidence of actual experiences.

The case analyzed in this chapter provides an opportunity to explore a widely reported outsourcing failure, and so to reconsider the "evidence" that has been used to promote outsourcing. The chapter discusses the methodology and some of the key findings, and then considers the implications of these findings for practitioners.

# Background

There is a relative shortage of negative case studies in the outsourcing literature — with the notable exception of the early work of Lacity and Hirschheim (1993, 1995) and a handful of more recent cases reported by Kern and Blois (2002), Kern, Willcocks, and Van Heck (2002) and Dalcher (2005). This probably reflects the political realities of case study research — organizations that have unhappy experiences with their outsourcing do not tend to talk about it "outside" for fear of appearing badly managed. Moreover, university ethics committees tend to insist that research participants should be free to withdraw from research at any time, and this, combined with a reluctance to publish anonymous cases, acts to prevent the publication of negative organizational experiences. The result of a process that favors the positive over the negative is that decision makers can be lulled into perceiving outsourcing as more successful, and less risky than it really is. As a result, it has almost become an article of faith that outsourcing business services saves money and improves service quality, even though the quantitative empirical evidence does not necessarily support this.

When the IT outsourcing literature is examined, it is also clear that the majority of IT outsourcing cases reported in the academic and trade literature has involved private sector organizations (illustrated in Dibbern, Goles, Hirschheim, & Jayatilaka, 2004). Yet substantial proportions of IT investment within western economies are made by the "not for profit" and public sectors, and over the past two decades governments all around the world have been outsourcing IT services as a key part of public sector reforms.

This chapter attempts to address the imbalance in the literature by reporting on a large-scale public sector outsourcing exercise that was widely reported in the literature to be a "failure", or even, in some cases a "fiasco" (Rouse & Corbitt, 2003). The case involved the attempt by the Australian Federal Government to outsource the provision of most of its IT infrastructure through a series of rolling contracts with large, multinational outsourcing vendors. These contracts, while large, involved selective outsourcing of particular IT services that were thought by decision makers to involve relatively low risk.

The case presents *audited* data on the costs of outsourcing that is rarely obtained. This is important because there have been virtually no studies of IT outsourcing that have involved detailed, forensic investigations of the cost assumptions and outcomes. Such studies would (as with the case reported here) take months, and cost in the realm of hundreds of thousands of dollars. Thus of the handful of IT outsourcing studies in the literature that have examined cost outcomes, none involved in depth audits. Instead, studies into cost outcomes have tended to rely on global judgments by either informants, or sometimes the interviewer, about whether or not cost expectations were met. Experienced auditors know that such surface judgments tend to understate the transaction costs substantially (Walker & Walker, 2000). Fortunately, because the Australian Auditor General examined the outsourcing arrangements in some depth the case provides a relatively unique opportunity to explore the issues thoroughly. It also provides an opportunity to investigate whether the rosy projections for outsourcing that are announced to the press actually unfold.

## Methodology

The chapter draws on a large number of public sources related to the case that were gathered over a four-year period. These were supplemented by in-depth interviews with 20 industry personnel, many of whom were consulted several times during the study period (individual interviews totaled more than 41 hours). The informants were highly placed within either Federal government agencies or vendors, but the interviews were conducted on the basis of confidentiality and anonymity for individuals and organizations (Rouse, 2002).

Public documents analyzed included:

- Press reports related to Australian IT outsourcing between 1997 and May 2001;
- A number of Federal and State government reports, particularly the 1997, 1998 and 2000 *Senate Finance and Public Administration References Committee Inquiries* into outsourcing initiatives (SFPARC 1997, 2001), the Auditor General's Report (ANAO, 2000); and the Humphry Report (cited as Humphry, 2001);
- Walker and Walker's (2000) broad based analysis of government outsourcing in Australia;
- A study of the Humphry and Auditor General's reports by Seddon (2001); and
- Analyses prepared for members of parliament by the Parliamentary Library Politics and Public Administration Group (Verspaandonk, 2001).

In addition, the authors draw upon notes (Rouse, 2002) from a series of Australian focus groups involving 56 respondents reporting on their experiences of IT outsourcing. These were conducted at the time the case was unfolding.

The case study was analysed using hermeneutic textual analysis. Hermeneutic analysis involves a cyclical interpretive analysis of textual materials and narrative. The textual material is repeatedly sifted and compared to find cross-verification and contradictions. Understanding emerges from the comparison between new and previous information. The strategy is akin to the work of a historian sifting through competing accounts of past events and motivations. Hermeneutic analysis has been used in several qualitative case studies in the information systems discipline (Myers, 2004).

## The Australian Federal Government Outsourcing Initiative

In 1997, the Australian Federal Government announced that by 1999 it intended to outsource the delivery of IT infrastructure (mainframe, server, desktop services and in some cases telecommunications) for most federal agencies. The Federal Government's Whole of Government IT Infrastructure Outsourcing Initiative, (referred in this chapter as "WOGITIOI"), was a key plank of the Federal Liberal Coalition party's 1995 election policy and amounted to some 50% of the Federal IT budget (SFPARC, 1997). The initiative was expected to save "up to $AUD 1billion" through the use of external vendors and the consolidation of requirements across government agencies which would be clustered to form cross-agency contracts.

The decision to outsource on this scale created considerable controversy and became the subject of examination by an ongoing Senate Inquiry (SFPARC, 1997). In 1999, the Auditor General independently decided to review the outcomes of the first four contracts under this WOGITIOI initiative. These four contracts totaled spending of about $1.04 billion dollars.

Table 1, below, summarizes the major outsourcing initiatives instigated by the Australian government throughout the 1990s. These initiatives included an early series of contracts amounting to something more than $AUD 295 million, and a later series of WOGITIOI policy initiatives amounting to around $AUD 1.521 billion. Over the decade, these IT outsourcing initiatives encompassed contracts to the value of some $AUD 1.816 billion overall. The four WOGITIOI arrangements that were reviewed by the Auditor General (ANAO, 2000) are highlighted.

## The WOGITIOI Context and Timing

The controversial WOGITIOI initiative was the subject of considerable attention and some criticism from the start. This particularly came from unions, Opposition parties, and the Opposition-dominated *Senate Finance and Public Administration References Committee Outsourcing Inquiry,* which first met in 1997 (SFPARC, 1997). A range of concerns was expressed, including worries about privacy provisions, effects on departmental business initiatives, industry development, and staffing implications[1]. Observations were made that the likelihood of substantial cost savings from such an initiative was low (Rouse & Corbitt, 2003). However, these concerns were largely presented in political terms, and were somewhat remote from the day-to-day issues affecting private sector decision-makers involved in IT sourcing decisions.

*Table 1. Federal government IT outsourcing initiatives 1994 – 2000*

| | | | |
|---|---|---|---|
| ***Early Outsourcing Initiatives*** | | | |
| Department of Veterans Affairs | ns* | Ferntree/GE | Feb 92 |
| Department of Veterans Affairs | $65m | IBM-GSA | Feb-97 |
| Department of Finance & Administration | $30m | IBM-GSA | Sep-97 |
| Australian Customs Service | $200m | EDS | Dec-97 |
| **"Whole Of Government IT Infrastructure Outsourcing Initiative"** | | | |
| "Cluster 3" - two large and four small agencies | $160m | CSC | Mar-98 |
| Department of Employment, Training and Youth Affairs | $300m | Cancelled | Jun-98 |
| Australian Tax Office (ATO) | $490m | IBM/GSA | Jun-99 |
| "Group 5" – five small agencies | $90m | Advantra | Jul-99 |
| "Group 2" – Department of Health, Health Insurance Commission, and Medibank Private | $351m | IBM/GSA | Jan –Jul 2000 |
| "Group 8" – seven small agencies | $130m | Ipex ITG | Jun-2000 |

This situation was to change when the Auditor General's Report of his inquiry into the first four of the Federal Government WOGITIOI contracts was released to the public in September 2000 (ANAO, 2000). The Australian Auditor General reports directly to Parliament, not to the Government, and has many statutory protections to ensure independence. His extensive 243 page review examined the goals, tender evaluations, implementation and outcomes of these first four arrangements, and was damning in its criticism of the IT outsourcing initiative.

The Auditor General's Report (ANAO, 2000) had enormous impact in public sector circles. Usually regarded as financially conservative, apolitical and on the side of the taxpayer, the Auditor General's scrutiny shed light on what, in private sector organizations is normally a commercial-in-confidence arrangement. According to informants we interviewed, the impact of these criticisms was also felt in the private sector. Unlike earlier Senate Inquiries, the strong community perception was that the Auditor General's Review findings were independent and highly credible. For the first time the shroud of secrecy and political point-scoring that surrounded both public and private outsourcing arrangements had been pierced (Mitchell, 2000), allowing the public to examine how the promised "savings" being reported by vendors, consultants and governments were being calculated.

The negative elements of the Auditor General's report were highly publicized, with vocal public criticism, coming from both the press and parliament, finally forcing the Federal government to act to avoid further political damage[2]. In response to both the Auditor General's findings and the negative publicity, the Federal government established another review of the initiative headed by Richard Humphry, Chairman of the Australian Stock Exchange, and a former member of the group that had initially recommended the outsourcing strategy - the 1997 IT & Telecommunications Advisory Committee (Humphry, 2001, p. 22).

This review in turn generated negative public reactions, and the *Review of the Whole of Government Information Technology Outsourcing Initiative* (the "Humphry Report") released in January 2001, led to the public abandonment of key aspects of the strategy.

Initially announced in April 1997, the WOGITIOI strategy was abandoned after four years when the Government announced that it would accept the recommendations of the Humphry Review (Humphry, 2001) and allow individual departments to decide whether to, and how to, outsource their IT services. The outsourcing experiment ended with the subsequent release of the Report of the *Senate Finance and Public Administration References Inquiry* in 2001.

## Outsourcing Expectations

Australia was a leader in public outsourcing during the 1990s, and the strategy was promoted on the basis of several arguments. First, outsourcing would save taxpayer funds (cost saving), perhaps even with better business service operations, and second, outsourcing would lead to the development and enhancement of an effective IT industry (Industry Commission, 1996). The industry development objectives were positively received by small Australian companies, but interviews with industry personnel revealed that the major rationale for outsourcing in the Federal arena was expected cost reductions, in both the long and short term (Rouse, 2002)[3].

The Federal Government sought savings of 20% or more by outsourcing IT infrastructure. This expectation was based on the advice of an industry-based expert panel, the IT Review Group (ITRG, 1995). The source for the Federal Government's bold announcement of savings of the order of $1 billion appears to be an economic business case for outsourcing undertaken in 1996. The Minister for Finance and Administration explained in 1998 "across budget funded agencies, potential savings in the order of $1 billion are realizable, over the term of multiple, seven year contracts." The Minister was confident, further stating that "the savings to the budget are robust and they are conservative" (Fahey, 1998, p. 1). In the end, a more conservative cost-savings target figure of 15% was adopted by government for a strategy that encompassed outsourcing and the consolidation and standardization of data centers and infrastructure services (ANAO 2000, p. 11, p. 195).

To this end, groups of departments ("clusters") that supposedly shared similar IT needs were created. This "clustering" appears to have been based on vendor arguments that consolidating similar service requirements into one contract would achieve greater economies of scale (Humphry, 2001). It was also, according to informants, heavily influenced by the analysis done by Lacity, Willcocks, and Feeny (1996) of the strategies that are likely to lead to cost savings: that is, consolidating data centers or standardizing other services. The Federal government was thus following Lacity, Willcocks, and Feeny's (1996, p. 17) "best practice" advice to "empower [management] to overcome the resistance of users" by encouraging users to "manage demand by consolidating data centers into one site or by standardizing software".

An important part of the strategy was that the government would not outsource "totally," as this was perceived as a high-risk strategy. Instead, it would selectively outsource infrastructure services, which at that time accounted for "about half of the Commonwealth's total IT expenditure of approximately $2 billion" p.a. (SFPARC, 1997 Chapter 2, final paragraph). The infrastructure to be outsourced included mainframe and midrange operations, operations of distributed servers and desktops, and in some cases, data networks.

Government decision-makers saw this as a conservative strategy, consistent with Lacity, Willcocks and Feeny's (1996) "best practice" recommendations that selective outsourcing (less than 80% of IT expenditure), and outsourcing of commodity-like services, would be most likely to achieve significant savings. The contracts were kept short, ranging from three to five years, in response to the "best practice" recommendations at the time[4] (e.g., Lacity, Willcocks and Feeny, 1996). The shorter contracts covered fast changing technology such as networks, while the longer contracts covered mainframe services.

Building on a belief that there were considerable inefficiencies in the delivery of IT services in many areas, and the reassurance that cost savings would be made, decision-makers within the government required agencies to accept budget reductions up front. They saw this strategy as consistent with practices suggested by Lacity and Hirschheim (1995) who demonstrated that organizations, whether in-sourcing, or outsourcing, can save considerably on their IT budgets by instituting unpopular reforms, like consolidating data centers, and restricting the rate of technology change by sticking with equipment that is one to two generations behind.

## Key Findings

After several inquiries and assessments, and the analyses conducted by Rouse (2002) and Rouse and Corbitt (2003), a number of central findings have emerged.

### *1. Large Cost-Savings Promised for the Initiative Were Not Delivered*

The Auditor General (ANAO 2000) found that expected costs had blown out substantially. As Rouse and Corbitt (2003, p. 82) put it, "Most of these cost blow outs were related to the costs of specialist international consultants, including "Big 5" accounting firms, outsourcing advisors, and the outsourcing legal specialists, Shaw Pitman ...".

While many reported outsourcing cases (e.g., those in Lacity & Hirschheim, 1993) have involved cost blowouts, the Auditor General also found that, contrary to the results of initial modeling, only one of the first four contracts, the contract for "Cluster 3", would *ever* have been likely to deliver any savings.

In their analysis of the auditor general's report, Rouse and Corbitt noted that despite relying on world-class consulting advice, the cost and savings projections were flawed. The Auditor General reported that decision makers had failed to take into account additional cash streams associated with equipment that would have been available at the end of the a contract if the services were not outsourced. They had also underestimated the costs of leasing risks absorbed by the agencies. As a consequence of this, the Auditor General determined that "only Cluster 3 was likely to make any substantial savings from the outsourcing arrangements" (ANAO, 2003, p. 83).

The Auditor General also reported that actual savings for the Cluster 3 contract amounted to around 12% rather than the 28% initially projected on the basis of detailed cost models. These had been prepared by the Office of the Asset Sales and IT Outsourcing organization (OASITO), with the help of specialist consultants. Whilst 5% of this discrepancy was accounted for by unexpectedly high initial redeployment costs, there was still a substantial gap between the remaining projected 23% savings and the actual 12% achieved (Rouse, 2002).

An important issue is that these cost savings calculations did not include the significant outlays spent by OASITO in searching out, briefing, and selecting vendors. These costs were viewed not as an additional cost to these four contracts, but as a separate sunk "overhead". Had these transaction costs been amortized over the life of the outsourcing contracts (as the costs were directly related to the decision to outsource) the costs of outsourcing the IT infrastructure would almost certainly have exceeded the cost of keeping the services in-house by a substantial margin.

A contemporary survey of other large organizations in Australia (Rouse, 2005) revealed that the Australian Government was not alone in failing to reap savings from IT outsourcing. Only a minority of the survey respondents (n = 240, from a survey of 1000 of the largest 1000 organizations in the country) reported any savings at all from outsourcing IT. The proportion reporting *substantial* savings from IT outsourcing (seen by focus group informants and interviewees as being about 12% or more of the IT budget) was only 7%. Furthermore, there was no statistical difference between organizations from the public and private sector in relation to financial outcomes (Rouse, 2005). Hence, the experiences of the Federal Government appear to be no different to those of other large Australian organizations.

## *2. "Failure" was Almost a Text Book Case of 'Best Practice' Outsourcing*

Industry analysts have suggested that a range of good practices will ensure that outsourcing failures are avoided. Seddon (2001) for instance defined a series "ten commandments" for succeeding at outsourcing, based largely on earlier work by Lacity and Hirschheim (1993, 1995). He implied (but did not provide evidence) that the WOGITIO was a failure because decision makers did not follow good practice. However, a detailed investigation of the case carried out by Rouse as part of her doctoral studies (2002) revealed that decision makers in this case study went to considerable trouble to follow "best practice" and recommended procedures.

The very fact that the Australian government spent $AUD 25 million on specialist consultant advice suggests that they were keen to make the arrangement work well. All the advice from the IT Review group (ITRG), the Information, The IT and Telecommunications (IT&T) Policy Advisory Committee, panels of industry specialists, and from the Australian Industries Commission supported the notion that if the process was carefully managed, the government could succeed in achieving the target 15% savings (and possibly more). More recent empirical data (Hodge, 2000) has revealed that cost savings of this order are common only for very simple, well-codified services, such as cleaning, catering, refuse collection.

Considerable time and effort went into planning for and implementing the initiative. Indeed, of Seddon's ten practices, nine were essentially followed (Rouse, 2002). These included:

- selective outsourcing (of around 50% of the IT budget),
- targeting of only "non-core" infrastructure services,
- short (three- to five-year) contracts,
- detailed contracts prepared under the advice of international and local specialists,
- retaining highly skilled staff to manage the arrangement,
- involving both line and IT management in decision making,
- conducting detailed analyses of vendor offerings, and
- implementing comprehensive post-contract management and monitoring structures.

The single practice not followed related to the option of allowing internal service groups to bid against external vendors. This option was judged as expensive, and it is easy to see that this practice would have been politically risky as well.

The adoption of recommended outsourcing practice in this case study was in marked contrast to many of the negative IT outsourcing cases reported in the early to mid-'90s. At that time, organizations often engaged in naïve behavior such as failing to know their own market costs and signing long term contracts with a single vendor for a large proportion of their IT budget (Lacity & Hirschheim, 1995). The Australian case study findings cast doubt on the plausible and attractive proposition that IT outsourcing fails to reap benefits largely because of poor management.

## *3. In Practical Terms, Large-Scale Outsourcing is Difficult to Reverse*

A third key finding, stemming largely from the individual interviews, is that in practical terms, outsourcing on this scale is almost impossible to reverse, even if it involves only "selective" outsourcing. It is essentially a one-way option, because the timeframe and costs (both financial and organizational) involved in re-establishing the arrangement are prohibitive.

At the end of the WOGITIOI contract periods, all of the reported outsourcing arrangements have now either been rolled over with the existing vendor, or have been broken up into a number of smaller contracts — described by consultants to the government as a "best in breed strategy" (Gartner, in ANAO, 2001). Smaller contracts are frequently reported in the press as examples of good management, as "selective" outsourcing is seen, almost ubiquitously, to be best practice, and by implication, expected to lead to greater cost savings. Yet the empirical evidence we do have on this is that, if anything, larger IT outsourcing contracts tend to lead to better outcomes than smaller contracts (Rouse, 2005). Certainly when the transaction costs associated with multiple, short-term contracts are taken into account, cost savings are by no means guaranteed.

However, the evidence for whether or not this multiple-vendor "best of breed" approach will lead to better outcomes than keeping the programs in-house, or in fact than the original larger contracts, will never be made available. There is no longer a base line for comparisons, and the costs and difficulties of auditing the plethora of new arrangements are prohibitive. Furthermore, such an audit would be politically unattractive. In intimating, in the press announcements, that selective outsourcing will be "better," no real evidence has been put forward. Economic theory (such as transaction cost economics) and practical experience suggests that these arrangements will prove substantially more expensive than the larger-scale prime-vendor arrangements they have replaced, because of the substantial transaction costs associated with managing multiple vendors and negotiating the gaps between them.

Rather than being examples of mature management strategy, as described by consultants, these new contracts reflect the reality that re-insourcing their IT services was practically and financially impossible for the government agencies involved. Several informants pointed out to us that, having let go their key IT staff to the vendor, and having spent substantial once-off sums associated with staff retrenchment, they were faced with prohibitively costly and time-consuming processes to regain the skills involved. Furthermore, new recruits would command a salary premium (as the agencies could no longer trade on their reputation as reliable and long-term employers). Thus, the costs of delivering the services in-house after re-insourcing would be substantially higher than the original in-house costs, and probably than the outsourced arrangements that were revealed to be more expensive than in-house delivery. There would be no simple reversal.

In several cases informants reported that the organizational knowledge embodied in the lost staff could not be retrieved once lost. In fact, this was an issue that vendors raised themselves in submissions to the Humphry report (Humphry, 2001, Appendix 1) — the vendors had wanted the Australian government to "force" skilled staff to join them to preserve organizational knowledge, but this was at odds with the industrial awards negotiated with unions. In addition, the business disruption and elapsed time to re-implement the lost functions "from scratch" were seen by all but one of the informants to be so great that re-insourcing (or "backsourcing") the outsourced functions were not organizationally possible.

Other informants advised us that they were effectively forced to renew the existing contracts with their existing vendor because of a thin vendor marketplace. This was because other potential vendors were unwilling to bid against the incumbent, whom competitors believed had an inside advantage in knowing the true business requirements and costs. The higher level of uncertainty for non-incumbent bidders required them to charge risk premiums, so effectively pricing them out of the market. Without competition, incumbent vendors could then afford to charge high premiums. The net effect was that seven (or in one case, nine) years after entering into the initial IT outsourcing arrangement, the purchaser had no choice but to continue with the existing vendor at prices that were tied to the original contract.

# Discussion

The Australian case study raises a number of cautionary points for organizations that are considering entering into, or rolling over existing, outsourcing arrangements.

## The Problems of Inaccurate Costing Models

Much outsourcing is entered into on the basis of faith — because it is difficult and costly to accurately project the cash flows associated with the new outsourcing arrangement. When such cash flow projections are made, they tend to be inaccurate, because of the likelihood of major changes during the life of the contract. It is even more difficult to project the costs that "would have" applied had the services not been outsourced (the "status quo" situation).

Even where organizations devote the time (and expense) to carry out such projections, the experience of the case reported here is that the figures are subject to large error margins of over 100%. It needs to be remembered that the Australian government had access to the best and most expensive technical advice available internationally (at a cost of many millions of dollars); as well as a highly skilled audit and review group (in the form of the Australian Auditor General's office). Few organizations have access to, or can afford, this level of advice and skill. Yet even with these resources, according to the Auditor General, their original business case was flawed.

It has been suggested that by entering into smaller "selective" outsourcing arrangements, the errors associated with projections are lower, and potential savings more accurately pinpointed (Lacity & Willcocks, 1998). However, on the basis of the focus group data gathered by the authors, the opposite seems to be true. This is because those organizations that entered into substantial outsourcing contracts brought in highly skilled accounting and costing specialists when contracts were large and strategic. On the other hand, focus group informants reported that smaller contracts were often "costed" by staff without the requisite managerial accounting skills to capture and allocate costs, particularly coordination and transaction costs. What's more, many focus group informants (both vendor and purchaser) reported that without technical expertise what they eventually understood would be delivered by an outsourced vendor was very different from what was initially specified. So the economic models ended up comparing "apples" with "oranges", even for selective outsourcing.

Another area in which outsourcing costing models are inaccurate is the quarantining of certain costs, particularly transaction costs associated with the initial investigation and search for partners. These were treated by the Federal Government (and many of the focus group members, who were not part of the case study) as outside the economic business case for comparing different sourcing options. The argument for doing this seems (as with the WOGITIOI case above) to be that these "search" "market testing" "contracting" and "analysis" costs are once-off, and are part of general good management.

In fact, as the case has illustrated, these costs are entered into every time that a contract is terminated or renegotiated, and the shorter the contract length, and the greater the number of "selective" contracts, the higher the search and contracting costs. Furthermore, at the renewal of a contract, the vendor can hold a substantial advantage over the purchaser, who faces major disruption and un-planned for costs if it does not renew the existing contract, even though the prices originally negotiated (uplifted for inflation) are by that stage substantially more expensive than market rates.

In the Australian case study, although there was a great deal of cautious academic research information available to government prior to the WOGITIOI initiative, this was discounted in the rush to contract-out IT to external providers. The economic business cases were complex and comprehensive, but also assumed idealistic "best case" outcomes rather than assuming a spread of more realistic outcomes. The adoption of such assumptions in the business cases led, according to the Auditor General, to overoptimistic, and essentially incorrect, predictions of the likely outcomes.

## Why Are Outsourcing Risks Downplayed?

It appears that outsourcing is often entered into with the expectation that, for well-managed organizations, it is a relatively low-risk undertaking, particularly if it is not the highly-condemned "total" outsourcing (Rouse, 2002). Yet this case study illustrates that the risks of outsourcing IT services can be substantially higher than is commonly acknowledged. Potential risks raised by the case include loss of organizational knowledge, redirection of organizational attention away from core business, loss of flexibility (because of contractual obligations), and financial risks (associated with blowouts in costs, or failure to achieve expected benefits). These risks need to be factored into the economic business case. The case study also raises the question of why, since the risks of outsourcing IT have been known for some time, were they discounted by organizations as well advised as the Australian government? Our analysis of this case study suggests several reasons:

There is a heavy reliance in the literature on theory, particularly economic theory, which is frequently misinterpreted to justify outsourcing. For example, transaction cost economics theory suggests that outsourcing will lead to reduced costs only where the production cost savings are not outweighed by additional transaction costs. The identification of all transaction costs requires substantial skill and training, as well as an open mind. Ang and Straub (1998) have reported that proponents of outsourcing tend to focus mainly on production cost savings, and to ignore the often-substantial transaction costs. Another source of theory is resource-based theory, which suggests that outsourcing IT will allow an organization to refocus on its core business. Yet the evidence provided to the various public reviews above suggested the opposite was true: unsatisfactory IT outsourcing drained organizational attention from core business — the major reason behind Humphry's recommendation that the WOGITIO initiative be discontinued.

Another reason is the dominance of illustrative or inappropriately-aggregated case studies in the literature. Large numbers of our informants told us that "selective" outsourcing was relatively low risk because they could cite example "successes". Often they referred to the aggregated cases reported by Lacity and Willcocks (1998). Yet most "successes" are reported publicly at the time an organization enters into the outsourcing arrangement; few are ever evaluated after the fact. Even fewer are evaluated systematically as was done with the WOGITIOI. Anecdotal individual successes, or even the ratios of success and failure for aggregations of opportunistic cases, provide no indication of success rates that could be expected in the field, despite the seductive appeal of numbers and proportions.

A striking feature of the IT outsourcing literature (and in fact, the outsourcing literature as a whole) is the shortage of theory-testing studies. As a result of this trend, so-called "proven practices" go unchallenged, leaving decision makers with a false understanding of the likelihoods of success and failure even if they follow these practices. Thus, the subtle, but generally unwarranted, messages coming from much outsourcing research to date — that well managed outsourcing is largely successful — leads many decision makers to be over-optimistic about their chances of making outsourcing work well. The empirical research conducted by Rouse and Corbitt (2003b), and by Aubert, Rivard and Patry (1996) indicates that well managed outsourcing arrangements can still be problematic.

## The Seductiveness of Simple Solutions

The failure of an organization that went to such trouble to manage its risks also raises questions about the "recommended practices" OASITO followed. These recommendations were drawn largely from the case studies carried out by Lacity and Hirschheim in the early '90s, and the post-hoc cross-case analyses done when Lacity and Willcocks began reviewing their combined research (c.f. Lacity et al., 1996; Lacity & Willcocks, 1998). Examination of the original case descriptions (for example, those in Lacity & Hirschheim, 1993) reveal complexity and richness, yet this richness was eventually distilled (Lacity et al., 1996; Seddon, 2001) into a number of relatively simple prescriptions that may not have captured the underlying causal factors.

As an example, the recommended practice "involve line management and IT management in the decision" came about because some of the problematic cases studied by Lacity and Hirschheim (1993) excluded one or other of these groups from the decision. In the Federal initiative, the Government did involve both line management and IT in their decisions. There was extensive consultation and discussion amongst OASITO and line and IT staff in all the agencies involved. Not all agreed with the decision, but stakeholders had many opportunities to express their reservations through this consultation, and through the Senate Inquiry that took place during 1997. When seeking to reconcile this observation it becomes apparent that the term "involvement" is very general. It does not, for example, necessarily imply that active support from all parties is required for success. There are many examples in the IS and management literatures of senior management instituting ultimately successful organizational programs that encountered disagreements and dissent. Furthermore, such simplicity is not apparent in Lacity and Hirschheim's original discussion of this practice, which was concerned, with the problems of excluding one or other viewpoint. The impact of this imprecision is that it is likely to be only in those (probably rare) organizations that actively exclude one or other group that decision-makers would not perceive themselves as involving both IT and line management. Consequently, the practical usefulness of this recommended practice is limited.

This case study suggests that many of the practices recommended by researchers are necessary, but not sufficient for achieving success, particularly as the probability of their not being followed at all is low. For example, it is unlikely that an organization involved in a multi-million dollar venture would not establish post management structures and processes of some kind, yet the federal initiative has illustrated that such processes, even when based on "international best practice" advice do not guarantee success. A similar observation can be made about careful market testing and crafting of detailed contracts. The conclusion that such practices are not sufficient to guarantee success implies that decision makers may be unwittingly led to under-estimate their own risks when outsourcing IT, because most would be able to reassure themselves that they were following recommended risk-minimizing practices.

## Conclusions and Final Observation

While the trade press, and some analysts (e.g., Seddon, 2001) generally viewed the WOGITIO case as an example of naivety and foolishness, the authors do not view the case as a "failure". Instead it reveals a strategic and far-reaching decision that was predicated on research and advice that was overoptimistic about likely benefits if IT outsourcing, and unrealistically confident that good management could overcome the associated risks. Many of the outcomes experienced by the Australian government were typical of those of contemporary Australian organisations, and probably of many large organisations elsewhere. The Australian case study suggests that IT outsourcing is far more risky than is commonly acknowledged.

The case study also confirms Ang and Straub's (1998) suggestion that those choosing to outsource frequently pay less attention to the transaction costs and risks associated with the strategy than to the expected production savings they will make. Although there was a great deal of academic research urging caution that was available to the government prior to the WOGITIOI initiative, this was discounted in the rush to contract-out IT to external providers. The economic business cases were complex and comprehensive, but also assumed idealistic "best case" outcomes rather than a spread of more realistic outcomes. The adoption of such assumptions in the businesses cases led, according to the Auditor General (ANAO, 2000), to incorrect predictions of the likely outcomes. In other words, cost savings were predicted which in fact would not occur.

The Australian case implies that decision-makers need to be much more focused on the relative risks and returns from IT outsourcing, which are far less optimistic than the proponents (often not disinterested players) suggest. The case reveals considerable uncertainty surrounding likely outcomes, and highlights the possibility that key assumptions about costs, savings, managerial effort, or the effects of outsourcing on operational performance might be incorrect.

The case also implies that organizations should consider their exit strategy when planning to outsource. This advice has particular implications for those deciding whether to outsource offshore or not. It is important that decision makers plan for (and cost into their economic model) the potential need to move their operations either back in-house, or to another vendor (and perhaps another country) should economic, political, or social conditions change, or should the vendor prove not to meet expectations. Outsourcing offshore only where there is a deep and vigorous marketplace of alternative vendors will help avoid this situation, though at the time the Australian government began its bold IT outsourcing initiative, they too thought that if arrangements proved problematic they would have the option of moving to alternate vendors. In real life, this may not be a realistic option.

## Acknowledgments

This research was funded in part by the management consultants Simsion Bowles & Associates and by the University of Melbourne's Department of Information Systems.

# References

Ang, S., & Straub, D. (1998). Production and transaction economics and IS outsourcing: A study of the U.S. banking industry. *MIS Quarterly, 22*(4), 535-552.

Aubert, B. A., Rivard, S., & Patry, M. (1996). Assessing the risk of IT outsourcing. *Proceedings of the Thirty-Fifth Annual Hawaii International Conference on Systems Sciences, Hawaii* [CD ROM].

Australian National Audit Office (ANAO). (2000). Implementation of whole-of-government information technology and infrastructure consolidation and outsourcing initiative. Audit Report No 9. Canberra, Australia.

Dalcher, D. (2005). From fixed contracts to dynamic partnerships: Successful outsourcing in a changing world. In P. Brudenalle, *Technology and offshore outsourcing strategies* (pp. 9-36). Basingstoke: Palgrave McMillan.

Davis, I. (1998, July 25). IT shifts from costs to better service. *Australian Financial Review*, 54.

Dibbern, J., Goles, T., Hirschheim, R., & Jayatilaka, B. (2004). Information systems outsourcing: A survey and analysis of the literature. *The DATABASE for Advances in Information Systems, 35*(4), 6-102.

Fahey, J. (1998, July 29). An address to the IT outsourcing seminar. IT Outsourcing Seminar at Freehill, Hollingdale and Page. Melbourne, Australia.

Hodge, G. A. (2000). *Privatisation: An international review of performance, theoretical lenses on public policy series* (P. A. Sabatier, Ed.). Colorado: Westview Press.

Humphry, R. (2001). Review of the whole of government information technology outsourcing initiative (Humphry Report). Canberra, Australia.

Industry Commission (Australian). (1996). Competitive tendering and contracting by public sector agencies. Report No. 48. Melbourne: AGPS.

Information Technology Review Group (ITRG). (1995). Clients first: The challenge for government of information technology: Report of the minister for finance's information technology review group. Canberra: Australia.

Kern, T., & Blois, K. (2002). Norm development in outsourcing relationships. *Journal of Information Technology, 17*(1), 33-42.

Kern, T., Willcocks, L., & Van Heck, E. (2002). The winners' curse in IT outsourcing: Strategies for avoiding relational trauma. *California Management Review, 44*, 47-69.

Lacity, M. C., & Hirschheim, R. (1993). *Information systems outsourcing: Myths, metaphors and realities*. Chichester: Wiley.

Lacity, M. C., & Hirschheim, R. (1995). *Beyond the information systems outsourcing bandwagon: The insourcing response*. New York: Wiley.

Lacity, M. C., & Willcocks, L. (1998). An empirical investigation of information technology sourcing practices: Lessons from experience. *MIS Quarterly, 22*(3), 363-408.

Lacity, M. C., Willcocks, L., & Feeny, D. F. (1996, Spring). The value of selective IT outsourcing. *Sloan Management Review, 37*(3), 13-25.

Loh, L., & Venkatraman, N. (1992). *Stock market reaction to IT outsourcing: An event study*. Working paper. Sloan School of Management, Massachusetts Institute of Technology.

Mitchell, S. (2000, December 9). Audit report slams federal outsourcing. *Australian IT: The Australian*, 31.

Myers, M. (2004). Qualitative research methods in information systems. Retrieved November 21, 2004, from http://www.qual.auckland.ac.nz/

Rouse, A., & Corbitt, B. (2003). The Australian government's abandoned infrastructure outsourcing program: What can be learned? *Australian Journal of Information Systems, 10*(2), 81-90.

Rouse, A. C. (2002). Information technology outsourcing revisited: Success factors and risks. Unpublished doctoral thesis. Melbourne: Department of Information Systems, University of Melbourne.

Rouse, A. C. (2005). *Testing some myths about outsourcing: Analysis of a survey of Australia's Top 1000 organizations*. Unpublished working paper. Deakin Business School. Available from http://www.deakin.edu.au/dbs

Rouse, A. C., & Corbitt, B. (2003b). Revisiting IT outsourcing risks: Analysis of a survey of Australia's Top 1000 organizations. *Proceedings of the 14th Australasian Conference on Information Systems*, 26-28 November, 2003, Perth, Australia.

Seddon, P. (2001). The Australian federal government's clustered-agency IT outsourcing experiment. *Communications of the Association for Information Systems, 5*(13), 1-33.

Senate Finance and Public Administration References Committee (SFPARC). (1997). *Contracting out of government services: First report: Information technology*. Canberra: Australia.

SFPARC. (2001). *Rebooting the IT agenda in the Australian public service: Final report on the government's information technology outsourcing initiative*. Canberra: Australia.

Verspaandonk, R. (2001). *Politics and public administration group: The whole-of-government IT outsourcing initiative*. Retrieved July 1, 2001, from http://www.aph.gov.au/library/intguide/pol/IT_outsourcing.htm

Walker, R., & Walker, B. C. (2000). *Privatisation: Sell off or sell out?* Sydney: ABC Books.

# Endnotes

[1] This statement is based on a review of newspaper reports, as well as the findings of the first Senate Inquiry into IT outsourcing (SFPARC, 1997).

[2] This statement is made on the basis of newspaper reports at the time.

[3] According to informants, the industry development goal, while important, was secondary to the cost savings goal. This observation was also supported by the reduction in attention paid to industry development in later WOGITIOI contracts (ANAO, 2000).

[4] While "short contracts" were described in Lacity et al (1996) as less than four years, informants suggested vendors could not accept such short contracts for many services, as they did not allow time for the vendor to recoup the significant cost of winning the contract.

# About the Authors

**Harbhajan Kehal** has recently retired from the position of senior lecturer in economics from the University of Western Sydney, Blacktown Campus, New South Wales, Australia. He has a PhD from the University of Western Australia, Perth. The author of chapters in various books that have been published in Australia and other countries, Dr. Kehal has received international recognition for his achievements in various facets of life. A well-travelled person, he has been a visiting fellow and visiting professor in many overseas universities and research institutions. His research interests centre around digital economy, outsourcing and offshoring, foreign investment in developing countries, economic relationships of Australia with Japan and other countries. An academician, researcher and philanthropist, his name has appeared in Australasian Who's Who since 1987, Who's Who in the World since 1995, Directory of International Biography since 1996, and many other publications. He is an Eminent Fellow of the American Biographical Institute. He is a member of a vast number of economic societies and is well known in the contemporary economic world for his leadership and active participation in international conferences. His recent travels have taken him to Toronto (Canada), Hawaii and San Francisco (USA) and Cancun (Mexico), not to mention his trips to Asia and other continents.

**Varinder Pal Singh** was born in 1974 in India and achieved his master's degree in commerce, specializing in information systems from the faculty of management, University of Western Sydney, Australia (2002). Earlier, he received his bachelor's and master's degrees in biochemistry from Panjab University, Chandigarh, India. He was co-editor of *Digital Economy-Impacts, Influences and Challenges*. He intends to pursue research in the less-explored field of health economics, emphasizing the financing and delivery of medical services, with extensive emphasis on federal and state legislation of current policy issues. His forthcoming projects include editing of the *Encyclopedia of Information Technology Global Sourcing* (Idea Group Reference, 2006).

* * *

**Michael Amberg** (born in 1961) is the head of the Department for Business Information Systems III at the Friedrich-Alexander-University of Erlangen-Nuremberg, Germany. Before he came to Nuremberg, he worked at the RWTH in Aachen and at the Otto-Friedrich-University of Bamberg. His major research interests are in the fields of IT outsourcing/offshoring, economics of IT investments, and competence management.

**Anthony S. Atkins** is a principal lecturer in information and applied business systems in the faculty of computing, engineering and technology at Staffordshire University, UK. He has a first degree in engineering and two Master of Science degrees in computing and engineering. He is a chartered engineer in both computing and engineering and has taught and supervised to the PhD level in both disciplines in the UK, Australia and the U.S. He also has a Churchill Fellowship in biotechnology and environmental engineering and has several patents in biotechnology with embedded real-time systems covering the UK, EU, Australia and the U.S. His main interests are in strategic management, outsourcing, knowledge management, visualisation, mobile computing and engineering application in computing/IT. He has more than 70 international journals, conference papers and book chapters.

**Parthasarathi Banerjee** is with the NISTADS, New Delhi, India, and is a visiting professor to a few management institutions. His research spans business strategy, technological changes, innovation management and information system strategy. Apart from undertaking consultancy/sponsored research projects and advising industry in these areas, he has contributed to teaching, training and has published large number of research papers, research reports and nine books. His last book has been *The Indian Software Industry: Business Strategy and Dynamic Coordination* (2004, Palgrave-Macmillan, London) and his forthcoming book from the same publisher is on *Biomedical Innovation in India.*

**Subhajit Basu** graduated from University College of Law, Calcutta University (India) in 1997. He was called to the West Bengal Bar and worked as an advocate specializing in corporate law. He did his PhD at the Liverpool John Moores University, on *Taxation of E-Commerce from a Global Perspective*. He worked as the research and administrative assistant for *Ethnic Minority Law Network (UKCLE Project)*. His research interest includes e-commerce, taxation of e-commerce, e-commerce and developing countries and WTO, e-government, cybercrime, intellectual property and developing countries, digital divide and corporate social responsibility, and legal issues of outsourcing. He is the book review editor for *International Review of Law Computers and Technology* and a reviewer of articles for *JILT (Journal of Information Law and Technology)* and *Inter-*

*national Review of Law, Computers and Technology*. He is an executive committee member of British & Irish Law, Education and Technology Association (BILETA). He is a member of the Tax Research Network (UK), member of the Legal Network of E-Commerce Law Professionals and a member of LEFIS (Legal Framework for the Information Society: Network, supported by the European Union as Erasmus Thematic Network). In addition, Dr. Basu is the author of a number of articles and chapters in scholarly journals and books covering a variety of topics, including e-commerce, cybercrime, intellectual property, outsourcing and e-government. Currently, he is a lecturer in information and technology law at the School of Law, Queen's University, Belfast, Northern Ireland.

**Nicholas B. Beaumont** (BSc, MBA, PhD) is a senior lecturer in the Department of Management at Monash University, Australia. He is a member of the Australian Society for Operations Research and the Australian Computer Society. He worked in the computer industry for 12 years and now teaches information systems management and electronic business. His research interests include the effect of information and communication technologies on individuals, organisations and society; a particular interest is electronic business and its ramifications. His major current project entails research on outsourcing in Australia. Other current projects are an investigation of service level management in Australia and the improvement of a particular kind of statistical analysis. He has published widely in operations research and management journals and presented at international academic conferences. He often presents at industry seminars on outsourcing and service level management. He welcomes opportunities to meet and work with people "at the coalface". He was heavily involved in negotiating Monash University's internal service level agreements.

**Sangeeta S. Bharadwaj** has an MSc (Hons.) in mathematics, an MMS (Master of Management Studies), an ME in systems and information and a PhD from Birla Institute of Technology and Science, Pilani, India. She has 10 years of experience in teaching and research and four years of entrepreneurial experience of managing a florist business in the U.S. Prior to joining Management Development Institute, India, she taught at BITS, Pilani. Her teaching interests are managing IT projects, software project management, knowledge management and MIS. She has published in *Opsearch, Indian Management* and *JITCA*. She is presently researching in the area of business process outsourcing, including strategic partnering of service providers with the clients and knowledge management in global software teams.

**Subrata Chakrabarty** is pursuing his PhD in information and operations management at Mays Business School, Texas A&M University, USA, since the fall of 2004. His research and consulting interests include global sourcing of information systems (IS), quality assurance & control, global project management, and business processes in the IS industry. Before pursuing his PhD, he had more than two years of work experience in the software services industry with Infosys Technologies (India), where he worked with large clients based in the U.S. and UK. In addition, he had worked for about half a year with Toyota (India) at their product design and development division. He also has one year of undergraduate research internship experience with National Aerospace Labs,

India. He is a certified software quality analyst (CSQA), indicating a professional level of competence in the principles and practices of quality assurance in the IT profession. He is willing to take up research and consulting assignments in areas related to his interests. His hobbies include swimming, painting and cartooning.

**Narendra S. Chaudhari** is with the Division of Information Systems, School of Computer Engineering (SCE), Nanyang Technological University (NTU), Singapore, as an associate professor since December 2001. He has obtained a PhD, an MTech in computer science, and a BTech in electrical engineering (with distinction) from I.I.T. Bombay (1988, 1983 and 1981, respectively). He has been a fellow at the Institute of Electronics and Telecom Engineers (IETE), India, since 2000, and is a member of many professional societies. He has varied experience in industry and R&D organizations, and he has been with Devi Ahilya University since 1988, and a professor of computer science since June 1990. He has been on various committees of the university, and he was a dean in the faculty of engineering sciences, Devi Ahilya University, from 1995-97. During this period, the university started the Institute of Engineering and Technology (IET), which currently offers BE programs in electronics and community engineering, computer engineering and mechanical engineering. He has more than 120 publications and four books to his credit. He has successfully guided nine PhDs in computer science and engineering. He was the chairman of the Computer Society of India (CSI), Indore Chapter, from 1997-99. He has been invited by various universities abroad to deliver colloquium lectures/research talks, as well as teaching assignments. The list of countries he has visited includes America, Australia, Germany, Hungary and Japan.

**Brian J. Corbitt** is currently a professor of management science at Shinawatra University in Thailand and also supervises research students as a professor of information systems at Deakin University in Melbourne, Australia. He has previously been a pro vice chancellor (Online Services) at Deakin University, JADE professor of eCommerce at Victoria University of Wellington in New Zealand. Prior to that, he lectured at the University of Melbourne, where he was also head of International House, and, before that, Monash University. Professor Corbitt specializes in IT policy development, analysis and implementation, in business modeling and electronic commerce trade relationships, and knowledge management. He has published six books on e-business, e-commerce and e-government, and another four books. He has also published more than 100 refereed scholarly papers and also numerous government reports to the governments of Thailand and New Zealand, and some 20 invited papers as a keynote speaker in Malaysia, Singapore, Thailand, New Zealand, Japan, Hong Kong and Australia. He has supervised 18 students to completed PhDs, and is an experienced PhD examiner.

**Glauco De Vita** is a reader in international business economics at Oxford Brookes University Business School (UK). Prior to joining academia, he worked as a senior analyst for an American multinational corporation. He has taught several subjects at both undergraduate and postgraduate levels, including international economics, econometrics, industrial economics, international business, international management and strategy. His research interests include international trade, FDI, international business, capital mobility and exchange rates. His research has been published in *Economics Letters*, *the Scottish Journal of Political Economy*, *Manchester School*, *Applied Economics*, *Energy Policy*, *Economic Issues* and other peer-reviewed academic journals.

**Abhinav Dhawan** is the president of team4U, an outsourced staffing services firm based in New Delhi, India. His company is one of the biggest players in this industry in India, with a more than 5,000-strong team located in more than 100 cities across India, handling a wide range of outsourced services including in-bound complaint management, loyalty programs, out-bound telesales, off-line direct sales and back-office business processes. Besides managing these widespread operations, Abhinav is also a member of several international organizations and attends all major international conferences in the BPO area.

**Alev M. Efendioglu** is a professor of management at the School of Business and Management (SOBAM), University of San Francisco (USF), USA. Having joined USF in 1977, he has served at various times as chair of SOBAM's many faculty committees (including peer review and academic standards committees), coordinator of the management teaching area, and the coordinator of USF-EMBA Program for Guangdong Enterprises in China (Hong Kong, Shenzhen and Guangzhou). He has extensive consulting experience, and is the author of two books, chapters in four other books (*Encyclopedia of E-Commerce, E-Government and Mobile Commerce, Encyclopedia of Online Learning, Digital Economy: Impacts, Influences and Challenges* and *Chinese Economic Transition and Its Impact on Marketing Strategy*), and articles in numerous professional publications, including *Business Horizons*, *Journal of American Academy of Business*, *Journal of Asia-Pacific Business*, *Journal of Small Business Strategy*, *Interacting with Computers* and *China International Review*. His research, "Acceptance and Use of Information Technology among Small Retail and Service Businesses," was awarded the best paper in the Small Business/Entrepreneurship Track award at the Western Decision Sciences Institute's Twenty-Sixth Annual Meeting in 1997. He holds leadership positions in a number of domestic and international professional organizations, including Academy of Management. He also serves as a member of the board of directors of Ameristock Mutual Fund companies. You can find more detailed information on Dr. Efendioglu at http://www.usfca.edu/alev/alev.htm.

**Ashima Goyal** is a professor at the Indira Gandhi Institute of Development Research, Mumbai, India. She has taught development theory and policy, advanced macroeconomics and open economy macroeconomics. She has been a faculty member in the Delhi School of Economics, Gokhale Institute of Politics and Economics, a visiting fellow at the Economic Growth Centre, Yale University, and a Fulbright Senior Research Fellow at Claremont Graduate University, USA. Her research interests are in institutional macroeconomics, the open economy, international finance, development and gender. She is the author of numerous international and national publications, and a book on developing economy macroeconomics. Her research has received national and international awards.

She is also active in the Indian policy debate. More details are available at http://www.igidr.ac.in/~ashima.

**Smita Gupta** works as an information technology (IT) consultant in St. Louis, MO, USA. She has extensive experience in IT software projects implementation for major corporates in the U.S. doing businesses in areas of telecommunications, financial, legal, education and health care. Software applications and project areas of her interest are: customer relationship management, pharmacy benefit management, point of sales, order management, business process improvement, software quality assurance, software configuration management, release management and visual modeling. Initial years of her career have been in academics in university education. Her first job was as a lecturer in the Department of Computer Science, Vikram University, Ujjain, India. Later, she joined as lecturer in the School of Computer Science, Devi Ahilya University, Indore, India, where she taught postgraduate students. She possesses a bachelor of engineering degree in electronics, a master of engineering degree in computer engineering, and a PhD degree in computer engineering from Devi Ahilya University, Indore, (MP), and India.

**Luke Ho** is a management consultant in the Centre for Organisational Decision Intelligence Studies (CODIS). He has previously worked with the Altria Group Inc. (formerly known as Philip Morris) and the Ministry of Defence (Singapore). He holds a masters degree in research, a BSc (Hons.) in computing science and was awarded two postgraduate scholarships from Staffordshire University, UK. His masters dissertation on "Strategic Frameworks for Outsourcing Decision-Making" was awarded the highest classification of "Distinction". Luke is currently undertaking a PhD which looks to develop a holistic framework to effectively address the complex multi-faceted nature of outsourcing decision-making. His research interests are in strategic management, outsourcing, infocomm security, computer forensics and electronic crime scene investigation (E-CSI).

**A. Hoecht** is a senior lecturer at the Business School, University of Portsmouth, UK. He is an economist and political scientist with a particular research interest in the role of trust in business relations. He holds a doctorate in economics (Budapest) and an M.A. in political science (Hamburg).

**Paula Luna Huertas** is a full professor at the University of Sevilla, Spain. She teaches information technologies and information systems in the faculty of managerial sciences. She holds graduate and doctoral degrees in economics and managerial sciences. She has been engaged as a principal researcher in several research projects in the area of MIS, supported by the Spanish government and the EU. She is currently the leading researcher of an alpha project of the European Union. She has also participated in several scientific summits in diverse Spanish, European and American institutions, and written more than 100 scientific documents — 12 books, 30 chapters, more than 30 articles and 50 research reports.

**Francisco Jose Martínez López** is a full professor at the University of Huelva, Spain. He teaches information technologies and information systems in the faculty of managerial sciences. He holds graduate and doctoral degrees in economics and managerial sciences (with extraordinary prize). He has imparted conferences in diverse institutions, courses and masters, as well as more than 30 doctorate courses in diverse universities in Spain, Europe and America. He has been the director and main investigator in numerous scientific projects, national and international, author and joint author of more than 100 scientific works; he has written 12 books, 29 chapters in books, more than 30 articles in scientific journals and more than 50 reports in national and international congresses.

**Rajiv Mathur** is a director with Percom Limited, an advertising and marketing services firm based at New Delhi, India. In his role as the head of media planning, consumer research and marketing services functions at Percom, he has a significant experience with local as well as overseas clients who outsource these services on a regular basis. Besides his professional responsibilities, Rajiv is an active participant in major marketing conferences in the Asia-Pacific region. He also shares his valuable experience with budding managers at many business schools in India as a seasoned guest faculty member.

**Arjun K. Pai** graduated with an honours degree in electronics & communications engineering from University of Mangalore with a distinction in 2001. After his short stint at Wipro-GE Medical Systems, Bangalore, as a graduate engineering intern, he moved to pursue his M.Sc. in system level integration at the University of Edinburgh, which he completed with a distinction in 2003. Arjun is currently a postgraduate research student in the School of Computer Science, at Queen's University Belfast, United Kingdom. He is a working member of a research cluster investigating programmable system-on-chip architectures for image and video processing applications, at the ECIT Institute in Northern Ireland Science Park. Arjun's commitment to professional development, academic excellence and involvement in community leadership activities has won him recognition and many laurels. His achievements have been honoured through an entry in the *Marquis Who's Who in the World®* in their 23rd edition to be published in 2006.

**Anne C. Rouse** is an associate professor in business strategy at the Deakin Business School, Melbourne, Australia. She previously taught IT strategy with the Monash Graduate School of Business, the University of Queensland/Mt Eliza Business School and the Helsinki School of Economics and Business Administration. Her Ph.D. into IT outsourcing risks and benefits won the Australasian "Best Ph.D." medal in 2003, awarded by the Association of Information Systems Professors and Heads of Schools. Her doctoral research was funded by a consortium of 10 large Australian organisations interesting in discovering outsourcing success factors, through the management consulting group, Simsion, Bowles & Associates. Her outsourcing research underpinned the Australian federal government's *Guide to ICT Sourcing* (which she co-authored in conjunction with the Boston Consulting Group and Consulting Insights). Dr. Rouse has more than 20 years industry experience in project management, business strategy consulting, and organizational psychology, and is licensed to practice as a psychologist in Australia. She has published widely in the areas of outsourcing and vendor-client relationships, and is currently supervising PhD students in the areas of enterprise software, quality management and customer relationship management.

**Fjodor Ruzic** is a doctor of information sciences at the University of Zagreb where he is lecturer in new media and interactive multimedia systems. He currently holds a position in the Croatian government office for e-Croatia as head of the information unit and a consultant in information-communications systems, interactive multimedia and information services (electronic documents). His recent research activities are covering the integration of information content and integration impacts on development of information theory and practice. He is in information sciences from 1975, and he is member of many national and international bodies relating to telecommunications systems integrity, information resources management and multimedia system environment. He was working on both research and implementation sides of networked databases, educational material, and digital media. He published more than 125 scientific and research papers in various international journals and he is author of several books dealing with graphical user interfaces, multimedia and Internet. After finishing work on Electronic Signature Law and related Ordinances in 2002, he wrote the Law on Electronic Document enacted in 2005.

**Jurgis Samulevièius** teaches at the Vilnius Gediminas Technical University of Lithuania. He graduated from the Vilnius University and did postgraduate work at The Kiev Institute of Trade, Ukraine. As a senior researcher, he worked at the Institute of Economics, Lithuanian Academy of Sciences. He published extensively in Lithuania and abroad; more than 80 publications at the latest count. His most recent publications in English include: *Introduction to Macroeconomics* (Vilnius, 2001), *Introduction to Modern Economics: Macroeconomics* (Vilnius, 2003) and China's Development: Foreign Direct Investment, Accession to the WTO and Future Perspectives, a chapter in the book *Foreign Investment in Rapidly Growing Countries: The Chinese and Indian Experiences* (Palgrave Macmillan, 2005), edited by Professor Kehal. His research interests include foreign investment in developing countries, environmental economics and management, economics of European integration, ITC, health care economy and the digital economy.

Educated in Poland, USA, the UK and elsewhere, **Val Samonis** (PhD, CPC) gained more than two decades of cross-functional research, teaching/training, and advisory experience combining theoretical and hands-on empirical approaches to business/finance, technology, and policy frontiers globally. Dr. Samonis worked with top reformers and business leaders in a number of countries (e.g., Polish Deputy PM L. Balcerowicz, Czech Deputy PM P. Mertlik), Nobel Laureates in economics (as part of the Stanford Economic Transition Group); lectured internationally on trade, investment/finance, knowledge economy, corporate governance, and other business reform issues in the global economy; and has been extensively published. He managed and/or worked in international research and advisory ("blue ribbon") teams sponsored by The Hudson Institute, World Bank, CASE Warsaw, EU (ACE, TEMPUS), USAID, Soros Foundations, The Center for

European Integration Studies (ZEI Bonn), Joint Committee on Corporate Governance (Canada), and a number of governments (e.g,. in the Baltic States, Ukraine, Poland and Canada). He served as an advisor to the Czech government, Lithuanian Parliament, international organizations (e.g., UNCTAD, ITC/WTO), and multinational corporations (e.g., Andersen Consulting, Medley Global Advisors). Professor Samonis taught executives globally online, onsite, and the dual mode; he is one of the two founding editors of *The Journal of East-West Business* (The Haworth Press, Inc).

**Carlos Piñeiro Sánchez** is a permanent lecturer of financial economics at the faculty of economics of the University of A Coruña, Spain, where he teaches financial management and MIS. He is also a permanent lecturer at several master and post-graduate programs. He got his postgraduate degree in 1994 in finance and a PhD degree in information systems in 1999 for a work on the use of group decision support systems by SMEs in Spain. He in involved in several research programs in Spain and the European Union, and has published more than 20 books and journal articles on finance and management information systems. He has also contributed about 30 works to academic summits, and collaborated as a reviewer for several Spanish academic journals.

**Piyush Sharma** is a research associate at Nanyang Business School, Singapore. He has more than 15 years of professional experience in heavy engineering, FMCG, health care and financial services with top Indian and multinational companies (e.g., BHEL, ITC (now Conagra India), Dabur and Becton Dickinson). For the last few years, he's been based in Singapore and actively engaged in teaching, academic research and executive education activities. He has presented his research in many top international conferences (e.g., ACR, AMS and AMA) and has a few papers under review at major marketing journals (e.g., JCR, JCP and JSM). Besides his academic efforts, he is also involved in consulting projects and executive education programs for major MNCs based in Singapore. His research interests are in consumer behavior (impulse buying, variety seeking and complaint behavior), international marketing (country-of-origin effects, consumer ethnocentrism, offshore outsourcing) and services marketing (healthcare services, service quality, inter-cultural service encounters and services outsourcing) areas.

**Varadharajan Sridhar** is a professor in information management at the Management Development Institute, Gurgaon, India. He received his PhD in management information systems from the University of Iowa. His current research interests include telecommunications management and policy, global electronic commerce, and global virtual teams. He has published articles in a number of journals including *Annals of Cases on Information Technology, European Journal of Operational Research, Journal of Heuristics, Telecommunication Systems,* and *The Journal of Regional Analysis and Policy*. He is an associate editor of *International Journal of Business Data Communications and Networking.*

**Kirk St.Amant** is an assistant professor in the Department of English at Texas Tech University, USA. He has a background in anthropology, international government and technical communication, and his research interests include intercultural communication via online media. He has taught online and conventional courses in technical and professional communication and in intercultural communication for Texas Tech University, Mercer University and James Madison University. He has taught courses in e-commerce, distance education and business communication in Ukraine as a part of the USAID-sponsored Consortium for the Enhancement of Ukrainian Management Education (CEUME).

**Siri Terjesen** received her Ph.D. from the Cranfield School of Management in the United Kingdom, and has published over a dozen refereed journal articles and book chapters in the areas of strategy and entrepreneurship. She is a research fellow at the Brisbane Graduate School of Business at Queensland University of Technology and a visiting research fellow at the Max Planck Institute of Economics in Jena, Germany. She also lectures at the London School of Economics Summer School in London and Beijing. Siri holds a BS in business administration from the University of Richmond, Virginia, and a master's degree in international business from the Norwegian School of Economics and Business Administration (NHH) in Bergen, Norway, where she was a Fulbright Scholar. Prior to her academic career, Siri worked in strategy consulting in the U.S. and Europe, in financial services, telecommunications and pharmaceuticals. She is an associate of Stratevolve Consulting and a member of Open World Initiative. In addition to her research and consulting, she is a keen runner and has represented the U.S. at the IAAF-sanctioned IAU World 100K Championships, holds three UK national championship titles, and was a member of England's Anglo-Celtic team.

**Felix R. Doldán Tié** is a professor of finance in the faculty of economics of the University of A Coruña, Spain, where he teaches financial management. He has two postgraduate degrees in business and computing from the Universities Complutense (Madrid) and Politécnica (Madrid); he got a PhD in business and finance from the University Complutense, for a work on "Quantitative Methods for Financial Management" As a researcher, he is an expert on financial management and management information systems, and is currently engaged in several research projects supported by the Spanish government and the European Union. He has also published 50 books and research papers, and taken part in several academic conferences. His main research concerns are information systems, decision theory, multicriteria analysis, uncertainty management and financial derivatives.

**P. Trott** is a principal lecturer at the Business School, University of Portsmouth, UK. He holds a PhD from Cranfield University. His research focuses on aspects of innovation management. His book, *Managing Innovation and New Product Development*, published by Pearson Education, is now in its third edition.

**Catherine L. Wang** is a senior lecturer in international strategic management at Oxford Brookes University Business School, UK. She holds a BA in economics, an M.Sc. in marketing management and a PhD in management. Prior to joining academia, she worked in industry for eight years, both in the UK and China, in the area of international trade and investment, small business support and consultancy. Currently, she teaches strategic management and research methods at both undergraduate and postgraduate level. Her research interests are in the fields of strategic management, knowledge management, innovation, the resource-based view, dynamic capabilities and organisational performance.

**Martin Wiener**, born in 1979, studied business information systems at the Friedrich-Alexander-University of Erlangen-Nuremberg, Germany. After residing in the United States for research purposes, he started working at the Department for Business Information Systems III, as a research associate and doctoral candidate in 2004. Martin's research activities concentrate on the field of IT offshoring. The topic of his dissertation is "Management of Critical Success Factors in Offshore Software Development Projects."

# Index

## T



## U

## V



## W

CPSIA information can be obtained
at www.ICGtesting.com
Printed in the USA
BVOW04*2236281016
466004BV00020B/27/P